W9-AXI-297

61-11?/ (2-27-6?)

GREEK
LYRIC POETRY

GREEK
LYRIC POETRY

From Alcman to Simonides

BY

C. M. BOWRA

WARDEN OF WADHAM COLLEGE
OXFORD

SECOND, REVISED EDITION

OXFORD
AT THE CLARENDON PRESS

WINGATE COLLEGE LIBRARY
WINGATE, N. C.

Oxford University Press, Ely House, London W. 1

GLASGOW NEW YORK TORONTO MELBOURNE WELLINGTON
CAPE TOWN SALISBURY IBADAN NAIROBI LUSAKA ADDIS ABABA
BOMBAY CALCUTTA MADRAS KARACHI LAHORE DACCA
KUALA LUMPUR HONG KONG TOKYO

© *Oxford University Press 1961*

FIRST PUBLISHED 1961
REPRINTED LITHOGRAPHICALLY IN GREAT BRITAIN
AT THE UNIVERSITY PRESS, OXFORD
FROM CORRECTED SHEETS OF THE SECOND EDITION
BY VIVIAN RIDLER
PRINTER TO THE UNIVERSITY
1967

PREFACE TO SECOND EDITION

THE first edition of this book was published in 1936 and went out of print during the war. Since then I have had many requests that it should be reprinted, but I have thought it better to wait until I could give the book a thorough revision. For this there were good reasons. First, in recent years our supply of Greek lyric poetry has been increased by a small but steady stream of new texts, and any book which deals with the subject must take note of them. Secondly, a great deal of work has been done on most of the poets, and some of it is too important to be neglected. Thirdly, in the light of criticism and discussion I have revised my own opinions on certain matters. I have therefore not so much revised the book as rewritten it. I have removed what now seem to me too many hasty conclusions and have allowed more space for legitimate doubt. I have taken notice of recent publications, at least in so far as they are relevant to my main subjects. Where I have changed my opinions or omitted passages from the first edition, I have not thought it necessary to say so in the text, as I see no point in troubling the reader with matters which I no longer regard as important. In general I have kept the main lines of the first edition, but I have omitted four of the Appendixes, since anything that matters in them can best be included in the main text. I have received invaluable help and encouragement from Professor Hugh Lloyd-Jones, who has read my typescript, removed many errors, and generously allowed me to make use of some of his own ideas. At an early stage Professor J. A. Davison read most of my chapters, and I have benefited greatly from his careful observations. I am deeply indebted to others who have given unstinted help. Mrs. Margaret Forrest has with great kindness compiled the Indexes. Mr. W. G. G. Forrest has helped in identifying references. Mr. C. E. Stevens has scrutinized my proofs with keen and scholarly eyes. The skilled staff of the Clarendon Press have removed many blemishes. For such as remain I have only myself to blame.

C. M. B.

Oxford, May 1960

37731

PREFACE TO FIRST EDITION

IN the last fifty years no comprehensive book on the early Greek lyric poets has been published, and in this period many new discoveries have been made. Papyri have increased our texts, and linguistic and historical research has raised new questions. This book is partly an attempt to review these poets in their historical development, partly a detailed criticism of their more important fragments. In it new theses are propounded in the hope that they will lead to a greater understanding of this unique phase of poetry, and to these I have devoted considerable space. But that the book may not be unduly one-sided I have also attempted to consider the different poets in a more general way and to analyse what seem important elements in their art. In this I have not consciously followed the work of others except where I have made acknowledgements, but in literary criticism repetition of earlier views is sooner or later inevitable, and I may have given as my own opinions held by others before me. In any case it is better to repeat a traditional judgement than to neglect some important quality in a poet's work.

In dealing with a fragmentary literature like this speculation and hypothesis are inevitable, and certainty seems an impossible ideal. I have therefore not refrained from occasionally putting forward views of whose rashness I am conscious. The best I can wish is that some of these speculations may be justified by future discoveries, but in the meantime I hope that they will help to make the poets more intelligible and raise legitimate questions about them. I have been at some pains to provide reasonably translatable texts, and though my work owes its foundations to E. Diehl's *Anthologia Lyrica* and E. Lobel's editions of Alcaeus and Sappho, I have often differed from them in my versions of familiar quotations and in my supplements of papyri. Most of my own suggestions will be found in an Appendix; they should be judged as attempts to make sense of difficult passages, not as emendations with any claim to finality. To most quotations made in the text I have added simple translations to show what meaning I attribute to them.

My obligations are many and various. I have learned much from H. W. Smyth's scholarly *Greek Melic Poets*, from several books and articles of U. von Wilamowitz-Moellendorff, from the masses of material collected in Schmid–Staehlin's *Griechische Literaturgeschichte* and in J. M. Edmonds's *Lyra Graeca*. I am particularly indebted to A. A. Blakeway, who has suggested many ideas to me and most liberally helped me with his great knowledge of history and archaeology; H. T. Wade-Gery has sustained me with unfailing support and thrown much light on problems whose solution was beyond my powers; E. Fraenkel and D. L. Page have each read some chapters in typescript and made valuable corrections. I am also gratefully indebted to B. D. Meritt, J. D. Beazley, Paul Maas, G. Zuntz, W. Schubart, and above all to R. H. Dundas, who with characteristic generosity has read my proofs and removed many blemishes. For such as remain he is in no way responsible.

C. M. B.

Oxford, July 1935

CONTENTS

SELECT LIST OF ABBREVIATIONS

A.J.A.	*American Journal of Archaeology.*
A.J.P.	*American Journal of Philology.*
Anz. Ak. Wien.	*Anzeiger der Öesterreichischen Akademie der Wissenschaften in Wien.*
An. Fil. Clas.	*Anales de Filología Clásica*
Beazley, *A.B.-F.V.*	J. D. Beazley, *Attic Black-figure Vase-painters*, Oxford, 1956.
Beazley, *A.R.V.*	J. D. Beazley, *Attic Red-figure Vase-painters*, Oxford, 1942.
Beazley, *A.R.V.A.M.*	J. D. Beazley, *Attic Red-figured Vases in American Museums*, Oxford, 1918.
B.C.H.	*Bulletin de correspondance hellénique.*
Bowra, *E.G.E.*	C. M. Bowra, *Early Greek Elegists*, Oxford, 1938.
Bowra, *Problems*	C. M. Bowra, *Problems in Greek Poetry*, Oxford, 1953.
C.A.H.	*Cambridge Ancient History.*
C.J.	*Classical Journal.*
C.P.	*Classical Philology.*
C.Q.	*Classical Quarterly.*
C.R.	*Classical Review.*
C.V.A.	*Corpus Vasorum Antiquorum.*
D.	Quotations from E. Diehl, *Anthologia Lyrica Graeca.*
Edmonds, *L.G.*	J. M. Edmonds, *Lyra Graeca*, 3 vols., London, 1922–7.
Färber	H. Färber, *Die Lyrik in der Kunsttheorie der Antike*, München, 1936.
Farnell, *Cults*	L. R. Farnell, *The Cults of the Greek States*, 5 vols., Oxford, 1896–1909.
Farnell, *G.H.C.*	L. R. Farnell, *Greek Hero Cults*, Oxford, 1921.
G.G.A.	*Göttingische Gelehrte Anzeigen.*
Haspels, *A.B.L.*	C. E. Haspels, *Attic Black-figured Lekythoi*, Paris, 1936.
Head, *H.N.*	B. V. Head, *Historia Nummorum*[2], Oxford, 1911.
J.D.A.I.	*Jahrbuch des Deutschen Archäologischen Instituts.*
J.H.S.	*Journal of Hellenic Studies.*
J.Ph.	*Journal of Philology.*
L.–P.	Quotations from E. Lobel and D. Page, *Poetarum Lesbiorum Fragmenta*, Oxford, 1955.
Lobel, *Ἀμ.*	E. Lobel, *Ἀλκαίου μέλη*, Oxford, 1927.
Lobel, *Σμ.*	E. Lobel, *Σαπφοῦς μέλη*, Oxford, 1925.

Mancuso, *Lir. cl. gr.*	U. Mancuso, *La lirica classica greca in Sicilia e nella Magna Grecia*, Pisa, 1912.
Page, *Alc. Parth.*	D. L. Page, *Alcman: the Partheneion*, Oxford, 1951.
Page, *S. and A.*	D. L. Page, *Sappho and Alcaeus*, Oxford, 1955.
Payne	H. G. Payne, *Necrocorinthia*, Oxford, 1931.
P.B.A.	*Proceedings of the British Academy.*
Pfuhl	E. Pfuhl, *Malerei und Zeichnung der Griechen*, 3 vols., München, 1923.
Powell	J. U. Powell, *Collectanea Alexandrina*, Oxford, 1925.
P.S.I.	*Pubblicazioni della Società Italiana.*
R.A.A.N.	*Rendiconti dell'Accademia di Archeologia, Lettere e Belle Arti di Napoli.*
R.A.L.	*Rendiconti della Classe di Scienze morali, storiche, e filologiche dell'Accademia dei Lincei*, Roma.
R.É.G.	*Revue des Études Grecques.*
Reitzenstein, *E.u.S.*	R. Reitzenstein, *Epigramm und Skolion*, Giessen, 1893.
R.F.I.C.	*Rivista di Filosofia e d'Istruzione Classica.*
Richter, *A.G.A.*	G. Richter, *Archaic Greek Art*, New York, 1949.
Rumpf	A. Rumpf, *Chalkidische Vasen*, 3 vols., Berlin, 1927.
Smyth, *G.M.P.*	H. W. Smyth, *Greek Melic Poets*, London, 1900.
Stud. It. Fil.	*Studi Italiani di Filologia Classica.*
Vürtheim	J. Vürtheim, *Stesichoros' Fragmente und Biographie*, Leiden, 1919.
Weber	L. Weber, *Anacreontea*, Göttingen, 1895.
Wide	S. Wide, *Lakonische Kulte*, Leipzig, 1893.
Wilamowitz, *A.u.A.*	U. von Wilamowitz-Moellendorff, *Aristoteles und Athen*, 2 vols., Berlin, 1893.
Wilamowitz, *Gr. Versk.*	U. von Wilamowitz-Moellendorff, *Griechische Verskunst*, Berlin, 1921.
Wilamowitz, *S.u.S.*	U. von Wilamowitz-Moellendorff, *Sappho und Simonides*, Berlin, 1913.
Wilamowitz, *T.G.L.*	U. von Wilamowitz-Moellendorff, *Die Textgeschichte der griechischen Lyriker*, Berlin, 1900.
W.Z.M-L.U.	*Wissenschaftliche Zeitschriften der Martin-Luther-Universität, Halle-Wittenberg.*

I. INTRODUCTION

IN modern English the title of lyric may be applied to almost any poetry which is not narrative or dramatic or philosophical. It is commonly used for any short poem, and it has nothing to do with either the subject or the performance of the poetry which it characterizes. It is applied equally to Shakespeare's songs and to Milton's *Lycidas*, to Gray's *Elegy* and to Wordsworth's sonnets. In the main it refers to personal poetry, and to poetry which, if not actually sung, has in itself an element of song. But the term is elastic and justified neither by history nor by current practice. For few of the English poems which are called lyrical ever had anything to do with the lyre. In so far as the term may be justified, it must be by a certain affinity which the many kinds of poetry have to one another—by that relation, however distant and theoretical, to song, which differentiates them from plays and narratives and meditations. Nor is the vagueness of the term confined to England. Most European culture since the Renaissance has employed the same useful, if incorrect, method of classification, and used words akin to 'lyrical'. The word may be misapplied, but it stands for something real and has passed into the common language of criticism. If we would find an origin for this modern usage, we may perhaps look to Horace, whose influence lies behind most personal poetry since the Renaissance. He wrote poems to be read in the study and not to be sung in company, but in obedience to his Greek models he assumed a convention that they should in theory be sung to the lyre.[1] He did not mean this to be taken literally; his purpose was rather to claim his spiritual and artistic descent from Alcaeus, Sappho, and Pindar. But he established a convention which posterity has accepted and found useful. Words like 'lyric' and 'lyrical' are serviceable labels, and criticism would be the poorer without them. But when we consider the character of Greek lyric poetry, we must rid ourselves of the associations which these words have for us. When applied to the Greeks, 'lyric' and 'lyrical' have a meaning more precise and more technical than when applied to the moderns.

[1] *C.* 1. 6. 10; 3. 3. 69; 4. 3. 23.

The word λυρικός makes its first important appearance at Alexandria.[1] In their classification of earlier poets the Alexandrian scholars made a list of the ἐννέα λυρικοί,[2] and this is implied by Horace when he expresses the hope that he himself will be accounted among the true lyric poets:

> quod si me lyricis uatibus inseres,
> sublimi feriam sidera uertice.[3]

It was known to Petronius, who speaks tantalizingly of 'Pindarus nouemque lyrici'.[4] Both he and Horace drew on Alexandrian scholarship, and we cannot doubt that the list of the Nine Lyric Poets existed before them. It was known to Antipater of Thessalonica,[5] who was a client of L. Calpurnius Piso Frugi, for whose sons Horace wrote his *Ars Poetica*, and it was familiar enough to be mentioned without further detail at the end of the first century B.C. A list of the Nine Poets is given in two anonymous Greek epigrams,[6] whose date is not known, but of which the first at least is not likely to be later than Antipater. Though the order of the names differs, the actual names are the same in both poems, and are Pindar, Bacchylides, Sappho, Anacreon, Stesichorus, Simonides, Ibycus, Alcaeus, and Alcman. It has been conjectured that this list was based on those poets whose works were brought to Alexandria, and there edited and known as οἱ πραττόμενοι,[7] but whether this is the case or whether the choice was made for aesthetic considerations of presumed excellence, the list shows what the Alexandrians understood by a λυρικός. He was a poet who was distinguishable equally from the writers of tragedies, of epic, of iambic verse, and of elegiacs. These other kinds might have their own lists; the nine λυρικοί formed a class of their own.

What constituted membership of this class is not hard to determine. The λυρικός was primarily a poet who composed poems

---

[1] The earlier word was μελοποιός: Aristoph. *Ran.* 1250; Plat. *Ion* 533 e, 534 a; *Prot.* 326 a.

[2] The evidence is assembled by H. Färber, *Die Lyrik in der Kunsttheorie der Antike*, ii, pp. 7-11.

[3] *C.* 1. 1. 35-36.

[4] *Sat.* 2. Wilamowitz, *T.G.L.* p. 4, points out that he is not to be taken too literally or assumed to include Corinna among the Nine.

[5] *Anth. Pal.* 7. 18. 3-4:
> ... Ἀλκμᾶνα λύρης ἐλατῆρα Λακαίνης
> ἔξοχον, ὃν Μουσέων ἐννέ' ἀριθμὸς ἔχει.

[6] Ibid. 9. 184 and 571.

[7] Bekker, *An. Gr.*, p. 751.

to be sung to the λύρα, which is first mentioned by Archilochus,[1] but closely resembled the instrument of seven strings which Hermes was said to have invented, and which may have gone back to Mycenaean times. The lyric poet was thus distinguished from the writer of plays, who was not in the first place concerned with the lyre, since much of his work was not sung but spoken; from the writer of trochaic and iambic verses, who wrote mainly for recitation; and from the writer of elegiacs, who originally at least composed for accompaniment by the flute.[2] So far the distinction was reasonably precise. Nor was it difficult to distinguish lyric poetry from epic, although at an early stage the epic bards accompanied their performances with a φόρμιγξ, which was a kind of lyre. The performance of an epic poem seems to have been more akin to recitative than to singing and to have involved not a recognizable tune but a simple chant. What might seem a greater difficulty is that lyric poets, as Alexandria classified them, did not confine themselves to the lyre and sometimes did not use it at all. Both Pindar[3] and Bacchylides[4] mention flutes as forming part, if not the whole, of their musical accompaniment, and the Prosodion or Processional Song is explicitly said to have been sung to the flute.[5] Since the flute was the distinctive instrument of the elegiac, this might seem to indicate some confusion in the definition of lyric poetry. But the answer is that the lyre was the normal accompaniment, and gave it its special character, while the flute was subsidiary and possibly brought into use later. The actual type of lyre might be altered and given a new name,[6] but it remained in essentials the same kind of stringed instrument. The Alexandrians were justified in drawing up a list of the nine λυρικοί, for each of them composed songs for the lyre, and this served to differentiate them from other poets who composed for other, or for no, instruments, or, if they used the lyre, used it in a different way.

The character, then, of Greek lyric poetry is decided by the

---

[1] Fr. 51. 47 D.
[2] Archiloch. fr. 123 Bergk; Theogn. 533, 1041; Paus. 10. 7. 5; see Bowra, *E.G.E.* pp. 4 ff.
[3] *Ol.* 7. 12; *Nem.* 9. 8; *Isthm.* 5. 27.
[4] 2. 12; 9. 68; fr. 4. 68.
[5] Procl. *Bibl. Phot.* 320 a 18 ff. Bekker.
[6] Ibycus invented the σαμβύκη, Athen. 4. 175 e; Terpander the βάρβιτος, Pind. fr. 110 Bo.; for Anacreon and his inventions see L. Weber, *Anacreontea*, pp. 72 ff.

nature of its musical accompaniment, but when we try to classify its different branches, we are faced by serious difficulties. The Greeks indeed used two forms of classification, which are not actually incompatible but indicate different approaches to the subject. The first is to be found in Plato, who distinguishes between monody and choral song.[1] He does not press the point or make much of it, and it plays almost no part in Greek poetical theory. The second comes from Alexandrian scholars, possibly Didymus,[2] and can be seen, for instance, in the arrangement of Pindar's poems in seventeen books according to their εἴδη.[3] This classification seems to have been applied also to Bacchylides, but not to Sappho, whose work, so far as we can see, is arranged on other principles.[4] Nor was the method very precise even with Pindar. Among his Epinicians there are pieces which were certainly not composed for victories in the games, such as Pythian III, which looks like a poetical letter, and Nemean XI, which celebrates the introduction of a young man into the Town Hall of Tenedos, and among his Maiden-songs one piece (fr. 84 Bo.) is a δαφνηφορικόν, which the Alexandrians classed as something special by itself.[5] This kind of classification may have been useful to editors and teachers, but in fact it does not tell us much about real distinctions inside lyric poetry. Nor is this surprising. The conditions for which songs were composed were so various and so different from place to place that it was not easy to force them into a schematic frame. We cannot hope for a precise classification, but we can at least see how the main forms worked and what their purpose was.

Both monody and choral songs may be almost as old as the Greek people, but the earliest evidence for them comes from Homer. He gives hints of the singing of solo songs, and these may be supplemented by small pieces of evidence from other sources. When he makes Hector say to Ajax

οἶδα δ' ἐνὶ σταδίῃ δηΐῳ μέλπεσθαι Ἄρηϊ[6]

the word μέλπεσθαι shows that Hector means a war-dance, like that which Achilles was said to have performed at the funeral of

---

[1] Laws 6ɨ 764 d–e. [2] Färber, i, p. 18.
[3] Vit. Ambr. (Schol. Pind. ed. Drachmann, i, p. 3). Somewhat different lists are given by 'Suidas', s.v. Πίνδαρος, and the metrical Life, op. cit., p. 9, 26 ff. Cf. A. E. Harvey, C.Q. N.S. 5 (1955), p. 161.
[4] See Page, S. and A., pp. 112–16.
[5] Färber, ii, pp. 55–56. [6] Il. 7. 241.

Patroclus[1] and which may well have been accompanied by words, like those in the Song of Hybrias. On the Shield of Achilles a boy sings the Linus song, and his companions dance, while he sings.[2] This must be a traditional song for a dying vegetation-god, and some kind of parallel to it may be seen in the Adonis song written by Sappho.[3] Homer also, naturally enough, knows of songs which have no special function or occasion, as when Calypso sings while she plies her golden shuttle.[4] Nor can we doubt that of the few specimens of popular Greek song which survive some are mono-dies, like the mill-song of Mytilene.[5] The songs of Alcaeus, Sappho, and Anacreon look as if they were in the first place composed to be sung by the poet to his friends, though there is no reason why some of them should not also be sung by a choir.

The Homeric evidence for choral songs is more abundant and more instructive. He records the existence, at an early stage, of four kinds, which were later developed and formalized and turned to ritual uses. First, in four passages he describes a θρῆνος or dirge—when Thetis and her Nereids lament for Patroclus,[6] when Achilles and his followers lament all night also for Patro-clus,[7] when the Trojan women lament for Hector,[8] and when the Muses lament for Achilles.[9] Secondly, he tells how the young men of the Achaeans sing all day of Apollo as παιήονα,[10] which suggests an early example of the Paean, which was closely con-nected with Apollo. Thirdly, on the Shield of Achilles there is a ὑμέναιος or wedding-song, which some sing, while others dance, to the music of pipes and lyres.[11] Fourthly, at the court of Alci-nous the song of Demodocus on Ares and Aphrodite is accom-panied by dancing,[12] and looks as if it were an early example of the ὑπόρχημα or song illustrated by mimetic steps and gestures. These four types were known to the Alexandrians and composed by Pindar. Homer certainly knew of some kinds of choral song in which a number of people took part.

At the same time Homer describes this art at an earlier stage of development than any which has come to us from later times. The ὑπόρχημα of Demodocus is not in the strict sense choral, since Demodocus is the only person who actually sings. In the

---

[1] Aristot. fr. 519 R.   [2] Il. 18. 570.   [3] Fr. 140 L.–P.
[4] Od. 5. 61–62.   [5] Plut. Sept. Sap. Conv. 14 e.   [6] Il. 18. 50–51.
[7] Ibid. 314–16.   [8] Ibid. 24. 723 ff.   [9] Od. 24. 60 ff.
[10] Il. 1. 472–4.   [11] Ibid. 18. 493 ff.
[12] Od. 8. 262 ff.; Athen. 5. 181 b says that the ὑπόρχημα was of Cretan origin.

various laments the normal form seems to be that one person
leads, ἐξῆρχε γόοιο, while the others do little more than utter
cries of sorrow. The leader may be Thetis or Achilles or in turn
Andromache, Hecuba, and Helen, while the rest στενάχοντο. Even
in the lament for Achilles, where the Nine Muses lament 'answer-
ing each other with beautiful voice', and we have an indisputable
reference to a choir, the daughters of the Old Man of the Sea
do no more than stand around and cry piteously, οἴκτρ' ὀλοφυρό-
μεναι. Homer relates conditions in which the choir has not found
its final duty, and much depends on the leader, who carries out
the main function, while the rest do little more than support him.
Their task is to carry out certain steps or gestures and to utter
appropriate cries at certain moments. These cries may have survived in such refrains as Ὑμὴν ὦ Ὑμέναιε, αἴλινον αἴλινον, ἰήϊε
Παιάν, which are to be found in Wedding-songs, Dirges, and
Paeans.

   The difference between choral song and monody is not absolute, and there is a certain overlap between them. A ὕμνος, or
hymn to the gods, could be sung by a choir, as in Pindar's Hymns,
or by a single person, as it must have been in some Hymns of
Alcaeus and Sappho. The σκόλιον or drinking-song might be
sung by individuals, like the Attic σκόλια, or by a company, like
those of Ibycus, Pindar, and Bacchylides. None the less the
distinction between choral song and monody is not valueless,
because the first was part of a complex activity which included
both song and rhythmical movements, while the second was only
a song. The difference helped to shape the development of Greek
lyric poetry. First, the stanzas of choral song were longer than
those of monody, or at least, while those of Sappho, Alcaeus, and
Anacreon are short, those of Alcman, Pindar, and Bacchylides
are normally long. The difference may be due to the part taken
by dance in the latter. Just because a set of complicated steps had
to be performed, the stanza must coincide with them and last till
they were finished. Secondly, the metres of choral songs are much
more elaborate than those of monody. Though Sappho and
Alcaeus use a wide range of stanzas, these can be divided into
various, easily recognizable classes, but the metres of Pindar and
Bacchylides, which can indeed be classified according to their
main principles, vary from poem to poem. So great indeed is their
variety that, when we find that the metre of *Isthmian* IV is the

same as that of *Isthmian* III, we suspect them of being a single poem or at least of being very closely related. Thirdly, though the choral poets often speak in the first person and are by no means shy of voicing their own opinions, they are less intimate and personal than the writers of monody, who speak without reserve of their innermost feelings and do not attempt to identify themselves with their company, or to speak for anyone but themselves. Though the distinction between choral song and monody is not absolute, it represents something which cannot be ignored, since it helped to foster a variety of form and temper in Greek lyric poetry.

The forms of choral song mentioned by Homer are not the only ancient forms. Others, which survived into Pindar's time, are clearly of considerable antiquity. First, is the ὕμνος or Hymn. A Hymn was regarded by Plato[1] as a song addressed to the gods in distinction from a song addressed to men, and the definition is sound enough. The word might be used in a general sense for any song to the gods and cover forms which were commonly treated separately, such as the Paean, the Dithyramb, and the προσόδιον, but it seems to have had a more technical meaning as a hymn sung to the gods to the accompaniment of the κιθάρα[2] by a choir which did not move but stood still.[3] In this respect it would be closer to monody than most choral songs, and that would help to explain why the two classes overlap at this point. An early example of such a Hymn was ascribed to a Lycian called Olen and was sung by women on Delos in honour of the legendary women who brought offerings from the Hyperboreans.[4] Olen may be a fabulous figure, but the Hymn was real enough and was probably ancient. Second is the προσόδιον, or Processional Song, which was sung on the way to altars or temples of the gods, and unlike the Hymn proper, was accompanied by the flute.[5] Two lines from such a song survive in a fragment attributed to Eumelus of Corinth and are said to have been composed for a

---

[1] *Rep.* 10. 607 a; *Symp.* 177 a.

[2] Menand. περὶ ἐπιδ. p. 331, 17 Spengler.

[3] Proclus, p. 320 a 20 ὁ δὲ κυρίως ὕμνος πρὸς κιθάραν ᾔδετο ἑστώτων. See Harvey, op. cit., p. 166, who compares *Et. Mag.* 690. 41 ff. with its division of μέλη καὶ ὕμνοι into προσόδια, ὑπορχήματα, στάσιμα.

[4] Hdt. 4. 35. 3; Paus. 9. 27. 2; cf. Callim. 4. 305; frs. 524 and 547 P.

[5] Procl. p. 320 a 18 ἐλέγετο δὲ τὸ προσόδιον, ἐπειδὰν προσίωσι τοῖς βωμοῖς ἢ ναοῖς, καὶ ἐν τῷ προσιέναι ᾔδετο πρὸς αὐλόν.

male choir sent by the Messenians to Delos.[1] Since the *floruit* of Eumelus is placed in 743 B.C. and he is said to have been a contemporary of Archias,[2] who founded Syracuse in 734 B.C.,[3] this is indeed an early relic:

τῷ γὰρ Ἰθωμάτᾳ καταθύμιος ἔπλετο Μοῖσα
ἁ καθαρὰ καὶ ἐλεύθερα σάνδαλ' ἔχουσα.[4]

Third, the Dithyramb, which was for a long time specially concerned with Dionysus, may well be equally old. Its first appearance is in Archilochus, who says of himself:

ὡς Διωνύσοι' ἄνακτος καλὸν ἐξάρξαι μέλος
οἶδα διθύραμβον οἴνῳ συγκεραυνωθεὶς φρένας.[5]

Unlike the προσόδιον, the Dithyramb has not yet taken a formal shape and still resembles the choral songs known to Homer in having an ἔξαρχος who did most of the purely poetical work. Since Dionysus is mentioned at Pylos in the Mycenaean age, the Dithyramb may have been very ancient, even if it did not attain a formal dignity until almost classical times.

The Greeks, from Plato onwards, differentiated between songs addressed to the gods and songs addressed to men and called the latter by the general name of ἐγκώμια.[6] Such songs are attributed to Simonides, Pindar, and Bacchylides, but there is no reason to think that the type was not earlier. Songs about the living form a natural counterpart to songs about the past, and were likely enough to have developed in Greece. Indeed Ibycus' poem to Polycrates seems, from what survives of it, to have been essentially an ἐγκώμιον in the sense that it was concerned with a living, human subject. From this kind of song developed a special form, the ἐπινίκιον, sung for men who won in the great games. This cannot have existed before the foundation of the Olympian Games in 776 B.C. and probably did not come into prominence until the foundation of other games in the sixth century at Delphi, Nemea, and the Isthmus. When it makes its first appearance, it is indeed

---

[1] Paus. 4. 33. 2.
[2] Hieron.–Euseb. p. 155. 4 Fotheringham. Clem. Al. *Strom.* I, p. 399 P.
[3] Thuc. 6. 3. 2.
[4] Fr. 13 Kinkel. So the text in Paus. 4. 33. 2. It is easy, but not perhaps necessary, to change to σάμβαλ' ἔχοισα. In 2 Bergk secured a second hexameter by reading ἁ καθαρὰν κιθάραν, but we cannot be certain that the song was in hexameters and not composed of different dactylic metra like Stesichorus, fr. 6. 1–2 D.
[5] Fr. 77 D.
[6] Plat. *Rep.* 10. 607 a; *Laws* 8. 822 b; for other passages see Färber, ii, pp. 42–44.

a form of ἐγκώμιον, but it has also some characteristics of a hymn in that it is often sung at the festival of a god and contains references and homage to him. Another form of the ἐγκώμιον was the choral σκόλιον, like that which Pindar wrote for Theoxenus of Tenedos.[1] The Alexandrian scholars also recognized a form called ἐρωτικόν,[2] which plainly had much in common with the choral σκόλιον and could easily come under the general heading of ἐγκώμιον. Poems to men seem to have taken a new prominence in the sixth century, and their development may have been encouraged by the tyrants, who patronized poets and liked to be praised by them.

The origins of Greek lyric poetry are lost in an irrecoverable past. From the earliest times there must have been some kinds, however simple, of μολπή and of solo song, but we can form no conception of them, since all that survives from the eighth century is two lines of Eumelus and before that we have nothing. Such evidence as we have suggests that between the fall of the Mycenaean world and the seventh century the dominating art was the epic. It suited the temper of the time, and was so accomplished that other forms of poetry may have been insignificant beside it. But when this age passed into another more civically minded, another means of expression was needed and was found in choral song. Its efflorescence in the seventh century shows that times had changed and that the epic no longer satisfied all the spiritual needs of men. Though the growth of choral song is wrapped in legend, there can be little doubt that its first great names are those of musicians and musical reformers who made a new poetry possible. The problems connected with these pioneers belong more to the history of music than to that of poetry, but because they started choral poetry on a career of extraordinary vitality, some aspects of their works must be noticed.

The chief result of these musical reforms was the establishment of a musical scale. Attributed to the Phrygian Olympus,[3] this gave to musical composition a new range, which began to realize its possibilities when Terpander of Lesbos fitted the scale to the lyre[4] and made it possible for an accompaniment to be played in any key. The result was that poets, who were also musicians, could compose songs in the knowledge that they would be sung

---

[1] Fr. 108 Bo. [2] Färber, ii, p. 49. [3] 'Plut.' *Mus.* 11.
[4] Timoth. *Pers.* 237–8; Aristot. *Probl.* 19. 32; 'Plut.' *Mus.* 28; 'Suid.' s.v. Τέρπανδρος.

as they wished. What Terpander did for the lyre, Clonas did for the flute,[1] and the two chief instruments of Greek music were liberated from the hazards of extemporary composition and brought under the discipline of deliberate art. In later times these musicians were remembered by their tunes, and other ancient tunes were attributed to them.[2] But because the same man wrote both the tune and the words, they were also promoters of lyric poetry. Almost nothing of their work survives. Even the few fragments ascribed to Terpander are not likely to be genuine.[3] Such words as he and his kind wrote may have been too simple for the cultivated taste of later ages and have perished long before the tunes with which they were originally associated. But the mere act of composing words specially for a given tune was of great importance. The foundations were laid for an art which had enormous possibilities of development and kept for some three centuries the main outlines which its founders made possible.

Because Greek choral songs were accompanied by music and dancing, their metrical character was different alike from that of the Greek epic and from that of modern lyrical poetry. Almost every Greek choral song is written on an individual metrical pattern, and though the underlying principles may be analysed and classified, the fact remains that the choral poet could and did compose in a far greater variety of forms than any other poet. If there is still uncertainty about the ultimate nature of these metres, that is largely because the music and the dances are lost, and without them we have only part of a complex whole. But even in their divorced state the words have an astonishingly melodious movement of their own, and this certainly owes much to the demands of their accompaniment. The quantitative nature of Greek verse, which seems to be an inheritance from a remote past, allows a far greater variety of rhythms than is possible in any purely accentual system, and it was undeniably stimulated to new and more varied effects by being forced to follow the changing movements of the dance and the music which emphasized them.

Since Greek music lacked harmony in the modern sense of the word, what mattered was the tune, and this set the metrical

[1] 'Plut.' *Mus.* 3.
[2] Id. 7 for the nomes of Olympus; 'Suid.' s.v. νόμος for the nomes of Terpander.
[3] Wilamowitz, *T.G L.* pp. 7–8.

pattern for the words. The simplest form of composition was to repeat the same tune several times, and this meant a series of strophes each of which was composed on precisely the same metrical plan. This seems to be the system in Alcman's Maidensong, and is often used by Pindar and Bacchylides. But there were ways of varying this, perhaps because it was thought more lively to introduce a change without spoiling the essential formality of the whole, perhaps because, as songs grew in length, a division between singers became necessary and called for some such adjustment. The main form of variation in choral poetry was to compose not in single strophes but in triads. Each triad was a whole which balanced metrically with every other triad, but inside it, while the strophe and the antistrophe were composed on one plan, the epode was composed on another. It is not likely that such an arrangement can be found in Alcman's Maidensong, but it appears in Ibycus' poem to Polycrates and may well have been the invention of Stesichorus,[1] who seems to have composed on a large scale and would have found it useful in relieving his choir of too prolonged an effort. A second variation, of which we have no example and know very little, was to change the metre in the second half of the poem. We hear on good authority that in a poem of fourteen stanzas Alcman made the first seven in one metre and the second seven in another.[2] Though, so far as we know, this did not appeal to Pindar and Bacchylides, it may ultimately be responsible for a third variation which we find in some choral songs of Attic tragedy, in which each pair of strophe and antistrophe has a new plan. But despite these variations choral song remained formal and regular until the latter part of the fifth century, when a revolution in music broke the old rules of composition and introduced a far greater freedom of movement.

The choral song was in origin and character largely religious. It was sung at festivals and solemn occasions, and to the end kept many marks of the hymn. Even when its secular forms attained a new dignity in the sixth century and human beings were celebrated as fully as gods, it still showed signs of its beginnings, and

[1] 'Suid.' s.v. τρία Στησιχόρου· στροφήν, ἀντιστροφήν, ἐπωδόν. ἐπῳδικὴ γὰρ πᾶσα ἡ τοῦ Στησιχόρου ποίησις. καὶ τὸν τελέως ἄμουσόν τε καὶ ἀπαίδευτον λοιδοροῦντες ἔφασκον ἂν οὐδὲ τρία τὰ Στησιχόρου εἰδέναι.

[2] Hephaest. p. 74, 17 Consbruch, γράψας γὰρ ἐκεῖνος δεκατεσσάρων στροφῶν ᾄσματα τὸ μὲν ἥμισυ τοῦ αὐτοῦ μέτρου ἐποίησεν ἑπτάστροφον, τὸ δὲ ἥμισυ ἑτέρου.

there can be no doubt that some of its most characteristic features are due to its religious connexions. Three main features, which may be seen in almost every surviving ode of Pindar and Bacchylides, all seem to be developments from ancient usage. First, there is a story or myth. Pindar sometimes omits the myth or reduces it to insignificant dimensions, but on the whole he employs it, even if its connexion with his main theme is not always clear to us. The myth nearly always tells of gods or heroes and seems to be a survival from a time when every choral song was directly concerned with them. The myth of Alcman's Maidensong, for instance, is surely relevant to the Spartan festival for which he writes, and the long heroic stories of Stesichorus may have been related to the cults of Sicily or the Peloponnese. Myths did for a choral song what sculpture did for a temple. They illustrated the importance of a rite by depicting episodes in legend which concerned the gods and their relations to men.

A second traditional characteristic was the maxim. It was commonly connected with the myth and made to underline its lessons. Pindar, like Alcman before him, likes to draw conclusions from his stories and to point out some universal truth in them. But maxims were not limited to this and might be introduced at any point on any issue. They were an integral part of Greek religious life. They taught men how to behave before the gods and before other men and were as necessary to poetry as lessons from the Bible were to the sculptors and glass-painters of the Middle Ages. If to a more sophisticated society they sometimes seem a little obvious, that is no argument against their sincerity or even their truth. The Greeks liked to drive them home in simple words or with an apt illustration. They may not always be instinct with poetry, but they provided something which the Greeks expected from their poets, who were concerned with religious occasions and would have neglected their duty as servants of the gods if they had not pronounced judgements on human duty and destiny. In this respect the choral poets are far removed from Homer, whose judgements are nearly all implicit and whose moral appeal is made more to the emotions than to the intellect. The difference exists because Homer composed not for religious occasions but for the pleasure of his patrons, who wished to hear of the heroic past and not to be told about his own notions of behaviour.

A third characteristic of choral poetry is personal references and remarks. The poet speaks freely about his patrons and his friends and even about himself, and in this too he differs from Homer, who hardly mentions himself and makes no allusion to existing society except indirectly through similes. Here the distinction is, perhaps, to be explained by the conditions in which the poems were sung. The choral poet composed for others to sing, and these represented not an individual but a society. So when the poet speaks of himself or praises his hosts or patrons, he speaks as one who interprets the meaning of the occasion and has behind him the authority of the gods. It is more his public than his private self which speaks. It is true that Alcman allows a greater degree of intimacy and even badinage than Pindar, but the difference is superficial. The praise which Alcman bestows on his young girls' beauty is relevant to the occasion of his songs. Even if his manner seems unduly familiar for a religious occasion, that is only because he interprets the festival as the right time for gaiety, and his mood would be shared by all who took part. The choral poet gave voice to the traditional and accepted meaning which a feast had for its participants. Therefore, when he spoke in the first person, he was in some sense the gods' spokesman, who stated what had to be stated and fulfilled the requirements of the ceremony.

Monody stands apart from choral song, although its development was roughly parallel. If it had a pioneer who opened new vistas to it, it was a great poet who was not strictly a λυρικός or included in the Alexandrian canon of the Nine. Archilochus of Paros expressed himself mainly in elegiac and iambic verse, but he helped the growth of lyrical poetry in two directions. First, he spoke unashamedly about himself. His frankness horrified, while it delighted, posterity, and his songs of hate struck Pindar as an awful example of the harm that a man's tongue can do to him.[1] But he also wrote freely of love and war, of simple affections and charming scenes. The matter of his poetry is not fundamentally very different from that of Alcaeus or Sappho or Anacreon. All these poets write of what is uppermost in their minds because they want to write about it and seldom for any other reason. Compared with them the writers of martial elegiacs like Callinus and Tyrtaeus are almost the voices of regiments, and even so delightful a poet of love as Mimnermus seems more to give a philosophy

[1] *Pyth.* 2. 54–56.

WINGATE COLLEGE LIBRARY
WINGATE, N. C.

of love than to recount his own personal feelings. Archilochus exploits his own personality as a subject for poetry. He is still sufficiently close to the heroic world to feel that his own honour and his own emotions are of paramount importance.[1] Like the injured Achilles, he broods upon his wrongs and feels that nothing can compensate for them. He speaks entirely for himself, and in this respect he anticipates personal monody. Secondly, Archilochus exploited the powers of vernacular speech as a vehicle for poetry. If in his elegiacs he uses the traditional language of the epic, in his other poems he uses a more vivid, contemporary speech, rich in metaphors and colloquialisms.[2] In this he was the forerunner of other notable poets. Greek monody kept on the whole to vernacular speech, and by this means maintained its contemporary character. Its poets were not primarily concerned with the heroic past or with the timeless truths of religion. They wrote for themselves and their friends, and they used a language which was closely related to their ordinary talk.

But though Archilochus did something important for lyric monody, some of its most characteristic features lay outside his art. Many of its themes are too traditional for his revolutionary and strongly personal taste. The songs which Sappho wrote for weddings or Alcaeus' lament of a love-sick girl go back to remoter origins than Archilochus' emphatically up-to-date themes. Moreover, his metres are not those of these poets. The metres of Sappho and Alcaeus, in all their melodious variety, are mostly developments of simple traditional metres such as the different forms of the Glyconic and the Ionic. Archilochus was a brilliant metrist, rich in invention, but he built his stanzas more from iambic, trochaic, and dactylic elements than from the traditional metres of song. His influence was greater on the tone and language of monody than on its technique, and his true successors were not Sappho and Alcaeus but Semonides and Hipponax. He put the self into poetry, but he himself preferred an art which was closer to speech than to song.

The two main classes of lyric poetry, choral song and monody, provide our best record for the two centuries in which Greece passed from the age of Homer into the scientific and critical fifth century. They record the thoughts and feelings of representative

---

[1] W. Jaeger, *Paideia*, i, pp. 164–6.
[2] A. Hauvette, *Archiloque*, pp. 266–78.

men and women who gave voice to what stirred their joy or
anger or prompted them to anxious meditation or high flights of
the imagination. They provide illuminating evidence for an age
which was both splendid in itself and pregnant with vast issues
for coming generations. Of this period we have, except for a few
inscriptions, no contemporary history, and even the rich remains
of its plastic and pictorial art tell us far less than the broken
remnants of its poetry. These scattered lines and incomplete
quotations are not only contemporary records, worth more than
the traditions preserved in later historians; they are in themselves
the relics of an art, which if it had survived complete, would be
one of the wonders of the world. If it lacks the imaginative scope
and the intellectual strength of Attic tragedy, it has a spontaneity
and freshness which are among the highest gifts of poetry. For
the student of literature the fragments present a double task. In
the first place they raise many problems that belong to literary
scholarship. Their development may be traced, their origins
examined, their meaning elucidated. In the second place, they
concern the historian. They may be set in their historical context
and related to the societies which produced them and on which
they are the most vivid commentary. They grew from the social
circumstances of their time, and without some consideration of
these they cannot be properly understood. These two branches
of inquiry are closely related and often overlap, but to neglect
either one or the other is to mutilate the subject and to give a
false impression of an art which was essentially part of life and
whose record calls for the literary critic no less than the historian.

II. ALCMAN

OUT of the bewildering tangle of names and dates which makes the early history of musical development at Sparta a man, and a poet, emerges. Alcman is the first choral poet of Greece of whose work anything solid survives, and he summarizes in himself the various activities which had gone to the making of lyric poetry and the mixed influences which shaped Spartan culture in the seventh century. His dates and his origin are matters of dispute, and certainty about them may well be out of reach. Yet it seems possible to pick our way through the confusing testimonies and to construct a tentative theory for them. His dates are variously given. First, 'Suidas' says: 'he lived in the 27th Olympiad (672–669 B.C.), when Ardys, the father of Alyattes, was king of the Lydians'.[1] This will not do as it stands, for Ardys was not the father of Alyattes. But if we assume that 'Alyattes' is a slip for 'Sadyattes', the entry is not impossible; for Ardys, according to Herodotus,[2] reigned from 679 to 630 B.C., and 'Suidas'' date for Alcman would fall early in the reign. It is true that the later chronographers put the reign from 663 to 626 B.C., but since 'Suidas' is known to follow Herodotus on this point, it is clear enough what he meant. The connexion between Alcman and Ardys cannot be lightly dismissed. It may mean that Alcman mentioned the king in some poem, and that the mention was dated by later scholars by some recognized event. Secondly, Eusebius places Alcman in the fourth year of the 30th Olympiad (657 B.C.). This is not inconsistent with 'Suidas'' date, but seems to have been determined by special considerations, and we may perhaps see what they were. 'Suidas'' date is the seventh year of Ardys by the Herodotean chronology, Eusebius' date the seventh year by another. It looks as if both knew of the seventh year but dated it differently.[3] In fact the seventh year of this reign was about 646 B.C., since we know from Assyrian records that Gyges, whom he succeeded, was killed fighting the Gimirrai, or

---

[1] s.v. Ἀλκμάν. ἦν δ' ἐπὶ τῆς κζ' 'Ολυμπιάδος, βασιλεύοντος Λυδῶν Ἄρδυος τοῦ Ἀλυάττου πατρός.　　　　　[2] I. 16. I.

[3] E. Rohde, *Rh. Mus.* xxxiii (1878), pp. 199 ff.

Cimmerians, in 652 B.C. But, despite these little variations, the evidence so far suggests that Alcman was alive and active in the middle of the seventh century. This would be as good as we could expect if Eusebius did not give a second date for him in the second year of the 42nd Olympiad (612 B.C.), and this is hardly consistent with the earlier date. We cannot surmise the reason for this, but it too may have been based on some passage in Alcman now lost to us. It is true that it is given as a minority opinion, 'ut quibusdam uidetur,' but there may none the less have been a reason for it, and even if Alcman referred to some event in the seventh year of Ardys, his reference need not necessarily have been contemporary. Between these two views we may perhaps mention the statement of 'Suidas' that Stesichorus was younger than Alcman,[1] and since Stesichorus' birth is put in 632 B.C., this would slightly favour the earlier date. There the matter must stay. It is at least clear that Alcman lived in the seventh century and may have been active in the middle of it.

Alcman's origin is also a matter of dispute. In antiquity there were two views of it. It was all very well for Antipater to say that 'many are the mothers of minstrels', πολλαὶ μητέρες ὑμνοπόλων,[2] but the matter was seriously discussed. On the one hand, Aristotle, followed by the Pergamene scholar Crates of Mallus, said that Alcman was a Lydian from Sardis,[3] and this view was familiar to Alexander (probably Aetolus),[4] Velleius Paterculus,[5] and Aelian.[6] On the other hand 'Suidas' reports the view that Crates was wrong and that Alcman was a Laconian from Messoa.[7] Leonidas of Tarentum knew of the controversy but did not take sides in it,[8] and Heraclides Ponticus says that Alcman was the slave of a Spartan called Agesidas, who gave him his freedom because of his skill,[9] and though we must not put too much trust in this, it suggests that Alcman may possibly have been a slave of foreign origin. In this controversy we may perhaps see how ancient scholars came to such opposing conclusions. In such a matter they would surely base their views on the poet's own words, and the words in question may be some which have survived:

[1] s.v. Στησίχορος.   [2] Anth. Pal. 7. 18. 6.
[3] Ox. Pap. 2389, fr. 9, col. i. 12; 'Suid.' s.v. Ἀλκμάν.
[4] Anth. Pal. 7. 709.
[5] 1. 18. 2.   [6] V.H. 12. 50.
[7] s.v. Ἀλκμάν.   [8] Anth. Pal. 7. 19.
[9] Const. 2.

οὐκ ἦς ἀνὴρ ἀγρεῖος οὐδὲ
σκαιὸς οὐδὲ πὰρ †σόφοισιν
οὐδὲ Θεσσαλὸς γένος,
Ἐρυσιχαῖος οὐδὲ ποιμήν,
ἀλλὰ Σαρδίων ἀπ' ἀκρᾶν.[1]

He was no rustic boor, nor a lubber, nor among the skilled (?), nor a Thessalian by race, nor a shepherd from Erysiche, but from lofty Sardis.

If here Alcman is really speaking of himself, then there is no doubt that he came from Sardis. That he could refer to himself in the third person is clear from frs. 49. 4; 51; and 92. 1. Indeed it was natural for him to do so, since, though he wrote the songs, they were sung by choirs of which he was not a practising member. That he came from Sardis can be argued on more than one ground. First, the lines about lofty Sardis come from the beginning of a Maiden-song,[2] and in such a place it might be appropriate to speak of himself in the third person. Secondly, Alcman knows something about Asia Minor and mentions Asiatic peoples like the Ἀννίχωροι, Εἰβηνοί, and Ἐσσηδόνες, places like Ἀσσός and Γάργαρος, and the river Xanthus, and uses foreign words like κακκαβίς and μαγαδίς. Thirdly, in the seventh century Sparta seems to have imported poets from abroad. Terpander came from Lesbos, Thaletas from Crete, and even Tyrtaeus' origins were connected with Athens. We cannot be certain that Alcman came from Sardis, but it is at least possible that he did. His name Ἀλκμάν is the Doric form of the Ionic Ἀλκμέων,[3] and when at one place he uses Ἀλκμάων,[4] it looks as if he were transliterating the original not into its true Doric equivalent but into a form that might pass muster at Sparta. On this whole topic we are not

---

[1] Fr. 13 D. In 1 ἀγρεῖος is Lobel's correction of the MSS. ἄγριος, and is justified by *Ox. Pap.* 2389, fr. 9, col. i. 14 and Aristoph. *Nub.* 655. In 2 παρὰ σόφοισιν of the MSS. is unmetrical, and πὰρ σόφοισιν at least restores the metre, as παρ' ἀσόφοισιν does not. But it is hard to give any cogent meaning to σόφοισιν unless Alcman means that he is neither a boor nor a professional bard. The right solution has not yet been found. Lobel deletes οὐδ' before Ἐρυσιχαῖος for metrical reasons. In general Alcman seems to be claiming that he is not a bumpkin. For this view of the Thessalians cf. Eur. *Phoen.* 1407 ff.; Aristoph. *Vesp.* 1271 ff. Erysiche is in Acarnania (Steph. Byz. s.v.); Schol. Ap. Rhod. 4. 972 interprets the reference ἐρυσίχαιον, τῷ χαίῳ ἐρύοντα ἤγουν ποιμαίνοντα.

[2] Steph. Byz. s.v. Ἐρυσίχη. παρ' Ἀλκμᾶνι ἐν ἀρχῇ τοῦ δευτέρου τῶν παρθενείων ᾀσμάτων.

[3] Bechtel–Fick, *Die griechische Personennamen*, p. 89.

[4] Fr. 51 D.

likely to learn much more. The dispute about Alcman's origins
was lively in antiquity, when Aristotle and others were thought
to have been misled by the lines just quoted about Sardis.[1] Nor is
it of great importance. In Sparta Alcman lived and worked, and
with it, and with no other place in Greece, his name is connected.
There he seems to have stayed till he died and was buried 'near
the plot of Sebrus'.[2]

The world in which Alcman lived has been in some small
measure unveiled by archaeology and discredits the familiar
notion of Sparta as a severe, repressive place. It had its own
delightful arts, its gay and charming ceremonies. It practised
song and dance to a high degree and expected its girls no less
than its boys to take part in them. Its trade extended to Phoenicia
and Egypt, and the cult of local deities favoured an indigenous
school of ivory-carving. Though we cannot recover the political
conditions which made it possible, it is clear enough that at some
period in the seventh century Sparta was occupied with the
Second Messenian War, but we do not know its date or whether
Alcman lived before or during or after it. One small hint suggests
that he knew something about it. A broken papyrus commentary
on him mentions $\Lambda\epsilon\omega\tau\upsilon\chi\iota\delta\alpha\varsigma$ $[\Lambda]\alpha\kappa\epsilon\delta\alpha\iota[\mu\text{ον}\iota]\omega\nu$ $\beta\alpha\sigma\iota\lambda\epsilon\upsilon\varsigma$,[3] and this
seems to indicate that this king appeared somehow and some-
where in Alcman's poetry. He is known to Herodotus as the six-
teenth in descent from Heracles and fourth back from his namesake
who was king of Sparta at the beginning of the fifth century.[4]
Rhianus adds that he was king of Sparta at the beginning of the
Second Messenian War,[5] and though Rhianus is not to be trusted
on all points, he may be right on this. If Alcman mentioned him,
it looks as if he touched on one personality connected with the
war, and we cannot assume that he ignored the war altogether in
his poetry. The fragments indeed say nothing explicit of it, and
Alcman does not seem to have celebrated war as Tyrtaeus did.
This may be because it was not a very suitable subject for his
Maiden-songs or because he himself found it uncongenial. His
claim is rather that he throws a light on Sparta which we should
not surmise from Tyrtaeus and that he is mainly concerned with
the ceremonies in which the Spartans relaxed and enjoyed themselves. Even when he says

[1] *Ox. Pap.* 2389, fr. 9. 11 ff.   [2] Paus. 3. 15. 2.
[3] *Ox. Pap.* 2390, fr. 2. col. ii. 14–15.   [4] 8. 131. 2.   [5] Paus. 4. 15. 2.

ἕρπει γὰρ ἄντα τῶ σιδάρω τὸ καλῶς κιθαρίδδην¹

'for against the steel comes the fine playing of the lyre', he may as well refer to the relief of song after military exercises as to peace after war. In his fragments we must not look for historical facts but for the expression of the Spartan spirit at its least formidable and most engaging.

Alcman inherited a flourishing tradition in music and poetry. In the seventh century the Spartans imported poets and musicians from abroad, and in Sparta two different streams met and united with remarkable results. One came from Crete, the other home of the Dorian people and ancient seat of Dorian ways. Little enough is known of Thaletas of Gortyn, who composed for the lyre songs which exhorted to civil obedience and unity,² and looks like a lyrical counterpart to Tyrtaeus. A second stream came from Aeolian and Ionian lands and must have owed much to music as it had developed in Asia. Terpander of Lesbos, Olympus of Phrygia, and Polymnestus of Colophon were all important figures at Sparta. They were primarily musicians who wrote famous tunes, and their disciples had great successes with winning prizes at the Spartan Carneia.³ Their musical innovations and the new opportunities which these created opened up unexploited possibilities for poetry. Polymnestus indeed seems to have been a poet of a very different character from Thaletas. His songs were said to be gay,⁴ and perhaps he favoured that festal element which is so attractive in Alcman. Since Alcman is known to have mentioned him,⁵ he may in some sense have been Alcman's master. In general the way for Alcman was prepared by a burst of musical innovation and invention. Tunes were composed for the flute and the lyre, and in the rich cycle of its festivals Spartan life offered full opportunities for a poet who could interpret the spirit of its rites and ceremonies.

If musical development extended the scope of choral poetry, Alcman seems also to have profited by other developments of a more strictly literary kind. In the seventh century the Ionian

¹ Fr. 100 D. The text is uncertain, and there is much to be said for Scaliger's change of ἕρπει to ῥέπει. Plutarch (*Lyc.* 24) quotes the words to show that the Spartans were μουσικωτάτους ἅμα καὶ πολεμικωτάτους.

² Plut. *Lyc.* 4. 1.   ³ 'Plut.' *Mus.* 6.

⁴ Hesych. s.v. Πολυμνήστειον ᾄδειν· εἶδός τι μελοποιίας . . . ἦν δὲ Κολοφώνιος μελοποιὸς ὁ Πολύμνηστος, εὐμελὴς πάνυ; Cratin. fr. 305 K; Aristoph. *Equ.* 1287.

⁵ 'Plut.' *Mus.* 5.

epic was becoming known at Sparta. Evidence for this may be seen in the discovery of an ivory comb, of the early seventh century, which depicts the Judgement of Paris, and though this is mentioned only once in the *Iliad*,[1] it is fundamental to the story, and its appearance at Sparta shows that the episode was known at an early date. The arrival of the epic art at Sparta lies behind two traditions, first that Terpander set Homer's lines to music to be sung at games,[2] and second that the Homeric poems were brought to Sparta by Lycurgus.[3] The first sounds likely enough, and though Lycurgus is largely a mythical figure, to whom almost anything Spartan can be attributed, at least the story suggests that the poems were established with some authority before the sixth century. These pieces of evidence mean not that the *Iliad* and the *Odyssey*, as we know them, were recited at Sparta in the seventh century, but that the art of Ionian epic, with its special, traditional language and its wide range of stories, found here a new public. That the epic style was widely known even in the eighth century is clear from its appearance on vases in places so widely apart as Athens, Ithaca, and Ischia. In all three cases hexameters appear which look Homeric in their manner, though not in their contents,[4] but are not sufficiently close to Homer to justify us in thinking that they are based on the *Iliad* or the *Odyssey*. They belong to the ancient and far-spread art of epic recitation, which Homer doubtless learned and practised, but which contained formulaic phrases and traditional stories beyond his own repertory. Even the Judgement of Paris must have been told before Homer, and its appearance on the comb implies no more than a knowledge of the story in some form or other. The spread of the epic, in this wide sense, is the historical fact behind the alleged appearance of the Homeric poems in Sparta in the time of Lycurgus. 'Homer' was the name to which most early heroic poetry was ascribed, and there is no need to think that such works were limited to the *Iliad* and the *Odyssey*.

Echoes of epic formulas may be seen in Alcman, and look like traditional phrases formed in the first case for the epic and then adapted to lyric. When he speaks of ἵππον παγὸν ἀεθλοφόρον καναχάποδα,[5] he does indeed recall the πηγοὺς ἀθλοφόρους which

---

[1] *Il.* 24. 25 ff.; K. Reinhardt, *Von Werken und Formen*, pp. 12 ff.
[2] 'Plut'. *Mus.* 3.   [3] Plut. *Lyc.* 4. 4; Ael. *V.H.* 13. 14; Dio Chrys. 2. 45.
[4] See C. M. Bowra, *Homer and his Forerunners*, pp. 6–7.   [5] Fr. 1. 48 D.

Agamemnon offers to Achilles,[1] but καναχάποδα is not a Homeric word, though it may belong to some epic tradition outside Homer, since it appears in the *Certamen* in the phrase καναχήποδες ἵπποι. Again, when Alcman says

$$Ζεῦ πάτερ, αἲ γὰρ ἐμὸς πόσις εἴη[2]$$

'Father Zeus, would that he were my husband', he inevitably recalls Nausicaa's words

$$αἲ γὰρ ἐμοὶ τοιόσδε πόσις κεκλημένος εἴη,[3]$$

but even here the form of words may have been in common usage and ready for such an occasion whenever it arose. Thirdly, when Alcman says

$$δύσπαρις, αἰνόπαρις, κακὸν Ἑλλάδι βωτιανείρᾳ[4]$$

'evil Paris, dread Paris, curse to Hellas nurse of men', not only is his Ἑλλάδι βωτιανείρᾳ a current epic phrase, since the adjective occurs in Homer, Hesiod, and the Hymn to Apollo,[5] but δύσπαρις, αἰνόπαρις suggests some connexion with the Homeric δύσπαρι, εἶδος ἄριστε.[6] Yet δύσπαρις may have been traditional to the story, and αἰνόπαρις, which does not occur in Homer, may be equally traditional and the ancestor of Aeschylus' Πάριν τὸν αἰνόλεκτρον[7] and Euripides' Πάρις αἰνόγαμος.[8] Alcman was certainly well acquainted with the epic manner and adapted its formulas to his own purposes. He was also aware of an episode familiar to us from the *Odyssey* but not necessarily current everywhere in the form that we know. When Alcman says

$$καί ποτ' Ὀδυσσῆος ταλασίφρονος ὦαθ' ἑταίρων$$
$$Κίρκα ἐπαλείψασα[9]$$

and Circe once, having anointed the ears of the companions of strong-hearted Odysseus,

he recalls the passage in the *Odyssey* where the sailors of Odysseus have their ears filled with wax to stop them from hearing the songs of the Sirens.[10] But there is a difference. Alcman says that Circe herself did this; Homer that Odysseus did it at Circe's instructions.[11] The difference is slight, but it suggests that Alcman

---

[1] *Il.* 9. 124, 266.   [2] Fr. 16 D.   [3] *Od.* 6. 244.
[4] Fr. 73 D.   [5] *Il.* 1. 155; *Ox. Pap.* 1369, col. i. 16; Hom. Hymn 3. 363.
[6] *Il.* 3. 39; 13. 769.   [7] *Ag.* 713.   [8] *Hel.* 1120.
[9] Fr. 80 D. The text and the metre are uncertain.   [10] *Od.* 12. 177.
[11] *Od.* 12. 47 ff.

followed a version of the story which was not quite the same as that in our *Odyssey*.

For Alcman this knowledge of epic language and subjects may have served a special purpose. He certainly wrote poems in hexameters, and it is possible that these were like the προοίμια κιθαρῳδικὰ ἐν ἔπεσιν which were attributed to Terpander.[1] These προοίμια must be like the Homeric Hymns, which are so called by Thucydides,[2] and would presumably be recited rather than sung, and performed not by a choir but by a single bard. Of the existing Homeric Hymns none shows any signs of a connexion with Sparta, but among the remains of Alcman's poetry are a few lines whose character is well explained if we regard them as coming from such 'preludes'. This form seems to have enabled the bard to forsake the impersonal anonymity of the epic and to say something about himself, as in the Delian Hymn to Apollo the poet goes out of his way to speak of 'the blind man who lives on rocky Chios' and to commend his verses to the audience.[3] On these famous lines centuries of legend depend, but whatever conclusions we draw, it is clear that the poet assumes for himself an importance such as Homer never does. We cannot but feel that when the Hymn was performed, the bard had become a public character, performing at a national occasion, and was free to make claims for himself which he would not have made if he were singing, like Demodocus or Phemius, at the court of some king. So too when Alcman speaks of himself in the first person in hexameters, it is likely that his lines come from a similar kind of prelude, sung before some other song, which need not have been narrative and may well have been choral. On this point four lines of his must speak for themselves:

> οὔ μ' ἔτι, παρθενικαὶ μελιγάρυες ἱμερόφωνοι,
> γυῖα φέρην δύναται· βάλε δή, βάλε κηρύλος εἴην,
> ὅς τ' ἐπὶ κύματος ἄνθος ἅμ' ἀλκυόνεσσι ποτῆται
> νηδεὲς ἦτορ ἔχων, ἁλιπόρφυρος εἴερος ὄρνις.[4]

no longer, maidens with honey tones and voices of desire, can my limbs carry me. Would, ah, would that I were a kingfisher, who flies with the halcyons over the flower of the wave, having a fearless heart, the sea-blue, sprightly bird!

---

[1] 'Plut.' *Mus.* 3.   [2] Thuc. 3. 104. 4.
[3] Hom. Hymn. 3. 166 ff.
[4] Fr. 94 D. In 4 εἴαρος of the MSS. cannot be a genitive, 'of the spring', and εἴερος is the suggestion of W. Schulze, *Quaestiones Epicae*, p. 212.

These exquisite and beautiful lines find an echo in so many hearts
that they are easily taken as a simple expression of the desire for
escape which runs through all romantic poetry and has, in its
imagery of birds, parallels in Anacreon[1] and Euripides.[2] But we
may well doubt whether Alcman wrote in this spirit. Antigonus
of Carystus, who quotes the lines, explains them in a different
way. He says that the males of the halcyons are called κηρύλοι,
and when they grow old and are no longer able to fly, their
females carry them. 'Even so', he continues, 'Alcman says that
he is weak from old age and unable to be whirled round with the
choir and the dancing of the maidens.'[3] In other words, Alcman
uses a half-mythical piece of bird-lore to express how he wishes
that he could still join in the dance, from which old age bars
him, and would like to be carried off by the maidens. The point of
the myth is perhaps strengthened by the belief that the halcyons
appeared in winter, and Alcman seems to compare his old age
with this. The words are surely written for a real situation, and
we can hardly avoid thinking that the girls taking part in the
dance acted the role of Ἀλκυόνες. Bird-dances were common in
Greece,[4] and there is no difficulty in thinking that in Sparta a
dance imitated halcyons. The meaning of the lines is then quite
clear. Alcman is unable to join in the dance and makes full use of
its symbolism to express his regrets and his vain hopes.

Another line, also a hexameter and also personal, and therefore likely to come from a προοίμιον, may be seen in

$$\text{Πολλαλέγων ὄνυμ' ἀνδρί, γυναικὶ δὲ Πασιχάρηα.}^{5}$$

This is interpreted by Aristides to mean—'let the man speak, and
the woman be content with whatever she hears',[6] and Blass conjectured that the words came at the end or the beginning of some
long piece by the poet, to which the maidens had to listen in
silence.[7] The piece would contain a story or lesson, and to keep
his audience in good humour Alcman invents the playful, nursery
names of Πολλαλέγων and Πασιχάρηα, 'Say-much' and 'Glad-at-
everything'. This interpretation depends on the assumption that

---

[1] Fr. 52 D.   [2] *Hipp.* 732 ff.   [3] *Hist. Mir.* 27.

[4] See L. H. Lawler, *C.J.* xxxvii (1942), pp. 351–62.

[5] Fr. 95 D.

[6] 15. 32. S. Wide, *Lakonische Kulte*, p. 245, suggests that the names belong to
'ein Chthonisches Götterpaar'.

[7] *Rh. Mus.* xl (1885), p. 24.

Πολλαλέγων is the same as πολλὰ λέγων, but this is not the only possibility. It might be the same as πολλ' ἀλέγων, and in support of this we may quote the Homeric name of an old man, Οὐκαλέγων,[1] which can mean nothing but 'Care-not'. This suggests that Πολλαλέγων could mean 'Care-much', and then the contrast between the man and the woman takes a different look. While the woman enjoys everything, the man has to take trouble about it and look after it, and surely this is what we might expect Alcman to say about his own relation with his women or girl singers. He carries the responsibility and has to see that everything is in order, while what they have to do is to enjoy the whole proceeding. In these preludes Alcman seems to have spoken or sung of his relations with his choir and of his own feelings. These self-revelations were not confined to these preludes, and Alcman, like Pindar, sometimes makes his choir speak for him in the first person as if they embodied him, or rather as if both embodied the Muse. If the line on Paris[2] comes from such a prelude, it suggests that mythological references were at home in them. In general the remains of these preludes suggest that Alcman has moved some distance beyond the art of the Homeric Hymns. His matter is more personal and more closely related to his choir, and in the fragments that survive, his technique is different in that it uses no spondees but pure dactyls throughout. This may of course be an accident, but it seems more likely to be deliberate, and perhaps the regularity of the metrical system suggests that these poems were sung in a more true sense than were the Homeric Hymns, which may have been merely intoned or even recited. By this means Alcman brought the προοίμια of Terpander closer to lyric art and may have made them part of it.

If Alcman derived some of his form and manner from προοίμια, he derived other matter, suited to lyrical presentation, from other kinds of hexameter verse. First, he seems to have been interested in cosmogonical questions, and for this he had a precedent in Hesiod's *Theogony*. But his approach, so far as we can recover it, seems to have been quite different. A papyrus commentary[3] on him gives the facts in rather a rambling and confused way, but the general theory seems to have been something

---

[1] *Il.* 3. 148; cf. Verg. *Aen.* 2. 311; Iuv. 3. 199. [2] Fr. 73 D.
[3] *Ox. Pap.* 2390, col. iii, with Lobel's commentary.

like this. In the beginning was ὕλη, which was 'troubled and unmade'. We can hardly believe that Alcman actually used the word ὕλη, but we do not know what word he used, unless it was πάντα. Next someone set this ὕλη in order, and to our surprise it is Thetis, who is said to work on it as a smith works on bronze, and here perhaps we may catch a glimpse of an image which Alcman himself used. After Thetis appeared πόρος, which is the way of contriving things and sets them going. Lastly comes τέκμωρ the 'boundary' or 'end'. In the relics of early Greek cosmogonies Alcman's stands independent and alone. It has a mythical side, but it also tries to relate myth to physical and mental processes. In his conception of an original ὕλη he is not far from Hesiod's Chaos, but when he sets Thetis to work he seems almost to anticipate Thales, who made water the ἀρχή of everything.[1] His introduction of πόρος is confirmed by another passage in his poetry, where Πόρος is closely related to Αἶσα[2] and seems to stand for initiative as opposed to destiny. Finally, τέκμωρ takes the place of τέλος in the later philosophers. The combination of πόρος and τέκμωρ secures the result that light and darkness exist and relics of Alcman's own words for this survive:

ἆμαρ τε καὶ σελάνα καὶ τρίτον σκότος.[3]

One of these powers was called πρέσγυς, 'old man', rather as elsewhere Αἶσα and Πόρος are called θιῶν γεραιτάτοι, and no doubt this was Alcman's way of asserting the seniority of the pre-Olympian deities whom he sets to work. His account of the creation is more than mythological and anticipates some of the methods of the first Greek physicists, and incidentally shows how much these owed to the speculations of poets. In Alcman we see the first rays of the Ionian enlightenment, and watch how he moves forward from Hesiod to something more abstract and more scientific.

Another kind of hexameter poetry which Alcman used for

---

[1] Diog. Laert. 1. 27. H. Lloyd-Jones suggests to me that Thetis may perhaps be introduced because of the apparent connexion of her name with τίθημι. Cf. schol. ad Lyc. 22 (p. 23 Scheer) Θέτις ἡ θάλασσα ὅτι εὐθεσίας αἰτία· συναχθέντος γὰρ κατ' ἀρχὰς τοῦ ὕδατος ἐφάνη ἡ ξηρὰ καὶ γέγονε τοῦ πάντος εὐκοσμία, Schol. T. Il. 1. 399 φησι . . . Θέτιν . . . τὴν θέσιν καὶ φύσιν τοῦ πάντος. The idea has of course been subjected to some changes, but it may well be ancient and go back to Alcman.

[2] Fr. 1. 14 D.

[3] The words cannot quite be Alcman's as they stand, if only for metrical reasons. But they may be an abbreviated version of his actual words.

lyric purposes was concerned with marvels and wonders and strange beings on the edge of the known world. The most famous example of such poetry was the *Arimaspea* of Aristeas of Proconnesus, who seems to have lived early in the seventh century.[1] We cannot be sure that Alcman knew this actual work, but he evidently knew the kind of tales that it told, which look as if they came from Asia, where Greeks learned them from barbarian peoples. Aristides says of him:

Elsewhere, in priding himself on the number of people where his renown is known, he gives a list of so many and so peculiar peoples that even now learned men try to find where in the world they exist.[2]

Some of these peoples were certainly mythical, like the Σκιάποδες[3] or Shadow-feet, who were said to use their feet as parasols,[4] and the Στεγανόποδες, whose name suggests some connexion with the sea and must mean 'Web-feet'.[5] Not much less legendary were the Rhipaean Mountains, which were said to be beyond Scythia on the boundary of the fabulous Hyperboreans and credited, according to Aristotle, with mythical attributes.[6] Alcman saw them with the eye of imagination and wrote:

$$\text{'Ρίπας ὄρος ἀνθέον ὕλᾳ}$$
$$\text{νυκτὸς μελαίνας στέρνον}^{7}$$

the mountain of Rhipe, aflower with forests, the breast of black night.

It is possible that he thought them to be shrouded in eternal night, rather as Homer's Cimmerians are shrouded in mist and cloud, and in this he was followed by Sophocles when he spoke of ἐννυχιᾶν ἀπὸ 'Ριπᾶν.[8] The forest of which Alcman speaks was known later to Herodotus.[9] Alcman also mentioned the Essedones, whom later geographers placed on the frontier of China,[10] and whom Herodotus places on the edge of the known world beyond the 'Bald Men'.[11] More curious and perhaps more instructive

---

[1] H. T. Wade-Gery, *The Poet of the Iliad*, p. 75.

[2] 2. 508. [3] Ibid.

[4] Strab. 43; 299; Scylax ap. Philostrat. *Vit. Apoll.* 3. 47; Plin. *N.H.* 7. 2. 23.

[5] This is the normal meaning of the word, and there is no need to connect them with the Σκιάποδες; see C. M. Bowra, *C.Q.* N.S. vi (1956), pp. 3–4.

[6] *Meteor.* 1. 13. 19. [7] Fr. 59 D.

[8] Soph. *O.C.* 1248. [9] 4. 22.1.

[10] Steph. Byz. 'Ισσηδόνες; Ptol. *Geogr.* 8. 24. 3.

[11] 4. 25–27.

is the adjective Κολαξαῖος, which Alcman gives to a horse.[1] It
would be wrapped in mystery if Herodotus had not recorded a
curious account of the first king of Scythia called Colaxais, from
whom the sea-faring section of the Scythians claimed descent.[2]
Alcman introduces the adjective so naturally that it must have
been familiar to his audience, and may have come from some
recent and popular work.

With this kind of education in music and song Alcman set
about his creative task with an obvious confidence. That he felt
himself in some sense inspired is clear from his references to the
Muses, but he also knew that he had to invoke them and that
they were indeed strange and powerful. We must take him
literally when he speaks of them, and though they had of course
been canonized by centuries of poets, Alcman deals with them
in a new way and shows that they have a special meaning for
him. They are in the first place 'Ολυμπιάδες,[3] and that connects
them with the gods. Others might make them the daughters of
Zeus and Mnemosyne, or Memory, but though at one place
Alcman seems to combine the two words in Μῶσαι Μναμοσύνα,[4]
we do not know the context, and it is unlikely that he made
Memory the mother. He certainly made the Muses the daughters
of Uranus and Ge, of Heaven and Earth,[5] and this not only gives
to them a revered position but proclaims their ancient place in
the scheme of things. Yet at times he seems to have felt that this
was not quite sufficient, and he calls them daughters of Zeus.[6]
For this inconsistency an explanation may be found. Mimnermus
is reported to have said that the earlier Muses were the daughters
of Uranus and the later of Zeus,[7] and no doubt in this he distinguished between the older and younger members of the divine
party which governed the nine arts. Some of these arts might
indeed be regarded as having less seniority than others, and
Alcman may have held the same view. In any case he exalts the
Muses to a high position and leaves no doubt of the importance
which he attaches to them. When he summons a Muse to help
him he does so with formality and respect, knowing that she is
not his servant and that he must rely on her good will in composition. He is aware that his songs are new, and that may be one

[1] Fr. 1. 59 D.   [2] Hdt. 4. 5. 2.
[3] *Ox. Pap.* 2387, fr. 1. 1.   [4] *Ox. Pap.* 2389, fr. 4, col. ii. 9.
[5] Diod. 4. 7. 1.   [6] Frs. 40 and 67 D.   [7] Paus. 9. 29. 4.

of the reasons why he does not connect the Muses with Mnemosyne, but goes straight to his own need:

> Μῶσ᾽, ἄγε, Μῶσα λίγηα, πολυμμελές,
> αἰενάοιδε, μέλος νεοχμὸν
> ἄρχε παρσένοις ἀείδην.[1]

Hither, Muse, clear-voiced Muse, singer for ever of many tunes, and begin a new lay for maidens to sing.

So he summons Calliope by name and explains to her the kind of song which he wishes to compose:

> Μῶσ᾽, ἄγε, Καλλιόπα, θύγατερ Διός,
> ἄρχ᾽ ἐρατῶν ἐπέων, ἐπὶ δ᾽ ἵμερον
> ὕμνῳ καὶ χαρίεντα τίθη χόρον.[2]

hither, Muse, Calliope, daughter of Zeus, begin the lovely songs, set desire on our hymn, and make our dance graceful.

Here the neat words convey a full weight of meaning. The Muse is to start the song going, but she has also to make the singers feel ἵμερος as they sing their hymn, and show χάρις in their dance which accompanies it. This is a true account of how the creative spirit works and of what the poet desires from it. Nor was Alcman unaware of what it does for a man when it comes to him. His words

> ἁ Μῶσα κέκλαγ᾽ ἁ λίγηα Σηρήν[3]

'the Muse has raised her voice, the clear-voiced Siren' mean that the Muse has answered his prayer and filled him with that sense, which the poet knows, of speaking through him, and the words which she gives him are like those of a Siren, in that they cast enchantment on all who hear them. Their clear tones leave no doubt of their appeal or their meaning, and it is impossible to resist them. Alcman speaks of the creative process with knowledge and insight and lays considerable emphasis on its divine origin and its powerful effects.

Alcman combines this main theory with another which is not very different from it and may be equally ancient, even if it comes from a rather less exalted outlook. In Greek legend the discovery of music was first made in imitation of the songs of birds,[4] and the myth not only embodies the simple truth that

---

[1] Fr. 7 D. [2] Fr. 67 D. [3] Fr. 10 D.
[4] Plut. *de Soll. Anim.* 20; cf. Lucr. 5. 1378 ff.; Chamael. ap. Athen. 9. 390 a.

every poet at some time or other sings for no reason except that he must, but also hints that the singer knows the secrets of nature, as did the famous birds and prophets of the past, like Calchas and Mopsus.[1] Alcman is aware of this belief and refers explicitly to it when he says:

$$οἶδα δ' ὀρνίχων νόμως$$
$$πάντων,[2]$$

'I know the tunes of all birds'. In this he proclaims both the wide range of his own song and the intimate knowledge of nature which is his. But there may be more in it than this. He may well suggest that it is from the birds that he has learned to sing. For this is the claim which he makes elsewhere, perhaps at the end of a long song, for himself:

$$ἔπη δέ γε καὶ μέλος Ἀλκμὰν$$
$$εὗρε γεγλωσσαμένον$$
$$κακκαβίδων στόμα συνθέμενος.[3]$$

Alcman found words and tune by giving heed to the tongued speech of partridges.

The partridge was known for its sharp chatter, indicated by the use of the word κακκαβίζειν,[4] and in comparing his own spate of words with it Alcman takes advantage of the old connexion between human songs and the songs of birds and half laughs at himself in the comparison. He may well have known something of shamanistic notions in which men understood the songs of birds, and he admits some relation to them, but he keeps any hint of it well in hand and is content for it to be little more than an image well suited to his own purpose.

Alcman was known to posterity chiefly as a writer of παρθένια or Maiden-songs. This type of choral hymn was known in Ionia and in Athens, but it found a distinctive form in Sparta, where girls were brought up to learn singing and dancing in honour of the gods.[5] The songs were accompanied by the flute,[6] and the choirs who performed them were chosen from the daughters of prominent families and enjoyed a delightful freedom of speech to each other or to their choir-master, Alcman. When he

---

[1] Hes. fr. 160 R.   [2] Fr. 93 D.
[3] Fr. 92 D.; see B. Marzullo, *Rh. Mus.* xcviii (1955), pp. 73–94.
[4] Aristot. *H.A.* 536 b 14.   [5] Schol. Theocr. 18. 22.
[6] Athen. 4. 176 f.

wrote words for them, no convention prevented him from putting
on their lips his own sentiments or ideas, but he was fully conscious of their claims and feelings and enjoyed an easy relation
with them, as when he makes them praise him for his skill with
the lyre:

ὅσαι δὲ παῖδες ἁμέων
ἐντί, τὸν κιθαριστὰν αἰνέοντι,[1]

'all of us who are young praise the lyre-player'. Conversely, just
as he makes his maidens speak freely of himself, so he makes
them speak freely of one another, and display their emotions
without restraint or shyness. His poetry conveys a happy air of
interchange between choir and choir-master, and it was perhaps
for this reason that in later times he was regarded as the originator
of love-songs. It may be doubted whether he ever wrote quite so
straight from the heart as Sappho did, but he certainly used the
language of love, even if he did so half playfully. Athenaeus
indeed says that he loved a poetess Megalostrata,[2] but some lines
which refer to her bear rather a different interpretation:

τοῦτο ϝαδηᾶν ἔδειξε Μωσᾶν
δῶρον μάκαιρα παρσένων
ἁ ξανθὰ Μεγαλοστράτα[3]

this gift of the sweet Muses has been revealed by one happy among
maidens, fair-haired Megalostrata.

The gifts of the Muses were many and various, and perhaps
Megalostrata had some special talent for song or dance which
delighted Alcman and made him praise her for it. In themselves
the words provide no evidence that he was in love with her.

At the same time Alcman gives to his maidens sentiments
which are essentially meant for them and not for himself. Since
at Sparta they lived on terms of free emotional intimacy with one
another, and no shame was felt about speaking frankly of their
attachments, we may suspect that words thought to describe
Alcman's own passions were in fact written for others. When, for
instance, he wrote

Ἔρος με δαῦτε Κύπριδος ϝέκατι
γλυκὺς κατείβων καρδίαν ἰαίνει,[4]

[1] Fr. 20 D.
[2] Athen. 13. 600 f. τῆς Μεγαλοστράτης οὐ μετρίως ἐρασθείς, ποιητρίας μὲν οὔσης
δυναμένης δὲ καὶ διὰ τὴν ὁμιλίαν τοὺς ἐραστὰς προσελκύσασθαι; cf. 'Suid.' s.v. Ἀλκμάν.
[3] Fr. 102 D. [4] Fr. 101 D.

'Io again, at the Cyprian's command sweet Eros distils and melts my heart', he may have been speaking about himself, but it is equally possible that, since the lines come from a choral poem, they were written for someone else and are in this sense dramatic. In either case they have their own distinction and aptness, and the image in them is original and charming. So too when Alcman writes

Ἀφροδίτα μὲν οὐκ ἔστι, μάργος δ' Ἔρως οἷα ⟨παῖς⟩ παίσδει
ἄκρ' ἐπ' ἄνθη καβαίνων, ἃ μή μοι θίγῃς, τῶ κυπαιρίσκω.[1]

It is not Aphrodite but wild Eros who plays like a child, as he comes down over the topmost flowers of the clover—touch them not, I beg,

he is surely not speaking of himself, since the comparison between the lover and the flowers which careless young Love treads down suggests that the lover is more probably a young girl than a grown man. This delicate art has an air of detachment and impartiality, as if the poet were writing not for himself but for others whom he understands and with whom, from a little distance, he sympathizes. He is therefore able to depict, as it were from the inside, what his maidens felt for one another and to display their emotions in a language and an imagery suitable to girls on the verge of womanhood. Since he wrote about girls who would be known to everyone in his audience, he had no need to introduce or explain them, and he moves straight into the heart of his matter with an ease which may leave us gasping to know what he really means. For instance, in a recently published papyrus the remains of a Maiden-song seem to celebrate the beauty of a single girl, and we are left with the impression that the whole company is in love with her, and no doubt this is what Alcman intended his audience to feel. The singers use the first person singular, and it does not matter whether each speaks for herself or for a composite, choral personality; for the aim of the song is the celebration of a girl's beauty and charm which everyone is assumed to feel. After addressing the Olympian Muses and referring to the coming song the choir speaks of the effect which it will have on others and themselves:

ὕπνον ἀπ]ὸ γλεφάρων σκεδ[ά]σει γλυκὺν
αἶψα, πόσο]ς δέ μ' ἄγει πεδ' ἀγῶ[ν'] ἴμεν,
ἔνθα μάλ]ιστα κόμα[ν ξ]ανθὰν τινάξω.[2]

[1] Fr. 36 D.
[2] Ox. Pap. 2387, fr. 1. 7-9. I have supplied αἶψα, πόσο]ς exempli gratia.

(The song) will scatter sweet sleep from their eyelids at once, and desire drives me to go to the contest, where in truth I shall toss my yellow hair.

The song will awake everyone, and the singers will toss their hair in the delighted excitement of singing. Then, after a gap whose length we cannot estimate, the papyrus continues with praise of a girl called Astymeloisa, and the language is infused with love:

> λυσιμελεῖ τε πόσῳ, τακερώτερα
> δ' ὕπνω καὶ σανάτω ποτιδέρκεται·
> οὐδέ τι μαψιδίως γλυκῆ[α κ]ήνα.
>
> Ἀ[σ]τυμέλοισα δέ μ' οὐδὲν ἀμείβεται,
> 5   ἀλλὰ τὸ]ν πυλεῶν' ἔχοισα
> ὤ] τις αἰγλά[ε]ντος ἀστὴρ
> ὠράνω διαιπετὴς
> ἢ χρύσιον ἔρνος ἢ ἁπαλὸ[ν ψίλ]ον
> – [ ] ‿ –
> 10 – ‿ ‿ –]διέβα ταναοῖς ποσί
> – ‿]ομος νοτία Κινύρα χ[άρ]ις,
> ἅ τ' ἐπὶ π]αρσενικᾶν χαίταισιν ἴσδει.
>
> – ‿‿ Ἀ]στυμέλοισα κατὰ στρατὸν
> – ‿ –]μέλημα δάμῳ
> 15 – ‿ – τι]μὰν ἐλοῖσα[1]

with longing that loosens the limbs, and she casts glances that are more melting than sleep and death, and not at all in vain is she sweet. Astymeloisa answers me not, but, holding the garland, like a star that falls through the glittering sky or a golden shoot or tender down ... she has come with long steps ... the moist charm of Cinyras which is set on maidens' hair. ... Astymeloisa in the host ... a darling to the people ... having won honour ....

There is no doubt that, despite all the gaps and uncertainties, Astymeloisa is praised in the language of powerful love. Her glances, more melting than sleep and death, the comparison of her in turn with a shooting star, a golden shoot, and tender down, and the statement of the general admiration and love for her leave no doubt of what the poet intends his audience to think. The language, more figurative than that of Sappho and more direct than that of Ibycus, conveys with passionate attention

---

[1] *Ox. Pap.* 2387, fr. 3. 1–15. I suggest τὸ]ν in 5, ἅ τ' in 12, and τιμὰν in 15.

what is felt about this girl, and though these may not be Alcman's own feelings, there is no doubt that he understands them
to the full and knows how to present them as if they were. The
occasion concerns everyone present to such an extent that Alcman
is able to speak for everyone and through his art to show what
such beauty in a girl really means.

The appearance of the word πυλεῶνα in this poem seems to
indicate that it was sung at a festival of Hera; for πυλεών could
be used in Sparta for a garland offered to Hera.[1] The situation is
that Astymeloisa carries it to the goddess, and the choir sings of
her as she does so. This is no doubt the implication of the words
διέβα ταναοῖς ποσί, and the public nature of the occasion is revealed by κατὰ στρατόν and δάμῳ. Hera was a goddess of birth
and of children, over whom she watched until they were married,
and was responsible for their strength and health. It was therefore appropriate that girls should bring offerings to her and quite
in order that they should commend the beauty of one of their
number chosen for the chief task. In what looks like a fragment of
another poem Alcman makes the girl who carries the πυλεών
speak of herself:

> καὶ τὶν εὔχομαι φέροισα
> τόνδ' ἐλιχρύσω πυλεῶνα
> κἠράτω κυπαίρω.[2]

to thee also I pray, as I bring this garland of casidony and lovely
galingale.

Fortunately some light on the ceremony is thrown by Pliny the
Elder, who says of *cyperus* that it is 'a root of present help against
the bites of serpents and scorpions. When drunk it opens the
veins',[3] and of *heliochrysus*, that 'others call it chrysanthemum; it
has white stems, sub-white leaves, like abrotonoum; its leaves of
three ounces in weight mixed in white wine stop the flux of
women'.[4] These pieces of popular lore help to explain the Spartan
ceremony. It was concerned with Hera as a goddess of health and
growth, and makes it easier to understand why the girls who take
part in it rejoice in the physical attractions of Astymeloisa.

Even more intimately connected with girls was Artemis, the
goddess of maidenhood and childbirth, of wild animals and wild
places. She is to women what Apollo is to men, the spirit of

---

[1] Athen. 15. 678 a; cf. Wide, p. 29. [2] Fr. 24 D.
[3] *N.H.* 21. 15 (71). 118. [4] Ibid. 25 (96). 168–9.

purity and independence, who appeals to the more austère and
ascetic side of the Greek character. At Sparta she played a large
part and, though she was worshipped under a large number of
titles, she had her most notable shrine as Artemis Ortheia. This,
dating back to the ninth century, has been uncovered, and the
mass of dedicated objects shows its enduring popularity. As the
goddess of unmarried maidens, she was honoured by them with
songs and dances, and some details of her rites survive. The
Lacedaemonian Women of Aristophanes' *Lysistrata* summon her
to join their celebrations over the conclusion of peace:

> ἀγροτέρα σηροκτόνε,
> μόλε δεῦρο, παρσένε σιά,
> ποττὰς σπονδάς.[1]

huntress, slayer of wild beasts, come hither, divine maiden, to our
libations.

In the country round Sparta feasts were held in honour of
Artemis at Diktynnaion[2] and Limnai.[3] At the temple of Ortheia
legend told that Helen was carried off by Theseus when she was
dancing there,[4] and this suggests that dances formed part of its
ceremonial. For other dances there is good evidence. As Κορυ-
θαλία Artemis was honoured by dancers called κορυθαλίστριαι.[5] If
κορυθάλη is really a synonym for δάφνη, the ceremony would be
a tree-cult, but this has been questioned, and it is thought that
it was held in honour of Artemis as the protectress of young
children.[6] At it dances were held of a lively and ridiculous character, and wooden masks were worn.[7] Another feast was celebrated
at Caryae on the Arcadian frontier, and at it there was an annual
performance of a local dance. καρύα means 'walnut tree' and the
dance was performed by Spartan girls of the best families, who
carried plaited baskets on their heads, presumably with offerings
for the goddess.[8] Another curious dance was that in which cakes
shaped like breasts were brought to her and a hymn of praise to
the 'Maiden' was sung by a choir of girls.[9] For ceremonies of
this kind Alcman must have written songs; for the rhetorician

---

[1] *Lys.* 1262–4.   [2] Paus. 3. 24. 9.
[3] Ibid. 4. 4. 2; 4. 31. 3; Strab. 362.   [4] Plut. *Thes.* 31. 3.
[5] Athen. 4. 139 a; Hesych. s.v. κορυθαλίστριαι· αἱ χορεύουσαι τῇ Κορυθαλίᾳ θεᾷ;
id. s.v. κυριττοί· οἱ ἑλόντες τὰ ξυλινὰ πρόσωπα κατὰ Ἰταλίαν, καὶ ἑορτάζοντες τῇ
Κορυθαλίᾳ γελοιασταί.   [6] Wide, p. 123.
[7] Hesych. s.v. κορυθαλίστριαι.   [8] Paus. 3. 10. 7; Poll. 4. 104.
[9] Athen. 14. 646 a.

Menander says that 'Alcman summons Artemis from countless mountains and countless cities and from rivers too.'[1] Allowing for a little exaggeration, we can hardly deny that Alcman wrote for a variety of festivals in honour of Artemis. Little enough survives of his songs, but some few facts can be put together.

He certainly wrote a hymn for her festival as 'Maiden'; for the line

$$\theta\rho\iota\delta\alpha\kappa\iota\sigma\kappa\alpha\varsigma \ \tau\epsilon \ \kappa\alpha\iota \ \kappa\rho\iota\beta\alpha\nu\omega\tau\dot{\omega}\varsigma^{2}$$

'cakes and baked loaves' is expressly referred to it. He seems to have called himself

$$\dot{A}\rho\tau\dot{\epsilon}\mu\iota\tau\sigma\varsigma \ \theta\epsilon\rho\dot{\alpha}\pi\sigma\nu\tau\alpha^{3}$$

'servant of Artemis', and he addresses her as

$$\dot{A}\rho\tau\epsilon\mu\iota, \ \dot{\rho}\dot{\upsilon}\tau\epsilon\iota\rho\alpha \ \tau\dot{\sigma}\xi\omega\nu^{4}$$

'Artemis, drawer of the bow'. It may be she whom he describes as

$$\dot{\epsilon}\sigma\sigma\alpha\mu\dot{\epsilon}\nu\alpha \ \pi\dot{\epsilon}\rho\iota \ \delta\dot{\epsilon}\rho\mu\alpha\tau\alpha \ \theta\eta\rho\dot{\omega}\nu^{5}$$

'clothed in the skins of wild beasts'. These fragments are the merest flotsam and jetsam, casual wreckage of poetry, but they show that Alcman saw Artemis as a goddess of hunting and wild creatures, and was at home in her cults and her ceremonies.

With Artemis neither Athene nor Aphrodite seems to compare in importance. Athene had indeed her Brazen House where she received a ritual procession of young warriors, and maidens danced in front of her.[6] Alcman may have addressed her in the words

$$\sigma\dot{\upsilon} \ \gamma\dot{\alpha}\rho \ \dot{\epsilon}\gamma\dot{\omega}\nu\gamma\alpha, \ \dot{\varphi}\dot{\alpha}\nu\alpha\sigma\sigma\alpha, \ \Delta\iota\dot{\sigma}\varsigma \ \theta\upsilon\gamma\dot{\alpha}\tau\epsilon\rho^{7}$$

'for not I, O queen, daughter of Zeus', and he seems elsewhere to have told of her sturdy handling of a Giant in battle.[8] But beyond this the fragments say nothing. Nor is there much evidence for Alcman's connexion with Aphrodite. She had her place in Sparta, and Lucian says that at dances held in her honour songs were sung which summoned her and the Loves to join in the festivities.[9] Alcman clearly composed such a song for her, of which the opening lines survive:

---

[1] Ed. Spengel, iii, p. 334.   [2] Fr. 63 D.; Athen. 3. 114 f.
[3] Fr. 64 D.   [4] Fr. 65 D.   [5] Fr. 62 D.
[6] Paus. 3. 17. 2; Polyb. 4. 35.2; Aristoph. *Lys.* 1300; Plut. *Lyc.* 5; Schol. Eur. *Hel.* 228; 245.   [7] Fr. 25 D.
[8] Fr. 28 D. The text is too uncertain to be restored.   [9] *de Salt.* 11.

Κύπρον ἱμερτὰν λιποῖσα
καὶ Πάφον περριρύταν[1]

'leaving lovely Cyprus and sea-girt Paphos'. In this she is not treated as a specifically Spartan goddess but invoked from her shrines on the eastern edge of the Greek world, and the poem must have been a κλητικὸς ὕμνος in which she was summoned from elsewhere to ceremonies held in her honour. Alcman may well have written hymns for the rites of Athene and Aphrodite, but the evidence for them is almost entirely lacking.

Outside this circle of goddesses, with whose worship girls were naturally concerned, there was a god who, despite his ancient status which goes back to Mycenaean times, never seems to fit very comfortably into the Olympian circle. Dionysus was accepted in Sparta and had a place there, and some remarkable lines of Alcman survive which have been persuasively connected with his ministrants:

> πολλάκι δ' ἐν κορυφαῖσ' ὀρέων, ὅκα
> θεοῖσι ϝάδη πολύφανος ἑορτά,
> χρύσιον ἄγγος ἔχοισα, μέγαν σκύφον,
> οἷά τε ποιμένες ἄνδρες ἔχουσιν,
> χερσὶ λεόντεον ἐγ γάλα θεῖσα
> τυρὸν ἐτύρησας μέγαν ἄτρυφον
> ἀργεϊφόνταν.[2]

often on the mountain-peaks, when the feast with its many torches delights the gods, holding a golden vessel, a great can, such as shepherd men carry, you set in it with your hands the milk of a lioness and make a great cheese, unbroken and shining white.

The lines are well explained as referring to nocturnal revels of Bacchants on the mountains.[3] like those described by Euripides in the *Bacchae*. The epithet πολύφανος 'with many torches', shows that the feast is at night, and as such it accords well with the Dionysiac love of παννύχιοι χοροί.[4] In it the person addressed

[1] Fr. 35 D.
[2] Fr. 37 D. The only serious problem is the last word. The MSS. of Athenaeus give ἀργειοφόνται, but *Gramm. Hamburg.* (*Rh. Mus.* x, p. 256) says τύρος ἐντηρήσας μέγαν ἀργύφαν ἀργιφόντα, which perhaps indicates that the word is an adjective which agrees with τυρόν. ἀργιφόνταν is wrong metrically; ἀργύφεόν τε of the Aldine edition of 1514 is good sense, but perhaps too remote from the MSS. In these uncertain circumstances we may perhaps read ἀργεϊφόνταν, which suits the metre and may be used not in the Homeric way, of which the meaning is really unknown to us, but as some variant on the theme of brightness.
[3] Bergk, *P.L.G.*[4] i, p. 50.   [4] Eur. *Bacch.* 862.

milks a lioness. Bacchants were credited with miraculous powers,
especially over wild beasts, and Tzetzes noted the milking of
lionesses as typical of the powers of Dionysus.[1] Adherents of his
cult drew a special strength from the flesh of wild animals, and
no doubt a lioness's milk would be equally beneficial, just as
Tzetzes, drawing on some unknown poet, says that Bacchants
ate lions raw.[2] So the person whom Alcman addresses milks a
lioness and makes cheese from the milk. But who is she? She can
hardly be a human being, since in his time there would be no
lions on Taygetus and such a feat would surely be beyond the
powers of any human Bacchant. She may be a nymph, for the
Nymphs were the usual companions of Dionysus,[3] or she may be
a goddess, for many goddesses are associated with him. It looks as
if Alcman were addressing some divine or half-divine being, and
of course such a part may have been acted by a human being in
a Dionysiac ceremony. The details certainly suggest a rite. The
cheese, which looks like an offering to the god, recalls the smooth,
flat cheeses which were offered in sacrifice in Crete,[4] and the great,
golden vessel recalls the vessels of the Athenian Panathenaea.
We may surmise that the lines describe a rite, and that this rite
embodied a myth about one of the less usual activities ascribed
to the companions of Dionysus.[5]

To this degree we can connect some fragments of Alcman's
poetry with the gods for whom it was written, and even see how
he fitted his maidens into it. Though he deals with many subjects, his poetry has an intimate character, which reveals how
well he understood these ceremonies from the inside and saw
what they meant to the participants. He is deeply interested in
the thoughts and feelings of his choirs and makes them an essential
part of his structure. The degree to which he does this, and the
difficulties which it causes to us, may be seen from the longest
extant example of his work, the remains of a Maiden-song on a
papyrus found in 1855 near the second pyramid of Sakkarah and
now in the Louvre. The poem consisted of at least ten strophes
composed on the same metrical plan, and though it is possible to
divide each into strophe, antistrophe, and epode, this is unlikely,

---

[1] Aristid. *Or.* 41. 7.   [2] ad Lyc. 143.
[3] Soph. *O.T.* 1105 ff.   [4] Athen. 14. 658 d.
[5] W. Den Boer, *Laconian Studies*, pp. 264 ff., connects the lines with Hermes,
who seems hardly suitable for such a part.

since it makes the epode unduly long, and this method of division was said to be the work of Stesichorus, whose career falls later than Alcman's. Of the eight surviving strophes the first three tell a myth; the second five are concerned with the immediate occasion and the girls who take part in it. While the first part is badly preserved, the second part presents difficulties of interpretation so formidable that almost every single sentence has been disputed. This poem is the earliest example of Greek choral song which is preserved on any scale, but it shows some characteristics which are familiar from Pindar—the illustrative myth, the instructive maxims, and the personal references. Though its temper is unlike almost anything in Pindar, it is an early example of a tradition which he inherited and maintained.

The main part of the myth, with which the papyrus begins, is concerned with the destruction of Hippocoön and his sons. The papyrus seems to begin with the eighth line of the third strophe, and in it Alcman clearly gave some account of the fighting and named the fallen. Supplements are unusually hazardous, and the text is best presented with those which are reasonably certain because they come from the marginal scholia or from ancient quotations. We start with what looks like a battle and end with general considerations to be drawn from it:

$$
\begin{array}{ll}
&]\Pi\omega\lambda\upsilon\delta\epsilon\upsilon\kappa\eta\varsigma \\
& o\dot{\upsilon}\kappa\ \dot{\epsilon}\gamma\dot{\omega}]\nu\ \Lambda\upsilon\kappa\alpha\iota\sigma o\nu\ \dot{\epsilon}\nu\ \kappa\alpha\mu o\hat{\upsilon}\sigma\iota\nu\ \dot{\alpha}\lambda\dot{\epsilon}\gamma\omega \\
& {}'E\nu\alpha]\rho\sigma\phi\dot{o}\rho o\nu\ \tau\epsilon\ \kappa\alpha\dot{\iota}\ \Sigma\dot{\epsilon}\beta\rho o\nu\ \pi o\delta\dot{\omega}\kappa\eta \\
&]\nu\ \tau\epsilon\ \tau\dot{o}\nu\ \beta\iota\alpha\tau\dot{\alpha}\nu \\
5 &]\ .\ \tau\epsilon\ \tau\dot{o}\nu\ \kappa o\rho\upsilon\sigma\tau\dot{\alpha}\nu \\
& E\dot{\upsilon}\tau\epsilon\dot{\iota}\chi\eta]\ \tau\epsilon\ \digamma\dot{\alpha}\nu\alpha\kappa\tau\dot{\alpha}\ \tau'\ {}'A\rho\dot{\eta}\ddot{\iota}o\nu \\
&]\dot{\alpha}\ \tau'\ \dot{\epsilon}\xi o\chi o\nu\ \dot{\eta}\mu\iota\sigma\dot{\iota}\omega\nu.
\end{array}
$$

$$
\begin{array}{ll}
&]\nu\ \tau\dot{o}\nu\ \dot{\alpha}\gamma\rho\dot{o}\tau\alpha\nu \\
&]\mu\dot{\epsilon}\gamma\alpha\nu\ E\ddot{\upsilon}\rho\upsilon\tau\dot{o}\nu\ \tau\epsilon \\
10 &]\pi\dot{\omega}\rho\omega\ \kappa\lambda\dot{o}\nu o\nu \\
& {}'A\lambda\kappa\omega\nu\dot{\alpha}]\ \tau\epsilon\ \tau\dot{\omega}\varsigma\ \dot{\alpha}\rho\dot{\iota}\sigma\tau\omega\varsigma \\
&]\pi\alpha\rho\dot{\eta}\sigma o\mu\epsilon\varsigma \\
&]\dot{\alpha}\rho\ A\dot{\iota}\sigma\alpha\ \pi\alpha\nu\tau\hat{\omega}\nu \\
& \kappa\alpha\dot{\iota}\ \Pi\dot{o}\rho o\varsigma]\ \gamma\epsilon\rho\alpha\iota\tau\dot{\alpha}\tau o\iota \\
15 & \sigma\iota\hat{\omega}\nu\cdot\ \dot{\alpha}\pi]\dot{\epsilon}\delta\iota\lambda o\varsigma\ \dot{\alpha}\lambda\kappa\dot{\alpha}\cdot \\
& \mu\dot{\eta}\ \tau\iota\varsigma\ \dot{\alpha}\nu\theta]\rho\dot{\omega}\pi\omega\nu\ \dot{\epsilon}\varsigma\ \dot{\omega}\rho\alpha\nu\dot{o}\nu\ \pi o\tau\dot{\eta}\sigma\theta\omega \\
& \mu\eta\delta\dot{\epsilon}\ \pi\eta]\rho\dot{\eta}\tau\omega\ \gamma\alpha\mu\hat{\eta}\nu\ \tau\dot{\alpha}\nu\ {}'A\phi\rho o\delta\dot{\iota}\tau\alpha\nu \\
& \digamma]\dot{\alpha}\nu[\alpha]\sigma\sigma\alpha\nu\ \ddot{\eta}\ \tau\iota\nu'
\end{array}
$$

]η παῖδα Πόρκω
20   Χά]ριτες δὲ Διὸς δ[ό]μον
]σιν ἐρογλεφάροι.[1]

Polydeuces. Among the dead I count not Lycaesus (but) Enar-
sphorus and swift-footed Sebrus and . . . the violent . . . and . . .
the helmeted, and Euteiches, and king Areius, and . . . greatest of
demi-gods . . . the gatherer . . . the great, and Eurytus, throng of . . .
the best . . . we shall (not) pass over. (They were conquered) by Doom
and Device, oldest of all gods. Their valour was without foundation.
Let not any man fly to the sky, nor try to marry Aphrodite . . . the
queen, or any . . . daughter of Porcus . . . and the Graces, with love in
their looks . . . the house of Zeus.

In the surviving text there are five names, and these may be
supplemented with some confidence by Εὐτείχη in 6, which comes
from an independent quotation from the poem, and by Ἄλκωνα
in 11, which is the only known name of a son of Hippocoön that
suits the metre at this point. Attempts have been made to find
other names in Apollodorus[2] and Pausanias,[3] who give eleven
between them. But we may doubt whether Alcman's list agreed
at all points with later traditions. First, the scholiast says that
Lycaethus, whom Apollodorus makes a son of Hippocoön, was
a son of Derites, and that must be why Alcman speaks of him as
he does. Secondly, neither Apollodorus nor Pausanias mentions
Ἀρήϊον of 6, but the scholiast says that he was known to Pherecydes under the name of Ἀρήϊτον. Thirdly, it is almost impossible,
for metrical reasons, to introduce any of the names, except that of
Alcon, given by Apollodorus and Pausanias into our text. We
must therefore rest content with what names we have, and not
attempt to increase the list.

The story of Hippocoön and his sons is told by Apollodorus,[4]
and turns on the vengeance which Heracles took on them for
killing Oeonus, the son of Licymnius and cousin of Heracles.
Pausanias confirms the main outlines of this tale, but adds that
Heracles in his first attack was wounded and withdrew. He then
returned and slew Hippocoön and his sons.[5] Our text does not
mention Heracles, and there is no place where he could easily be
introduced, but we can hardly doubt that he was. Sosibius, the

---

[1] Fr. 1 D. Supplements are 2 οὐκ ἐγὼν Schol. Pind. *Ol.* 11. 15 a. 6 Εὐτείχη An.
Ox.; Cramer, 1. 158. 31. 11 Ἄλκω]να Bergk. 14 καὶ Πόρος e scholl. Blass. 15 σιῶν Blass.
[2] *Bibl.* 3. 10. 5.   [3] 3. 15. 3 ff.
[4] *Bibl.* 2. 7. 3.   [5] 3. 15. 5.

Laconian commentator on Alcman, speaks of the wounding of
Heracles in the fight with the sons of Hippocoön and says that it
was told by Alcman in his Book I,[1] and this must surely be our
poem. On the other hand none of the later versions of the story
mentions Polydeuces, who certainly had a place in Alcman's
version of it, and this suggests that Alcman told the tale differently. From him surely comes the story of the wounding of
Heracles and the consequent division of the struggle into two
parts. From him too may come a rather different version of the
reasons for the struggle. In referring to what seems to be this
poem Clement says that the sons of Hippocoön were ἀντιμνηστῆρες
of the Dioscuri, and this theme must also come from the poem.[2]
It would explain the fight, as well as the appearance of Polydeuces, in the text of Alcman. We do not know how far this was
combined with other motives that Heracles may have had for
the destruction of Hippocoön and his sons, and we cannot even
be certain that any other motive was given. The remains point to
a scene of slaughter but do not explain its cause.

In the second stanza the destruction seems to have been followed and perhaps concluded by general considerations of a kind
familiar in choral poetry. First Αἶσα and Πόρος clearly played
a part, and it must have been in deciding the issue against
Hippocoön. They seem to have been called γεραιτάτοι σιῶν, and
this would accord well with what the papyrus commentary on
Alcman says about Πόρος. Just as somewhere else he makes it
a shaping power in his cosmology, and evidently means it to
signify 'Device' in the sense of the intelligence which shapes
situations, so here he must have done something of the same
kind. Αἶσα must be fate or doom, just as for Homer it is the
destiny with which a man is born and which in the end settles
his death for him.[3] When Αἶσα and Πόρος are combined, it
means that what has to be happens, but the means by which it
happens is the wits of men, in this case the wits of Heracles and
the Dioscuri. Secondly, this is followed by the mysterious words
ἀπέδιλος ἀλκά. It is natural to take ἀπέδιλος in the sense of
'unsandalled', but if we do, the meaning is hard to find. Page

<hr />

[1] Clem. Alex. *Protr.* 36 Σωσίβιος δὲ καὶ τὸν Ἡρακλέα πρὸς τῶν Ἱπποκωντιδῶν
κατὰ τῆς χειρὸς οὐτασθῆναι. Schol. in *Protr.* i, p. 308 Stählin ὁ Ἡρακλῆς . . . αὐτὸς
τήν χεῖρα ἐπλήγη. μέμνηται καὶ Ἀλκμὰν ἐν α′.

[2] J. A. Davison, *Hermes*, lxxiii (1938), p. 433; Page, *Alc. Parth.* 32.

[3] *Il.* 20. 127.

suggests that it should be taken in a single sentence with the next line,[1] but it seems exaggerated to make ἀλκά fly. A second possibility is that ἀπέδιλος ἀλκὰ is a complete phrase which stands on its own and implies some kind of helplessness in that an unshod warrior cannot fight. But why are the sons of Hippocoön unshod, or indeed what has such a meaning to do with battle? A third possibility is that the words means 'hurried', and this at least has the support of the only other occasion where it appears in Greek poetry.[2] But this would imply that the sons of Hippocoön took to flight, whereas in fact they stood their ground and were killed. It looks as if all these suggestions were on the wrong lines and that ἀπέδιλος has in fact nothing to do with sandals. It can be far better explained by Pindar's ἀδαμαντοπέδιλοι κίονες, 'based on adamant'.[3] In that case ἀπέδιλος ἀλκά is 'valour unfounded'. The sons of Hippocoön had their share of courage, but it was not properly based on heroic worth, and that is why they were killed. Finally, Alcman proceeds to give warnings against flying to the sky or marrying Aphrodite or 'a daughter of Porcus', and his admonitions anticipate later poets. Pindar warns a young victor in the Pythian Games

ὁ χάλκεος οὐρανὸς οὔ ποτ' ἀμβατὸς αὐτῷ[4]

'he may never climb the brazen sky', and by the image stresses the limits of mortal achievement and glory. In the *Prometheus Bound* of Aeschylus the Chorus, shocked by the spectacle of Io, say

μήποτε, μήποτέ μ', ὦ
πότνιαι Μοῖραι, λεχέων Διὸς εὐνά-
τειραν ἴδοισθε πέλουσαν.[5]

never, O never, O mistress Fates, may ye behold me a bride of the bed of Zeus.

To aspire beyond the limitations of the mortal state is to invite disaster, and this is what the sons of Hippocoön seem to have done. Yet it is possible that Alcman means his advice to be rather more precise than the parallels in Pindar and Aeschylus might suggest. If indeed they were suitors, and presumably violent suitors, for the daughters of Tyndareüs, they might well be thought guilty of presumption, and the maxims would apply

---

[1] *Alc. Parth.* p. 34. [2] Aesch. *P.V.* 135.
[3] Pind. fr. 78–79. 13 Bo. I owe this suggestion to H. Lloyd-Jones.
[4] *Pyth.* 10. 27. [5] *P.V.* 894–6.

to them with special force. Who the daughter of Porcus was we do not know, but she too must have been beyond the reach of ordinary men and was perhaps some daughter of a sea-god.[1] The section ends with a reference to the Graces doing something to or in the house of Zeus, and though we cannot say what they do, we may presume that the contrast is between the disastrous failures of the sons of Hippocoön and the untroubled life on Olympus.

The third strophe is much more fragmentary even than the second, and very little can be made of it. It clearly refers to more destruction, as 27 ὦλεσ᾽ ἤβα and 32 Ἀΐδας show. Since it refers to an arrow, ἰῷ, at 30 and to a marble millstone, μαρμάρῳ μυλάκρῳ, at 31 Diels ingeniously suggested that it dealt with the war of the Gods against the Giants;[2] for in the war Poseidon tore off a great block of rock from the island of Cos and with it overwhelmed the Giant Polybotes. The rock became the island of Nisyrus,[3] and Strabo says that the island was rich in millstones and like one to look at.[4] Yet both arrows and big stones were used in heroic warfare by men,[5] and the word ἤβα does not seem very appropriate to the Giants. The battle may have been human after all, and it may not have been one battle but a series of examples to enforce the lesson already drawn from the sons of Hippocoön. It can hardly refer to them, since they have been settled and dismissed, but it may well have referred to others not unlike them, from whom another severe lesson may be drawn:

ἄλαστα δὲ
35 ϝέργα πάσον κακὰ μησαμένοι.

for their evil machinations they suffered things not to be forgotten.

The lesson of the dangers of violence is evidently emphasised and driven home with new examples, and that is the end of the part of the poem which deals with a myth.

The remaining five strophes of the poem take us to within four lines of its close and are concerned with personal matters relevant to the occasion at which the song is sung and to the girls who take part in the ceremony. Even when it is well preserved, it bristles with problems and must be approached with circumspection from the start:

[1] Page, *Alc. Parth.* pp. 38–42.   [2] *Hermes,* xxxi (1896), p. 347.
[3] Apollod. *Bibl.* 1. 6. 2.   [4] 489.
[5] *Il.* 7. 270; 12. 161; Pind. *Nem.* 10. 67; Apollod. *Bibl.* 3. 12. 2.

36 ἔστι τις σιῶν τίσις·
ὃ δ' ὄλβιος ὅστις εὔφρων
ἀμέραν [δι]απλέκει
ἄκλαυτος· ἐγὼν δ' ἀείδω
40 Ἀγιδῶς τὸ φῶς· ὁρῶ
ϝ' ὤτ' ἄλιον, ὅνπερ ἇμιν
Ἀγιδὼ μαρτύρεται
φαίνην· ἐμὲ δ' οὔτ' ἐπαινῆν
οὔτε μωμήσθαι νιν ἁ κλεννὰ χοραγὸς
45 οὐδ' ἁμῶς ἐῇ· δοκεῖ γὰρ ἤμεν αὐτὰ
ἐκπρεπὴς τὼς ὥπερ αἴ τις
ἐν βοτοῖς στάσειεν ἵππον
παγὸν ἀεθλοφόρον καναχάποδα
τῶν ὑποπετριδίων ὀνείρων.

50 ἦ οὐχ ὁρῆς; ὁ μὲν κέλης
Ἐνητικός· ἁ δὲ χαίτα
τᾶς ἐμᾶς ἀνεψιᾶς
Ἀγησιχόρας ἐπανθεῖ
χρυσὸς [ὡ]ς ἀκήρατος·
55 τό τ' ἀργύριον πρόσωπον
διαφάδαν τί τοι λέγω;
Ἀγησιχόρα μὲν αὕτα·
ἁ δὲ δευτέρα πεδ' Ἀγίδω τὸ ϝεῖδος
ἵππος Ἰβηνῷ Κολαξαῖος δραμήται·
60 ταὶ Πεληάδες γὰρ ἇμιν
ὀρθρίαι φάρος φεροίσαις
νύκτα δι' ἀμβροσίαν ἅτε σήριον
ἄστρον ἀϝηρομέναι μαχόνται.

οὔτε γάρ τι πορφύρας
65 τόσσος κόρος ὥστ' ἀμύναι,
οὔτε ποικίλος δράκων
παγχρύσιος, οὐδὲ μίτρα
Λυδία, νεανίδων
ἰανογ[λ]εφάρων ἄγαλμα,
70 οὐδὲ ταὶ Ναννῶς κόμαι,
ἀλλ' οὐ[δ'] Ἀρέτα σιειδής,
οὐδὲ Συλακίς τε καὶ Κλεησισήρα,
οὐδ' ἐς Αἰνησιμβρότας ἐνθοῖσα φασεῖς·
Ἀσταφίς [τ]έ μοι γένοιτο
75 καὶ ποτιγλέποι Φίλυλλα
Δαμαρ[έ]τα τ' ἐρατά τε ϝιανθεμίς·
ἀλλ' Ἀγησιχόρα με τείρει.

οὐ γὰρ ἁ κ[α]λλίσφυρος
Ἀγησιχ[ό]ρ[α] πάρ' αὐτεῖ,
80 Ἀγιδοῖ [δὲ π]αρμένει,
θωστήρ[ια τ'] ἄμ' ἐπαινεῖ;
ἀλλὰ τᾶν [εὐχὰς,] σιοί,
δέξασθε· [σι]ῶν γὰρ ἄνα
καὶ τέλος. [χο]ροστάτις,
85 ϝείποιμι κ', [ἐ]γὼν μὲν αὐτὰ
παρσένος μάταν ἀπὸ θράνω λέλακα
γλαύξ· ἐγὼ[ν] δὲ τᾷ μέν Ἀώτι μάλιστα
ϝανδάνην ἐρῶ· πόνων γὰρ
ἇμιν ἰάτωρ ἔγεντο·
90 ἐξ Ἀγησιχόρ[ας] δὲ νεανίδες
[ἰρ]ήνας ἐρατ[ᾶ]ς ἐπέβαν.

τῷ] τε γὰρ σηραφόρῳ
αὐ]τῶς ἐδ . . . .
τ[ῷ] κυβερνάτᾳ δεχ.η
95 κ[ἠ]ν ναῖ μά[λιστ' ἀκούεν·]
ἁ δὲ τᾶν Σηρην[ί]δων
ἀοιδοτέρα μ . . . .
σιαὶ γάρ· ἀντ[ὶ δ' ἔνδεκα
παίδων δεκ[ὰς ἅδ' ἀείδ]ει·
100 φθέγγεται δ' [ἄρ'] ὥ[τ' ἐπὶ] Ξάνθω ῥοαῖσι
κύκνος· ἁ δ' ἐπιμέρῳ ξανθᾷ κομίσκᾳ . . .[1]

There is a vengence of the gods. Blessed is he who with glad heart
weaves his day without tears. I sing the light of Agido. I see her like
the Sun, which Agido summons to shine in witness for us. To praise
or blame her I am not allowed in any way by our famous leader of
the Choir. For she herself seems to be supreme, as if one were to set
among the herds a prize-winning courser, strong, with ringing hooves,
of the race of winged dreams.

Do you not see? The racer is Venetic; the hair of my kinswoman
Hagesichora blossoms on her like undefiled gold; and her silver face—
why should I tell you openly? Such is Hagesichora. She who is second
after Agido in beauty will run like a Colaxean horse for an Ibenian.
For the Pleiads of the dawn rise through the ambrosial night like the
star of Sirius and fight against us as we bear the plough.

For we have neither such abundance of purple to protect us, nor
dappled snake all of gold, nor Lydian coif, the delight of soft-eyed
maidens, nor even Nanno's hair, nor Areta like a goddess, nor Sylacis

[1] I am greatly indebted to D. L. Page's presentation of the text.

nor Cleësisera, nor shall you go to Aenesimbrota's house and say:
'May Astaphis be mine, and may Philylla look upon me, and Damareta, and lovely Vianthemis', but Hagesichora wears me out.

For is not Hagesichora, of the lovely ankles, here at my side? She
waits by Agido and commends our festival. O Gods, accept their
prayers. For to the gods belong the accomplishment and the fulfil-
ment. Teacher of the choir, I shall say, I, who am myself a maiden,
have screeched in vain like an owl from the roof-beam. But I wish
most of all to please the Lady of the Dawn. For she has been the healer
of our pains, and because of Hagesichora the maidens have found the
peace which they desired.

For the trace-horse in the same way . . . the helmsman in a ship must
be obeyed above all. Our Ten (may not be) more tuneful than the
Sirens, but instead of eleven girls it sings. Its voice is like that of the
swan on the streams of Xanthus. And she with her lovely yellow
hair . . .

This part of the poem begins with an abrupt change of tone. The
myths of pride and presumption are dismissed in the adage that
the gods send vengeance, and Alcman prepares his way for the
present occasion with a statement that joy and happiness are a
better state. He then plunges into allusions to the actual occasion
which naturally take much knowledge for granted, and we are
confounded at every turn by ignorance not only of Spartan
religion but of the actual personal references. It is natural and
tempting to advance hypotheses which cannot be fully proved,
but we must recognize that we are unlikely ever to know all that
the lines mean, and in discussing them we may perhaps try to
distinguish between what is less speculative and what is more.

This song is sung at a θωστήρια (81), a festival of some god or
goddess. The word is hardly known elsewhere, but Hesychius
explains it as εὐωχητήρια, and this indicates that it is a joyful
occasion, but of course a joyful occasion may have its serious
side and there is no need to decry what the singers say. From 99
it is clear that there are ten of them, and it is a natural conclusion
that all ten sing. It is true that the singular ἐγών is used at 40, 85,
87, ἐμέ at 43, με at 77, μοι at 74, ἐμᾶς at 52, while ἇμιν appears at
41, 60, 89. But if we may argue back from Pindar, choirs seem
not to discriminate between the first person singular and the
first person plural. This may be because they speak in some sense
both for the poet and for themselves, or that each speaks for his

or her self and at the same time recognizes that all are engaged in saying the same thing. It is clear that here singular and plural are interchangeable, unless we like to find some slight difference of nuance between them, in that the singular reflects a personal view held by each singer and the plural refers to the joint activity. We may presume that the song was sung by all ten members. That they are maidens can hardly be doubted, since it is assured by νεανίδων at 68, νεανίδες at 90, and παρσένος at 86. These maidens stand in a close relation to one another. When at 52 Hagesichora is called ἀνεψιᾶς, it hints that all are in some sense kin. This is not surprising, since in Pindar's δαφνηφορικόν for Agasicles, which is also a Maiden-song, the whole festival is a family affair.[1] In Alcman the ten girls probably form an ἀγέλα, such as Pindar refers to in Λάκαινα μὲν παρθένων ἀγέλα[2] and comparable to those male ἀγέλαι in powerful and important Cretan families.[3] In such an ἀγέλα, even if the members were not actually related by blood, they were spoken of in such terms as κάσιοι, ἀδελφοί, and ἀνεψιοί.[4] In an ἀγέλα of this sort, whether male or female, the members might be bound by ties of warm affection and use freely the language of love, and when Hagesichora is called κλεννά at 44, the word may have a connexion with Hesychius' entry κλεινοί· οἱ εἰς τὰ παιδικὰ ἐπὶ κάλλει ἁρπαζόμενοι παῖδες, though we should not of course press the parallel in detail. A parallel to such an ἀγέλα in Sparta may be seen in Theocritus' *Epithalamium for Helen*, where the wedding-song is sung by twelve maidens:

δώδεκα ταὶ πρᾶται πόλιος, μέγα χρῆμα Λακαινᾶν[5]

twelve, the first of the city, the flower of Lacedaemonian girlhood.

Alcman's Choir may have been drawn from the same class.

Though Alcman's Choir clearly consists of ten girls, there is a mysterious reference at 98 to its singing ἀντὶ δ' ἕνδεκα. This cannot mean 'against eleven' and must mean 'instead of eleven'. But what does this imply? The scholiast was aware of the difficulty and says διὰ τὸ τὸν χορὸν ὁτὲ μὲν ἐξ ἕνδεκα παρθένων ὁτὲ δὲ ἐκ δέκα. This makes sense and suits the Greek. The Choir sometimes

---

[1] Wilamowitz, *Pindaros*, pp 432–9.
[2] Fr. 101 Bo.   [3] Strab. 483.
[4] Hesych. s.v. κάσιοι· οἱ ἐκ τῆς αὐτῆς ἀγέλης ἀδελφοί τε καὶ ἀνεψιοί. καὶ ἐπὶ θηλείων οὕτως ἔλεγον Λάκωνες. s.v. κάσης· ἡλικιώτης.
[5] 18. 4. See Kaibel, *Hermes*, xvii, pp. 211 ff.

has eleven members, sometimes ten, and at the moment it
clearly has ten, but it manages to sing as well as if it had eleven.
The only trouble with this is that it may seem a little feeble, and
for this reason hypotheses have been built to explain the weak-
ness away. But it is dangerous to assume either that a Choir of ten
differed in age from a Choir of eleven,[1] or that the Choir is sometimes of eleven, when Hagesichora sings, and only of ten when
she devotes herself to prayer or other rites.[2] So far as the text
goes, the Choir has ten members on this occasion, though it
might have had eleven, and it feels at some disadvantage. From
this it is tempting to try to reconstruct the names of the ten. At
70–75 if we omit Aenesimbrota, who is clearly not a girl or a
member of the Choir, there are eight names, and if we add to
these the names of Agido and Hagesichora, we have ten, and all
looks well. But in this there are difficulties. First, it is quite clear
that Agido and Hagesichora are busy with other activities, which
would prevent them from joining in the song at the same time.
At 41–42 Agido conducts some rite and presumably offers prayers
to the sun. 58–59 suggests that both Agido and Hagesichora will
take part in some race, though of course this may be after the
song is finished. At 78 ff. it looks as if Hagesichora had been
moving about before taking her place by Agido, which is not
necessarily in the Choir. It looks as if neither Agido nor Hagesichora was actually singing, but both were busy conducting some
other kind of activity relative to the occasion, rather as in *Ox.
Pap.* 2387 Astymeloisa conducts a rite with the πυλεών while
the other girls sing of her. Secondly, the context in which the
girls' names are given in 70–76 does not encourage the view that
they are members of the choir. If we take the reference to Aenesimbrota's household at its face-value, it can only mean that
Astaphis, Philylla, Damareta, and Vianthemis are not present,
and that it is useless to ask for them to be. Moreover, the girls'
names follow closely on the mention of advantages in equipment
which the Choir has not got, and it follows that the girls named
are equally not in its number. Indeed, if we assume that they are,
the whole structure of the sentence is inordinately artificial.
Alcman is not likely to change suddenly from describing what the

---

[1] Page, *Alc. Parth.* p. 99.
[2] van Groningen, *Mnemosyne*, iii (1936), p. 259; Bruschi, *R.F.I.C.* xxiii (1895),
p. 557.

Choir lacks to saying that what it has is not good enough for its purpose. This involves an anti-climax of which he is hardly capable.

The actual Choir, then, consists of ten unnamed girls, and stands in some close relation to Agido and Hagesichora. We do not know what title, if any, Agido has, but Hagesichora seems to be χοραγός. At least this is the natural deduction from 43 ff., which follow the high praise of Agido for resembling the sun. As χοραγός, Hagesichora would presumably act, while the singing takes place, as a conductor and leader, who need not necessarily take part in it herself and is busy seeing that the right movements are performed and that the actual singing members of the choir do their task properly. This follows from 93 ff., where the references first to the trace-horse and then to the helmsman suggest that the Choir is compared first to a chariot and then to a ship, each of which has its leading figure who must be followed or obeyed. This leaves unsolved the question of χοροστάτις at 84. The form indicates that she must be a girl or perhaps a woman and certainly not Alcman, who would be χοροστάτας. The word cannot be in the nominative singular, since the post would be held by a single person and, as the whole Choir is singing, each member cannot claim to be χοροστάτις. It must therefore be a vocative, and it is not impossible that then it is addressed to Hagesichora, whom it suits well if she is not herself singing, and who could without much difficulty be called both χοραγός and χοροστάτις. It follows that while Agido conducts rites, Hagesichora looks after the Choir, and this seems a fair division of duties. But the two are compared in more than one respect through the poem, and the comparison invites analysis. It seems that Agido is the more beautiful, since she is compared with the sun, and it is hard to think of any brilliance which will defeat this. On the other hand Hagesichora seems to be ἐκπρεπής like a racing horse among the herds (45 ff.), and here the comparison is not of beauty but of something else, presumably of speed. This forecasts the race which is to take place after the song. The point is emphasized at 50 ff., where Agido is compared to a κέλης Ἐνητικός, while Hagesichora is praised for her beauty. Then comes the crucial point when the race is foreshadowed:

ἁ δὲ δευτέρα πεδ' Ἀγίδω τὸ ϝεῖδος
ἵππος Ἰβηνῷ Κολαξαῖος δραμήται.

The two kinds of horses, Ibenian and Colaxaean, are indeed mysterious. The first seems to be Lydian, the second Scythian, but about their respective merits we are in the dark. The papyrus commentary on the poem, *Ox. Pap.* 2389, fr. 6, col. i. 8 ff., seems to say something like ἀμ[φότερ]α γένη ἵπ[πων -]ικα; λέ[γ-]δὲ ἀμφοτέρω[ν τάχει διαπρε]πόντων [προ]φέρειν τὸν [᾽Ι]βην[όν. This tells, as we already knew, that there are two kinds of horses, and that both belong to a single, larger class, but what this is eludes us, since all that survives in the papyrus is the termination -ικα, which tells nothing. The papyrus then adds that of the two kinds the Ibenian is better, and since this information comes from Aristarchus, it calls for attention, but it raises some awkward questions.

First, who in 58 is second to Agido in beauty? We should surely expect it to be Hagesichora, but this has been denied on the ground that Hagesichora is undoubtedly pre-eminent in beauty.[1] But is she? Can she really be said to surpass Agido who shines like the sun? Nor is it fair to argue that Hagesichora is for the moment dismissed in the line

Ἀγησιχόρα μὲν αὖτα

and that therefore we must think of someone else. For though her appearance has for the moment received high praise, the theme now is a different matter—her speed, and this is what matters. If Hagesichora is not in question, we are left in the dark. It is surely impossible to assume the existence of some third, unnamed maiden, or even to assume that 'the second in beauty' is any other member of the choir.[2] Apart from its shaky sense, the introduction of the rest of the choir spoils the strophe, which at this point is concerned with Agido and Hagesichora and their competing claims. There seems indeed no reason to reject the notion that it is indeed Hagesichora who is the subject here, and the point is that, in the sustained comparison with Agido, she is likely to put up a good show in the race as a horse of a parallel, if not quite so pre-eminent, breed. Secondly, if we assume that Agido is going to run as the Ibenian horse, what is the relation of the Colaxaean to her, and what is the precise significance of the dative ᾽Ιβηνῷ? It cannot mean 'against', since Greek has no construction comparable to the English 'Hyperion to a Satyr'.

---

[1] Page, *Alc. Parth.* pp. 47 ff.   [2] Ibid., p. 49.

The only possible sense is 'for', and then Hagesichora will run as a Colaxaean horse for an Ibenian, that is, as a pace-maker, whose own speed will provoke Agido to make her utmost efforts.

Before we consider the nature of the race, we must go back to what precedes it, the actual occasion when the song is sung. This is clearly before dawn, and Agido signifies the time by summoning the sun to shine. The ceremony concerns a goddess, who appears at 87 in the dative as Ἀώτι. Nothing is known of any goddess with this name or title, and speculation has enjoyed itself at her expense. She cannot be the same as the Dawn, who is Ἀώς, but she is evidently closely connected with her and in some sense a goddess related to the Dawn. She may indeed have some other name but it is not mentioned. In this uncertainty and obscurity it is not surprising that scholars should have had recourse to help provided by the scholia, which on 61, where the text reads ὀρθρίαι, provide, either as a variant or a comment, the word ὀρθίαι. It is then assumed that the song was sung to Artemis Ortheia, who seems an excellent candidate for more than one reason. She is pre-eminently the patroness of maidens; the shrine of Artemis Ortheia at Sparta has been excavated and revealed centuries of a rich and popular cult; if the goddess is Artemis, then Ἀώτι refers to her and is said to be paralleled by a cult of her as προσηῴα in Euboea.[1] Such arguments have popularized the notion that the hymn is to Artemis, but when we examine the arguments in detail, they betray certain defects. First, the reading ὀρθρίαι in the text makes perfectly good sense as it stands, and there is no good reason for altering it. The text is, after all, better testimony than the scholia, which are demonstrably wrong on one or two other points, as when they quote the Homeric people of dreams to illustrate 15 or say that Agido and Hagesichora are compared with doves at 60. Moreover, the change to ὀρθίᾳ is open to the charge of being unmetrical. The word appears in inscriptions variously as ϝορθείαι, ϝορθαίαι.[2] The omission of the digamma in the papyrus need cause no surprise, as it is careless in this respect, but the second syllable is long as we know from a Spartan inscription:

> ϝωρθείαι τάδ' Ἀρήξιππος νικῶν ἀνέσηκε
> ἐν συνόδοις παίδων πᾶσιν ἱορῆν φανερά.[3]

[1] Plut. *Them.* 8. 2.   [2] *I.G.* v. 1. 252 a, b; 1572.
[3] Ibid. 255.

If we read the correct form ϝορθείαι at 61, we get a long syllable in the second place of a trochaic dipody, and this is against the metrical practice of the poem. Nor can we argue that this syllable can in fact be short. In theory perhaps it might sometimes be, but the evidence shows that in practice it was long.

Secondly, there is no good reason for identifying Artemis with τᾷ Ἀώτι of 87. The quotation of Ἄρτεμις προσηᾠα is not to the point, because the normal meaning of προσῆᾠος, as we see, for instance, in Theocritus' καὶ τὸ ποτάϙον τὸ Λακίνιον,[1] is 'facing the east', and Ἄρτεμις προσηᾠα is Artemis whose temple faces the east. The argument for Artemis would be stronger if any case could be found where she is associated or identified with the dawn. But no such case has been found, and the evidence points in the opposite direction; for, at least by the time of Aeschylus, Artemis was already a moon-goddess:

ᾶς οὔτε πέμφιξ ἡλίου προσδέρκεται
οὔτ' ἀστερωπὸν ὄμμα Λητᾠας κόρης.[2]

on whom neither the ray of the sun looks nor the starry eye of Leto's daughter.

If Artemis was a goddess of the moon, she is not likely to have been also a goddess of the dawn, and there is no evidence that she was. Nor do the excavations at the shrine of Artemis Orthia throw any light on the problem. The existence of one cult does not disprove the existence of others, and though Artemis was certainly a patroness of maidens, there were others who rivalled her even in this capacity.

An important rival of Artemis at Sparta as the patroness of maidens was Helen. She had her feast of the Ἑλένεια,[3] at which maidens took part and drove to it in wagons called κάνναθρα.[4] She had one shrine near the Colonnade[5] and another outside the city.[6] The excavations of the temple of Menelaus, with whom she was jointly worshipped, show that she was conceived as having wings, and many votive offerings were made to her. She had little to do with Homer's Helen in character or attributes, and she was in fact a goddess of unmarried maidens, who paid rites to her at certain times of the year. If Helen is concerned in

[1] 4. 33.
[2] Fr. 170 N., with Bentley's correction of ἀστέρων στόμα to ἀστέρωπον ὄμμα.
[3] Hesych. s.v. Ἑλένεια.   [4] Id. s.v. κάνναθρα.
[5] Paus. 3. 15. 3.   [6] Hdt. 6. 61. 3.

Alcman's poem, the significance of the myth becomes clearer. The Dioscuri were her brothers; her father feared Hippocoön for her sake; her shrine behind the Colonnade was near the shrine of Heracles where the sons of Hippocoön were said to have been killed. These general considerations make Helen a possible candidate, but perhaps something more cogent may be found in the song of the Laconian Women at the end of the *Lysistrata*:

> ᾇ τε πῶλοι ταὶ κόραι
> πὰρ τὸν Εὐρώταν
> ἀμπάλλοντι πυκνὰ ποδοῖν
> ἀγκονίωαι,
> ταὶ δὲ κόμαι σείονθ' ᾇπερ Βακχᾶν
> θυρσαδδωᾶν καὶ παιδδωᾶν.
> ἀγεῖται δ' ἁ Λήδας παῖς
> ἁγνὰ χοραγὸς εὐπρεπής.[1]

And the maidens, like fillies, beside Eurotas twinkle to and fro with nimble feet; and their tresses wave as they go, like the tresses of the Bacchanals sporting and flourishing their thyrsus-wands. Leda's daughter leads them, a pure and seemly ruler of the dance.

Here Helen is presented among her votaries, who are maidens 'like fillies'. The comparison is striking, for it seems to hide a ritual use of πῶλος. At Sparta πῶλος was used in reference to a guild of priestesses called Λευκιππίδες. Hesychius, in describing a bronze ornament called πωλία, says that on it were depicted the πῶλοι of the Leucippides, and he adds δύο δὲ εἶναι παρθένους φασίν, which can only mean that the πῶλοι were maidens, two in number, who belonged to or were associated with the Leucippides.[2] At a later date, when the cult of Demeter and Persephone was revived after long disuse in Sparta, their priestesses were called πῶλοι,[3] and the name was presumably taken over from earlier usage in other cults.

This use of πῶλοι for the two maidens associated with the Leucippides the remarkable way in which Alcman at four places compares his girls to horses, 47 ff., 50, 58–59, 92. This may of course not be intentional, and he may mean no more than when Anacreon compares a girl with a Thracian filly (fr. 88 D.), but the repetition of the figure is certainly striking, and if the two leaders were called πῶλοι, it would have a great deal more point. There is a possibility that Alcman's Choir were the

[1] *Lys.* 1308–15.　　[2] Wide, p. 331.　　[3] *I.G.* v. 1. 594. 2; 1444 a.

Leucippides, and its two leaders were called πῶλοι. The case is strengthened by the fact that the Leucippides were attached to Helen. In Euripides' *Helen*, where the Chorus address Helen on the delights which await her in her own land of Laconia, they sing:

ἦ που κόρας ἂν ποταμοῦ
παρ' οἶδμα Λευκιππίδας ἢ πρὸ ναοῦ
Παλλάδος ἂν λάβοις
χρόνῳ ξυνελθοῦσα χοροῖς.[1]

Perhaps you will find the Leucippides by the river's water or before the shrine of Pallas, and join in time with their dances.

The occasion is like that described by Aristophanes. Helen leads a dance of maidens by the river, but the important detail is added that the maidens were called Λευκιππίδες. The Leucippides are attached to Helen; their leaders are called πῶλοι. They are therefore possible candidates for Alcman's choir.

Yet though this theory has its attraction, it has also its difficulties. In what sense can Helen deserve the title Ἀῶτις? Is she ever connected with the Dawn? A very tenuous connexion may be seen in Theocritus' *Epithalamium for Helen* which is sung by Spartan maidens who acclaim her beauty:

Ἀὼς ἀντέλλοισα καλὸν διέφανε πρόσωπον,
πότνια Νύξ, τό τε λευκὸν ἔαρ χειμῶνος ἀνέντος·
ὧδε καὶ ἁ χρυσέα Ἑλένα διεφαίνετ' ἐν ἁμῖν.[2]

Beautiful, Lady Night, is the face that the rising Dawn reveals, or the bright spring when winter is over; and so among us did golden Helen shine.

This may be something, but it is very little, and certainly gives no evidence for a cult of Helen as Ἀῶτις. A second shred of evidence might perhaps be found in Hesychius' entry Ἄωοι· θεοὶ οἱ ἐκ δρόμου μετακομισθέντες εἰς Σαμοθράκην καὶ Λῆμνον. The gods moved ἐκ δρόμου and called Ἄωοι may be Castor and Polydeuces, who had their shrines by the δρόμος at Sparta,[3] while Helen had her shrine near it,[4] and her connexion with it is shown by the statement of Theocritus' Spartan maidens that they will go ἐς Δρόμον in the spring and gather flowers, remindful of Helen.[5] It looks as if the gods transferred from the δρόμος at Sparta to

---

[1] *Hel.* 1465–7.   [2] 18. 26–28.   [3] Paus. 3. 14. 6.
[4] Ibid. 3. 15. 3.   [5] 18. 39–40.

Lemnos and Samothrace included Castor and Polydeuces, and it is just possible that Helen was taken with them. If they were called Ἄωοι, the title may have been connected with Helen's title of Ἀῶτις. But this again is only a speculation. It is possible, but there is not enough evidence to prove it. Helen may not fail quite so completely as Artemis for the post of Ἀῶτις, but she does not make her claims good. We are left as we started with the knowledge that the goddess was called Ἀῶτις, and that is something. We must be content with it.

The ceremony is held in honour of Aotis, but its details are as obscure as she is. It is just before dawn, and the Choir carry an object which appears in the text of the papyrus as φᾶρος and as φάρος in the scholium, which attributes the reading to Sosiphanes, and a parallel from Antimachus is quoted by Herodian (fr. 118 Wyss). So far as the sense is concerned either is perfectly possible. The carrying of a φᾶρος or robe to a goddess is paralleled by the women of Troy in the *Iliad*,[1] the presentation to Athene of a πέπλος in the Panathenaea at Athens, the worship of Artemis as Χιτώνη,[2] the presentation to Iphigeneia at Brauron of the clothes of women who died in childbirth.[3] If Aotis is Artemis or Helen, she might well be treated like some other goddesses elsewhere and receive a robe in her honour. The presentation of a φάρος or plough is a much rarer event, and there is no close parallel. Yet there is no inherent objection to it. There is no need to think that it was too heavy for the maidens to carry, or that they carried it throughout the dance. If the goddess was Artemis Ortheia, a plough may be quite as suitable an offering as the iron sickles, prizes of victory, which were dedicated to her by the winners of competitions. If she was Helen, who as δενδρῖτις was worshipped as a goddess of nature,[4] it would be hardly less suitable. Nor can we really doubt that φάρος is right and φᾶρος wrong. The tradition represented by the quotation of Sosiphanes in the scholia is independent of the text and comes from Alexandrian scholars, who would know about the ceremony from other sources than the poem, and if they said that the word was φάρος and that it meant ἄροτρον, we are wise to take their word for it.

Though the presentation of the plough is part of the rite, it is not the whole of it, and Alcman does not give it much attention.

[1] 6. 90 ff.   [2] Callim. *Hymn* 3. 225; Steph. Byz. s.v. Χιτώνη.
[3] Eur. *I.T.* 1464 ff.   [4] Paus. 3. 19. 10; Theocr. 18. 48.

His song indicates rather some kind of contest, which is suggested by such words as μάχονται at 63, ἀμύναι at 65, πόνων at 88, and ἰρήνας ἐρατᾶς at 91. The question is what can this contest be, and though there is endless opportunity for disagreement on details, the main point to be settled is whether Alcman's Choir is competing against another choir or fighting some quite different kind of battle. The vital passage is that which is connected with the plough:

ταὶ Πεληάδες γὰρ ἇμιν
ὀρθρίαι φάρος φεροίσαις
νύκτα δι' ἀμβροσίαν ἅτε σήριον
ἄστρον ἀϝηρομέναι μάχονται. (60–63)

There is obviously something to be said for the view that the Πεληάδες are a rival Choir, and at the start we need not trouble to make fine discriminations between alternative meanings for 'the Doves' and 'the Pleiads'; for after all the Pleiads were still doves, who had once been the daughters of Atlas and were then turned into doves and set in the sky. The word means 'the Doves' and is equally applicable to birds and to stars. Nor is it difficult to surmise why such a name should be given to a Choir of Spartan maidens. One at least of the Pleiads, Taygeta, was a Spartan girl, and such a local association would be a good justification for giving the name of 'Doves' to a Choir. But there may have been a better reason than this. The rising of the Pleiads was an important date in the Greek calendar because it marked the season for beginning the reaping.[1] Such an occasion justified a festival, and a Choir which took part in it might reasonably call itself after the star-cluster which fixed the date. The members of the Choir could wear some emblem or clothing that suggested doves. Bird-dresses were common enough in Attic rites at a somewhat later time,[2] and may well have been customary in Sparta for similar purposes. More important is the traditional connexion between the Pleiads and dancing. Callimachus says that they were the daughters of the Queen of the Amazons and were the first to establish dancing and night-long festivals for maidens.[3] A Choir called Πεληάδες would therefore be well fitted

[1] Hes. Op. 383–4.
[2] See A. W. Pickard-Cambridge, Dithyramb, Tragedy, and Comedy, pp. 245–6.
[3] Fr. 693 P. αἱ Πελειάδες. φησὶ Καλλίμαχος, ὅτι τῆς βασιλίσσης τῶν Ἀμαζόνων ἦσαν θυγατέρες, πρῶτον δ' αὗται χορείαν καὶ παννυχίδα συνεστήσαντο

to dance on an occasion like that which Alcman celebrates, and
if he knew of a choir of 'Halcyons', he may equally have known
of a choir of 'Doves'.

If there was a contest between Alcman's Choir and another
Choir called 'the Doves', we must ask of what it consisted. There
is no hint in the text that dancing is the point at issue, and though
such a song would certainly be accompanied by rhythmical
movements like a dance, this does not seem to have assumed any
great prominence. We find instead other points which suggest a
competition. First, in 65 ff. when the maidens deplore, no doubt
playfully, their lack of rich ornaments, we may assume that in
assessing the result the judges took such matters into account.
The words suggest that, though Alcman's Choir has neither
purple raiment nor ποικίλος δράκων παγχρύσιος, that is gold bracelets shaped like snakes, nor a Lydian coif, their opponents may
have them and rely upon them to get marks. With this competition in appearance goes another closely related to it—in looks.
This is certainly the best interpretation of the girls' names in
70 ff. The girls mentioned are clearly renowned for their beauty,
and Alcman's girls modestly say that they have no one of this
kind in their number and that it is useless for them to apply to
Aenesimbrota, who seems to be some sort of teacher of girls, for
reinforcements from her household. Secondly, though dancing is
only hinted at in 92 ff., where the need for discipline and order
is stated through the familiar figures of the trace-horse and the
steersman, song is certainly emphasized towards the end of the
poem. It is unfortunate that in 97 we are not sure who is compared with the Sirens for song, or how the comparison is made,
but at least the Sirens would not have been mentioned unless the
choir prided itself on its singing, and this is reinforced in 100,
where the group sings like the swan on the streams of Xanthus.
The subject of φθέγγεται may well be δεκάς from the preceding
line, and the change of subject that follows accompanies a change
of theme from the strength of the Choir's singing to the beauty of
some individual member of it, presumably either Hagesichora or
Agido. Thirdly, it seems clear that after the song and the presentation of the plough which is closely connected with it, as the
present participle φεροίσαις shows, there is some sort of race.

παρθενεύουσαι; for the dancing of the Pleiads cf. Eur. *El.* 467; Hor. *Carm.* 4. 14.
21; Prop. 3. 5. 36.

This suits nicely the imagery of horses, and is made clear by δραμῆται in 59. Races of such a kind were not uncommon. In Sparta eleven maidens called Διονυσιάδες held a δρόμου ἀγῶνα,[1] and Hesychius[2] mentions a δρόμος παρθένων ἐν Λακεδαίμονι. These are not quite parallel to our case since the race is between the members of a single company. But more relevant is what took place every fourth year by the temple of Hera at Olympia. In connexion with the weaving and offering of a robe to Hera games called Heraea were held, and a race was run by unmarried girls of different ages. The whole was organized by sixteen women, who also got up two choruses, of which one was called the Chorus of Physcoa and the other the Chorus of Hippodamia.[3] The combination of a girls' race with the existence of two choruses looks very like the situation in Alcman, and just as at Olympia the race was somehow connected with a dedication to Hera, so in Sparta it was connected with a dedication to Aotis. There is, then, no difficulty in thinking that Alcman's Choir has, among its other duties, to run a race. Alcman does not explicitly say that the whole Choir has got to run, and indeed his references to the actual race might suggest that only two maidens have to. But the recurring comparison with fillies suggests that all are involved, and the emphasis on the Ibenian and Colaxaean horses is simply a way of mentioning the two girls who are expected to run fastest.

There is then something to be said for the view that Alcman's Choir competes against another choir called 'the Doves', and that the competition consists of appearance, singing, and running. Since the competition is also a rite, some members of the Choir, notably Agido and Hagesichora, have, at least at the beginning, other duties to perform, but these need not interfere with the competition itself. The advantage of this theory is that it takes note of the obvious elements of action mentioned by the song, and that it conforms to the Greek love of good looks, song, and running. Yet this theory is open to a serious objection. What does Alcman mean when he says that the Doves μάχονται against his choir? This is certainly a very unusual word to use of one Choir competing against another,[4] and no parallel for it has been found. It is useless to quote Herodotus' description of a ritual

---

[1] Paus. 3. 13. 7. [2] s.v. ἐνδριῶνας. [3] Paus. 5. 16. 2 ff.
[4] Davison, *Hermes*, lxxiii (1938), p. 449.

contest between two bands of maidens, who δίχα διαστᾶσαι μάχονται πρὸς ἀλλήλας λίθοισί τε καὶ ξύλοισι,[1] since after all the use of
stones and sticks really justifies the name of a fight. It is quite
true that μάχεσθαι can be used metaphorically, as in the Homeric
μαχεσσαμένω ἐπέεσσιν,[2] but even in this an element of violence is
implied which is surely absent from Alcman. This consideration
has led to the view that the Πεληάδες are not another Choir but
simply the actual Pleiads, and that Alcman's choir somehow
sees itself as challenged by them. In that case the song performs
some kind of magical action against what seems to be their baleful
influence. This notion calls for serious attention. It is true that we
do not know why the Pleiads should be regarded as hostile, but
that is no reason why they should not be. If the Choir are dealing
with the Pleiads, the case for another Choir vanishes, and such
competition as takes place is between the separate members of the
Choir, certainly in racing and perhaps in beauty.

It cannot be held against this theory that it leaves too many
points obscure. That after all is to be expected if the poem treats
of what is essentially a magical performance, and we must
acquiesce in ignorance of what lies behind it. Nor can we com-
plain that the comparison of the Pleiads with Sirius is inept,
because they are a not very distinguished cluster, ὀλίγαι καὶ
ἀφέγγεες,[3] while it is a bright, single star. The comparison must
be on the point of their common balefulness, and since Sirius
is notoriously baleful, the parallel is fully justified. But there
remain serious objections to this theory. First, if the song is intended in some way to avert the hostility of the Pleiads, its tone
is wrong. We must of course expect Alcman to combine a gay
exterior with more serious thoughts, but we can hardly believe
that he makes his Choir indulge in light badinage when his occasion is of some gravity. Since the lines on the Pleiads follow
immediately the comparison between Agido and Hagesichora,
this argument is formidable. Secondly, if the Pleiads are the
star-cluster, there is a certain incoherence in the development of
Alcman's thought. He is not indeed a man to make all his mental
movements immediately obvious, but we expect him to be reasonably intelligible, and here he seems not to be. The theme of the
Pleiads is introduced by γάρ, and this suggests that their menace,

[1] 4. 180. 2; Page, Alc. Parth. p. 54.
[2] Il. 1. 304. [3] Arat. Phaen. 264.

μάχονται, is a reason why the two girls should run as fast as possible. This may indeed, in our ignorance of the rite, be possible, but what is not possible is that the emphasis should be laid not on the fact of running, which could be relevant, but on the comparative merits of the two runners, which cannot. Though the notion that the Πεληάδες are the star-cluster is undoubtedly attractive and must be treated seriously, it seems not to fit our needs. If we reject it, we must still recognize that μάχονται is used in a very unusual way if it refers to a competition, but it seems easier to think that Alcman is capable of this than to accept the difficulties inherent in the war waged by the Pleiads.

We may then try to see what light the theory of a contest against another Choir called 'the Doves' throws on the poem, and indeed on how Alcman presents his subject. In this contest between two Choirs in beauty, speed, and singing Alcman mentions all three, but his special concern is with the first two as they are exemplified in Agido and Hagesichora, who seem to have special functions, rather as Astymeloisa has in the presentation of the πυλεών, and to be busy with other activities, mentioned at 40 ff., where Agido summons the sun to rise, and hinted at in 78 ff., where Hagesichora has completed some movement which brings her back to the Choir. These two girls are clearly Alcman's chief concern, and it is mainly of them that the Choir sings. In the references to them there is a certain amount of inconsistency, which must be deliberate and calls for explanation. Both are clearly beautiful, and both fleet of foot. But they are played off against each other with competing praises. First, at 39 ff. Agido is compared with the sun, and this suggestion of radiance must certainly include the notion of beauty, but at 51 ff. the hair of Hagesichora is compared with unmixed gold, and this implies a very similar praise. Secondly, in 45 ff. the suggestion that Hagesichora is like a courser of dreams hints at her speed, but this is matched in 50–51 where the Enetic horse is Agido, while at 58–59 the comparison between the Ibenian and the Colaxaean horses means that there is almost nothing to choose in point of speed between them, and indeed if anything, Agido, as the Ibenian, is the faster. This playful treatment of the claims of the two girls leaves us guessing which is the more beautiful and which the faster, and this no doubt is what Alcman intends to do. In 78 he brings them together, and though Hagesichora is said to commend the feast, and is to this degree more prominent, she seems to do so at the side of Agido, since in 80 the reading must be something like Ἁγιδοῖ δὲ παρμένει. This kind of playful treatment is quite in place in the part of the poem which deals with intimate matters and is very much what the Choir, divided in their admiration for the two girls, might be expected to think and to say.

There remain, however, two problems. The first is in 77, when, after saying that it is no good going to Aenesimbrota's household for reinforcements, the Choir says:

ἀλλ' Ἁγησιχόρα με τείρει.

There is no doubt that τείρει is the reading of the papyrus, and it is not surprising that it has caused trouble. The word means 'wears out'. This might of course be a tribute of love,[1] but no word about love is said, and the word by itself would more naturally have some other meaning—but what? The sentence occurs at the end of the strophe in which the Choir speaks of its lack of advantages, and we may presume that these are compensated by the presence of Hagesichora. Yet τείρει almost suggests that Hagesichora is a liability. A possible solution is that in a contest where so much counts Hagesichora 'wears out' her fellows in the sense that they are tired of praising her and saying what an asset she is to them. The word is purely playful, and in the strophe which follows it is put in its right place, when the Choir welcomes her back in its ranks. The use of τείρει implies that the Choir have really no more to say about Hagesichora, because she is obviously so pre-eminent. This certainly means that she is in the last resort more important than Agido, though she takes her place by Agido immediately afterwards.

A second problem comes after the mention of Aotis. The Choir, speaking in depreciative language of its own capacities in singing and comparing its voice to an owl from the rafter (86–87), goes on to say that its chief desire is to please Aotis. Since the song must be sung at her ceremony, this is easy enough. But what follows is less easy:

πόνων γὰρ
ἇμιν ἰάτωρ ἔγεντο·
ἐξ Ἁγησιχόρας δὲ νεανίδες
ἰρ]ήνας ἐρατ[ᾶ]ς ἐπέβαν. (88–91)

[1] Page, *Alc. Parth.* pp. 67, 91.

The aorist ἔγεντο suggests that in the past Aotis has healed the
πόνοι of the singers, and by πόνων they may well mean their
efforts in such contests as the present; for such a use of the word
was common in reference to games[1] and would be quite appropriate here. Then the last words mean that the peace which the
maidens desire is that peace of mind which comes from success in
such contests, and for this use of the word we may quote a line
which has been ascribed to Alcman and may conceivably come
from his hand:

ἁμὲς δ' εἰρήναν· τόδε γὰρ θέτο Μῶσα λίγεια.[2]

Just as in the past the maidens have had peace after toil, so presumably they hope to have it again. But they ascribe their past
successes in winning the favour of Aotis to Hagesichora, and this
leaves it clear beyond doubt that she is in the last resort more
important than Agido.

   If we accept these main propositions, and of course every one
of them has been questioned and may rightly be questioned
again, we may form an idea of how the poem moves and develops its intimate, almost domestic subject of the relation
between the Choir and its chief performers or accomplices,
Hagesichora and Agido. It may then be helpful to attempt an
expanded analysis of what is said in the hope that this may throw
some light on the structure which lies behind the nimble and
wayward movements of Alcman's thought.

1st Section (36–49)

   From the story of vengeance exacted by the gods, the Choir
turns to the present moment as an example of that happiness
which may befall those who have avoided the temptation of
seeking too much. In the present ceremony Agido, who summons
the sun to shine by some ceremonial not described, is compared
with the sun for brightness, which certainly includes the notion
of beauty, and is very high praise. The Choir breaks off its praise
of her on the ground that the χοραγός, who must be Hagesichora,
does not allow either praise or blame for Agido, and the reason
for this is that she herself is so pre-eminent that she is like a fast
race-horse of dreams among pasturing cattle. This indicates that

---

[1] Pind. *Ol.* 11. 4; *Pyth.* 8. 73; *Nem.* 4. 1; 7. 74; 10. 24; *Isthm.* 6. 11; Bacch.
13. 56.   [2] Fr. Mel. Chor. Adesp. 2 Diehl. Cf. Pind. *Nem.* 1. 69.

Hagesichora is more important than Agido, but of course it does not stop the Choir from continuing to praise Agido, if only to tease Hagesichora.

2nd Section (50–63)

The Choir draws attention to the two girls and elaborates the themes of beauty and speed. Agido may indeed resemble an Enetic horse, but Hagesichora is truly beautiful with her golden hair, and her face silver, we may presume, in the moonlight. She may be second to Agido in beauty, and this is not meant too seriously, but in the race she will act as pace-maker to her, and her performance will be at the high level of a Scythian horse. This combination of speed and beauty, exemplified in the two maidens, is needed in a contest against the rival choir of Doves, who appear through the darkness with all the brilliance and menace of Sirius as it rises, and it is in competition against them that the Choir must contend as it carries its plough in the dawn.

3rd Section (64–77)

The Choir proclaims its deficiencies, with a modesty suited to a religious festival but not necessarily to be treated too seriously. They have no purple, golden armlets, or Lydian coifs, nor can they summon to their help girls renowned for their beauty, whom they name, or others, no less beautiful, also named and associated with Aenesimbrota. Then abruptly and dramatically the Choir announces that it is being worn out by Hagesichora, and by this it means that though she is its chief hope and defence, it has no more for the moment to say in praise of her.

4th Section (78–91)

Hagesichora, who has been conducting movements, has now joined the Choir and taken her place at the side of Agido, and this adds dignity to the occasion. She, or they, have been offering prayers to the gods, which the gods are asked to accept, for the gods control the result. The Choir then addresses Hagesichora, and with some mock modesty about its own incapacity, speaks of its desire to please the goddess Aotis, to whom presumably the two girls have been praying along with other gods. Just as in the past Aotis has given victory, so it is hoped that she will give it

again, and in its hopes that she will the Choir places its chief
trust in Hagesichora as an intermediary with the gods.

5th Section (92–101)

The Choir begins with stressing the need for order and discipline
in a song as in a chariot or a ship. Its ten members may not be such
singers as the Sirens, who are, after all, goddesses, but though they
are short of one member they put up a fine performance, which
may be compared with that of a swan on the river Xanthus. Their
first hope, then, is that their singing will make them victorious,
and their second hope seems to be in the beauty of Hagesichora,
whose yellow hair is the last thing mentioned before the papyrus
breaks off four lines before the end of the poem.

If, while admitting that we cannot be certain on many points
in this poem, we try to make sense of it on these lines, we can to
some degree appreciate how Alcman works, and one or two
characteristics of his style emerge. First, it is clear that though his
Choir sings with one voice and is regarded as a unit, its members
are permitted to have different views which look like personal
opinions and almost suggest that some of the singers favour
Hagesichora while others favour Agido. This is neatly dealt with
by the slight shifts of praise from one to the other, and though we
might expect this to be handled by two semi-choirs, each of which
states its own case, there is no need to think that Alcman does
this, and indeed it is difficult to arrange the semi-choirs in any way
that will win acceptance. Secondly, Alcman preserves throughout a certain unity of tone, which is indeed a kind of gaiety, in
which praise, badinage, self-depreciation, and a keen eye for
physical things all play a part. The most serious moment is when
Aotis is mentioned, but this is done rapidly and effectively at the
end of a strophe and does not disturb the general level of gaiety.
Rather it fits in with it, for in their hopes of victory the maidens
maintain before the goddess their trust that all will be well.
We can hardly deny that these strophes are meant to make a
strong contrast with the myths of violence and requital which
come before them. At 36, when he begins the second part of his
poem, Alcman adroitly changes his tone and keeps up the new
temper to the end. In this he displays an art which is much
simpler than that of Pindar with his abrupt shifts of mood and

his complex interweaving of themes round a central situation. Alcman's art may to this degree be more archaic, but the maintenance of tone is no mean achievement and accounts for much that is most attractive in his song. Thirdly, the imagery in which Alcman presents his most vivid points is conceived with considerable originality. The least original image seems to be in 92 ff., where the chariot and the ship may be echoes from Homer,[1] but elsewhere Alcman relies on other less familiar sources with admirable effect. The language about horses may have been suggested to him by the maidens bearing some such title as Λευκιππίδες, but if so, he advanced bravely forward from it and made his own use of its possibilities. The great courser in 47 ff. is new not only in its glory as a splendid creature of dreams, seen only for a fleeting moment, but in its contrast with the slow, pasturing cattle among which it moves. The difference between the Ibenian and the Colaxaean horses at 59 may not mean much to us, but to Alcman's audience they would suggest associations of rare and even royal splendour. In contrast with them we may set the homely image of the owl screeching from the roof-beam at 86. This has no connexion with the later notion of the owl as a bird of ill omen, but anticipates another bird-fancier, Aristophanes, who against the musical cry of τοροτοροτοροτοροτίξ sets the owl's unmusical κικκαβαῦ κικκαβαῦ,[2] and speaks of owls as κακκαβαζουσῶν.[3] Alcman draws his images from any source that he thinks appropriate, and makes his effect without any trouble about precedent or convention. They add greatly to the enchanting freshness of his manner and accord exactly with the gaiety which he feels and evokes.

The fragments of Alcman's other poems do not contradict the notion of him which we get from this Maiden-song, but they supplement it, and indicate that he worked on certain lines, which allowed him plenty of variation in tone and temper as well as in subject and detail. Just as he makes his maidens speak candidly about one another, so he speaks candidly about himself. He moves without pride or self-consciousness or solemnity among innocent, happy girls, and introduces himself into his songs with an easy sense of his own comedy. He makes his choirs speak of his habits, just as in the Maiden-song the girls speak of each other. These personal touches take us straight into Alcman's world.

[1] *Il.* 23. 316 ff. [2] *Aves*, 261. [3] *Lys.* 761.

For all its pride and power Sparta of the seventh century was a simple, human place; its pleasures were natural, convivial pleasures; and since Alcman realized their charm and knew their worth, he made his choirs sing of them. The feasts for which he composed his songs were no doubt feasts in the real sense of the word, and it was highly appropriate that he should touch on the pleasures of eating and drinking. He knew all the wines of the Laconian land and what he said about them has been reconstructed from Athenaeus' expanded quotation:

⟨ἢ⟩ Πέντ' ἐκ Λόφων
ϝοῖνον ⟨ἢ⟩ ϝοινωντίδαν ἢ Δένθιν ἢ Καρύστιον
ἢ ῎Ονογλιν ἢ Σταθμίταν ἄπυρον ὄσδοντ' ἀνθέων.[1]

whether from the Five Hills or from Oenus or Denthian or Carystian or from Onogle or from Stathme wine unfired with the scent of flowers.

This taste in local wines was balanced by a healthy love of simple food. One fragment shows where Alcman's appetites lay:

καὶ ποκά τοι δώσω τρίποδος κύτος,
ᾧ κ' ἔνι ⟨σιτί' ἀολ⟩λέ' ἀγείρῃς.
ἀλλ' ἔτι νῦν γ' ἄπυρος, τάχα δὲ πλέος
ἔτνεος, οἷον ὁ παμφάγος Ἀλκμὰν
ἠράσθη χλιαρὸν πεδὰ τὰς τροπάς·
οὔτι γὰρ ἦὖ τετυγμένον ἐσθίει,
ἀλλὰ τὰ κοινὰ γάρ, ὥσπερ ὁ δᾶμος,
ζατεύει.[2]

And some day I shall give you a great cauldron on a tripod, and in it you may gather food of every kind. Now it is unfired, but soon it will be full of porridge, such as Alcman, who eats everything, loves hot after the solstice. For he does not eat what is well confectioned, but, like the people, seeks the common fare.

Here Alcman stresses his own simple taste in food and classes himself as παμφάγος, which means not so much 'glutton', as Athenaeus suggests,[3] as 'not fastidious'. Aristotle classes animals as ζωοφάγα, καρποφάγα, and παμφάγα,[4] and though there is no need to think that Alcman anticipates this, he belongs to the class of eaters who take what they can get and enjoy it. The lines are more than a tribute to his simplicity and his appetite. When he says that he shares the tastes of the δᾶμος, he throws

[1] From Athen. i. 31 c by Wilamowitz, *Hermes*, lx, pp. 127 ff. (fr. 53 D).
[2] Fr. 49.   [3] 10. 416 c.   [4] *Pol.* 1256 a 25.

some light on the conditions of his life. If in his professional capacity he mingled with noble families who ate daintily, he has no contempt for the δᾶμος, who are country people living quietly off the produce of their fields and enjoying copious, if unpretentious, fare. Alcman finds that their tastes are the same as his. The lines refer to a time of year πεδὰ τὰς τροπάς, when food is abundant, and this must be towards the end of summer, when it is changing to autumn and the harvest has been gathered in.[1]

The lines present a nice problem of interpretation. Who sings them, to whom are they addressed, and what is the exact point of Alcman's invitation, if such indeed it be? Welcker thought that they were addressed by the poet in his own person to some girl whom he loved,[2] and compared the promise made of a milking-vessel and a cup by the shepherd to a girl in Theocritus.[3] To this there are two objections. First, if Alcman is really addressing a girl in his own person, he would hardly use the third person Ἀλκμάν to do so. Secondly, the lines come from his Third Book, and this seems to have been composed of choral songs, and though he was fully capable of speaking of himself in them, we may doubt if he would use such a song to make a proposal of love. Romagnoli too thinks that it is a personal song, but that it has a humorous point, which is that while Alcman will provide the cooking-pot, he expects his guest to produce the food,[4] about which he promises not to be faddy. If so, Alcman anticipates a theme exploited by Catullus[5] and Horace,[6] and in itself this is by no means impossible. But here too the theme seems to be rather too personal for a choral song, though the spirit of such a suggestion certainly accords with what we know of Alcman's temperament. A third suggestion is that of Edmonds, that the lines are intended for the judge of a contest who is made to address the choir-leader and tell him or her what can be done with the prize when it is won.[7] This meets the situation quite well, and explains why Alcman's name is introduced in the third person. In a small society, where intimacies were common and every one was known to every one else, it would be easy for Alcman, the poet and the instructor, to insert a mention of himself in this way.

[1] Cf. Plat. Laws 12. 945 e μετὰ τροπὰς ἡλίου τὰς ἐκ θέρους εἰς χειμῶνα.
[2] Kleine Schriften, iv, pp. 63–66.　　　　[3] 5. 104.
[4] Quoted by A. Garzya, Alcmane, p. 119.　　　[5] C. 13.
[6] C. 4. 12.　　　　　　　　　　　　[7] L.G. i, p. 83.

Alcman's account of simple pleasures usually has some ulterior purpose and is not meant simply to record what happens. The details are relevant because they call up the occasion, but we are entitled to examine them with care. For instance, one fragment describes a feast:

κλῖναι μὲν ἑπτὰ καὶ τόσαι τράπεσδαι
μακωνιᾶν ἄρτων ἐπιστέφοισαι
λίνω τε σασάμω τε κἠν πελίχναις
παίδεσσι χρυσόκολλα.[1]

seven couches and as many tables crowned with poppy-cakes and linseed and sesame, and among the flagons are honey-cakes for the boys.

This looks like a wedding. Cakes of sesame were the ancient equivalent of wedding-cakes. In the *Peace* of Aristophanes the Slave of Trygaeus announces the forthcoming celebrations with the words:

ὁ πλακοῦς πέπεπται, σησαμῆ ξυμπλάττεται[2]

'the cake is kneaded, and the sesame is being beaten up with it', and the scholiast quotes Menander to say that sesame was added because it helped to get children, διὰ τὸ πολύγονον. The golden cups for drinking are in the true tradition of weddings, as we know from Pindar,[3] and the boys must be those who accompany the bridal couple from the bride's home to the bridegroom's— the κοῦροι ὀρχηστῆρες of Homer[4] and the νέοι of the *Shield of Heracles*.[5] A feast of this kind has a special purpose, and Alcman is well aware of it as he mentions the main features of the occasion.

The fare which Alcman describes at Spartan feasts is simple enough, and there is no sign of luxury.[6] Indeed at one place he humorously picks up a traditional point in order to make a small complaint about the nature of things. Homer and Hesiod admit only three seasons, spring, summer, and winter,[7] and the existence of four makes its undisputed appearance in Hippocrates[8] and Euripides.[9] Alcman too knows of four seasons but treats them

[1] Fr. 55 D, μακωνιᾶν suggested by Chantraine and Irigoin for μακωνίδων.
[2] *Pax*, 869. Cf. *I.G.* v. 1. 364. 9. [3] *Ol.* 7. 1 ff.
[4] *Il.* 18. 494. [5] *Scut.* 281.
[6] See P. Von der Muehll, *Festschrift K. Meuli*, pp. 208–14.
[7] See Smyth, *G.M.P.* p. 202.
[8] *Aph.* 1. 18. [9] Fr. 990 N.

in his own fanciful way. They are indeed made by Zeus, who is
the subject of his sentence:

> ὥρας δ' ἔσηκε τρεῖς, θέρος
> καὶ χεῖμα κὠπώραν τρίταν,
> καὶ τέτρατον τὸ ϝῆρ, ὄκα
> σάλλει μέν, ἐσθίην δ' ἄδαν
> οὐκ ἔστιν.[1]

Three seasons he made, summer and winter and autumn the third,
and a fourth the spring, when things grow but a man cannot eat
his fill.

Alcman hesitates between the old notion of three seasons and
the new notion of four, but he goes his own way by making the
doubtful season not autumn but spring, and his reason for this is
that though in spring food grows abundantly, there is still not
enough to eat, presumably because the winter's stores have been
consumed and the new crops have not yet come. He judges the
divine arrangements for the year's cycle by the food which they
provide, and enters his complaint against spring. He did not ask
for very much, but what he asked for he really liked and felt no
lack of dignity in writing such lines as

> ἤδη παρέξει πυάνιόν τε πόλτον
> χίδρον τε λευκὸν κηρίναν τ' ὀπώραν.[2]

Now he will provide raisin porridge and white frumenty and the
harvest of the honey-comb.

This is unlikely to come from the same poem as the preceding
fragment, but it seems to be on a similar topic. If the subject of
παρέξει is Ζεύς, then the situation is later in the year, and Alcman
speaks of the delicacies of full summer.

Alcman's taste for food and drink was matched by his liking
for pretty ornaments. The Sparta of his day had not yet banished
gold from its treasuries, and the carvings in ivory found in ex-
cavation show what a lively sculpture it possessed. So Alcman
mentions the gold bracelets, worn by his maidens, and compares
the hair of Hagesichora to pure gold. He speaks of someone who
wears a golden necklace:

> χρύσιον ὅρμον ἔχων ῥαδινᾶν πετάλοισι καλχᾶν.[3]

'wearing a golden chain with petals of dainty flowers'. The same

---

[1] Fr. 56 D.   [2] Fr. 50 D.   [3] Fr. 105 D.

kind of craft must have belonged to the ear-ring called ἀάνθα,[1] where the name suggests the shape of a flower. This art was close to nature and found its models in animals and flowers. Just as the painters of Spartan vases in the next century filled their empty spaces with pictures of living creatures, such as scorpions, snakes, and birds, so Alcman not only liked the imitations of such creatures in metal but used them himself to adorn and illustrate his poetry. To one person he says

εἶκας μὲν ὡραίῳ λίνῳ[2]

'you are like ripe flax', and of someone or something:

μῆον ἢ κοδύμαλον[3]

'smaller than a medlar'. After comparing Astymeloisa with a falling star and a golden shoot, he adds a third comparison with soft down.[4] He compares Eros with a boy who treads down the flowers of the clover.[5] When he needs a simile to convey the flutter and fright of maidens in some sudden crisis, he finds it in birds on the appearance of a hawk:

λῦσαν δ᾽ ἄπρακτα νεάνιδες, ὧτ᾽
ὄρνις ἱέρακος ὑπερπταμένω[6]

'the maidens left their work undone, like birds when a hawk flies above them'. The simile is exact, illuminating, and delightful for its own sake, and it is derived from Alcman's own observation. He lived so close to nature that he took it almost for granted until, when something touched him, he expressed it with an apt comparison from some quite simple, natural thing.

That Alcman marked and loved the natural scene in which he lived is clear from some remarkable lines which describe a night. They may be set out in R. Pfeiffer's neat version:

εὕδουσιν δ᾽ ὀρέων
κορυφαί τε καὶ φάραγγες,
πρώονές τε καὶ χαράδραι
ὕλα θ᾽ ἑρπετά θ᾽ ὅσσα
τρέφει μέλαινα γαῖα,
θῆρές τ᾽ ὀρεσκῷοι
καὶ γένος μελισσᾶν

[1] Hesych. s.v. ἀάνθα.
[2] Fr. 107 D.
[3] Fr. 114 D.
[4] *Ox. Pap.* 2387, fr. 3, 6–8.
[5] Fr. 36 D.
[6] Fr. 15 D.

καὶ κνώδαλ' ἐν βένθεσσι πορφυρέας ἁλός,
εὕδουσιν δ' οἰωνῶν
φῦλα τανυπτερύγων.[1]

The peaks and the gullies of the mountains are asleep, the headlands
and the torrents, the forest and all four-footed creatures that the
black earth nourishes, the wild beasts of the mountains and the race
of bees and the monsters in the depth of the dark-blue sea, and the
tribes of the long-winged birds are asleep.

We do not know what the context of this was, but there is not the
slightest need to assume that it is the first known example of a
famous poetical theme in which the sleep of nature is contrasted
with the busy doings of men and which makes its first appearance
in the opening scene of Euripides' *Iphigenia in Aulis* and has a
long and distinguished history thenceforward.[2] Alcman presents
a natural scene, and it is entirely satisfying in itself. It may of
course be a prelude to some nocturnal rite, and it would be
perfectly appropriate as such, but we cannot say that it is.

The notion that nature sleeps is as old as Homer who uses it in
a restricted form for the north wind, ὄφρ' εὕδῃσι μένος Βορέαο,[3] and
it reappears in Simonides' εὑδέτω δὲ πόντος.[4] But Alcman goes
much farther than either of these, and his conception is different.
While Homer and Simonides speak of the slumber of wild elements like wind and sea, Alcman is concerned with the whole
of nature, animate and inanimate, fierce and friendly. Though
here Alcman relies on Homer for his language more than he
usually does,[5] the effect is not in the least Homeric. Even the conventional epithets come to life, and play their part in the whole
picture.

Alcman's reliance on his fine and perceptive senses was
strengthened by his taste for ideas. Like most Greek poets, he had
his own view of life and events, and stated it in a half mythological
way. Just as he works out his cosmology through such abstract
but perfectly recognizable powers as Πόρος and Τέκμωρ, and
just as the sons of Hippocoön are defeated by Αἶσα and Πόρος, so
when he comes to Fortune, who has so large a career in Greek

---

[1] Fr. 58 D; *Hermes*, lxxxvii (1959), pp. 1–6.
[2] A rich collection of passages may be found in A. S. Pease, *Vergil: Aeneid IV*,
pp. 434 ff.
[3] *Il.* 5. 524.   [4] Fr. 13. 18 D.
[5] Page, *Alc. Parth.* p. 161.

poetry and invites so many different explanations, Alcman sums her up in a neat genealogy:

$$Εὐνομίας καὶ Πειθῶς ἀδελφὰ$$
$$καὶ Προμαθήας θυγάτηρ.^1$$

'sister of Good Order and Persuasion, and daughter of Forethought'. Fortune is already the sister of Persuasion in Hesiod,[2] but Alcman has given her a more typically Spartan pedigree by making her the sister of Εὐνομία, which is the abstraction that typifies the so-called Lycurgan constitution, and the daughter of Προμαθεία, which well reflects how the Spartan leaders laid their plans in advance and carried them out as they intended. Alcman's maxim contains much truth to fact, but leaves little place for the guidance of the gods. Pindar would have given a very different judgement on the influence of Fortune in politics. The same sound sense may be seen in another maxim:

$$πῆρά τοι μαθήσιος ἀρχά^3$$

'experiment is the beginning of learning'. Its context is not known, and it may be referred variously to learning, art, athletics, song, dancing, or some heroic tale. But here too the emphasis is put on human experience. Alcman saw the issue clearly and set out his solution in a neat precept.

Alcman's world was simple, even small. Its literature was limited to the old epics and its own songs. It had no science or history. Its religion was that of local cults which were as yet little influenced by foreign ideas or rationalistic simplification. Its landscape was that of a valley flanked by high, majestic mountains and bounded on one side by the sea. But because this life was simple, it was clear and easy to understand. Alcman extended his knowledge to include all that he could find in legend and travellers' tales and adapted myths to suit his new ideas of cosmology. From his own past he knew of a different world on the eastern shores of the Aegean, but he accepted and loved the life which he found in Sparta, and many delightful aspects of it found their way into his verse. He understood its heroic temper when he wrote of Heracles and the Sons of Hippocoön, and he conveyed its gospel of hard effort in such a line as

$$λεπτὰ δ' ἄταρπος, νηλεὴς δ' ἀνάγκα.^4$$

[1] Fr. 44 D.	[2] *Theog.* 349, 360.
[3] Fr. 109 D.	[4] Fr. 110 D.

'narrow is the path, and Necessity is pitiless'. He saw the reasons of its political greatness, and he knew its powerful, no less than its pleasant, gods. But above all, he knew its hours of relaxation and pleasure, the dainty simplicity of its festivals, the honest enjoyment of its feasts. He marked with keen and loving eyes its landscapes, its animals, its birds. In the intervals between the the challenges of ambition and discipline he caught the spirit of Spartan happiness and turned it into melodious song.

III. STESICHORUS

IN the early history of Greek poetry looms the shadow of a great name. Few fragments of Stesichorus survive, and these are for the most part short and not very illuminating. But so great was his reputation and so strong, apparently, his influence, that he calls for the same attention as those more fortunate writers whose works are better preserved.[1] On his date the tradition gives information which, if not very precise, seems reasonably tenable. 'Suidas' places his birth in the 37th Olympiad (632–629 B.C.) and his death in the 56th (556–553 B.C.).[2] This is not inconsistent with another notice in 'Suidas' that he was a contemporary of Sappho,[3] nor in such a matter need we worry about minor inconsistencies, as when Lucian says that he died at the age of eighty-five.[4] The ancients noted that the date of his death was that of Simonides' birth,[5] and if the coincidence need not be taken too literally, it is likely enough that Stesichorus belonged to a generation or more before Simonides, who referred to him, along with Homer, as an authority on the Funeral Games of Pelias.[6] Against this chronology, which may be slight but is certainly credible, two objections call for a passing notice. The first is a statement in mathematical writers that Stesichorus had a brother called Mamertius, who flourished between Thales and Pythagoras,[7] that is in the middle of the sixth century. This looks too late for a brother of the poet, but the tradition, which comes from Hippias of Elis, need not be treated too seriously, since Hippias was not a careful historian. The second is more difficult. The Parian Marble has two entries for the name Stesichorus, and neither can be fitted into the traditional scheme. To the year 485 B.C. it assigns the first tragic victory of Aeschylus, the birth of Euripides, and the arrival of the poet Stesichorus in

---

[1] The fragments are excellently collected and discussed by J. Vürtheim, *Stesichoros' Fragmente und Biographie*, to which I am greatly indebted.

[2] s.v. Στησίχορος.   [3] s.v. Σαπφώ.   [4] *Macr.* 26.

[5] Cic. *Rep.* 2. 10. 20; Euseb. I, p. 106; II. 302 Helm.

[6] Fr. 32 D.

[7] Procl. in Eucl. 65. 11 Friedl.; Heron, *Defin.* 103. 1, vol. iv p. 108 Heiberg; see P. Maas, *R.-E.* iii A, p. 2459.

Greece, Στησίχορος ὁ ποιητὴς εἰ[ς] τὴν Ἑλλάδα ἀ[φίκετ]ο.[1] Later, at 370 or 369 B.C.—the marble is mutilated at this point—we hear that Stesichorus the second won at Athens, Στησίχορος ὁ Ἱμεραῖος ὁ δεύτερος ἐνίκησεν Ἀθήνησιν.[2] It looks as if the authority used by the Marble regarded the Stesichorus of 485 B.C. as the first Stesichorus, and since he is called ὁ ποιητής, there can be no question of his identity. This date is about a century later than that given for him by 'Suidas' and is certainly troublesome; for it might be thought that there existed in antiquity quite a different chronology for him. Wilamowitz tried to solve the difficulty by postulating the existence not of two but of three poets called Stesichorus,[3] but, though there is no inherent improbability in this, since Στησίχορος looks like a title which might be held by more than one man, yet, if three poets were so called, they were not known to the authority of the Parian Marble, which expressly calls the third of Wilamowitz's trio ὁ δεύτερος and shows no acquaintance with a third bearer of the name. It is easier to suppose that the Marble has made a mistake in the date of the first Stesichorus and put him in the wrong place. That it was capable of this is clear from its attribution of a poetical victory to Simonides 'the grandfather of the poet, being himself also a poet' in 489 B.C.[4] Since in 489 our Simonides was himself sixty-seven years old, his grandfather cannot have won a competition at this date. A similar confusion may have happened with Stesichorus, who has been brought down much lower than he ought to be. It is true that some feeble support for this later date might be claimed from a story which connects Stesichorus with Gelon,[5] but this is patently a variant of another story which connects him with Phalaris, and need not be taken seriously. The dates given by 'Suidas' suit what little evidence we have for an earlier date for Stesichorus. Aristotle connects him with Phalaris,[6] and Phalaris' period of power may be placed with some assurance towards the middle of the sixth century.[7] Moreover, Stesichorus lived sufficiently before Simonides to be regarded by him as an established authority on heroic legend,[8] and his mention of an eclipse, known to Pliny,[9] may have been that of 585 B.C. Indications of

[1] *Mar. Par.* 50. [2] Ibid. 73. [3] *S.u.S.* pp. 233–9.
[4] *Mar. Par.* 49. [5] Conon, 26 F 42 Jacoby. [6] *Rhet.* 1393 b.
[7] Jerome puts him in 565–549 B.C., and 'Suidas' in the 52nd Olympiad (572–569 B.C.).
[8] Fr. 32 D. [9] *N.H.* 2. 12 (9). 54.

this character tend to confirm the view that Stesichorus lived in the last quarter of the seventh century and the first half of the sixth. He was presumably younger than Alcman, certainly older than Simonides, and that is where Greek historians placed him.

Stesichorus' name and home are also matters of dispute. 'Suidas' says that 'formerly he was called Teisias' and that later he was called Stesichorus 'because he first established a choir of singers to the lyre'.[1] Στησίχορος looks like a title and Τεισίας like a real name; so there is really no problem. Nor need his home cause much trouble. He seems at one time to have lived at Mataurus, a Locrian colony in southern Italy,[2] but his main activities were in Sicily, whether at Acragas, where he came into conflict with Phalaris, or at Himera.[3] For Plato he was 'the man of Himera',[4] and since Himerius says that 'he adorns Himera with speech',[5] and his image appears on its coins,[6] there is reason to think that he was closely connected with it. He was buried at Catane, where his octagonal tomb excited interest in later times.[7]

Stesichorus is the first poet of Magna Graecia from whose work anything survives, and we cannot but relate what we know of it to his circumstances and his background. Both in Italy and in Sicily cultural forces received a peculiar direction from the facts of colonization. Locri was an Achaean colony from the Peloponnese,[8] and to some extent independent alike of Dorian and of Ionian influences, while Himera had a mixed population of Dorian and Chalcidian origins,[9] and since it lay on the north coast of Sicily, away and apart from the other Greek colonies and exposed to native and Carthaginian forces, it developed an independent life in which several threads were united. It is therefore impossible to attach Stesichorus strictly to either Dorian or Ionian tradition. He owed something to both, and something perhaps to indigenous influences also. In him various currents met, and his poetry, like Sicilian sculpture, was a new creation.

---

[1] s.v. Στησίχορος. ἐκλήθη δὲ Στησίχορος ὅτι πρῶτος κιθαρῳδίᾳ χόρον ἔστησεν, ἐπεί τοι πρότερον Τεισίας ἐκαλεῖτο.

[2] Steph. Byz. s.v. Μάταυρος.

[3] Cic. Verr. 2. 2. 35. 87; Pollux 9. 100; I.G. xiv. 1213.

[4] Phaedr. 244 a.   [5] Or. 27. 24 Colonna.

[6] Head, H.N. p. 147.

[7] Phot. s.v. πάντα ὀκτώ; Antipater of Sidon, Anth. Pal. 7. 75.

[8] Strab. 259.   [9] Thuc. 6. 5. 1.

He owed something to the epic, whether Homeric or Hesiodic or less strictly defined, something to Dorian choral poetry, and something to local legends and beliefs. To the first he owed some of his stories and his broad handling of them; to the second his poetical form; to the third some of his more unusual themes. The different elements were united in him, and though any separation of them is artificial, it is necessary because it shows from what origins he developed his art and in what directions he shaped it.

We cannot say that Stesichorus knew the *Iliad* and the *Odyssey* in any form like that in which we know them. For those who believe that the Homeric poems were brought to the west by Cynaethus about 504 B.C.,[1] Stesichorus clearly can have known nothing of them. But the epic style and the epic stories were in currency in the west long before Cynaethus. Two mysterious hexameters on a cup from Ischia speak of what seems to be a love-charm in the language of the epic, and are earlier than 700 B.C.[2] But we need not rely on such general considerations as this. That Stesichorus knew something about an episode very like one in our *Odyssey*, and that he treated it with a full respect for the epic language, is clear from a papyrus fragment which has been thought to come from his *Νόστοι*. Before the publication of the papyrus almost nothing was known of this poem except that, as its title indicated, it dealt with the epic theme of the returns of the Achaean heroes from Troy. The new fragment describes a situation:

θε[ῖ]ον ἐ[ξ]αίφνας τέρας ἰδοῖσα νύμφα,
ὧδε δ' ἔ[πειθ'] Ἑλένα φωναῖ ποτ[ὶ] παῖδ' Ὀδύσειο[ν]·
Τηλέμαχ', [ἦ] τις ὅδ' ἁμὶν ἄγγελ[ο]ς ὠρανόθεν
δι' αἰθέρο[ς ἀτ]ρυγέτας κατέπαλτο βαδ[
5   ].ε φοινᾶι κεκλαγγώ[ς
        ]... ἐς ὑμετέρους δόμους προφα[νεὶς Ὀδυσε]ύς,
                 μ]άν[τ]ις ἀνὴρ
             βο]υλαῖς Ἀθάνας
           μὴ φ]ῆις· αὖτα λακέρυζα κορώνα.
10   ].μ' οὐδ' ἐγώ σ' ἐρύ[ξ]ω
        Παν]ελόπα σ⟨ε⟩ ἰδοῖσα φίλου πατ[ρ]ὸς υἱόν
         π]ό[ροι] τ[έλ]ος ἐσθλ[όν.[3]

---

[1] H. T. Wade-Gery, *Studies in Greek History*, pp. 31 ff.
[2] G. Buchner and C. F. Russo, *R.A.L.* x (1955), pp. 215-34.
[3] *Ox. Pap.* xxiii, no. 2360; cf. W. Peek, *Philologus*, cii (1958), pp. 169-77; H. Lloyd-Jones, *C.R.* N.S. viii (1958), p. 17. 2 ἔπειθ' Lloyd-Jones. 3 ἦ Lloyd-Jones. 4 βαδιζέμεναι, suggested by Peek, seems hardly suitable for a journey by chariot or

The situation here recalls at once that in *Odyssey* 15. 43–181, where Telemachus takes elaborate farewells of Menelaus and Helen, and when he is on the point of departure, an eagle flies overhead carrying a goose, and Helen interprets this to mean that Odysseus will return home and exact vengeance from the Suitors. In both poems an omen is interpreted by Helen to mean that Telemachus can safely return home and that his father will be there. If μάντις ἀνήρ is right in Stesichorus at 7, it would echo Helen's μαντεύσομαι at *Od*. 15, 172, and the words οὐδ' ... σ' ἐρύξω at 10 recall what Menelaus says to Telemachus at *Od*. 15. 68, Τηλέμαχ', οὔτι σ' ἐγώ γε πόλυν χρόνον ἐνθάδ' ἐρύξω. In the second column of the papyrus there are clearly references to a gift:

> ἀργυρέαν τε π[ε
> χρυσῷ ὕπερθε[
> ἐκ Δαρδανίδ[α Πριάμου
> 5 Πλεισθενίδας α[
> καὶ τὰ μὲν εὐ[ξεστ-
> σὺν [θεράποντι
> χρυσ[¹

and we are reminded of the bowl of silver and gold which Menelaus gives to Telemachus at *Od*. 15. 155 ff. On the other hand there are some differences, real or suspected, between Stesichorus and Homer. In Homer the bowl is a gift from the king of the Sidonians; in Stesichorus it seems to be loot from Priam's palace. In Homer Helen's prophecy turns entirely on the sight of the eagle and the goose; in Stesichorus we hear of an ἄγγελος, who κατέπαλτο through the sky. This looks as if it were Hermes or Iris or some other messenger of the gods, but this impression is perhaps counteracted by the appearance of φοινᾶι in the next line, which would suit an eagle but not a god. In Stesichorus the words αὖτα λακέρυζα κορώνα at 9 have no counterpart in Homer, but there is no need to assume that a crow has actually appeared, and what Helen means is that what she says is not nonsense. Finally, in Stesichorus it must surely be she, and not Menelaus as in Homer, who says that she will not keep

ship. 5 With φοινᾶι Peek suggests ὀπί after κεκλαγγώς on the lines of θυμὸς φοινός in Hom. Hymn 3. 361–2, but the missing word might just as well have meant 'throat' or 'beak'. 6 The line may have begun with some word like ἥξει; the rest is supplied by Peek. 7 μάντις makes excellent sense, especially if prefixed by ἅτε, but is perhaps against the evidence of the papyrus. 11 σ⟨ε⟩ ἰδοῖσα Lloyd-Jones. 12 π]ό[ροι] Peek.

¹ Πριάμου in 3, εὐ[ξεστ- in 5, and [θεράποντι in 6 are Peek's suggestions.

Telemachus from going. These differences are slight enough, but they suggest that either Stesichorus knew something very like our version of the *Odyssey* and made his own innovations in it, or that he knew a somewhat different version, which he followed of his own choice. We cannot say which solution is right, but in any case Stesichorus certainly knew something close to the episode in our *Odyssey*.

It is also clear that Stesichorus was familiar with the epic manner of narrative and the epic language. Actual echoes from Homer are few. When he calls Helen νύμφα, he recalls νύμφα φίλη of *Il*. 3. 130, and his δι' αἰθέρος ἀτρυγέτας is close enough to δι' αἰθέρος ἀτρυγέτοιο of *Il*. 17. 425, but some other phrases suggest that the epic language which he used covered a wider field than that of Homer. Thus neither τέλος ἐσθλόν nor παῖδ' 'Οδύσειον is Homeric, though the first has some resemblance to κλέος ἐσθλόν at *Il*. 5. 273; 18. 121, and the second is formed on the same lines as Καπανήϊον υἱόν at *Il*. 5. 108. More significantly Πλεισθενίδας is not known to Homer in any form, and λακέρυζα κορώνα is an echo from Hesiod (*Op*. 747; fr. 71.1). Stesichorus was certainly acquainted with the epic in its advanced stage, and drew on much more than the Homeric poems for his themes and his language.

Stesichorus' acquaintance with the Hesiodic school of narrative poetry can be seen in several themes, notably the cowherd Eurytion, who kept the cattle of Geryon,[1] the presence of an εἴδωλον of Helen at Troy,[2] the oath sworn by Helen's suitors,[3] and the births of Typhos[4] and Athene.[5] More significantly he seems to have known in some form the *Shield of Heracles*; for Hypothesis A to this poem says Στησίχορος δέ φησιν 'Ησιόδου εἶναι τὸ ποίημα. Fortunately we are able to control this statement to some degree by the scholiast on Pindar *Ol*. 10. 19:

The great Heracles turned back and retreated in his fight against Cycnus because Cycnus was stirred on by Ares. Heracles fought because Cycnus was cruel to strangers and, living in a pass in Thessaly, used to cut off the heads of travellers in order to build a shrine to Apollo from them, and, when Heracles came, wished to treat him

---

[1] Strab. 148; Hes. *Theog.* 293.
[2] Plat. *Rep.* 9. 586 c; Hes. fr. 266 R.
[3] Schol. ad *Il.* 2. 339; Hes. frs. 94–96.
[4] *Et. Mag.* 772. 49; Hes. *Theog.* 821 ff.
[5] Schol. Ap. Rhod. 4. 1310 and *Ox. Pap.* 2260, ii. 19–23; Hes. *Theog.* 895.

in the same way. After joining battle with them, Heracles fled, because Ares helped the young Cycnus. But later Heracles killed him
also. Stesichorus tells this in the work called *Cycnus*.

The story, as told by Stesichorus, bears obvious resemblances to
the Hesiodic *Shield of Heracles*, which has been dated to the early
part of the sixth century[1] and could have been known to Stesichorus. If the poem was so near to him in time, it is odd that he
should have attributed it to Hesiod, who lived some generations
earlier, and it is possible that Stesichorus knew the poem either
in a slightly different form or used 'Hesiod' in a generic sense as
early writers used 'Homer'.[2] In any case it is instructive to compare what we know of the Κύκνος with the *Shield*. In the latter
poem Cycnus tries to stop Heracles from passing through Thessaly and is helped by Ares; Heracles attacks and kills Cycnus,
defeats Ares, and goes, laden with booty, to Trachis. It is the
story of a tough fight in which hard blows are dealt by both sides,
and Heracles wins. Any possible impiety which we might feel
to be implicit in the fight with Ares is countered by the old
assumption that Ares was a fair foe for men.[3] This is the Hesiodic
version, and on the whole Stesichorus followed it, but he made
two diversions from it, and each illustrates his method of treating
traditional myths.

First, Stesichorus was not content to recount a straightforward
fight ending in victory but said that on the arrival of Ares Heracles turned tail and fled, but later returned and killed Cycnus.
This temporary set-back struck the imagination of Pindar who,
in a poem for a man from Locri, says with reference to his victory in the Olympian games:

τράπε δὲ Κύκνεια μάχα καὶ ὑπέρβιον
'Ηρακλέα,[4]

'even Heracles of surpassing strength was routed in his fight with
Cycnus'. This is surely a deliberate reference to Stesichorus, since
it occurs in a poem for a Locrian and is introduced without further
explanation or development. The purpose of this set-back was
no doubt to enhance the tension of the story, and it shows how

---

[1] R. M. Cook, *C.Q.* xxxi (1937), pp. 204–13; J. L. Myres, *J.H.S.* lxi (1941),
pp. 17–38.
[2] J. A. Davison, *Eranos*, liii (1956), pp. 135 ff.
[3] *Il.* 5. 889 ff.   [4] *Ol.* 10. 15.

Stesichorus, in his desire to tell a good tale, does not confine himself to what his epic precedents provide. Secondly, in Stesichorus Cycnus kills travellers because he wishes to make a shrine for Apollo from their heads. On this gruesome detail the *Shield* says not a word, but Apollo has a place in it. Cycnus kills pilgrims on their way to offer sacrifices at Delphi,[1] and though he meets Heracles in Apollo's precinct and hopes that the god will help him, he is sadly deceived; for Apollo urges Heracles to fight him.[2] His relations with Apollo are at least ambiguous, and the Hesiodic poet gives good enough reasons for Apollo to urge Heracles against him. Stesichorus must have been aware of the connexion between Cycnus and Apollo and decided to make more of it. It was not sufficiently dramatic that Cycnus should kill pilgrims; he must do something more blood-curdling, and what better than make a shrine of their skulls? The detail emphasises that, though Cycnus appeals to Apollo, he likes to insult and deride him and show his independence of him. It stresses the personality of Cycnus as one of the monstrous highwaymen, like Sinis or Procrustes, who had their own disgusting ways of killing strangers. The temple of skulls is not a tribute but an insult to Apollo, and Stesichorus, who may have picked it up from local folk-lore, uses it to increase the horror with which Cycnus inspires us.

What we know of Stesichorus' Νόστοι and Κύκνος indicates that he was well versed in the material of epic poetry,[3] but that he must have known it in its later days when its language was moving away from the more strictly formulaic style of oral epic and its themes could be treated with some freedom in the interests of surprise and novelty. The stories which he learned from it he transferred to lyrical, choral odes, and if the epic provided him with much of his matter, the ode provided him with his form. In principle his poems belong to the same class as Alcman's, and though there seem to have been substantial differences both in language and in the manner of telling a story, both poets used the form which was gaining popularity and prestige in the seventh century. There is no evidence that Stesichorus owed

---

[1] *Scut.* 479–80. [2] Ibid. 68 ff.

[3] Aristotle fr. 565 records the legend that Hesiod was the father of Stesichorus, and this at least indicates some close connexion between their two kinds of poetry.

his style to Alcman or that he even handled the same tales. His predecessors seem to have come from his own world, and we may surmise who two of them were. The first is Xenocritus of Locri, who played a prominent part in the second musical κατάστασις at Sparta.[1] Like his fellow workers, Thaletas, Polymnestus, and Sacadas, he was more important for his music than for his poetry, but his musical innovations gave a new importance to the choral ode. His Locrian origin suggests that in the seventh century Locri had already its own musical art which spread to Sparta at a time of artistic experiment and change. The Locrian mode was ascribed to Xenocritus, but he was also credited with narrative odes which were called Dithyrambs,[2] and it certainly looks as if Stesichorus inherited from him the main character of his art. Of the second figure, Xanthus, we do not know the home, but he was earlier than Stesichorus, who referred to him,[3] and since, like Stesichorus, he wrote an Ὀρέστεια, we may well conclude that he was in some sense a predecessor of the poet of Himera, who is said to have taken a good deal from him.[4] The chances are that he too came from Magna Graecia, and his art of lyrical narrative looks as if it came from the same kind of school as that of Xenocritus.

Just as choral lyric in the Peloponnese owed something to the example of poets from the eastern Aegaean, so it is possible that Stesichorus may have learned from a famous and influential Lesbian poet. The poems of Arion may never have reached the libraries of Alexandria,[5] and that would explain why no single fragment of them survives, but at an earlier date something was known of them and Herodotus speaks of him as the man who first gave a proper composition to Dithyrambs.[6] He seems to have found in existence an improvised, ecstatic song to Dionysus and to have transformed it into a formal, choral hymn attached to definite festivals and accompanied by regular dancing. Though nothing is known of the contents of his poems, it is possible that he was responsible for the element of narrative which was later to predominate in Dithyrambs. Indeed this is the only satisfactory explanation of the word ὀνομάσαντα, which Herodotus uses in

---

[1] 'Plut.' *Mus.* 9.   [2] Ibid. 10.   [3] Athen. 12. 513 a.

[4] Ibid. πολλὰ δὲ τοῦ Ξάνθου παραπεποίηκεν ὁ Στησίχορος.

[5] Wilamowitz, *T.G.L.* p. 6.

[6] 1. 23 διθύραμβον πρῶτον ἀνθρώπων τῶν ἡμεῖς ἴδμεν ποιήσαντά τε καὶ ὀνομάσαντα καὶ διδάξαντα ἐν Κορίνθῳ; cf. Hellanic. 4 F 66 Jacoby.

reference to him. It suggests that just as Dithyrambs by Pindar or Bacchylides were called ‘Ηρακλῆς or ’Ηΐθεοι, so the Dithyrambs of Arion also had names derived from the stories which they told. He may have influenced Xenocritus in the composition of dithyrambs and Xanthus in the emphasis given to stories in song. The possibility of his influence is the more likely in view of his famous and profitable tour of Italy and Sicily.[1] His traditional date is in the last quarter of the seventh century,[2] and since Herodotus explicitly connects him with Periander,[3] he must have been busy before 600 B.C. When he visited the West, Stesichorus would still have been quite a young man, and his high reputation may have reached the ears of the younger poet and inspired him to compose in somewhat the same manner.

A third influence on the art of Stesichorus may have been in the local songs of Locri, which Clearchus compared with the work of Sappho and Anacreon.[4] Pindar, who was not an enthusiastic admirer of contemporary poetry, twice pays a tribute to that of Locri, and on each occasion suggests that it is an established and well founded art, whether he calls the Locrians στρατὸν ἀκρόσοφον,[5] with the suggestion that they practise the true σοφία of poetry, or says of them

μέλει τέ σφισι Καλλιόπα.[6]

The only surviving specimen of Locrian poetry may perhaps show of what it was capable:

ὦ τί πάσχεις; μὴ προδῷς ἄμμ’, ἱκετεύω.
πρὶν καὶ μολεῖν κεῖνον, ἀνίστω, μὴ κακὸν
μέγα ποιήσῃ σὲ κἀμὲ τὰν δειλάκραν.
ἀμέρα καὶ δή· τὸ φῶς διὰ τῆς θυρίδος οὐκ εἰσορῇς;[7]

O what is the matter? Do not betray us, I beseech you. Get up before he comes, lest he do a great evil to you and to me, poor wretch. It is already day. Do you not see the light through the window?

This song is not likely to be old, but it looks as if it came from an ancient tradition, since its subject is to be found in many parts of the world. It is an *alba* or *aubade*, a dawn-song, such as appealed to the troubadours and the Minnesinger, and has a far

[1] Hdt. 1. 24. 1.
[2] Eusebius gives Ol. 40. 4 (617 B.C.) and ‘Suidas’ Ol. 38 (628-625 B.C.).
[3] 1. 23.   [4] Athen. 14. 639 a.
[5] *Ol.* 11. 19.   [6] *Ol.* 10. 14.   [7] *Carm. Pop.* 43 D.

older counterpart in the Chinese Book of Songs.[1] It is popular
in nearly every sense and comes from an almost vulgar tradition,
but it shows that Locrian poetry had its own individuality, and
that Xenocritus and Stesichorus may have learned some of their
craft from humbler models than choral odes.

A love-song of this kind is close to folk-song, and something of
a folk-spirit may lie behind two poems of Stesichorus, the Δάφνις
and the Καλύκα, whose subjects lie outside his usual preference
for heroic tales. According to Aelian,[2] Stesichorus was the first
to compose βουκολικὰ μέλη, and though Aelian is not an accurate
scholar, and his words must not be pressed into meaning that
Stesichorus wrote idylls like Theocritus, we can at least see from
his words what the Δάφνις was, and his account is supplemented
and confirmed by Diodorus.[3] Daphnis, the neatherd, was the
son of Hermes and a nymph, and he tended the cattle of the
Sun. He was loved by a jealous nymph and swore faithfulness
to her, but once, overcome by wine, he was unfaithful, and she
blinded him for it. In this version the story looks like an Alexandrian tale. Theocritus locates Daphnis near Syracuse, and Diodorus in the middle of Sicily among the Heraean Hills, but
Timaeus sets him in the neighbourhood of Himera,[4] and here
Theocritus, contradicting himself, places him when he writes of
the trees who mourn his death:

$$καὶ ὡς δρύες αὐτὸν ἐθρήνευν$$
$$Ἱμέρα αἵτε φύοντι παρ' ὄχθαισιν ποτάμοιο.[5]$$

and how he was lamented by the oaks which grow by the banks of the
river Himeras.

The story belonged to Stesichorus' own region of Himera, and
who Daphnis was is clear from two points. First, his name.
When Aelian says that he was called Δάφνις because he was born
ἐν δάφνῃ in a bay-tree, and Diodorus because he lived in a place
where bay-trees abounded, we need not treat them too seriously.
The name indicates that Daphnis was some sort of tree-spirit,
like Dionysus ἔνδενδρος or Helen δενδρῖτις, and this conclusion
is strengthened by the second point. Diodorus, forgetful of his
nymph, says that Daphnis accompanied Artemis on her hunting,
much to the pleasure of the goddess. He was, then, a counterpart

[1] Arthur Waley, *The Book of Songs*, p. 37.
[2] *V.H.* 10. 18.   [3] 4. 84.
[4] 566 F 83 Jacoby.   [5] 7. 74–75.

of Hippolytus, a chaste young man who attended the virgin
goddess. But such attendants come to violent ends, as Hippolytus
is killed through the panic of his own horses. Aelian and Diodorus
agree that Daphnis was blinded by his nymph for being unfaithful, and this is an indubitable piece of folk-lore, since there were
chthonic powers called Παλικοί who blinded those who broke
their oaths.[1] Others say that Daphnis flung himself from rocks
into the sea,[2] and Theocritus hints at something like this:

χὠ Δάφνις ἔβα ῥόον· ἔκλυσε δίνα
τὸν Μοίσαις φίλον ἄνδρα, τὸν οὐ Νύμφαισιν ἀπεχθῆ.[3]

and Daphnis has gone down the flood. The eddy has overwhelmed
him, whom the Muses loved and the Nymphs did not abhor.

Nor is the scene of the story unknown. Servius says that near
Himera there was a cliff jutting into the sea, called Cephaloe-
dium, on which a rock which resembled a man was said to be
Daphnis turned into stone,[4] while others added that in his blindness he fell into the sea.[5] This indeed suggests that in Stesichorus'
poem his blindness may have brought him to such a death, and
his true character emerges. He is a nature-spirit, who perishes in
the sea, and when he perishes, nature laments him because life
passes from the trees. We cannot be sure how much of this was to
be found in Stesichorus but Aelian and Diodorus make it clear
what Daphnis' character was, and we may draw the conclusion
that his cult was connected with Himera and that Stesichorus
wrote his poem for it.

The Καλύκα also seems to have been based on Sicilian lore;
for so good an authority as Aristoxenus says:

Of old, women had a song called *Calyce*. It was a poem of Stesichorus,
in which a maiden called Calyce prayed to Aphrodite that she might
be wedded to a youth called Euathlus, whom she loved, and when
he despised her, she threw herself over a cliff. The action was set
near Leucas. The poet gave the maiden a very virtuous character;
for she did not wish to be joined to the youth at all costs, but
prayed to be the wife of Euathlus, or failing that to die.[6]

The theme suggests some general resemblance with the Δάφνις,
but the poem may have been more informal and closer to the

---

[1] Diod. 11. 89. 5. [2] Philargyr. ad Verg. *Buc.* 5. 20.
[3] 1. 140–1. [4] ad Verg. *Buc.* 8. 68.
[5] Schol. Theocr. 8. 93. [6] Athen. 14. 619 d.

later Locrian love-songs; for Athenaeus classes it with the νόμιον, attributed to the poetess Eriphanis, which told of a hopeless love for Menalcas[1] and contained the line

μακραὶ δρύες, ὦ Μενάλκα.

Since this recalls folk-song in its metre and its theme, the Καλύκα may have been a lover's lament or at least have contained such a subject in it. It seems to have been attached to mythology, since Euathlus, whom Calyce loved, was a king of Elis and father of Endymion.[2] If the story started on the mainland, it evidently found a home in Sicily and may be a distant ancestor of the love-lorn songs of the Theocritean shepherds. Its most striking quality seems to have been the virtuous character of Calyce, to which Aristoxenus draws attention. Was this a heritage from folk-lore or the contribution of a poet who liked to maintain a noble, heroic tone?

It is possible that Stesichorus came even closer than this to the Locrian tradition of love-songs. Athenaeus says that he wrote παίδεια καὶ παιδικά[3] and this finds some support in a passage of Eupolis:

τὰ Στησιχόρου τε καὶ Ἀλκμᾶνος Σιμωνίδου τε
ἀρχαῖον ἀείδειν· ὁ δὲ Γνήσιππος ἔστιν ἀκούειν.
κεῖνος νυκτέριν' εὗρε μοιχοῖς ἀείσματ' ἐκκαλεῖσθαι
γυναῖκας ἔχοντας ἰαμβύκην τε καὶ τρίγωνον.[4]

It is old-fashioned to sing the songs of Stesichorus and Alcman and Simonides. But Cnesippus is there to be heard. He discovered nocturnal songs for adulterers to call for when they have women and an *iambyce* and a triangular harp.

Since Alcman was regarded as ἡγεμὼν ἐρωτικῶν μελῶν,[5] the appearance of Stesichorus in his company suggests that he too wrote love-songs, and this may get some support from Lucian who makes choirs of boys and girls sing his songs in the Elysian fields.[6] This is not necessarily inconsistent with Dio Chrysostom's remark that, while it is improper for kings to sing the songs of Sappho and Anacreon, they may sing those of Stesichorus and Pindar;[7] for this may refer to the normal, serious songs of Stesichorus. But on this question we must recognize the serious doubt

---

[1] Athen. 14. 619 c.　　　　　　　　[2] Schol. Ap. Rhod. 4. 57.
[3] 13. 601 a.　　　　[4] Fr. 139 K.　　　　　　[5] Athen. 13. 600 f.
[6] *V.H.* 2. 15.　　　　　　　[7] 2. 28.

that these songs were composed not by our Stesichorus but by the poet of the same name who lived in the fourth century and in his *Rhadine* told the sad tale of lovers killed by a despot.[1] We may doubt whether Stesichorus abandoned his choral style for such personal measures as these, but we can hardly doubt that in some of his poems, notably the Δάφνις and the Καλύκα, he told of stories which lay outside the heroic sphere and were close to local cults and beliefs.

Though Stesichorus absorbed different elements into his art, there is no reason to think that the result was not homogeneous. If specifically local legends took him off the beaten path in the Δάφνις and Καλύκα, there is no doubt that the greater part of his work was concerned with heroic themes presented in a lyrical form. The themes came from the epic in a wide sense, and the form must have been capacious enough to present them in some detail. Indeed the small fragment of the Νόστοι shows in how straightforward and even leisurely a way he told a story. If Pindar's *Pythian* IV had not survived, we might wonder how Greek choral song was able to deal with a long story and, within its limits to compete with the epic; but just as Pindar told the story of the Argonauts in an extensive and expansive manner, so Stesichorus must have done something of the same kind. He may well have been less allusive and less circuitous than Pindar, but what we know of his songs suggests that he put a good deal into them and transformed into lyric shape much matter that was well known from the epic. Indeed his special position is at the point where the lyric succeeds the epic as a main means of expressing what concerns a Greek audience, and starts on its task by re-shaping and bringing up to date much that the epic had told in a simpler and less ingenious manner. The transference from epic to lyric was made easier for Stesichorus by the existence of dac-tylic metres which could contain without much adjustment epic phrases, and he never shows such metrical complexities as we find in Pindar and Bacchylides. No doubt the foundations of his work had been laid by his predecessors, but his name and his achieve-ments eclipsed theirs. He represents the western version of the movement which Alcman epitomizes on the mainland, but he seems to have been at once more straightforward and more fluent than Alcman. We do not know for what purposes he

[1] H. J. Rose, *C.Q.* xxvi (1932), pp. 88-92.

wrote, but the manner of his writing suggests the call of high occasions, such as the feast of a god or hero or some other important celebration.

A notable feature of Stesichorus' work is that in later times his poems were known by names which referred to their mythological subjects. This was probably the case with Arion before him, and was certainly the case after him with the Dithyrambs of Pindar and Bacchylides. Though we cannot say with any assurance that the poems of Stesichorus were Dithyrambs, we can assume with some confidence that the ascription of names indicates a larger element of narrative than is to be found, for instance, in the Epinicians of Pindar or even in the Maiden-songs of Alcman. At least thirteen names of his poems survive, and we cannot doubt that these express what the main themes of these poems were. In trying to recapture some of their contents from the few quotations and references which concern them we may well be facing an almost hopeless task. The quotations too often are made by ancient scholars for any interest but their contents, and the references are often too short to be really informative. Nor is it always safe to supplement them by what we know of later handling of the same stories. Greek poets might indeed owe much to tradition and have few qualms about repeating what had already been said by others before them, but at least they made their own improvements and variations on familiar themes, and we cannot be sure that, when Stesichorus had told a story, they repeated it in the same way. Yet we can to some degree supplement what we know of his stories by a critical use of two kinds of evidence. First, the art of his time, whether in sculpture or in vase-painting or in more ambitious works lost to us but known from descriptions, bears so close a relation to Stesichorus' work that it may be used, with due caution, as evidence for what he said in certain stories. Secondly, some of his themes are referred to by later poets and mythographers in a way so incidental and allusive that they look like direct allusions to him. With a cautious use of these two kinds of evidence we may hope to know a little more about Stesichorus than we do from the fragments and the references.

Four of Stesichorus' titles indicate that the poems told of episodes in the life of Heracles. This is not surprising in view of the large part which the hero played in the myths and cults of Magna

Graecia. Dionysius of Halicarnassus says that it would be difficult to find any part of Italy in which he was not honoured,[1] and
a follower of Aristotle confirms this when he records that there
were memorials of Heracles in several parts of Italy along the
roads by which he travelled.[2] The reason for this popularity was
partly that Heracles was the foundation-hero of some towns, as at
Croton he was worshipped as οἰκιστής.[3] Early metopes depict his
labours. In the second quarter of the sixth century B.C. the Cretan
Bull appears on Temple Y at Selinus,[4] and the struggle for the
Delphic tripod and the bringing of the Erymanthian boar[5] on
the temple of Argive Hera at Sele near Paestum (Posidonia). In
the middle of the century the Cercopes appear on Temple C at
Selinus.[6] Heracles was worshipped at Tarentum[7] and Acragas,[8]
and the hot baths at Himera were associated with him.[9] If
in the Peloponnese Heracles was the type of enduring, suffering,
heroic manhood, in Magna Graecia he was almost the ideal
embodiment of the Greek settler, who destroyed aboriginal
monsters and gave peace to the regions which he traversed. Of
all heroes he stood nearest to Greek colonists, and it is not
surprising that the audiences of Stesichorus were ready to hear
about him.

Himera, the town of Stesichorus, lay among barbarian peoples
on the northern coast of Sicily, an outpost of Hellenism that
looked to the far west for its adventures and its trade. The early
date of its first coins shows that it found prosperity before many
other Greek colonies in Sicily, and it must have been a ready
home for stories told by travellers. Something from these has
found a way into Stesichorus' Γηρυονηίς, in which he told of the
voyage of Heracles to the west in search of the cattle of Geryon,
and elaborated a subject on which Hesiod had touched in the
Theogony.[10] Hesiod had set the scene on a sea-girt island, Erytheia,
beyond the stream of Ocean, and that was as much as his geo-
graphical knowledge permitted, but Stesichorus, who knew about
the discovery of Tartessus, localized it more precisely and set
Eurytion, the keeper of Geryon's cattle,

---

[1] *Ant. Rom.* 1. 40. 6.   [2] *de Mir. Ausc.* 97.
[3] Head, *H.N.* p. 100.   [4] G. Richter, *Archaic Greek Art*, p. 126.
[5] Ibid. p. 128.   [6] Ibid. p. 126.
[7] Plut. *Fab. Max.* 22. 6.   [8] Cic. *in Verr.* 2. 4. 43. 94.
[9] Aesch. fr. 32 N.   [10] 287–94.

σχεδὸν ἀντιπέρας κλεινᾶς Ἐρυθείας,
Ταρτησσοῦ ποταμοῦ παρὰ παγὰς ἀπείρονας ἀργυρορίζους,
ἐν κευθμῶνι πέτρας.[1]

hard over against famous Erytheia, by the inexhaustible silver-rooted
springs of the river Tartessus, in the hollow of a rock.

Tartessus, the biblical Tarshish, had been discovered by the
Greeks when Stesichorus was a boy, and rather than set Geryon
vaguely in the middle of a fabulous Ocean he placed him in a
country of which he must have heard from sailors. He pays his
tribute to tradition by calling Erytheia κλεινά, and then strengthens
the picture by adding circumstantial details which owe nothing
to legend. When, however, in the same poem he mentioned the
'island of Sarpedon', which the *Cypria* placed as the home of the
Gorgons in the Ocean,[2] he yielded to tradition and kept it there.[3]
Discovery had indeed extended his horizon, but he had to rely
on legends for some of his details.

An important episode in the Γηρυονηΐς was the voyage of
Heracles to the west. He had to get there somehow, and Stesichorus hit on a splendid expedient for it. There was an im-
memorial story that the Sun travelled in a cup from his setting
in the west to his rising in the east. Mimnermus, who was older
than Stesichorus, knew of this and brought it into his lines on the
ever-labouring Sun, telling how he is borne over the water in a
winged, golden vessel, made by Hephaestus, from the Hesperides to the land of the Aethiopians, where his horses and chariot
await him.[4] The charming fancy has its parallels in the folk-
lore of many lands, and the cup has been found in Egyptian,
Lithuanian, and German tales.[5] The probability is that at one
time the Sun was thought of as a cup and that later the cup
became his symbol or attribute. Stesichorus is not likely to have
known the origins of the story and certainly disregards them.
He uses the cup for its dramatic possibilities. Instead of taking
Heracles a long journey to the west over land, he transports him
in the Sun's cup, on the reasonable assumption that it travelled
empty daily from east to west by its own propulsion. The brilliance of the idea certainly impressed the Greeks, and it is

---

[1] Fr. 4 D.   [2] Fr. 21 Kinkel.
[3] Schol. Ap. Rhod. I. 211 Στησίχορος δὲ ἐν τῇ Γηρυονηΐδι καὶ νῆσόν τινα ἐν τῷ
Ἀτλαντικῷ πελάγει Σαρπηδονίαν φησί.
[4] Fr. 10. 5-10 D.   [5] Roscher, *Lex. Myth.* 1. 2014.

significant that when, soon after Stesichorus, Pisander of Rhodes wrote his epic on Heracles he repeated the theme,[1] as did Aeschylus after him.[2] If the cup itself belongs to cosmological myth, the way in which Stesichorus made Heracles get it from the Sun seems to have been in the grand heroic tradition. It is likely that his version appears in Pherecydes,[3] who says that Heracles threatened the Sun with his bow, but desisted when the Sun ordered him to do so. For this the Sun lent him the cup, and on it he fared to Erytheia. On the way Ocean rocked the cup, but again Heracles threatened with his bow, and Ocean calmed the sea. This double defiance of gods by a hero is not a mere reduplication of a stock theme. In both cases Heracles threatens them as almost he alone may. On both occasions he gets his way, first by yielding to the Sun, then by persisting against Ocean. The difference of treatment reflects a difference of status between the Sun and Ocean. The Sun was an Olympian, who could not be threatened too violently, but Ocean, the son of Uranus and Gaea and the brother of the Giants,[4] could perhaps be defied with less risk. Yet in repeating the theme of defiance Stesichorus shows that he is closer to the old epic world in which men fight against gods than to the coming age which insisted that this should never happen.[5] Indeed later poets, in telling the story, remodelled it to avoid any implications of impiety. Pisander said that the cup was a gift from Ocean,[6] and Panyassis that it was a gift from Nereus.[7] Such changes made any struggle with the Sun unnecessary and brought Heracles into line with more respectable standards of conduct.

In the cup Heracles came to Erytheia, and some lines survive in which Stesichorus tells how the Sun takes it back and leaves Heracles to make his way by land:

Ἀέλιος δ' Ὑπεριονίδας δέπας ἐσκατέβαινε
χρύσεον, ὄφρα δι' Ὠκεανοῖο περάσας
ἀφίκοιθ' ἱερᾶς ποτὶ βένθεα νυκτὸς ἐρεμνᾶς
ποτὶ ματέρα κουριδίαν τ' ἄλοχον παῖδάς τε φίλους·
ὃ δ' ἐς ἄλσος ἔβα
δάφναισι κατάσκιον ποσσὶ πάϊς Διός.[8]

---

[1] Fr. 5 Kinkel. For the date of Pisander see Wilamowitz, *Herakles*, p. 67.
[2] Fr. 69 N.   [3] 3 F 18 Jacoby.
[4] Hes. *Theog.* 133.   [5] Pind. *Ol.* 9. 29 ff.
[6] Fr. 5 Kinkel.   [7] Fr. 7 Kinkel.
[8] Fr. 6 D. In 3 Vürtheim suggests διὰ βένθεα instead of ποτὶ βένθεα.

The Sun, Hyperion's child, went down into the golden cup, that he might cross over the Ocean and come to the depths of black, holy night, to his mother and his young wife and his dear children. But he, the son of Zeus, entered on foot the wood, shadowy with laurel-trees.

The lines mark a turning-point in the story. Adventure at sea is over, and adventure on land begins. The hero marches into a shadowy grove at the end of the world and pursues his search for Geryon's cattle. We can see where Stesichorus places the home of Geryon. It may be near Tartessus, but it is also near the Garden of the Hesperides; for it is from their home, χώρου ἀφ' Ἑσπερίδων, that Mimnermus makes the Sun start his voyage in the cup, and it is here that Stesichorus lands Heracles.

After this Heracles slew the monstrous Geryon. His origin is unknown, but he may once have been a god of death and the underworld. As such he appears on the Etruscan Tomba del Orco at Corneto,[1] and Apollodorus says that his successor 'pastured the cattle of Hades'.[2] Stesichorus knew that he was a monster and made him even more monstrous than tradition told. Hesiod had given him three heads,[3] and in Protocorinthian art, dated before 640 B.C., he has three bodies as well.[4] He is already that τρισώματος Γηρυών to whom Clytaemestra's fancy compares her wounded husband.[5] Stesichorus went farther and gave him not only six hands and six feet but wings.[6] This improvement in his monstrous character shows how boldly Stesichorus altered ancient stories. The touch appealed to Aristophanes. When Lamachus puts on his gorgeously plumed helmet, Dicaeopolis answers him by producing the four feathers of a cock and says:

βούλει μάχεσθαι Γηρυόνῃ τετραπτίλῳ;[7]

Will you join fight with four-winged Geryon?

If Lamachus' helmet recalls the three pairs of wings on Geryon, Dicaeopolis will try to rival them. Of the rest of the encounter between Heracles and Geryon we know nothing, except perhaps one small detail. Pindar, speaking of Heracles, says:

θρασεῖαι τόν ποτε Γαρυόνα φρίξαν κύνες.[8]

[1] *Mon. d. Inst.* ix. 15.   [2] *Bibl.* 2. 5. 10.
[3] *Theog.* 287.   [4] H. G. Payne, *Necrocorinthia*, p. 130.
[5] Aesch. *Ag.* 869 ff.
[6] Schol. Hes. *Theog.* 287 Στησίχορος δὲ ἐξ χεῖρας ἔχειν φησὶ καὶ ἐξ πόδας καὶ ὑπόπτερον εἶναι.
[7] *Ach.* 1082.   [8] *Isthm.* 1. 13.

'at whom Geryon's bold dogs once shivered'. The words are slipped in almost haphazard in order to praise the formidable character of Heracles, and this suggests that Pindar draws from some well-known source, which may be Stesichorus, since it would be nicely in character with the redoubtable personality which he gives to Heracles that the dogs of Geryon should be frightened of him.

In the Γηρυονηίς Stesichorus also included a scene in which Heracles drank with the centaur Pholus. We do not know the circumstances, but the mere introduction of the theme suggests the generous scale of the poem. Two lines tell of the mighty cup offered to Heracles by his host:

σκύπφειον δὲ λαβὼν δέπας ἔμμετρον ὡς τριλάγυνον
πῖνεν ἐπισχόμενος, τό ῥά οἱ παρέθηκε Φόλος κεράσας.[1]

he took the vessel like a cup, three flagons deep, which Pholus had mixed and set before him, and put it to his lips and drank.

Theocritus had either these lines or their occasion in mind when he wrote:

ἆρα γέ τοι τοιόνδε Φόλῳ κατὰ λάϊνον ἄντρον
κρατῆρ' Ἡρακλῆι γέρων ἐστάσατο Χίρων;[2]

Was such a bowl set before Heracles by old Chiron in the stony cave of Pholus?

The entertainment described by Stesichorus must have been part of a famous story. The other Centaurs smelt the wine, came to the cave, and an ugly fight followed.[3] The theme was popular in Protocorinthian and in Early Corinthian art,[4] and must have been well established in poetry, either epic or lyric, before Stesichorus took it up. If he dealt with it at any length, he may have helped to start on its career the conception of Heracles as a man of prodigious appetites, which often caused him trouble and came from another side of his character than that which made him a great hero. This conception is not known to Homer, but seems to have been developed in farce and comedy as in Epicharmus' Ἡρακλῆς παρὰ Φόλῳ and Aristophanes' Δράματα ἢ Κένταυρος, and it has a place in Euripides' Alcestis. Its origins may be older than Stesichorus, and it is sad that we cannot estimate how much he contributed to it.

[1] Fr. 5 D.
[2] 7. 149–50.
[3] Apollod. Bibl. 2. 5. 4.
[4] Payne, p. 129.

Heracles was also the main figure of Stesichorus' Κύκνος, and we have seen how he gave a new turn to the story. A third poem about Heracles was the Κέρβερος, which must have told how he brought the hound of Hades to the upper world. Homer knew of the story,[1] and Hesiod mentions Cerberus without saying that Heracles went to fetch him.[2] A representation of it may be seen on a Middle Corinthian kotyle (600–575 B.C.) from Argos.[3] Hades turns away behind his throne, and in front of it Persephone, stately and defiant, prevents Heracles from attacking him. Behind Heracles are Hermes and a single-headed, prancing Cerberus, from whose body five snakes grow. An episode so dramatic and so detailed implies dependence on literature, and we cannot doubt that the subject had been treated in poetry from which the artist profited. Of Stesichorus' own treatment we know in effect nothing except that in the poem he used the word ἀρύβαλλος in the sense of 'wallet'.[4] Little enough can be deduced from this, but Vürtheim[5] suggests that here we have an anticipation of the comic treatment which Heracles' appearance in the underworld received in Aristophanes' *Frogs* and less certainly in Sophocles' satyric play Ἡρακλῆς ἐπὶ Ταινάρῳ. He thinks that the wallet contained Heracles' journey-money, which he needed for the various pleasures retailed in the *Frogs* by Dionysus, and concludes that the poem was in some sense burlesque. This is a weighty conclusion for so little evidence, and we can hardly accept it with comfort. It is more likely that Aristophanes, not Stesichorus, is responsible for the element of burlesque, and after all wallets may contain other things than money, nor do we know that this wallet belonged to Heracles. Indeed we may doubt whether Stesichorus is likely to have made fun of the heroic tales which elsewhere he treated in so exalted a spirit, and there is certainly no hint from antiquity that he did.

A fourth poem concerned with Heracles may have been the Σκύλλα. At least, without naming Stesichorus as his authority, an ancient writer says that on his way home with the cattle of Geryon Heracles was robbed of a beast by Scylla and killed her.[6] It is then possible that the Σκύλλα was a kind of sequel to the Γηρυονηΐς, but the only detail known from it is that Stesichorus

---

[1] *Il.* 8. 368. [2] *Theog.* 311 ff. [3] Payne, p. 10.
[4] Pollux 10. 152 ἀρύβαλλος . . . καὶ ἐν Στησιχόρου Κερβέρῳ.
[5] Op. cit. p. 27. [6] Schol. Lyc. 46. 879. See Vürtheim, p. 27.

made Scylla the daughter of Lamia.[1] In this he went against Homer, who made her Crataiis,[2] and Hesiod who made her Hecate.[3] Nor are Stesichorus' reasons hard to surmise. Lamia was an ogress, whose original home seems to have been Libya and who stole and killed children.[4] Later writers identified or associated her with the bogey Mormo.[5] She was therefore well suited to be the mother of Scylla, who stole sailors from ships and killed them. The story was perhaps known in Sicily, where a place called Λαμίας μασθοί owed its name to two hills being called after her breasts, and in later Greek lore her breasts were said to be used for cleaning out ovens.[6]

Stesichorus' poems about Heracles may have some connexion with Sicily, but other poems of his certainly spring from the heroic tradition of the mainland. The plot of his Συοθῆραι was the hunting of the Calydonian boar and had some past behind it. Homer retailed it in a simple form, in which Atalanta is not mentioned and Meleager dies in battle.[7] Yet Atalanta does not seem to have been a late addition to the story, since Hesiod speaks of ποδώκης δι᾽ Ἀταλάντη . . . Χαρίτων ἀμαρύγματ᾽ ἔχουσα and refers to her refusal to be married.[8] The hunt is presupposed in the metope of the boar from the Sicyonian treasury at Delphi, which dates from the second quarter of the sixth century, and is depicted with much life and skill on the François Vase of the painter Clitias, which is not much later.[9] The vase gives the names of twenty-seven hunters, which is more than it actually portrays. An essential ingredient of the story was the gathering of heroes from all parts of Greece to hunt the boar, and it may have been from a list of these that Hesiod's mention of Atalanta comes. The hunters belonged to the older generation before the Trojan War. It is this gathering which has been thought to be the subject of a papyrus fragment of the Συοθῆραι, in which the first column gives the names of some heroes:

[1] Eustath. 1714. 33 Στησίχορος δὲ Λαμίαν αὐτῆς μητέρα ποιεῖ; Schol. Ap. Rhod. 4. 828 Στησίχορος δὲ ἐν τῇ Σκύλλῃ Λαμίας τὴν Σκύλλαν φησὶ θυγατέρα εἶναι.
[2] Od. 12. 124.
[3] Fr. 150 R.
[4] Lyc. Al. 44 with scholl.
[5] Schol. Bas. Greg. Naz. Or. 35, p. 563 c; Philostrat. Vit. Ap. 4. 25; Lucian, Philops. 2.
[6] V. Mancuso, La Lirica classica greca, p. 235.
[7] Il. 9. 538 ff.
[8] Fr. 21. 2–3 R.
[9] See J. D. Beazley, The Development of Attic Black-figure, p. 32.

Θεσ]τιάδαι
]αρ ὀψιγόνοι τε καὶ ἀσπάσι-
οι μένο]ν ἐν μεγάρ[ο]ισιν· ἀτὰρ πόδας
ὠκέες ....] τ' ἀγαθο[ὶ] Προκάων Κλυτί-
5   ος τε ...... ἱκέ]σθαν.
      ἐκ Φθί]ας δὲ μόλ' [Ε]ὐρυτίων
        ]ς τανυπ[έ]πλου
        ]ας
        ] . Εἰλατίδαο δαΐφρονος[1]

This cannot be the whole list of hunters, but those named are
of some interest. First come the sons of Thestius, who are the
brothers of Althaea and the uncles of Meleager. We hear that
some of these remained at home, presumably because they were
too young, but that Procaon and Clytius went. Their connexion
with the hunt is stated by only one other ancient source,[2] though
a fragment, variously ascribed to Pindar and Bacchylides, mentions them together with Meleager.[3] They seem to be the only
sons of Thestius who went to the hunt in this poem, and it must
be they who were later killed. After them Eurytion is named, and
presumably with him his mother, unknown to us, to establish his
genealogy. Eurytion is of some importance in the story since he
was killed in mistake by Peleus.[4] The third name is not quite so
easy. The genitive Εἰλατίδαο would seem to suggest that this was
a grandson of Elatus, and that is chronologically awkward. His
son, Caeneus, was included in some accounts of the hunt, and it
must surely be he to whom Stesichorus refers, and in that case
the awkward genitive of the patronymic may, as Page suggests,
be explained by the loss of some such word as βία.

The names given by Stesichorus throw an instructive light
on the nature of Greek poetical tradition. Not only are Procaon
and Clytius not mentioned in the usual accounts of the huntsmen,

[1] *Ox. Pap.* xxiii. 2359, fr. 1, col. i. See D. L. Page, *C.R.* n.s. vii (1957), p. 192.
H. Lloyd-Jones, ibid. viii (1958), p. 17, suggests the possibility that the lines may
come from the Ἄθλα ἐπὶ Πελίᾳ, which, according to Stesichorus fr. 3 D, must have
taken place earlier than the hunt. The careful mention of the sons of Thestius may
perhaps weigh the scales in favour of the Συοθῆραι. B. Snell, *Hermes*, lxxxiv (1956),
pp. 249–50, attempts to recover the metre, but the state of the papyrus hardly
allows any sure conclusions. 3 μένο]ν Lobel. 4 ὠκέες Page, who continues with
αἰχματαί. 5 ἱκέ]σθαν Lloyd-Jones, νεέ]σθαν Page.
[2] Schol. T. ad *Il.* 9. 567.
[3] Pind. fr. 343. 28 Snell; Bacch. fr. 25. 8 Snell.
[4] Apollod. *Bib.* 1. 8. 2.

but not one of Stesichorus' names is to be found among the
twenty-seven on the François Vase.[1] The vase evidently followed
one source, and Stesichorus another. Nor was Stesichorus much
followed by later poets. Bacchylides makes the brothers of Althaea Iphiclus and Aphares,[2] and in this later authorities on the
whole agree with him, though it is worth noting that neither of
them is mentioned on the François Vase. On the other hand
something of Stesichorus' account may have passed into the
brilliant episode of the hunt which Ovid gives in the *Metamor-
phoses*. He provides a full list of hunters, and among them we can
identify some who are close to Stesichorus. First he mentions 'duo
Thestiadae' without giving their names, then 'impiger Eurytion',
and 'iam non femina Caeneus'.[3] On the other hand, when he
develops his story later, he certainly makes the sons of Thestius
Plexippus and Toxeus.[4] Ovid of course draws from more than
one source, and his account of Meleager's love for Atalanta may
come from Euripides, who is partial to this kind of thing and is
likely to have invented it.[5] Yet it is surprising how little influence
Stesichorus' list of the huntsmen had, and how each poet and
mythographer seems to have gone very much his own way. The
Calydonian boar-hunt was evidently so popular a theme that
poets took liberties with it and introduced their own casts of
heroes into it.

Of the actual hunt, as the Συοθῆραι described it, only one
fragment survives:

κρύψαι δὲ ῥύγχος
ἄκρον γᾶς ὑπένερθεν.[6]

'and hid the tip of his snout underneath the ground'. We do not
know why the boar does this, and we might conjecture equally
that it is preparing for the fight or that it has been wounded and
gives it up. Nor in view of the varieties of the story can we
surmise how Stesichorus developed the theme of the kill. Our
next evidence is the second, fragmentary column of the papyrus,
and it tells of the struggle between the heroes for the skin of the
dead boar:

ἔνθεν μὲν Λοκρ[οὶ
ἱζάνον αἰχματαὶ[

---

[1] The inscriptions are given in J. C. Hoppin, *A Handbook of Greek Black-figured
Vases*, p. 152.   [2] 5. 128–9.   [3] 8. 301 ff.
[4] 8. 440 ff.   [5] M. C. van der Kolf, *R.-E.* xv. 453.   [6] Fr. 7 D.

τέκνα φίλα[ἐρί-
ηρες Ἀχαιοὶ[
5   καὶ ὑπερθύμοι[
     θ' ἱαρὰν Βοιωτίδ[α ν]αίον[
     χθόνα πυροφόρ[ον.

     ἔνθεν δ' αὖ Δρύοπ[ές] τε κα[ὶ Αἰτω-
     λοὶ μενεχάρμα[ι

The words ἔνθεν μέν . . . ἔνθεν δέ indicate two parties, the one consisting of at least Locrians, Achaeans, and Boeotians, the other of Dryopians and Aetolians. Since the nature of the fight is very variously told by different authors, we can deduce nothing about it from them, and must try to see what Stesichorus says. One point looks clear. The word ἵζανον can only mean 'sat', and suggests that anyhow the first party were not combatants but onlookers. The balance between ἔνθεν and ἔνθεν hints that the other party were also onlookers, even if they backed a different side. These slight indications may perhaps provoke the hypothesis that the fight was not yet a full-scale mellay but between Meleager and his party against his uncles and their party. If so, here also Stesichorus went his own way, which was quite different from the war of the Curetes and Calydonians in Homer, but Bacchylides may have followed Stesichorus when he said of the fight:

περὶ δ' αἴθωνος δορᾶς
μαρνάμεθ' ἐνδυκέως
Κουρῆσι μενεπτολέμοις,[1]

for the bright skin we fought strenuously with the Curetes steadfast in battle.

Meleager, the son of Oeneus, is supported by the Calydonians, and the uncles, who come from Pleuron, by the Curetes.[2] Bacchylides implies rather a larger struggle than we need assume in Stesichorus, who seems to place Aetolians among the onlookers, but in general he may have set his fight between the parties of Meleager and his uncles. This is about as much as we are likely to know at present about Stesichorus' treatment of the Calydonian boar-hunt. It is unlikely that he introduced the theme of Meleager's love for Atalanta, and there is no evidence that he used the theme of the log whose existence is coterminous

[1] 5. 124–6.   [2] For the distinction see Schol. Il. 9. 529.

with that of Meleager and whose destruction brings him to death.

Though the fragments of the Συοθῆραι show that Stesichorus went his own way in handling a very popular story, we do not know what his motives were or what he gained by his originality. We can see this more clearly in two poems which must have been based on the Theban cycle of legends, the Εὐρώπεια and the Ἐριφύλα. The first, as the title indicates, must have told the story of Europa, sister of Cadmus, who was carried off by Zeus disguised as a bull. About it two interesting pieces of information survive. First, Stesichorus told of the sowing of the dragon's teeth at Thebes. Ordinary tradition ascribed this to Cadmus, but Stesichorus ascribed it to Athene.[1] Of course he may have composed the poem for a festival of Athene and thought such a change suitable, but we can see what he gained by it. The whole action becomes more majestic and more mysterious by being transferred from human to divine agency. The curious thing is that it had very little effect on subsequent literature. It was indeed known but modified and brought into harmony with the usual version, as when Euripides says that the sowing was done Παλλάδος φράδαισιν,[2] and Apollodorus, perhaps following him, says that Athene suggested the idea to Cadmus.[3] It looks as if the name of Cadmus was too closely associated with the dragon's teeth for any new version of the story to be accepted.

In the same poem Stesichorus dealt with the death of Actaeon and made two important points. First, though he told that Actaeon saw Artemis bathing, he made this the excuse rather than the reason for his death, which was that he should not marry Semele.[4] Semele, like Europa, was a daughter of Cadmus and would be appropriately mentioned in the Εὐρώπεια. The role of Artemis is not unlike that which Pindar gives to her in the doom of Coronis, whose unfaithfulness to Apollo makes him get Artemis to kill her.[5] This version was known to Acusilaus,[6] but did not gain much popularity, and posterity was content that Actaeon was killed for having seen Artemis naked. Secondly, Stesichorus made a special point in the actual death of Actaeon. The words that Artemis ἐλάφου περιβαλεῖν δέρμα Ἀκταίωνι have

---

[1] Schol. Eur. *Ph.* 670 ὁ μὲν Στησίχορος ἐν Εὐρωπείᾳ τὴν Ἀθηνᾶν ἐσπαρκέναι τοὺς ὀδόντας φησίν.　　[2] *Ph.* 667.　　[3] *Bibl.* 3. 4. 1.
[4] Paus. 9. 2. 3.　　[5] *Pyth.* 3. 24 ff.　　[6] 2 F 33 Jacoby.

been taken to mean that this is the later story,[1] familiar from Ovid's brilliant handling of it,[2] that Actaeon was actually turned into a stag, and for this use of περιβαλεῖν support is claimed in Aeschylus' account of the transformation of Philomela into a nightingale:

περέβαλον γάρ οἱ πτεροφόρον δέμας[3]

'for the gods cast round her a winged body'. The conclusion is that the transformation of Actaeon into a stag was the creation of Stesichorus. But there are difficulties in this view. First, δέρμα is not the same as δέμας, and Pausanias' words do not easily bear the interpretation so given to them. Their natural meaning is that Artemis flung a skin round him, and this is what we see in the middle of the fifth century on a metope from Temple E at Selinus.[4] Secondly, the complete transformation of Actaeon, if we may judge by its representation in art, seems to be later than his wearing a stag's skin.[5] What Stesichorus did was to start the story on a new line of development by providing a reason why Actaeon's dogs should devour their master, and he did this by making Artemis cover him with a stag's skin.

The 'Εριφύλα told another Theban legend, the betrayal by Eriphyle of her husband Amphiaraus. The story was connected with the cycle of the Seven against Thebes and was known to the author of the Homeric Νέκυια, who speaks of

στυγερὴν 'Εριφύλην
ἣ χρυσὸν φίλου ἀνδρὸς ἐδέξατο τιμήεντα.[6]

Nothing is known of Stesichorus' treatment of the main theme, but our information contains one or two items of interest. Legend told that Asclepius had once raised a man from the dead and was punished by the gods for this impious act. Whom he raised was a matter for dispute. Some said Hippolytus, others Glaucus, others Tyndareüs; Stesichorus said that he raised Capaneus and Lycurgus.[7] The choice is illuminating. The resurrection was a godless

[1] H. J. Rose, *Mnemosyne*, lix, pp. 431–2.
[2] *Met.* 3. 131 ff. [3] Aesch. *Ag.* 1147.
[4] G. Richter, *The Sculpture and Sculptors of the Greeks*, fig. 411.
[5] P. Jacobsthal, *Aktaions Tod*, p. 2.
[6] *Od.* 11. 326–7.
[7] Apollod. *Bibl.* 3. 10. 3 εὗρον δέ τινας λεγομένους ἀναστῆναι ὑπ' αὐτοῦ, Καπανέα καὶ Λυκοῦργον, ὡς Στησίχορός φησιν ἐν 'Εριφύλῃ. Cf. Schol. Pind. *Pyth.* 3. 96; schol. Eur. *Alc.* 2.

act, and Stesichorus makes it worse by applying it to Capaneus, who was the type of pride and presumption,[1] and to Lycurgus, who must surely be the king who defies Dionysus in the *Iliad*.

From a somewhat different source Stesichorus drew his Ἄθλα ἐπὶ Πελίᾳ. The Funeral Games of Pelias formed part of the Argonautic cycle and belonged by origin to Thessaly. The theme was popular for the variety of its incidents and for the select company which took part in them. The poem was known to Simonides, who wrote:

> ὃς δουρὶ πάντας
> νίκασε νέους δινάεντα βαλὼν
> Ἄναυρον ὕπερ πολυβότρυος ἐξ Ἰωλκοῦ·
> οὕτω γὰρ Ὅμηρος ἠδὲ Στασίχορος ἄεισε λαοῖς.[2]

who surpassed all the young men with the spear, when he cast it over the eddying Anaurus from Iolcus rich in grape-clusters; for so did Homer and Stesichorus sing to the peoples.

Simonides finds a precedent for Stesichorus' story in 'Homer', and by this he must mean an epic poem which, like many others, was vaguely attributed to Homer, though we cannot guess what it was.[3] The games were evidently described by Stesichorus in detail, though not necessarily on an equal scale throughout. Meleager, who won the spear-cast, also won the javelin-cast, but the event seems to have been dismissed with some curtness:

> θρῴσκων μὲν ἄρ' Ἀμφιάραος, ἄκοντι δὲ νίκασεν Μελέαγρος,[4]

'Amphiaraus won in the leap, Meleager with the javelin', and the brief, factual notice recalls the way in which Pindar dismisses five athletic events in eight lines.[5] The boxing may have been a little more generous in scale, since the words

> χειροβρῶτι δεσμῷ[6]

'with bonds that gnaw the hands' must come from it and refer to the harm which such bonds did both to the boxer himself and to his adversary.[6] Though both Apollonius and Theocritus tell of a boxing-match between Polydeuces and Amycus,[7] it is not clear that Stesichorus did, since the nearest contemporary evidence to him, a Late Corinthian crater, shows a match between

---

[1] Aesch. *Sept.* 422 ff.; Soph. *Ant.* 128 ff.
[2] Fr. 32 D.
[3] See J. A. Davison, *Eranos*, liii (1956), pp. 132–3.
[4] Fr. 3 D.
[5] *Ol.* 10. 64 ff.
[6] Zenob. 6. 44.
[7] Ap. Rhod. 2. 67 ff.; Theocr. 22. 80 ff.

H

Peleus and Hippalcimus.[1] Nor was the poem entirely concerned with games. There was some kind of feast in it, and two lines show that Stesichorus, like Alcman, enjoyed to retail tasty foods:

$$\sigma \alpha \sigma \alpha \mu \acute{\iota} \delta \alpha \varsigma \; \chi \acute{o} \nu \delta \rho o \nu \; \tau \epsilon \; \kappa \alpha \grave{\iota} \; \acute{\epsilon} \gamma \kappa \rho \acute{\iota} \delta \alpha \varsigma$$
$$\mathring{a} \lambda \lambda \alpha \; \tau \epsilon \; \pi \acute{\epsilon} \mu \mu \alpha \tau \alpha \; \kappa \alpha \grave{\iota} \; \mu \acute{\epsilon} \lambda \iota \; \chi \lambda \omega \rho \acute{o} \nu.[2]$$

'sesame-cakes, groats, sweet-oil cakes, other pasties, and yellow honey'. This seems to have been a wedding-feast, since Athenaeus speaks of $\tau \mathring{\eta} \; \pi \alpha \rho \theta \acute{\epsilon} \nu \omega \; \delta \mathring{\omega} \rho \alpha$,[3] and $\sigma \eta \sigma \alpha \mu \acute{\eta}$ or $\sigma \eta \sigma \alpha \mu \acute{\iota} \varsigma$, a cake made of honey and sesame and olive-oil, was especially connected with weddings $\delta \iota \grave{\alpha} \; \tau \grave{o} \; \pi o \lambda \acute{\upsilon} \gamma o \nu o \nu$,[4] because it was thought to promote fertility. The wedding may have been that of Pelias' daughter, Alcestis; for both she and it were depicted on the Chest of Cypselus,[5] and her husband, Admetus, was a competitor in the chariot-race.[6]

The $\mathring{A} \theta \lambda \alpha$ looks as if it was composed on some scale, and it is possible that its account of the chariot-race was less summary than that of the jumping and javelin-throwing. Stesichorus describes the horses of the Dioscuri:

$$\acute{E} \rho \mu \epsilon \acute{\iota} \alpha \varsigma \; \mu \grave{\epsilon} \nu \; \acute{\epsilon} \delta \omega \kappa \epsilon \nu$$
$$\Phi \lambda \acute{o} \gamma \epsilon \acute{o} \nu \; \tau \epsilon \; \kappa \alpha \grave{\iota} \; \mathring{A} \rho \pi \alpha \gamma o \nu, \; \mathring{\omega} \kappa \acute{\epsilon} \alpha \; \tau \acute{\epsilon} \kappa \nu \alpha \; \Pi o \delta \acute{\alpha} \rho \gamma \alpha \varsigma,$$
$$\mathring{H} \rho \alpha \; \delta \grave{\epsilon} \; \Xi \acute{\alpha} \nu \theta o \nu \; \kappa \alpha \grave{\iota} \; K \acute{\upsilon} \lambda \lambda \alpha \rho o \nu.[7]$$

Hermes gave Phlogeus and Harpagus, swift children of Podarge, and Hera gave Xanthus and Cyllarus.

Stesichorus follows Homeric tradition in giving each chariot only two horses, and his choice of names recalls Homeric practice. Yet it is possible that he got two horses' names from a source nearer than Homer. A Virgilian scholiast says that, according to Alcman, Poseidon gave to Hera two horses called Cyllarus and Podargus, and he then goes on to connect these with Polydeuces.[8] It looks as if Stesichorus took over the horses from Alcman and brought them into his chariot-race.

The scale of the $\mathring{A} \theta \lambda \alpha$ may have been matched or even surpassed by that of the $\mathring{I} \lambda \acute{\iota} o \upsilon \; \pi \acute{\epsilon} \rho \sigma \iota \varsigma$, whose title shows that it must have had some sort of relation to the epic poem of the same name attributed to Arctinus, though its episodes must often have been

[1] Payne, no. 1471.   [2] Fr. 2 D.   [3] 4. 172 d.
[4] Menand. ap. schol. Aristoph. *Pax* 869.   [5] Paus. 5. 17. 11.
[6] Id. 5. 17. 9.   [7] Fr. 1 D.   [8] Schol. Bern. ad *Georg.* 3. 89.

told and a poem on the main theme had been written by
Sacadas.[1] What we know of Stesichorus' treatment suggests that
he tried to give new life to old subjects by ingenious innovations.
For instance, the *Odyssey* had told of Epeüs, son of Panopeus, the
maker of the Wooden Horse, and the *Iliad* said that he was a
good athlete and called him by the stock epithets of δῖος and
μεγάθυμος.[2] Stesichorus was more specific about his social station
and made it lower than the Homeric epithets might suggest, by
telling that he carried water for the Atridae,[3] a humble, if not
a slavish, task. A surviving line tells how Athene pitied his condition:

ᾤκτειρε γὰρ αὐτὸν ὕδωρ αἰεὶ φορέοντα Διὸς κούρα βασιλεῦσιν.[4]

for the daughter of Zeus pitied him as he ever carried water for the
kings.

Now Homer said that it was Athene who suggested to Epeüs the
idea of the Wooden Horse,[5] and it looks as if Stesichorus, anxious
to emphasize by contrast the later fame of Epeüs, started his
career in a very humble station. Stesichorus certainly dealt with
the Wooden Horse, and though he did not follow Sacadas in
giving a list of the warriors in it,[6] he said that there were a
hundred, whereas the usual version was that there were twelve.[7]
A simple increase of numbers was an easy way of enhancing the
Horse's size and dramatic interest.

Of more importance is Stesichorus' invention that, when the
Achaeans went to stone Helen, as soon as they saw her face, they
let the stones fall from their hands.[8] This story seems to have
had little following, since there is no trace of it on the Chest of
Cypselus or in Euripides, and posterity preferred the version of
Ibycus that Menelaus dropped his sword in front of Helen because of her beauty. Stesichorus had to face the problem why, if
Helen was the villain she seemed to be, she was not killed by the
Achaeans. Homer's silence may have been dictated by his obvious admiration for her, but later generations felt more sternly,
and some explanation was needed. Stesichorus found one, and
Ibycus another, but both made her beauty a reason and filled
the gap left by Homer. The almost romantic colouring of the

---

[1] Athen. 13. 610 c. [2] *Il.* 23. 694, 838, 839. [3] Athen. 10. 456 f.
[4] Fr. 9 D. [5] *Od.* 8. 493. [6] Athen. 13. 610 c.
[7] Eustath. 1698. 1. [8] Schol. Eur. *Or.* 1287.

episode must have reduced what would otherwise have been a brutal tension, and it looks as if Stesichorus was concerned with easier emotions than those of the epic. In the same way he avoided the story that Hecuba was turned into a dog, and said that she was transported by Apollo to Lycia.[1] This looks like a variation on the Homeric episode in which Sleep and Death transport the dead body of Sarpedon to Lycia,[2] but Stesichorus could justify it. Homer had made Apollo the god of Troy, and Hesiod knew of some connexion between him and the family of Priam, claiming that Ileus was the son of Apollo and a Nymph.[3] Stesichorus went a step farther and made Hector the son not of Priam but of Apollo,[4] and this would explain and justify his treatment of Hecuba. He seems indeed to have tempered some of the more barbarous episodes in the epic. In Arctinus' *Sack of Troy* Astyanax was thrown alive from the walls,[5] but Stesichorus said that he was dead first.[6] Such variations of familiar epic themes show the scope and manner of Stesichorus' handling. They show too that the Ἰλίου πέρσις must have been of considerable length to contain not only the different episodes of the Wooden Horse, the fate of Hecuba, and the death of Astyanax, but to treat them in what looks like some detail. Indeed evidence for such a scale of treatment can be seen in the preservation of the names of two minor characters, who would hardly have been mentioned if the poem had not been of considerable length. First, Stesichorus said that Priam had a daughter called Medusa,[7] and in this he was followed not only by the mythographers Hyginus[8] and Apollodorus,[9] but by Polygnotus in his picture of the Sack of Troy.[10] Secondly, among the Trojan women captured by the Greeks he named Clymene,[11] and for this he had good reasons, since Homer had made her a handmaiden of Helen.[12]

Our knowledge of Stesichorus' Ἰλίου πέρσις has been thought to receive reinforcements from a Roman monument of the first century A.D., found at Bovillae on the Appian Way and known

---

[1] Paus. 10. 27. 2.   [2] *Il.* 16. 681 ff.   [3] Fr. 116. 1 R.

[4] Tzetz. ad Lyc. 266 Στησίχορος γὰρ καὶ Εὐφορίων καὶ Ἀλέξανδρος ὁ Αἰτωλὸς ποιηταί φασι τὸν Ἕκτορα υἱὸν εἶναι τοῦ Ἀπόλλωνος.

[5] Schol. Eur. *Andr.* 10.

[6] Ibid. Στησίχορον μὲν γὰρ ἱστορεῖν ὅτι τεθνήκοι.

[7] Paus. 10. 26. 9.   [8] *Fab.* 90.

[9] *Bibl.* 3. 12. 5.   [10] Paus. 10. 26. 9.

[11] Id. 10. 26. 1.   [12] *Il.* 3. 144.

as the Tabula Iliaca.[1] The monument seems to be based on an earlier work by a sculptor called Theodorus, who was evidently a Greek and well acquainted with Greek literature. He depicts scenes from other poems than the Ἰλίου πέρσις, and since his scenes from the *Iliad* keep fairly close to the known text, he seems to have been a well-educated man who respected his literary authorities. The central section of the Tabula is inscribed Ἰλίου πέρσις κατὰ Στησίχορον, and has naturally been taken to display the contents of Stesichorus' poem. It falls into three main parts. The top shows Troy girt with walls and towers, the middle the tombs of Achilles and Hector, the bottom two harbours separated by a tongue of land, in both of which there are ships. All three sections have human figures, some of whom have names attached. In the top section several scenes can be identified. In front of a temple Aias seizes Cassandra; below him a warrior comes out of the Wooden Horse; in Priam's palace Neoptolemus kills the old king, while Hecuba tries to protect him; before a temple labelled ἱερὸν Ἀφροδίτης Menelaus takes a sword to Helen; round and among these scenes are various encounters and combats, and below them Aeneas carries his father and leads Ascanius, while Hermes shows the way. In the middle section Hector's burial takes place before a concourse of distinguished, if not always distinguishable, Trojans, while at the tomb of Achilles Polyxena is sacrificed in the presence of Odysseus and Calchas. The bottom section shows the Greek ships in one harbour, and in another the departure of Aeneas, ἀπόπλους Αἰνήου. With him is his helmsman Misenus, and the riddling and disturbing inscription Μισῆνος, Αἰνήας ἀπαίρων εἰς τὴν Ἑσπερίαν. In the interstices and on the edges of these scenes are many others of violence or death, for which various interpretations have been found.

Such, in general, is the Tabula Iliaca, and such, it has been claimed, must have been the contents of Stesichorus' Ἰλίου πέρσις. If the sculptor really followed the poem so closely as he implies, then indeed Stesichorus' poem must not only have been a truly epic tale with a wealth of circumstantial episodes but also have introduced into poetry the story of Aeneas' voyage to the west, with all its incalculable consequences not merely for literature but even for history. The problem, however, is extremely difficult. Our broken and scanty evidence makes it hard to say

[1] M. Paulcke, *De Tabula Iliaca Quaestiones Stesichoreae*. (Diss. Königsberg, 1897).

whether all this was in Stesichorus' poem. It is true that the
Wooden Horse and the death of Astyanax are known to have been
in it and appear on the Tabula, but they would be almost indispensable to any representation of the sack of Troy. It is also
true that an artist who followed Homer with a reasonable degree
of accuracy might be expected to be equally faithful to Stesichorus. But despite these arguments, we may doubt if the sculptor
was right in ascribing all these episodes to the 'Ιλίου πέρσις of
Stesichorus, and we suspect that he attributed to it episodes
which occurred in the *Little Iliad* of Lesches, the *Sack of Troy* of
Arctinus, and even Virgil's *Aeneid*. It is not merely that there
seem to be too many episodes for the compass of a single lyrical
poem; after all an ingenious artist might have extracted almost
an equal number from Pindar's *Pythian* IV. But it is certainly
suspicious that the episodes of the 'Ιλίου πέρσις should tally so
closely with those of *Aeneid* II and especially that Stesichorus
should have dealt with the departure of Aeneas from Troy. But
perhaps the best evidence against the trustworthiness of the
Tabula lies in quite a small point. Stesichorus, as we have seen,
told that the Achaeans went to stone Helen but dropped the
stones when they saw her in her beauty. Now the Tabula shows
Menelaus pursuing her with a sword, and this is the version not
of Stesichorus but of Ibycus. Since the sculptor does not acknowledge this debt, it is likely that he does not acknowledge others,
and his accuracy is open to serious doubt. Even if he knew and
used the 'Ιλίου πέρσις of Stesichorus, he seems to have made it
a peg for a whole series of episodes in the sack of Troy, some of
which came from elsewhere. The Tabula cannot be taken to
prove that Stesichorus started the career of Aeneas as an immi-
grant to Italy.

In the poems which we have so far examined there is almost no
indication of the manner or place of their performance. It is
likely enough that they were performed in Magna Graecia, since
the Sicilian and South Italian Greeks took pleasure in stories
which stressed their ancient connexion with the mainland. With
Heracles they were fully at home; the Argonauts and the heroes
of the *Νόστοι* were connected with their own legends of colonization; the 'Ιλίου πέρσις mentioned heroes like Neoptolemus
who had adventures in the west, and the Ἆθλα ἐπὶ Πελίᾳ dealt
with the popular demi-gods Castor and Polydeuces. It looks as if

Stesichorus found the main material of his poems in stories current in his own land, and supplemented them from the epic and
other literary sources. But his two most famous and most influential poems, the Ἑλένη and the Ὀρέστεια, are perhaps best understood on the view that he wrote them on the Greek mainland and
that religious and political considerations influenced his treatment of them. That he should have visited the mainland is no
matter for surprise. In the last years of the seventh century Arion
had travelled in Italy and Sicily, and we can assume the possibility that Stesichorus paid, as it were, a return visit. This may lie
behind the entry in the *Marmor Parium* that he 'came to Hellas'
and the statement of 'Suidas' that he went to Catane when
banished from Pallantium in Arcadia.[1] This has indeed been
thought to be a misunderstanding of a mention of Pallantium in
the Γηρυονηίς,[2] but it too, as we shall see, may be based on fact.
Confirmatory evidence for Stesichorus' visit to the mainland is to
be found in certain features of his Ἑλένη and Ὀρέστεια, and
though such a visit need not have had any political consequences,
it is important for the comprehension of certain peculiarities in
both poems.

The details of the Ἑλένη are so confused with myth and legend
that it is hard to disentangle the facts. On the one side is the
famous story that the poet insulted Helen and was blinded for it
until he apologized in a Palinode and received his sight back.
This looks more like legend than history and provides neither
a date nor an explanation for the Palinode. It has parallels in
Greek and Hebrew folk-lore, and we need only remember such
cases as the blinding of Teiresias and Phineus, of St. Paul and
St. Zacharias. When the gods deal intimately with men either
in wrath or in display, they are liable to blind them. In the case
of Stesichorus the story seems to have had a western origin. In
the battle of Sagra between Locri and Croton—the date is not
known—a Crotoniate soldier, Leonymus, was wounded by Aias,
who was helping the other side. He was transported to the island
of Leuce in the Euxine Sea, where he met the two heroes called
Aias and also Patroclus, Antilochus, and Helen. Here he was

---

[1] s.v. Στησίχορος. οἱ δὲ ἀπὸ Παλλαντίου τῆς Ἀρκαδίας φυγόντα αὐτὸν ἐλθεῖν φασιν
εἰς Κατάνην κἀκεῖ τελευτῆσαι. For his presence at Sparta see also Philodem. 1. 30.
35–42 and 4. 20. 8.

[2] Vürtheim, p. 102; Paus. 8. 3. 2 Παλλαντίου μὲν δὴ καὶ ὁ Στησίχορος ὁ Ἱμεραῖος
ἐν Γηρυονηίδι ἐποιήσατο μνήμην.

healed, and on his departure Helen, who was now the wife of Achilles, told him to warn Stesichorus of his insults to her.[1] A very similar story is told by Conon, who calls the Crotoniate warrior Autoleon, and it looks as if the tale came from Croton.[2] The question is whether Stesichorus himself made any reference to his temporary blindness. He certainly recanted what he said of Helen, but the stories of the blindness smack too much of folklore to suggest that he told them himself. They may indeed be due to misunderstanding of some words of his in which, speaking of his former attitude to Helen, he called himself τυφλός[3] in a figurative sense. But the story of the blindness remains outside the scope of the actual poem, and it is this which we must try to understand.

In his Ἑλένη Stesichorus evidently told the story of Helen in his usual expansive manner and covered a wide sweep of narrative from the fatal beginning, when Tyndareos forgot to sacrifice to Aphrodite and incurred her wrath against his daughters, to the arrival of Helen at Troy.[4] It must have been a full affair and contained some important episodes. Before Helen's marriage to Menelaus Tyndareüs made all her suitors take an oath that if the successful suitor suffered wrong through her, the others would come to his aid.[5] The theme had been treated in the Hesiodic ἢ Οἶαι[6] and we do not know what innovations, if any, Stesichorus introduced. Soon after it must have come the actual wedding, and three lines survive from this, which show the skill with which Stesichorus caught the spirit of the occasion:

πολλὰ μὲν Κυδώνια μᾶλα ποτερρίπτευν ποτὶ δίφρον ἄνακτι,
πολλὰ δὲ μύρσινα φύλλα
καὶ ῥοδίνους στεφάνους ἴων τε κορωνίδας οὔλας.[7]

Many Cydonian quinces they cast on the chariot of the prince, and many leaves of myrtle, and crowns of roses, and twisted wreaths of violets.

The scene must be the bridal procession in which the married pair go on their chariot from the bride's home to the bridegroom's, and the crowd follows joyfully and throws fruit and flowers. Nor was this the only attention that Stesichorus paid to the

[1] Paus. 3. 19. 13.   [2] 26 F 1. 18 Jacoby.
[3] Cf. Pind. Nem. 7. 23; Soph. O.T. 371, 389; Parm. fr. 6. 7 D–K.
[4] Schol. Eur. Or. 249.   [5] Schol. Il. 2. 339.
[6] Fr. 96. 40 ff. R.   [7] Fr. 10 D.

wedding. Since we hear that certain things in Theocritus' Ἐλένης Ἐπιθαλάμιος are taken from Stesichorus,[1] and since this poem is concerned with the song sung outside the bridal chamber, it seems likely that a similar scene had a place in the Ἐλένη. The foundations of the story were evidently laid with care and attention, but after this we can only guess what happened. One thing is clear, and it is that Stesichorus must have told the story on roughly Homeric lines. What these were can best be deduced from his own words in the Παλινῳδία as Plato quotes them:

οὐκ ἔστ' ἔτυμος λόγος οὗτος,
οὐδ' ἔβας ἐν νηυσὶν εὐσέλμοις
οὐδ' ἵκεο Πέργαμα Τροίας.[2]

This tale is not true. You did not go on well-benched ships, nor did you come to the citadel of Troy.

This can only mean that in the original Ἐλένη Stesichorus had told of Helen's flight to Troy, and that in the second part or sequel he withdrew what he had said and substituted a new version. In the Παλινῳδία Stesichorus said emphatically that Helen neither embarked on a ship nor went to Troy, but presumably stayed at home at Sparta. This is plain both from Plato's quotation and from the statement of Dio Chrysostom that, according to Stesichorus, Helen never went anywhere: καὶ τὸν μὲν Στησίχορον λέγειν ὅτι τὸ παράπαν οὐδὲ πλεύσειεν ἡ Ἑλένη οὐδαμόσε.[3] It is clear that Stesichorus' reformed Helen went neither to Troy nor indeed to Egypt, and that statements which imply that he told the same story as Euripides in the Helen[4] are not based on his text. Two questions then arise: what happened to Helen in the Ἐλένη, and what were Stesichorus' reasons for recanting what he had said?

At this point Horace comes to the rescue. In his recantation to Canidia for earlier bad behaviour, he plainly has Stesichorus' Palinode in mind when he says:

tu pudica, tu proba
perambulabis astra sidus aureum.
infamis Helenae Castor offensus uice
fraterque magni Castoris, uicti prece,
adempta uati reddidere lumina.[5]

---

[1] Hypoth. Theocr. 18.   [2] Fr. 11 D; Plat. Phaedr. 243 a.
[3] 11. 182.   [4] Notably Schol. Aristid. 3, p. 150; Tzetz. ad Lyc. 113.
[5] Epod. 17. 40-44.

Just as Stesichorus was pardoned for his insults to Helen, so Horace hopes to be pardoned for his to Canidia, and when he says that Canidia will become a star, he must be following his master, who must have placed Helen in the sky with her divine brethren. If Stesichorus had not said something of the sort, there would be little point in Horace's words, and that such a myth existed is clear from two passages of Euripides. At the end of the *Helen* the Dioscuri say to their sister:

$$\text{ὅταν δὲ κάμψῃς καὶ τελευτήσῃς βίον,}$$
$$\text{θεὸς κεκλήσῃ καὶ Διοσκόρων μέτα}$$
$$\text{σπονδῶν μεθέξεις.}^{1}$$

When you have closed and finished your life, you shall be called a goddess and share libations with the Dioscuri.

At the end of the *Orestes* Apollo says of Helen to Menelaus and Orestes:

$$\text{Κάστορί τε Πολυδεύκει τ' ἐν αἰθέρος πτυχαῖς}$$
$$\text{σύνθακος ἔσται, ναυτίλοις σωτήριος.}^{2}$$

She shall sit with Castor and Polydeuces in the folds of the sky and bring safety to sailors.

These two passages show that Euripides knew of a belief that Helen took a place beside her brothers in the sky, and since he agrees with Horace on this point, it is probable that he too is following Stesichorus. But if Helen stayed at Sparta before being translated to the sky, Stesichorus had still to account for her alleged presence at Troy. He solved this problem, as we know from Plato, by saying that not Helen herself but an εἴδωλον or phantom went to Troy.[3] This was a bold idea which had far-reaching consequences, but it may not have been an original invention of Stesichorus. It was attributed to Hesiod,[4] and though it is not the usual Hesiodic version, it may have appeared in some poem of the Hesiodic school. By this means Stesichorus got himself clear of the ordinary story which he had told in his Ἑλένη, and said that, while Helen stayed at home, a phantom of her went to Troy.

This, then, was the change of story which Stesichorus introduced into his Palinode. But what were his real reasons for it? The stories of his blindness are not very satisfactory, even if we admit

---

[1] *Hel.* 1666-8.   [2] *Or.* 1636-7.
[3] *Rep.* 9. 586 c.   [4] Fr. 266 R.

that they may be based on something that he said. We have still
to discover what Stesichorus said about Helen that gave offence,
and if we can find a rationalistic explanation of his recantation,
it may avoid certain difficulties in the old myth. Now the particular glory which Stesichorus gives to Helen in the Palinode was
appropriate to Sparta and to almost nowhere else in the Greek
world. At Sparta she had her festivals and special duties, and was
ἀγνά and εὐπρεπής,[1] words curiously reminiscent of Horace's
pudica and *proba*. There indeed she was unlike the Helen of epic
tale. In his Ἑλένη Stesichorus not only followed Homer but
passed moral judgements such as Homer did not, as we can see
from a fragment which must come from the poem:

> οὕνεκα Τυνδάρεος
> ῥέζων ποτὲ πᾶσι θεοῖς μούνας λάθετ᾽ ἠπιοδώρου
> Κύπριδος, κείνα δὲ Τυνδαρέου κόραις
> χολωσαμένα διγάμους τε καὶ τριγάμους τίθησιν
> καὶ λιπεσάνορας.[2]

how Tyndareüs one day, when sacrificing to all the gods, forgot alone
the Cyprian, who gives gentle joys, and she, in wrath with the
daughters of Tyndareüs, made them to be wed twice and thrice and
to forsake their husbands.

This is certainly not the Spartan ideal of a chaste Helen but anticipates Aeschylus' idea of her as πολυάνωρ.[3] Such an account of
her would cause offence at very few places outside Sparta, but
there it might well cause very great offence. Nor does Stesichorus
seem to have confined himself to this. Pausanias tells of a temple
of Ilithyia at Argos, which was dedicated by Helen at a time when
she was with child by Theseus. This child she gave to the care of
Clytaemestra, and she was in fact Iphigeneia.[4] Pausanias suggests that Stesichorus was the author of this story, and since
Helen was not at the time married, he must have made her a
good deal worse than could be deduced from Homer. If Stesichorus told stories of this kind about her, we can understand that
he got into trouble in a place where she was held in high regard,
and found it prudent to retract. He then made her stay at Sparta
and eventually become a goddess. The natural conclusion is that
in his Ἑλένη Stesichorus offended Spartan sentiment and that his
Παλινῳδία was intended to take back what he said and to give

---

[1] Aristoph. *Lys.* 1315.   [2] Fr. 17 D.
[3] *Ag.* 62.   [4] Paus. 2. 22. 6.

a more acceptable view of Helen. That his denial of the first poem was complete follows from the words μάτας εἰπών which are attributed to Stesichorus[1] and seem to come from the Palinode.

The technical relation of the Παλινῳδία to the Ἑλένη is not without interest. Philostratus calls the first part πρότερος λόγος[2] and Dio the later ἡ ὕστερον ᾠδή.[3] The two look distinct, and Isocrates tells a story that Stesichorus was blinded early in the performance of the first part, ἀρχόμενος τῆς ᾠδῆς,[4] and then composed the Palinode. The two parts clearly stood in a close relation, but we need not assume that they formed two separate poems of which the latter, beginning with the words οὐκ ἔστ' ἔτυμος λόγος οὗτος, denied what had come before and gave an alternative story. The Palinode may have been in some sense a new start, which seems to have begun with an apology which Aristides paraphrases as μέτειμι δ' ἐφ' ἔτερον προοίμιον.[5] Nor need we be surprised that Stesichorus spoke of himself in this frank way. Just as in *Olympian* I Pindar first at 26–27 mentions the old version of the story of Pelops, and then proceeds to tell another, so Stesichorus makes his second start with a topic which he knows to be in everybody's mind, his previous treatment of Helen, and withdraws it.

The case for Stesichorus' relations with Sparta gets some additional support from what we know of his Ὀρέστεια. In this renowned and influential work Stesichorus went considerably beyond the bare outlines of the story as they are sketched in the *Odyssey*, and seems to have made use of a poem by Xanthus, of whom almost nothing but this is known.[6] But his shaping of the tale may none the less be largely his own and has a character suited to Spartan claims and ambitions in the early part of the sixth century, when she was extending her control over Arcadia and the relics of the Argive kingdom of Pheidon. To justify herself she revived stories that the House of Pelops had once reigned from Sparta over the whole of the Peloponnese. By this means she thought to supersede the claims of Argos, which were based on the possession of Agamemnon's capital and kingdom, by other claims based on descent and ancient rights. A good example of her methods may be seen in her treatment of Tegea. Having failed to subdue Tegea in war, she brought her into an

---

[1] Fr. 47 Bergk. [2] *Vit. Ap.* 6. 11. [3] 11. 40.
[4] *Hel.* 64. [5] 2. 572. [6] Athen. 12. 512 f.

alliance, and part of the procedure consisted of finding the bones of Orestes at Tegea and bringing them to Sparta,[1] somewhat as the Venetians brought the bones of St. Mark to Venice and established him as a patron saint in their midst. With the bones of Orestes in her possession, Sparta could point to her spiritual descent from Agamemnon. The duration and the potentialities of this policy may be seen in the fifth century when Cleomenes, king of Sparta, in answer to the priestess of Athene on the Acropolis at Athens, who told him that he could not enter the shrine, replied ὦ γύναι, ἀλλ᾽ οὐ Δωριεύς εἰμι ἀλλ᾽ Ἀχαιός,[2] meaning that he was no mere Dorian but the successor of Achaean kings like Agamemnon. So too Herodotus makes the Spartan envoy, Syagrus, say to Gelon of Syracuse ἦ κε μέγ᾽ οἰμώξειε ὁ Πελοπίδης Ἀγαμέμνων πυθόμενος Σπαρτιήτας τὴν ἡγεμονίην ἀπαραιρῆσθαι ὑπὸ Γέλωνός τε καὶ Συρηκοσίων.[3] The Spartan kings sometimes found it convenient to forget their descent from Heracles and to boast of their descent from Agamemnon. For this some manipulation of tradition was indispensable, and in it Stesichorus collaborated. If the Spartans could persuade the other inhabitants of the Peloponnese that Agamemnon and Orestes had ruled from Sparta, they had done something to assert their claim to be the real descendants of the Achaean kings who had been the overlords of a united Hellas.

The political tendencies of Stesichorus' Ὀρέστεια are revealed in three different ways. First, he placed the home of Agamemnon in Lacedaemon.[4] Homer placed it in Mycenae,[5] and the transference looks like a deliberate innovation of Stesichorus. Pindar indeed went a step farther and placed it at Amyclae,[6] but this was probably because at Amyclae there was an alleged tomb of Agamemnon.[7] Nor is it perhaps straining the point to say that the difference between the versions of Pindar and Stesichorus is significant because it illustrates the growth of a legend. Pindar is more precise in that he names not a district but a town, and Stesichorus does not seem to have reached such a point. His main concern was to detach the murdered king from Argos, and he did this by placing the palace and the murder in Lacedaemon. This

---

[1] Hdt. 1. 68.   [2] Id. 5. 72. 3.   [3] Id. 7. 159.
[4] Schol. Eur. Or. 46 Ὅμηρος δὲ ἐν Μυκήναις φησὶν εἶναι τὰ βασίλεια τοῦ Ἀγαμέμνονος, Στησίχορος δὲ καὶ Σιμωνίδης ἐν Λακεδαίμονι.
[5] Od. 3. 304.   [6] Pyth. 11. 32.   [7] Paus. 3. 19. 6.

was claimed as his home, and here he must have come to his end. In saying this Stesichorus condoned and assisted the Spartan propaganda of his time.

Secondly, in his Ὀρέστεια Stesichorus gave a role to the Nurse of Orestes,[1] and in this he was followed both by Aeschylus[2] and by Pindar,[3] although there was no authority for her in Homer. Pindar called her Arsinoa, Aeschylus Cilissa, and Stesichorus Laodameia. Reasons for this variety are not easy to find. Of Arsinoa and Cilissa nothing else is known, and both names may be pure inventions. But Laodameia has at least a place in Spartan story. Pausanias mentions a Laodameia, who was the mother of Triphylus and the daughter of Amyclas, king of Lacedaemon.[4] The genealogy is plainly fictitious, but its purpose may be surmised. Triphylus was an Arcadian hero and the eponymous ancestor of the Triphylians, who had been added to the Spartan empire in the seventh century. The tradition which provided Triphylus with Amyclas for a grandfather implies that the Spartans claimed Triphylia on the grounds of racial relationship, and when he was given a mother, Laodameia, of whom almost nothing else is known, it looks as if she appealed to Stesichorus as a suitably national figure to save the child Orestes from death. Pindar, writing for Thebans, and Aeschylus, writing for Athenians, abandoned a detail that meant nothing to them or their audiences and seem to have invented other names for the Nurse to suit their own taste.

Thirdly, in his account of Clytaemestra's dream of a snake, Stesichorus called either Agamemnon or Orestes, and more probably Orestes, βασιλεὺς Πλεισθενίδας, just as in the Νόστοι he applied Πλεισθενίδας to either Menelaus or Agamemnon.[5] The place of Pleisthenes in the genealogy of the House of Atreus is certainly awkward. There is no room for him in the descent Tantalus, Pelops, Atreus, Agamemnon, and it is not convincing to argue that Pleisthenes was the father of Agamemnon but died young, and so Agamemnon was called the son of Atreus.[6] It looks as if Πλεισθενίδας implied some other, alternative descent for Agamemnon, which was superseded by the more popular Homeric version. Ibycus, who was irresponsible in matters of mythology,

[1] Schol. Aesch. *Cho.* 733.
[2] *Cho.* 731 ff.
[3] *Pyth.* 11. 17 ff.
[4] 10. 9. 5.
[5] *Ox. Pap.* 2360, col. ii. 4.
[6] Hes. fr. 98 R.

calls Agamemnon both Πλεισθενίδας and Ἀτρέος παῖς,[1] but that is a light-hearted acquiescence in confusion. Pleisthenes may well have been a son of Pelops and had his own place in tradition outside the Homeric scheme, but when he appeared as the father of Agamemnon in Stesichorus' 'Ορέστεια, it was probably due to the poet's desire to avoid any associations with Argos and the name of Atreus. Atreus was not merely a discreditable ancestor; he had no standing at Sparta, and his grave was at Mycenae.[2] If Spartan interests demanded a glorification of Agamemnon, some other father than Atreus had to be found, and Pleisthenes supplied the need. To this piece of manipulation Stesichorus gave his support.

The *Oresteia* must have been composed on some scale, since the Alexandrian editors divided it into two books. It looks as if it was composed for some Spartan festival, and the opening lines may give a hint of when this took place:

> τοιάδε χρὴ Χαρίτων δαμώματα καλλικόμων ὑμνεῖν
> Φρύγιον μέλος ἐξευρόντας ἁβρῶς ἦρος ἐπερχομένου,[3]

'Such popular songs of the fair-tressed Muses must we sing, finding a Phrygian tune, when the spring comes delicately on', and this is confirmed by another fragment:

> ὅταν ἦρος ὥρᾳ κελαδῇ χελιδών,[4]

'when the swallow babbles in the spring season'. It may not be an accident that the story of Orestes was told at such a time. For a papyrus of Corinna is sufficiently well preserved to show that it had a title 'Ορέστας and was sung in the spring,[5] and it is possible that Pindar's *Pythian* XI was sung at a similar occasion. Stesichorus composed the music in the Phrygian mode, and we may presume that the song was accompanied by the flute in the manner popularized by Olympus and presumably brought by him or his disciples to Sparta.[6] More significant is Stesichorus' reference to the subjects of his song as δαμώματα, which suggests that, though he repeats stories told in Sparta, he claims no personal responsibility for them. This suits the mood in which he begins the poem and has an air of gaiety very unlike the gravity of Pindar or the Attic tragedians in their treatment of Orestes. Something more of his opening movement can be gathered from the *Peace* of Aristophanes in which the Chorus sings:

[1] Fr. 3. 31–32 D.   [2] Paus. 2. 16. 6.   [3] Fr. 14 D.
[4] Fr. 13 D.   [5] Fr. 5 B D.   [6] 'Plut.' *Mus.* 5.

Μοῦσα, σὺ μὲν πολέμους ἀπωσαμένη μετ' ἐμοῦ
τοῦ φίλου χόρευσον,
κλείουσα θεῶν τε γάμους ἀνδρῶν τε δαῖτας
καὶ θαλίας μακάρων· σοὶ γὰρ τάδ' ἐξ ἀρχῆς μέλει.[1]

Muse, put aside wars and dance with me whom you love, singing of
the weddings of gods and the feasts of men and the carousals of the
Blessed Ones; for from the beginning these are your concern.

Commenting on this passage the scholiast says *σφόδρα δὲ γλαφυρὸν
εἴρηται καὶ ἐστὶ (ἡ πλοκὴ) Στησιχόρειος*. Since the song contains
two quotations (frs. 14 and 15 D) from Stesichorus' *Oresteia*, these
words must surely be either a quotation or an adaptation from
the poem. If so, they shed some light on its contents. The note of
joy is stressed because the occasion is one of respite from war, and
though we do not know what war this is, we can imagine that it
was one in which Sparta had been recently engaged or was still
engaged. What follows seems to have no very definite relevance
to the story of Orestes, but it is simply a statement of the kind
of topics about which poets sing and may convey the note of
exhilaration which belongs to some feast of the gods at which the
poem is performed. The *Oresteia* of Stesichorus clearly began in a
mood of high exaltation before moving on to its more disturbing
and more sinister elements.

Between the story of Orestes as it is sketched by Homer and its
full treatment by the Attic tragedians a great development took
place, and some of the enlargement and enrichment is the work
of Stesichorus. At two points we can test his influence, and both
are instructive. All three Attic tragedians make some play with
menacing dreams which frighten Clytaemestra. In the *Choephori*
Aeschylus tells how she dreams that she suckles a snake, only to
find that it has drawn blood. This Orestes interprets as referring
to himself; he is the snake and will kill his mother:

ἐκδρακοντωθεὶς δ' ἐγὼ
κτείνω νιν, ὡς τοὔνειρον ἐννέπει τόδε.[2]

I turn into a snake and slay her, as this dream says.

In his *Electra* Sophocles also makes Clytaemestra have a dream,
but it is of a different kind.[3] She sees her dead husband on the
hearth, and from his sceptre a branch grows which shadows the
whole land and portends the return of Orestes. In his *Orestes*

---

[1] *Pax* 775-8.   [2] *Cho.* 549-50.   [3] *El.* 417 ff.

Euripides is less explicit and says simply that the queen has dreams of Agamemnon.[1] Such dreams, fearful and threatening, are not mentioned by Homer, but they had a part in Stesichorus' *Oresteia*. There Clytaemestra has a dream, and the poet describes it:

τᾷ δὲ δράκων ἐδόκησε μολεῖν κάρα βεβροτωμένος ἄκρον·
ἐκ δ' ἄρα τοῦ βασιλεὺς Πλεισθενίδας ἐφάνη.[2]

There seemed to come to her a snake with the crest of his head dabbled in blood, and from it a king, son of Pleisthenes, appeared.

This must be the source of the snake in Aeschylus and have something of the same intention, but Stesichorus treats the theme a little differently. The snake with the bloody crest is surely Agamemnon, who has blood on his head because of the blows with which he was killed. The second line can be treated in one of two ways. Either the snake turns into the human form of Agamemnon and reveals its true identity, or out of it grows an offspring, Orestes. The use of ἐφάνη might seem to favour the first interpretation, but on the whole the second seems more convincing. The vague phrase βασιλεὺς Πλεισθενίδας is meant to inspire a sense of majesty and awe and refers to a scion of the royal line who will take the place of the dead Agamemnon. Clytaemestra sees a snake, which is a symbol of vengeance and the Furies, and out of it rises the figure of a prince of the House of Pleisthenes, threatening and royal.

A second episode treated by Stesichorus reveals its full results in the *Orestes* of Euripides. In the scene where Orestes is haunted by hallucinations, he cries out for a bow to keep off the Furies:

δὸς τόξα μοι κερουλκά, δῶρα Λοξίου,
οἷς μ' εἶπ' Ἀπόλλων ἐξαμύνεσθαι θεάς,
εἴ μ' ἐκφοβοῖεν μανιάσιν λυσσήμασιν.[3]

Give me the curved bow, the gift of Loxias, with which Apollo bade me keep off the goddesses, if they should frighten me with raving madness.

For Euripides both the bow and the Furies are creations of Orestes' fevered fancy, but the scholiast on the passage says that here Euripides follows Stesichorus, who made Orestes receive the bow from Apollo.[4] What is hallucination in Euripides is literal fact in Stesichorus. How real and fearsome the Furies of

[1] *Or.* 618.   [2] Fr. 15 D.   [3] *Or.* 268-70.
[4] Schol. *Or.* 268 Στησιχόρῳ ἑπόμενος τόξα φησὶν αὐτὸν εἰληφέναι παρὰ Ἀπόλλωνος.

I

Stesichorus were may perhaps be deduced from a metope of the temple of the Argive Hera at Sele, now at Paestum, dating from the end of the sixth century. On it a vast coiled snake, like a python, threatens a young man, who must be Orestes,[1] since another metope depicts the murder of Agamemnon. It was against such an enemy that Stesichorus made Orestes beg Apollo for a bow to defend himself. From this an important conclusion follows. The Furies who pursue Orestes are so familiar from Aeschylus that we almost take their presence in the story for granted, but we may now doubt whether, without Stesichorus to help, they would have had this central part.

The character of the Ἑλένα and the Ὀρέστεια indicates that the *Marmor Parium* may be right in saying that Stesichorus came to the mainland, even if it gets the date wrong. His presence in Sparta is confirmed by a piece of local knowledge. Somewhere he mentioned the Spartan dancers called βρυαλίκται, who danced in a warlike manner and also masked themselves indecently as women and sang songs,[2] presumably at some fertility festival. They were hardly known outside Sparta, and Stesichorus' reference to them, which was repeated by Ibycus, indicates that he knew them in their home. Nor need we dismiss as a fabrication the story that he was exiled from Pallantium in Arcadia. No reason for it can be given, but it is quite conceivable in the disturbed politics of the time. It receives some small support from the statement of Philodemus that he called Iphigeneia Hecate.[3] The identification had, it is true, been made in the Hesiodic Catalogue of Women,[3] but Pausanias says that it was Arcadian,[4] and in Arcadia Stesichorus may have picked it up. It looks as if Stesichorus visited Arcadia but, for political reasons, was not allowed to stay there. He seems also to have known something about Boeotia, since the story dramatized by Euripides in his *Heracles*, that Heracles went mad and killed his children, seems to have belonged to Thebes, and Pausanias says that it was told by Stesichorus.[5] If he visited the mainland, Stesichorus returned to the West, where he died in 556–553 B.C. and was buried at Catane,[6] and a Pythagorean story told that he had inherited the

---

[1] P. Zancani Montuoro, *R.A.A.N.* xxvi (1951), pp. 270–9.

[2] Hesych. βρυαλίκται· πολεμικοὶ ὀρχησταί· μενέδουποι, Ἴβυκος καὶ Στησίχορος; id. βρυλλιχισταί· οἱ αἰσχρὰ προσωπεῖα περιτιθέμενοι γυναικεῖα καὶ ὕμνους ᾄδοντες; Poll. 4. 104.   [3] περὶ εὐσεβείας 24.   [4] 1. 43. 1.

[5] 9. 11. 2.   [6] 'Suid.' s.v. Στησίχορος.

soul of Homer.[1] The period of Phalaris' rule in Acragas comes
before this, and his seizure of power may have been the cause of
Stesichorus' departure from Sicily to Greece. Aristotle says that
Stesichorus opposed the election of Phalaris as general,[2] and to
this time must belong the fable, which is no more than a local
tale, that Stesichorus told the men of Himera, as a warning
against Phalaris, of the horse and the stag, and how the horse,
in its eagerness to get rid of the stag, is enslaved by a man.[2] In
the same spirit he may have made his enigmatic remark to the
Locrians that they must not become arrogant 'or the crickets
would chirp from the ground',[3] that is, their trees would be
destroyed by enemies. Stesichorus' opposition to Phalaris failed,
and he may not have returned to Sicily until after the tyrant's
death.

A remarkable feature of Stesichorus' poems is that, although
our knowledge of their contents is lamentably fragmentary, their
subject-matter has much in common with that of late-seventh-
century and early-sixth-century art as we know it from the extant
monuments and from Pausanias' description of the Chest of
Cypselus and the Amyclean Throne. Almost every one of these
poems may be illustrated by the art of this period. When we
consider the hesitation with which Greek artists chose subjects
from the *Iliad* and the *Odyssey*, the popularity of themes from
Stesichorus is all the more remarkable. In some cases the poet
and the artist must draw from a common tradition. When, for
instance, Protocorinthian artists paint the triple-bodied Geryon[4]
or Heracles' fight with the Centaurs,[5] both painters and poets
must have got their subject from established legends, and the
illustrations show versions of stories told in poetry, probably epic,
which is now lost. But the themes of seventh-century art are
limited, and, except for these two cases, have not much relation
to Stesichorus. On the other hand the great efflorescence of
the sixth century raises more intricate problems. This was the
time of Middle and Late Corinthian ware, of Attic black-
figure, and of the fine ware known as Chalcidian. It was also
a period of rapid and inventive development in sculpture, and
though the evidence of extant remains is limited, descriptions
of lost works like the Chest of Cypselus and the Amyclean

[1] *Anth. Pal.* 7. 75.   [2] *Rhet.* 1393 b.   [3] Ibid. 1395 a.
[4] Payne, p. 130.   [5] Id. p. 129.

Throne bear important testimony. In these different depart-
ments we may see connexions with Stesichorus, and it seems
more likely that artists drew on Stesichorus than that he drew
on them.

We may first consider those subjects which are treated both by
Stesichorus and by artists but are not demonstrably taken from
him, because they may well have been popular before he gave
them a new currency. Such is the Middle Corinthian kotyle of
Heracles fetching Cerberus, to which reference has already been
made.[1] This may be dated 600–575 B.C. and therefore belongs
to the time of Stesichorus' mature manhood. The dramatic
story which it portrays implies poetical influence, but we cannot
be certain whether this was Stesichorus' *Cerberus* or some epic
about Heracles. The story was ancient, and not enough is known
of the *Cerberus* to allow a decision. Against this doubtful case we
may set a general consideration of a more positive kind. It is
remarkable how many of Stesichorus' subjects appeared on the
Chest of Cypselus. It displayed the Funeral Games of Pelias,[2]
which were described in the Ἆθλα ἐπὶ Πελίᾳ, the combat between
Heracles and a triple-bodied Geryon,[3] as in the Γηρυονηΐς, the
story of Eriphyle,[4] and the figure of Alcestis,[5] who belonged to
Pelias' funeral-games. If the Chest was really dedicated by
Cypselus himself, the resemblances between it and the poetry
of Stesichorus present an insoluble problem; for the Chest
would have been made when Stesichorus was only a child. But
it seems highly improbable that so intricate and complex a
work of art should have been made in the seventh century,
and the nature of its scenes recalls the François Vase in the
middle of the sixth. In that case there is no difficulty about
the artist learning his subjects in part from Stesichorus and
making full use of them.

Hardly less relevant is the Amyclean Throne, which may be
dated to the same period. Here were the fight of Heracles with
Cycnus,[6] the Calydonian Boar-hunt,[7] Heracles with Geryon's
cattle,[8] and the fetching of Cerberus.[9] The throne was made by
an Ionian artist, but he may have chosen his subjects to suit his
patrons, and he certainly seems to have found Stesichorus a

---

[1] See p. 94.   [2] Paus. 5. 17. 9.   [3] Id. 5. 19. 1.
[4] Id. 5. 17. 7.   [5] Id. 5. 17. 11.   [6] Id. 3. 18. 10.
[7] Id. 3. 18. 15.   [8] Id. 3. 18. 13.   [9] Id. 3. 18. 13.

congenial source. The evidence of the Chest and the Throne may
be supplemented by actual objects which show how artists treated
their subjects. A fine Late Corinthian crater in Berlin (575–550
B.C.) presents two themes handled by Stesichorus, the departure
of Amphiaraus from Eriphyle and the chariot-race at the Funeral
Games of Pelias.[1] Both themes were on the Chest of Cypselus,
and the vase helps to clarify the relations of the artists to the
poet. The departure of Amphiaraus, as the Chest showed it, is
closely described by Pausanias, and this shows that there was
much in common between it and the vase. In view of this resemblance Payne concludes that 'the two designs are roughly
contemporary and go back to a common origin'. From this a
small advance may be made. The vase shows the boy Alcmaeon,
who also appeared as a naked child on the Chest, but the Chest
showed another child, Amphilochus, carried by a nurse. Both
boys, as the future punishers of Eriphyle, were indispensable to
the story, and both may have had a place in Stesichorus' 'Εριφύλα. Their presence on the Chest indicates that the sculptor
knew the story as the poet told it, but the absence of Amphilochus from the vase means the omission, for reasons of space or
design, of a character who was thought relatively unimportant,
and the Chest was apparently closer than the vase to Stesichorus.

    In Stesichorus' account of the chariot-race both Castor and
Polydeuces competed, each in a two-horsed chariot. On the
Chest also there were two-horsed chariots, but though Polydeuces competed, Castor did not. On the other hand the vase
shows four-horsed chariots and Castor but not Polydeuces. The
vase-painter did not follow the Chest faithfully, if indeed he followed it at all. The Chest showed five competitors, and the vase
shows ten; only Euphamus and Admetus are common to both,
and these are indispensable because Euphamus won the race
and Admetus married Pelias' daughter Alcestis. There is, then,
a considerable divergence between the two presentations of the
story, but here too a common origin would account for the
divergences. If both the Dioscuri competed, it would be reasonable
for artists pressed for space to depict only one of them; if there was
a large number of competitors, it is likely that one artist would
make one selection, and the other another; if four-horsed chariots
were usual in the vase-painter's day he might well depict them in

[1] Payne, pp. 139–41.

defiance of legend. A common source could be found either in Stesichorus' poem or in some work of art inspired by it. It is in itself significant that a single vase should depict two scenes treated by Stesichorus. The stories of Amphiaraus and the Funeral Games of Pelias have little connexion with one another, and a natural reason for associating them would be that a single poet had told of both. Their popularity endured through the later part of the sixth century, and the departure of Amphiaraus can be seen on Attic black-figure fragments and on a Tyrrhenian fragment from the Acropolis.[1] Themes treated by Stesichorus emerge during his own lifetime and remain current after his death, and we can hardly doubt that artists drew on him for them.

The combat of Heracles and Cycnus was also an epic theme, but its first appearance as a subject for art seems to be in the second quarter of the sixth century. It was on the Amyclean throne,[2] and it may be seen on a Late Corinthian amphora,[3] a Chalcidian amphora,[4] and often on Attic black-figure vases,[5] of which the earliest are before 550 B.C. Its first appearance, then, is about contemporary with the two themes just considered. Since the Hesiodic *Shield* survives, the vase representations may be compared with it, and certain results follow. First, the Late Corinthian amphora shows some sort of building, and Payne suggests that this may be the temple of Apollo. The *Shield* says nothing about a temple and mentions only an altar and sacred grove in Apollo's precinct.[6] On the other hand the temple built by Cycnus was integral to the Stesichorean version. Secondly, the *Shield* limits the fighting to Cycnus, Heracles, and Ares, with Apollo as a malevolent neutral. But in early Attic black-figure the characters are more numerous. An oenochoe of Lydos,[7] for instance, introduces Athene as an ally of Heracles, and in later representations she is normally there. Of course for artists a figure of Athene provided symmetry for the figure of Ares, but it seems possible that Stesichorus had introduced her. Once she was there, the characters were often reinforced, and a crater of Nicosthenes adds Zeus, Ares, Eris, and Phobos to the company.[8]

[1] Payne, p. 139. [2] Paus. 3. 18. 10. [3] Payne, p. 131.
[4] Rumpf, *Chalkidische Vasen*, Taf. xi.
[5] Beazley, *A.B.-F.V.* pp. 60, 109, 110, 111, 122, &c.
[6] *Scut.* 70, 99. [7] Beazley, *A.B.-F.V.* p. 110.
[8] Ibid., p. 229.

The theme grew as painters handled it, but both its inception and some at least of its details may be due to Stesichorus.

In these cases Stesichorus seems to have given a new popularity to themes already known to some extent in poetry, but in other cases his unusual inventiveness directly influenced artists, and details of his creation passed into their repertories. A signal example may be found in his treatment of the birth of Athene. He improved on the tradition that she came out of the head of Zeus by saying that she was fully armed.[1] The birth of an unarmed Athene can be seen in a late Protocorinthian relief from Delphi,[2] but in the second quarter of the sixth century a fully armed Athene bursts from the head of Zeus on Attic black-figure.[3] An excellent example is the Phrynus cup in the British Museum, admirably described by J. D. Beazley: 'Zeus is seated on his throne: Athena bursts from his head on fighting trim, shield on arm: Zeus brandishes his thunderbolt in his emotion; Hephaistos, axe in hand, turns to leave, quite the surgeon satisfied with an operation.'[4] Pindar may well have some echo of Stesichorus in his mind when he treats the same theme in *Olympian* vii. 35–38. But the debt of the Phrynos Painter to Stesichorus in this case may be seen also on the other side of the cup, which shows the apotheosis of Heracles. Again to quote Beazley; 'The scene is again Heaven, and two of the figures are the same as on the reverse, for Athena is introducing Herakles to her father. The hero, on him all he owns (white shirt, lion-skin, sword, bow, and arrow, and club), is drawn rapidly forward by his guide: Zeus on his throne, with his sceptre, extends a gracious hand'.[4] Here not the subject but certain details seem to be due to Stesichorus. Megaclides, quoted by Athenaeus, says that Stesichorus was the first to clothe Heracles with club, lion-skin, and bow.[5] Before Stesichorus his usual clothing had been that of any other hero, and his only weapon a bow and arrows. This is certainly substantiated by the literary evidence. Homer says nothing of club or lion-skin, and in the Νέκυια Heracles goes on his way

γυμνὸν τόξον ἔχων καὶ ἐπὶ νευρῆφιν ὀϊστόν.[6]

---

[1] Schol. Ap. Rhod. 4. 1310 πρῶτος Στησίχορος ἔφη σὺν ὅπλοις ἐκ τῆς τοῦ Διὸς κεφαλῆς ἀναπηδῆσαι τὴν Ἀθηνᾶν; Ox. Pap. 2260 ii. 19–23.

[2] *Fouilles de Delphes*, v, pl. 2.   [3] Payne, p. 142.

[4] *Attic Black-Figure: a Sketch*, p. 7.   [5] Athen. 12. 512 f.

[6] *Od.* 11. 607.

A fragment attributed to Alcman speaks of κὠ τοξόταs 'Ηρακλέηs,[1]
and the *Shield of Heracles* clothes the warrior in full Homeric
panoply. This view of Heracles is reflected in early works of art.
In the Protocorinthian vase of the fetching of Cerberus the hero
is naked except for his bow;[2] in Early Corinthian vases Heracles
slays the hydra with sword or arrows and wears little except a
quiver;[3] on the Nessus amphora, painted in the seventh century,
Heracles wears a chiton and uses a sword.[4] Then early in the
sixth century a change comes over the treatment of Heracles.
Henceforward his normal clothing is the skin of the Nemean lion,
and he carries a club as well as bow and arrows. An early
example is a Cycladic amphora, on which he abducts a bride.[5]
After this the clothing is common, even normal. Most painters of
Attic black-figure depict it, and it may be seen on the work of the
Amasis Painter, Lydos, Nicosthenes, the Achelous Painter, and
others. The date of its first appearance agrees with the heyday
of Stesichorus, and its combination with the birth of Athene on
the Phrynos Cup makes it additionally likely that both themes
come from him.

We have seen that Stesichorus followed tradition in giving
Geryon three bodies, but he also gave him wings,[6] and this looks
like an innovation. In Protocorinthian art Geryon has no wings,
and Pausanias' description of him on the Chest of Cypselus as
τρεῖs ἄνδρεs ἀλλήλοιs προσεχόμενοι[7] seems to exclude any possibility of them. So too painters of Attic black-figure such as
Lydos, Execias, and the Leagros Group,[8] do the same. But two
splendid Chalcidian amphorae, painted before 550 B.C., show
Geryon not only with three bodies but with three pairs of great
curved wings.[9] This touch surely comes from the Γηρυονηίs, and
the comparative rarity of the winged Geryon makes these cases
more impressive. It looks as if the painter, eager to break new
ground and to improve upon Corinthian models, added this
decorative detail, and we can hardly doubt that he got it from
Stesichorus. Nor was the popularity of the Γηρυονηίs limited to
Chalcidian vases. Two of its more dramatic themes were used by

---

[1] Fr. 12 D.   [2] Payne, p. 130.   [3] Ibid., p. 127.
[4] Beazley, *Attic Black-Figure: a Sketch*, p. 9, pl. 3.
[5] Pfühl, iii, Taf. 110.   [6] See p. 92.   [7] 5. 19. 1.
[8] Beazley, *A.B.-F.V.* pp. 108, 111, 131, 147, 361, 379.
[9] Rumpf, Taf. vii and xiii.

Attic painters who were not interested in the winged Geryon. A lekythos of the Leagros Group shows Heracles threatening the Sun,[1] and a wine-jug from the same group shows him travelling in the Sun's bowl.[2] In the fifth century both themes became more popular, but it is noteworthy that Stesichorus' Γηρυονηίς was appreciated in Athens almost in his own life-time.

These examples, with the possible exception of the Chalcidian vases,,come from the mainland, but Stesichorus was not unnoticed in his own land of Sicily. A metope from temple Y at Selinus, from the middle of the sixth century, shows one of the earliest representations of Europa on her bull,[3] a theme which must have had a prominent place in the Εὐρώπεια. The same theme occurs on a metope of the Sicyonian Treasury at Delphi,[4] which probably comes from the second quarter of the sixth century, and two Caeretan hydrias, which may be Ionian work but are of a kind that was common in the west, each give different representations of the scene c. 550 B.C.[5] In one Europa looks at a flower while she rides; on the other she gallops gaily over the sea, while fishes tumble about the bull's hooves. At about the same time the scene is portrayed on Attic blackfigure, on two lekythoi and an oenochoe.[6] In all these versions the charming and constant element is the completely untroubled air of Europa who rides on her remarkable beast as if she were going quietly over a meadow and not over the sea. The theme did not attain a vast popularity, but it appealed to artists in several places and inspired them to produce their own individual versions of it.

Stesichorus' ingenious idea of clothing Actaeon in a stag's skin does not seem to have caught the imagination of many artists, but an Attic black-figured lekythos takes full advantage of it, when it shows Actaeon, clothed in the skin, being attacked by seven dogs, one of whom has seized the dead beast's leg.[7] In the second quarter of the fifth century it appears on a metope from temple E at Selinus, where Actaeon wears the skin over his shoulders, and the dogs seem to be going for it before they go for him.[8] A little earlier the Pan Painter treated the scene in an

---

[1] Beazley, *A.B.-F.V.* p. 380. [2] Id. p. 378. [3] F. Poulsen, *Delphi*, fig. 22.
[4] Ibid., p. 124, fig. 19. [5] Ibid., figs. 20 and 21.
[6] Beazley, *A.B.-F.V.* pp. 380, 422, 478. [7] Ibid., p. 586.
[8] G. Richter, *The Sculpture and Sculptors of the Greeks*, fig. 411.

early work, on a red-figure crater, and made Actaeon wear the skin like a closely fitting coat and present himself as an easy prey to his attackers.[1] Later, when the same artist painted the magnificent crater in Boston, he made Actaeon naked, as if he felt that not even a skin was needed to emphasize the whole horror of the episode.[2] It is clear that though Stesichorus invented the detail and had his own reasons for doing so, it need not necessarily have a wide appeal for artists, though it provided them with something rather unusual and unexpected. Some of these points of resemblance may seem sketchy and others insufficiently founded, but the cumulative impression from them is that Stesichorus brought into the presentation of heroic subjects new details which appealed to artists for their pictorial potentialities, and that this influence spread far beyond his own land in his own lifetime.

On the general character of Stesichorus' poetry the verdict of posterity leaves no doubt. Critics so varied as 'Longinus',[3] Dio Chrysostom,[4] and Synesius[5] all compare him with Homer, and Quintilian supports their verdict when he speaks of him as 'maxima bella et clarissimos canentem duces et epici carminis onera lyra sustinentem,'[6] while a more popular judgement was embodied in the fancies that he was the son of Hesiod[7] or the incarnation of Homer.[8] This consensus of opinion indicates more than one quality in his work. In the first place he evidently composed on a generous scale. His whole collected works were arranged at Alexandria in twenty-six books,[9] and this implies a far greater scale of creation than Alcman, who was represented by six,[10] or Ibycus by five.[11] Moreover, the mere fact that his Ὀρέστεια was divided into two books shows that it was of a magnitude that we do not expect from Greek lyric poetry. His individual poems must often have contained varied and lengthy plots, and that is why their incidents made such an impression on artists. They must have provided episodes and details far beyond the usual scope of choral song. If, for instance, we knew more of his Ὀρέστεια, we might well see in it the source of the metope from Sele which depicts the slaying of Aegisthus, and the capacious contents of the Ἰλίου πέρσις or the Ἆθλα ἐπὶ Πελίᾳ must

[1] Beazley, Der Pan-Maler, Taf. 12. 2.   [2] Ibid., Taf. 1.
[3] De Sub. 13. 3.   [4] Or. 2. 25.   [5] Insomn. 158 b.
[6] 10. 1. 62.   [7] Aristot. fr. 565 R.   [8] Anth. Pal. 7. 75.
[9] 'Suid.' s.v. Στησίχορος.   [10] Id. s.v. Ἀλκμάν.   [11] Id. s.v. Ἴβυκος.

have included much more than we know of, though this is illuminating enough. Stesichorus evidently told stories with something of a Homeric breadth and richness, and did not anticipate Pindar's method of alluding briefly and elliptically to them. No other extant lyric poet does this on the scale indicated for Stesichorus, and though there is flowing narrative in Bacchylides and perhaps in Alcman, it does not seem to be so whole-hearted or so informative as that in Stesichorus. Stesichorus seems to represent, as no other poet does, the transition from epic to lyric, in that he keeps much of the narrative of the epic even though he presents it in a lyric form.

Secondly, as we have seen from the fragment of the Νόστοι, Stesichorus owes much to the epic manner, and though this extends well beyond Homer, it merely shows that Stesichorus was acquainted with the full vocabulary and formulas of the epic in its later stages. At times he keeps close to this in a whole phrase, as when he says of the sons of Thestius who were too young to go to the Calydonian boar-hunt that they were ὀψιγόνοι τε καὶ ἀσπάσιοι and recalls the words of a Homeric Hymn:

> τηλύγετος δέ οἱ υἱὸς ἐνὶ μεγάρῳ εὐπήκτῳ
> ὀψίγονος τρέφεται πολυεύχετος ἀσπάσιός τε.[1]

There are obvious echoes from the epic in such standard phrases as τανυπέπλου applied to a woman, δαΐφρονος applied to a man, κουριδίην ἄλοχον παῖδάς τε φίλους, ναυσὶν εὐσέλμοις, Ἥλιος Ὑπεριονίδας, χθόνα πυροφόρον, and less obvious but no less genuine echoes in Ταρτάρου ἠλιβάτου, ἀπειρεσίου κυναλαγμοῦ, ὑπερθυμέστατον ἀνδρῶν, which suggest either loans from epics lost to us or adaptations of the epic manner to new uses. Stesichorus' epithets tend to be less distinctive than those of Alcman or Pindar, and that is because they still keep some of their original formulaic character which aims at helping the poet to compose rather than at adding a special distinction to the context where they occur. So when he speaks of κλεινᾶς Ἐρυθείας, he is not talking nonsense but he may not expect us to read very much into it. The texture of his poetry seems to be less close and less carefully worked than that of later lyric poets, and his taste for the epic expansiveness may account for Quintilian's reservation about him, 'sed redundat atque effunditur, quod ut est reprehendendum, ita copiae

[1] Hom. Hymn 2. 164–5.

uitium est'.[1] He evidently lacked the concentration of power which can be so impressive in Alcman or Pindar, but he must have made up for it by his easy flow and ample invention.

Thirdly, Stesichorus must have had something like a heroic temper. This is what Horace means when he refers to his 'graues Camenae'[2] or Statius when he calls him 'ferox'.[3] He was certainly capable of a heroic majesty, and there is a truly Greek ring in some of his lines about death, as when he says with sorrowful resignation

$$\theta\alpha\nu\acute{o}\nu\tau o\varsigma\ \mathring{\alpha}\nu\delta\rho\grave{o}\varsigma$$
$$\pi\mathring{\alpha}\sigma' \mathring{\alpha}\pi\acute{o}\lambda\lambda\upsilon\tau\alpha\iota\ \pi o\tau' \mathring{\alpha}\nu\theta\rho\acute{\omega}\pi\omega\nu\ \chi\acute{\alpha}\rho\iota\varsigma,[4]$$

'when a man dies all his glory perishes from men', but he does not waste tears on it and says elsewhere

$$\mathring{\alpha}\tau\epsilon\lambda\acute{\epsilon}\sigma\tau\alpha\tau\alpha\ \gamma\grave{\alpha}\rho\ \kappa\alpha\grave{\iota}\ \mathring{\alpha}\mu\acute{\alpha}\chi\alpha\nu\alpha\ \tau o\grave{\upsilon}\varsigma\ \theta\alpha\nu\acute{o}\nu\tau\alpha\varsigma\ \kappa\lambda\alpha\acute{\iota}\epsilon\iota\nu,[5]$$

'it is most useless and helpless to weep for the dead'. This is in the true Homeric vein, and fits well with the gravity of his themes. But this was only the background of his imaginary world. In the foreground he sets his brilliant and varied scenes of action and pleasure and his attitude may be seen from his own words:

$$\chi o\rho\epsilon\acute{\upsilon}\mu\alpha\tau\acute{\alpha}\ \tau o\iota\ \mu\acute{\alpha}\lambda\iota\sigma\tau\alpha$$
$$\pi\alpha\iota\gamma\mu o\sigma\acute{\upsilon}\nu\alpha\varsigma\ \langle\tau\epsilon\rangle\ \phi\iota\lambda\epsilon\hat{\iota}\ \mu o\lambda\pi\acute{\alpha}\varsigma\ \tau'\ \mathring{A}\pi\acute{o}\lambda\lambda\omega\nu$$
$$\kappa\acute{\alpha}\delta\epsilon\alpha\ \delta\grave{\epsilon}\ \sigma\tau o\nu\alpha\chi\acute{\alpha}\varsigma\ \tau'\ \mathring{A}\acute{\iota}\delta\alpha\varsigma\ \mathring{\epsilon}\lambda\alpha\chi\epsilon\nu.[6]$$

Apollo loves dances and games and songs most of all, but mourning and lamentations belong to Hades.

Against the final darkness of death Stesichorus sets the sunlit present, and it is not surprising that for him Apollo counts for so much. It is he who protects Heracles, who gives a bow to Orestes, who is the father of Hector, who takes Hecuba to Lycia. He is the god of light and song, and his presiding presence illuminates even the most gloomy and murderous tale. Stesichorus' delight in gay occasions, such as feasts and dances, is as obvious as his inventiveness in varying old tales, and both tendencies reflect his pleasure in the living scene and the keen eye which he had for its variety and its drama. He may have lacked authentic magical moments, and his style may have been a little more traditional than would have appealed to a later century, but Hermogenes admits that

[1] 10. 1. 62.   [2] C. 4. 9. 11.   [3] Silu. 3. 3. 154.
[4] Fr. 24 D.   [5] Fr. 23 D.   [6] Fr. 22 D.

he was 'extremely sweet because of his abundant use of epithets',[1] and in addition to this incidental sweetness he seems also to have possessed strength and creative invention and a keen instinct for making the old stories live again.

[1] *de Id.* 3. 322 ταῦτά τοι καὶ ὁ Στησίχορος σφόδρα ἡδὺς εἶναι δοκεῖ διὰ τὸ πολλοῖς χρῆσθαι τοῖς ἐπιθέτοις.

IV. ALCAEUS

THE island of Lesbos is well fitted by nature to be the home of a distinctive culture. Its southern shore looks across the sea to Chios, the traditional dwelling-place of Homer and those 'sons of Homer' who recited his poems and composed preludes to them in the form of Hymns. In full view from Mytilene and the eastern shore lies the coast of Asia Minor, which had begun in the seventh century to come under the sway of the Lydian kings and to absorb some of their oriental ways. To the north lies the Adramyttian promontory and the site of Troy, where Greek story-tellers placed the deeds of their heroic ancestors. In contrast with its neighbours Lemnos and Chios Lesbos is a rich land. Olive-trees grow up to the tops of the high hills; an abundance of natural springs fills the valleys with plane-trees and lush grass; in the spring the ground is covered with anemones, orchids, and wild tulips. The island still deserves the epithet of ἠγαθέη given to it by the Chian poet who wrote the Delian Hymn to Apollo[1]. Protected by the sea and well supplied with means of subsistence, its inhabitants developed a lively and independent life, based on ancient traditions which went back to the heroic age and the Trojan War. Here Orestes was said to have led the first colonists;[2] here in later centuries noble families traced their descent from men who had fought for Helen.[3] In surroundings favourable to ease and security, Lesbian society reached its zenith in the seventh and sixth centuries, and the record of that life is its poetry.

Lesbian poetry seems to have been helped, if not begotten, by religious needs. In the seventh century two Lesbian musicians, who were also poets, Terpander and Arion, won a wide renown. While Terpander composed 'preludes' in hexameters, which suggest a resemblance to the Homeric Hymns,[4] Arion composed

---

[1] Hom. Hymn 3. 37. For doubts on the meaning of ἠγαθέη see F. Bechtel, *Lexilogus zu Homer*, pp. 149–50. For a romantic but not entirely false picture of the Lesbian landscape cf. Longus i. 1 κτῆμα κάλλιστον, ὄρη θηροτρόφα, πεδία πυροφόρα, γήλοφοι κλημάτων, νομαὶ ποιμνίων. [2] Strab.582.

[3] Aristot. *Pol.* 1311 b 27; Plut. *de Soll. An.* 36.

[4] 'Plut.' *Mus.* 4 πεποίηται δὲ τῷ Τερπάνδρῳ καὶ προοίμια κιθαρῳδικὰ ἐν ἔπεσιν.

dithyrambs and gave a new significance to the form.[1] Much of their work seems to have been done away from their own home, but even before this date Lesbos was already famous for its songs. Archilochus specifically associates the Paean with it:

αὐτὸς ἐξάρχων πρὸς αὐλὸν Λέσβιον παιήονα,[2]

and his words show that well before the time of Alcaeus and Sappho Lesbos was renowned as a home of song. Perhaps Sappho referred to this, as well as to her own eminence, when she wrote

πέρροχος ὡς ὅτ' ἄοιδος ὁ Λέσβιος ἀλλοδάποισιν[3]

'towering as the Lesbian singer over foreigners'. The idea passed into a proverb and was known to Cratinus.[4] When Alcaeus began to write, the art of song was not only well established in Lesbos but had a considerable fame abroad.

Among the poems composed by Terpander Pindar included σκόλια.[5] We do not know precisely what these were, nor has any hint of their contents survived, but we may assume that they were in some sense convivial songs, intended for social occasions. If they were solo songs, they would help to account for the special direction which Lesbian poetry took with Alcaeus and Sappho. Though both Terpander and Arion wrote for choruses, Alcaeus and Sappho on the whole did not. The more characteristic part of their work is monody, composed in short stanzas and in varied but simple metres. Nor is there much evidence that it was attached to formal ceremonies. A large part of it had a social, rather than a ritual, background, and is the work of poets who felt the need to express their feelings and thoughts in song and had a brilliant technique for doing so. They could hardly have done this if they had not inherited some kind of tradition and been helped by favourable circumstances. What this tradition was we hardly know, but one or two hints suggest that it owed something to popular song.

A precious example of such a song is the Mill Song, which, Plutarch says, was sung at Eresus:[6]

---

[1] Hdt. 1. 23 διθύραμβον πρῶτον ἀνθρώπων τῶν ἡμεῖς ἴδμεν ποιήσαντά τε καὶ ὀνομάσαντα καὶ διδάξαντα ἐν Κορίνθῳ; 'Suid.' s.v. Ἀρίων. In general see A. W. Pickard-Cambridge, *Dithyramb, Tragedy, Comedy*, pp. 19–22.   [2] Fr. 76 D.
[3] Fr. 106 L.–P.
[4] Fr. 243 K.; Zenob. 5. 9 μετὰ Λέσβιον ᾠδόν· παροιμία ταττομένη ἐπὶ τοῖς τὰ δεύτερα φερομένοις.
[5] 'Plut.' *Mus.* 28 ἔτι δέ, καθάπερ Πίνδαρός φησι, καὶ τῶν σκολιῶν μελῶν Τέρπανδρος εὑρετὴς ἦν.   [6] *Conv. Sept. Sap.* 14.

ἄλει, μύλα, ἄλει·
καὶ γὰρ Πίττακος ἄλει,
μεγάλας Μυτιλήνας βασιλεύων.

Grind, mill-wheel, grind;
Even Pittacus ground,
Who was king of great Mytilene.

Tryphon, quoted by Athenaeus,[1] gives a list of different kinds of song, among which is the ἱμαῖος or Mill Song, which men sang while they ground corn; for the word ἱμαῖος seems to be connected with ἱμάλις, the 'return' or 'over-measure' of wheat-flour. Pollux goes a step farther and distinguishes between the ἐπιμύλιος ᾠδή and the ἱμαῖος καὶ ἱμαλίς, of which the first was sung over the mill-wheel and the second was more formal and sung by a ἱμαοιδός.[2] Our song evidently belongs to the first class. Its mention of Pittacus means that it cannot be earlier than 600 B.C., and its first known appearance was when it was heard by Clearchus, the pupil of Aristotle,[3] but of course it may have been old when he heard it. Even if it is later than Alcaeus and Sappho, it is relevant to their art for two reasons. First, it is a truly popular song and, like all such songs, it may have a long past behind it. Its metrical units have not yet fully matured into those of lyric verse, and the first line is certainly puzzling, but the second line is a Pherecratean and the third is Ionic.[4] To this degree it shares, at a humbler level, the metrical practice of the Lesbian poets. Secondly, it has a political reference, such as we often find in Alcaeus. We can hardly believe that the notion of grinding is as innocent as it appears, or that Pittacus ground simply for exercise or pleasure, and though we need not necessarily assume that there is an obscene reference,[5] we may suspect at least some deliberate ambiguity, such as that Pittacus ground the faces of the rich.[6]

[1] 14. 618 d.   [2] 4. 53.
[3] Wilamowitz, *Hermes*, xxv, p. 227.
[4] Id. *Gr. Versk.* p. 401 rewrites the poem

> ἄλει, μύλα, ἄλει·
> καὶ γὰρ βασιλεύων
> μεγάλας Μυτιλήνας
> Πίττακος ἄλει,

and claims that this gives three Reiziana, followed by an Adonius. But this reduces the emphatic βασιλεύων to comparative impotence.

[5] A. von Blumenthal, *Hermes*, lxxv (1940), pp. 225 ff.
[6] Cf. Sext. Emp. *Adv. Math.* 1. 287. ὀψὲ θεῶν ἀλέουσι μύλαι, ἀλέουσι δὲ λεπτά.

Even if we add to these examples of popular songs in Lesbos those which are mentioned by Longus[1] and may have some basis in local practice, they do not take us very far. More illuminating are two poems, one by Alcaeus and one by Sappho, which look as if they were modelled on traditional folk-songs. Hephaestion preserves a line from Alcaeus, which he says was the beginning of a poem:[2]

ἔμε δείλαν, ἔμε παῖσαν κακοτάτων πεδέχοισαν[3]

'me, poor woman, who have a part in every misery . . .'. If this is the start, the poem is dramatic in the sense that it is spoken by a woman in the first person without introduction or preliminary, and we suspect that this is a traditional theme of a love-lorn girl. This impression is confirmed when, after three fragmentary lines, we have

ἐλάφω δὲ βρόμος ἐν στήθεσι φυίει φοβέροισιν

'the belling of the deer grows in the timid heart'. Though ἐλάφω can be either masculine or feminine,[4] its connexion with βρόμος suggests that here it is masculine, and that the girl who speaks recalls her lover. His mating-cry remains with her and grows stronger in her breast. Deer are a traditional image in more than one country,[5] and we may surmise that here the girl speaks of the violent emotions which assail her, as she contrasts her

---

[1] 2. 31 songs in praise of nymphs; 2. 35 songs of herdsmen; 2. 36 Dionysiac songs.
[2] p. 65. 17 Consbruch.   [3] Fr. 10 L.–P.
[4] For a full discussion see Page, S. and A. pp. 291–4.
[5] A Chinese example, before 600 B.C. is given by A. Waley, *The Book of Songs*, p. 60:

> In the wilds there is a dead doe;
> With white rushes we cover her.
> There was a lady longing for the spring;
> A fair knight seduced her.
>
> In the wood there is a clump of oaks,
> And in the wilds a dead deer
> With white rushes well bound;
> There was a lady fair as jade.

The Portuguese poet, Pero Meogo, c. A.D. 1250, associates deer with unsatisfied love:

> En as verdes ervas
> vi anda-las cervas,
> meu amigo!
>
> en os verdes prados
> vi os cervos bravos,
> meu amigo!

K

present misery with the excitement which her lover's desires
have awoken in her. Alcaeus would not have written this poem,
even as a literary exercise, if he had not been well acquainted
with songs on such subjects among his own people.

Beside this we may set two lines from Sappho. They too make
a girl speak in the first person. We do not know that it is the
beginning of a poem, though this is not impossible, since Hephaestion quotes it for its metre:

> γλύκηα μᾶτερ, οὔτοι δύναμαι κρέκην τὸν ἴστον,
> πόθωι δάμεισα παῖδος βραδίναν δι' Ἀφροδίταν.[1]

Sweet mother, I cannot weave my web; for because of slender Aphrodite I am overcome with desire for a boy.

This too is a song of an ancient and widespread kind, a *chanson de
toile*, such as girls sang over the loom, lamenting their loves.
We recognize Sappho's characteristic touch both in δάμεισα and
in the attachment of the adjective βραδίναν to Aphrodite, but we
cannot doubt that, like the lines of Alcaeus, it is derived ultimately
from a popular tradition.

These two fragments suggest that, whatever Alcaeus and
Sappho learned from pioneers like Terpander and Arion, they
also learned something from songs which they heard around
them. It is permissible to speak of these as folk-songs, but we need
not assume that they were sung only by humble people. It is
more likely that they were popular songs in the sense that all
kinds of people composed and sang them. They would probably
be quite simple in form and in content, but none the less they
may account for some features in Lesbian song as we know it.
First, the use of the short stanza, so unlike the long stanza of the
choral ode, looks as if it were a popular inheritance. Secondly, the
way in which Alcaeus and Sappho both write largely in their
local vernacular suggests that they worked in a Lesbian tradition
and did not look outside it for models. Thirdly, though their
metres are indeed varied with many happy combinations, they
are not so complex or so various as those of choral poetry, and
their dominating *metra*, whether μέτρα μονοειδῆ, such as dactyls,
ionics, and choriambs, or μέτρα ἐπισύνθετα, such as the Glyconic
and the various expansions of it, are essentially based on easy
rules and a simple practice. We may assume that both poets

---

[1] Fr. 102 L.–P. Heph. p. 34. 9 Consbruch.

learned something from popular art, but transformed it to their own needs and standards, rather as the courtly Portuguesé poets of the thirteenth century took popular forms and themes and made graceful and accomplished poems from them. This art was essentially aristocratic and showed the trained taste of men and women who had a natural feeling for style and saw that a refined simplicity is a remarkable instrument for self-expression. Above all, Alcaeus and Sappho wished to speak freely for themselves and had enough self-knowledge and self-command to do so without either rhetoric or defensive irony. In them different tendencies met in harmony and produced an art which moves confidently within its own chosen boundaries.

The poetry of Alcaeus is to a large extent the immediate re-flection of a life given to action, especially to politics and civil war. He may have been born c. 630 B.C., and he lived through a period when Lesbos, free from foreign invasion, was convulsed by intestine feuds. This was partly the result of the collapse of the old monarchy not later than the middle of the seventh century.[1] Its obvious successors were the noble families, who were in a position to divide its powers between themselves, but failed to do so because one or other man or group aimed at getting supreme power. This meant a series of struggles, in which Alcaeus was usually in opposition to the rising or risen power. When c. 612–608 B.C. the tyrant Melanchros was overthrown by Pittacus and the brothers of Alcaeus, he himself seems to have been too young to take part,[2] but soon afterwards he fought on the side of Pittacus against the Athenians at Sigeum.[3] Then the coalition broke up, and Alcaeus turned against Pittacus, who had found an ally in Myrsilus and seems to have governed Mytilene with him.[4] The result was that Alcaeus retired into exile, not far away, at Pyrrha,[5] and it may have been here that he heard of Myrsilus' death.[6] He returned from Pyrrha, but before long his opposition to Pittacus sent him again into exile, and between 604 and 591 he seems to have gone so far as Egypt,[7] while his brother Antimenidas took service with the army of Babylon.[8] From 590 to 580 Pittacus

---

[1] A. Andrewes, *The Greek Tyrants*, p. 92. Some details of the fall are given by Aristot. *Pol.* 1311 b.   [2] Fr. 75 L.–P.
[3] Hdt. 5. 94 ff.; frs. 306 (7) 15 ff.; 167 L.–P.   [4] Fr. 70. 7 L.–P.
[5] Schol. ad fr. 113 L.–P.; fr. 130.   [6] Fr. 332 L.–P.
[7] Strab. 37 Ἀλκαῖος ... φήσας ἀφῖχθαι καὶ αὐτὸς εἰς Αἴγυπτον.
[8] Fr. 350 L.–P.

governed Mytilene, and in due course is said to have forgiven Alcaeus,[1] who must have returned from exile and lived again in his native city. In 580 Pittacus retired from power and lived as a private citizen until his death in 570.[2] This provides the bare outline of Alcaeus' career, and though the details and the dates are uncertain, it shows the kind of life that he lived and the circumstances in which he wrote his poetry. Much of it must have been composed in the excitement of civil war and political conspiracy, almost on the spur of the moment, and it reflects what this passionate, uncompromising aristocrat thought of the events in which he took so active and so futile a part. Through his political poems Alcaeus found a vent for violent feelings and a means to bind his supporters more closely to his cause.

Though Alcaeus' political life consisted largely of a struggle for power against men who wanted it for themselves, we must not assume that the different parties did not have some kind of principles or convictions. In the case of Pittacus we can see why Alcaeus failed. While Alcaeus based his claims on hereditary rights,[3] Pittacus had some degree of popular backing. He was not a tyrant in the sense that he seized power by violence, but an αἰσυμνήτης chosen by the people to restore order with a limited tenure of office.[4] When Alcaeus says that the choice was unanimous and made by the city,[5] he admits that it was not arbitrary or unpopular. We do not know what comprised the δᾶμος in Mytilene or how large it was, but it was presumably the whole body of citizens who had political rights. Even if Pittacus himself was not of humble birth, his power may have depended to some degree on others who were, and it cannot be by accident that Alcaeus more than once refers to κακοπάτριδαι in the plural.[6] The achievement of Pittacus was not that, like Solon, he created a new political system, but that he restored the existing system and made it work.[7] In this process his sumptuary legislation against expensive funerals and offences committed in drunkenness[8] shows that he disapproved of the rich displaying their wealth too arrogantly and that to this extent he marked a stage in the movement towards a more democratic government. Nor can we

[1] Diog. Laert. i. 76. [2] Id. i. 79. [3] Fr. 130. 19 ff. L.–P.
[4] Aristot. Pol. 1285 a 35. [5] Fr. 348 L.–P. [6] Frs. 67. 4 and 75. 12.
[7] Aristot. Pol. 1274 b 18 νόμων δημιουργὸς ἀλλ' οὐ πολιτείας.
[8] Ibid. b 20; Id. Rhet. 1402 b 12; Plut. Sept. Sap. Conv. 13; Diog. Laert. i. 76; Cic. de Leg. 2. 26; Stob. 44. 22.

absolve Alcaeus of designs against law and order. Strabo, who is well informed on the whole business and got information from Alcaeus' own poems, says that 'Alcaeus is not himself clear of the suspicion of revolutionary ambitions',[1] and we may be certain that Alcaeus' idea of a revolution was not to give more power to the people. He seems rather to have fought for hereditary privileges which had been taken from him and to have had no liking for the rule of law which Pittacus gave to Mytilene. We can hardly be surprised that Alcaeus was not successful.

Alcaeus' στασιωτικά show how the old heroic temper, as we see it in the Homeric poems, had been assimilated into an aristocratic world without losing its chief characteristics. The cult of personal honour and glory is still of paramount importance, but it is tempered in different ways to suit a society in which men of the same class live closely together and have the same conventions and manners. The fragments of Alcaeus do not tell much about actual fighting or what he thought about it, but one piece is concerned with preparations for it, and presents from the inside the kind of scene which Homer presents from the outside, when he describes a warrior arming himself. Alcaeus relates in detail the stock of weapons which he and his friends have in readiness before action:

μαρμαίρει δὲ μέγας δόμος χάλκωι, παῖσα δ' ἄρ' εὖ κεκόσμηται
στέγα

λάμπραισιν κυνίαισι, κὰτ τᾶν λεῦκοι κατέπερθεν ἴππιοι λόφοι
3 νεύοισιν, κεφάλαισιν ἄνδρων ἀγάλματα· χάλκιαι δὲ πασσάλοις

κρύπτοισιν περικείμεναι λάμπραι κνάμιδες, ἄρκος ἰσχύρω βέλεος,
5 θόρρακές τε νέω λίνω κοίλαί τε κὰτ ἄσπιδες βεβλήμεναι·

πὰρ δὲ Χαλκίδικαι σπάθαι, πὰρ δὲ ζώματα πόλλα καὶ κυπάσσιδες.
7 τῶν οὐκ ἔστι λάθεσθ' ἐπεὶ δὴ πρώτιστ' ὑπὰ τῶργον ἔσταμεν τόδε.[2]

The great house glitters with bronze, and the whole roof is well decked with gleaming helmets, from which white plumes of horsehair hang waving, to deck the heads of men. Bright greaves of bronze lie round pegs and hide them—a protection against the strong arrow, —and corslets of new linen and hollow shields lie thrown upon the

---

[1] Strab. 617 οὐδ' αὐτὸς καθαρεύων τῶν τοιούτων νεωτερισμῶν.
[2] Fr. 357 L.–P. with Page's correction of ἄρ' εὖ for Ἄρηι of the MSS. in 1 and a suggestion of Lobel at the end of 7.

floor. With them are swords from Chalcis, and with them many belts and tunics. These we may not forget, ever since we first stood to this task.

Alcaeus marks the arms and the armour with a keen eye and registers each item in turn. Though such an armoury is clearly intended for use, it has its own charm for him, and he delights in it as an aristocrat delights in the apparatus of his sport. The arms so described are contemporary and the best that money can buy. If the helmets, with their horse-hair plumes, are not so up to date as the plumeless Corinthian helmet, which was already in full use on the Greek mainland,[1] but have a Homeric air, the 'hollow' shields came into existence with the introduction of hoplite tactics in the seventh century,[2] and the adjective is much to the point. The linen corslets are not so much a means of protection as a military elegance; they recall those which Amasis of Egypt dedicated in the temple of Athene at Lindos[3] and sent to Sparta.[4] The ζώματα and the κυπάσσιδες complete the inventory of what a full uniform required. The whole passage suggests an officer who enjoys the inspection of kit and looks forward with confidence to the good use that will be made of it.

Yet though Alcaeus enjoys the panoply of war, he does not seem always to have treated war itself with the gravity which we might perhaps expect from him. When as a young man he fought on the same side as Pittacus at Sigeum against the Athenians, he dropped his weapons and ran away. That he was not ashamed of this is clear from the poem which he sent to his friend Melanippus saying in effect: 'Alcaeus is safe; his weapons are not. The Athenians hung them up in the temple of the grey-eyed goddess.'[5] In allowing himself this degree of candour Alcaeus may have owed something to the precedent of Archilochus, who in somewhat similar circumstances wrote:

> ἀσπίδι μὲν Σαίων τις ἀγάλλεται, ἣν παρὰ θάμνῳ
> ἔντος ἀμώμητον κάλλιπον οὐκ ἐθέλων.
> αὐτὸς δ' ἐξέφυγον θανάτου τέλος. ἀσπὶς ἐκείνη
> ἐρρέτω· ἐξαῦτις κτήσομαι οὐ κακίω.[6]

---

[1] H. L. Lorimer, *Homer and the Monuments*, p. 250.
[2] Tyrtaeus fr. 1. 11 D and Mimnermus ap. B. Wyss, *Antimachi Colophonii Reliquiae*, p. 83, both of whom speak of κοίληισ' ἀσπίσι φραξάμενοι.
[3] Hdt. 2. 182. 1.   [4] Id. 3. 47. 2.
[5] Fr. 428 (a) L.–P.   [6] Fr. 6 b D.

Some Saian rejoices in my shield, which unwillingly I left by a bush,
a piece of armour unspoiled. But I myself escaped the end of death.
Let that shield go. I shall soon get another no worse.

Archilochus liked to deride himself, but we hardly expect it
from Alcaeus. It is true that the new hollow shield, which gave a
great advantage in attack, was nothing but a nuisance in retreat,[1]
and that Alcaeus was probably wise to throw his away, but the
same would not apply to his other arms. At this point he shows
his difference from the Homeric heroes, who fight over armour
as if to lose it were a fearful dishonour. He knows that his friends
will judge his action correctly and be pleased that he is alive at
the cost of his weapons.

A similar touch of gaiety in the treatment of war may be seen
in some lines which Alcaeus wrote for his brother Antimenidas,
when he came home from soldiering in foreign parts. Antimenidas
seems to have fought as a mercenary in Palestine[2] with the army
of Nebuchadrezzar, king of Babylon, in the campaigns which
culminated in the capture of Jerusalem on 15/16th March, 597 B.C.
Alcaeus is proud of his brother's exploits and welcomes him
home with a tribute to one particular feat:

> ἦλθες ἐκ περάτων γᾶς ἐλεφαντίναν
> λάβαν τὼ ξίφεος χρυσοδέταν ἔχων . . .
> συμμάχεις δ' ἐτέλεσσας Βαβυλωνίοισ'
> ἄεθλον μέγαν, εὐρύσαο δ' ἐκ πόνων
> 5 κτέννais ἄνδρα μαχαίταν βασιληίων
> παλάσταν ἀπυλείποντα μόναν ἴαν
> παχέων ἀπὺ πέμπων.[3]

You have come from the ends of the earth with an ivory hilt, bound
with gold, on your sword. Fighting with the Babylonians you achieved
a great feat, and saved them from their troubles by killing a warrior
who lacked only a single span from five royal cubits in height.

Here affection and admiration are disguised with a playful
familiarity. The man slain by Antimenidas was certainly a giant,
for the royal cubit was twenty-one inches, and the height here

---

[1] A. Andrewes, *The Greek Tyrants*, p. 32.
[2] Fr. 48. 10-11 L.–P.]Βαβύλωνος ἴρας
]ν Ἀσκάλωνα
Ascalon was destroyed by Nebuchadrezzar in 604 B.C., D. J. Wiseman, *Chronicles
of Chaldaean Kings*, p. 69; for Jerusalem see ibid, p. 73.
[3] Fr. 350 L.–P. I have reconstructed 3 from Strab. 617 τὸν ἀδελφὸν Ἀντιμενίδαν
. . . φησιν Ἀλκαῖος Βαβυλωνίοις συμμαχοῦντα τελέσαι.

indicated is eight feet four inches. This was taller by some four inches than the traditional height of Heracles,[1] and shorter by a span than the five cubits credited to the Giants.[2] No doubt Alcaeus improves on the truth, as befits his welcome to a returning brother, but it is curious that Herodotus says that the tallest man in the army of Xerxes lacked four inches from five royal cubits.[3] The East had its giants like Goliath, and perhaps Herodotus, half-conscious of Alcaeus' lines, made a contribution to the height of Artachaies. Alcaeus is proud of his brother's exploit, but treats it lightly and gaily.

Though the actual conduct of war provoked a variety of responses in Alcaeus, he was serious enough about his own cause and the calls which it made on his companions. He believed in it without qualm or question, and saw nothing but baseness in his adversaries. If he stood for anything, it was for the aristocratic order in which he had been brought up and which he did not wish to be changed. Though he speaks of the δᾶμος, it is not clear that he has its interests at heart. No doubt he felt that it was best for himself and his friends to be in power, and that others could do little but harm. His honour, as that of an individual and an aristocrat, was engaged. His violent feelings seem to have blinded his political vision, and he shows little sign of understanding what was happening to his world. On one point he can be checked. Two mysterious stanzas refer to the Lydians, in what we may assume to be the reign of Alyattes:

Ζεῦ πάτερ, Λύδοι μὲν ἐπα[σχάλαντες
συμφόραισι διοχελίοις στά[τηρας
ἄμμ' ἔδωκαν, αἴ κε δυνάμεθ' ἴρ[αν
4 ἐς πόλιν ἔλθην,

οὐ πάθοντες οὐδάμα πῶσλον οὐ[δ' ἔ]ν
οὐδὲ γινώσκοντες· ὁ δ' ὡς ἀλώπα[
ποικ[ι]λόφρων εὐμάρεα προλέξα[ις
8 ἦλπ[ε]το λάσην.[4]

Father Zeus, the Lydians, in distress at our misfortunes, gave us two thousand gold pieces, if we could enter the holy city, though they had never yet had anything good from us, and did not know us; but *he,*

[1] Schol. Pind. *Isthm.* 4. 87; Apollodor. *Bibl.* 2. 64; Schol. Lyc. 663.
[2] Philostrat. *Vit. Ap.* 2. 4.   [3] 7. 117. 1.
[4] Fr. 69 L.–P.

like a crafty fox, foretold easy success and thought that we should not mark him.

We are hampered at the start by not knowing either what is the 'holy city' or who is the 'crafty fox'. Though there was a city called Hira on Lesbos,[1] and we might read either Ἴρας ἐς πόλιν or Ἴραν, ἐς πόλιν, this may perhaps be counted out, since Alcaeus does not seem to attach πόλις to the name of a place. It is more likely that he refers to Mytilene, since he calls it simply πόλις elsewhere,[2] though of course there is always a possibility that it is some other place, even on the Asiatic mainland. The Fox is a suitable enough epithet for Pittacus, as Alcaeus saw him, but no less suitable for anyone else whom Alcaeus thought to be double-faced. He seems to have discouraged Alcaeus and his friends from taking Lydian money, on the grounds that they would easily get what they wanted without it. If this refers to an attempt to return to Mytilene, the Fox is not likely to be Pittacus, who would hardly wish to have Alcaeus and his companions in his own city, and it looks as if it were some other man who had more political sense than Alcaeus. For it is clear that the Lydians were trying to buy a place in Lesbos. The sum of two thousand staters is very large indeed, since Croesus is said to have raised an army with half the amount,[3] and the offer implies that the goal was worth the expense. Indeed we are almost forced to the conclusion that Alyattes was trying to further his policy of bringing the coastal Greeks under his dominion. For this end he made a treaty with Thrasybulus of Miletus,[4] attacked Clazomenae, and captured Smyrna.[5] That he had an eye on Lesbos may be inferred from his colonization of Adramyttium with men from Sardis[6] and his establishment of a fortress in Bithynia.[7] That he tried to establish relations with Pittacus may be deduced from the story that he wrote Pittacus a haughty, dictatorial letter and that Pittacus replied telling him to eat onions and new bread,[8] no doubt with the implication that he should keep his wind to himself. In his hatred of local opponents Alcaeus regarded the Lydians as friends and saw in their offer of money no more than an act of noble

---

[1] Plin. N.H. 5. 31 (39). 139; Steph. Byz. s.v. Ἰρά; Eustath. 743. 17.

[2] Frs. 70. 7; 129. 24; 141. 4; 348. 2 L.-P.

[3] Nic. Dam. 90 F 65 Jacoby; see Page, S. and A., p. 232. [4] Hdt. 1. 21. 1.

[5] Id. 1. 16. 2. [6] Strab. 613. [7] Steph. Byz. s.v. Ἀλυάττα.

[8] Conv. Sept. Sap. 10 ἀποκρινάμενος οὐδὲν ἀλλ' ἢ μόνον κελεύσας κρόμμυα καὶ θερμὸν ἄρτον ἐσθίειν.

generosity. The Fox, whether he was Pittacus or another, knew better.

Just as in his dealings with the Lydians Alcaeus was moved by purely personal considerations of what he thought to be a generous offer of help, so in his opposition to Pittacus it was primarily personal considerations that counted. The alliance with him first against Melanchros and then against the Athenians broke up, and Pittacus joined Myrsilus. What Alcaeus felt can in part be deduced from a song of hate which this provoked:

$$] . ρά . α τόδε Λέσβιοι$$
$$. . .] . . . . εὔδειλον τέμενος μέγα$$
$$ξῦνον κά[τε]σσαν, ἐν δὲ βώμοις$$
$$\text{4} \qquad ἀθανάτων μακάρων ἔθηκαν,$$

$$κἀπωνύμασσαν ἀντίαον Δία,$$
$$σὲ δ' Αἰολήίαν [κ]υδαλίμαν θέον$$
$$πάντων γενέθλαν, τὸν δὲ τέρτον$$
$$\text{8} \qquad τὸν Σεμελήϊον ὠνύμασσ[α]ν$$

$$Ζόνυσσον ὠμήσταν. ἄ[γι]τ' εὔνοον$$
$$θῦμον σκέθοντες ἀμμετέρα[ς] ἄρας$$
$$ἀκούσατ', ἐκ δὲ τῶν[δ]ε μόχθων$$
$$\text{12} \qquad ἀργαλέας τε φύγας ῥ[ύεσθε.$$

$$τὸν ″Υρραον δὲ πα[ῖδ]α πεδελθέτω$$
$$κήνων 'Ε[ρίννυ]ς ὤς ποτ' ἀπώμνυμεν$$
$$τόμοντες ἄ. .[\qquad . .]ν . .$$
$$\text{16} \qquad μηδάμα μηδ' ἔνα τὼν ἑταίρων,$$

$$ἀλλ' ἢ θάνοντες γᾶν ἐπιέμμενοι$$
$$κείσεσθ' ὑπ' ἄνδρων οἳ τότ' ἐπικ. .ην$$
$$ἤπειτα κακκτάνοντες αὔτοις$$
$$\text{20} \qquad δᾶμον ὑπὲξ ἀχέων ῥύεσθαι.$$

$$κήνων ὀ φύσγων οὐ διελέξατο$$
$$πρὸς θῦμον, ἀλλὰ βραϊδίως πόσιν$$
$$ἔ]μβαις ἐπ' ὀρκίοισι δάπτει$$
$$\text{24} \qquad τὰν πόλιν ἄμμι δέδ[.]. .[.]ί.αις$$

$$οὐ κἀν νόμον[.]ον . .[$$
$$γλαύκας ἀ[$$
$$γεγρά.[$$
$$\text{28} \qquad Μύρσιλ[ο¹$$

¹ Fr. 129 L.-P.; see Page, *S. and A.* pp. 161-9. In 8 I follow A. J. Beattie in reading τὸν Σεμελήϊον for the unintelligible τόνδε κεμήλιον of the papyrus.

The Lesbians established this precinct, conspicuous, large, for all to share, and in it set altars of the immortal Blessed Ones. Zeus they named the God of Suppliants, and you, the Aeolian, glorious goddess, Mother of All, and third they named the son of Semele, Dionysus, eater of raw flesh. Come with friendly spirit and hearken to our prayer, and deliver us from these toils and grievous exile. Let *their* Fury pursue the son of Hyrrhas, since once we took a solemn oath, . . . and swore that never any comrade of ours . . . but either dead and clothed in earth we would lie conquered by men who were then in power (?), or else would kill them and deliver the people from its woes. Of these things the Pot-belly did not discourse to his heart, but trod the oaths lightly underfoot and devours the city . . . against the law . . . Myrsilus . . . .

These lines were evidently composed in a place which held the shrines of the three great divinities of Lesbos, Zeus, Hera, and Dionysus.[1] φύγας in 12 shows that Alcaeus is in exile, but whether at Pyrrha or elsewhere we do not know. The whole is a curse upon Pittacus for breaking his oath to his former companions, and it looks as if the gods who are now called on for vengeance were the same as those who presided over the oath. The seriousness of the occasion is emphasized by the way in which Alcaeus gives the gods their full titles and invokes them through this solemn approach before proceeding to the supplication which follows. At 11 the object of the prayer becomes clear. Through the treachery of Pittacus Alcaeus and his friends have been made to suffer sorrows and exile, and for this they demand vengeance. The vengeance is an Ἐρίννυς, an avenging Fury, who is qualified by κήνων as the representative of those men whom Pittacus has most grievously harmed.

This impressive introduction leads up to a brief summary of the oath which the companions took. It was that they would go on fighting until either they died, or, preferably, succeeded in delivering the people from its troubles. Before this in 15 there must have been some general undertaking that no one would forsake the rest until one of these things occurred.[2] Presumably the oath contained a clause that anyone who broke it should be punished, probably by death.[3] Alcaeus does not seem to mention

[1] Sappho refers to the same three deities at fr. 17 L.–P.
[2] This means that the last word of 15 was probably a future infinitive with some such meaning as 'betray'. προδώσην is said not to suit the traces.
[3] See Ziebarth, *R.-E.* v. 2076 ff.

this, but perhaps that is because he takes it for granted and his mention of the Ἐρίννυς is all that he needs. His wrath against Pittacus is based on his conviction that he has been betrayed, and he conforms to Homeric and heroic standards when he demands that a Fury should punish the perjurer.[1] So far he speaks with power and authority, but when in 25–28 he moves on to speak of Pittacus' actual breach of his oath, he abandons his majestic tone and adopts a special and almost colloquial sharpness. His point is that Pittacus has acted all the worse because he gave no thought at all to the matter and 'never discussed it with his heart'. Here the θῦμος is not the mere intelligence, but the spirit which makes a man what he is and informs his actions,[2] and the charge against Pittacus is that he has paid no attention to his sworn obligations, but has trodden them underfoot, as Menelaus claims that the Trojans have in his duel with Paris,[3] or as Archilochus, if it be he, charges a friend with falseness.[4] A man who can do this may be expected to turn against his city and devour it, δάπτει, as a lion[5] or a wolf[6] devours its prey. After the solemn invocation of the gods the anger, which has been kept in control during it, comes to the surface, and we see how violent Alcaeus' feelings were.

Alcaeus not only hates Pittacus; he also despises him. He accuses him of perjury, but he also calls him a φύσγων, or 'pot-belly'. This seems to have been characteristic of the abuse which Alcaeus flung at Pittacus after their quarrel. Diogenes Laertius gives a striking list of epithets,[7] which recall a capacity for mud-slinging worthy of Archilochus or Hipponax and show that Alcaeus did not spare his opponent's physical or social defects. He strikes hard and low. Pittacus is called σαράπους because of his splay toes, χειροπόδης because of the cracks in his feet, γαύρηξ because of his boastful bearing, φύσκων (φύσγων) and γάστρων because of his big belly, ζοφοδορπίδας because of his midnight carousals, and ἀγάσυρτος because of his unkempt appearance. If we may judge by our piece, such words were not limited to special poems of

---

[1] Il. 19. 258–60; Hes. Op. 803 ff.

[2] For the phrase cf. Theocr. 30. 11 πολλὰ δ' εἰσκαλέσαις θῦμον ἐμαύτῳ διελεξάμαν, and its Homeric precedent φίλος διελέξατο θυμός Il. 11. 497; 17. 97, and in general such cases as when a man, speaking to himself, addresses his θυμός, Archiloch. fr. 67, 1 D; Pind. Ol. 2. 89; Nem. 3. 26; Theogn. 695, 877, 1029; Aristoph. Ach. 480.　　　[3] Il. 4. 157.　　　[4] Fr. 79. 13–14 D.

[5] Il. 11. 481.　　　[6] Il. 16. 159.　　　[7] 1. 81.

abuse but might be introduced into serious and even solemn situations. The point is of interest because it shows how Alcaeus' poetical spirit worked. His changes of temper in a single poem are matched by changes of style, and the whole effect is of a man passing through a rapidly shifting series of moods. Alcaeus is carried by his strong temperament from august solemnity to vulgar abuse, and yet there is nothing inappropriate or in-artistic in the process. The purpose of the poem is to express as forcibly as possible what Alcaeus feels, and if the occasion itself is varied, his reactions are hardly less so.

A similar variation of moods and effects may be seen from some other lines, also written from exile in Lesbos and con-ceivably from the same place, since they mention a μακάρων τέμενος θέων which may be the same precinct of Zeus, Hera, and Dionysus. The lines are exceedingly obscure, and much of their interpretation eludes us. We do not know where the poem begins, and, though we know that it ended on the papyrus, the last four lines yield almost nothing. What seems fairly clear is that Alcaeus is almost alone, since he mentions no companions, and addresses the poem to a friend, who may have been with him, or to whom he may have sent it:

> ἀγνοισ . . σβιοτοισ. .ıς ὁ τάλαις ἔγω
> ζώω μοῖραν ἔχων ἀγροϊωτίκαν
> ἰμέρρων ἀγόρας ἄκουσαι
> 19   καρυ[ζο]μένας, ὦγεσιλαΐδα,
>
> καὶ β[ό]λλας· τὰ πάτηρ καὶ πάτερος πάτηρ
> καγγ[ε]γήρασ' ἔχοντες πεδὰ τωνδέων
> τὼν [ἀ]λλαλοκάκων πολίταν
> 23   ἔγ[ωγ' ἀ]πὺ τούτων ἀπελήλαμαι
>
> φεύγων ἐσχατίαισ', ὡς δ' Ὀνυμακλέης
> ἔνθα[δ'] οἶος ἐοίκησα λυκαιμίαις
>   ]ον [π]όλεμον· στάσιν γὰρ
> 27   πρὸς κρ.[. . . .]. οὐκ †ἄμεινον ὀννέλην·
>
> .].[. . .].[. .]μακάρων ἐς τέμ[ε]νος θέων
> ἐοι[. . . . .] με[λ]αίνας ἐπίβαις χθόνος
> χλι.[.].[.].[.]ν συνόδοισί μ' αὔταις
> 31   οἴκημ⟨μ⟩ι κ[ά]κων ἔκτος ἔχων πόδας,
>
> ὄππαι Λ[εσβί]αδες κριννόμεναι φύαν
> πώλεντ' ἐλκεσίπεπλοι, περὶ δὲ βρέμει.

ἄχω θεσπεσία γυναίκων
35 ἶρα[ς ὀ]λολύγας ἐνιαυσίας

].[.].[.]. ἀπὺ πόλλων πότα δὴ θέοι
].[   ]σκ...ν 'Ολύμπιοι
           ].....
39   .να[   ]... μεν.[1]

... I, poor wretch, live with a yokel's lot, longing to hear the Assembly summoned, and the Council, o Agesilaidas; what my father and my father's father have grown old possessing, among these citizens who do evil to one another, from all these things I have been driven forth, an exile on the boundaries; and like Onomacles, I have settled here a lonely wolf-man, (plotting?) war; for it is not good (?) to give up rebellion against the . . . to the precinct of the Blessed Gods, . . . treading the black earth; . . . assemblies . . . I dwell, keeping my steps out of troubles, where Lesbian girls, with trailing robes, go to and fro, being judged for their beauty, and around rings the wonderful echo of the holy cry of women in every year . . . from many (woes?) when will the Olympian gods (deliver me)?

In his rustic exile Alcaeus thinks of his normal life in Mytilene, and especially of the Council and the Assembly, of which he must have been a member. We know very little about them, but it is reasonable to assume that they were not unlike the similar institutions in Homer and had survived from the collapse of the monarchy into the aristocratic age. Alcaeus feels warmly towards them because they represent the political life which he enjoyed before everything was spoiled by the tyrants. In so far as he had any political theory, it was that things were best managed by men like himself and his father through institutions of this kind in which their opinions carried weight. He regards his deprivation of them as a personal wrong. His contempt and disapproval of his countrymen come out in the epithet ἀλλαλοκάκων, which contrasts with his own pride of birth in the preceding lines. From this he turns to his present situation and compares himself with Onomacles, of whom nothing is known, but who must come from fable or legend or folk-lore as a wild man of the woods. The word λυκαιμίαις is no easier to explain, but whether it means a man who frequents thickets, αἰμοί, where wolves live,[2] or a man

---

[1] Fr. 130 L.–P.; see Page, S. and A. pp. 198–209. In 27 ἄμεινον cannot be right as the metre requires – ∪ ∪. Page's κάλλιον is open to the objection that it is a comparative when we expect a positive with some sense like 'good'.

[2] So Page, S. and A. p. 205, quoting Hesych. αἰμοί· δρυμοί.

who is thought to have the blood of wolves in his veins, it indicates someone savage and solitary and alien to the haunts of men. So exile forces Alcaeus to compare himself first with a yokel and then with some creature which is as much beast as man.

In his exile Alcaeus enjoys the spectacle of the girls who compete for prizes in beauty in an annual competition. His mind turns happily to this from his regrets and his complaints, and for a moment he catches its excitement and its clamour. Then, presumably, he closes the poem with a question asking when the gods are going to deliver him from his troubles. The poem records a sequence of different moods, each one of which arises from the unusual situation in which Alcaeus finds himself, and, because he is alone and not with his companions, he is quieter and more reflective than usual. Here, as in the previous poem, he touches on each theme with remarkable concentration and economy and gives to it its right place in a complex whole. His method is different from Sappho's straightforward development of a single topic and creates its own dramatic effect by approaching its subject from more than one angle.

This technique creates considerable difficulties in the interpretation of the less well-preserved poems of Alcaeus. His habit of moving abruptly from one theme to another may confound us if clues are lacking. Such is a poem which has, reasonably enough, been connected with Pittacus. Pittacus enacted that, if drunkards committed a misdemeanour, they should pay a bigger penalty than if they had been sober.[1] Alcaeus, who liked wine, naturally attacked him for this, not, as we might expect, for undue puritanism, but for hypocrisy, for being himself given to habits which he penalized in others. Some such situation seems to lie behind some lines which refer to junketings on a large scale:

λάβρως δὲ συν στεί[.]..[..]ειαπ..
πίμπλεισιν ἀκράτω [τὸ δ᾽ ἐ]π᾽ ἀμέρα[ι
καὶ νύκτι παφλάσδει [λάτ]αχθεν,
6   ἔνθα νόμος θάμ᾽ ἐν.....νην.

κῆνος δὲ τούτων οὐκ ἐπελάθετο
ὤνηρ ἐπεὶ δὴ πρῶτον ὀνέτροπε,
παίσαις γὰρ ὀννώρινε νύκτας,
10   τὼ δὲ πίθω πατάγεσκ᾽ ὀ πύθμην.

[1] Aristot. *Pol.* 1274 b 20; *Rhet.* 1402 b 9.

σὺ δὴ τεαύτας ἐκγεγόνων ἔχηις
τὰν δόξαν οἴαν ἄνδρες ἐλεύθεροι
ἔσλων ἔοντες ἐκ τοκήων . . . ;[1]

Violently . . . he fills . . . with unmixed wine, and by day and night it
seethes as it is thrown, where often the law. . . . But that man did not
forget these things once he had upset them; for he kept every night
awake, and the bottom of the jar kept on ringing. Do *you*, who are
born of such a woman, have the renown which men bred of noble
parents . . . ?

The gaps in the text add to the difficulties of interpretation, which
are already formidable enough owing to Alcaeus' abrupt changes
of theme. D. L. Page has advanced a theory which takes full note
of the text and introduces three different characters.[2] This makes
Pittacus σὺ δή, his father κῆνος ὤνηρ, and his mother τεαύτας, and
the sequence of thought is that in the first stanza a general habit
of revelry is described, in the second we hear of the debauches
of Pittacus' father, and in the third Alcaeus turns to Pittacus
himself and asks him: 'Have you, the son of such a woman, the
repute which free nobles have?' We thus get a piece of family
history, a drunken father, whose propensities the son inherits,
and a mother, whose low parentage should make him realize
that he has no right to behave like the son of noble parents.
This imaginative flight is not backed by much evidence. First,
we know nothing about Pittacus' mother except that she was
a woman of Lesbos,[3] and this tells us nothing about her social
origins. Secondly, there is no scrap of evidence that his father was
a drunkard. Thirdly, in the extant fragments Alcaeus nowhere
addresses Pittacus as σύ or speaks of him except in the third person. Indeed he seems to reserve σύ for friends or gods. Fourthly,
even if the third stanza is cast as a question, which is not certain,[4]
we do not know the force of ἐκγεγόνων, whether it is causal or
concessive. Fifthly, both ὀνέτροπε and ὀννώρινε are transitive
verbs but are left in the air without clear objects, and lastly,
τούτων is thought to mean 'these barbarous manners', which is,
to say the least, adventurous. This chapter of family history is
a happy work of fiction but hardly a serious hypothesis.

In the presence of so many unknown factors, it is not easy to

---

[1] Fr. 72 L.–P. In 4 [τὸ δ' ἔ]π' is Page's suggestion.
[2] *S. and A.* pp. 172–5.   [3] 'Suid.' s.v. Πίττακος· μητρὸς δὲ Λεσβίας.
[4] For the use of σὺ δή in questions cf. J. D. Denniston, *The Greek Particles*, 2nd ed.
p. 207, 'the emphasis is often ironical, contemptuous, or indignant in tone'.

provide an alternative explanation, but perhaps some few points may be established. The first stanza describes in the present tense continual drinking by day and night. That Alcaeus should ascribe this to Pittacus is at least probable, since the note of disapproval in λάβρως implies that he speaks of an enemy. In the second stanza there is no reason why κῆνος ὤνηρ should not refer to Pittacus, whom Alcaeus calls ὤνηρ οὗτος at one place[1] and κῆνος at another,[2] and if we feel that the phrase is too emphatic for someone of whom Alcaeus has just been speaking, that is just what happens in fr. 70, where an account of lavish drinking precedes the mention of Pittacus as κῆνος. In the second stanza Alcaeus proceeds to say that this revelry is no new thing, but began when Pittacus first ὀνέτροπε. Since elsewhere the word is used with reference to the city in the sense of 'upset' or 'overturned',[3] it must surely have a similar sense here. It is not easy to take it absolutely in the sense of 'caused the upset', and we should probably supply either τὰν πόλιν from the general context or ταῦτα from the preceding τούτων, 'upset these things', and the reference would then be to such Lesbian customs as drinking in the Prytaneum, which Pittacus has indeed not forgotten but to which he has given a new and vulgar prominence by his addiction to them. The notion of the 'upset' is followed by a reference to his behaviour from the first, when he παίσαις ὀννώρινε νύκτας, and since ὀννώρινε is transitive, παίσαις νύκτας must be its object, and the sense is 'stirred up all the nights', that is, he made them loud with carousal and the noise of the wine-butt struck when the wine was running out. In the third stanza Alcaeus turns from the third person to the second and addresses someone as σὺ δή. It is impossible to say who this is. It may of course be Pittacus, but there is no evidence that it is, and the change from the third person to the second is certainly unexpected. Nor do we know the precise intonation of τεαύτας upon which so much depends. It could be derogatory and refer to someone of low birth who claims and gets the glory that is the right of free men, but it might equally be perfectly straightforward, and then Alcaeus asks a friend why he, who comes of a good family, dishonours the name which one of his birth should have. The words then look like a reproof, and their point may be that such a man should have nothing to do with the revelries of Pittacus.

[1] Fr. 141 L.-P. [2] Fr. 70 L.-P. [3] Fr. 141 L.-P.

L

Alcaeus' στασιωτικά are too passionate and too unpremeditated to deserve the name of propaganda, but they have some of its qualities in their ability to ram a point home and to give it considerable force and appeal. His direct and unqualified approach to his problems is characteristic of his unrestrained and outspoken nature. When Solon foresaw the approaching tyranny of Peisistratus in Athens, he spoke of it in allusive words as snow and hail coming from the storm-cloud,[1] but Alcaeus has none of this oracular gravity. His forecast of the tyranny of Pittacus goes straight to the point:

> ὤνηρ οὗτος ὁ μαιόμενος τὸ μέγα κρέτος
> ὀντρέψει τάχα τὰν πόλιν· ἀ δ' ἔχεται ῥόπας.[2]

In his desire for the great power this fellow will soon upset the city. It hangs by a thread.

His approach is direct and immediate and realistic. He sees the situation with the clarity that comes from dislike and fear, and expresses himself with instinctive power.

In this struggle Alcaeus took a low view of Pittacus and his supporters and attacked them from more than one angle. When Pittacus was elected, or acclaimed, as αἰσυμνήτης by the Mytileneans, Alcaeus turned with passion against them:

> τὸν κακοπατρίδαν
> Φίττακον πόλιος τὰς ἀχόλω καὶ βαρυδαίμονος
> ἐστάσαντο τύραννον, μέγ' ἐπαίνεντες ἀόλλεες.[3]

One and all praising him greatly, they have made the low-born Pittacus tyrant of the city, which has no bile and is cursed by a heavy fate.

Each word does its duty. Pittacus may not have been a τύραννος in the worst sense of the word, but he was an autocrat, and for Alcaeus that was the same thing. The people who choose him are treated contemptuously, as having no bile and, pityingly, as being the victims of a δαίμων, which drives them to such an action. The combination of adjectives shows Alcaeus' feelings towards the δᾶμος. While he despised them, he also in some sense pitied them, no doubt feeling that they did not know what they were doing. The implications of κακοπατρίδαν are more interesting.

[1] Fr. 10 D.　　　[2] Fr. 141 L.–P.　　　[3] Fr. 348 L.–P.

This can only mean 'low-born'.[1] That Pittacus really was of
humble origin is on the whole unlikely. The man who was an
ἕταιρος of Alcaeus and his brothers in the struggle against
Melanchros and who married into the royal family of the Penthi-
lids could hardly be low-born in any real sense. On the other
hand he need not have belonged to quite the same social group
as Alcaeus. His father was in fact a Thracian,[2] who is said once
to have been a 'king', that is, some kind of magistrate, in Mytilene.[3]
The foreign origin of Pittacus may have made Alcaeus despise
him, and the gibes at his drinking unmixed wine in fr. 72 may
indicate that he followed his native customs in Mytilene; for this
was notoriously a Thracian habit.[4] But probably Alcaeus' real
reason for using κακοπατρίδαν was that Pittacus was against the
circle of aristocrats who had held power and wished to continue
to hold it. Such an ambition would be enough to unclass him and
to justify abuse of him for his coarse ways. It is significant that
Alcaeus applies the word to other men and uses it once at least
in the plural,[5] as if he regarded his opponents as a low lot. This
does not necessarily mean that they were, but it shows what
Alcaeus felt about them.

Once Alcaeus threw himself into this struggle he did not question either his ends or his means. His attitude is revealed in some
lines which must have been written when Pittacus was already
in power:

> κῆνος δὲ παώθεις Ἀτρεΐδα[ν γένει
> δαπτέτω πόλιν ὡς καὶ πεδὰ Μυρσί[λ]ω,
> θᾶς κ' ἄμμε βόλλητ' Ἄρευς ἐπὶ τ[ε]ύχε[α
> 9 τρόπην· ἐκ δὲ χόλω τῶδε λαθοίμεθ' αὖ.
>
> χαλάσσομεν δὲ τὰς θυμοβόρω λύας
> ἐμφύλω τε μάχας, τάν τις Ὀλυμπίων
> ἔνωρσε, δᾶμον μὲν εἰς ἀνάταν ἄγων,
> 13 Φιττάκωι δὲ δίδοις κῦδος ἐπήρ[ατ]ον.[6]

Let him, who has married a daughter of the race of the Atridae,
devour the city as he did with Myrsilus, until Ares consents to turn

---

[1] J. Wackernagel, *Glotta*, xiv (1925), 50 ff.
[2] Diog. Laert. 1. 74; 'Suid.' s.v. Πιττακός.
[3] Schol. Dion. Thrac. p. 368. 15 Hilg. Ύρρας δὲ Μυτιληναίων ἐγένετο βασιλεύς,
οὗ υἱὸς ὁ Πιττακός.
[4] Athen. 9. 432 a.   [5] Frs. 67. 4 L.-P.
[6] Fr. 70.; see Page, *S. and A.* pp. 233–6. In 6 I supply γένει as the simplest word
that meets the needs of the sense and the metre.

us to our weapons; and may we forget again this our wrath. Let us abate our heart-eating discord and intestine fighting, which some Olympian has aroused among us, bringing the people to ruin, but giving to Pittacus the glory which he desires.

In this there is no concession to Pittacus, still less any forgiveness for him. Alcaeus merely expresses his intention to wait until the military situation is more in his favour. The strife to which he refers is the στάσις in Mytilene, for which he and his friends are in fact largely responsible, but he does not see it like that. He sees himself as the champion of a cause, whose admirable plans have been frustrated by the gods and the doom which they have laid on the people. His hope is simply that in due time he will win his way by arms and that then the intestine strife will cease. Since, according to Aristotle,[1] the people elected Pittacus αἰσυμνήτης against the menace of the exiles led by Antimenidas and Alcaeus, the hope was illusory, and perhaps Alcaeus may be excused for ascribing the existing state of affairs to the inscrutable will of the gods which fooled the people into preferring Pittacus to himself.

The operations and conspiracies in which Alcaeus engaged excited in him emotions which have an almost heroic quality. It was this which Horace had in mind when he wrote:

> et te sonantem plenius aureo,
> Alcaee, plectro dura nauis,
> dura fugae mala, dura belli.[2]

Things that were *dura*, hard, brought out the best in Alcaeus, and he turned his talents to convey the severe nature of the struggle in which he delighted. For him the efforts which he and his friends made were aptly compared with a ship in trouble at sea. He transposed his own knowledge of seafaring to situations in which the imagery of ships represents the strain and the dangers of his struggle. In this he was not, as has been claimed for him, a pioneer,[3] but he developed a theme which had already been exploited by Archilochus.[4] Alcaeus uses the image for a wider variety of purposes and perhaps with a greater sense of its implications. His passages on ships are not strictly concerned with the 'Ship of State', which was later to become a commonplace of

[1] *Pol.* 1285 a 35.   [2] *C.* 2. 13. 26–28.
[3] Page, *S. and A.* p. 182.
[4] Fr. 56 D; see F. Rodríguez Adrados, *Aegyptus*, xxxv (1955), pp. 206–10.

poetry and rhetoric, nor with the comparison of his own party
with a ship. He uses seafaring to convey the significance of more
than one situation and to present it in a new light. So in one
place he speaks of a ship in a rough sea and draws the conclusion
that the crew must patch up the timbers and get at once into
harbour.[1] The point is that the situation is getting out of hand,
and that it is wise to find some refuge, not as an escape from
action but as a good base for future operations. The imagery is
applicable to his position. The mounting waves indicate growing
danger; the need to bale out implies foresight, the strengthening
of the timbers the strengthening of their resources, and the safe
harbour a proper base for action. From this Alcaeus moves easily
to an appeal for courage, and the image has done its work by
showing how serious the danger is and what action is needed at
once. To a seafaring people each word would strike home,
and they would respond to the need for courage in such a crisis.

In another poem Alcaeus develops the theme of a ship with
more elaboration and with such an air of actuality that we can
understand Heraclitus asking 'Who would not think this to be
a picture of men in trouble at sea?',[2] if he himself had not told
us that the subject is Myrsilus and the stirring of a tyrannical
conspiracy at Mytilene. Here too Alcaeus seems to be speaking of
his own friends and political colleagues when he describes their
situation as that of a ship troubled by contrary winds:

> ἀσυννέτημι τὼν ἀνέμων στάσιν·
> τὸ μὲν γὰρ ἔνθεν κῦμα κυλίνδεται,
> τὸ δ' ἔνθεν, ἄμμες δ' ὂν τὸ μέσσον
> νᾶϊ φορήμμεθα σὺν μελαίναι,
>
> χείμωνι μόχθεντες μεγάλωι μάλα·
> πὲρ μὲν γὰρ ἄντλος ἰστοπέδαν ἔχει,
> λαῖφος δὲ πὰν ζάδηλον ἤδη,
> καὶ λάκιδες μέγαλαι κὰτ αὖτο.[3]

I do not understand the strife of the winds; for one wave rolls from
this side, and another from that, and in the middle we are borne in
our black ship, much vexed by the great storm; for the bilge is over
the masthold, and the sail is all transparent, and there are great
rents in it.

---

[1] Fr. 6 L.–P.; see Page, *S. and A.* pp. 182–5.

[2] *Quaest. Hom.* 5.

[3] Fr. 326 L.–P.; see Page, *S. and A.* pp. 185–6, for the connexion with frs. 305
and 208.

Alcaeus describes a difficult feat of sailing, for much damage has been done to the ship, but, as appears from the fragmentary lines that follow, she is still saved by the sheets holding firm. The image can be pressed in its details. The conflicting winds are the different political forces through which he has to pass and which he does not understand. He has been badly buffeted and is in trouble, but he still continues his voyage. The method is not really that of allegory, still less of a 'one–one correspondence', but of a poetical imagery which gives a concrete precision and imaginative significance to events which might otherwise remain somewhat vague and indeterminate. We identify Alcaeus' struggle with that of a ship in a storm, and it excites similar responses from us.

Just because Alcaeus had to fight for his position and his beliefs, on the whole without success, he was occasionally forced to conclusions which were to become characteristic of his century and of the class to which he belonged, when it found itself on the losing side. In spite of his belief in birth and its privileges, in spite of his contempt for the 'low-born' Pittacus, he was forced by hard facts to recognize that the aristocratic creed did not conform to realities. He saw especially that, if a man was poor, his birth was useless to him:

ὡς γὰρ δήποτ' Ἀριστόδαμον φαῖσ' οὐκ ἀπάλαμνον ἐν Σπάρται λόγον
εἴπην, χρήματ' ἄνηρ, πένιχρος δ' οὐδ' εἶς πέλετ' ἔσλος οὐδὲ τίμιος.[1]

For, as they say, Aristodemus spoke no foolish saying once in Sparta, 'Money makyth Man', and no poor man is noble or held in honour.

So long as the old nobles were entrenched in power, they could assume that wealth and nobility were almost synonymous terms. Facts supported them, and exceptions did not shake the general validity of their belief. But all was changed when men of low birth expropriated men of ancient lineage. Alcaeus saw the change and realized that the values of established society were being severely tested by events. Of course the Greeks, like everyone else, had always known that poverty robs a man of everything desirable, but Alcaeus makes a good point when he says that, if a man is poor, he is no longer ἔσλος. The theme was dear to Theognis, who shared Alcaeus' views and put them epigrammatically:

[1] Fr. 360 L.-P.

Πλοῦτε, θεῶν κάλλιστε καὶ ἱμεροέστατε πάντων,
σὺν σοὶ καὶ κακὸς ὢν γίνεται ἐσθλὸς ἀνήρ.[1]

Wealth, most beautiful and most desired of all the gods, with you even a base man becomes noble.

The sixth century was a time of social struggles, and though in Lesbos the results do not seem to have been very notable, Alcaeus represents the older point of view and acknowledges that it does not always work.

This conviction forced on Alcaeus another almost political theory. He had to explain the apparent slavishness of the Mytilenaeans, who preferred the rule of Pittacus to that of himself and his friends. He may have found comfort in the thought that some god had infatuated them, but he was not so blind as to shirk a more realistic appraisal of the situation. The people were servile because they were poor:

ἀργάλεον Πενία κάκον ἄσχετον, ἁ μέγαν
δάμναι λᾶον Ἀμαχανίαι σὺν ἀδελφέαι.[2]

Poverty is a grievous thing, an uncontrollable evil, who with her sister Helplessness subdues a great people.

Theognis again tells the same story, when he warns Cyrnus against the way in which poverty breaks a man's spirit:

ἄνδρ' ἀγαθὸν πενίη πάντων δάμνησι μάλιστα
καὶ γήρως πολιοῦ, Κύρνε, καὶ ἠπιάλου·
ἢν δὴ χρὴ φεύγοντα καὶ ἐς βαθυκήτεα πόντον
ῥιπτεῖν καὶ πετρέων, Κύρνε, κατ' ἠλιβάτων.
καὶ γὰρ ἀνὴρ πενίη δεδμημένος οὔτε τι εἰπεῖν
οὔθ' ἔρξαι δύναται, γλῶσσα δέ οἱ δέδεται.[3]

Poverty, Cyrnus, most of all things, breaks a good man, more than hoary age or fever. You must fly from it, Cyrnus, and hurl yourself into the yawning sea from sheer rocks. For a man bound by poverty cannot do or say anything. His tongue is tied.

Nobody can say that Alcaeus and Theognis were wrong. It was the hardness of Greek life which forced the less privileged to dispute the power of their traditional rulers and to expect too much from changes of government. Alcaeus saw the process with unsympathetic eyes, but at least he saw it and, from his own angle, understood it.

As an alternative to the new conditions Alcaeus offered his

---

[1] 1117–18.　　　[2] Fr. 364 L.-P.; cf. Hdt. 8. 111. 3.　　　[3] 173–8.

aristocratic creed. He emphasized the value of courage and loyalty, and in this too he resembles Theognis. Experience taught him that the life of a community depends on them, and in this spirit he wrote

ἄνδρες γὰρ πόλιος πύργος ἀρεύιος[1]

'For *men* are a city's warlike tower', and said elsewhere that 'it is not stones nor timbers nor the craft of craftsmen, but wherever there are men knowing how to defend themselves, there are walls and a city.'[2] If he was not the inventor of this notion, he gave it an impressive form, and in later times it appealed alike to Sophocles[3] and to Nicias.[4] Alcaeus' interest and belief in personality were the natural results of his upbringing and of his heroic scale of values. The same conviction underlies his statement that weapons are useless if the bearer of them is not brave.[5] It finds a vivid form in the oath which he took with Pittacus against their common opponents,[6] and even more emphatically when, having spoken of himself and his companions as a crew in trouble at sea, he appeals to them to show courage worthy of their ancestors:

καὶ μή τιν' ὄκνος μόλθ[ακος ἀμμέων
λάχηι· πρόδηλον γὰρ μέγ' [ἀέθλιον.
μνάσθητε τὼ πάροιθα μ[όχθω·
νῦν τις ἄνηρ δόκιμος γε[νέσθω,

καὶ μὴ καταισχύνωμεν [ἀναλκίαι
ἔσλοις τόκηας γᾶς ὔπα κε[ιμένοις...[7]

And let not soft fear take hold of any one of us; for a great task lies clear before us. Remember our earlier labour. Now let a man prove himself steadfast, and let us not dishonour by cowardice our noble forefathers who lie under the earth.

It is this mood which gives distinction to Alcaeus' unsuccessful enterprises and shows what really lay behind them. He felt the need to show through a display of ἀρετή that he was an ἀνὴρ

---

[1] Fr. 112. 10 L.–P.   [2] Fr. 426 L.–P.
[3] *O.T.* 56–57 ὡς οὐδέν ἐστιν οὔτε πύργος οὔτε ναῦς
ἐρῆμος ἀνδρῶν μὴ ξυνοικούντων ἔσω.
[4] Thuc. 7. 77. 7 ἄνδρες γὰρ πόλις, καὶ οὐ τείχη οὐδὲ νῆες ἀνδρῶν κεναί.
[5] Fr. 427 L.–P.   [6] Fr. 129. 17–20 L.–P.
[7] Fr. 6. 9–14 L.–P. The supplements are not certain but give what seems to be the right kind of sense.

ἀγαθός, and it is a pity that he did not find a more distinguished
field in which to prove himself.

The strength of Alcaeus' poetry of action lies in his immediate
and powerful response to events. He is not subtle, nor even very
imaginative, but he has a gift for saying firmly and impressively
certain things which have always belonged to a masculine outlook and concern all who feel the call of adventure and risk and
struggle. Even when he relaxes and takes his pleasure, the same
spirit is at work. He passes without effort from war to conviviα-
lity, and treats a drinking-party with the same energetic attention with which he treats politics. He throws himself wholly into it,
and at one place seems quite happy to let the ship of state founder
while he takes to drink.[1] At another he dismisses the thought of
some trouble or disaster and says:

> οὐ χρῆ κάκοισι θῦμον ἐπιτρέπην,
> προκόψομεν γὰρ οὐδὲν ἀσάμενοι,
> ὦ Βύκχι, φαρμάκων δ' ἄριστον
> οἶνον ἐνεικαμένοις μεθύσθην.[2]

We must not surrender our heart to evils; for we shall do no good by
vexing ourselves, Bycchis, and the best of medicines is to send for wine
and get drunk.

Conversely, when the news is good, the same remedy is sought, as
when he hears of the death of Myrsilus:

> νῦν χρῆ μεθύσθην καί τινα πὲρ βίαν
> πώνην, ἐπεὶ δὴ κάτθανε Μύρσιλος . . .[3]

Now must a man get drunk and drink with all his strength, for Myrsilus has died . . .

Alcaeus gave to relaxation the same whole-hearted, practical
attention that he gave to more violent kinds of action.

Alcaeus' drinking-songs have an air of being spontaneous and
almost extemporary. He looks to the immediate occasion and not
to some ideal drinking-party, and speaks of it as it is or as he
wishes it to be. He enjoys its correct ceremonial and likes to dwell
on the details of the arrangements or the time of day or the
season of the year. An excuse can always be found for a party,
and Alcaeus is an adept at it. So he calls for wine because the day
is coming to an end:

[1] Fr. 73 L.–P.; see Page, S. and A. p. 190.
[2] Fr. 335 L.–P.   [3] Fr. 332 L.–P.

πώνωμεν· τί τὰ λύχν' ὀμμένομεν; δάκτυλος ἀμέρα.
2 κὰδ δάερρε κυλίχναις μεγάλαις αἶψ' ἀπὺ πασσάλων.
οἶνον γὰρ Σεμέλας καὶ Δίος υἶος λαθικάδεον
4 ἀνθρώποισιν ἔδωκ'. ἔγχεε κέρναις ἔνα καὶ δύο
πλήαις κὰκ κεφάλας, ⟨ἀ⟩ δ' ἀτέρα τὰν ἀτέραν κύλιξ
6 ὠθήτω.[1]

Let us drink. Why do we wait for the lamps? The day has but an inch to go. Lift down the big cups at once from the pegs. For the son of Semele and Zeus gave wine to men to forget their cares. Mix one of water and two of wine, pour them in to the brim, and let one cup jostle another.

Here is the essential ritual of Greek drinking—the mention of the time of day, the drill of taking the cups from their pegs, the justification of wine because it gets rid of cares, the precise proportions of wine and water, and the call to keep the proceedings going by emptying the cups quickly and calling for more. All is in order, but not quite usual. The drink is a good deal stronger than normally. When Alcaeus says ἔνα καὶ δύο he can only mean one part of water to two of wine, since in such phrases the water comes first and the wine second.[2] This is evidently a special occasion when the wine is not only abundant but taken strong. That perhaps is why Alcaeus prepares the way by invoking the patronage of Dionysus.

Another excuse for drink could be found in the weather. So when rain and frost keep him indoors, Alcaeus sees no alternative to convivial relaxation:

ὔει μὲν ὁ Ζεῦς, ἐκ δ' ὀράνω μέγας
χείμων, πεπάγαισιν δ' ὑδάτων ῥόαι. . . .

κάββαλλε τὸν χείμων', ἐπὶ μὲν τίθεις
πῦρ, ἐν δὲ κέρναις οἶνον ἀφειδέως
μέλιχρον, αὐτὰρ ἀμφὶ κόρσαι
μόλθακον ἀμφι⟨τίθεις⟩ γνόφαλλον.[3]

Zeus rains. From the sky comes a great storm, and the water-streams are frozen. . . . Put down the storm, pile up the fire, and mix the sweet wine without stint, putting a soft pillow about your brows.

The physical scene is conjured up in a few dexterous words, and we feel the sense of relief and comfort which Alcaeus has in

[1] Fr. 346 L.–P. In 2 I read Ahrens's αἶψ' ἀπὺ πασσάλων for the meaningless αιταποικιλλις of the MSS.
[2] Page, S. and A. p. 308, quoting Hes. Op. 596; Anacr. fr. 43. 3 D; Athen. 10. 430 d.   [3] Fr. 338 L.–P.

defying the elements safely indoors. By this we may set a song from the high heat of summer:

τέγγε πλεύμονας οἴνωι, τὸ γὰρ ἄστρον περιτέλλεται,
2 ἀ δ' ὤρα χαλέπα, πάντα δὲ δίψαισ' ὑπὰ καύματος,
ἄχει δ' ἐκ πετάλων ἄδεα τέττιξ, πτερύγων δ' ὔπα
4 κακχέει λιγύραν ⟨πύκνον⟩ ἀοίδαν, ⟨θέρος⟩ ὄπποτα
φλόγιον †καθέταν πεπτάμενον πάντα καταυάνηι
6 ⟨   ⟩
ἄνθει δὲ σκόλυμος· νῦν δὲ γύναικες μιαρώταται,
8 λέπτοι δ' ἄνδρες, ἐπεὶ ⟨δὴ⟩ κεφάλαν καὶ γόνα Σείριος
ἄσδει.[1]

Soak your lungs with wine, for the Star is on the turn, and the season is harsh, and everything thirsts with the heat. From the leaves the cicada chirps sweetly, and from under its wings pours down a shrill song incessantly, when the blazing summer is spread abroad and withers everything. . . . The golden thistle is in bloom; now women are at their worst, and men are feeble, for the Dog-star shrivels their head and knees.

The poem is a close adaptation of some lines by Hesiod which also describe the high summer and suggest that it calls for wine. Each item in Alcaeus has its source in Hesiod, and the imitation shows not only how little Greek poets worried about borrowing from others, but with what ease Alcaeus transforms Hesiod's hexameters into Asclepiads:

ἦμος δὲ σκόλυμός τ' ἀνθεῖ καὶ ἠχέτα τέττιξ
δενδρέῳ ἐφεζόμενος λιγυρὴν καταχεύετ' ἀοιδὴν
πυκνὸν ὑπὸ πτερύγων, θέρεος καματώδεος ὤρῃ,
τῆμος πιόταταί τ' αἶγες καὶ οἶνος ἄριστος,
μαχλόταται δὲ γύναικες, ἀφαυρότατοι δέ τοι ἄνδρες
εἰσίν, ἐπεὶ κεφάλην καὶ γούνατα Σείριος ἄζει,
αὐαλέος δέ τε χρὼς ὑπὸ καύματος· ἀλλὰ τότ' ἤδη
εἴη πετραίη τε σκιὴ καὶ βίβλινος οἶνος.[2]

[1] Fr. 347 L.–P.; see Page, S. and A. pp. 303–6. In 5 Bergk's καταυάνηι seems the best proposal yet made.

[2] Op. 582–9. The Shield of Heracles, 393–9, also develops the theme, but in rather a different way:

ἦμος δὲ χλοερῷ κυανόπτερος ἠχέτα τέττιξ
ὄζῳ ἐφεζόμενος θέρος ἀνθρώποισιν ἀείδειν
ἄρχεται, ᾧ τε πόσις καὶ βρῶσις θῆλυς ἐέρση,
καί τε πανημέριός τε καὶ ἠώιος χέει αὐδὴν
ἴδει ἐν αἰνοτάτῳ, ὅτε τε χρόα Σείριος ἄζει,
τῆμος δὴ κέγχροισι πέρι γλῶχες τελέθουσι
τούς τε θέρει σπείρουσιν, ὅτ' ὄμφακες αἰόλλονται.

Though everything comes from Hesiod, Alcaeus' own imprint can be seen when he puts the summons to drink emphatically at the start instead of keeping it to the end. That after all is to be expected from the imperative temper of a drinking-song. Alcaeus has indeed been forced by the difference of metre to change one or two important words, and μαχλόταται becomes μιαρώταται and ἀφαυρότατοι becomes λέπτοι. It is not clear whether by λέπτοι he means 'thin' or 'weak'. Though the first is a normal usage and would suit the hot weather, the second is closer to Hesiod's ἀφαυρότατοι and provides a better contrast with μιαρώταται. This is a word of moral disapproval, not necessarily very harsh but a colloquial equivalent of the epic μαχλόταται, which recalls Homer's use of μαχλοσύνη for Paris.[1] In both substitutions Alcaeus keeps the main purport of his original. It is also perhaps worth noting that he delays the mention of the flowering of the σκόλυμος until later than Hesiod and makes it come immediately before his account of the summer condition of men and women. For Hesiod it merely indicates the time of year, and perhaps it does no more for Alcaeus, who may have kept it till late simply because his beginning is occupied with a summons to drink. Pliny, however, uses this passage to argue that the σκόλυμος mixed with wine is an aphrodisiac.[2] It is just possible that Alcaeus may have gone on to say something of the kind, but we must reckon that, since Pliny says the same of Hesiod and is plainly wrong in doing so, he may also be wrong about Alcaeus.

Alcaeus has his own philosophy of wine and forms maxims about it. As a landowner he appreciated the value of vines and said

μηδ' ἒν ἄλλο φυτεύσῃς πρότερον δένδριον ἀμπέλω[3]

'Do not plant any other tree before the vine', and no doubt he meant what he said. But he knew that drink had its social justification, and was an early proponent of the thesis that wine reveals the true man. When he wrote

οἶνος, ὦ φίλε παῖ, καὶ ἀλάθεα[4]

---

[1] *Il.* 24. 30.

[2] *N.H.* 22. (43). 86–87, 'traditur (scolymus) . . . Venerem stimulare in uino Hesiodo et Alcaeo testibus, qui florente ea cicadas acerrimi cantus esse et mulieres libidinis auidissimas uirosque in coitum pigerrimos scripsere, uelut prouidentia naturae hoc adiumento tunc ualentissimo'.

[3] Fr. 342 L.–P. Cf. Hor. *C.* 1. 18. 1 'nullam, Vare, sacra uite prius seueris arborem'.

[4] Fr. 366 L.–P. Cf. Theocr. 29. 1 with Gow's note.

'Wine, dear boy, and also truth', or

οἶνος γὰρ ἀνθρώπω δίοπτρον¹

'Wine is a spy-hole into a man', he justifies drink by an argument
which was well suited to a society which attached paramount
importance to truthfulness and candour between friends. Greek
poetry often plays with the notion that men need some means of
testing one another's fidelity, and Alcaeus found his own answer
to it.

Alcaeus seems also to have been one of the first to use wine as
an element in the theme of *carpe diem* and to insist that, since life
is short, it is wise to spend it in pleasure and especially in drink.
Mimnermus had indeed put forward his own philosophy on
these lines, but love, not wine, was the centre of his interest.
Though Alcaeus was an inveterate man of action, or even perhaps because he was one, when he relaxed, he relaxed fully, and
found consolation in the thought that, since we shall soon be
dead beyond recall, it is wise to drink:

πῶνε [καὶ μέθυ', ὦ] Μελάνιππ', ἄμ' ἔμοι· τί [φαῖς
2 †ὅταμε[. . . .]διννάεντ'† Ἀχέροντα μέγ[

ζάβαι[ς ἀ]ελίω κόθαρον φάος [ἄψερον
4 ὄψεσθ'; ἀλλ' ἄγι μὴ μεγάλων ἐπ[ιβάλλεο·

καὶ γὰρ Σίσυφος Αἰολίδαις βασίλευς [ἔφα
6 ἄνδρων πλεῖστα νοησάμενος [θάνατον φύγην,

ἀλλὰ καὶ πολύιδρις ἔων ὑπὰ κᾶρι [δὶς
8 διννάεντ' Ἀχέροντ' ἐπέραισε, μ[έμηδε δ' ὢν

ἀ]ύτωι μόχθον ἔχην Κρονίδαις βα[σίλευς κάτω
10 μελαίνας χθόνος· ἀλλ' ἄγι μὴ τά[δ' ἐπέλπεο.

θᾶς] τ' ἀβάσομεν, αἴ ποτα κἄλλοτα, [νῦν πρέπει
12 φέρ]ην ὅττινα τῶνδε πάθην τά[χα δῶι θέος.

. . . .] ἄνεμος βορίαις ἐπι[.²

Drink and get drunk, Melanippus, with me. Why do you think that
when you have crossed (?) eddying Acheron you will see the clean
sunlight again? Come, aim not at great things. For even king Sisyphus, son of Aeolus, who was the wisest of men, claimed that he had

¹ Fr. 333 L.–P. Cf. Theogn. 500; Aesch. fr. 393 N; Ion fr. 1. 12 D.
² Fr. 38 L.–P.; Page, *S. and A.* pp. 300–3, whose readings and suggestions I
follow except in 6 and 11. Line 2 must have been corrupt in the papyrus as διννάεντ' cannot stand at this place in the metre.

fled from death, but despite all his cunning he twice crossed whirling Acheron at the orders of fate. And the king, the son of Cronus, devised for him a labour to have under the black earth. But come, hope not for these things. While we are young, now, if ever, is it fit to endure whatever of these things the gods give us to suffer . . . the wind Boreas . . .

It is not certain that the last line belongs to this poem, and it may be the first line of another. So we cannot press its relevance. What is clear is Alcaeus' view that a man has only one life and must make the best of it. But this best, though for the moment it is to be found in drink, is to be found mainly in taking whatever the gods send and getting the most from it, whether it is good or bad. Alcaeus drives home his point by the story of Sisyphus, who escaped once from the dead but nevertheless died in due course. His cunning earned him the title of κέρδιστος ἀνδρῶν from Homer,[1] and similar tributes from Hesiod,[2] Theognis,[3] and Pindar.[4] The story was told by Pherecydes.[5] When Zeus carried off Aegina, Sisyphus told her father, Asopus. Zeus sent Death to Sisyphus, but Sisyphus chained him up, with the result that nobody could die. Ares freed Death, and Sisyphus was surrendered to him, but before dying he told his wife Merope to omit the funeral rites. So Hades sent him back to remonstrate with her and, once he was back, he did not return but lived to an old age. For this, in his second sojourn below earth, he was punished by having to roll a boulder up hill, which rolled down as soon as it reached the top. The story is a warning against trying to escape from death, and Alcaeus uses it as an example of the dangers of asking for too much. If Melanippus is wise, he will make the most of the passing hour and be content with it. The poem looks as if it were written when Alcaeus and Melanippus were both young, and it has a certain youthful seriousness and elegance. It may even be more or less complete, in the sense that it had no more than twelve lines, and in that case we can see how neatly and effectively Alcaeus makes his point.

The theme of wine is closely allied to the theme of love. The fragments contain almost nothing about women, except a

---

[1] *Il.* 6. 153.
[2] Fr. 7. 4 R. Σίσυφος αἰολόμητις.
[3] 701 ff. οὐδ' εἰ . . . πλείονα δ' εἰδείης Σισύφου Αἰολίδεω.
[4] *Ol.* 13. 52 Σίσυφον μὲν πυκνότατον παλάμαις ὡς θεόν
[5] 3 F 119 Jacoby.

remark on the futility of giving anything to a harlot[1] and a reference to 'lovely Abanthis'.[2] More revealing is the line

δέξαι με κωμάσδοντα δέξαι, λίσσομαί σε λίσσομαι[3]

Welcome me, welcome me, the reveller, I beg you, I beg.

This is an early example of a favourite Greek custom, when young
men, after their wine, would roam the streets and sing serenades,
παρακλαυσίθυρα. Such songs would normally be addressed to
women of easy character, and Alcaeus' line evidently was composed for such an occasion. But so far as love was concerned, he
seems to have been more interested in boys and young men than
in women. At least this is the impression that he left on Horace:

> Liberum et Musas Veneremque et illi
> semper haerentem puerum canebat
> et Lycum nigris oculis nigroque
> crine decorum.[4]

But the fragments do not mention Lycus and indeed say very
little about love. It is true that Bycchis is addressed in two drinking-songs,[5] and he may have been an ἐρώμενος, but there is no
evidence for it. More substantial are the claims of Menon, who is
mentioned in two lines:

> κέλομαί τινα τὸν χαρίεντα Μένωνα κάλεσσαι,
> αἰ χρῆ συμποσίας ἐπόνασιν ἔμοιγε γένεσθαι.[6]

I bid someone call the charming Menon, if I am to take pleasure in
our drinking together.

So too the scholiast says that two other lines were written εἰς τὸν
ἐρώμενον, and they seem to concern some friend who has deserted
Alcaeus, though he once enjoyed the pleasures of his hospitality:

> φίλος μὲν ἦσθα κἀπ' ἔριφον κάλην
> καὶ χοῖρον· οὕτω νομίσδεται.[7]

You were my friend, to be invited to kid and pork. This is what
happens.

In these scanty fragments there is little trace of emotion, still
less of love. Nor should we treat as serious evidence for Alcaeus
the παιδικὰ Αἰολικά of Theocritus, in which he uses an imitation

---

[1] Fr. 117 (b) 26 L.–P.   [2] Fr. 261 (b) i. 8 L.–P.
[3] Fr. 374 L.–P.; see Headlam–Knox, *Herodas*, p. 83.
[4] *C.* i. 32. 9–12.   [5] Frs. 73 and 335 L.–P.
[6] Fr. 368 L.–P.   [7] Fr. 71 L.–P.

of the Aeolic dialect and two favourite metres of Alcaeus, the Aeolic Dactylic Pentameter and the Greater Asclepiad, to speak of the misery which his boy-loves bring him. Though he quotes Alcaeus at the beginning of *Idyll* XXIX and plainly treats him as a model, his mawkish spirit is alien to anything that we know of Alcaeus and seems characteristic of the Alexandrian age. That Alcaeus wrote erotic poems we cannot doubt, but we do not know what they were like.

Alcaeus saw his life against a background of gods and goddesses, who gave or withheld their favours as they chose, and were for him an indispensable part of the daily round. In the poems that he wrote for them he shows that he had his own vivid vision of them and gave them an intimate place in his life. His hymns were written in the same style and the same metres as his other poems and show little affinity with the choral hymns of Alcman or Stesichorus. They may well have been quite short, since Alcaeus is economical of words and makes his effects in a brief compass. To Apollo he wrote a hymn in the Alcaic stanza, and the first line survives:

ὦναξ Ἄπολλον, παῖ μεγάλω Δίος[1]

'King Apollo, son of mighty Zeus'. This simple but stately opening may be supplemented by the account which Himerius gives of the poem:

When Apollo was born, Zeus decked him with a golden head-band and a lyre and gave him also a chariot to drive, and swans drew the chariot. He sent him to Delphi and the streams of Castalia, thence to speak as a prophet of justice and right to the Hellenes. He mounted on the chariot and made the swans fly to the Hyperboreans. When the Delphians heard of this, they composed a Paean and a tune and established dances of young men round the tripod, and summoned the god to come from the Hyperboreans. But for a whole year he gave laws to the men there, and when he thought that it was time for the Delphian tripods to give sound, he ordered his swans to fly back from the Hyperboreans. It was summer, indeed midsummer, when Alcaeus brings Apollo back from the Hyperboreans. Hence with the summer blazing forth and Apollo in the land the lyre also puts on a summer wantonness about the god. To him the nightingales sing the sort of song that you expect birds to sing in Alcaeus, and the swallows and cicadas also sing, not announcing their own fortune among men but voicing all their tunes at the god. Castalia, in poetic

[1] Fr. 307 L.–P.

style, flows with silver streams, and Cephisus rises great with purple waves, imitating Homer's Enipeus. For, like Homer, Alcaeus is forced to make the water know the presence of gods.[1]

The paraphrase shows that Alcaeus treated Apollo in an original and striking way. He accepts the belief of his time that he is the god of law and order. Such a notion is mentioned three times in the Homeric Hymn to Apollo,[2] and Plato says that Minos and Lycurgus established the laws of the Pythian Apollo.[3] In historical times Zaleucus, the law-giver of Locri, was nominated by Apollo,[4] and Delphi gave a constitution to Cyrene.[5] Alcaeus, despite his own lawless instincts, accepts and celebrates this side of Apollo's character. But we suspect that it means less to him than another side in which Apollo is the god of song and music. As such he is given the lyre at birth, and it may have been in this hymn that he was presented by Alcaeus as the inventor of lyre-playing and flute-playing.[6] Certainly music was associated with the Hyperboreans, and it may have been from Alcaeus that Pindar ultimately derived his notion of their gay life at the end of the world:

> Μοῖσα δ' οὐκ ἀποδαμεῖ
> τρόποις ἐπὶ σφετέροισι· παντᾷ δὲ χόροι παρθένων
> λυρᾶν τε βοαὶ καναχαί τ' αὐλῶν δονέονται.[7]

And the Muse never leaves that land,
For this is their life:—
Everywhere the girls are dancing
And the sound of the lyres is loud
and the noise of the flutes.

Though Alcaeus appreciated Apollo's function as a law-giver, his imagination seems to have been more splendidly fired by his functions as the lord of song.

Against the Hymn to Apollo we may set the Hymn to Hermes. It began with an invocation:

> χαῖρε Κυλλάνας ὁ μέδεις, σὲ γάρ μοι
> θῦμος ὕμνην, τὸν κορύφαισιν ἄγνα
> Μαῖα γέννατο Κρονίδαι μίγεισα
> παμβασίληϊ.[8]

---

[1] Or. 48. 10–11 Colonna; see Page, S. and A. pp. 244 ff.   [2] 253, 293, 394.
[3] Laws 1. 632 d.   [4] Aristot. fr. 548 R.   [5] Hdt. 4. 161. 1.
[6] 'Plut.' Mus. 4.   [7] Pyth. 10. 37–39.
[8] Fr. 308 (b) L.-P. In 2 no sense can be made of αὔγαις, and I suggest ἄγνα as a suitable epithet for Maia.

M

Hail, ruler of Cyllene; for it is of you that I would sing, whom on the mountains holy Maia bore, when she had lain with the son of Cronus, the king of all.

Alcaeus seems to have told how Hermes was brought to birth by the Graces and nursed by the Hours,[1] but the episode of which we know most is that in which Hermes stole Apollo's bow and arrows at the very moment when Apollo threatened to punish him for having stolen his cattle. It is a delightful addition to the adventures of the mischievous young god and shows how little he cared for authority. It is this to which Horace refers in his poem to Mercury:

> te, boues olim nisi reddidisses
> per dolum amotas, puerum minaci
> uoce dum terret, uiduus pharetra
> risit Apollo.[2]

Porphyrio, who says that the whole of this poem is a 'hymnus in Mercurium ab Alcaeo lyrico poeta', need not be taken too literally, but he may well be right, within the limits of his knowledge, when he calls the stanza just quoted 'fabula . . . ab Alcaeo ficta'. Yet we can perhaps see how the episode was born. The Homeric Hymn to Hermes is concerned at length with the theft of the cattle, but, when they have been returned, Apollo is still suspicious of Hermes and says to him:

> δείδια, Μαιάδος υἱέ, διάκτορε, ποικιλομῆτα,
> μή μοι ἅμα κλέψῃς κίθαριν καὶ καμπύλα τόξα.[3]

The theme is not developed because Hermes swears that he will not steal the bow. Alcaeus took the point and gave it a new intention and importance. It added something to the rascally youth of Hermes and ended happily with Apollo laughing at the young god's mischief. The Hymn to Hermes was evidently less majestic than the Hymn to Apollo, as was natural with a very different god. But it too appealed to something in Alcaeus, to his admiration of cunning and his love of gay adventure.

---

[1] Fr. 308 (a) L.-P.; Philostrat. *Vit. Ap.* 5. 15. See Wilamowitz, *S.u.S.* p. 311; Page, *S. and A.* p. 256.

[2] *C.* 1. 10. 9–12.

[3] Hom. Hymn 4. 514–15. See L. Radermacher, *Der homerische Hermeshymnus*, p. 162.

These two Hymns dealt with two of the great Olympians, and the contrast between them conformed to the contrast which we find in Homer's treatment of the gods, sometimes as figures of august majesty, sometimes as delightful and irresponsible pleasure-seekers. Another Hymn written by Alcaeus probably comes from nearer home since it embodies a real experience and would suit many occasions in his active life:

δεῦτέ μοι νᾶ]σον Πέλοπος λίποντε[ς,
παῖδες ἴφθ]ιμοι Δ[ίος] ἠδὲ Λήδας,
εὐνόω]ι θύ[μ]ωι προ[φά]νητε, Κάστορ
4   καὶ Πολύδε[υ]κες,

οἲ κὰτ εὔρηαν χ[θόνα] καὶ θάλασσαν
παῖσαν ἔρχεσθ' ὠ[κυπό]δων ἐπ' ἴππων,
ῤήα δ' ἀνθρώποι[ς] θα[ν]άτω ῥύεσθε
8   ζακρυόεντος,

εὐσ[δύ]γων θρώισκοντ[ες ὸν] ἄκρα νάων
πήλ]οθεν λάμπροι πρό[τον' ὸν]τρ[έχο]ντες,
ἀργαλέαι δ' ἐν νύκτι φ[άος φέ]ροντες
12   νᾶϊ μ[ε]λαίναι.[1]

Come hither, leaving Pelops' island, strong sons of Zeus and Leda, appear with kindly heart, Castor and Polydeuces; who go on fast horses over the broad earth and all the sea, and easily rescue men from freezing death, leaping on the peaks of their well-benched ships, shining from afar as you run up the fore-stays and bring light to the black ship in the night of horror.

The whole poem had six stanzas, of which these are the first three, invoking the Dioscuri in the first stage of a prayer. Of the rest we know nothing. The Dioscuri are addressed in their special function of watching over men at sea. Their visible presence was thought to be manifest in the 'fuoco di Sant' Elmo', the natural electric lights which are familiar in the Mediterranean and thought to portend the passing of a storm.[2] Whether Alcaeus wrote this poem as a thanksgiving after returning from a rough voyage, or before setting out to sea, or even at sea, or for some

[1] Fr. 34 L.–P. Page's εὐνόωι in 3 gets support from fr. 129. 9–10 εὔνοον θῦμον. For my πρό[τον' ὸν]τρ[έχο]ντες in 10 cf. Et. Gud. 483. 13 for the neuter form.
[2] For the phenomenon in antiquity cf. Eur. Hel. 1495 ff.; Lucian Deor. Dial. 26. 2; Plin. N.H. 2. 101. The verbal similarities between Alcaeus' poem and Hom. Hymn 33 and Theocr. 22 probably indicate that certain themes were common in praise of the Dioscuri.

festival of the Dioscuri we do not know. But it is clear that Alcaeus speaks from experience and through it gives a special touch of intimacy and reality to the Dioscuri.

Alcaeus' Hymns to the gods introduced myths incidentally to illustrate some special aspects of divine power, but elsewhere he uses myths with a somewhat different intention, to point what is in effect a moral lesson. This is clear from two places where he speaks of Helen. Homer passes no judgements on her and treats her with a compassionate understanding, but in the sixth century she is treated in a new spirit, and to this Alcaeus made his contribution:

> ὡς λόγος κάκων ἄ[χος ἔννεκ' ἔργων
> Περράμωι καὶ παῖσ[ί ποτ', ᾿Ωλεν', ἦλθεν
> ἐκ σέθεν πίκρον, π[ύρι δ' ὤλεσε Ζεῦς
> 4   ᾿Ίλιον ἴραν.
>
> οὐ τεαύταν Αἰακίδαι[ς γύναικα
> πάντας ἐς γάμον μάκ[αρας καλέσσαις
> ἄγετ' ἐκ Νή[ρ]ηος ἔλων [μελάθρων
> 8   πάρθενον ἄβραν
>
> ἐς δόμον Χέρρωνος· ἔλ[υσε δ' ἄγνας
> ζῶμα παρθένω· φιλό[τας δ' ἔγεντο
> Πήλεος καὶ Νηρείδων ἀρίστ[ας,
> 12 ἐς δ' ἐνίαυτον
>
> παῖδα γέννατ' αἰμιθέων [φέριστον
> ὄλβιον ξάνθαν ἐλάτη[ρα πώλων·
> οἱ δ' ἀπώλοντ' ἀμφ' 'Ε[λέναι Φρύγες τε
> 16 καὶ πόλις αὔτων.[1]

As story tells, bitter woe came once because of evil doings, Helen, from you to Priam and his sons, and Zeus destroyed holy Ilium with flame. Not such was the woman whom the son of Aeacus, summoning all the Blessed Ones to his wedding, married, when he took from the halls of Nereus a delicate maiden to the house of Chiron. He loosed the chaste maiden's girdle, and the love was accomplished of Peleus and the best of Nereus' daughters. In a year she bore him a son, the

---

[1] Fr. 42 L.-P.; Page, S. and A. pp. 278–81. I accept his choice of supplements, except in 5, where γύναικα gives a better balance to the sentence than some such epithet as ἄγανος, and in 10, where ἔγεντο avoids the not very pointed metaphor implicit in ἔθαλε.

mightiest of demigods, happy driver of tawny horses. But they, the Phrygians and their city, were destroyed for Helen's sake.

The moral is pointed plainly, and the chief aim of the poem seems to be the emphasis which it gives to the good wife, Thetis, in antithesis to the faithless Helen. An attempt has been made to read more into it, and the claim made that it is eristic and gives the answer to a poem just sung in which Helen's beauty has been praised; Alcaeus replies by pointing out its disastrous consequences and setting Thetis as an alternative to Helen.[1] On this view the song resembles the Attic σκόλια in that one singer caps another. It is also claimed that there is a riddling element in the style, which refers both to Thetis and to Achilles by periphrasis instead of by name. This seems unjustified as the periphrases are familiar and immediately intelligible. In the main the theory fails; for the words ὡς λόγος can hardly refer to a preceding poem, and the emphatic κάκων is unsuitable if that poem has praised Helen. ὡς λόγος seems rather to be the tradition which told what disaster Helen brought to Troy, and this is what Alcaeus is concerned to demonstrate. He does not dispute the facts but draws a moral from them, which is simply that an evil action leads to disaster.

This poem is supplemented by another which also speaks of Helen and the destruction which she caused. The legible portion does not allow us to say what the subject of the first sentence is, though it may be Aphrodite or love or something of the kind:

κ'Αλένας ἐν στήθ[ε]σιν [ἐ]πτ[όαισε
θῦμον Ἀργείας, Τροΐω δ' ὑ]π' ἄν[δρος
ἐκμάνεισα ξ[εν]ναπάτα 'πὶ π[όντον
6 ἔσπετο ναΐ,

παῖδά τ' ἐν δόμ[ο]ισι λίποισ' [ἐρήμαν
κἄνδρος εὔστρωτον [λ]έχος ὦ[ς ϝ' ὑπείκην
πεῖθ' ἔρωι θῦμο[ς διὰ τὰν Διώνας
10 παῖ]δα Δ[ίο]ς τε

]πιε . . μανι[
κ]ασιγνήτων πόλεας μ[έλαινα
γα]ῖ ἔχει Τρώων πεδίωι δά[μεντας
14 ἔν]νεκα κήνας,

[1] H. J. Jurenka, *Wien. Stud.* xxxvi, p. 229.

πόλ]λα δ' ἄρματ' ἐν κονίαισι[
ἤρι]πεν, πό[λ]λοι δ' ἐλίκωπε[ς ἄνδρες
ὔπτι]οι 'στείβοντο. φόνωι δ' [ἔχαιρε
18 δῖος Ἀ]χί[λλ]ευς.[1]

and fluttered the heart of Argive Helen in her breast; driven mad by the man from Troy, who betrayed his host, she followed in a ship over the sea, leaving her child desolate at home, and her husband's richly decked bed, since her heart persuaded her to yield to love because of the son of Dione and Zeus. . . . Many of his brothers the dark earth holds, laid low on the Trojan plain for her sake, and many chariots fell in the dust . . . and many dark-eyed men were trampled as they lay on their backs, and god-like Achilles delighted in the slaughter.

In Helen's unfaithfulness Alcaeus sees the cause of a huge slaughter, and the view is characteristic of him. With his strong loyalties and hatred of treachery he was likely to draw such a moral from the old story. In this he represents a change in the literary tradition. Helen, who excited the loyalty and chivalry of heroic Greece, was herself a traitress and brought the fall of Troy. Alcaeus sees the issue clearly, and, true to his standards, draws his own conclusions.

Alcaeus does not make that straight appeal to universal emotions which Sappho does, and some of the issues which meant so much to him cannot mean so much to others. He suffers because he writes too directly for his friends, and at times he fails to capture our full interest because his subjects are too transitory or too narrow. But if we make allowances for this, he remains a poet of considerable power and charm. His foursquare personality passes without distortion into his verse and displays all the vigour and passion with which he responded to anything that concerned him. Though his poetry is often obscure to us, it is mainly the fault of our incomplete texts and our ignorance of the events through which he lived. Even so his masculine strength is manifest everywhere. He is a master of plain statement, and often uses it, but when he wants to drive something home, he uses imagery with a firm understanding of its worth, as in his various accounts of ships, and at times he builds up a picture with care and precision.

[1] Fr. 283 L.–P.; Page, *S. and A.* pp. 275–8. The supplements are mostly his, but in 16 I see no objection to ἄνδρες, even if it does not specify whether they are Greeks or Trojans, and in 17 I suggest ὔπτι]οι and [ἔχαιρε as giving the right kind of sense.

For instance, at one place he compares a failure in some action with that of men who are disappointed in their vintage:

> σοὶ μὲν [γ]ὰρ ἤ[δ]η περβέβα[τ]αι χρό[νος
> κ]αὶ κάρπος ὄσσ[ο]ς ἦς συνα[γ]άγρετ[αι,
> τὸ κλᾶμμα δ' ἐλπώρα, κάλον γά[ρ,
> 12 ο]ὐκ ὀλ[ί]γαις σταφύλαις ἐνείκη[ν,
>
> ἀλλ]' ὄψι· τοιαύτας γὰρ ἀπ' ἀμπέ[λω
> βότρ]υς γ......ι σκοπιάμ[ενοι
> τά]ρβη⟨μ⟩μι μὴ δρόπ[ω]σιν αὔταις
> 16 ὄμφ]ακας ὠμοτέραις ἐοίσαις.[1]

For already the time has passed for you, and all the fruit there was has been gathered. The hope was that the vine-branch, which was good, would bear not a few clusters, but it is too late; for I am afraid lest the ... after expecting bunches from such a vine, gather grapes which are too sour.

The imagery, which would be completely familiar to his hearers, is worked out with precision and neatness, and the implications of the unsuccessful vintage hit the temper of a chance which has been missed and brings only disappointment.

Alcaeus varies his style with phrases which may be either colloquial or traditional but have a smack of the spoken word. He says for instance:

> οἶδ' ἦ μὰν χέραδος μὴ βεβάως ἐργάσιμον λίθον
> κίνεις καί κεν ἴσως τὰν κεφάλαν ἀργαλέαν ἔχοι.[2]

I know indeed, that if a man moves silt, stone not firmly to be worked, he may perhaps have a sore head.

There seems to have been a proverbial saying μὴ κίνη χέραδος, known to Sappho,[3] and Alcaeus develops it in a practical way, no doubt with reference to some ill-chosen task which will bring trouble to him who undertakes it. Even more colloquial, and no doubt equally proverbial, is

> πάλιν ἀ σῦς παρορίνει[4]

'Again the sow stirs a little.' The image, which comes from the

---

[1] Fr. 119, 9–16 L.–P. I still hanker for γεώμοροι or for some word with a like meaning in 14, but yield to Page's pronouncement, *S. and A.* p. 242, that 'it is an impossible form in Lesbian'.
[2] Fr. 344 L.–P.   [3] Fr. 145 L.–P.
[4] Fr. 393 L.–P. Cf. Diogen. 8. 64 ὖς ὀρίνει. ἐπὶ τῶν βιαίων λέγεται καὶ ἐριστικῶν.

farm, is said to have been applied to violent and quarrelsome
people. More literary but perhaps equally familiar is

κεῖται πὲρ κεφάλας μέγας, ὦ Αἰσιμίδα, λίθος[1]

'About my head, Aesimides, hangs a great stone.' This comes
from the myth of the stone which was supposed to hang over the
head of Tantalus in the underworld and was an early equivalent
of the sword of Damocles. It had already been used by Archilochus of impending danger:

μηδ' ὁ Ταντάλου λίθος
τῆσδ' ὑπὲρ νήσου κρεμάσθω,[2]

and was used later by Pindar soon after the Persian Wars to
express the relief which he felt at the peril having passed.[3] When
an image, whether homely or literary, will clinch a point, Alcaeus
will use it, and vary his texture by these brief, vivid divagations
from his more usual manner.

Alcaeus' attachment to the visible world meant that he noticed
many things in it, and, when nature caught his attention, he
spoke of it with truth and sensibility, as we might expect from a
man who spent much of his life in the open air. He must have
visited Thrace, for he describes, as only an eye-witness could, the
river Hebrus as it flows into the sea:

Ἔβρε, κ[άλ]λιστος ποτάμων πὰρ Α[ἶνον
ἐξί[ησθ' ἐς] πορφυρίαν θάλασσαν
Θραικ[ίας ἐρ]ευγόμενος ζὰ γαίας . . .[4]

Hebrus, you are the most beautiful of rivers, as you flow past Aenus
into the purple sea, surging through the Thracian land. . . .

He describes in lively and appropriate words a flight of birds
which are so unfamiliar to him that they seem to come from the
edge of the world:

ὄρνιθες τίνες οἴδ' Ὠκεάνω γᾶς ἀπὺ πειράτων
ἦλθον πανέλοπες ποικιλόδειροι τανυσίπτεροι;[5]

What birds are these that have come from Ocean, the limits of the
earth, widgeon with dappled necks and long wings?

---

[1] Fr. 365 L.–P.   [2] Fr. 55 D.
[3] *Isthm.* 8. 10–12. ἐπειδὴ τὸν ὑπὲρ κεφαλᾶς
                         λίθον γε Ταντάλου παρά τις ἔτρεψεν ἄμμι θεός,
                         ἀτόλματον Ἑλλάδι μόχθον.
[4] Fr. 45 L.–P.
[5] Fr. 345 L.–P. See Thompson, *Greek Birds*, pp. 147–8.

In a moment of unexpected insight he fancies that he has heard the spring coming:

ἦρος ἀνθεμόεντος ἐπάϊον ἐρχομένοιο,[1]

'I heard the flowery spring coming.' He is no less conscious of something quite gentle and quiet, like a soft wind:

βλήχρων ἀνέμων ἀχείμαντοι πνόαι[2]

'The stormless breaths of gentle winds.' Alcaeus was not primarily interested in nature, but at moments it became more to him than a background for action or an excuse for drink. He would suddenly notice something and record it in happy, exact, and lively words.

Alcaeus differs from Sappho, and still more from Anacreon, in his attachment to certain phrases which he learned from the epic repertory. Though at times he hits on just the right unusual and unforeseen word, at other times he is content with a short, conventional phrase, which does not add very much to his immediate effect. Homeric influence is apparent in such combinations as εὔρηαν χθόνα, ἐν στήθεσιν θῦμον, Ἴλιον ἴραν, ναῖ μελαίναι, μέγαν ὄρκον, οἴνοπα πόντον, ἄρματ' ἐν κονίαισι, μελαίνας χθόνος, πολέμω δότερραν, ὠκυπόδων ἵππων, θέων μακάρων, πολίας ἅλος, εὔστρωτον λέχος, Τρώων πεδίωι, ὄρνιθες τανυσίπτεροι. But though such phrases fall naturally from him because he is soaked in the epic and relies on its help in dealing with heroic themes, they do not interfere with the straightforward movement of his poetry and are never misfits. As he was ready sometimes to admit an epic phrase like Ἀΐδαο δῶμα in defiance of Lesbian local usage, so too he admitted Lesbian adaptations of epic formulas because they fitted his subjects and his temper. Just because they make no great demand from us, they help the easy movement of his verse, and it is notable that, when he deals with strictly contemporary subjects, he uses them less. They are part of his mental and artistic equipment, and on certain matters he falls naturally into them.

Alcaeus differs from most known Greek poets in being an aristocrat in an aristocratic age, whose ideas and ideals he embodies with almost unquestioning conviction. He has indeed something of Archilochus, but Archilochus was always rather a misfit and had no such position as Alcaeus in society. He has also

---

[1] Fr. 367 L.–P. [2] Fr. 319 L.–P.

much that reminds us of the poems ascribed to Theognis, but
shows a more confident and less melancholy temper. Though the
world which he represents was already on the defensive and was
soon after his death to be absorbed by Persian overlords, he shows
how vigorous it was even in its intestine convulsions. As a poet,
he was an amateur, as the Homeric rhapsodes before him were
not, and as many poets after him were equally not, whether,
like Ibycus and Anacreon, they were the clients of tyrants, or,
like Simonides and Pindar, the guests of rich patrons in different
parts of Greece. Alcaeus sang not for money but because he
wished to, and if he had any ulterior purpose, it was to make his
views known to his contemporaries and to win adherents for his
cause or to comfort his companions in their troubles. Sometimes
he seems to write in a hurry without undue care, as when he
repeats the same word within a few lines; at other times he is so
carried away by controversy that he may not rise to a high level
of poetry and deserves what Dionysius says of him: 'Often if you
were to remove the metre, you would find political rhetoric.'[1]
He has not the imagination of Alcman or the concentrated power
of Sappho. His gifts are circumscribed by his outlook, and at
times his prejudices and his spleen make him unsympathetic.
Even as a poet of hate, he has not the nip and bite of Archilochus. But at his best he has a rare quality of directness, of going
straight to the point and hitting his target with apt and lively
words. He is all sinew and muscle and goes into action with an
effortless confidence. If we pick odd lines almost at random, they
may indeed serve very different purposes, but they all have the
same kind of balance and clarity and unaffected vigour, whether

> ὄλβιον ξάνθαν ἐλάτηρα πώλων

or

> πάμπαν δ' ἐτύφωσ' ἐκ δ' ἔλετο φρένας

or

> τερένας ἄνθος ὀπώρας

or

> τὼ δὲ πίθω πατάγεσκ' ὁ πύθμην

or

> αἴ κ' εἴπηις τὰ θέλῃις ⟨καί κεν⟩ ἀκούσαις τά κεν οὐ θέλοις.

---

[1] de Imit. 421 πολλαχοῦ γοῦν τὸ μέτρον τις εἰ περιέλοι ῥητορικὴν ἂν εὕροι πολιτικήν.

The straitness of his outlook, after all, made Alcaeus see things more clearly and feel them with undivided emotions. He does not attempt themes beyond his power or lose himself in subjects which do not mean very much to him, and even in his most savage moods his verse has a toughness which keeps it well above the level of any prose. He wrote because he had something to say. Sometimes he tumbles roughly into poetry; at other times he rides easily and lightly over his obstacles with a power that is the more admirable because it is unadorned.

V. SAPPHO

ALCAEUS was a friend and a contemporary of a woman whose fame was to surpass his own and win a very special place in the estimate of posterity. Sappho cast such a spell on Greece and Rome that even now it is hard to distinguish fact from fiction in her story or to see clearly how she lived and worked. The few ascertainable facts about her life are soon stated. Though some said that she was born in the Lesbian town of Eresus,[1] her home was at Mytilene.[2] Her father's name was Scamandronymus,[3] her mother's Cleïs.[4] The date of her birth is uncertain. 'Suidas' says γεγονυῖα κατὰ τὴν μβ′ Ὀλυμπιάδα.[4] If γεγονυῖα means 'born', her birth would fall in 612–609 B.C., but it is more commonly used to mean 'flourished',[5] and in that case she would be of much the same age as Alcaeus, with whom, as with Pittacus, she is connected.[6] There is no need to doubt that she was married to Cercylas of Andros, reputed to be a rich man;[7] she certainly had a daughter, whom she called Cleïs after her own mother.[8] Presumably she came from a noble family, since her brother Larichus served wine in the town-hall of Mytilene, an office reserved for young men of good birth and handsome appearance.[9]

---

[1] 'Suid.' s.v. Σαπφώ (a′); Dioscorides, *Anth. Pal.* 7. 407. It is worth noting that Strabo 618, in speaking of Eresus, mentions it as the birthplace of Theophrastus and Phanias but not of Sappho.

[2] Athen. 10. 424 e; Strab. 617; *Mar. Par.* 36; 'Suid.' s.v. Σαπφώ (β′).

[3] Hdt. 2. 135. 1. The name may be recognized on a broken inscription from the island of Halone in the Sea of Marmara, Wilamowitz, *Nordionische Steine*, pp. 63–64, but there is no assurance that this is Sappho's father. 'Suidas' gives eight other names for her father, and perhaps they are inventions of Middle or New Comedy. In any case none has authority comparable to that of Herodotus.

[4] 'Suid.' s.v. Σαπφώ (β′).

[5] Rohde, *Rh. Mus.* xxxiii (1878), pp. 161 ff., shows that in 'Suidas' γεγονυῖα usually refers to the *floruit*, but in exceptional cases means 'was born.' He gives 88 certain cases of *floruit* against 6 of 'was born'. In Sappho's case the meaning of *floruit* receives some support from the dates given by Eusebius.

[6] Strab. 617.

[7] 'Suid.' s.v. Σαπφώ (β′).

[8] Frs. 98 (b) 1; 132 L.-P.; 'Suid.' s.v. Σαπφώ (a′); *Ox. Pap.* 1800.i. 14; 'Ov.' *Ep. Sapph.* 69–70.

[9] Athen. 10. 425 a; Schol. *Il.* 20. 234.

About 600 B.C. she went into exile in Sicily,[1] whence in later years a statue of her by Silanion was looted by Verres.[2] Of this exile her poetry bears almost no traces, since even the line

$$\mathring{\eta} \ \sigma\epsilon \ K\acute{\upsilon}\pi\rho\sigma\sigma \ \kappa\alpha\grave{\iota} \ \Pi\acute{\alpha}\phi\sigma\sigma \ \mathring{\eta} \ \Pi\acute{\alpha}\nu\sigma\rho\mu\sigma\sigma[3]$$

'whether thee Cyprus and Paphus or Panormus . . .' may indicate no more than the limits of the world known to her. She probably returned soon afterwards, and when the two versions of Eusebius offer a choice of dates for her fame in 603–2 and 596–5,[4] they suggest that she was already well known at the end of the seventh century. She seems to have passed most of her life in Lesbos, and her name is indissolubly connected with it. She was said to be small and dark,[5] but the three pictures of her on vases and the representations on coins cannot be anything but works of fancy. The date of her death is not known, and the story that she killed herself, in love for Phaon, by throwing herself from the Leucadian Rock looks like an invention of Middle or New Comedy, based perhaps on a misunderstanding of some of her own words.[6]

The remains of Sappho's poetry are almost entirely concerned with her own sex. Apart from her brothers and perhaps Alcaeus, she does not seem to have written for or about men. Her devoted interest was chiefly given to girls, and to this degree she deserves Horace's comment:

> Aeoliis fidibus querentem
> Sappho puellis de popularibus.[7]

She was stirred by powerful emotions towards them, and they

---

[1] *Mar. Par.* 36 ἀφ' οὗ Σαπφὼ ἐγ Μυτιλήνης εἰς Σικελίαν ἔπλευσε φυγοῦσα. Then follows a lacuna. The previous entry is 603/2 and the next 591/0.

[2] Cic. *in Verr.* 2. 4. 126–7. This of course proves nothing about Sappho's stay in Sicily.

[3] Fr. 35 L.–P.; cf. fr. 98 (b) for a possible reference to exile.

[4] Jerome gives *Ol.* 45. 1, the Armenian version *Ol.* 46. 2.

[5] Max. Tyr. 18. 7 καίτοι μικρὰν οὖσαν καὶ μέλαιναν. Schol. Lucian. *Imag.* 18 ὅσον εἰς σῶμα εἰδεχθεστάτη ἡ Σαπφώ, μικρά τε καὶ μέλαινα ὁρωμένη, καὶ τί γὰρ ἄλλο ἢ ἀηδὼν ἀμόρφοις τοῖς πτίλοις ἐπὶ σμικρῷ τῷ σώματι περιειλημμένη; 'Ov.' *Ep. Sapph.* 31 ff. J. D. Beazley, *Greek Vases in Poland*, pp. 8–10, gives 1, a hydria in Goluchow, not later than the last decade of the sixth century; 2, kalathos in Munich *c.* 480; 3, hydria in Athens *c.* 440. He adds: 'No bronze, marble, or gem has the slightest claim to represent her.'

[6] Wilamowitz, *S.u.S.* pp. 25 ff.

[7] *C.* 2. 13. 24–25. *querentem* seems to be justified by the existing fragments: *popularibus* need mean no more than 'of her country'.

inspired her to write with a remarkable intimacy and candour. It would be wrong to regard this as a feminine counterpart to the way in which Ibycus and Anacreon wrote about boys; for they were to some degree influenced by the tastes of Polycrates and the conventions of his court. She wrote about girls because they touched her deeply. But that this had a social background we can hardly dispute. Though men and women may have mixed freely enough in Lesbos, yet, while men pursued their own masculine tastes, women must have developed their own lives with one another. In Sappho's case this partial segregation was strengthened by the Lesbian cult of beauty in girls. Just as, according to Theophrastus, there were καλλιστεῖα or contests in beauty in Tenedos,[1] and Cypselus founded similar contests at the altar of Demeter Eleusinia among the Parrhasians,[2] so too they were held in Lesbos.[3] The best evidence comes from Alcaeus, who watched them when he was in exile at Pyrrha:

> ὄππαι Λ[εσβί]αδες κριννόμεναι φύαν
> πώλεντ' ἐλκεσίπεπλοι, περὶ δὲ βρέμει
> ἄχω θεσπεσία γυναίκων
> ἴρα[ς ὀ]λολύγας ἐνιαυσίας.[4]

Where Lesbian girls in trailing robes go up and down, being judged for their beauty, and about them rings the marvellous sound of the holy cry of women in every year.

Sappho accepted this cult of beauty with the seriousness and the passion of genius. It was a main inspiration in her art and gave her the subjects of many songs. She turned into poetry something inherent in the Lesbian admiration of young womanhood and seems to have fashioned much of her life in its service.

That Sappho was not unique in her devotion to girls is clear from the existence of rival women who shared her tastes. Maximus of Tyre says:

What his rival craftsmen, Prodicus, Gorgias, Thrasymachus, and Protagoras were to Socrates, that Gorgo and Andromeda were to Sappho, who sometimes takes them to task and at other times refutes them and dissembles with them just like Socrates.[5]

---

[1] Athen. 13. 610 a.   [2] Id. 609 f.
[3] Schol. *Il.* 9. 129; Hesych. s.v. πυλάιδες· αἱ ἐν κάλλει κρινόμεναι τῶν γυναικῶν καὶ νικῶσαι, from which it has been inferred that the contests took place near Mt. Pylaion, Tümpel, *Phil.* iv (1891), pp. 566–7; cf. also *Anth. Pal.* 9. 189.
[4] Fr. 130. 32–35 L.–P.   [5] 18. 9.

There was eager rivalry between Sappho and these women for the affection of various girls, and in it Sappho shows a sharp side of her character. She derides Andromeda for being attracted by some country wench who does not yet know how to draw her dress properly about her ankles:

τίς δ' ἀγροΐωτις θέλγει νόον...
ἀγροΐωτιν ἐπεμμένα σπόλαν...
οὐκ ἐπισταμένα τὰ βράκε' ἔλκην ἐπὶ τῶν σφύρων.[1]

What country woman charms your mind ... clad in country clothes ... not knowing how to draw her gown over her ankles?

It was for Andromeda that Atthis deserted Sappho, and Sappho felt that the girl had come to hate her:

Ἄτθι, σοὶ δ' ἔμεθεν μὲν ἀπήχθετο
φροντίσδην, ἐπὶ δ' Ἀνδρομέδαν πόται.[2]

Atthis, you have come to hate the thought of me, and you fly to Andromeda.

At another time she mentions Andromeda as if she had been properly punished by making a bad bargain, and though we know no details, we can feel the scornful temper of her words:

ἔχει μὲν Ἀνδρομέδα κάλαν ἀμοίβαν.[3]

'Andromeda has made a fine bargain.' Of Gorgo we know rather less, but at one place Sappho speaks of people

μάλα δὴ κεκορημένοις
Γόργως,[4]

'fully sated with Gorgo', and at another she says that Archeanassa 'will be called wife to Gorgo'.[5] In Lesbos girls were cultivated by more than one older woman, and the relations between the rivals were not always cordial. We need no better evidence for the prevalence of the cult of girlhood and of the strong emotions which it aroused.

Towards these girls Sappho felt what can only be called love. When she speaks of it, she refers to ἔρος and uses the verb ἔραμαι. That it meant more than anything to her and gave her a kind of philosophy of life is clear from a poem on Anactoria,

[1] Fr. 57 L.–P. The first two lines are incomplete. In 1 we should expect νῶν for νόον, but the general sense is clear. Lobel ad loc. compares Heliod. Aethiop. 3. 1 ἀνδρῶν ἀγροικότερον βίον τε καὶ στολὴν ἐφελκομένων.
[2] Fr. 131 L.–P. Cf. Page, S. and A. p. 134 n. 1.
[3] Fr. 133. 1 L.–P.   [4] Fr. 144 L.–P.   [5] Fr. 213 L.–P.

which despite gaps in the papyrus looks as if it had a beginning and an end:

> ο]ἰ μὲν ἰππήων στρότον, οἰ δὲ πέσδων,
> οἰ δὲ νάων φαῖσ' ἐπ[ὶ] γᾶν μέλαι[ν]αν
> ἔ]μμεναι κάλλιστον, ἔγω δὲ κῆν ὄτ-
> τω τις ἔραται.

> 5 πά]γχυ δ' εὔμαρες σύνετον πόησαι
> π]άντι τ[ο]ῦτ', ἀ γὰρ πόλυ περσκέθοισα
> κάλλος [ἀνθ]ρώπων Ἐλένα [τὸ]ν ἄνδρα
> τὸν [πανάρ]ιστον

> καλλ[ίποι]σ' ἔβα 's Τροίαν πλέοι[σα
> 10 κωὔδ[ὲ πα]ῖδος οὐδὲ φίλων το[κ]ήων
> πά[μπαν] ἐμνάσθη, ἀλλὰ παράγαγ' αὔταν
> αὔτικ' ἴδοι]σαν

> Κύπρις· εὔκ]αμπτον γὰρ[
>] . . . κούφως τ . . οη . . ν
> 15 . .]με νῦν Ἀνακτορί[ας ὀ]νέμναι-
> σ' οὐ] παρεοίσας,

> τᾶ]ς ⟨κ⟩ε βολλοίμαν ἔρατόν τε βᾶμα
> κἀμάρυχμα λάμπρον ἴδην προσώπω
> ἢ τὰ Λύδων ἄρματα κὰν ὄπλοισι
> 20 πεσδομ]άχεντας.[1]

Some say that a host of horsemen is the fairest thing on the black earth, others of foot-soldiers, but I say that it is what one loves. It is very easy to make this understood by everyone. For she, who surpassed all human beings in beauty, Helen, left her most noble husband and went sailing to Troy with not a thought for her daughter or her dear parents. But the Cyprian led her astray at the first glance; for easily swayed . . . and lightly . . . as (?) now it has reminded me of Anactoria who is away. I would rather see her lovely gait and the bright sparkle of her face than the chariots of the Lydians and men in arms fighting on foot.

Here Sappho sets her own feminine ideal against the masculine

---

[1] Fr. 16 L.–P. In 12 I have followed Milne's αὔτικ' ἴδοι]σαν. In 13–14 there must have been some reference to love, whether as ἔρος 'or πόθος or, less probably, Κύπρις, and the connexion of thought was presumably that this same power, which ruled Helen, rules Sappho. The first word of 15 is then ὄς or ὤς or ἄ. In 19 I have kept the reading of the papyrus. It is certainly unexpected to find the first syllable of ὄπλοισι short in Sapphics, but it is arbitrary to dismiss it as impossible. καὶ πανόπλοις of Lobel–Page does not go easily with πεσδομάχεντας, since it is not clear which is the adjective and which the noun.

ideal of such as Alcaeus who delight in war. She claims to go her own way to her own ends, while they obey the call to action and enjoy its glittering splendours. To her the sight of Anactoria is worth more than armies, and the story of Helen is not, as it was for Alcaeus,[1] a warning, but an example, readily understood, of the power of love to break familiar bonds and force its victims to risk everything for it. Sappho makes it the centre of her life, because it is not only radiant and enthralling but in the end irresistible.

This poem is a poem of love, not of qualities incidental or subsidiary to it, but of love itself. What Sappho wants is the physical presence of Anactoria, and this makes the climax and the crisis of the poem. The statement of it is indeed extraordinarily simple, but the words are so apt and powerful that each makes its point at once. In a not dissimilar mood an Elizabethan song-writer mentions the qualities of his beloved:

> Her gesture, motion, and her smiles,
> Her wit, her voice, my heart beguiles,

but while he gives five, Sappho confines herself to two. To each she gives its flawless, satisfying epithet and lets the words do their work without further trimming, Anactoria's gait is ἔρατον, and the word is much more than a mere term of praise. It means that it is because of her way of walking that Sappho loves her. Then she adds ἀμάρυχμα λάμπρον προσώπω. The word ἀμάρυχμα is used of quick, sparkling motion. Hesiod wrote of some goddess or heroine Χαρίτων ἀμαρύγματ' ἔχουσαν,[2] and later Apollonius used the word for the flashing of Medea's eyes.[3] Sappho uses it for the changing brilliance of Anactoria's face and enhances it by the adjective λάμπρον. The girl's expression is bright and radiant, and Sappho catches this with her adjective.

This is the core of the poem, but Sappho shows art and elaboration in moving to her climax. In the first verse, before she comes to her main point, she uses a paratactic trope not uncommon in Greek poetry.[4] A parallel may be found in a couplet attributed to Theognis and known to Aristotle as the 'Delian epigram':[5]

[1] Frs. 42 and 283 L.–P.   [2] Fr. 94. 6 R.; cf. fr. 21. 3.
[3] 2. 288.
[4] See F. Dornseiff, Die archäische Mythenerzählung, pp. 3 ff. and 78 ff.; W. A. A. Otterlo, Mnemos. 1939–40, pp. 149 ff.; Page, S. and A. pp. 55–56.
[5] Nic. Eth. 1099 a 25; cf. Soph. fr. 356 P.

N

κάλλιστον τὸ δικαιότατον, λῷστον δ' ὑγιαίνειν,
πρᾶγμα δὲ τερπνότατον τοῦ τις ἐρᾷ τὸ τυχεῖν.¹

Fairest is justice, and best is health, but the sweetest thing is to find
what one loves.

But whereas this balances moral and physical excellences against
the delights of love and leaves the question unsettled by its
adroit choice of different superlatives, Sappho comes to a firm
decision. She is concerned only with what is κάλλιστον, and she
has no doubts what it is for her. In this she resembles Socrates,
with whom Maximus compares her;² for he said ὁ μὲν γάρ τις
ἵππους ἐπιθυμεῖ κτᾶσθαι, ὁ δὲ κύνας, ὁ δὲ χρυσίον, ὁ δὲ τιμάς·
ἐγὼ δὲ . . . βουλοίμην ἄν μοι φίλον ἀγαθὸν γενέσθαι.³ The point of
this device is that it normally stresses what apparently different
things have in common. So when Pindar begins *Olympian* I first
with a mention of water and then of gold, and goes on to say
that nothing surpasses the splendour of the Olympian Games,
he gives examples of splendour.⁴ When Tyrtaeus speaks of the
strength of the Cyclops, the swiftness of Boreas, the beauty of
Tithonus, the wealth of Midas, and goes on to say that none is to
be compared with the brave soldier, he gives different examples
of ἀρετή.⁵ In her own way Sappho does the same thing, but she
chooses her examples from the sphere of τὸ κάλλιστον and inside
it she makes a sharp contrast. The device is plainly traditional
and may well be ancient.⁶ Sappho weaves it into her poem

¹ Theogn. 255–6.   ² 18. 9.   ³ Plat. *Lysis* 211 d–e.
⁴ In *Isthm.* 5. 4 ff. Pindar uses ships and chariots as parallels to athletic games.
That both were traditional follows from Alcman fr. 1. 92–95 D.
⁵ Fr. 9. 1–20 D.
⁶ A later example is a song by Gil Vicente (*c.* 1470–c. 1536) in Spanish:

Muy graciosa es la doncella,
¡cómo es bella y hermosa!

Digas tú, el marinero,
que en las naves vivías,
si la nave o la vela
o la estrella es tan bella.

Digas tú, el caballero
que las armas vestías,
si el caballo o las armas
o la guerra es tan bella.

Digas tú, el pastorcico
que el ganadico guardas,
si el ganado o las valles
o la sierra es tan bella.

without any loose threads. Her last verse picks up the first and reiterates her conviction as to what is κάλλιστον, and in so doing puts the masculine ideal of military splendour in what she believes to be its right place.

Sappho makes her case by drawing on spectacles familiar enough in her day. For her, as for Alcaeus, the great military power of the time was Lydia, and its cavalry had already made a vivid impression on the Greeks of Asia Minor. Not many years earlier the Colophonian poet, Mimnermus, had written:

> οὐ μὲν δὴ κείνου γε μένος καὶ ἀγήνορα θυμὸν
> τοῖον ἐμεῦ προτέρων πεύθομαι, οἵ μιν ἴδον
> Λυδῶν ἱππομάχων πυκινὰς κλονέοντα φάλαγγας
> Ἕρμιον ἂμ πέδιον φῶτα φερεμμελίην.[1]

Not such were his might and his noble heart, as I learn from my forbears, who saw him routing the serried ranks of the Lydian cavalry on the plain of Hermus with his spear.

Against such cavalry the Greeks might use either the infantry phalanx or their own horsemen. An Attic black-figured dinos of about 550 B.C. depicts an encounter on horseback between Greeks in brimmed hats who hurl javelins and barbarians in hooded caps who reply with the same weapons.[2] Such methods would certainly appeal to Alcaeus and his friends, who would admire Lydian cavalry almost as much as their own. The chariots mentioned at the end were probably a speciality of the Lydians. In most Greek regions, except Cyrene[3] and Cyprus,[4] the chariot went out of use quite early, but in certain Asiatic countries it survived until the Persian Wars, when the Lydians are said to have used it,[5] and later, when it was known to Xenophon.[6] Sappho chooses chariots for mention as one of the most stylish elements in the masculine world of war.

In this poem, so far as we know, Sappho says nothing of the anguish of love, though she stresses its power. She certainly knew this anguish and wrote of it in decisive words. Her art did not shrink from describing the onslaughts of passion and was able to rise fully to its challenge. At times she uses her own kind of imagery, which is perhaps derived from the similes of the epic,

---

[1] Fr. 13. 1–4 D.
[2] J. D. Beazley, *Attic Black-figure: a Sketch*, p. 14 and pl. 4. In Athens.
[3] Xen. *Cyr.* 6. 1. 27.
[4] Hdt. 5. 113. 1.
[5] Aesch. *Pers.* 45 ff.
[6] Loc. cit.

but applied to a more subjective and more personal range of subjects. So when Love has fallen on her, she says

$$\text{Ἔρος δ' ἐτίναξέ μοι}$$
$$\text{φρένας, ὡς ἄνεμος κὰτ ὄρος δρύσιν ἐμπέτων,}^1$$

Love shook my heart, like a wind falling on oaks on the mountain.

The image is single and consistent. Love shakes Sappho as the wind shakes the oak-trees, and the point of comparison is that the assault is both violent and physical. The sudden gust is like the kind of passion to which she refers. Something of the same kind but expressed with more elaboration may be seen in

$$\text{Ἔρος δηὖτέ μ' ὀ λυσιμέλης δόνει,}$$
$$\text{γλυκύπικρον ἀμάχανον ὄρπετον}^2$$

Again Love, the looser of limbs, shakes me, a creature bitter-sweet, inescapable.

The word λυσιμέλης is traditional,[3] but Sappho gives it a new force by combining it with what follows. Love is seen as an ὄρπετον, and the word is, no doubt intentionally, vague. It can mean almost any creature that walks on all fours or creeps, from a snake[4] to the giant Typhos imprisoned under Etna.[5] Its associations may well be sinister, and therefore it is called ἀμάχανον, since there is no defence against it. This notion is combined with another, that the creature shakes Sappho and loosens her limbs. Just because the image in ὄρπετον is left vague, it is easily assimilated into the whole effect. Finally, it is γλυκύπικρον, and in this word, not found again till Hellenistic times, Sappho distils her divided feelings about love. The degree of her concentration can be seen from a comparison with the more diffuse methods of Theognis, who says of Love:

$$\text{πικρὸς καὶ γλυκύς ἐστι καὶ ἁρπαλέος καὶ ἀπηνής.}^6$$

In a very few words Sappho conveys the turmoil of her state, which is both physical and mental and which she both welcomes and hates.

In these passages Sappho reveals an unshrinking observation of herself. So far from obscuring or hampering her insight, her emotions set it more keenly to work. We cannot and need not

---

[1] Fr. 47 L.–P.
[2] Fr. 130 L.–P.
[3] Archil. fr. 118 D.; Hes. *Theog.* 121.
[4] Eur. *Andr.* 269.
[5] Pind. *Pyth.* 1. 25.
[6] 1353.

believe that such pieces were written in the very moment of passion, but they imply only a short interval of recollection from its first onslaught, and indicate that it is still at work in Sappho's whole being. It is this combination of passion and detachment which gives a special force to some lines in which she describes her sensations on seeing and hearing a girl and leaves no doubt about the violence of her love:

> φαίνεταί μοι κῆνος ἴσος θέοισιν
> ἔμμεν' ὤνηρ, ὄττις ἐνάντιός τοι
> ἰσδάνει καὶ πλάσιον ἆδυ φωνεί-
> σας ὑπακούει
>
> 5 καὶ γελαίσας ἰμέροεν, τό μ' ἦ μὰν
> καρδίαν ἐν στήθεσιν ἐπτόαισεν·
> ὡς γὰρ ἔς σ' ἴδω βρόχε', ὤς με φώναι-
> σ' οὐδ' ἔν ἔτ' εἴκει,
>
> ἀλλ' ἄκαν μὲν γλῶσσα πέπαγε, λέπτον
> 10 δ' αὔτικα χρῶι πῦρ ὑπαδεδρόμηκεν,
> ὀππάτεσσι δ' οὐδ' ἔν ὄρημμ', ἐπιρρόμ-
> βεισι δ' ἄκουαι,
>
> κὰδ δέ μ' ἴδρως κακχέεται, τρόμος δὲ
> παῖσαν ἄγρει, χλωροτέρα δὲ ποίας
> 15 ἔμμι, τεθνάκην δ' ὀλίγω 'πιδεύης
> φαίνομ' ἀλαία.[1]

That man seems to me to be the equal of the gods, who sits opposite you and, near to you, listens to you as you speak sweetly and laugh your lovely laughter; that in truth has set my heart fluttering in my breast. For whenever I look at you for a moment, then nothing comes to me to say, but my tongue is frozen in silence, straightway a subtle flame has run under my skin, I see nothing with my eyes, and my ears are buzzing. Sweat pours down over me, and trembling seizes me all over, and paler than grass am I, and a little short of death I seem in my distraught wits.

It is not by any means certain that this is the complete poem. The MSS. of 'Longinus', who quotes it, continue after φαίνομαι

---

[1] Fr. 31 L.–P. In 8 εἴκει seems more likely to mean 'comes' (cf. Hesych. s.v. εἴκει· παρεγένετο, Epicharm. fr. 35, 13 K) than 'it is possible', as in the Attic παρείκει. In 9 Cobet's πέπαγε gives sense and may have some, not very reliable, support in Catullus' lingua sed torpet, C. 51. 9. In 13 no solution is certain, and I follow Lobel in his earlier text p. 16. In 16 the last syllable of φαίνομαι must have been elided. A. G. Page's ἀλαία (cf. Hesych. s.v. ἀλαιός· ἄφρων) keeps close to the ductus litterarum, but perhaps φαίνομαι demands an infinitive.

in 16 with ἀλλὰ πᾶν τολματὸν, ἐπεὶ καὶ πένητα, which has been assumed to be a corrupt version of what came next. It looks as if it was the beginning of another verse, and since 'Longinus' does not say that he quotes the poem in its entirety, this is in principle possible. On the other hand, there are difficulties. First, even if we emend with Wilamowitz to ἐπεί κεν ᾖ τά, there is still a gap after φαίνομ'. Secondly, 'Longinus' quotes the lines for their account of physical sensations, and it is hard to see what this line has to do with them. Thirdly, even allowing for a considerable corruption in the manuscripts, it is odd that the quotation of the poem should break off after the first line of a strophe. In these conditions, we cannot say whether the poem is complete or not, or where the quotation ends. If the words ἀλλὰ πᾶν τολματόν, ἐπεὶ καὶ πένητα are corrupt, there is no reason why they should not be a corruption of a comment of 'Longinus'[1] as much as of Sappho's text. What we have for certain are four stanzas dealing with love, and we must be content with them.

'Longinus' quotes the poem for a definite reason. He precedes his quotation with the remarks:

> For instance, Sappho everywhere chooses the emotions that attend delirious passion from its accompaniments in actual life. Wherein does she demonstrate her supreme excellence? In the skill with which she selects and binds together the most striking and vehement circumstances of passion.

After quoting the poem, he goes on to comment:

> Are you not amazed how at one instant she summons, as though they were all alien from herself and dispersed, soul, body, ears, tongue, eyes, colour? Uniting contradictions, she is, at one and the same time, hot and cold, in her senses and out of her mind, for she is either terrified or at the point of death. The effect desired is that not one passion only should be seen, but a concourse of passions. All such things occur in the case of lovers, but it is, as I said, the selection of the most striking of them and their combination into a single whole that has produced the singular excellence of the passage.[2]

'Longinus'' words, τὰ συμβαίνοντα ταῖς ἐρωτικαῖς μανίαις παθήματα, show that he regarded this as a love-poem, and as such it was regarded in antiquity. Plutarch knew it and assumed that it

---

[1] Bergk, P.L.G. iii[4], p. 90, suggests ἀλλὰ πᾶν τολματόν, ἐπεῖπεν· εἶτα οὐ θαυμάζεις κτλ.

[2] de Sub. 10, trans. W. Rhys Roberts.

described Sappho's feelings on the appearance of her beloved,
τῆς ἐρωμένης ἐπιφανείσης.[1] Catullus translated it, even if freely and
incompletely, as a poem of love to his Lesbia.[2] Its different
elements were often used by Greek and Roman poets to describe
the pathology of love.[3] There is no doubt that it is a love-poem
and that it represents a personal experience. 'Longinus' indeed
suggests that it is simply a work of art, that Sappho has deliberately brought together a series of sensations in order to give a
powerful effect. But this is surely to underestimate or to misjudge
the impression which the poem makes. Its powerful impact comes
from its air of reality, of being derived immediately and directly
from Sappho's own experience. Nor does the poem rely very
much on the union of contradictions. Indeed we hardly notice
any, and though we might claim that the fire under her skin and
the sweat which flows down her are a kind of union of opposites,
it is entirely natural and easy. The real and remarkable strength
of the poem is that Sappho is able to observe her passions with
unfaltering insight and to express them in all their overmastering
power. The concentration and economy of her words catch the
concentration of her love as it obsesses and dominates her.

The poem is a triumph of art, but of an art so well controlled
that it responds exactly to the poet's feelings. The scene which it
presents is quite simple. A man sits opposite a girl and listens to
her voice and her laughter. We do not know who either is, and it is
quite possible that no names were given. Nor do we know what
kind of occasion it is. It has been surmised that the intimacy
between the girl and the man implies that it is their wedding-
feast,[4] but there is no clear evidence that it is, and we know too
little about the social relations of the sexes in Lesbos at this date
to say whether they were likely to mix on other occasions so
freely as the poem implies.[5] As Sappho hears and sees what is
happening, she is overwhelmed by violent sensations of passionate
love. But she has too her intellectual reaction. The man is for her
'an equal of the gods', and though the words may be based on

---

[1] *Erot.* 18.   [2] *C.* 51.

[3] A. Turyn, *Studia Sapphica*, pp. 41–57.

[4] Wilamowitz, *S.u.S.* pp. 56 ff.; B. Snell, *Hermes*, lxvi (1931), pp. 71 ff.

[5] Page, *S. and A.* p. 32, quotes with approval the statement of A. Setti, *Stud. It. Fil.*
xvi (1939), pp. 195 ff., that 'I Lesbi non erano musulmani'. Indeed they were
not, but that does not mean that they did not practise some segregation of the
sexes.

such traditional formulas as θεοειδής and θεοείκελος, they have a different intention. When Homer applies these adjectives, they refer to physical appearance, whether to the royal style of old Priam[1] or to the heroic beauty of Achilles.[2] Sappho's φαίνεται shows that she does not mean this. She means rather that in her eyes the man seems to enjoy a divine felicity and is at this moment like the gods in the inestimable happiness of holding the girl's attention. Against this celestial moment, of which she is the witness, Sappho sets her own all too human state, which makes her feel that she is at the point of death. Her φαίνομ' in 12 answers φαίνεται in 1 and suggests the contrast between the man and herself. Both are at the same level of appearance, even, in a sense, of unreality, and both get their special importance from Sappho's emotional state. Towards him she shows no jealousy or complaint. She sees him as a divine being beyond the reach of human suffering. By starting the lines as she does, Sappho gives a standard of reference by which she can set her own situation more clearly and forcibly.

Such a description of the physical symptoms of love was not entirely new. Archilochus had done something of the same kind, and it is possible that Sappho learned from his firm handling of the theme. At one place he says:

δύστηνος ἔγκειμαι πόθῳ,
ἄψυχος, χαλεπῆσι θεῶν ὀδύνῃσιν ἕκητι
πεπαρμένος δι' ὀστέων.[3]

Miserable I lie in longing, lifeless, pierced through the bones with bitter pains by the will of the gods.

In stressing his sense of lifelessness and the physical pain in his bones, Archilochus does something new in Greek poetry, but for both he is to some extent indebted to Homer. In calling himself ἄψυχος he suggests the grief of Andromache when she sees the dead body of Hector dragged behind the chariot of Achilles:

τὴν δὲ κατ' ὀφθαλμῶν ἐρεβεννὴ νὺξ ἐκάλυψεν,
ἤριπε δ' ἐξοπίσω, ἀπὸ δὲ ψυχὴν ἐκάπυσσε.[4]

Black night fell on her eyes and covered her, and she fell backward, and breathed out her life.

Archilochus picks up a hint from the last words and applies it to

[1] Il. 24. 217.
[3] Fr. 104 D.
[2] Il. 1. 131.
[4] Il. 22. 466–7.

himself not for grief but for love. So too his πεπαρμένος δι' ὀστέων recalls the Homeric ὀδύνῃσι πεπαρμένος,[1] but gives to it a more precise character by localizing the pains. Another fragment deals directly with the actual onslaught of love:

τοῖος γὰρ φιλότητος ἔρως ὑπὸ καρδίην ἐλυσθεὶς
πολλὴν κατ' ἀχλὺν ὀμμάτων ἔχευεν,
κλέψας ἐκ στηθέων ἀπαλὰς φρένας.[2]

For such was the desire for love that twisted itself under my heart and shed a thick mist over my eyes, stealing the tender spirit from my breast.

Here too the main symptoms owe something to Homer. The mist falling on the eyes is a common Homeric way of describing death or a swoon which resembles death,[3] and the stealing of the spirit suggests the simile in which a lion takes the ἀπαλὸν ἦτορ out of the kids which it devours.[4] Both phrases come from the language of death, but are applied by Archilochus to the way in which his desire seems to kill him. By doing this he prepares the way for Sappho. But she differs from him in the fuller enumeration of her symptoms and her lack of any verbal echoes from Homer. She has forged her own manner, and made it the immediate vehicle of her emotions. If Archilochus used some Homeric themes dealing with events as seen from without and applied them to his own sensations, Sappho fashioned a more selective technique in which everything is seen firmly from within.

With this poem of Sappho in our minds it is something of a surprise to find the Greek critic Demetrius speaking of her poetry in quite a different way. In his discussion of various kinds of literary χάρις he says that some of them may be found in the subject, οἷον νυμφαῖοι κῆποι, ὑμέναιοι, ἔρωτες, ὅλη ἡ Σαπφοῦς ποίησις,[5] as if the whole of Sappho's poetry were concerned with a special kind of enchantment. Much of it is, especially when it tells of the life which Sappho passed with her girls. That she was interested in even the small details of their doings is clear from some lines in which Gongyla is set a-flutter by someone's dress, and Sappho is delighted:

πόθος τ.[
ἀμφιπόταται

[1] Il. 5. 399.   [2] Fr. 112 D.   [3] Il. 5. 696; 20. 321, 421; Od. 22. 88.
[4] Il. 11. 115.   [5] de Eloc. 132.

τὰν κάλαν· ἀ γὰρ κατάγωγις αὖτα[ν
ἐπτόαισ᾽ ἴδοισαν, ἔγω δὲ χαίρω . . .[1]

Desire floats about the beautiful girl; for the gown set her fluttering when she saw it, and I rejoice.

So she tells Dica to crown herself with flowers:

σὺ δὲ στεφάνοις, ὦ Δίκα, πέρθεσθ᾽ ἐράτοις φόβαισιν
ὄρπακας ἀνήτω συναέρραισ᾽ ἀπάλαισι χέρσιν.[2]

Set lovely garlands on your hair, Dica, weaving stems of anise with tender hands.

But the fullest evidence for the pleasures of Sappho and her friends comes from a poem written in grief after one of them has left her. Shaken by the bitter pangs of parting, Sappho looks back on the times which they have passed together and enumerates activities which must have made the common round of their lives:

τεθνάκην δ᾽ ἀδόλως θέλω·
2　　ἄ με ψισδομένα κατελίμπανεν

πόλλα καὶ τόδ᾽ ἔειπ[έ μοι·
ὤιμ᾽ ὡς δεῖνα πεπ[όνθ]αμεν,
5　　Ψάπφ᾽, ἦ μάν σ᾽ ἀέκοισ᾽ ἀπυλιμπάνω.

τὰν δ᾽ ἔγω τάδ᾽ ἀμειβόμαν·
χαίροισ᾽ ἔρχεο κἄμεθεν
8　　μέμναισ᾽, οἶσθα γὰρ ὥς σε πεδήπομεν·

αἰ δὲ μή, ἀλλά σ᾽ ἔγω θέλω
ὄμναισαι [. . . . .] . [. . . .] . . αι
11　　ὄσ[σα μόλθακα] καὶ κάλ᾽ ἐπάσχομεν·

πό[λλοις γὰρ στεφάν]οις ἴων
καὶ βρ[όδων σφα]κίων τ᾽ ὔμοι
14　　κἀ[νήτω] πὰρ ἔμοι περεθήκαο,

καὶ πό[λλαις ὐπα]θύμιδας
πλέκ[ταις ἀμφ᾽ ἀ]πάλαι δέραι
17　　ἀνθέων [ἔβαλες] πεποημμέναις,

καὶ πάνται [λιπάρως] μύρωι
βρενθείωι . [　　　　]ρυ[. .]ν
20　　ἐξαλείψαο κα[ὶ βασ]ιληίωι

[1] Fr. 22. 11–14 L.–P.
[2] Fr. 81 (b) L.–P. The next two lines, which refer to the Graces, have not yet been satisfactorily emended.

καὶ στρώμν[αν ἐ]πὶ μολθάκαν
ἀπάλαν πα.[   ]...ων
23 ἐξίης πόθο[ν αἶψα νεα]νίδων,

κωὔτε [τις χόρος οὔτε] τι
ἶρον οὐδ' υ[   ]
26 ἔπλετ' ὄππ[οθεν ἄμ]μες ἀπέσκομεν,

οὐκ ἄλσος.[   ].ρος
                    ]ψόφος
29   ]...οιδιαι[1]

Honestly I wish to die. She left me with many tears, and this she said
to me: 'Alas, how sad is our plight; Sappho, truly I leave you unwillingly.' And these words I answered to her: 'Go gladly and remember me; for you know how we cared for you. If not, I would
remind you . . . of all the gentle and beautiful times we had. For many
garlands of violets and roses and vine-tendrils you put round yourself
at my side, and many necklaces woven of flowers you flung round
your soft neck, and everywhere with royal scent made from flowers
you anointed smoothly . . . and on soft beds, gentle . . . you put away
at once longing for maidens, and there was no dance and no shrine
nor . . . from which we were absent . . . no precinct . . . noise . . . .'

Despite all the gaps and the uncertainties this gives a picture of
Sappho's life with a favourite girl. Such were the delights which
they shared—the wearing of flowers as garlands or necklaces, the
use of rich scent, visits to shrines and temples, no doubt because
ceremonies were held in them. That this life was entirely satisfying
and happy seems clear enough. Even in 21–23 the soft beds seem
to indicate no more than that the girl was so absorbed by her
activities that she put away all longing for other girls who did not
share them.[2] If we had the full works of Sappho, they would surely

---

[1] Fr. 94 L.–P. See G. Zuntz, Mnemos. 3rd ser. vii (1938), pp. 83–92. The lines
contain many uncertainties, and I have merely printed what seem to me the best
available supplements, notably as follows: In 11 Zuntz's μόλθακα, after Wilamowitz's μάλθακα, gives a suitable sense. In 13 Sitzler's σφακίων is better than his
κροκίων, which is an unknown form. In 14 Blass's κἀνήτω is at least in character in
the context. In 17 Theander's ἔβαλες provides a verb where one is needed. In 18
πάνται is Zuntz's reading of the papyrus. In 23 Lobel's νεανίδων seems to be the
only word possible, and I have added αἶψα to fill the gap. In 24 a possible alternative to Zuntz's χόρος is γάμος.

[2] The words ἐξίης πόθον recall the Homeric ἔρον ἔντο, εἶναι, εἴην in the sense of
'put away desire for' food and drink, dance and song. But πόθος is not the same as
ἔρος, and though the Homeric phrases indicate satiety after the appetites have been
indulged, πόθος indicates desire for someone absent, and the notion is that even
this is set aside.

contain many references to this kind of existence. In the grief of separation Sappho sees the past with the clarity of vivid recollection and almost lives it again. The catalogue of happy occasions might in less skilful hands have become trivial, but Sappho skims lightly through them and evokes their happiness. The simplicity of her manner has some of the qualities of the conversation which she claims to record, and it is hard not to believe that some such conversation took place, and that its substance was not entirely different from this record of it.

The lines with which our text begins strike an almost tragic note. They are what Sappho feels now that the parting is over and its painfulness comes fully back to her. The convention that lovers wish to die has been common in poetry since the Hellenistic age, and though it reflects a genuine emotion, it is often a cliché that lacks sincerity. But we feel that when Sappho says it, she means it. Her words are so unadorned that we take them literally and believe her when she claims to speak ἀδόλως. It looks as if her feeling of desertion, of isolation, had so taken the life out of her that annihilation seemed desirable. It may have been in a similar mood that she wrote the lines:

κατθάνην δ' ἴμερός τις [ἔχει με καὶ
λωτίνοις δροσόεντας [ὄ-
χ[θ]οις ἴδην Ἀχέρ[οντος.[1]

A desire to die possesses me, and to see the lotus-covered dewy shores of Acheron.

The vision of Acheron, with its vivid details, implies a less violent grief. Sappho is at least able to ask what death means, but in our poem the thought of it is too strong to allow any close forecast of its nature, and she can escape from it only by memories of the recent past.

The hint in this poem that Sappho shared the feelings and the interests of her young companions is confirmed by the remains of another poem which is concerned, if not with parting, at least with absence. After two broken lines, which seem to refer to a girl in Sardis, the papyrus continues:

ὠσπ . . . . . ώομεν, ... χ . . -
σε θέαι σ' ἰκέλαν ἀρι-
5 γνώται, σαι δὲ μάλιστ' ἔχαιρε μόλπαι·

[1] Fr. 95. 11–13 L.–P.

νῦν δὲ Λύδαισιν ἐμπρέπεται γυναί-
κεσσιν, ὡς ποτ' ἀελίω
8 δύντος ἀ βροδοδάκτυλος σελάννα

πάντα περ⟨ρ⟩έχοισ' ἄστρα· φάος δ' ἐπι-
σχει θάλασσαν ἐπ' ἀλμύραν
11 ἴσως καὶ πολυανθέμοις ἀρούραις·

ἀ δ' ⟨ἐ⟩έρσα κάλα κέχυται, τεθά-
λαισι δὲ βρόδα κἄπαλ' ἄν-
14 θρυσκα καὶ μελίλωτος ἀνθεμώδης·

πόλλα δὲ ζαφοίταισ' ἀγάνας ἐπιμνάσθεισ' Ἀτθιδος ἰμέρωι
17 λέπταν ποι φρένα· κᾶρ ⟨δ'⟩ ἄσαι βόρηται.[1]

She (thought) you like a manifest goddess, and in your song was her
chief delight. But now she stands out among the women of Lydia, as,
after the sun has set, the rosy-fingered moon surpassing all the stars. It
sheds light alike over the salt sea and the flowering fields. The dew is
spread in beauty, the roses bloom, and tender chervil and blossoming
melilot. She wanders to and fro, remembering gentle Atthis with
longing in her young heart, and her spirit is heavy with longing.

The 'you' in the poem must surely be the same as Atthis who is
named in 16; for it is unlikely that Sappho, having said that the
absent friend delights in 'your song', should so soon mention
another girl in so strong terms. Of Atthis we know something.
We have seen that she was chidden by Sappho for turning to
Andromeda, and this poem may have been composed before that
happened. It should, too, be earlier than the lines which Sappho
wrote after she had ceased to love her:

ἠράμαν μὲν ἔγω σέθεν, Ἄτθι, πάλαι ποτά . . .
σμίκρα μοι πάις ἔμμεν' ἐφαίνεο κἄχαρις.[2]

I loved you Atthis once on a time . . . You seemed to me a little girl
without charm.

---

[1] Fr. 96 L.–P. See Zuntz, op. cit. pp. 92–108. In 4 it looks as if -σε were the end
of an aorist verb with some such meaning as 'thought'. Page's ἔτι|σε would re-
quire ὡς. In 8 the papyrus gives μῆνα, which is unmetrical. Schubart's σελάννα
restores the metre, but raises difficulties of sense. In 15 I follow Zuntz in taking
ζαφοίταισ' to be the 3rd person of the present indicative, ζαφοίταισι, for which there
is a good parallel in Alcaeus fr. 347. 2 L.–P., δίψαισι. The alternative is to take it as
a present participle, but this is clumsy in the proximity of ἐπιμνάσθεισ'. In 17 I
follow Wilamowitz in inserting δ' to avoid asyndeton, and take βόρηται to be related
to βαρέομαι. [2] Fr. 49 L.–P.

Though the two lines probably come from the same poem,[1] it is hard to believe that they are consecutive; for the statement that Atthis seemed to be without charm is an inconsequent anticlimax after Sappho's declaration of her former love for her. It seems more likely that in this poem Sappho told how Atthis, who at first did not appeal to her, later won her love. We do not know who the absent girl is who thinks of Atthis, or indeed much more than that she is in Lydia. In antiquity Atthis was connected both by Maximus of Tyre[2] and by the author of the *Epistle of Sappho*[3] with Anactoria as chief among Sappho's maidens, and since Anactoria's absence is associated by Sappho with Lydian chariots, the absent girl may possibly be she. What stirs Sappho is the love of the two girls for one another. The absent girl used to think Atthis a manifest goddess, and the tribute must be to her beauty and her charms. It recalls the words which Homer makes the old men of Troy say about Helen:

$$\alpha \grave{\iota} \nu \hat{\omega} s \ \grave{\alpha} \theta \alpha \nu \acute{\alpha} \tau \eta \sigma \iota \ \theta \epsilon \hat{\eta} s \ \epsilon \grave{\iota} s \ \mathring{\omega} \pi \alpha \ \mathring{\epsilon} o \iota \kappa \epsilon \nu^4$$

'she is terribly like the immortal goddesses to look upon.' Sappho may have had this in her mind, but she transposed it into her own medium by adding the important word ἀριγνώται, which Homer uses of gods who reveal themselves to men and force their divine character on human notice.[5] So here, when Sappho says that the absent friend regarded Atthis as a manifest goddess, it is the highest possible tribute. The girl who once seemed to lack charm has become a rival in her beauty to divine beings. In the later part of the poem, which is for the most part too broken to yield any sense, Sappho seems to pick up the comparison with a goddess:

$$\epsilon] \mathring{\nu} \mu \alpha \rho [\epsilon s \ \mu] \grave{\epsilon} \nu \ o \mathring{\nu} \kappa \ \mathring{\alpha} \mu \mu \iota \ \theta \acute{\epsilon} \alpha \iota \sigma \iota \ \mu \acute{o} \rho -$$
$$\phi \alpha \nu \ \grave{\epsilon} \pi \acute{\eta} \rho [\alpha \tau] o \nu \ \grave{\epsilon} \xi \acute{\iota} \sigma \omega -$$
23 $\quad \sigma \theta \alpha \iota \ \sigma \upsilon [\ . \ .] \rho o s \ \mathring{\epsilon} \chi \eta \iota \sigma \theta' \ \grave{\alpha} [\ . \ . \ . \ .] \nu \acute{\iota} \delta \eta o \nu$

it is not easy for us to rival goddesses in loveliness of form, but you (?). . . .

Sappho knows that the praise is high, but none the less insists upon it.

Eight lines of this poem are taken up by a simile in which the

---

[1] Of the nine ancient authorities who quote the lines only Terentianus Maurus, *de Metr.* 2154-5 (vi. 390 Keil), suggests that they are consecutive.
[2] 18. 9.   [3] 17-18.
[4] *Il.* 3. 158.   [5] *Il.* 13. 72; 14. 490.

absent girl among the women of Lydia is compared with the
moon among the stars. This simile does not occur in Homer, who
indeed at one point suggests that the stars shine most brightly
when the moon is among them.[1] Sappho relies on her own observation, and we can surmise what is in her mind. In Mytilene
the moon rises across the sea over the Asiatic mainland, and its
appearance might well remind her of the girl in Sardis. But the
chief interest of the simile is the way in which it is developed. It
begins simply enough by illustrating how a girl's beauty outshines all around her; then it tells how the moon sheds light over
sea and land and suggests that this beauty is λάμπρον, rather as is
the ἀμάρυχμα of Anactoria's face. Finally, Sappho picks up the
common notion that the moon nourishes the dew,[2] and the
implication is that in a like way the girl gives life to all around her.
Unlike many Homeric similes, which advance beyond the immediate point of comparison to something purely decorative and
even irrelevant, Sappho's comparison of the girl with the moon
may be pressed in its main details. She does not identify the moon
with the girl, but she sees her as like it in the brilliant and re-
viving power of her beauty.

With her powerful inclinations and the way of life which they
fostered, Sappho formed her own approach to the gods. Though
she mentions Artemis, Apollo, and Hera[3], the chief divinity in
her life was Aphrodite. Though there is no evidence that she held
any official post as priestess, Sappho was deeply concerned with
Aphrodite simply because she was the goddess of love. But
Aphrodite is not merely the goddess of love, or, rather, because
she is, she is also much besides. She is as much the goddess of
beauty as of the desire for it. She is the goddess of flowers and
of the smiling, incalculable sea. Her power lies in the enchantment which she throws over visible things, and therefore her
attendants are Eros and Peitho, Desire and Attraction, as Phei-
dias depicted them at Olympia.[4] But since the strongest of all
enchantments is that of the human form, the goddess who gives it
is responsible for the spell which it lays on all who see it. In her
own way Aphrodite stands for an absolute value, for the magic

---

[1] *Il.* 8. 555 f.
[2] See the passages quoted by Housman on Man. 4. 501, especially Ptol. *Tetr.* p. 5;
Plut. *de Fac. in Orb. Lun.* 25; *Qu. Symp.* 3. 10. 14 ff.; Hermipp. 71; Verg. *G.* 3. 337;
Macr. *Sat.* 7. 16. 21.   [3] Frs. 84. 6; 208; 17. 2 L.–P.   [4] Paus. 5. 11. 8.

light which falls at times on life and makes someone or something seem so desirable that men are driven almost to madness. Therefore the Greeks regarded the gifts of Aphrodite as akin to madness and thought that her girdle contained those arts of enticement 'which steal away the wits even of the wise'.[1] In the beauty of girls, and the enchantment which it laid upon her, Sappho saw the work of Aphrodite, and because she was the presiding deity of her own powerful longings, she found in her both strength and consolation.

For Sappho, as for other Greeks of her time, the gods were real beings, not abstractions but divine personalities, with whom it was possible to form almost intimate relations. The varieties of religious experience are so multifarious, and belief so imposes its own interpretation on them, that we must take Sappho at her word and accept what she says as the record of what she believes to have happened. In two poems she treats of Aphrodite at some length, and in both she is concerned with an epiphany of the goddess. The first, which is abominably preserved on a potsherd of the third century B.C., has certainly an air of cult about it, and though Sappho's position may not be official, she certainly officiates. The situation seems to be that, with her friends about her, she summons Aphrodite to their midst:

δεῦρύ μ' ἐκ Κρήτας ἐπ[ὶ τόνδ]ε ναῦον
ἄγνον, ὄππ[αι τοι] χάριεν μὲν ἄλσος
μαλί[αν], βῶμοι δὲ τεθυμιάμε-
4   νοι [λι]βανώτωι.

ἐν δ' ὕδωρ ψῦχρον κελάδει δι' ὔσδων
μαλίνων, βρόδοισι δὲ παῖς ὁ χῶρος
ἐσκίαστ', αἰθυσσομένων δὲ φύλλων
8   κῶμα κατέρρει.

ἐν δὲ λείμων ἱππόβοτος τέθαλεν
ἠρίνοισιν ἄνθεσιν, ἐν δ' ἄηται
μέλλιχα πνέοισιν[
12   [   ]

ἔνθα δὴ σὺ στέμματ' ἔλοισα, Κύπρι,
χρυσίαισιν ἐν κυλίκεσσιν ἄβρως
ὀμμεμείχμενον θαλίαισι νέκταρ
16   οἰνοχόαισον.[2]

---

[1] Il. 14. 216–17.
[2] Fr. 2 L.–P In the main I reproduce the text as given by Page, S. and A. p. 34,

Come hither from Crete to this holy temple, where is your graceful grove of apple-trees, and altars smoking with frankincense. In it cool water sounds through apple-boughs; all the place is shadowed with roses, and from the quivering leaves sleep comes down. In it a meadow blossoms with spring flowers, where horses pasture, and there the breezes breathe sweetly. . . . There, Cyprian, take chaplets and pour softly in gold cups nectar mingled with our feasting.

We do not know what preceded or followed these verses, but, as they stand, they give a clear and charming picture of a religious occasion in which Sappho seems to play a leading part.

The song takes the form of a κλητικὸς ὕμνος and summons the goddess from the shrine where she is believed to be to a place where rites await her. In this case Aphrodite is summoned from Crete, which was claimed by its inhabitants to be the original home of her worship.[1] Since she was worshipped at Cnossus as Ἄνθεια[2] and had in general a connexion with gardens, as at Athens ἐν Κήποις,[3] the spring was a special season for her. So Sappho chooses a time and a place which suit her character. Though Sappho plainly delights in the charming setting, each element in it is relevant to the worship of Aphrodite. The apple was one of her emblems, and at Magnesia on the Maeander she was worshipped as Ἀφροδίτη μηλεία.[4] Horses too had a place in her system and ἔφιππος was one of her titles.[5] In making her hymn tell of the place where the rite is to be held, Sappho suggests to the goddess that it is well suited to her different functions, and implies that at such a place and in such a season she will enjoy a proper welcome.

The fourth stanza gives the inner meaning of the occasion. When the goddess comes, she is to take part in some kind of feast. The presence of gods at feasts was common enough. Pindar composed his *Olympian* III for one at Acragas, when the Dioscuri

---

but in 8 Sitzler's κατέρρει seems a better correction of the meaningless κατάγριον of the sherd than Page's καταίρει. For κατέρρει cf. Erinna fr. 1. 2 D. καταρρεῖ, quoted by Hermog. π. ἰδ. β 4 (p. 331 Rabe), is not a Lesbian form. In 10 Lobel's ἐν δ' ἄηται gets rid of an awkward definite article in αἰ δ' ἄηται. In 13 Norsa's στεμματ' gives the right kind of sense and has some support on the sherd.

[1] Diod. Sic. 5. 77.
[2] Hesych. Ἄνθεια . . . καὶ Ἀφροδίτη, παρὰ Κνωσίοις.
[3] Κῆποι was the name of a district, Paus. 1. 19. 2, but must have been in some sense descriptive.
[4] B. Head, *Hist. Num.* p. 502; Farnell, *Cults*, ii, p. 743.
[5] Schol. *Il.* 2. 820.

were believed to be present. Other such θεοξένια were held in honour of Apollo at Pellene,[1] of Leto at Delphi,[2] and of Dionysus in Crete.[3] On such occasions the god was thought to be invisibly present at the feast given in his honour. Sappho goes farther than this. She calls Aphrodite not merely to be present but to pour nectar in golden chalices. It is surely impossible to believe that by 'nectar' Sappho means something else such as her song[4] or the sweetness of love.[5] Her clear, concrete vision does not work in this way, and when she calls for nectar, she must mean the drink of the gods. In another place she seems to have told how Aphrodite pours nectar from a golden vessel,[6] and no doubt such an idea was natural to her. The action asked of the goddess gives the religious meaning of the rite. While Sappho and her companions celebrate their feast, Aphrodite is thought to be among them and to mingle nectar with their wine. The earthly occasion has a divine significance.

As a counterpart to this poem we may set another, which is probably the only complete poem by Sappho which has come down to us. In discussing ἡ γλαφυρὰ σύνθεσις 'the smooth mode of composition', Dionysius quotes in illustration an ode of Sappho:

> ποικιλόθρον' ἀθανάτ'Ἀφρόδιτα,
> παῖ Δίος δολόπλοκε, λίσσομαί σε,
> μή μ' ἄσαισι μηδ' ὀνίαισι δάμνα,
> 4 πότνια, θῦμον·
>
> ἀλλὰ τυίδ' ἔλθ', αἴ ποτα κἀτέρωτα
> τὰς ἔμας αὔδας ἀίοισα πήλοι
> ἔκλυες, πάτρος δὲ δόμον λίποισα
> 8 χρύσιον ἦλθες
>
> ἄρμ' ὑπασδεύξαισα· κάλοι δέ σ' ἆγον
> ὦκεες στροῦθοι περὶ γᾶς μελαίνας
> πύκνα δίννεντες πτέρ' ἀπ' ὠράνωἴθε-
> 12 ρος διὰ μέσσω·

---

[1] Schol. Pind. Ol. 9. 146; Paus. 7. 27, 4.
[2] Polemo ap. Athen. 9. 372 a.
[3] Callim. fr. 43. 86 P. (θεοδαίσια).
[4] C. Theander, Philol. xcii (1937), p. 466 n. 1.
[5] P. Von der Mühll, Mus. Helv. iii (1946), p. 25.
[6] Fr. 96. 26–28 L.–P.   ]ος Ἀφροδίτα
   καμ[   ]νέκταρ ἔχευ' ἀπὺ
   χρυσίας[

αἶψα δ' ἐξίκοντο· σὺ δ', ὦ μάκαιρα,
μειδιαίσαισ' ἀθανάτωι προσώπωι
ἤρε' ὄττι δηὖτε πέπονθα κὤττι
16   δηὖτε κάλημμι,

κὤττι μοι μάλιστα θέλω γένεσθαι
μαινόλαι θύμωι· τίνα δηὖτε πείθω
ἆψ †σάγην ἐς σὰν φιλότατα; τίς σ', ὦ
20   Ψάπφ', ἀδικήει;

καὶ γὰρ αἰ φεύγει, ταχέως διώξει,
αἰ δὲ δῶρα μὴ δέκετ', ἀλλὰ δώσει.
αἰ δὲ μὴ φίλει, ταχέως φιλήσει
24   κωὔ κε θέλοισα.

ἔλθε μοι καὶ νῦν, χαλέπαν δὲ λῦσον
ἐκ μερίμναν, ὄσσα δέ μοι τέλεσσαι
θῦμος ἰμέρρει, τέλεσον· σὺ δ' αὔτα
28   σύμμαχος ἔσσο.[1]

Immortal Aphrodite, of the patterned throne, daughter of Zeus, weaver of wiles, I beseech you, subdue not my heart, lady, with pangs or sorrows, but come hither, if ever before at other times you heard my voice from afar and hearkened to it, and left your father's house and came, yoking your golden chariot. Beautiful swift sparrows brought you, fluttering their multitudinous wings, over the black earth from the sky through the middle air, and swiftly they came. And you, Blessed One, with a smile on your immortal face, asked what again is the matter with me, and why again I call, and what most of all in my frenzied heart I wish to happen: 'Whom now am I to persuade to come (?) into your friendship? Who wrongs you, Sappho? Even if she flees, soon shall she pursue; if she receives not gifts, yet shall she give, and if she loves not, soon shall she love, even though she would not.' Come to me now also, and deliver me from harsh cares, and all that my heart longs to accomplish, accomplish it, and be yourself my fellow-fighter.

This is not a public but a private poem, not a hymn for a festival but a personal appeal from Sappho to her goddess. Later of course Sappho must have made it known to others, but the mood and the situation of which it tells concern nobody but herself and Aphrodite.

[1] Fr. 1 L.–P. The only serious crux is 19, where *Ox. Pap.* xxi. 2288 seems to give ἆψ. The solution ἄψ σ' ἄγην ἐς ϝὰν φιλότατα, following Edmonds *L.G.* i, p. 186, gives an awkward sense, as ἄγην must mean something like 'lead'. Page's τάγην is not sufficiently to the point and smacks too much of the parade-ground. It looks as if σάγην hid some word for 'come'.

The poem is cast in the form of a prayer and obeys the usual rules for entreating the gods to do something. It may be illustrated by an early and simple example, the prayer of Achilles to Zeus, when Patroclus goes out to battle:

Ζεῦ ἄνα, Δωδωναῖε, Πελασγικέ, τηλόθι ναίων,
Δωδώνης μεδέων δυσχειμέρου· ἀμφὶ δὲ Σελλοὶ
σοὶ ναίουσ᾽ ὑποφῆται ἀνιπτόποδες χαμαιεῦναι.
ἠμὲν δή ποτ᾽ ἐμὸν ἔπος ἔκλυες εὐξαμένοιο,
τίμησας μὲν ἐμέ, μέγα δ᾽ ἴψαο λαὸν Ἀχαιῶν,
ἠδ᾽ ἔτι καὶ νῦν μοι τόδ᾽ ἐπικρήηνον ἐέλδωρ.[1]

King Zeus, lord of Dodona, Pelasgian, dwelling afar, ruler of stormy Dodona; about you dwell the Selli, your interpreters, who wash not their feet and sleep on the ground. Once indeed you hearkened to my word when I prayed, and brought honour to me, and oppressed greatly the people of the Achaeans; now again accomplish this prayer for me.

The straightforward procedure is what we might expect in a religion which allowed a considerable element of contract in the relations of gods and men.[2] First, comes the Invocation. The god is addressed with a suitable accumulation of epithets and references to his powers and places, as befit him in his majesty and show the range of his rule. This is what courtesy and respect demand, and is indispensable for the formal opening. Second comes the Sanction. The person who prays refers to services which he has rendered to the god or the god has rendered to him. This establishes his credentials, his qualifications, his right to receive help again. Third there is the Entreaty. The god is asked to do something suited to his sphere and well within his scope. Sappho observes this form and follows its principles, but at each stage she makes her own individual variations and gives her personal touch.

First, in the Invocation Sappho calls Aphrodite ποικιλόθρον᾽ and suggests that she imagines Aphrodite seated on her throne on Olympus, as Zeus and Hera are depicted on the François vase.[3] No doubt the adjective suggests that such a throne is finely wrought as befits the throne of a goddess, but the whole conception is of Aphrodite enthroned on high in the seat of divine power.

[1] Il. 16. 233–8.
[2] T. Zielinski, The Religion of Ancient Greece, p. 135.
[3] G. M. A. Richter, Ancient Furniture, pp. 3 ff.; Page, S. and A. p. 5.

That she is 'immortal' goes almost without saying, but is not without a point. It is this which gives Aphrodite her power and sets her above the troubles and uncertainties of humankind. Then she is called δολόπλοκε. 'Theognis' liked the idea and gave his own interpretation of it:

Κυπρογενὲς Κυθέρεια δολοπλόκε, σοί τι περισσὸν
Ζεὺς τόδε τιμήσας δῶρον ἔδωκεν ἔχειν·
δαμνᾷς δ' ἀνθρώπων πυκινὰς φρένας, οὐδέ τίς ἐστιν
οὕτως ἴφθιμος καὶ σοφὸς ὥστε φυγεῖν.[1]

Born in Cyprus, Cytherean, weaver of wiles, Zeus, honouring thee, gave to thee in over-abundance this gift to keep; thou subduest the prudent minds of men, nor is there anyone strong and wise enough to escape from thee.

If Sappho is to get what she desires, she will need the goddess's craft as well as her power, and she is not afraid or ashamed of saying so. These adjectives are not cult-epithets. They express what Sappho sees in Aphrodite and what hopes she places in her.

The Sanction occupies the greater part of the poem and occupies the second to the fifth verse inclusive. In it Sappho appeals not to services which she has rendered to the goddess but to services which the goddess has rendered to her,[2] and thus invokes her generosity rather than her gratitude. She assumes that because Aphrodite has helped her in the past, she will be willing to do it again, and she asks for it almost as an obligation on the goddess. That is why she tells at length how in the past Aphrodite came to her, and repeats what she then said. The first reminds the goddess clearly of the occasion; the second implies that, if she then promised to give help, the promise still holds. The whole approach is almost between friends. Sappho feels that she stands in a special relation to Aphrodite, and that Aphrodite regards her with special favour.

The Entreaty is no more than a single stanza, but each word counts and shows what Sappho means by her request. As the goddess of love, Aphrodite is responsible for its pangs and sorrows, and Sappho asks her to take them away. She means of course that she wishes her love to be fulfilled, but she states this vaguely, and perhaps modestly. The words ὅσσα δέ μοι τέλεσσαι θῦμος

---

[1] 1385-8.
[2] So too Diomedes, *Il.* 5. 115 ff.; 10. 284 ff.; Soph. *O.T.* 163 ff.; Pind. *Isthm.* 6. 42 ff.

ἰμέρρει, τέλεσον suggest that her unrevealed desires are known to
the goddess and that it is unnecessary and almost impertinent to
state them openly. If Aphrodite does what Sappho asks, she will
relieve her of the μέριμναι which harass her, and will fight on her
side. The metaphor from the battlefield has its point. Aphrodite
was notoriously ἄμαχος, a goddess against whom even gods do
not fight.[1] It was important to have her as an ally, and this is
what Sappho asks of her.

In this poem Sappho describes with circumstantial detail
Aphrodite's appearance to her. This is not a conventional or
common theme of Greek poetry, but it is not without precedents
or parallels. In the *Iliad*, when Achilles is on the point of drawing
his sword on Agamemnon, Athene appears to him alone and
stops him.[2] In the *Odyssey* Athene often appears to Odysseus, and
the poet recognizes that the gods do not appear in bodily presence to all men.[3] Sappho tells of herself what Homer tells of
especially chosen heroes, and we have no reason to doubt her
word. The appearance of Aphrodite must be treated as a genuine
experience, even if it is hardly possible to translate it into modern
terms. There is no hint that it is a dream, and indeed it can hardly
be one; for it comes in answer to a prayer which Sappho presumably made in her conscious, waking hours. It is certainly
more like a vision, and a vision in which something is revealed
with unusual clarity and force. The golden chariot, the sparrows
which draw it, the smile on the face of Aphrodite, are precisely
and carefully related. Such an experience is by no means impossible for a woman who believed implicitly in the existence of
Aphrodite and passed hours of imaginative communion with her.
The poem shows that Sappho thought herself to be specially
favoured, and this would strengthen her belief in the visitations
of the goddess. It is never easy to get to the heart of religious
experience, but we have no reason to assume that the Greeks did
not sincerely believe themselves to be visited at times in visible
presence by gods. Pindar claims that he saw the hero Alcmaeon
on the road to Delphi,[4] and it is hard not to suspect some personal experience behind his account of the appearance of Poseidon to Pelops in the darkness,[5] while all Greece believed that

---

[1] Soph. *Ant.* 800; fr. 941 P.; Eur. *Hipp.* 530 ff.
[2] *Il.* 1. 194 ff.   [3] *Od.* 16. 161.   [4] *Pyth.* 8. 56–60.
[5] *Ol.* 1. 71 ff.; cf. 6. 61 ff. where Iamus hears the voice of Poseidon.

Philippides saw Pan on Mount Cyllene in Arcadia in 490.[1] It is not after all surprising that Sappho believed that she had seen Aphrodite and spoken with her.

Though this poem tells of an unusual and highly intimate experience, it is not solemn. It is of course serious, because it is passionately sincere, but it lacks the absorbing self-importance which makes for solemnity. There is in it a touch almost of gaiety, of friendly humour, of smiling comprehension between Aphrodite and Sappho. This appears at the start when Sappho calls the goddess δολόπλοκε. It might seem irreverent or discourteous or at least unsuitable for the moment of supplication, but it is none of these. Simonides goes even farther when he calls Eros σχέτλιε παῖ δολόμηδες Ἀφροδίτας.[2] The gods are known for what they are, and guile was part of the character of Aphrodite and Eros. Sappho refers to it without impertinence and even with a kind of admiration. Her regard for the majesty of Aphrodite is mixed with an appreciation of her wiliness, and she speaks to her in almost the same spirit as Athene speaks admiringly to Odysseus:

> κερδαλέος κ' εἴη καὶ ἐπίκλοπος ὅς σε παρέλθοι
> ἐν πάντεσσι δόλοισι, καὶ εἰ θεὸς ἀντιάσειε.[3]

Cunning would he be, and a trickster, who would outdo you in all wiles, even though it were a god who came against you.

Sappho is intimate enough with Aphrodite to be able to speak freely to her without any false reservations or unjustified humility.

This candour is repaid by Aphrodite in what is almost a humorous tolerance. After her passage through the sky in her golden chariot, her first act is to smile on Sappho. It is indeed the smile of a goddess familiarly known as φιλομμειδής, and we must imagine it in all the enchantment which it implies, but it is not merely a smile of friendliness or favour. It anticipates what Aphrodite is going to say. She asks what she can do, and says firmly that the situation is not new. The thrice repeated δηῦτε shows that she has already had experience of Sappho's troubles and helped her in them.[4] She wishes to know what the new trouble is and what she can do about it. She goes even farther than this. When she asks Sappho whom she can bring back into her love, she must already know the answer. The whole episode is

---

[1] Hdt. 6. 105. 1.
[2] Fr. 24 D.; cf. Ox. Pap. 2432. 9–10.
[3] Od. 13. 291–2.
[4] Page, S. and A. pp. 13–15.

at a level of affectionate understanding. Aphrodite knows Sappho and anticipates what her request will be. Then, with a quick change of mood, in the sixth stanza she promises help and speaks with perfect seriousness. Whatever her quiet amusement may have been, she is ready to help and knows what Sappho needs. She speaks with a consciousness of her own powers, which can subdue someone even against her own will, κωὔ κε θέλοισα, to do what Sappho wants. So in the finale, when Sappho turns from the memory of the past visitation to the present crisis, she speaks with an unaffected simplicity and candour and an unhesitating trust in the goddess's help. In this unusual drama of a goddess and a woman, with its cross-currents of past promises and present needs, Sappho marks the changes of mood with effortless ease and records them in words which fly straight to the target and hit the mark. Her relations with Aphrodite may not be religious in any sectarian sense, but no Greek would dispute their seriousness. Sappho speaks of the goddess who rules her life through love, and knows how much comes from her.

This poem throws some light on Sappho's methods of composition. It tells us nothing about the length or the structure of her other poems, and may well differ from them, since it is cast in the form of a prayer and has to suit special demands. But such as it is, it is evidence for her art in composition and suggests more than one conclusion. First, it has a formal balance. The requirements of a prayer are observed both internally and externally. The Invocation receives one complete stanza at the beginning, the Entreaty one complete stanza at the end; the Sanction occupies the rest. The Invocation introduces the theme of Sappho's anguish in ἄσαισι and ὀνίαισι, while the Entreaty picks up the same theme in χαλέπαν μερίμναν. At the start the goddess is asked not to subdue Sappho's θῦμος, and at the end Sappho asks that she may have what her θῦμος desires. The word is important and almost central. It is the spirit which keeps Sappho alive, and she fights for it. Secondly, the Sanction is in effect a single sentence, varied indeed with pauses, but with no complete break at any point. Aphrodite's past visitation is a single memory and experience, and Sappho presents it in its unity. It begins with a prayer of Sappho and ends with words of Aphrodite; it passes from the majesty of Olympus to an earthly scene; it moves from affectionate humour to a solemn promise. The changes rise so naturally from the situation that we hardly notice them, but in the end we see how many different notes have been struck and how easily we pass from one to another. Thirdly, though the Sapphic stanza gives its rhythmical movement to the poem, the sentences run almost counter to its regular progress. There is a heavy stop only at the end of the first, sixth, and last stanzas, that is of the Invocation, the Sanction, and the Entreaty; the rest are linked together by the passage of the sentences from one to another. When a sub-clause occupies a line to itself like

μειδιαίσαισ' ἀθανάτωι προσώπωι

our attention is at once drawn to it and notices its importance. When the rhythm of one line matches exactly that of another, as

καὶ γὰρ αἰ φεύγει, ταχέως διώξει

matches

αἰ δὲ μὴ φίλει, ταχέως φιλήσει,

we see that the two promises are parallel and presented as such. We may doubt whether Sappho always worked in this way, but when she does so here, we appreciate how full her control of her technique is and how skilfully she makes it serve both her powerful emotions and her detached insight into them.

That love was the mainspring of Sappho's poetry we can hardly doubt. Of course she wrote of other matters, but love set her powers to work in a special degree, and she knew it. For with it she associated the Χάριτες or Graces and the Μοῖσαι or Muses. Their close connexion with one another is clear from such a line as

δεῦτέ νυν ἄβραι Χάριτες καλλίκομοί τε Μοῖσαι[1]

'Come hither, gentle Graces, and lovely-haired Muses', which looks like a summons to song, and from another line, whose context is not known, since it is one of a series of quotations in a bibliographical fragment:

ἄγναι Χάριτες Πιέριδές τε Μοῖσαι[2]

'the holy Graces and the Pierian Muses.' The connexion of the Graces with Aphrodite is clear from Himerius' account of a wedding-song, in which Sappho 'brings Aphrodite in a chariot of Graces and a choir of Loves to play with them'.[3] For Sappho the Graces meant, as they did to most Greeks, the divine powers who

---

[1] Fr. 128 L.–P.   [2] Fr. 103. 8 L.–P.   [3] *Or.* 46. 6 Colonna.

shed or reveal the beauty of the world. Since they are concerned with beauty in all forms, they are concerned with the beauty of those whom Sappho loves, and with the Muses, who transform her anguish and her delight into song. Just as she summons the Graces and calls them the daughters of Zeus, as if they were the worthy sisters of Aphrodite,

βροδοπάχεες ἄγναι Χάριτες δεῦτε Δίος κόραι[1]

'Come hither, rosy-armed, holy Graces, daughters of Zeus', so she also summons the Muses from what looks as if it were the golden house of Zeus:

δεῦρο δηῦτε Μοῖσαι χρύσιον λίποισαι. . .[2]

'Come hither again, Muses, leaving the golden . . . .' We can hardly question that in these summonses Sappho wished the Graces and Muses to aid her in song. If the mainspring of her art was love sent by Aphrodite, it was turned into song by the help of the Graces and the Muses. However earthly some of its matter might be, her song had the sanction and the assistance of the gods.

Through song Sappho mastered her troubles by turning them into melody. But it meant so much to her that she saw more in it than this and regarded it as more than an end in itself. It was a source of pride to her that she would be remembered in times to come:

μνάσεσθαί τινά φαιμι καὶ ἄψερον ἀμμέων[3]

'I say that someone will remember us afterwards', but the full implications of such a conviction can be seen more forcibly in four lines in which she speaks, not without scorn, to a woman who will not be so remembered:

κατθάνοισα δὲ κείσηι, οὐδέ ποτα μναμοσύνα σέθεν
ἔσσετ' οὐδὲ πόθα εἰς ἄψερον· οὐ γὰρ πεδέχηις βρόδων
τῶν ἐκ Πιερίας, ἀλλ' ἀφάνης κἀν Ἀίδα δόμωι
φοιτάσηις πεδ' ἀμαύρων νεκύων ἐκπεποταμένα.[4]

---

[1] Fr. 53 L.–P.　　　　　　　　　　　　[2] Fr. 127 L.–P.

[3] Fr. 147 L.–P., with Lobel's correction of ἔτερον to ἄψερον.

[4] Fr. 55 L.–P. In 2 I keep Wilamowitz's οὐδὲ πόθα εἰς as giving better sense than Page's οὐδ' ἴα τοίς, which is a little overweighted. Aristid. Or. 28. 51 may refer to these lines, οἶμαι δέ σε καὶ Σαπφοῦς ἀκηκοέναι πρός τινας τῶν εὐδαιμόνων δοκούσων εἶναι μεγαλαυχουμένης καὶ λεγούσης ὡς αὐτὴν αἱ Μοῦσαι τῷ ὄντι ὀλβίαν τε καὶ ζηλωτὴν ἐποίησαν καὶ ὡς οὐδ' ἀποθανούσης ἔσται λήθη.

When you have died, you shall lie there, and there will never be memory of you or longing hereafter; for you have no share in the roses from Pieria; but in the House of Death also you shall walk unseen with the unsubstantial dead, when you have flown from here.

Obviously Sappho compares herself with this woman and marks the difference between those who have cultivated the Muses and those who have not. The woman will be forgotten after death and for this reason have but a dim and unsubstantial after-life, but Sappho, it is clear, expects something better. She assumes that she will be remembered, rather as Theognis says that the name of Cyrnus will live on the lips of men[1] or Pindar that even great acts of prowess have a deep darkness if they lack song.[2] Sappho believes that her own song will save her from oblivion and from too shadowy an existence after death. Perhaps she thought that, like Orpheus, she would be translated to some Elysian fields;[3] more probably that she would have some kind of life in the memories of men. Her song was the centre of her being, her pride and delight and consolation, and she trusted in it to keep her spirit alive when her body had perished.

Though Sappho seems to have found her chief subjects and her strongest inspiration in the girls whom she loved, she had too her domestic and family life, and when she wrote about it, revealed other sides of her nature. She is said to have praised often her brother Larichus, who poured wine in the Town Hall of Mytilene.[4] She once mentions her mother in an indecipherable context.[5] We know more about her feelings for her daughter Cleïs, to whom she speaks in some lines, which may not be correctly preserved but make impeccable sense:

> ἔστι μοι κάλα πάις χρυσίοισιν ἀνθέμοισιν
> ἐμφέρην ἔχοισα μόρφαν Κλέις ἀγαπάτα,
> ἀντὶ τᾶς ἔγωὐδὲ Λυδίαν παῖσαν οὐδ' ἐράνναν. . . .[6]

I have a beautiful child in form like golden flowers, Cleïs, my beloved, for whom I would not (take) all Lydia or lovely . . . .

[1] 237 ff.   [2] *Nem.* 7. 11–16.   [3] Plat. *Apol.* 41 a.
[4] Athen. 10. 425 a; Schol. T. *Il.* 20. 234; *Ox. Pap.* xv. 1800, col. i. 1–14.
[5] Fr. 98 (b) 1 L.–P.
[6] Fr. 132 L.–P. The real difficulty is that the lines do not conform to Hephaestion's account of the metre, p. 53. 16. Consbruch. Page, *S. and A.* p. 132, suggests rewriting 3 as

> ἀντὶ τᾶς ἔγωὐδὲ Λύδαν ἄπαισαν οὐδ' ἐράνναν,

which makes it correspond with 1.

Sappho values her daughter above kingdoms, and names the richest known to her, Lydia, which had, under the rule of Alyattes, extended its frontiers and begun to accumulate that wealth which later brought Croesus such renown. When Sappho compares Cleïs to flowers, she may base the image on some traditional phrase like ἥβης ἄνθος,[1] but she has freed it from its conventional limits and made it live again in its own right. And she does more than this. When she adds the epithet 'golden', she does not mean that Cleïs is like the flower called χρυσάνθεμον,[2] which seems to have been the same as the ἐλίχρυσος,[3] but suggests that on such flowers as she imagines there is a divine light, as Pindar imagines that the Hyperboreans bind their hair δάφνᾳ χρυσέᾳ[4] or that in the Island of the Blest ἄνθεμα χρυσοῦ φλέγει.[5] The beauty of Cleïs is divine in its brilliance.

That Sappho shared some of her interests with Cleïs seems to follow from two lines which are said to have been addressed to her:

οὐ θέμις γὰρ ἐν μοισοπόλων δόμωι
θρῆνον ἔμμεν'· οὔ κ' ἄμμι τάδε πρέποι.[6]

For it is not right that there should be lamentation in the house of those who serve the Muses; it would not be seemly for us.

It looks at least as if Cleïs sometimes took part in songs in her mother's house, and was here told that neither of them should conduct a lament. Another poem is more intimate and more domestic. In the latter part of it, which is too fragmentary to allow even tentative restoration, Sappho seems to speak of her poverty, which prevents her from giving a gay headband to Cleïs, and since a little later she mentions Κλεανακτίδαν, who looks like the tyrant Myrsilus, it is possible that the lines were written in or after exile, and that her poverty was due to it. 'Ovid' echoes some such conditions when he makes Sappho say:

et tamquam desint, quae me sine fine fatigent,
accumulat curas filia parua meas.[7]

---

[1] Il. 13. 484; cf. Hom. Hymn 2. 108 ὥς τε θεαὶ κουρήιον ἄνθος ἔχουσαι.
[2] Dioscor. 4. 58. See Perrotta Saffo e Pindaro, p. 53.
[3] See Gow on Theocr. 1. 30.
[4] Pyth. 10. 40.   [5] Ol. 2. 72.
[6] Fr. 150 L.–P. In 1 I have transposed οὐ γὰρ θέμις of the MSS. to get an exact metrical correspondence. δόμωι is Hartung's correction of the MSS. οἰκίαι. In 2 Lobel transposes πρέποι τάδε to avoid keeping the second syllable of ἄμμι short before πρέποι.   [7] Ep. Sapph. 69–70.

In the earlier part of the poem Sappho discusses a subject suitable to a young girl—what kind of headband should she wear:

> ...] . θος· ἀ γάρ με γέννα[τ’ ἔφα ποτὰ
>
> σ]φᾶς ἐπ’ ἀλικίας μέγ[αν
> κ]όσμον, αἴ τις ἔχηι φόβαις
> 4   πορφύρωι κατελιξαμέ[να πλόκωι,
>
> ἔμμεναι μάλα τοῦτο δ[ή·
> ἀλλὰ ξανθοτέραις ἔχη[ν
> 7   ταῖς κόμαις δάιδος προ[φέρει πόλυ
>
> σ]τεφάνοισιν ἐπαρτία[ις
> ἀνθέων ἐριθαλέων·[
> 10   μιτράναν δ’ ἀρτίως κλ[
>
> ποικίλαν ἀπὺ Σαρδίω[ν
> .... αονίας πόλεις[1]

For she who bore me said that in her day if one had hair bound with a purple headband, that was truly a great ornament; but it is far better to have hair yellower than a torch, fitted with wreaths of blossoming flowers. Lately ... lately a patterned headband from Sardis ... cities

From what follows the point seems to be, that though Sappho cannot afford an expensive headband, she thinks that anyhow for Cleis flowers are better. This is a domestic poem, written for her home, and shows Sappho in her maternal and parental responsibilities.

Another side of Sappho's character may be seen in her relations with her brother Charaxus. Herodotus tells the story. Charaxus went to the Greek colony of Naucratis in the Egyptian Delta, and there he met and loved a famous courtesan called Rhodopis. For a large sum of money he bought her freedom, and, when he returned home, he was severely rated for it by Sappho in a poem.[2] That the burden of Sappho's attack was directed against his extravagance is likely enough, but that she combined this with other criticism follows from 'Ovid''s words:

> sparsit opes frater meretricis captus amore
> mixtaque cum turpi damna pudore tulit.[3]

---

[1] Fr. 98 L.-P. I follow Page, *S. and A.* pp. 97, in his reconstruction of the text, except in 6, where Lobel's suggestion seems neater.

[2] 2. 134 ff. Cf. Strab. 808; Athen. 13. 596 b; *Ox. Pap.* xv. 1800, i. 7–13; Phot. s.v. Ῥοδώπιδος ἀνάθημα.

[3] *Ep. Sapph.* 63–64.

We have nothing of this poem, but since the woman whom Herodotus knew as Rhodopis was known to Sappho by the name of Doricha,[1] her appearance in another poem suggests that Sappho did not relent towards her for being the authoress of her brother's undoing. But she evidently forgave Charaxus. For when he was about to sail home to Lesbos from Egypt, Sappho wrote a poem of which we have some remains:

Κύπρι καὶ] Νηρήϊδες, ἀβλάβη[ν μοι
τὸν κασί]νητον δ[ό]τε τυίδ᾽ ἴκεσθα[ι
κὤσσα ϝ]οι θύμωι κε θέληι γένεσθαι
4 πάντα τε]λέσθην,

ὄσσα δὲ πρ]όσθ᾽ ἄμβροτε πάντα λῦσα[ι,
καὶ φίλοισ]ι ϝοῖσι χάραν γένεσθαι
δάϊόν τ᾽ ἔ]χθροισι, γένοιτο δ᾽ ἄμμι
8 μήποτα μ]ηδ᾽ εἶς·

τὰν κασιγ]νήταν δὲ θέλοι πόησθαι
ἔμμορον] τίμας, [ὀν]ίαν δὲ λύγραν
ἐκλάθοιτ]ο, ταῖσι π[ά]ροιθ᾽ ἀχεύων
12 θῦμον ἐδάμ]να.[2]

Grant, Cyprian and Nereids, that my brother may come here unharmed, and that all that he wishes in his heart to happen may be accomplished; and that he may redeem all his former errors and be a delight to his dear ones, and deadly to his enemies, and may no one ever be deadly to us. May he wish to give honour to his sister, and may he forget the lamentable sorrows with which he laboured before and vexed his spirit.

This is a prayer to Aphrodite and the Nereids for the safe voyage of Charaxus, an early example or an anticipation of a type which was afterwards to become popular, a προπεμπτικόν written for someone about to put out to sea. Erinna seems to have written one for Baucis,[3] and Horace wrote one for Virgil.[4] With time the

---

[1] Fr. 15 (b) 11. Cf. Strab. 808.

[2] Fr. 5 L.–P. See Page, S. and A. pp. 45 ff. In 7 I find κωνίαν difficult to accept, partly because it is too near to ὀνίαν in 10, partly because I feel that a masculine word is needed to explain μηδ᾽ εἶς. I have hesitantly printed δάϊον as the best that I can think of. Sappho prays that she and her brother may not have an enemy who does them harm. In 11 ἐκλάθοιτο gives excellent sense, but can be kept only by altering τοῖσι of the papyrus to ταῖσι. Page's δέσμ᾽ ὄλοιτο introduces a rather inept metaphor. In 12 θῦμον ἐδάμνα gets some justification from fr. 1. 3–4.

[3] Fr. 2 D.

[4] C. 1. 3. See also Theocr. 7. 52–89; Stat. Silu. 3. 2; Callim. fr. 400 P.; Theogn. 691–2; Eur. Hel. 1451 ff.

form became stereotyped, and the rhetorician Menander lays down rules for the proper construction of speeches on such occasions.[1] Sappho knows nothing of such rules and writes from her natural feelings. The Nereids are real divinities. As Εὔπλοια[2] and Γαλανεία,[3] Aphrodite was worshipped as a sea-goddess, and it was natural to associate the Nereids with her. Sappho prays to her own goddess, but invokes her in her special capacity as a goddess of the sea.

In this poem Sappho has evidently forgiven Charaxus and wishes him nothing but good. Hints of his past mistakes may be seen in ἄμβροτε, and of his estrangement from his sister in 6–8. So when we hear of τίμας in 10, Sappho may be referring to the slur which his conduct has brought upon her. She hints too that his infatuation for Doricha is at an end. The word ὀνίαν in 10 suggests love, and Sappho hopes that this, which has been painful and burdensome, may pass away. Towards Doricha she seems to have been less forgiving. For it is probably to this poem that we should assign another fragment:

> Κύ]πρι, κα[ί σ]ε πι[κροτέρ]αν ἐπεύρ[οι,
> μη]δὲ καυχάσ[α]ιτο τόδ' ἐννέ[ποισα
> Δ]ωρίχα, τὸ δεύ[τ]ερον ὡς πόθε[ννον
> εἰς] ἔρον ἦλθε.[4]

Cyprian, may Doricha find you even harsher, and not boast, saying this, that she (he) came a second time to the love which she (he) desired.

It is not certain at the end whether the subject of ἦλθε is Doricha or Charaxus. If it is the second, the point would be that he has not gone back to her; if the first, that she has failed to win him back. Perhaps this is the more likely in view of the absence of any word for 'he', but in either case Sappho wishes that Doricha will be in no position to boast of her continued hold on the man whom she has fleeced of his money.

The passages which we have considered so far are personal and at times almost private and must have been composed by Sappho to be sung in the company of friends. But she wrote other poems of a more formal character in which there was no need to speak of her own feelings or for the performance to be confined to a few companions. Songs were required for more than one kind of

---

[1] *Rhet. Gr.* iii, p. 395 Spengel.
[2] Paus. 1. 1. 3; Anyte, *Anth. Pal.* 9. 144.
[3] Eur. *I.A.* 546. [4] Fr. 15 (b) 8–11 L.–P.

religious ceremony, and Sappho sometimes composed them. Connected with the cult of Aphrodite was that of her young lover, Adonis. He was a vegetation-deity, said to be born from the myrtle-tree, which became his emblem.[1] Autumn fruits were offered to him, and beds of flowers were called 'gardens of Adonis'.[2] Every year he died in the autumn, and in due course was born again. Though in Athens his cult was unimportant, in Lesbos, with its Asiatic connexions, he had a place. That Sappho wrote songs for his ceremonies was known to Dioscorides, who says of her:

> ἢ Κινυρέω νέον ἔρνος ὀδυρομένη Ἀφροδίτῃ
> σύνθρηνος μακάρων ἱερὸν ἄλσος ὁρῇς.[3]

Or, sharing Aphrodite's laments, when she weeps for the young offspring of Cinyras, you behold the holy grove of the Blessed Ones.

The lament for Adonis was connected with the passing of life from orchards and gardens, and the type of song which Sappho wrote for it may have contained some primitive elements. One fragment survives. It is a dialogue between Aphrodite and the nymphs, and it looks as if the priestess took the part of Aphrodite, and her companions that of the nymphs. There is no evidence that Sappho herself took a part or that she did any more than write the song for the occasion.[4] It has the simple directness which we should expect from a song of this kind:

> (Νύμφαι). κατθναίσκει, Κυθέρη', ἄβρος Ἄδωνις· τί κε θεῖμεν;
> (Ἀφροδίτη). καττύπτεσθε, κόραι, καὶ κατερείκεσθε κίθωνας.[5]

Nymphs. Tender Adonis is dying, Cytherea. What should we do?
Aphrodite. Beat your breasts, maidens, and rend your garments.

The tone of lament which characterized such songs may be recognized in the quotation ὦ τὸν Ἄδωνιν,[6] and it is possible that some far, faint echo from Sappho may be heard in Bion's *Lament for Adonis*, where, in spite of the rich and redundant manner, traces of something older and simpler can be seen in the repeated ἀπώλετο καλὸς Ἄδωνις. It is, too, noteworthy that Sappho com-

---

[1] Ov. *Met.* 10. 512.
[2] Plat. *Phaedr.* 276 b; Theophr. *H.P.* 6. 7. 3; cf. Praxilla fr. 2 D.
[3] *Anth. Pal.* 7. 407. 7–8.
[4] Dioscorides indeed implies that she did, but he may be taking too literally the events related in such poems and assuming that Sappho took part in them.
[5] Fr. 140 (a) L.–P.   [6] Fr. 168 L.–P.

bined laments for Adonis with a lament for Linus.[1] Linus, like Adonis, came from the east, and was also a vegetation-god who died yearly. In calling him Οἰτόλινος Sappho indicates that her song was a lament.[2] Such a song was of ancient origin, since it seems to have some relation with the song of the boy in the harvesters' scene on the Shield of Achilles.[3] No doubt the rites and ceremonies of the two gods were sufficiently similar for Sappho to be able to honour them both.

Such songs, composed for ceremonial needs, may perhaps be the origin of the stories of Sappho's death. She was said to have loved a young man called Phaon and to have killed herself for it.[4] In this form the story looks like a creation of Middle and New Comedy,[5] but behind it must have lain some poems of Sappho which afforded material for misunderstanding. The solution is that Phaon was another name for Adonis. Like Adonis, he was loved by Aphrodite, and, like Adonis, he was on some occasion laid among lettuces.[6] He has the marks of a vegetation-deity who was loved and then died. It looks as if Sappho wrote a song in which Aphrodite declared her love for him, and this was misunderstood as being Sappho's love for a living man. The climax of the legend may be seen in the 'Ovidian' *Epistle of Sappho to Phaon*, where he is presented as a beautiful young man, which looks like a variation of the legend, itself a reflection of his annual birth and death, that once he was old but was transformed by Aphrodite into a young man because of a kind service done to her.[7] The confusion was worse confounded by attaching to the story of Phaon another story that Sappho flung herself from the Leucadian Rock into the sea.[8] This was probably due to a misunderstanding or misinterpretation of some proverbial phrase in which Sappho spoke of leaping off the Leucadian rock as the kind of thing that despairing lovers did.[9] So Phaon was located in

---

[1] Fr. 140 (b) L.–P. [2] Ibid.

[3] *Il.* 18. 570.

[4] 'Suid.' s.v. Φάων; Menand. fr. 312 K.

[5] Comedies called Σαπφώ are ascribed to Ameipsias, Amphis, Antiphanes, Diphilus, Ephippus, and Timocles, and with the title Φάων to Plato and Antiphanes. Cratinus ap. Athen. 2. 69 d also dealt with Phaon, but not with Aphrodite's love for him.

[6] Ael. *V.H.* 12. 18; Athen. 2. 69; Comes Natalis, *Mythol.* 5. 16.

[7] 'Palaeph.' *de Incred.* 48; Apostol. 17. 80.

[8] 'Suid.' s.v. Σαπφώ (β') and s.v. Φάων; Strab. 452.

[9] Wilamowitz, *S.u.S.* pp. 25 ff.; cf. Anacr. fr. 17 D.

Leucas and turned into a ferryman there. The truth is that he
was a god, probably to be identified with Adonis, and if she wrote
words of love for him, they were in all likelihood intended to be
spoken by Aphrodite.

Another type of ceremonial song was the ἐπιθαλάμιον or wedding song. Sappho wrote enough of these to occupy a whole book
in her works as they were known at Alexandria. That she should
be asked to write them was almost inevitable. Her chosen goddess, Aphrodite, had the title γαμήλιος,[1] and marriage was after
all the natural and usual destiny of the girls whom Sappho
admired:

> Lesbides aequoreae, nupturaque nuptaque proles.[2]

Though wedding-rites may well have differed in Greece from
place to place and from time to time, they seem to have had certain features which may be recognized in Sappho's verses and
provide some sort of background to them. We must not press too
strongly the precise implications of the word ἐπιθαλάμιον, which
strictly stands for songs at one stage only of the proceedings.
Sappho seems to have written for other stages also, and we must
give a liberal interpretation to ἐπιθαλάμια as wedding-songs in all
their range.

The proceedings began with a feast in the house of the bride's
father and with sacrifices to the gods of marriage.[3] It is of such a
feast that Pindar speaks when a young bridegroom is pledged with
wine in a golden bowl οἴκοθεν οἴκαδε,[4] and it is likely that some
lines of Sappho were composed for such a feast. They tell of a
wedding in which the gods take part, and whether it is of Zeus
and Hera, or Heracles and Hebe, or Peleus and Thetis, it looks
as if it were a divine counterpart to a human occasion and gave
significance to rites which were being held:

> κῆ δ' ἀμβροσίας μὲν
> κράτηρ ἐκέκρατ᾽·
> Ἔρμαις δ' ἔλων ὄλπιν θέοισ᾽ ὠινοχόαισε.
>
> κῆνοι δ' ἄρα πάντες
> καρχάσι᾽ ἦχον
> κἄλειβον· ἀράσαντο δὲ πάμπαν ἔσλα
> τῶι γάμβρωι.[5]

[1] Eur. fr. 781. 17 N.   [2] *Ep. Sapph.* 199.
[3] Athen. 4. 185 b; Lucian *Symp.* 8. 5; Bekker, *An. Gr.* i, pp. 200 and 390.
[4] *Ol.* 7. 1 ff.   [5] Fr. 141 L.–P.

There a bowl of ambrosia had been mixed, and Hermes took the wine-jug and poured for the gods. They all held their beakers and made libations, and wished good things in every way to the bridegroom.

At such a feast the proceedings seem to have been decorous and formal. The bride was veiled and sat apart among her maidens, and ceremonies took place which ended in her being presented by her friends and relatives to the bridegroom. It was perhaps at such a feast that Sappho wrote some lines, in which she speaks of going to a wedding and tells someone to send maidens to it:

σ]τείχομεν γὰρ ἐς γάμον, εὖ δὲ[
κα]ὶ σὺ τοῦτ', ἀλλ' ὅττι τάχιστα[
πα]ρ[θ]ένοις ἄπ[π]εμπε, θέοι[
]εν ἔχοιεν.[1]

For we are going to a wedding, and do you . . . this also well; but send the maidens forth with haste, and may the gods have . . .

She is perfectly serious and treats the occasion with some solemnity. What follows is more mysterious. The broken words give no clear sense:

]όδος μέ[γ]αν εἰς "Ολ[υμπον
ἄ]νθρω[π   ]αικ.[

but the 'way to great Olympus' suggests perhaps a hint either of bridal happiness or a warning against asking for too much, since both Alcman[2] and Pindar[3] use the phrase in such a context.

The second stage consisted of a procession in which the bride rode to her new home in a chariot with her husband[4] and the best man or παράνυμφος.[5] This was a joyful and even rowdy affair, and its character may have been like what Homer describes on the Shield of Achilles.[6] At this stage the ὑμέναιος proper was sung with its refrain of 'Υμὴν ὦ 'Υμέναι' ὦ. Aristophanes composes such songs both in the *Peace* and the *Birds*, and the difference between them shows how wide a range they could cover; for while the first is frank and even bawdy, the second has an exalted gaiety as befits Zeus and Hera whom it celebrates. One fragment of

---

[1] Fr. 27. 8–11. L.–P.
[2] Fr. 1. 16 D. μή τις ἀνθρώπων ἐς ὠρανὸν ποτήσθω.
[3] *Pyth.* 10. 27 ὁ χάλκεος οὐρανὸς οὔ ποτ' ἀμβατὸς αὐτῷ.
[4] Phot. 52. 22; Eur. *Hel.* 723 ff.
[5] Pollux 3. 40.   [6] *Il.* 18. 491–6.

Sappho seems to come from this stage, since it has the Hymeneal refrain and speaks of the bridegroom's arrival:

ἴψοι δὴ τὸ μέλαθρον,
ὑμήναον,
ἀέρρετε, τέκτονες ἄνδρες·

γάμβρος εἶσ' ἴσ' Ἄρευι,
ὑμήναον,
ἄνδρος μεγάλω πόλυ μέζων.[1]

lift high the roof—hail Hymen!—ye skilled craftsmen. A bridegroom comes like Ares—hail Hymen!—far bigger than a big man.

This is neither bawdy nor exalted, but playful. If the humour is a bit primitive, that is due to tradition, which expected jokes at this level.

The third stage was reached when the bride and bridegroom reached the bridal chamber. This came as the evening advanced, and was accompanied by torches. We have two accounts of it. The first comes from Himerius and gives some account of how Sappho treated the occasion:

Most of the poets, when it came to the rites of Aphrodite, left it to Lesbian Sappho alone to sing to the lyre and make a song for the bridal chamber. After the contests, she enters the chamber, weaves the bower, strews the bed, brings the maidens into the bridal-room, brings Aphrodite also on a chariot of Graces with a choir of Loves to play with them. She adorns the bride's hair with hyacinths, except for what is parted by the brow, and leaves the rest to float in the breezes if they strike it. She decks the wings and the hair of the Loves with gold and makes them go before the chariot to escort it and shake torches in the air.[2]

That gives one side of the picture, and so Sappho certainly must at times have presented it. But another view comes from Longus, who need not owe anything to her, but who had his own idea of what a rustic wedding should be:

Then, night having come, all the guests sent them to the nuptial chamber, some with whistles, some with flutes, some lifting great torches. And when they were near the doors they sang with voices harsh and rude, as if they were breaking the earth with mattocks, not singing a wedding-song.[3]

---

[1] Fr. 111 L.–P. with Lobel's εἶσ' ἴσ' Ἄρευι in 5 instead of the MSS. εἰσέρχεται ἴσος Ἄρευι.

[2] *Or.* 9. 4 Colonna.   [3] 4. 40.

This gives the other side of the picture, but it is a useful corrective to Himerius. Neither weddings nor wedding-songs need be quite so lyrical as Himerius suggests, and Sappho herself was well aware of their mixed character.

The arrival at the bridal chamber was an occasion for jests, and in her songs Sappho was not above introducing colloquial or familiar elements; for as Demetrius says:

Very different is the style in which she mocks the clumsy bridegroom or the keeper of the wedding door. It is quite commonplace, and the words are better suited to prose than to poetry. Indeed these poems of hers can better be spoken than sung, and would not be suitable for the chorus or the lyre, unless for a kind of talking chorus.[1]

There was evidently in these songs something like the *Fescennina iocatio* which Catullus put into one of his wedding-songs.[2] Known as κτυπία,[3] this joking abuse was probably meant to avert evil fortune by making out the happy couple to be less fortunate than they were. It may already have been present in the songs sung during the procession, but now in the real ἐπιθαλάμια it took a prominent place. Here too Sappho seems to avoid bawdry but is not averse from rather elementary jokes. A suitable target was the θύρωρος or door-keeper, who locked up the couple in their bridal chamber and was expected to keep out the bride's friends from helping her if she called out.[4] The choir, which consisted of the bride's friends, might well make fun of him, and it is quite in place for Sappho to mock his big feet:

θυρώρωι πόδες ἑπτορόγυιοι,
τὰ δὲ σάμβαλα πεμπεβόηα,
πίσυγγοι δὲ δέκ᾽ ἐξεπόναισαν.[5]

The door-keeper's feet are seven fathoms long; his sandals are made of five hides; ten cobblers laboured to make them.

This is the same kind of humour as that in which she mocks the bridegroom, simple and primitive and traditional. It reflects popular rejoicing and has no trace of Sappho's more intimate and more private manner.

---

[1] *de Eloc.* 167. [2] *C.* 61. 120.
[3] Hesych. s.v. κτυπία· ὁ ἐπιθαλάμιος κτύπος.
[4] Pollux 3. 42 καλεῖται δέ τις τῶν τοῦ νυμφίου φίλων καὶ θυρωρός, ὃς ταῖς θύραις ἐφεστηκὼς εἴργει τὰς γυναῖκας τῇ νύμφῃ βοώσῃ βοηθεῖν. Hesych. s.v. θυρωρός· ὁ παράνυμφος, ὁ τὴν θύραν τοῦ θαλάμου κλείων. Cf. Xen. Eph. 1. 8. 3.
[5] Fr. 110 (a) L.-P.

These passages from the ἐπιθαλάμια show how Sappho conformed to the spirit of wedding celebrations rather as Longus
describes them. But there was another side to this poetry, which
conforms to what Himerius says of it. Mockery was demanded by
custom, but it could be mixed with praise, and especially with
praise of the bride, whom her friends were present to honour.[1]
Some such spirit must have inspired such a line as

ού γὰρ ἦν ἀτέρα πάις, ὦ γάμβρε, τεαύτα[2]

For, bridegroom, there was no other girl like her.

The bridegroom too might receive compliments as well as gibes,
as when Sappho compares him to Achilles,[3] or says to him:

τίωι σ', ὦ φίλε γάμβρε, κάλως ἐικάσδω;
ὄρπακι βραδίνωι σε μάλιστ' ἐικάσδω.[4]

To what, dear bridegroom, am I to compare you well? To a slender
sapling I most compare you.

So both bridegroom and bride are brought together in generous
congratulations:

ὄλβιε γάμβρε, σοὶ μέν δὴ γάμος ὡς ἄραο
ἐκτετέλεστ'· ἔχηις δὲ πάρθενον ὡς ἄραο...
σοὶ χάριεν μὲν εἶδος, ὄππατα δ' ⟨αὖτε νύμφας⟩
μέλλιχ', ἔρος δ' ἐπ' ἰμέρτωι κέχυται προσώπωι
⟨μειδιάων⟩· τετίμακ' ἔξοχά σ' Ἀφροδίτα.[5]

Happy bridegroom, your wedding has been accomplished as you
prayed, and you have the maiden as you prayed. You have a charming beauty, but the eyes of your bride are honey-sweet, and smiling
love is shed on her lovely face. Aphrodite has honoured you exceedingly.

Even here in the repeated ὡς ἄραο there is a touch of the colloquial
manner, but the whole has a truly lyrical ring. Sappho has left
her badinage for something nearer to her heart and more suited
to her gifts.

---

[1] Pind. *Pyth.* 3. 17 ff.
[2] Fr. 113 L.-P. ἦν ἀτέρα is Blomfield's correction for the MSS. ἐτέρα νῦν.
[3] Fr. 105 (b) L.-P.   [4] Fr. 115 L.-P.
[5] Fr. 112 L.-P. In 2 ὡς is a necessary correction for ἀν, since the Lesbian form
would be τάν and spoil the metre. In 3, if σοί is right, it must be addressed to the
bridegroom. I have therefore supplied αὖτε νύμφας. In 5 μειδιάων is a possible
supplement on the analogy of Hom. Hymn 10. 2 ἐφ' ἰμερτῷ δὲ προσώπῳ αἰεὶ
μειδιάει καὶ ἐφ' ἰμερτὸν θέει ἄνθος.

On Sappho's wedding-songs we have some additional but elusive evidence from the sixty-second poem of Catullus, which in places seems to reproduce certain elements of her ἐπιθαλάμια. Catullus has indeed transformed the setting and introduced some purely imaginary themes,[1] but his debt to her is none the less clear. The poem, written in dactylic hexameters, claims to be sung with the approach of evening at the end of the wedding feast, and so belongs to the first stage of the proceedings. This may account for its graceful and dignified character, and its lack both of bawdry and of badinage. It begins with an address to the evening star:

> Vesper adest, iuuenes, consurgite; Vesper Olympo
> exspectata diu uix tandem lumina tollit.[2]

The words are a summons to all to leave the feast and join in the cries to Hymen. Sappho too addresses the Evening Star, and though her second line is corrupt beyond hope of restoration, it is clear that she regards this as a critical moment in the complex sequence of ceremonies:

> Ἔσπερε, πάντα φέρων ὅσα φαίνολις ἐσκέδασ' Αὔως,
> †φέρεις ὄιν, φέρεις αἶγα, φέρεις ἄπυ† μάτερι παῖδα.[3]

Hesperus, who bringest all that the shining dawn scattered, you bring the sheep, you bring the goat, you bring the child back to its mother.

It is not clear how Sappho fitted this into a song, but possibly she went on to say that Hesperus brings also the bride to the bridegroom. They have both been present at the feast, but the bride has sat apart from the bridegroom.[4] If so, the lines refer to the close of the feast; for the bride and bridegroom will now go forth together. A second comparison between Sappho and Catullus may be seen in the contrasted similes which both use to present different points of view on marriage. Catullus' song is divided between young men and maidens. First, the maidens lament the loss which marriage brings to a girl:

---

[1] E. Fraenkel, *J.R.S.* xlv (1955), pp. 3 ff.

[2] *C.* 62. 1–2.

[3] Fr. 104 (a) L.–P. Wilamowitz, *T.G.L.* p. 72, arranges the lines as a hexameter, followed by an iambic dipody, and a catalectic dactylic pentameter, but (a) there is no parallel for this metrical pattern and (b) it is against the evidence from Catullus.

[4] This was not the case at Rome. For Catullus' skilful treatment of it see Fraenkel, op. cit. p. 7.

ut flos in saeptis secretus nascitur hortis,
ignotus pecori, nullo conuolsus aratro,
quem mulcent aurae, firmat sol, educat imber;
multi illum pueri, multae optauere puellae:
idem cum tenui carptus defloruit ungui,
nulli illum pueri, nullae optauere puellae.[1]

After this charming comparison, they point out that, while a girl is a virgin, all admire her, but when she loses her virginity, no one admires her. The lines suggest a comparison with a simile of Sappho's, which is reasonably presumed to make a similar point:

οἴαν τὰν ὑάκινθον ἐν ὤρεσι ποίμενες ἄνδρες
πόσσι καταστείβοισι· χάμαι δέ τε πόρφυρον ἄνθος...[2]

Even as shepherd-men tread down with their feet the hyacinth on the hills, and on the ground the purple flower....

So far Catullus models himself to some degree on Sappho, though he prefers the domestic flower of the garden to the wild hyacinth on the hills. But beyond this point the difference in the method of performance takes him farther away from his model. In the early stages of a wedding in Greece both sexes took part,[3] but when it came to singing outside the bridal chamber, it seems that the main duty fell to girls.[4] This means that Catullus is able to develop a contrast which Sappho cannot. In a second simile his men praise wedlock in the image of the vine, which gains strength by being fastened to an elm, and draw the moral:

cum par conubium maturo tempore adepta est,
cara uiro magis et minus est inuisa parenti.[5]

Sappho does not go so far as this, but seems rather to have made her young women cling to the notion that girlhood is indeed a delightful state and should not be broken until it is ripe. This she expresses in a brilliant simile:

[1] C. 62. 38–44. Cf. Calvus fr. 4 Morel, '(lilium) uaga candido nympha quod secat ungui'.
[2] Fr. 105 (c) L.–P. The lines are not explicitly attributed to Sappho by Demetrius, de Comp. 106, but he is well acquainted with her wedding-songs. Neither καταστείβοισι nor πόρφυρον is a normal Lesbian form, but Sappho admits such anomalies in her hexameters.
[3] Pind. Pyth. 3. 17–18; Theocr. 18. 1 ff.; Aesch P.V. 556; Eur. I.T. 366.
[4] Il. 18. 495 ff.; Hes. Scut. 274 ff.
[5] C. 62. 57–58.

οἶον τὸ γλυκύμαλον ἐρεύθεται ἄκρωι ἐπ' ὕσδωι,
ἄκρον ἐπ' ἀκροτάτωι, λελάθοντο δὲ μαλοδρόπηες·
οὐ μὰν ἐκλελάθοντ', ἀλλ' οὐκ ἐδύναντ' ἐπίκεσθαι.[1]

As the sweet apple reddens on the top bough, on the top of the top-most bough; the apple-gatherers forgot it—no, they did not quite forget it, but they could not reach so far.

The context and the point of this are given by Himerius:

Sappho compared the girl to an apple which has delighted those who were eager to pluck it so much that they could not taste it with the tip of a finger, but kept its youth blooming for him who in season intends to gather the apple.[2]

Sappho evidently admits that marriage must come, but at the right time, and until it comes, girlhood has its own peculiar beauty.

The three stages of wedding-songs, at the feast, in the procession, and outside the bridal chamber, may account for most of them, but even so they did not always stop here, but in the morning a song called ἐγερτικόν was sung outside.[3] Of such a song there is no clear trace in Sappho, but at one place she seems to have written about maidens who sing all through the night and to have told the bridegroom to call his comrades. She seems to suggest that he should leave his bride and join his friends in merriment:

πάρθενοι δ[
παννυχίσδ[οισ]α[ι
σὰν ἀείδοιεν φ[ιλότατα καὶ νύμφας ἰοκόλπω,

ἀλλ' ἐγέρθεις ἠϊθ[έοις
στεῖχε σοῖς ὐμάλικ[ας, ὡς κ' ἐλάσσω
ἤπερ ὄσσον ἀ λιγύφω[νος ὄρνις
ὕπνον [ἴ]δωμεν[4]

May maidens . . . all night long . . . sing the love of you and your violet-girt bride. Come wake up, go (and summon) the young men who are your comrades, that we may see less sleep than the clear-voiced nightingale.

It is not quite clear what Sappho means by this, but it looks like a song sung outside the bridal chamber, and in it the choir of

[1] Fr. 105 (a) L.-P.   [2] *Or.* 9. 16 Colonna.
[3] Hypoth. Theocr. 18; cf. Aesch. fr. 43 N.
[4] Fr. 30. 2–9 L.-P.; Page, *S. and A.* p. 125.

maidens mock the bridegroom and tell him to come out and join his old friends, as if he would really prefer to do so. The song is not a true ἐγερτικόν, but it shows how easily songs sung at night could become songs of awakening.

So far the fragments of Sappho's wedding-songs seem to fit into a ceremonial ritual in which we can distinguish the different stages and their appropriate tones and tempers. But there remains another kind of song, to which there is no Greek parallel outside her works. It is a dialogue between the bride and someone else who takes the part of her maidenhood. Only two lines survive, and the second is woefully corrupted:

(νύμφη). παρθενία, παρθενία, ποῖ με λίποισ᾽ ἀποίχηι;
(παρθενία); οὐκέτ᾽ †ἤξω πρὸς σέ,† οὐκέτ᾽ ἤξω.[1]

Bride. Maidenhood, maidenhood, whither do you go away and leave me?
Maidenhood. Never again shall I come to you, never again shall I come.

This is indeed a primitive ritual, in which the Bride presumably took her own part, while that of her Maidenhood was taken by some friend. Its popular character may be illustrated by a song from Moravia, in which bride and bridegroom sing a duet on the same theme:

Bride. Shepherds, shepherds, have you in any place found my crown? I have lost a green crown, and so beautiful was its brightness.
Bridegroom. We have not found it in any place. But we saw it, we saw it, when the birds carried it far away over the mountain.
Bride. Alas, my crown is lost! If I had a pair of swift coursers like the wind to get it back, they would never bring it back; it would never more be mine. If I sought it with a hundred wagons, I should never recover it; it would never more be mine.
Bridegroom. Ah, do not lament so, my treasure, but be glad. Instead of a green crown I wish to give you a crown of gold.
Bride. Ah, is such the crown of gold instead of my green crown? What is the glitter of pure gold in place of its fresh brightness?[2]

It is possible that from such a song come Sappho's words

ἦρ᾽ ἔτι παρθενίας ἐπιβάλλομαι;[3]

'Do I still long for maidenhood?' But the whole subject is obscure, and we can hardly even surmise at what stage of the wedding

---

[1] Fr. 114 L.–P. The second line may, very tentatively, be restored as οὐκέτ᾽ ἤξω πρός σε πάλιν, νῦν πάλιν οὐκέτ᾽ ἤξω.   [2] H. Usener, *Rh. Mus.* lv, pp. 288 ff.
[3] Fr. 107 L.–P.

proceedings such songs were sung. Were they perhaps sung later, and who took the place of the Maidenhood in the dialogue?

The greater part of Sappho's poetry was concerned with her immediate surroundings. Her personal poems reflected its sorrows and its glories; her more impersonal poems were demanded by its ceremonies, especially those which had something to do with Aphrodite. Compared with other Greek poets, Sappho is sparing in apophthegms and maxims, and though this may be an accident due to the haphazard way in which her fragments are preserved, it is possible that she was not very much interested in general ideas, since in the presence of strong passions it is absurd to argue or to preach. She even lacks references to politics except when she refers to Myrsilus in the case of her poverty[1] or condemns Mika because she has chosen the friendship of women in the house of Penthilus.[2] This does not mean that she had not her own standards of conduct. She certainly had, and sometimes discloses them, though we suspect that there is usually an immediate, personal application in them. In one she shows how she assessed beauty and goodness:

ὁ μὲν γὰρ κάλος ὄσσον ἴδην πέλεται ⟨κάλος⟩,
ὁ δὲ κἄγαθος αὔτικα καὶ κάλος ἔσσεται.[3]

He who is beautiful, is beautiful to see, but he who is also good, will forthwith be beautiful also.

This woman, who was so moved by beauty, put it second to true nobility. So too she did not accept the possession of wealth as an unqualified good in itself, but saw its dangers and realized its obligations:

ὁ πλοῦτος ἄνευ τὰς ἀρέτας οὐκ ἀσίνης πάροικος·
ἀ δ' ἀμφοτέρων κρᾶσις εὐδαιμονίας †ἔχει τὸ ἄκρον.†[4]

Wealth without goodness is not a harmless neighbour; but the mingling of both has the top of happiness.

She, who certainly knew what anger was when her brother or her rivals provoked her, could issue a warning against it:

σκιδναμένας ἐν στήθεσιν ὄργας
μαψυλάκαν γλῶσσαν πεφύλαχθαι.[5]

---

[1] Fr. 98 (b) 7 L.–P.   [2] Fr. 71. 3 L.–P.

[3] Fr. 50 L.–P. In 1 ⟨κάλος⟩ is supplied by Hermann.

[4] Fr. 148 L.–P. 2 is perhaps past repair but may have been something like
ἀ δ' ἀμφοτέρων κρᾶσις ἔχει εὐδαιμονίας ἄωτον.

[5] Fr. 158 L.–P. The MSS. give πεφύλαχθαι γλῶσσαν, which Seidler rearranged as two Adonii.

When anger spreads in the breast, beware of a tongue that babbles at random.

These are the merest accidents, and though they tell us something about Sappho, we learn more about her when she follows her emotions and speaks freely of them.

In one place, however, it is possible that Sappho speaks with an unusually critical sense of behaviour, not to a girl or a rival, but to her distinguished contemporary Alcaeus. Aristotle quotes some lines, which he attributes to Alcaeus and Sappho.[1] If we take him at his word, and clearly it must be treated with respect, Alcaeus first said:

θέλω τί τ᾽ εἴπην, ἀλλά με κωλύει
αἴδως . . .

'I wish to say something to you but shame prevents me . . .' and Sappho answered:

αἰ δ᾽ ἦχες ἔσλων ἵμερον ἢ κάλων
καὶ μή τί τ᾽ εἴπην γλῶσσ᾽ ἐκύκα κάκον,
αἴδως κέ τ᾽ οὐ κάτηχεν ὄππα-
τ᾽, ἀλλ᾽ ἔλεγες περὶ τὠδικαίως.[2]

If you had a desire for noble and beautiful things, and your tongue were not brewing some evil thing to say, shame would not hold your eyes, but you would speak about what you claim.

According to Aristotle there were two poems, the one by Alcaeus, the other in answer to it by Sappho, both in the Alcaic stanza. Though Sappho is not known to have used this stanza anywhere else, there is no good reason why she should not have done so on this occasion in addressing Alcaeus. The two poems would presumably have survived separately in the works of Alcaeus and Sappho, and Aristotle would have known their connexion and quoted from both. If we look at the fragments with his view in mind, it is clear that while Alcaeus speaks with a becoming enough restraint, Sappho answers him sharply. She tells him that his intentions cannot be good, and that he must be concocting something evil; otherwise he would not shrink from speaking.

---

[1] *Rhet.* 1367 a 8 ff. ὥσπερ καὶ Σαπφὼ πεποίηκεν εἰπόντος τοῦ Ἀλκαίου κτλ.

[2] Fr. 137 L.–P. In 5 I follow Hermann in reading κάτηχεν (κάτειχεν) and in 6 Lobel in τὠδικαίως (meaning περὶ τούτω, τὸ ἐδικαίως) instead of τὼ δικαίω of the MSS.

Her words are certainly chilly, if not harsh and disapproving, and the metaphor in ἐκύκα, which suggests cooking or brewing, is more colloquial than we should expect from her in such company. Her tone is all the more surprising since the only other line which Alcaeus is said to have written to her expresses unmixed admiration and high praise.[1] None the less if we pin our faith in Aristotle, this is the only possible conclusion.[2]

Happily the situation is not so simple as this. An anonymous commentator on Aristotle, who looks reliable and well informed, says that Sappho wrote the lines ascribed to Alcaeus.[3] Presumably he knew the complete text, and gave his own account of it. In that case we have a different tradition, that Sappho wrote a single poem, purporting to be a dialogue between Alcaeus and herself, in which she appears in no very favourable light. We need not necessarily accept this, but the commentator's evidence shows that the alleged authorship of Alcaeus was not universally accepted and may not have been at all obvious. In view of this uncertainty it is not surprising that attempts have been made to jettison Aristotle's account of the two poems, and to postulate that there was a single poem, written indeed by Alcaeus or Sappho but not concerned with their personal relations. This notion first appears in Stephanus, who says that the poem is a dialogue between ὁ ἐρῶν and τὴν ἐρωμένην, and leaves undecided its relation to Alcaeus.[4] This may be no more than a conjecture, for on such a matter Stephanus is not a weighty authority,[5] but at least he may have found the idea elsewhere, and if he got it from someone who had the full text of the poem, we could put some trust in it. Without indulging in these possibilities, we may still ask whether Stephanus's conception has something to be said for it or not. His case has been restated by Wilamowitz, who thinks that the poem is not a dialogue between Alcaeus and Sappho but between a man and a woman, or rather between a suitor and a rather unwelcoming maiden.[6] In favour of this view some points may be

---

[1] Fr. 384 L.–P.   [2] Page S. and A. pp. 106–9.

[3] Schol. Anon. in Rhet. p. 51 Rabe πεποίηκε γὰρ ἡ Σαπφὼ λέγοντα τὸν Ἀλκαῖον θέλω κτλ.

[4] p. 280 Rabe εἴτε ὁ Ἀλκαῖος ὁ ποιητὴς ἤρα κόρης τινὸς ἢ ἄλλος τις ἤρα, παράγει οὖν ὅμως ἡ Σαπφὼ διάλογον· καὶ λέγει ὁ ἐρῶν πρὸς τὴν ἐρωμένην· θέλω τι εἰπεῖν πρός σε, ἀλλ' ἐντρέπομαι, αἰδοῦμαι, αἰσχύνομαι· εἶτ' αὖθις ἀμοιβαδὶς ἡ κόρη λέγει πρὸς ἐκεῖνον· ἀλλ' ἐὰν ἦς ἀγαθὸς καὶ ὃ ἔμελλες πρός με ἦν ἀγαθόν, οὐκ ἂν ἦδου καὶ ἠσχύνου οὕτως, ἀλλὰ μετὰ παρρησίας ἔλεγες ἂν βλέπων πρός με ἀνερυθριάστως.

[5] P. Maas, Sokrates, viii (1920), pp. 20 ff.   [6] S.u.S. p. 41.

made, though none is perhaps final. First, such a dialogue was
a literary form in Greek poetry, as we may surmise from Horace's
Donec gratus eram tibi[1] and know from the song found in an
inscription at Marissa between Jerusalem and Gaza.[2] Secondly,
the tone of the woman's reply seems much more suited to a
popular song of this kind than to Sappho addressing the other
great poet of Lesbos. Thirdly, since the poem was written in
Alcaics, it was natural to ascribe some part in it to Alcaeus.
Even if we add to these the undoubted ambiguity of the tradition
about authorship, the case is not final. Everything depends on
how far we are prepared to go in disowning the authority of
Aristotle. On this we may at least say that not all his ascriptions
of authors may be accepted without question, and his pupils,
like Chamaeleon, went out of their way to invent stories about
poets such as that Anacreon was in love with Sappho.[3] It is
possible, but of course far from certain, that Aristotle, finding this
poem in the works of Sappho and seeing that it was written in
Alcaics, assumed for himself, or repeated from another, that it was
the work of both poets. There the problem stops. We can either
accept Aristotle's statement, and in that case we may feel uncomfortable that Sappho should treat Alcaeus in this way, or we
can reject it, with all the difficulties that such a rejection implies.

Most of Sappho's poetry, as we know it, is personal. Even the
cult-songs which she wrote for Aphrodite rose naturally from her
devotion to the goddess. She wrote on the whole about herself
and her feelings, and though she touches on mythological subjects, they seem often to be used to illustrate some point, as when
Helen is an example of the power of love,[4] or a beautiful companion is compared with her and Hermione,[5] or a friendship
between women receives an august precedent:

Λάτω καὶ Νιόβα μάλα μὲν φίλαι ἦσαν ἔταιραι[6]

'Lato and Niobe were very dear companions.' Even when we do
not know what the context is, we surmise that it concerns her
own feelings, as the story of Tithonus may illustrate something
to do with old age,[7] or the Moon's love for Endymion the divine
quality of love,[8] or the children of Niobe the beauty of some girls.[9]

---

[1] *C*. 3. 9.   [2] Powell, *Coll. Alex.* p. 184; cf. Aristoph. *Eccles.* 952–75.
[3] Athen. 13. 599 c.   [4] Fr. 16 L.–P.   [5] Fr. 23 L.–P.
[6] Fr. 142 L.–P.   [7] Fr. 58 L.–P.   [8] Fr. 199 L.–P.
[9] Fr. 205 L.–P.

We might easily think that she was not given to writing narrative poems for their own sake, if one of the most substantial pieces recovered from papyri did not tell in some detail a story. The poem tells of the wedding of Hector and Andromache, or rather of their home-coming to Troy after it. That it was the last poem in her Book II is stated by two papyri[1] and is partly confirmed by Athenaeus.[2] There is no doubt that it was included in Sappho's collected works and regarded in antiquity as hers. It is none the less unusual. Here are at least some thirty-five lines of undiluted narrative with no personal or topical references. Of course there may have been such in parts which have not survived, but even so the scale of narrative is surprising. It has been suggested that it was a wedding-song, and for this its subject is well suited.[3] If so, it would more probably be sung at the bridal feast than in the procession or outside the bridal chamber; for it has no popular or jocose elements. But we know too little to be able to say whether it was such a song or not.

The poem is anomalous both in its language and its prosody.[4] Though elsewhere Sappho sometimes allows divagations from the Lesbian dialect and from her own standard prosody, here abnormal elements abound. We find such non-Lesbian forms as ὄσα (ὄσσα), ἰέρας (ἴρας), ἐνί (ἐν), κατά (κάτ), πτόλιν (πόλιν), φίλοις (φίλοισι), ὀνκαλέοντες (ὀνκάλεντες), and such variations from her usual practice as epic correption in συνέταιροι ἄγοισ', the keeping of a short vowel before the combination of a mute and a liquid in ἐλίγματᾰ χρύσια and ὄχλος, the presence of a final short vowel in hiatus between the end of a line and the beginning of the next in ἀθύρματα ἀργύρα, the scansion εὐτρόχοις. Yet for most of these there is some parallel in other fragments, notably in the ἐπιθαλάμια, and a likely explanation is that, when she told a story in a dactylic metre, Sappho used epic forms and licences far more freely than she did elsewhere. Most of these anomalies are to be found in Homer, and that no doubt is why they are here. None of this need trouble us. What is troubling is the presence of the forms πορφύρα and ἀργύρα in 9 and 10. As they stand, they are Attic, and nothing else, and we may well ask what they are doing in a Lesbian poem. They cannot have replaced Lesbian forms, for these would be πορφύρια and ἀργύρια and would not fit into

[1] Ox. Pap. 1232 and 2076.   [2] 11. 460 d.   [3] B. Snell, Hermes, lxvi (1931), p. 73.
[4] Lobel, Σμ. pp. xxv ff. and Ἀμ. pp. x ff.

the metre. It has therefore been claimed that the work is sup-
posititious, the work not of Sappho but of an Athenian imitator.[1]
We know so little of the methods by which the Alexandrian
editors collected the works of early poets that we cannot say
whether this is likely or not. It is true that *Olympian* V, which
appears in our MSS. of Pindar, may conceivably not be genuine,[2]
but at least in antiquity it was known not to be contained ἐν τοῖς
ἐδαφίοις.[3] It is also true that certain Idylls appear in the work of
Theocritus, which are almost certainly not from his hand, and if
this could happen with an Alexandrian poet, it may also have
happened with a poet writing over three hundred years earlier.
Perhaps the editors had doubts about our poem and indicated
them in its beginning in the papyrus, but for that we have no
evidence, since the beginning is lost. It is not impossible that an
Athenian poet should, at quite an early date, imitate Sappho. In
the sixth century Athens had little poetry of her own, and the
Attic σκόλια, which begin towards the end of the century, are
undeniably influenced by Lesbian models and even include
a badly treated stanza of Alcaeus. The case for authenticity can
be impugned, but it is not necessarily hopeless.

Though πορφύρα and ἀργύρα are Attic forms, they may have
replaced some other forms which were not Attic. This was quite
likely to happen when Athens became the centre of the Greek
book-trade and imposed some of its local linguistic peculiarities
on texts. There are undeniably Attic forms in Homer, and there
is no *a priori* reason why there should not be in Sappho. They are
indeed hard to find elsewhere, but that may be because they are
not so metrically important as here. The question is what have
they replaced. The epic forms would be πορφύρεα and ἀργύρεα,
but since Homer does not need the scansion - ᴗ -, these do not
have their final two syllables contracted. It is conceivable that
Sappho so contracted them because she needed such a scansion,
as Anacreon, writing in his native Ionic, does in πορφυρέη[4] and
probably in ἀργυρέη.[5] If Sappho wrote πορφύρεα and ἀργύρεα and
contracted the final syllable of each, it would not be difficult for
Athenian editors to substitute, with perfect metrical propriety,
their own forms πορφύρα and ἀργύρα. This is not, however, the

---

[1] Lobel, op. cit.   [2] Wilamowitz, *Pindaros*, pp. 420 ff.
[3] *Ol.* 5. Inscr. a αὕτη ἡ ᾠδὴ ἐν μὲν τοῖς ἐδαφίοις οὐκ ἦν, ἐν δὲ τοῖς Διδύμου ὑπο-
μνήμασιν ἐλέγετο Πινδάρου.   [4] Fr. 2. 3 D.   [5] Fr. 59 D.

whole matter. It remains a mystery why Sappho should have used Ionic forms at all, especially since they are not Homeric, and the mystery becomes deeper when we find her using an alternative form to both πορφύριος and πορφύρεος when she writes πόρφυρον ἄνθος[1] and πορφύρωι πλόκωι.[2] We can only answer that, if she used two different forms of a word, there is no good reason why, if metre called for it, she should not use a third.

The case against the authenticity of the poem is at least 'not proven', since it turns on a point too slight to be pressed against the tradition, which is strongly for the defence. The poem still remains unusual and unexpected, but largely because it differs from Sappho's other, personal poetry. Yet, if we look at it closely, we see that it is the kind of poem which we might expect Sappho to write on such a subject. It does not so much tell a story as describe a situation, or a series of situations, the arrival of Hector and Andromache at Troy after their wedding. The news is brought by a herald:

5   Ἔκτωρ καὶ συνέταιρ[ο]ι ἄγοισ' ἐλικώπιδα
     Θήβας ἐξ ἰέρας Πλακίας τ' ἀπ' ἀ[ϊν]νάω
     ἄβραν Ἀνδρομάχαν ἐνὶ ναῦσιν ἐπ' ἄλμυρον
     πόντον· πόλλα δ' [ἐλί]γματα χρύσια κάμματα
     πορφύρ[α] κὰτ ἀύτ[με]να, ποίκιλ' ἀθύρματα,
10   ἀργύρα τ' ἀνάρ[ι]θμα [ποτή]ρ[ια] κἀλέφαις.[3]

Hector and his comrades bring dark-eyed, tender Andromache from holy Thebes and ever-flowing Plakië in ships over the salt sea; many are their golden bracelets and purple robes on the wind, cunningly wrought playthings and silver cups beyond counting, and ivory.

Sappho's feminine touch is present in the adjectives given to Andromache and in the absence of them from Hector. Hers too is the taste for rich and beautiful objects, for purple and gold and silver and ivory and for the sense of wealth and prosperity which they evoke. On hearing the news Troy springs into action, and everyone prepares to meet the couple:

     ὢς εἶπ'· ὀτραλέως δ' ἀνόρουσε πάτ[η]ρ φίλος·
     φάμα δ' ἦλθε κατὰ πτόλιν εὐρύχορον φίλοις.
     αὔτικ' Ἰλίαδαι σατίναι[ς] ὑπ' ἐντρόχοις

[1] Fr. 105 (c) 2 L.–P.   [2] Fr. 98. 4 L.–P.
[3] Fr. 44 L.–P. In 6 ἐ[ϊν]νάω is a possible alternative to ἀ[ϊν]νάω. In 9 I print Lobel's κὰτ ἀύτ[με]να, which seems well authenticated, but does not give an easy sense, since we expect a verb.

Q

ἆγον αἰμιόνοις, ἐπ[έ]βαινε δὲ παῖς ὄχλος
15 γυναίκων τ' ἄμα παρθενίκα[ν] τ' [ἀπαλο]σφύρων,
χῶρις δ' αὖ Περάμοιο θύγ[α]τρες . . . .[1]

Thus spake he, and quickly Hector's dear father arose, and the tidings
came to his friends through the broad places of the city. Straightway
the sons of Ilos led mules under the well-wheeled carriages, and all the
multitude of women and tender-ankled maidens went forward and
apart from them the daughters of Priam . . . .

The couple arrive, and there are rejoicings in Troy, notably
song and music:

αὖλος δ' ἀδυ[μ]έλης [κίθαρις] τ' ὀνεμίγνυτο
25 καὶ ψόφο[ς κ]ροτάλ[ων, λιγ]έως δ' ἄρα πάρθενοι
ἄειδον μέλος ἄγν[ον, ἴκα]νε δ' ἐς αἴθ[ερα
ἄχω θεσπεσία . . . .

The sweet tones of the flute and the lyre were mingled and the noise
of cymbals, and the maidens sang clearly a holy song, and the
wonderful echo came to the sky . . . .

Then rapidly the poem comes to its close with the raising of the
ὀλολυγή, a hymn to Apollo, and a song in honour of the bridal
pair:

30 μύρρα καὶ κασία λίβανός τ' ὀνεμείχνυτο
γύναικες δ' ἐλέλυσδον ὄσαι προγενέστεραι,
πάντες δ' ἄνδρες ἐπήρατον ἴαχον ὄρθιον
Πάον' ὀνκαλέοντες ἐκάβολον εὐλύραν,
ὔμνην δ' Ἔκτορα κ' Ἀνδρομάχαν θεοεικέλο[ις.

Myrrh and cassia and frankincense were mingled. The older women
all raised a glad cry, and all the men sang a loud, lovely song, calling
on Paean, the far-archer, lord of the lyre, and they sang of Hector
and Andromache like the gods.

The poem ends, with no external reference and no general sentiment. If it is some sort of hymn, the god whom it concerns has
been forgotten in the pleasure of the story.

Despite its Homeric air and its use of some Homeric forms and
devices, the art of this poem is not Homeric. It is indeed objective
in that it tells of events from the standpoint of an imaginary onlooker, but it pursues a different technique of narrative.
First, it does not so much describe a continuous action as dwell

[1] In 15 Pfeiffer's [ἀπαλο]σφύρων may not be right; see Page, S. and A. p. 65, but
it is at least closer to the papyrus than [ταυι]σφύρων.

affectionately on certain chosen episodes—the news brought by
the herald, the rush to welcome the bridal pair, the rejoicings that
celebrate their arrival. Secondly, its appeal is not so much dramatic
as pictorial. The carefully described details, the sense of visible
splendour, and the unfailingly happy tone give the poem a remarkable unity of temper, and reflect a mood of festive joy. But
there is nothing that recalls Homer's gift of varying a tale by
making one kind of effect succeed another. Thirdly, though the
story comes from the heroic cycle and is ultimately based on a
mention, in the *Iliad*, of Andromache's home,[1] it must be largely
Sappho's own invention. There is no hint that the epic told of it
except perhaps very incidentally, and its scale is perhaps beyond
what Homer would have allowed. It is Sappho's own expansion
of a hint in Homer, and she fashions it in her own way. Though
some of her material is indeed Homeric, the rest comes from her
own time and her own observation. The silver cups, the carriages
in which the women ride, the noise of the cymbals, the myrrh
and cassia and frankincense, all belong to her own world and
help to make the scene from the past lively and contemporary.

The language and the metrical technique of this poem are not
usual in Sappho's poetry. She seems indeed to have had at least
two manners and to have kept them more or less distinct. In one
she confined herself to her own Lesbian dialect and eschewed
even such devices as hiatus and epic correption; in the other
she used some words and forms which are not Lesbian, and had
no aversion from epic devices in prosody. A similar distinction
may be seen in Archilochus, who in his iambic and trochaic verse
keeps to his Ionic vernacular, but in his elegiacs draws freely on
the epic. That the epic should have such an influence is natural
enough, since it was the basis of poetical education and poets
inevitably exploited its rich resources. It was more likely to affect
dactylic verses than iambic, for its phrases were coined for this
purpose, and that must be why Archilochus shows traces of it in
his elegiacs. So too Sappho seems to have kept it mainly for
dactylic hexameters and pentameters. But in her case the distinction seems to have deeper roots than in the external form of
a poem. She drew upon the epic for poems performed in public,
notably marriage-songs, and kept her own vernacular for her
more private and more intimate pieces. The remarkable thing is

[1] *Il.* 6. 394 ff.

that from her own vernacular she formed a strictly consistent language. We may surmise that she used it in this class of songs partly because she owed something to earlier Lesbian song-writers, whom she and Alcaeus totally eclipsed, partly because it was the right kind of speech for poems which dealt not with a remote past but with events in her own life and her own circle. In using it she secured a high degree of immediacy and directness. The traditional style of the epic had already found a new range of activity in choral song, which was essentially public and formal; Sappho needed something closer to the spoken word and found it in the speech of her own island.

Though Sappho's vernacular poems have little that recalls the abundant formulas of the epic which were created to meet the needs of improvisation in oral recitation, she is not without Homeric echoes. But she shows her independence in her use of them. She applies βροδοδάκτυλος not to the dawn but to the moon,[1] καλλίκομοι not to mortal women but to the Muses,[2] λυσιμέλης not to death but to love,[3] λιγύφωνος not to a woman or a sea-bird but to the nightingale,[4] ἱππόβοτος not to Argos but to a meadow.[5] She has too her own small mannerisms and idiosyncrasies, and seems to have felt no great objection to using the same words more than once if they met a real need. She writes both φαίνεταί μοι κῆνος[6] and φαίνεταί ϝοι κῆνος,[7] both γᾶς μελαίνας[8] and γᾶν μέλαιναν;[9] she twice writes χρόα γῆρας ἤδη[10] and οὐ δύνατον γένεσθαι.[11] She has her favourite words like ἄβρος, ἄπαλος, βράδινος, χρύσιος, ἵμερος, πόθος. More strikingly she has an affection for an emphatic kind of comparative, as when she speaks of something as ὤιω πόλυ λευκότερον[12] or of some woman who snatches girls as worse than a legendary bogey, Γέλλως παιδοφιλωτέρα,[13] or of some source of musical sound as πόλυ πάκτιδος ἀδυμελεστέρα[14] or of what seems to be a girl as χρύσω χρυσοτέρα.[14] We cannot be sure whether these comparisons are based on current speech, but it is possible that they are, since they owe nothing to the epic and hardly occur outside Sappho and, it is said,[15] Anacreon, who certainly enjoys

---

[1] Fr. 96. 8 L.–P.   [2] Fr. 128 L.–P.
[3] Fr. 130. 1 L.–P.   [4] Fr. 30. 8 L.–P.
[5] Fr. 2. 9 L.–P.   [6] Fr. 31. 1 L.–P.   [7] Fr. 165 L.–P.
[8] Fr. 1. 10 L.–P.   [9] Fr. 16. 2 L.–P.   [10] Fr. 21. 6; 58. 13 L.–P.
[11] Fr. 16. 21; 58. 18 L.–P.   [12] Fr. 167 L.–P.   [13] Fr. 178 L.–P.
[14] Fr. 156 L.–P.
[15] Greg. Cor. in Hermog. π. μεθ. δειν. xiii (vii. 1236 Walz) οἷον τὰ Ἀνακρέοντος,

the use of vernacular phrases. They appeal to her because they have a playful, fanciful element, which reveals some hidden charm in ordinary things without distracting attention too far from them. They have become part of her individual utterance, which, despite its directness and straightforward character, is not unsophisticated, but the creation of a highly discriminating and discerning art. No doubt she proclaimed her own position when she praised the poetry of her island:

πέρροχος, ὡς ὄτ᾽ ἄοιδος ὁ Λέσβιος ἀλλοδάποισιν[1]

'Pre-eminent, as the Lesbian singer is among foreigners', and she was sure of her fame. Whatever the Muses and the Graces brought to her, she shaped to an exacting and deeply considered art.

The ancient critics have much of interest to say about Sappho, but do not all approach her from the same angle or praise her for the same reasons. First Demetrius praises her for her sweetness:

When Sappho sings about beauty, she is herself sweet and uses beautiful words. So too when she sings of love and the spring and the halcyon. Indeed every beautiful word is woven into her poetry, and some are of her own invention.[2]

In this tribute Demetrius incidentally praises Sappho's senses. Though there is no evidence that she wrote about nature for its own sake, she certainly used it as a background and as a means of comparison. What she noticed, she recorded deftly and briefly, catching just what is most striking and characteristic. Two isolated lines, of unknown context, illustrate her skill. The first speaks of the nightingale:

ἦρος ἄγγελος ἱμερόφωνος ἀήδω[3]

'the herald of the spring, the lovely-voiced nightingale', and the second of pulse growing:

χρύσειοι δ᾽ ἐρέβινθοι ἐπ᾽ αἰόνων ἐφύοντο,[4]

'the golden pulse grew upon the shores.' Though both lines are stray survivals, each has its own poetry and appeals to the senses,

τὰ Σαπφοῦς, οἷον γάλακτος λευκοτέρα, ὕδατος ἀπαλωτέρα, πηκτίδων ἐμμελεστέρα, ἵππου γαυροτέρα, ῥόδων ἀβροτέρα, ἱματίου ἑανοῦ μαλακωτέρα, χρυσοῦ τιμιωτέρα.
[1] Fr. 106 L.-P.   [2] de Eloc. 166.
[2] Fr. 136 L.-P. A possible alternative is the accusative ἄγγελον ἱμερόφωνον ἀήδων.   [4] Fr. 143 L.-P.

the first to the ear, the second to the eye. Nature could also be
the scene for some rite which takes place at night:

> πλήρης μὲν ἐφαίνετ᾽ ἀ σελάννα,
> αἰ δ᾽ ὡς περὶ βῶμον ἐστάθησαν....[1]

The moon shone in its fullness, and they, as they stood about the
altar. . . .

We might feel that the moon calls for more attention than this,
but it gives the right setting, and no more is needed. It was but
a small step from this art of quiet description to making natural
things serve as similes and comparisons. Just as the girl who has
gone to Lydia outshines other girls as the moon outshines the
stars, so Sappho must surely have a like notion in her mind when
she writes:

> ἄστερες μὲν ἀμφὶ κάλαν σελάνναν
> ἂψ ἀπυκρύπτοισι φάεννον εἶδος,
> ὅπποτα πλήθοισα μάλιστα λάμπηι
> γᾶν. . . .[2]

The stars around the beautiful moon hide back their shining face,
when she is at the full and shines most brightly over the earth . . . .

In the same poem perhaps she called the moon ἀργυρία,[3] 'silver',
and though the notion is familiar to us, it was new in her day,
and shows how she looked with fresh eyes on the most familiar
phenomena.

This keen observation served Sappho in good stead when she
wished to speak of those powers, in some sense divine, whom she
believed to be at work in the world about her. It was natural and
easy for her to take Homer's ῥοδοδάκτυλος Ἠώς and to translate
it, with due regard for the needs of metre, as βροδόπαχυν Αὔων.[4]
It was perhaps equally natural to call the Dawn χρυσοπέδιλλος
Αὔως,[5] when Homer[6] and Hesiod[7] had used the epithet of Hera.
It was certainly well suited to the Dawn who rises in gold. But
Sappho could be more adventurous than this. When she calls the
Graces βροδοπάχεες,[8] it is a tribute to their physical beauty and
suggests that they have in a divine degree the charms of those
whom they favour on earth. Even more remarkable, and certainly

---

[1] Fr. 154 L.–P.   [2] Fr. 34 L.–P.
[3] Ps. Julian *Ep.* 19 (*Ep.* 194, p. 264 Bidez–Cumont) Σαπφὼ . . . τὴν σελήνην
ἀργυρέαν φησὶ καὶ διὰ τοῦτο τῶν ἄλλων ἄστρων ἀποκρύπτειν τὴν ὄψιν.
[4] Fr. 58. 19 L.–P.   [5] Frs. 103. 13; 123 L.–P.
[6] *Od.* 11. 604.   [7] *Theog.* 454.   [8] Fr. 53 L.–P.

more mysterious, is her βροδοδάκτυλος σελάννα.[1] The moon is not 'rosy-fingered' in the same sense as the Dawn; she does not throw out rosy shafts of light into the darkness. But when the moon rises in Greece, she is often rosy, and if she is a goddess, as of course she is, it is a bold but not impossible extension of an old image to call her 'rosy-fingered'. If Sappho saw Aphrodite driving through the sky in a golden chariot drawn by sparrows, she saw Eros coming in splendour, like a young prince:

ἔλθοντ' ἐξ ὀράνω πορφυρίαν περθέμενον χλάμυν,[2]

'coming from the sky clad in a purple mantle.' When she told how Apollo went to Helicon to dance with the Muses and the Graces, she gave him hair of gold and a lyre and sent him on a chariot drawn by swans.[3] Her vivid visual imagination was all the more powerful because she believed implicitly in the divine powers of whom she wrote, and saw them as possessing the same kind of beauty and splendour that she loved in human beings. Her sense gave colour and brilliance to her poetry, and provided it with a magical appeal to the eye of the mind.

A second approach to Sappho's poetry is that of Dionysius of Halicarnassus, who treats it from a technical angle as a notable example of the 'smooth' type of composition. The essence of this type is that its choice of subjects demands a free, flowing style. Dionysius indeed begins by agreeing with Demetrius, when he says:

> As for figures, it is wont to employ not the time-honoured sort, nor those marked by stateliness, gravity, or mellowness, but rather for the most part those which are dainty and alluring, and contain much that is seductive and fanciful.

But this choice of subjects is best treated with a special class of words:

> It requires that all its words should be melodious, smooth, soft as a maiden's face; and it shrinks from harsh, clashing syllables, and carefully avoids everything rash and hazardous.[4]

This general doctrine, which is in his view applicable also to Anacreon and Simonides, Dionysius applies to Sappho, with a wealth of technical phraseology, in his criticism of ποικιλόθρον'

---

[1] Fr. 96. 8 L.–P.
[2] Fr. 54 L.–P.
[3] Himer. *Or.* 46. 6 Colonna.
[4] *de Comp.* 23, trans. W. Rhys Roberts.

ἀθανάτ᾽Ἀφροδίτα. In this poem he finds that the euphony and the grace of the language lie in the skilful collocation of vowels with 'mutes' (β, γ, δ, κ, π, τ, θ, φ, κ) and 'semi-vowels' (λ, μ, ν, ρ, σ, ζ, ξ, ψ) and the avoidance of other collocations. By this he means in effect that Sappho avoids too many consonants and so gives her verse 'an easy flow and softness'. If we compare her sound-effects with those of Pindar's Dithyramb for Athens,[1] which Dionysius quotes earlier as an example of the αὐστηρὰ ἁρμονία or 'austere composition', we get some idea of what he means. Sappho's choice of words makes her movement smoother and lighter, and it is this which Dionysius admires, though he does not think it the highest kind of poetry. It is unfortunately impossible for modern ears to hear Sappho's verses as Dionysius heard them, but we can at least see that ease of movement is one of her most striking qualities, and that it is well matched by her clarity of expression and her ability to move from one topic to another. But we need not conclude that this manner means some limitation or diminution of power. Indeed the remarkable thing is that through it Sappho displays her power all the more effectively because everything is clear and straightforward. Just because it lacks the occasional harshness of the αὐστηρὰ ἁρμονία, it is able to do its full work unhampered.

A third quality in Sappho's work which appealed to the ancients was its passion. It is this that 'Longinus' stresses in his praise of φαίνεταί μοι, even if his analysis seems a little formal and does not make all the points that it might. It was this too that appealed to a very different man, who understood Sappho's genius with a truly imaginative sympathy. Horace speaks more than once about her, and if his 'mascula Sappho'[2] is no more than a tribute to the strength of her creative powers, which are such as are usually possessed by men, in another place he uncovers the heart of his admiration:

> spirat adhuc amor
> uiuuntque commissi calores
> Aeoliae fidibus puellae.[3]

Still breathes the love and live the passions which the Aeolian maiden confided to her strings.

[1] Fr. 63 Bo.
[2] *Ep.* 1. 19. 28; see E. Fraenkel, *Horace*, p. 346.
[3] *C.* 4. 9. 11–12.

Sappho's passion is indeed remarkable not only for its strength but for its range. If love was her first concern, she wrote about its different manifestations with equal power and pursued its consequences with unflinching self-observation. This is not to say that she confines herself to the description of physical symptoms. Her true strength is that she can crystallize a whole situation or state of mind into a very few, extremely forceful words. At such a point she sometimes leaves behind her the imagery and decoration which so often give colour to her verse and speaks in the plainest possible way and makes every word carry a full weight of meaning. So, when in her desire to see Anactoria, she says

κἀμάρυχμα λάμπρον ἴδην προσώπω[1]

the line breathes the whole enchantment which the girl has for her. When she wishes that she were dead, she says so with the most poignant simplicity:

τεθνάκην δ' ἀδόλως θέλω,[2]

and indeed there is no more to be said than this. It is soon balanced by other words no less simple and heart-stricken, when the girl, from whom she is to be parted, says:

ὤιμ', ὡς δεῖνα πεπόνθαμεν,
Ψάπφ', ἦ μάν σ' ἀέκοισ' ἀπυλιμπάνω.[3]

No less powerful is passion when memory sees it in retrospect and gives to it the perspective of something very distant and very clear:

ἠράμαν μὲν ἔγω σέθεν, Ἄτθι, πάλαι ποτά . . . .[4]

If Sappho's χάρις is largely instrumental in setting her stage and keeping her poetry brilliant and attractive, and if her mastery of sounds enables her lines to move swiftly and lightly, it is passion which gives body and substance to her work. The ancient critics all had something percipient to say about her, but it is in the combination of what they praise that her true strength lies. The passion which assailed and inspired her was purified by her art and exalted to a peculiar beauty by her association of it with beautiful things.

Though Sappho wrote on other subjects, it was love that meant most to her. She knew that it was the gift of Aphrodite, who

---

[1] Fr. 16. 18 L.–P.   [2] Fr. 94. 1 L.–P.
[3] Ibid. 4–5.   [4] Fr. 49. 1 L.–P.

furthered and fostered it, and through it led her to the Graces
and the Muses. It was indeed something sent by the gods, and
at moments it brought Sappho close to them, not merely in her
vision of Aphrodite, but in her belief that the girls whom she loved
were divine in their beauty. She did not exaggerate when she
compared one to the famous beauties of the past, Helen and
Hermione, in whom flowed the blood of the gods:

> ὡς γὰρ ἄν]τιον εἰσίδω σ[ε,
> φαίνεταί μ' οὐδ'] Ἑρμιόνα τεαύτα
> ἔμμεναι,] ξάνθαι δ' Ἐλέναι σ' ἐΐσ[κ]ην
> οὐδὲν ἄει]κες.[1]

For when I look straight at you, I think that even Hermione was not
such as you are, and that it is in no way unbecoming to liken you to
golden-haired Helen.

When she says that one girl thinks another 'like a goddess'[2] she
states the case as she sees it. It is this conviction of a divine sanction for the passions which gives to Sappho's work a peculiar
quality and distinction. Through it she is able to transcend her
own anguish and to give to violent physical sensations a redeem-
ing pathos and a noble exaltation. In later times, when Aphrodite
had lost much of her original brightness, Sappho's emotions were
misjudged and hard names were given to her,[3] and even today
some scholars seem to be less interested in her passions, of which
we know something, than in her physical expression of them, of
which we know nothing.[4] Even if we were better informed it
would not matter, since what counts is the quality of Sappho's
actual poetry about love. For her love had something divine in
it, and she had no qualms or misgivings about its rightness. Nor
had her contemporaries. One stray line from the past is indeed
illuminating. Hephaestion, who quotes it, does not ascribe it to an

---

[1] Fr. 23. 3–6 L.–P. Supplements by Page, S. and A. pp. 138–9.

[2] Fr. 96. 4 L.–P.

[3] 'Ov.' Ep. Sapph. 19 'quas non (v.l. hic) sine crimine amaui'; 201 'Lesbides in-
famem quae me fecistis amatae'; Martial 7. 69; 10. 35. 15; Didymus, ap. Sen. Ep. 88.
3 'an Sappho publica fuerit?' 'Suid.' s.v. Σαπφώ (α') διαβολὴν ἔσχεν αἰσχρᾶς φιλίας;
Tatian, Adv. Gr. p. 34. 20 S. On the other hand Ox. Pap. xv. 1800, fr. 1, col. i. 16 ff.
κατηγόρηται ὑπ' ἐνίων ὡς ἄτακτος οὖσα καὶ γυναικεραστρία, indicates that it was a
matter for dispute. It is clear that Sappho's poetry did not provide final evidence
against her on the matter. The charges are implicitly dismissed by Strab. 617 ἡ
Σαπφώ, θαυμαστόν τι χρῆμα and Maximus of Tyre, 18. 9, when he compares her
with Socrates.

[4] Page. S. and A. pp. 143–6.

author, but he calls it an 'Alcaic dodecasyllable',[1] and we cannot
doubt that it was written by Alcaeus, since there is nobody else
whose words to her would have survived. It says nobly and
emphatically

ἰόπλοκ' ἄγνα μελλιχόμειδε Σάπφοι[2]

'Violet-crowned, holy, sweetly-smiling Sappho', and it is a
tribute of the highest praise. For in it Sappho is implicitly compared to a goddess and even to Aphrodite.[3] Elsewhere ἁγνός is
not applied to human beings before the fifth century. ἰόπλοκε
recalls ἰοστέφανος given to Aphrodite by a Homeric Hymn and
by Solon.[4] μελλιχόμειδε is another version of the Homeric φιλομμειδής and the later γλυκυμείλιχος.[5] The accumulation of epithets
is a heritage from prayer and recalls Sappho's own address to
Aphrodite. Nor is it conceivable that such words were intended
otherwise than in perfect seriousness. To suspect irony is out of the
question. That a woman should be so addressed is indeed remarkable, but it is a tribute to her unique gifts. In her power of
song and her devotion to Aphrodite Sappho has come so close to
divinity that she deserves to be honoured with something like the
same respect.

Sappho's remarkable temperament was united to a no less
remarkable gift for poetry. What she did shows no sign of effort,
and if composition ever came slowly to her, she hid any traces of
the strain. The sense of her poems goes so well with the metre and
falls so readily into its movement that they look like ordinary
words raised to the highest level of melody and expressiveness.
In her wide range of different metres there is not one which does
not move with effortless ease and receive her words as if they
were ordained for it. Only perhaps in some epigrams of Simonides
does the Greek language show anything so inevitably right in the
ordering of words. Even understatement, of which Simonides
makes so effective a use, is alien to her; for Sappho says just what
she feels, no more and no less. Such accomplishment and such
assurance were to some degree made possible by her certainty

[1] p. 45. 12 Consbruch.
[2] Fr. 384 L.–P. The form Σάπφοι is against the practice of the papyri, but nowhere is initial Ψ in her name guaranteed by the metre; see G. Zuntz, *Mus. Helv.*
viii (1951), pp. 12–35.
[3] Ferrari *Stud. It. Fil.* xvii (1940), pp. 33 ff.
[4] Hom. Hymn. 6. 18; Solon fr. 7. 4 D.
[5] Hom. Hymn. 6. 19.

about herself and her aims. She had an unfaltering conviction that song and the emotions were what mattered most. In this she is a true child of the aristocratic age, and, though it may seem paradoxical, a feminine counterpart of Archilochus. For Sappho finds the criterion of what should most matter not in tradition or convention or law but in her own feelings. Archilochus had done the same, and though his feelings took him in a very different direction, he resembles Sappho in his attachment to them and his firm conviction that nothing in the world is more important. Both poets assert their individuality and are far removed from the elegists like Tyrtaeus or Solon who speak as the voice of a class or a people or a public conscience. In her self-consciousness and self-reliance Sappho represents a ripe development of the aristocratic age. She keeps its unity of outlook and its social standards, but she relies on her own intuitions and is determined to be fully herself. Her cult of Aphrodite and the Muses was no doubt based on ancient traditions, but she transformed it into a cult of beauty and the emotions which it arouses. In her independence she stands apart from preceding generations, but equally in her self-assurance she stands apart from the courtly and ironical generation which followed her. At the parting of the ways she found an exquisite moment, and tradition and individuality were united in her.

In the end it is the experience which Sappho brings that matters. The pleasure to be found in her artistry is surpassed by that to be found in the emotional and imaginative power of her work, which is the reflection of her sensitive, suffering, passionate self. Her words are as fresh today as when she wrote them, and though we have only a pathetically small portion of what she wrote, and much even of this has survived for reasons other than its poetical merits, she still deserves the reputation of being the most gifted woman who ever wrote poetry. Her unfailing senses, her delightful fancy, her scrupulous sincerity, her passionate strength, even her outbursts of anger or scorn, are the qualities of a character endowed beyond mortal measure by the Muses and the Graces. To them, and to Aphrodite, she dedicated her life and her art, and their life-giving inspiration filled her verse. To read it is to understand that this woman was, as Alcaeus called her, holy.

VI. IBYCUS

SAPPHO and Alcaeus wrote while Stesichorus was developing the different art of the choral ode in the West. They owed nothing to him, and he owed nothing to them. But soon afterwards the art of the West was to be brought to Ionia, and the fusion of the two styles marked a new stage in Greek poetry. For Stesichorus left a disciple, who began by writing in the master's manner and then turned to other purposes and made his poetry the vehicle for his own private, or public, emotions. Ibycus was a native of Rhegium on the Italian side of the strait of Messina,[1] and must have been born in the first part of the sixth century. His father, Phytius,[2] has been identified with a famous Pythagorean of the name,[3] who made laws for Rhegium and received divine honours after his death.[4] But a man who was old enough to be father of Ibycus is unlikely to have been a Pythagorean, since Pythagoras did not leave Samos till after the assumption of power by Polycrates.[5] Since the name Ibycus is also known to have belonged to a Pythagorean,[6] it looks as if both names were fairly common in Rhegium, and of course the different men who bore them may have been related. Ibycus himself betrays no signs of Pythagoreanism, except that he is the first Greek poet to say that the Morning and the Evening Star are the same,[7] and this discovery, already made in Babylon, was first popularized by Pythagoras. All we can say is that Ibycus seems to have been of a noble family[8] and may have belonged to the aristocratic circle which governed the city until the assumption of power by Anaxilas in 494 B.C.

[1] 'Suid.' s.v. Ἴβυκος; Athen. 4. 175 e; Anth. Pal. 7. 714; Cic. Tusc. Disp. 4. 7.
[2] 'Suid.' ibid. He also gives as alternatives Polyzelus of Messene, 'the historian', and Cerdas. An 'historian' at this period is impossible, and Cerdas looks like a creation of New Comedy; see Mancuso, Lir. cl. gr. p. 296. I.G. xiv. 116 refers to a Phytius, father of Ibycus.
[3] Schmid–Stählin, Gr. Lit.-Gesch. i, p. 489.
[4] Iambl. Vit. Pyth. 27. 130; 30. 172.
[5] Porph. Vit. Pyth. 9; Diog. Laert. 8. 3.
[6] Athen. 2. 69 e.
[7] Cram. An. Ox. iii. 413. 16; see Meissner, Babylon und Assyrien, ii, pp. 25 ff.; A. Rehm, R.-E. viii. 1251.
[8] 'Plut.' pro Nob. 2; Strab. 257.

For the personal association of Ibycus with Stesichorus there is no evidence. In one story he is vaguely connected with Himera, in that it was said that on his way thither from Catane he fell out of his chariot and broke his wrist, played for some time out of tune, but did not dedicate his lyre to Apollo. It is hard to say what lies behind this, and we have no right to assume that he was visiting Stesichorus. Himerius, who reports it,[1] was well read in lyric poetry, but this is hardly a story we should expect in a poem. It looks more like an episode from a more or less apocryphal biography.[2] On the other hand there is no doubt of Ibycus' poetical debt to Stesichorus. It can be seen from the uncertainty in later times as to which of the two wrote the Ἆθλα ἐπὶ Πελίᾳ,[3] and though there is no good reason to dispute the Stesichorean authorship, which was accepted by Simonides,[4] the doubt shows that at least in some of his work Ibycus resembled Stesichorus as he does not in most of his extant fragments. Thus a broken text, which deals with various matters concerning Athene, states that he told of her birth in the same way as Stesichorus.[5] Though no names of his poems are preserved, he may have written something like an Ἰλίου πέρσις to which belong the lines

> γλαυκώπιδα Κασσάνδραν,
> ἐρασιπλόκαμον κούραν Πριάμου,
> φᾶμις ἔχησι βροτῶν.[6]

Bright-eyed Cassandra, the lovely-haired daughter of Priam, is kept in the speech of men,

and the remarkable episode in which Menelaus finds Helen hidden in the temple of Aphrodite, and though he means to kill her, is so overcome by love for her that he drops his sword.[7] Later critics called this a Dithyramb,[8] and this is not impossible. Again, just as Stesichorus told of the Calydonian boar-hunt in his Συοθῆραι, so Ibycus touches on the same story when he refers to Ἀλθαία Μελεαγρίς.[9] The influence of various episodes in the Νόστοι may be seen in two departures from ordinary tradition: in one Ibycus told how Diomedes was worshipped in a holy

---

[1] Or. 69. 5 Colonna.
[2] P. Maas, R.-E. ix. 1. 817.
[3] Athen. 4. 172 d.
[4] Fr. 32 D.
[5] Ox. Pap. xx. 2260, col. ii. 19 ff.; D. L. Page, C.R. iii, n.s. (1953), pp. 1–2; J. A. Davison, J.H.S. lxxiv (1954), p. 207.
[6] Fr. 16 D.
[7] Schol. Aristoph. Vesp. 714.
[8] Schol. Eur. Andr. 630.
[9] Fr. 28 D.

island called Diomedeia in the Adriatic,[1] and in the other how
Achilles wed Medea in the Elysian fields.[2] There are signs that
Ibycus dealt with episodes in the career of Heracles, who was a
favourite subject of Stesichorus. The quotation ἥλσατο βοῦς[3] may
conceivably refer to the cattle of Geryon, and it may have been
in connexion with some such adventure that Ibycus told how
Heracles refreshed himself in warm baths provided by Hephaestus.[4] Heracles was of course a popular figure in the West, and
too much influence must not be conceded to Stesichorus. It is,
however, more curious that certain words were used by both
poets. The unusual ἔξοθεν is ascribed to Stesichorus[5] but found in
Ibycus,[6] and the ancient grammarians ascribe to both poets
ἄτερπνος in the sense of ἄγρυπνος,[7] βρυαλίκται meaning 'war-
dancers',[8] and χάρμα in the sense of 'spear-head'.[9] This similarity
of usage may partly be attributed to local dialect, since the use of
ἄτερπνος is said to have been current at Rhegium.[10] But, though
the ancients may have confused quotations from the two authors,
they would not have done so if there had not been considerable
similarities between them.

Though it is impossible to assign any fragments of Ibycus with
certainty to his first, Italian period, he uses some themes which
belonged to the West and suggest that he found them there.
When he said that Diomedes was honoured as a god in the
Adriatic,[11] he exploited a genuine piece of information. The island
lay off the coast of Apulia, but Diomedes was also the chief hero
of Metapontum; his cult spread to the Adriatic, and in its
northern corner the Veneti sacrificed horses to him,[12] which indicates that they regarded him as a god. The baths which Hephaestus provided for Heracles are the warm baths of Himera, which
Pindar connects with the Nymphs[13] and Aeschylus mentioned in
his *Glaucus Pontius*.[14] Ibycus certainly saw Syracuse with his own

---

[1] Schol. Pind. *Nem.* 10. 12.　　　　[2] Schol. Ap. Rhod. 4. 814.
[3] *Et. Mag.* 428. 28.　　　　　　　　[4] Schol. Aristoph. *Nub.* 1051.
[5] Schol. Dion, Thrac. Bekker, *Anec. Gr.* ii. 945, 25.
[6] Fr. 30 D.　　　　　　　　　　　　[7] *Et. Gud.* 89. 31.
[8] Hesych. s.v. βρυαλίκται.　　　　　[9] Schol. Pind. *Ol.* 9. 129.
[10] *Et. Gud.* 89. 31.　　　　　　　　[11] Schol. Pind. *Nem.* 10. 7.
[12] Strab. 215, For Diomedes in the West cf. Pind. *Nem.* 10. 12; Strab. 283–4;
August. *C.D.* 18; *de Mir. Ausc.* 840 b.
[13] *Ol.* 12. 19 θερμὰ Νυμφᾶν λουτρά.
[14] Fr. 32 N. καλοίσι λουτροῖς ἐκλελουμένος δέμας
　　　　εἰς ὑψίκρημνον Ἱμέραν ἀφικόμην.

eyes; for he described the district of Ortygia, which was once an island but later joined to the mainland by the work of man:

λίθινον παρὰ χέρσον
ἔκλεκτον παλάμαις βροτῶν·
πρόσθε δέ νιν πεδ᾽ ἀνηριτᾶν
ἰχθύες ὠμοφάγοι νέμοντο.[1]

By the stony land, picked out by the hands of men; of old, flesh-eating fishes and sea-snails pastured there.

The junction of Ortygia to Achradina was probably completed in the middle of the sixth century and was new in Ibycus' day. There too he may have heard the story that Arethusa was the same as the Alpheus, which flowed thither under the sea.[2] A humbler Sicilian relic is Ibycus' story of the Ass and the Snake. The Ass has a charm to avert old age, but, being thirsty, wants to drink at a spring, guarded by a poisonous snake. The snake makes a bargain by which the ass gets a drink and the snake gets the charm.[3] Since this simple tale was told by the Sicilian Deinolochus,[4] the rival of Epicharmus, and is not common in other parts of Greece, it looks like a local variant on the common theme of plants which enable men to live for ever.

Though Ibycus may rightly be regarded as a follower of Stesichorus, he seems to have developed his own way of telling stories and to have diversified them with his own ingenious inventions. He certainly exploited a love-interest beyond the usual conventions of legend. For instance, he made Idomeneus love Helen, although she was growing grey.[5] Hesiod had indeed made Idomeneus one of Helen's suitors,[6] but this touch looks like Ibycus' own. More striking is the way in which he makes Achilles marry Medea in the Elysian fields.[7] This is so unusual that we might suspect some cult or ritual behind it, but it may equally have been Ibycus' own invention. So too, when the ancient critics praised his account of Menelaus' failure to kill Helen because he was so moved by her beauty'[8] they preferred his version to that of Euripides in his *Andromache*. Ibycus' interest

---

[1] Fr. 21 D. The text of the first two lines is very uncertain; see Wilamowitz, *Pindaros*, p. 226 n. 3. ἀνηριτᾶν may possibly be a Sicilian word, since it occurs at Epicharm. fr. 42. 5 K.

[2] Schol. Theocr. 1. 117; cf. Pind. *Nem.* 1. 1 on Ortygia, ἄμπνευμα σεμνὸν Ἀλφεοῦ.

[3] Ael. *N.H.* 6. 51. [4] Fr. 8 K.

[5] Schol. *Il.* 13. 516. [6] Fr. 96. 16 R.

[7] Schol. Ap. Rhod. 4. 814. [8] Schol. Eur. *Andr.* 628.

in love extended to his treatment of old stories and seems to have given them almost a romantic air to which we can find no parallel in the remains of Stesichorus. This desire and ability to improve upon his material by making it more unusual can be seen in his account of the 'Siamese Twins', Cteatus and Eurytus. They were known to Homer,[1] and to Hesiod, who touches lightly on their physical peculiarity.[2] Ibycus finds in them something that tickles his fancy and shirks no oddity when he makes Heracles tell how he has killed them:

> τούς τε λευκίππους κόρους,
> τέκνα Μολιόνας κτάνον,
> ἅλικας ἰσοκεφάλους ἐνιγυίους,
> ἀμφοτέρους γεγαῶτας ἐν ὠέῳ
> ἀργυρέῳ.[3]

I slew the white-horsed lads, the children of Molione, of the same age, equal-headed, single-bodied, both born in a silver egg.

For Ibycus they are almost of the same class as the three-bodied Geryon, and their birth recalls that of Helen and Clytaemestra. Their destruction by Heracles, which is a violent exploit in Pindar,[4] is used by Ibycus as an occasion for drawing attention to their highly eccentric physiology.

A turning-point came in Ibycus' life when he left Rhegium and went to Samos. In antiquity this was connected with a story that he could have been tyrant at home but went away instead to Ionia.[5] To this apparently inexplicable choice posterity referred proverbs such as ἀρχαιότερος Ἰβύκου and ἀνοητότερος Ἰβύκου,[6] 'more old-fashioned than Ibycus' and 'more stupid than Ibycus', implying that his foolish attachment to outmoded conventions lost him the sweet fruits of power. What little we know of Ibycus suggests that he was wise to make such a decision, and it certainly accords with one of his few statements about himself:

---

[1] Il. 23. 638.   [2] Fr. 110 R.
[3] Fr. 2 D. There is no good reason to dispute ἰσοκεφάλους, which gives good sense and is metrically acceptable; see E. Fraenkel, Rh. Mus. lxxii, pp. 17 and 343. In general see Wilamowitz, Pindaros, p. 513. A close parallel to Ibycus' conception is provided by Schol. T. ad Il. 11. 709 ἄμφω ἐν ἑνὶ σώματι ἦσαν.
[4] Ol. 10. 27 ff.
[5] Diogen. Paroem. 2. 71 Ἴβυκος γὰρ τυραννεύειν πολιτῶν δυνάμενος ἀπεδήμησεν εἰς Ἰωνίαν.
[6] Id. 5. 12.

δέδοικα μή τι πὰρ θεοῖς
ἀμβλακὼν τιμὰν πρὸς ἀνθρώπων ἀμείψω.[1]

I am afraid that I may win honour from men at the price of sinning
before the gods.

On the other hand the proverbs may after all not refer to the
poet but to his namesake the Pythagorean. In any case Ibycus
left Italy and found hospitality and a new home in the Ionian
island of Samos.

At some stage of his career Ibycus seems to have had relations
with Sicyon, and two of his references to it are sufficiently unusual
to suggest that they come from a poem or poems written by him
for Sicyonians. The first concerns the parentage of the eponymous
hero Sicyon. Hesiod, Eumelus, and local legend in Sicyon agreed
at least in connecting him with the Athenian Erechtheus, though
they disagreed whether he was his son or his grandson.[2] Ibycus
contradicted this account and said that Sicyon was the son of
Pelops.[3] An explanation may be found in the political situation in
the Peloponnese in the middle of the sixth century. After a period
of successful independence, Sicyon had entered into the alliance
led by Sparta in her attempt to secure as subjects or allies the
different cities which had once formed part of the Argive kingdom of Pheidon. In this process she made use of the story that
not Argos but Sparta was the true inheritor of Agamemnon's
realm. Just as Stesichorus accepted the notion in his *Oresteia*, so
Ibycus supported it by making Sicyon's father Pelops instead of
some scion of the house of Erechtheus. The attachment brought
additional justification for Spartan supremacy and helped to discredit the connexion, hitherto accepted, with Athens. This connexion had counted for something in the first part of the century
when Cleisthenes of Sicyon combined with an Athenian contin-
gent under Alcmaeon in the Sacred War of 590 B.C.[4] and later
married his daughter Agariste to Alcmaeon's son, Megacles.[5]
But this happy association was destroyed when Peisistratus
seized power and found his chief adversaries in the Alcmaeonids.
Athens, the former friend of Sicyon, became its enemy, and a
traditional connexion with Athens was undesirable when Sicyon

---

[1] Fr. 22 D; see Mancuso, *Lir. cl. gr.* p. 298.
[2] Paus. 2. 1. 1.   [3] Id. 2. 6. 5.
[4] Schol. Pind. *Nem.* 9. 2; Paus. 10. 37. 6; Polyaen. 3. 5.
[5] Hdt. 6. 130. 2.

had transferred her allegiance to Sparta. Ibycus, seeing how the situation lay, accommodated himself to it and manipulated mythology to suit it.

Ibycus' other reference to Sicyon is more mysterious. Strabo, in a discussion of rivers which flow under the sea, mentions that Ibycus made the Sicyonian Asopus flow under sea from Phrygia.[1] In doing so Ibycus was perhaps airing newly learned science, but his reference to Phrygia may have other intentions. The river Asopus played some part in Greek mythology, and though it was often confused or identified with its namesake in Boeotia, it was regarded as the father of many cities, of whom over twenty are known.[2] We cannot really see what was in Ibycus' mind, but he may have meant to suggest some kind of connexion between Sicyon and Phrygia, and perhaps the simplest solution is that, since Pelops came from Asia, so did the river Asopus and was a kind of physical example of an ancient connexion. Ibycus may even have hinted at a more recent relation. At some date between 560 and 541 Croesus, king of Lydia, had made an attempt to form an alliance with Sparta, because he heard that it was the most powerful state in Greece.[3] The Spartans welcomed his offer, and though they were of little use to him in his struggle against Cyrus, the accession of so rich and powerful a friend was not to be despised, and Ibycus may have had it in mind when he attached the Asopus to Phrygia. If these two references indicate some respect for Sparta, they are likely to come from poems written before Ibycus arrived in Samos, and it is possible that he wrote them on the way thither.

The date of Ibycus' arrival in Samos is not known, but we can hardly doubt that he was invited by Polycrates, who knew what fame the presence of a renowned poet might bring to his court. Polycrates was a remarkable man, and the court which he created at Samos was one of the most brilliant achievements of an age which appreciated princely magnificence. His ships controlled the sea, and by a happy combination of trade and piracy he amassed wealth which was the envy of his contemporaries. The visible monuments of his glory were the masterpieces of Greek architects. His palace, majestic though in ruin, stirred the envy

---

[1] Strab. 271.
[2] See Bowra, *Problems*, pp. 54 ff.
[3] Hdt. 1. 69; see H. T. Wade-Gery, *C.A.H.* iii, p 656.

of Caligula.[1] The foundations of his enormous temple of Hera
may be seen on the southern shore of Samos, a few miles from the
breakwater which sheltered his ships and from the underground
aqueduct which brought water to his capital. He was the patron of
jewellers like Theodorus[2] and of doctors like Democedes.[3] Statues
set up in his time still delight by their firm archaic beauty. This
man, who ruled the seas with a ruthlessness worthy of his
Genoese and Venetian successors, had a genuine love of beauty.
Like Sigismondo Malatesta and Lodovico il Moro he liked to
employ his hard-earned leisure in feasting and song. If Anacreon
gives the convivial spirit of the court, Ibycus also takes us into the
happy life which Polycrates fostered at Samos on the edge of the
menacing Persian Empire. Ibycus' style and manner are very
different from Anacreon's, but he moved in the same world and
reflected something of its spirit. Not without reason did Aristophanes couple the two names together, when he made Agathon
say that a poet should dance and sing as these two did in Ionia.[4]

That Ibycus went to Samos is beyond question. But when he
went is a vexed problem, complicated by the muddled entry in
'Suidas',[5] who says that he came there from Rhegium ὅτε αὐτῆς
ἦρχεν ὁ Πολυκράτης ὁ τοῦ τυράννου πατήρ· χρόνος δὲ ἦν οὗτος ἐπὶ
Κροίσου Ὀλυμπίας νδ'—'when Polycrates, the father of the tyrant
ruled it; it was in the time of Croesus in the 54th Olympiad'
(564–560 B.C.). This statement, which makes Ibycus almost a
generation older than Anacreon, is open to grave doubts. First,
Jerome's version of Eusebius says that Ibycus 'agnoscitur' in the
61st Olympiad (536–533 B.C.), and this would place him in the
heyday of Polycrates' reign. It is not absolutely incompatible
with the earlier date given by 'Suidas', but it deserves respect as
coming from a good authority and being consistent with the
known facts, since it is unlikely that Polycrates secured power
before 536.[6] Secondly, 'Suidas' makes a mistake when he calls the
father of Polycrates by the same name; for we know from Herodotus that the father's name was not Polycrates but Aeaces.[7]
Thirdly, 'Suidas' makes this father rule Samos, and this is contradicted by Herodotus, who says that Polycrates won his position

[1] Suet. *Cal.* 21.   [2] Hdt. 3. 41. 1.   [3] Id. 3. 125.
[4] *Thesm.* 159–63.   [5] s.v. Ἴβυκος.
[6] A. Andrewes, *The Greek Tyrants*, p. 118, puts the seizure of power by Polycrates about 535. For a view that his father was also a tyrant see Mary White,
J.H.S. lxxiv (1954), pp. 36 ff.   [7] Hdt. 2. 182. 2; 3. 39. 1.

by revolt, ἔσχε Σάμον ἐπαναστάς,[1] and this certainly precludes succession by inheritance. Suidas' entry is demonstrably wrong on these points, and we may regard his dating of Ibycus with some suspicion. What we can say is that Ibycus went to Samos when Polycrates was in power, and this would be not far from the date which Jerome gives as his 'agnoscitur'.

On the other hand there is good reason for thinking that Ibycus, like Anacreon, had a favoured position at the court of Polycrates. The two were associated by Aristophanes, but the most interesting evidence comes from Himerius, who in an address to an unnamed Roman says:

Now Polycrates of Rhodes loved music and song, and urged his father to help him to indulge his love of music. So his father sent for the lyric poet Anacreon and gave him to his son to teach him his heart's desire; and under him the boy, labouring with the lyre at royal virtue, seemed likely to fulfil the prayer of which Homer speaks, by surpassing his father Polycrates in all accomplishments.[2]

This not only shows that the tyrant Polycrates had a son with the same name, and in so doing perhaps explains the mistake of 'Suidas' in giving this name to the father of the tyrant, but, in calling the son 'Polycrates of Rhodes', helps to clear a literary problem. The younger Polycrates is called τῆς ʽΡόδου, and though it is easy to change the words to ὁ νεώτερος[3] or the like, there is no reason to do so, and if they are taken as they are, they provide some relevant information. The exact extent of the tyrant Polycrates' rule is not known, but Herodotus, who was well informed about him, says that he συχνὰς μὲν δὴ τῶν νήσων ἀραιρήκεε, πολλὰ δὲ καὶ τῆς ἠπείρου ἄστεα—'he had seized many of the islands and many cities of the mainland also'.[4] In an empire of this kind the possession of Rhodes would be almost indispensable. It is not more than two days' sailing from Samos, and the north wind, which prevails in the summer, would easily bring Samian ships to Lindus or Camirus. Rhodes was indeed of strategic importance. Lindus was an essential port of call for any Persian fleet sailing from Phoenician ports to the Aegean, and its Temple Chronicle records an offering made by Darius' general, Datis, who was besieging the town when a miraculous fall of rain

[1] 3. 39.
[2] *Or.* 29. 22 ff. Colonna.
[3] Edmonds, *L.G.* ii, p. 122.
[4] 3. 39.

occurred.[1] The entry Δαρείου . . . ἐπὶ καταδουλώσει τῆς Ἑλλάδος ἐκπέμψαντος μεγάλας δυνάμεις suggests that this was for the campaign of 490, and it shows the importance of Rhodes to the Persians, and therefore to Polycrates, who was threatened by them. In this struggle Rhodes was also an invaluable link with Egypt, with whose king, Amasis, Polycrates was allied.[2] It seems to have been one of the islands which he conquered, and it follows that when his son is called 'Polycrates of Rhodes', he held a position of importance, like that of the sons of Periander and Peisistratus,[3] at an important outpost of his father's empire.

An echo of the Samian occupation of Rhodes may perhaps be seen in a fragment of Anacreon. The text is almost beyond doubt:

οὗτος δ' Ἰηλυσίους
τίλλει τοὺς κυανασπίδας.[4]

This man pulls out the hair of the blue-shielded men of Ialysus.

Since we are told that here τίλλει means σκώπτει,[5] it follows that someone is deriding the people of Ialysus, who look as if they were being troublesome. Since Anacreon wrote for the tyrant Polycrates, it is conceivable, but not capable of proof, that he here refers to the tyrant's son and praises his conduct of his office in Rhodes. The remarkable κυανασπίδας is too rare to be a stock epithet, and suggests that it is drawn from reality, perhaps from some Rhodian art in decorating metal. The lines betray a knowledge of Rhodes and confirm our notion that it was part of Polycrates' dominions.

These considerations are relevant to the consideration of a poem found at Oxyrhynchus.[6] The papyrus gives no name of an author, but we can hardly doubt that it is the work of Ibycus. For this perhaps the best argument is that there is no other poet, whose works are likely to have survived to Alexandria, to whom we can ascribe it. The metre, with its predominant dactylic rhythm, is quite in Ibycus' style, and so are the accumulated epithets. It deals with love in his manner, and has a certain superficial element of Doric dialect, notably in ἐλεύσαν and ἐγήνατο.

[1] C. Blinkenberg, Die lindische Tempelchronik, pp. 34–36.
[2] Hdt. 3. 39. 2.
[3] Lycophron at Corcyra, Hdt. 3. 53; Hegesistratus at Sigeum, id. 5. 94. 1.
[4] Fr. 15 D.   [5] Et. Mag. 713. 7.
[6] Fr. 3 D.; Ox. Pap. xv. 1790; D. L. Page, Aegyptus, xxxi (1951), pp. 158–9; Wilamowitz, Pindaros, pp. 508 ff.

Its purpose emerges at the end with an elaborate compliment:
beautiful as was the son of Hyllis (of whom we know nothing at
all), Troilus was even more beautiful,[1] and with him must
Polycrates be praised:

41   τῷ δ' [ἄ]ρα Τρωίλον
       ὡσεὶ χρυσὸν ὀρει-
       χάλκῳ τρὶς ἄπεφθο[ν] ἤδη

       Τρῶες Δ[α]ναοί τ' ἐρό[ε]σσαν
45   μορφὰν μάλ' ἐίσκον ὅμοιον.
       τοῖς μὲν πέδα κάλλεος αἰέν,
       καὶ σύ, Πουλύκρατες, κλέος ἄφθιτον ἑξεῖς
       ὡς κατ' ἀοιδὰν καὶ ἐμὸν κλέος.

To him Trojans and Danaans compared Troilus in his lovely beauty
as thrice-refined gold to brass. For ever will they be fair; and you
too, Polycrates, shall have undying renown, such as will be mine also,
in song.

The conclusion of the whole matter is that Polycrates is compared
to Troilus, and the point is neater if he too is a prince. All falls
into place if we assume that this is the tyrant's son, Polycrates
'of Rhodes', and that Ibycus, like Anacreon, was employed at
Samos to satisfy the boy's taste for music and song.

The poem is not complete, but we have the best part of four
triads, each composed in strophe, antistrophe, and epode. This
means that the poem was sung by a choir and is probably a
choral ἐγκώμιον, whose main point was the glorification of the
tyrant's son. What remains is purely secular. There is no address
to a god, and no hint of performance at a religious festival. Of
course there may have been something of the kind in what is
lost, but it has evidently ceased to matter in the part which survives. It is meant to please and flatter powerful men. We may
attribute its secular character to Ionian enlightenment or to the
personal predilections of Polycrates or to the atmosphere of the
court, but whatever the explanation may be, the poem has an
unashamedly secular air. Ibycus uses the form and the language
of a choral hymn to pay an elaborate compliment to a young
prince.

The final compliment is the climax and the main point of the

[1] For the beauty of Troilus see Athen. 13. 564 f.; Schol. Lyc. 307; Serv.
ad *Aen.* 1. 47; and Phrynichus fr. 13 N., a line admired by Sophocles:
     λάμπει δ' ἐπὶ πορφυρέαις παρῇσι φῶς ἔρωτος.

poem, but the three preceding triads, clear and lively as they are, present a problem. If the chief point is praise of the young Polycrates, why does Ibycus devote whole triads not to compliments or myths or maxims, such as we expect in a choral ode, but simply to saying what he will *not* say? When a poet like Ibycus makes such a fuss about what he proposes to omit, he must have some reason for it, but what is it? Why this long parade of high events and heroic names, this catalogue of the tale of Troy, punctuated at intervals by such remarks as

> 10   νῦ]ν δέ μοι οὔτε ξειναπάταν Π[άρι]ν
>   ἔστ'] ἐπιθύμιον οὔτε τανί[σφ]υρ[ον
>   ὑμ]νῆν Κασσάνδραν

But now it is not my heart's desire to sing of Paris who tricked his host or of slender-ankled Cassandra,

or

>   οὐδ' ἐπ[ανέρχομαι
> 16   ἡρ]ώων ἀρετάν

Nor do I assay again the valour of heroes.

This is not the way to tell a myth, and there is no real parallel to it in Greek choral poetry. If we possessed the earlier stanzas, we might be better informed on Ibycus' intentions, but even as it stands, there is sufficient material to justify some speculation. The long and cheerful disowning of any real interest in heroic themes must have an explanation, and it may be found in what we know of Ibycus' poetical development.

Though Ibycus may never have known Stesichorus, the poetry which he wrote in the West was clearly influenced by the master. His first themes were epic themes, such as Stesichorus had already treated. In this art of lyrical narrative Ibycus served his apprenticeship. Stray relics of it survive among his fragments, and the papyrus which contains the poem to Polycrates contains also the scanty remains of another poem which seems to tell of war.[1] Lyrical narrative was the product of Magna Graecia, and it may be doubted whether it flourished in Ionia. The home of the Homeric poems presented its narratives in a different medium, and when Ibycus, who was used to writing choral songs, came to Samos, he had to change his manner. And in this lies a clue to his treatment of mythology in this poem. The rapid survey of epic

[1] *Ox. Pap.* 1790, frs. 4–5.

themes is a kind of leave-taking by a poet who has decided to
adopt another style. The crowded episodes of the tale of Troy
are mentioned only to be dismissed, because Ibycus is through
with them. He has now something else to sing of, the beauty and
the glory of the young Polycrates.

If we look at the poem in this light, it becomes more intelligible.
First, it appears that some of the themes mentioned as unsuitable
or impossible for song were actually themes treated by Ibycus
or by Stesichorus before him. The fragment opens with a rapid
account of the sack of Troy:

> οἳ κ]αὶ Δαρδανίδα Πριάμοιο μέγ᾽
> ἄ]στυ περικλεὲς ὄλβιον ἠνάρον
> Ἄργ]οθεν ὀρνυμένοι
> Ζη]νὸς μεγάλοιο βουλαῖς
>
> .5 ξα]νθᾶς Ἑλένας περὶ εἴδει
> δῆ]ριν πολύυμνον ἔχ[ο]ντες
> πό]λεμον κατὰ δακρ[υό]εντα,
> Πέρ]γαμον δ᾽ ἀνέ[β]α ταλαπείριο[ν ἄ]τα
> χρυ]σοέθειραν δ[ι]ὰ Κύπριδα.
>
> 10 νῦ]ν δέ μοι οὔτε ξειναπάταν Π[άρι]ν
> ἔστ᾽] ἐπιθύμιον οὔτε τανί[σφ]υρ[ον
> ὑμ]νῆν Κασσάνδραν
> Πρι]άμοιό τε παῖδας ἄλλου[ς
>
> Τρο]ίας θ᾽ ὑψιπύλοιο ἁλώσι[μο]ν
> 15 ἆμ]αρ ἀνώνυμον . . . .

They sacked the great, famous, wealthy city of Dardanian Priam,
stirring from Argos by the plans of mighty Zeus, maintaining for fair-
haired Helen's beauty in tearful war strife that is sung in many songs;
and doom came upon patient Troy because of the golden-haired
Cyprian. But now it is not my desire to sing of Paris, who tricked his
host, or of slender-ankled Cassandra, and Priam's other children, nor
of the nameless day when Troy of the tall gates was taken . . . .

Stesichorus had written an Ἰλίου πέρσις, and Ibycus may have
followed his example. To such poems the lines just quoted seem
to refer, for of the names there mentioned some appear elsewhere
in his fragments and look as if they came from an Ἰλίου πέρσις
resembling that of Stesichorus. The existence of some such poem
is presupposed in our passage. Ibycus has made his name by
narrative on the Stesichorean model, but now he intends to sing

in a different way, and he announces the change by reviewing his own kind of work and saying that this is not what he now proposes to do.

Some such explanation may account for two peculiarities in the manner of this poem. The first is Ibycus' apparent indifference to nice points of mythology. We might of course attribute this to ignorance or carelessness, but it is strangely out of character in a poet who enjoyed tinkering with old tales, as when he made Sicyon the son of Pelops[1] or Hector the son of Apollo.[2] Yet this same poet describes Agamemnon with an unusual confusion:

> 20   τῶν] μὲν κρείων Ἀγαμέ[μνων
>   ἆ]ρχε Πλεισθ[ενί]δας βασιλ[εὺ]ς ἄγος ἀνδρῶν
>   Ἀτρέος ἐσ[θλοῦ] πάϊς ἐκ π[ατρό]ς.

They were led by lord Agamemnon, the king, son of Pleisthenes, prince of men, a scion sprung from noble Atreus as sire.

Here mythology is confounded, when Agamemnon is made the scion of both Atreus and Pleisthenes. The two versions were current in the sixth century, but they were mutually opposed and incompatible, for while the claims of Atreus were supported by Homer and by local tradition at Argos and Mycenae, the claims of Pleisthenes were acclaimed at Sparta, where Agamemnon was honoured as a local hero. To this version Stesichorus had given his support in his *Oresteia*, with the intention of dissociating Agamemnon from Atreus. No doubt it was possible to fashion a genealogy in which Agamemnon could be descended from both, but it would at the best be confusing, and it would call for more explanation than Ibycus gives. In his old days Ibycus might have been interested in such questions, but now he has something better to sing about. A second example of this affected indifference may be seen in the account of the sailing of the Greek fleet for Troy:

> 27   ὠ[ς Μενέ]λαος ἀπ᾽ Αὐλίδος
>   Αἰγαῖον δι[ὰ πό]ντον ἀπ᾽ Ἄργεος
>   ἠλύθον [ἐς Τροία]ν
> 30   ἱπποτρόφο[ν οἵ τ]ε φῶτες . . .

how Menelaus and his men came over the Aegean sea from Aulis from Argos to horse-rearing Troy.

If by Argos Ibycus means the city, he simply contradicts himself;

---

[1] Paus. 2. 6. 5.   [2] Schol. *Il.* 3. 314.

if by it he means some larger area, as in Homer, he expresses himself with remarkable clumsiness. By this appearance of vagueness he seems to say that he has lost touch with his subject.

A second oddity is Ibycus' abundant use of decorative epithets. This would not indeed be surprising if these epithets were charming or illuminating in themselves, but they are unusually conventional. Most of them come straight from Homer like πόλεμον κατὰ δακρυόεντα, πόδας ὠκὺς Ἀχιλλεύς, μέγας Τελαμώνιος Αἴας, κλέος ἄφθιτον. Worse than this, he seems to go out of his way to use the flattest epithet possible, as when he calls Cassandra τανίσφυρον, when almost anything else would have been more suitable, and he himself treats her elsewhere with far more sympathy. At times the epithets are piled with a reckless profusion, which is indeed unlike his usual selection of them. We may well feel that he is slipshod when he speaks of

1   Πριάμοιο μέγ᾽
    ἄ]στυ περικλεὲς ὄλβιον

or θνατὸς ἀνὴρ διερός or calls Agamemnon βασιλεὺς ἀγὸς ἀνδρῶν. Yet perhaps even this redundancy is not to be interpreted by the serious standards of choral poetry but indicates a special purpose for the occasion. The epithets are, as it were, in inverted commas, familiar echoes from heroic tale and the heroic style, hints of what Ibycus might once have sung but will sing no more. It is by such means that he says good-bye to his earlier manner and dismisses it with a cheerful and playful mockery.

This air of unconcern, of studied ignorance, may be seen in Ibycus' statement that the whole subject of the sailing of the Achaeans is beyond his powers:

23   καὶ τὰ μὲ[ν ἂν] Μοῖσαι σεσοφ[ισμ]έναι
    εὖ Ἑλικωνίδ[ες] ἐμβαίεν λόγ[ῳ,
    θνατὸς δ᾽ οὔ κ[ε]ν ἀνὴρ
    διερὸ[ς] τὰ ἕκαστα εἴποι.

On these themes the Muses, daughters of Helicon, might well embark, since they have sung of them, but no living mortal man could tell each point.

The word σεσοφισμέναι is important. σοφίζεσθαι is closely connected with σοφία and σοφιστής in their sense of 'art' and 'artist' and itself means to 'practise an art'.[1] So Theognis speaks of himself

---

[1] See T. W. Allen, *Theognis*, p. 5; E. Harrison, *Studies in Theognis*, p. 227.

in his poetry as σοφιζομένῳ,[1] and so Xenophon uses the word of
the art of speech.[2] Pindar calls himself a σοφιστής,[3] and Aeschylus applies the word to a player of the lyre,[4] and Euripides to
Thamyris.[5] When Ibycus uses the verb σοφίζεσθαι and puts it
into the perfect participle with reference to the Muses, he means
that they have often sung of these themes, and are therefore well
equipped to sing of them again, and by this he refers to the
poetical tradition in which he was educated. He dissociates himself from it and assumes a mock modesty when he dignifies the
Muses by the Hesiodic title of Ἑλικωνίδες and says that no mortal
man can do what they can. He has found another theme for
poetry, the beauty of the young Polycrates, and by these dis-
claimers, which are of course not meant to be taken too solemnly,
he takes leave of his old manner and prepares his audience, who
may have expected that he would tell some old tale, for something new.

The praise of the young Polycrates is characteristic of the life
which Ibycus found at Samos, where the personal proclivities of
the tyrant[6] encouraged the paying of amatory compliments to
youths and boys. The unaffected passions of an earlier generation were here succeeded by something less spontaneous. Posterity
misunderstood the convention and overestimated the desires of
Ibycus. When 'Suidas' says that he was ἐρωτομανέστατος περὶ
μειράκια,[7] he took him too literally. No doubt Ibycus felt the
emotions of which he sang, but he was encouraged to feel them
and to sing of them. He had to work them up and make the
most of them in a way that suited his patron and his court. We
need not doubt his honesty, but equally we need not think that
he was always the victim of some devouring desire. The Samian
society of Polycrates had a cult of youth and its beauty and
attached importance to it. It provided an impulse and a subject
for songs when men relaxed over the wine, and added drama and
interest to their lives. It recalls the Athenian habit of writing
love-names on vases. Just as the young Polycrates was praised in
song, so the young Hipparchus was celebrated by the inscription
of Ἵππαρχος καλός on the vases of Epictetus.[8] In these courtly

---

[1] 19.   [2] *Mem.* 1. 2. 46.   [3] *Isthm.* 5. 28.
[4] Fr. 314 N.   [5] *Rhes.* 924.
[6] Athen. 12. 50 e; Ael. *V.H.* 9. 4; Apul. *Flor.* 15. 54; Philostrat. *Epist.* 8. 1.
[7] s.v. Ἴβυκος.   [8] Beazley, *A.R.V.*, p. 925.

circles compliments were called for, and this particular form of compliment was much to the taste of Polycrates and the family of Peisistratus.

When all consideration is made for circumstances, it must be admitted that the poem to the young Polycrates is not an unqualified success. Not only does it lack the qualities which delight us in Ibycus' other fragments, but even in its own way it is not very amusing. Of course Ibycus assails an esoteric subject of ephemeral interest, and cannot be expected to convey to us the thrill which he may have conveyed to Polycrates. He assumes a knowledge of poems known to his audience but not to us, and we can see his effect but dimly. But when all allowances are made, the humour of the poem is not of first-rate quality, and the discovery of the papyrus has not added to Ibycus' reputation. Even when he warms to his real task at the end and tries to close with a heart-felt tribute of praise, his words have not the strength or the concentration of his other fragments. The compliments are ingenious and graceful, but no more. It looks as if he was not inspired by his subject and wrote almost mechanically to answer the demands of an occasion which did not stir his heart.

How differently Ibycus could treat an amatory subject can be seen from other fragments. His method may be illustrated by some lines addressed to Euryalus:

Εὐρύαλε γλαυκέων Χαρίτων θάλος,
καλλικόμων ⟨Μουσῶν⟩ μελέδημα, σὲ μὲν Κύπρις
ἅ τ' ἀγανοβλέφαρος Πειθὼ ῥοδέοισιν ἐν ἄνθεσι θρέψαν.[1]

Euryalus, shoot of the blue-eyed Graces, darling of the lovely-haired Muses, thee did the Cyprian nurse, and tender-lidded Attraction, among the rose-blossoms.

We have only to compare this rich, enamelled opening with any love-poem of Sappho to see what a difference there is between her and Ibycus. Sappho's poetry is intimate and strictly personal, but Ibycus' lines proclaim his passion candidly to the world. No doubt such declarations were expected from him, and there is

[1] Fr. 8 D. In 1 it is tempting to alter γλαυκέων with Jacobs to γλυκέων, as it gives a more emphatic dactylic rhythm, but γλαυκέων is more precise and less obvious. In 2 it seems unlikely that καλλικόμων would by itself suggest any very clear meaning, and something like Hecker's Μουσῶν is needed, unless with Bergk we postulate the loss of a line between 1 and 2. The passage seems to have been in the mind of Aristophanes at *Eccl.* 973-4. In general see Wilamowitz, *Pindaros*, pp. 509 ff.

nothing shy or secret about them. For the theme of love Ibycus
has adapted the grand choral style which had been developed for
songs to the gods. These accumulated epithets, these divinities
named in their visible splendour, belong ultimately to a world of
solemn invocations and prayers, but Ibycus has secularized them.
The manner and even the matter of hymns are annexed to his
personal passion. He addresses Euryalus almost as an earlier poet
might have addressed a god, and spends on him the rich resources of choral song. No earlier poet known to us treats love in
this way, and when Ibycus so indulges himself, he shows that in
Samos the conventions of song were being broken and replaced
by others more courtly and more extravagant.

It may not surprise us that in these three lines the Graces,
Aphrodite, Attraction, and the Muses are all named, but it is
largely in such a combination of appropriate powers that Ibycus'
originality lies. Once love had become a theme irrespective of
cult or ceremony, it needed its own emblems and symbols, and
Ibycus found these by exploiting divine powers traditionally
connected with it. Sappho had invoked all these powers separately
at different times and in different poems, but Ibycus brings them
together to proclaim the urgency of his passion. Moreover, what
were real divinities to Sappho, powers to be invoked or placated,
have become half-abstractions to Ibycus. Instead of describing
the physical effects of love, he sees the object of his desire as
someone divinely blessed and gifted, endowed with those qualities which men commonly regard as the special blessing of
Aphrodite. For him Euryalus is less a creature of earth than someone brought up among roses in some garden of the gods. He
can express his feelings only by attempting to leave the immediate scene for an Olympian splendour, and to this extent he
displays what we may call a romantic tendency in him.

No complete love-poem by Ibycus survives, but we know
enough of him to see how he used myth to enlarge and illuminate
his themes. Apollonius Rhodius tells how Eros leaves Olympus
and gives a brilliant, imaginative account of his journey:

> αὐτὰρ ἔπειτα πύλας ἐξήλυθεν Οὐλύμποιο
> αἰθερίας· ἔνθεν δὲ καταιβάτις ἐστὶ κέλευθος
> οὐρανίη· δοιὼ δὲ πόλοι ἀνέχουσι κάρηνα
> οὐρέων ἠλιβάτων, κορυφαὶ χθονός, ᾗχί τ' ἀερθεὶς
> ἠέλιος πρώτῃσιν ἐρεύθεται ἀκτίνεσσιν.

νειόθι δ' ἄλλοτε γαῖα φερέσβιος, ἄστεα δ' ἀνδρῶν
φαίνετο καὶ ποταμῶν ἱεροὶ ῥόοι, ἄλλοτε δ' αὖτε
ἄκριες, ἀμφὶ δὲ πόντος ἀν' αἰθέρα πολλὸν ἰόντι.[1]

Then he passed through the gates of Olympus high in air; hence is
a downward path from heaven; and the twin poles rear aloft steep
mountain-tops—the highest crests of the earth, where the risen sun
grows ruddy with his first beams. And beneath him there appeared
now the life-giving earth and cities of men and sacred streams of rivers,
and now in turn mountain-peaks and the ocean all around, as he
swept through the vast expanse of air.[2]

This passage, says the scholiast, is paraphrased from 'what Ibycus
says in his description of the rape of Ganymede in his poem to
Gorgias. Ibycus adds there how the Dawn carried off Tithonus.'
This information shows how Ibycus set to work. He wrote a poem
to the boy Gorgias and decorated it with the myth most suitable
to it, that of Ganymede. The glory of the poem seems to have been
the vision of the world seen from on high, whither the eagle
carried the stolen boy. Ibycus' imagination was caught by the
pictorial possibilities of the story. A single line survives to show
his style in the poem:

πόταται δ' ἐν ἀλλοτρίῳ χάει[3]

'flies in the alien void'. This is reasonably taken to refer to the
eagle as it soars above the highest familiar tract of air, and the
word which Ibycus uses for this, χάος, is delightfully bold and
right. It hits off the vast unfamiliar region, and once at least
another poet, seeing how good it was, appropriated it for his own
use. When Bacchylides describes the flight of the eagle of song
over sea and land to Sicily, he says

νωμᾶται δ' ἐν ἀτρύτῳ χάει[4],

and his effect recalls that of Ibycus. Nor is the reference to Dawn
and Tithonus, to which the scholiast refers, without a point.
There was a parallel between him and Ganymede in that both
were loved by divine beings and transported from earth to
Olympus. By such parallels Ibycus was able to emphasise the
more than human beauty of Gorgias.

If this gives some hint of how Ibycus wrote a love-poem, his

---

[1] 3. 159–66.   [2] Trans. R. C. Seaton.
[3] Fr. 28 Bergk, from Schol. Aristoph. Av. 192.   [4] 5. 26–27.

most famous fragment shows how he could speak of himself as
a lover:

> ἦρι μὲν αἴ τε Κυδώνιαι
> μαλίδες ἀρδόμεναι ῥοᾶν
> ἐκ ποταμῶν, ἵνα παρθένων
> κᾶπος ἀκήρατος, αἴ τ' οἰνανθίδες
> 5   αὐξόμεναι σκιεροῖσιν ὑφ' ἔρνεσιν
> οἰναρέοις θαλέθοισιν, ἐμοὶ δ' ἔρος
>   οὐδεμίαν κατάκοιτος ὥραν·
> ⟨ἀλλ' ἄθ'⟩ ὑπὸ στεροπᾶς φλέγων
> Θρηίκιος βορέας ἀίσ-
> 10   σων παρὰ Κύπριδος ἀζαλέαις μανί-
> αισιν ἐρεμνὸς ἀθαμβὴς
>   ἐγκρατέως πεδόθεν τινάσσει
> ἀμετέρας φρένας.[1]

In the spring the Cydonian quinces bloom, watered from the flowing
rivers where is the maidens' inviolate garden, and the vine blossoms
swell to strength under the shady sprays of the vine; but for me Love
sleeps at no season. But like the North Wind from Thrace, aflame with
the lightning, it comes with a rush from the Cyprian, dark and shameless with shrivelling madness, and masterfully shakes my heart from
the roots.

The general drift is clear. There is a contrast between the spring-
like peace and innocence in which maidens live, and the unseasonable passion which vexes Ibycus. But his exact implications
call for some unravelling if we are to understand his thought and
his method.

These lines are metaphorical and even symbolical in the sense
that they consist entirely of images which stand for something
else. The images are carefully chosen, and each makes its own
contribution. In the first part, which tells of the state of maidenhood, Ibycus uses three different images, all of them familiar,
and combines them into a single pattern and a single picture.
The Cydonian quince-trees are related to the awakening of love.
When Stesichorus wrote of the wedding of Helen and Menelaus,

---

[1] Fr. 6 D. In 2 there is no need to alter ῥοᾶν of the MSS. to ῥοαί τ' with Wilamowitz, since the quince-trees and the streams are hardly like enough to be associated
in the nominative. In 8 ἀλλ' ἄθ', supplied by Hermann, not only mends the metre
but provides a necessary transition in the sense. In 12 the change from παιδόθεν
to πεδόθεν is metrically necessary, and perfectly easy. The MSS. reading φυλάσσει
is perhaps tenable in the sense of 'keeps watch over', but the image of the wind
seems to demand something like Schoemann's τινάσσει or Naeke's σαλάσσει. In
general see Wilamowitz, S.u.S. pp. 122 ff.

he told how πολλὰ Κυδώνια μᾶλα were cast before the bridegroom's throne.[1] Two epigrams, attributed to Plato, make a man throw a quince or an apple at a girl.[2] It is a sign of love and is to be found in countries far removed from Greece.[3] Ibycus puts it in the forefront of his poem because it is a familiar symbol of love which swells to ripeness as girls grow to maidenhood.

The second symbol is 'the inviolate garden of the maidens'. Of this we know something from Euripides. His virginal Hippolytus offers to Artemis a garland of flowers gathered in just such an inviolate meadow, and says as he makes his offering:

> σοὶ τόνδε πλεκτὸν στέφανον ἐξ ἀκηράτου
> λειμῶνος, ὦ δέσποινα, κοσμήσας φέρω,
> ἔνθ᾽ οὔτε ποιμὴν ἀξιοῖ φέρβειν βοτά,
> οὔτ᾽ ἦλθέ πω σίδαρος, ἀλλ᾽ ἀκήρατον
> μέλισσα λειμῶν᾽ ἠρινὴ διέρχεται,
> Αἰδὼς δὲ ποταμίαισι κηπεύει δρόσοις.[4]

For thee this woven garland have I braided
And bring it, lady, from a virgin field,
Where never shepherd dares to feed his flocks
Nor ever comes the scythe; that virgin field
Is traversed only by the vernal bee
And nursed with river-dew by Modesty.

The emphatically repeated ἀκήρατος λειμών shows that Euripides is determined to make his point clear. His meadow is not a real meadow in the common world; it belongs to fancy and fable and myth. Like other mythological inventions, it stands for an idea— the idea of unsoiled innocence, and Hippolytus, himself the patron of unmarried girls, makes it the centre of his religious life. The same idea, less fancifully but not less forcibly expressed, may be seen in Deianira's account of girlhood:

> τὸ γὰρ νεᾶζον ἐν τοιοῖσδε βόσκεται
> χώροισιν αὐτοῦ, καί νιν οὐ θάλπος θεοῦ,
> οὐδ᾽ ὄμβρος, οὐδὲ πνευμάτων οὐδὲν κλονεῖ,
> ἀλλ᾽ ἡδοναῖς ἄμοχθον ἐξαίρει βίον.[5]

The delicate plant grows in the sheltered place
That is its own. And it the sun-god's heat
Shakes not, nor rain, nor any wind that blows;
It lifts its heart up in untroubled joys.

[1] Fr. 10 D.   [2] Nos. 2–3 Diehl.
[3] For a Chinese example before 500 B.C. see A. Waley, *The Book of Songs*, p. 31.
[4] Eur. *Hipp.* 73–78.   [5] Soph. *Trach.* 144–7.

These two passages illustrate what Ibycus has in mind. He sees girlhood as passing its time in an inviolate meadow, which is of course an image of innocence.

Ibycus completes his picture with an image of vines swelling and has in mind the comparison of youth to a vine. Just as Pindar calls the down on a young man's face τερείνας ματέρ' οἰνάνθας ὀπώραν[1] or Sappho compares a bridegroom to a tender shoot,[2] so Ibycus conveys the natural growth from innocence to love through the figure of grapes swelling to fullness. This finishes his first part, and his picture, formed from three separate images, is complete and consistent. The first gives the ripening of girlhood towards love, the second the secure innocence in which it lives, the third the moment before it is ready for wedlock. The sequence is natural and coherent, and each image catches something essential in the subject. It is seen as a natural process, regular and orderly, in which nature does her work quietly and well.

With this process Ibycus contrasts his own case. His passion is not regular and orderly but unseasonable. It comes without warning and assails him without abatement. He is, presumably, past his first youth, when the onslaught of such a passion might be expected, but now it is the opposite of the growth of womanhood and love in girls. It is at once untimely, irregular, and violent. In the striking image of the North Wind he portrays its effects. What Sappho only hints at in

ἔρος δηὖτέ μ' ὁ λυσιμέλης δόνει,[3]

Ibycus develops and elaborates. The wind blows from Thrace as it does in Homer;[4] it is not a winter wind, which can at least be foreseen, but a stormy wind that may blow in or out of season, the modern μελτέμι that scourges the Aegean even in summer. It is ἀθαμβής, that is ἀναιδής;[5] it is aflame with lightning, because it brings sudden storms; it is ἐρεμνός, because it darkens the sky. Each detail comes directly from nature but is no less effective as imagery, and may be pressed for its meaning in the context. Ibycus is scourged and smitten by love; his spirit is struck by its lightning and clouded by its gloom, until he quivers all over like a tree shaken from its roots by the wind. At each point Ibycus

[1] *Nem.* 5. 6.   [2] Fr. 115 L.–P.   [3] Fr. 130. 1 L.–P.
[4] *Il.* 9. 5.   [5] Wilamowitz, *S.u.S.* p. 124.

compares his own state with that of maiden love. It is untimely, violent, and anything but a steady, ripening growth.

These lines show Ibycus' art at its strongest and richest. He might in them be called almost a metaphysical poet, because he describes an abstract and subjective situation in images drawn from the visible and sensible world. The passion that stirs him is seen with insight and understanding, but because it is complex, it is conveyed in images each of which has its own beauty as well as its aptness. The same method, used rather more simply, may be seen in some other lines written by Ibycus when he was growing old and found himself falling in love against his will:

"Ερος αὖτέ με κυανέοισιν ὑπὸ
βλεφάροις τακέρ' ὄμμασι δερκόμενος
κηλήμασι παντοδάποισ' ἐς ἄπειρα
δίκτυα Κύπριδι βάλλει.
ἦ μὰν τρομέω νιν ἐπερχόμενον,
ὥστε φερέζυγος ἵππος ἀεθλοφόρος ποτὶ γήραι
ἀέκων σὺν ὄχεσφι θοοῖσ' ἐς ἅμιλλαν ἔβα.[1]

Yet again Love with melting looks beneath dark eyelids drives me with manifold charms into the Cyprian's boundless net. Ah, I tremble at his approach, as a champion horse bearing its yoke in old age goes unwillingly with its swift car to the race.

Here there are two main images, of which the second supplements and completes the idea behind the first. The first picture, of Love driving Ibycus into his net, is drawn from hunting. Ibycus himself is the prey; Aphrodite holds the net and Eros, who acts as her ἀρκυωρός,[2] lures him into it. Both Aphrodite and Eros are seen in human shape performing the functions of hunters, and Eros lures the victim with melting looks. This touch is perhaps slightly outside the strict limits of the simile, but it serves a special purpose. Eros resembles the boy with whom Ibycus has fallen in love, and his task amplifies how dangerous this is. The second picture, of the old, unwilling champion horse, gives the other side of Ibycus' feelings. Though he feels himself impelled irresistibly into love, he is not altogether willing. He goes on because it is his habit and practice to do so, but he knows that he is really too old for it. The success of the image in a world which knew and loved horses can be seen from the mark which it

[1] Fr. 7 D; see Wilamowitz, *S.u.S.* pp. 125 ff.
[2] Ibid. p. 125.

seems to have made in different ways on Plato,[1] Sophocles,[2] and Ennius.[3]

Ibycus was regarded in antiquity as pre-eminently a poet of love, and his extant remains confirm this view. We do not know if he wrote much about current politics or local affairs. That he was conscious of the Persians across the narrow strait from Samos is clear from his line

οὐδὲ Κυάρας ὁ Μηδείων στραταγός[4]

'not even Cyaras, the general of the Medes', which ancient philologists took to refer to Cyaxares,[5] but the identification is almost impossible, since so famous a name is unlikely to have been transformed to this degree. It may, however, refer to Cyrus, whose shadow had begun to fall over the eastern Aegean after his capture of Sardis c. 540 B.C. But we have no idea in what context Ibycus used the words. It is also possible that, when he called Spartan girls φανομηρίδας,[6] Ibycus meant to denigrate them, since the Ionian world disapproved of the way in which they took part naked in games and dances.[7] But we have almost no political references in the remains, and we may doubt if Ibycus often made them.

Love was certainly his main concern. Cicero considered that he was even more amorous than Alcaeus or Anacreon,[8] and his judgement was based on far more evidence than is at our disposal. This predisposition gives to Ibycus' poetry its special quality, but is liable to blind us to other qualities for which he is less renowned. Although he was deeply concerned with the emotions, he expressed them through images derived from visible things, which his acute sensibility marked and his memory stored up for use. His love of nature has something in common with that of Sappho, notably when he speaks of flowers:

μύρτα τε καὶ ϝία καὶ ϝελίχρυσος
μᾶλά τε καὶ ῥόδα καὶ τέρεινα δάφνα.[9]

Myrtles and violets and gold-flowers and apples and roses and glossy bay-leaves.

In his love of birds he follows the tradition of Sappho and Alcaeus,

[1] *Parm.* 137 a.   [2] *El.* 25–26.   [3] *Ann.* fr. 374 V.
[4] Fr. 18 D.   [5] *Et. Mag.* 542. 51.
[6] Plut. *Comp. Lyc. et Num.* 3. 3; cf. Pollux 2. 187; 7. 55.
[7] Anacr. fr. 35 D.; Eur. *Androm.* 595–600.
[8] *Tusc. Disp.* 4. 33. 71, 'maxime uero omnium flagrasse amore Rheginum Ibycum apparet ex scriptis'.   [9] Fr. 13 D.

but goes farther in his detailed presentation of them. There is a touch of magic in his

τᾶμος κλυτὸς ὄρθρος ἄυπνος
ἐγείρησιν ἀηδόνας,[1]

When the glorious dawn that ends sleep awakes the nightingales.

Some of his critics have tried to change Ibycus' nightingales into swallows on the ground that the nightingale is not the bird of dawn,[2] but he knew what he was saying and had at least Euripides on his side, who in the *Phaethon*[3] and *Rhesus*[4] makes the nightingale sing at daybreak. Nor has any Greek poet except Aristophanes given so lively a picture of bird-life as Ibycus gives in

τοῦ μὲν πετάλοισιν ἐπ' ἀκροτάτοισ'
ἰζάνοισι ποικίλαι
πανέλοπες καιολόδειροι λασιπορφυρίδες καὶ
ἀλκυόνες τανυσίπτεροι.[5]

On its highest leaves sit pied wild-ducks and dapple-necked shag-purples and long-winged halcyons.

We do not know the context of these lines, but they prove that Ibycus looked at birds with more than a general or passing interest and marked each with its own delightful and distinguishing epithet long before Aristotle had begun the systematic study of them. We can hardly question that for him the halcyon is not a fabulous but a real bird. No doubt myths collected round it, but, even if it never sings,[6] and Ibycus does not say that it does, it may still be the Spotted Kingfisher, which is still found near the coast in Greece.[7] Birds could also provide him with imagery, as one tantalizing fragment shows:

αἰεί μ', ὦ φίλε θυμέ, τανύπτερος ὡς ὄκα πορφυρίς[8]

'always, o dear heart, as when the long-winged purple bird . . .'. We cannot say what it was with which he compared this bird, and

---

[1] Fr. 11 D.   [2] See Wilamowitz, *S.u.S.* p. 127 n. 1.
[3] Fr. 773. 23 ff. N.   [4] 546 ff.
[5] Fr. 9 D. D'Arcy W. Thompson, *A Glossary of Greek Birds*, p. 148, calls the πηνέλοψ 'a kind of Wild Duck or Goose' and compares Aristot. *H.A.* 8. 593 b; Aristoph. *Av.* 298, 1302 with scholl.; Ion of Chios fr. 11 v. B. On p. 149 he says that the λασιπορφυρίς has not been identified.
[6] Aristot. *H.A.* 8. 593 b says that one kind sings sitting on reeds.
[7] Thompson, op. cit. p. 29.   [8] Fr. 10 D.

the bird itself has not been satisfactorily identified.[1] Of course it may have something to do with love, and since he is speaking to himself, we suspect that the coming of love is like that of the bird. But that is only a guess.

Ibycus wrote in the composite, artificial language of choral poetry, and the few recognizable traces of Doric dialect are unimportant. But he did not lack invention in enriching the standard vocabulary. He seems to have invented a new form of the third personal singular of the present indicative, since neither ἐγείρησιν nor ἔχησιν is a real form, and both look like artificial archaisms built on a false analogy from verbs in -μι. He also used heteroclite forms hardly less dubious, such as ἀλίτροχα for ἀλίτροχον,[2] ἀετώσιος for ἐτώσιος,[3] ἤλσατο for ἠλάσατο,[4] κλαγγί for κλαγγῇ.[5] He coined a monstrous form Λιβυαφιγενής[6] to mean 'born in Libya', and thought nothing of creating adjectives with a genitival sense like Ἀνακώσιος,[7] 'belonging to the Dioscuri' and χαριτώσιος,[7] 'belonging to the Graces'. His language was determined by a desire to keep his poetry lively. He extends the use of the form proper to patronymics to cover other purposes, and for him Ἑλένα Μενελαΐς[8] is 'Helen the wife of Menelaus', and Ἀλθαία Μελεαγρίς[8] is 'Althaea the mother of Meleager'. He takes conventional, formulaic phrases and transposes them into synonyms, so that Homer's ὄζον Ἄρηος becomes κλάδον Ἐνναλίου,[9] which keeps the original metaphor and makes the idea more impressive. At times he gets just the right word in the right place. In the lines

> οὐκ ἔστιν ἀποφθιμένοις
> ζωᾶς ἔτι φάρμακον εὑρεῖν,[10]

'for the dead there is no drug to win back life again', the success comes from the masterly use of φάρμακον, which is unexpectedly used not as a drug which averts but as a drug which brings something, as Pindar writes φάρμακον κάλλιστον ἑᾶς ἀρετᾶς[11] of a drug which secures success. Something of the same surprise

---

[1] Callim. fr. 414 P. says that the πορφυρίς is not the same as the πορφυρίων which is known from Aristot. fr. 38 R. and identified by Thompson, op. cit. p. 150, with the Purple Gallinule.

[2] Choerobosc. 4. 267. 17

[3] Et. Mag. 20. 13.

[4] Ibid. 428. 28.

[5] Cramer, An. Ox. I. 65. 15.

[6] Herodian. π.μ.λ. 2. 943. 26 Lentz.

[7] Cramer, An. Ox. IV. 9. 22.

[8] Diomed. Ars Gr. 1. 393 Keil.

[9] Schol. Pind. Isthm. 8. 43.

[10] Fr. 23 D.

[11] Pyth. 4. 187.

comes when he calls the pillars of heaven ῥαδινούς,[1] 'slender', or when he writes of some shining object

φλεγέθων ᾆπερ διὰ νύκτα μακρὰν
σείρια παμφανόωντα[2]

'flaming, as in the deep night the all-illuming dog-stars.' There is only one Dog-star, but Ibycus felt the need for hyperbole, and against nature he found it in the plural σείρια.

We do not know if Ibycus survived Polycrates and the disasters which befell Samos after the tyrant's death. Tradition records that he was killed by robbers in a lonely place, but the birds who saw the murder led to the apprehension and punishment of the murderers.[3] Greek legend liked to create dramatic ends for poets, and Ibycus was no doubt one of its victims, but in his case we may surmise how the story arose. It is a folk-tale in which an association between ἶβυξ[4] and ἰβύειν[5] is related to the name Ἴβυκος.[6] We may perhaps put more confidence in an anonymous epigram which tells of his grave in Rhegium, and, even if we must not treat it too seriously as evidence that he died in his own land, it deserves quotation because it is a sympathetic estimate of his life:

Ῥήγιον Ἰταλίης τεναγώδεος ἄκρον ἀείδω
αἰεὶ Θρινακίου γενομένην ὕδατος,
οὕνεκα τὸν φιλέοντα λύρην φιλέοντά τε παῖδας
Ἴβυκον εὐφύλλῳ θῆκεν ὑπὸ πτελέῃ
ἡδέα πολλὰ παθόντα· πολὺν δ᾽ ἐπὶ σήματι κισσὸν
χεύατο καὶ λευκοῦ φυταλίην καλάμου.[7]

I sing of Rhegium, that at the point of Italy tastes always the Sicilian sea, because under the leafy poplar she laid Ibycus, lover of the lyre, lover of boys, who had known many pleasant things; and on his tomb she shed abundant ivy and the plant of the white reed.

---

[1] Schol. Ap. Rhod. 3. 106.   [2] Fr. 12 D.
[3] 'Suid.' s.v. Ἴβυκος; Plut. Garr. 14; Antip. Sid. A.P. 7. 745; Stat. Silu. 5. 3. 153.
[4] Hesych. ἶβυξ· ὀρνεοῦ εἶδος.   [5] Id. ἰβύει· τύπτει, βοᾷ.
[6] Wilamowitz, S.u.S. pp. 243–5.   [7] Anth. Pal. 7. 714.

VII. ANACREON

SAPPHO and Alcaeus left no literary descendants in Lesbos. Their achievement could not be repeated, and if they had any imitators or disciples, their names and their works have perished. Perhaps, too, the social changes of the sixth century destroyed the conditions which made such an art possible. It was the age of tyrants, and the concentration of power and wealth in the hands of a few individuals meant that the old aristocratic equality and frankness were replaced by a more courtly spirit, in which men were less ready to speak frankly about themselves and conformed to the tastes and wishes of their patrons. A strong personality like Polycrates could impose his idiosyncrasies on the men around him, and, though he was a gifted and generous friend of the arts, he knew what he liked in them and saw that he got it. This age seems to have been more ironical and more light-hearted than the preceding. The emotions, which Sappho and Alcaeus had treated so candidly and so seriously, were now largely the subject of fancy and wit, as befitted a generation which had learned that enterprise and intelligence can defeat established power and that the most charming things are often the most precarious. It is characteristic of the time that its most distinctive poetry came not from Lesbos but from Ionia and that its leading exponent was Anacreon. Just as Ibycus transformed the choral ode, so Anacreon transformed the personal monody to suit the requirements of the time.

Anacreon's home was Teos,[1] an Ionian town on the northern shore of the Caystrian Gulf. It was an ancient seat of Dionysus,[2] and echoes of its happy life may be heard in the fame of its cakes and fish[3] and in a special kind of cup known to Alcaeus.[4] In the genial air of Ionia poetry grew on its own lines and developed certain characteristics which distinguished it from its Aeolian counterpart. Ionia had long had its tradition of heroic poetry, and from this it had fashioned its own charming art of elegy. Its

---

[1] Strab. 1. 644; 'Suid.' s.v. Ἀνακρέων; *Anth. Pal.* 7. 24 and 25; Himer. *Or.* 17. 2; 27. 34 Colonna.   [2] W. Ruge, *R.-E.* v a, 1. 560.
[3] Athen. 4. 160 a; 7. 325 e.   [4] Fr. 322 L.–P.

lyrical poetry must have been influenced by the great musician, Polymnestus of Colophon, who in the seventh century composed tunes which were sung generations later.[1] If, as is probable, he used the mixed Lydian mode,[2] he would be among those who later earned Plato's condemnation for fostering intoxication, softness, and sloth.[3] Such music promoted a poetry which was intended more for relaxation than for public affairs and state occasions and did not shrink from a love of ease and luxury. That it had its worldly side may be seen from the only surviving line of Pythermus, who was himself a man of Teos and may have been a precursor of Anacreon:

οὐδὲν ἦν ἄρα τἆλλα πλὴν ὁ χρυσός[4]

'after all, everything but gold is of no account.' This was the artistic world into which Anacreon was born, and he remained faithful to its spirit.

Anacreon, the son of Scythines,[5] was born about 572 B.C.[6] In Teos he grew to manhood, but soon after the sack of Sardis c. 541 his home was threatened by the Persians under Harpagus. When the enemy had taken the outer wall, the Teans embarked on their ships and sailed to Abdera on the Thracian coast, which had been unsuccessfully colonized by the Clazomenians and was taken over from them by the Teans.[7] With these exiles went Anacreon. Echoes of regret for the loss of his home may perhaps be detected in the line

νῦν δ' ἀπὸ μὲν πόλεος στέφανος ὄλωλεν,[8]

'but now from the city its crown is destroyed', which looks as if it might refer to the capture of Teos by Harpagus. Perhaps too the same struggle inspired a couplet, composed not as a sepulchral

---

[1] Pind. fr. 178 Bo.; Cratin. fr. 305 K.; Aristoph. *Equ.* 1287.

[2] 'Plut'. *Mus.* 29.

[3] Plat. *Rep.* 3. 398 e.

[4] Heracl. Pont. ap. Athen. 14. 625 c says that Pythermus composed in the Ionian mode and was mentioned 'by Ananius or Hipponax in the Iambics'. If the *floruit* of Hipponax is put 540–537 (Plin. *N.H.* 36. (5) 11), it looks as if Pythermus was senior to Anacreon.

[5] 'Suid.' s.v. Ἀνακρέων.

[6] The date is not certain, but depends on 'Suidas'' statement γέγονε κατὰ Πολυκράτην τὸν Σάμου τύραννον, 'Ολυμπιάδι νβ' with Rohde's correction of νβ' to ξβ', *Rh. Mus.* xxxiii, p. 190, and the reasonable assumption that γέγονε, as often, means *floruit*.

[7] Strab. 644; Hdt. 1. 168; Scymn. 670 f.

[8] Fr. 67 D; see M. Treu, *Von Homer zur Lyrik*, p. 288.

epitaph but as a commemorative σκόλιον in honour of a man who fell fighting for his country:

> ἀλκίμων σ', Ὠριστοκλείδη, πρῶτον οἰκτίρω φίλων·
> ὤλεσας δ' ἥβην ἀμύνων πατρίδος δουληΐην.[1]

First of gallant friends I pity you, Aristoclides; you lost your youth warding off slavery from your land.

But neither of these quotations can be referred with certainty to Teos, and the early part of Anacreon's life remains obscure. It was in Abdera that he passed his first manhood and wrote his first identifiable verses. The country was rich—Pindar called it ἀμπελόεσσαν καὶ εὔκαρπον and χθόνα πολύδωρον[2]—but it lay among savage Thracian enemies and had a violent history. Relics of its struggles may be seen in an epitaph attributed to Anacreon. It is open to the usual doubts which affect all such epitaphs, since, being written on stone without any author's name, they were liable to be attributed to any suitable poet. But this has at least an Ionian elegance and concerns Abdera. Nor is it unworthy of Anacreon:

> Ἀβδήρων προθανόντα τὸν αἰνοβίην Ἀγάθωνα
> πᾶσ' ἐπὶ πυρκαϊῆς ἥδ' ἐβόησε πόλις·
> οὔ τινα γὰρ τοιόνδε νέων ὁ φιλαίματος Ἄρης
> ἠνάρισεν στυγερῆς ἐν στροφάλιγγι μάχης.[3]

Strong Agathon, who died for Abdera, was mourned at his pyre by the whole of this city; for Ares, who loves blood, never in the eddy of hateful battle slew such a young man as he was.

Though Anacreon's tastes were for peace and pleasure, he respected the brave in battle but saw them as chosen by gods who were not his own first concern:

> ὀρσολόπος μὲν Ἄρης φιλεῖ μεναίχμην.[4]

Ares, eager for the fray, loves a man who stands fast in battle.

He seems to feel that there is something strange about the taste for battle when he says of someone:

---

[1] Fr. 90 D. Wilamowitz, *S.u.S.* p. 106, refers it to Abdera.

[2] *Paean* 2. 25 and 60.

[3] Fr. 100 D. Fr. 101, on Timocritus, seems more dubious, partly because it contains no indication of place, partly because the form σᾶμα is suspicious in an Ionian poet. It expresses a sentiment known from Aesch. fr. 100 N. and Soph. *Phil.* 436 and fr. 724 P.

[4] Fr. 74 D.; see Weber, *Anacreontea*, p. 91.

δακρυόεσσάν τ' ἐφίλησεν αἰχμήν,[1]

'he fell in love with the tearful spear-point', as if this were not the kind of love which he himself would feel. But he accepted it as part of human nature, and said tolerantly:

ὁ μὲν θέλων μάχεσθαι,
πάρεστι γάρ, μαχέσθω.[2]

'He that wishes to fight, for he may, let him fight.' At Abdera Anacreon saw what war was, but there is no indication that he shared the liking of Archilochus and Alcaeus for it.

Life in Abdera left other marks on Anacreon. He kept his eyes open, and a few memories of his Thracian surroundings have survived. It must have been here that he saw in their native haunts the Διονύσου σαῦλαι Βασσαρίδες,[3] 'the prancing Bassarids of Dionysus', and perhaps it was from an early distaste for the gross drinking of northern peoples that he himself preached later, not very convincingly, the virtues of moderation.[4] It must too have been here that he fell in love with a Thracian girl and wrote some enchanting lines to her:

πῶλε Θρηικίη, τί δή με λοξὸν ὄμμασι βλέπουσα
νηλεῶς φεύγεις, δοκεῖς δέ μ' οὐδὲν εἰδέναι σοφόν;

ἴσθι τοι καλῶς μὲν ἄν σοι τὸν χαλινὸν ἐμβάλοιμι,
ἡνίας δ' ἔχων στρέφοιμί ⟨σ'⟩ ἀμφὶ τέρματα δρόμου.

νῦν δὲ λειμῶνάς τε βόσκεαι κοῦφά τε σκιρτῶσα παίζεις·
δέξιον γὰρ ἱπποπείρην οὐκ ἔχεις ἐπεμβάτην.[5]

Thracian filly, why do you look askance at me with your eyes and

[1] Fr. 57 D.; cf. Weber, p. 49.
[2] Fr. 82 D. Weber, p. 12 n. 6, argues that the metre precludes it from being the genuine work of Anacreon, but that he used this metre surely follows from its name Ἀνακρεόντειον, Hephaest. p. 16. 17 Consbruch. We cannot, however, rule out the possibility that the words are metaphorical and come from an erotic or convivial context.
[3] Fr. 48 D. Cf. Weber, pp. 74 ff., 95 ff.
[4] Fr. 43. 7 D.
[5] Fr. 88 D. In 1 there is no need to read ὄμμασιν, since the final syllable is lengthened before the combination of a mute and a liquid. In 6 the Aldine ἱπποσείρην, which implies the use of a lasso, spoils the consistent imagery of the poem. See Wilamowitz, S.u.S. p. 118. Anacreon may possibly refer to the same girl in fr. 98 D:

οὐκέτι Θρηικίης ⟨παιδὸς⟩ ἐπιστρέφομαι.

But I am not persuaded that the words form a dactylic pentameter, since there is no need to add παιδός, and Θρηικίης could be a trisyllable, as in fr. 88. 1.

cruelly flee from me and think that I have no sense? Know that I could nicely put a bridle on you and hold the reins and turn you about the limits of the course. But now you graze over the meadows and skip lightly; for you have no skilled horseman to mount you.

This strikes a new note in Greek poetry; for it is both lyrical and witty, both passionate and fanciful. The comparison of the girl with a filly recalls Alcman's treatment of Hagesichora and her friends, but the skill and precision with which the image is developed and completed shows that Anacreon has found his own individual voice. The wit comes in the amatory undertones. Anacreon proclaims his desire to 'ride' the girl, and the final word has a double meaning comparable to the Aristophanic κελητίζειν,[1] κέλης[2], ἱππικός.[3] He faces the facts, and smiles while he sings of his desire, and a note of sly mockery is audible among words which are perfectly apt and delicate. The technique is new. Anacreon, like Alcman and Alcaeus, develops an image in its full implications, but he goes farther in making a whole poem from it. Every word may be pressed; the whole hangs together until the last word strikes home. The old fire and strength are here, but they are kept firmly in control. Anacreon enjoys the situation and knows that others will enjoy it too. His head understands his heart, but refuses to make too many overt concessions to it.

Anacreon stayed long enough in Abdera for his fame to spread abroad. When Polycrates needed an instructor in music and poetry for his son, he summoned Anacreon to Samos.[4] His invitation may have been part of the same policy which determined his invitation to Ibycus, and the lives of the two poets in Samos must have been very similar. But while Ibycus brought with him the Western art of choral song, and adapted it to courtly needs, Anacreon came already equipped with an art of monody which was well suited to his new circumstances. His relations with his host seem to have been excellent. His poems are said to have been full of references to Polycrates,[5] and though the tyrant's name does not appear in the extant fragments, there is no need to doubt the truth of the statement. His intimacy with Polycrates may be inferred from the story told by Herodotus that, when the fatal messenger came from Oroetes to fetch the tyrant to his death, he

---

[1] *Thesm.* 153; *Vesp.* 501.   [2] *Pax* 901; *Lys.* 60.
[3] *Lys.* 677; cf. Theogn. 1249–52.   [4] Himer. *Or.* 29. 24 Colonna.
[5] Strab. 638.

found Polycrates and Anacreon reclining in the banqueting-hall.[1]
Himerius mentions that Anacreon 'sang the praise of Polycrates
when the Samians gave offerings to the goddess',[2] and it looks
as if he used some festival of the Samian Hera, such as that described by Asius of Samos,[3] to turn a solemn occasion into a means
for praising his patron. But on the whole it is unlikely that he
wrote many hymns to the gods. It is told that, when he was asked
why he did not write them, he replied 'Because our loves are our
gods',[4] and this suggests that his works contained little of an undeniably religious character.

Here and there, however, a few contemporary references may
be detected. In the first poem of his first book he wrote:

> γουνοῦμαί σ', ἐλαφηβόλε,
> ξανθὴ παῖ Διός, ἀγρίων
>   δέσποιν' Ἄρτεμι θηρῶν,
> ἥ κου νῦν ἐπὶ Ληθαίου
> δίνῃσιν θρασυκαρδίων
> ἀνδρῶν ἐσκατορᾷς πόλιν
> χαίρουσ'· οὐ γὰρ ἀνημέρους
>   ποιμαίνεις πολιήτας.[5]

Thee I beseech, huntress of deer, flaxen-haired daughter of Zeus,
Artemis, queen of wild beasts, who now above the eddies of Lethaeus
lookest down upon a city of bold-hearted men, gladly; for not savage
are the citizens whom thou shepherdest.

The lines are too slight and too informal to come from a choral
hymn; they are a personal prayer, and their occasion may be inferred from their contents. Artemis, whose temple stood above the
river Lethaeus, was Artemis Λευκοφρυήνη, the famous goddess of
Magnesia. The city and its temple had been destroyed in the seventh
century by the Cimmerians, but were rebuilt by the Ephesians.[6]
It is this goddess who is honoured by Anacreon, and he performs
his task with unobtrusive skill. The destruction of Magnesia had
become a classic case of the pride which is punished by the gods,[7]

[1] Hdt. 3. 121. 1.
[2] Or. 28 Colonna.
[3] Fr. 3 Kinkel.
[4] Schol. Pind. Isthm. 2. 1.
[5] Fr. 1 D; see Wilamowitz, S.u.S. p. 11. M. Kehrhahn, Hermes, xlix (1914)
p. 481, points out that the lines are unlikely to be a complete poem, and J. A.
Davison suggests that they may have been followed by three more lines like fr. 2.
If so, the missing lines would presumably contain the substance of Anacreon's
actual request to Artemis, to which the extant words prepare the way.
[6] Strab. 647.
[7] Callinus and Archilochus ap. Athen. 12. 525 c; Theogn. 603–4; 1103–4.

and this insinuation Anacreon quietly dismisses, when he calls its inhabitants by the old-fashioned but honourable epithet of θρασυκαρδίων and suggests that they are what men ought to be. Moreover, the goddess whom he addresses was worshipped with Asiatic symbols such as lions and sphinxes and showed her alien character by being 'multimammia'.[1] As such she might well seem foreign to thoroughbred Greeks, but Anacreon ignores this by treating her as if she were simply Artemis πότνια θηρῶν and by giving her such unexceptionable epithets as ξανθὴ παῖ Διός and ἐλαφηβόλε, which make her resemble Artemis as when Homer compares Nausicaa with her.[2] From this he proceeds to make the point that the Magnesians are οὐκ ἀνήμεροι, not barbarians but Greeks.[3] For all this he must have had his reasons. Magnesia was the seat of the Persian satrap, Oroetes, and it looks as if Polycrates cherished designs on it. For he sent Maeandrius there to spy out the land, but Oroetes saw through his intentions and outwitted him.[4] Anacreon's song stresses the Hellenic traditions and affinities of the Magnesians and their goddess, and may well have been associated with some plan of Polycrates to establish closer relations with them.

In Samos Polycrates did not lack enemies, and an echo of his troubles may be heard in some words of Anacreon:

μυθιῆται δ'
ἀνὰ νῆσον, ⟨ὦ⟩ Μεγίστη,
διέπουσιν ἱρὸν ἄστυ,[5]

In the island, Megistes, the Chatterers hold sway over the sacred town.

The μυθιῆται were a political party in Samos, consisting of ἁλιεῖς and led by a man called Herostratus.[6] In this passage they seem to be in power in Polycrates' capital, the modern Tigani, and their name suggests a parallel with the Attic party of πάραλοι, who were led by Megacles, son of Alcmaeon, in opposition to Peisistratus[7] and must have consisted largely of seafaring

---

[1] Farnell, *Cults*, ii, p. 48.   [2] *Od.* 6. 102–6.

[3] H. Fränkel, *Wege und Fromen*, p. 59, n. 4, sees no point in the words and suggests a change to οὐ γὰρ ἂν ἡμέρους ποιμαίνοις πολιήτας, 'denn sanfter Bürger würdest du nicht walten wollen'. But the point is surely that Artemis, who is a Greek goddess, keeps her flock well in hand in accord with Greek traditions.

[4] Hdt. 3. 123.   [5] Fr. 25 D.

[6] Antig. Caryst. p. 30 Keller; see E. Lobel, *C.Q.* xxi (1927), p. 51.

[7] Hdt. 1. 59. 3; Aristot. *Const. Ath.* 13; Plut. *Sol.* 29. 4.

folk. That Polycrates had open enemies is clear from the existence of those discontented Samians whom he hoped to frustrate by sending them on a ship to Egypt, but who went instead to Syria, where they collected help against him.[1] The name μυθιῆται looks as if it were given to opponents of Polycrates by his supporters, and in using it Anacreon seems to speak in the familiar, half-esoteric language of the court.

A third political reference may be seen in a line ascribed by good authority to Anacreon:

$$\pi \acute{\alpha} \lambda \alpha \iota \ \kappa o \tau' \ \mathring{\eta} \sigma \alpha \nu \ \mathring{\alpha} \lambda \kappa \iota \mu o \iota \ M \iota \lambda \acute{\eta} \sigma \iota o \iota^2$$

'of old the Milesians were valiant'. That this occurred in his works is clear enough, but it may have been quoted by him from some earlier work or proverbial usage. It is said to have been given as an oracle, which is in itself not impossible, but while one account says that the oracle was given to Polycrates,[3] the other says that it was given to the Carians in a war against Darius.[4] In either case it passed into common currency as a proverb,[5] and would certainly be relevant to the activities of Polycrates. Early in his reign he attacked Miletus, and though the Lesbians came to its help, the Milesians were defeated at sea, and the prisoners taken by Polycrates were forced, while wearing bonds, to dig the trench round the wall of his city in Samos.[6] This was indeed a case of departed glory, and our line, whether Anacreon composed or merely quoted it, is surely an echo of the humiliation of the Milesians.

Even if we add to these passages that in which Anacreon seems to refer to the rule of the younger Polycrates in Rhodes,[7] they remain a small part of his extant work, and it is clear that his first interest was not in politics. Most of his fragments are concerned with pleasure and look as if they came from songs composed for the amusement of Polycrates and his court when they relaxed on convivial occasions. Posterity liked to tell tales of the drunken habits of Anacreon,[8] and his poetry certainly proves that he enjoyed wine. We need not press him too seriously when he says

[1] Hdt. 3. 41. 2. [2] Fr. 86 D.
[3] Schol. Aristoph. *Plut.* 999. [4] Zenob. 5. 80.
[5] Aristot. fr. 557 R. καὶ παροιμία τις ἐγεννήθη ἀπ' αὐτῶν.
[6] Hdt. 3. 39. 4. [7] Fr. 15 D. See *supra*, p. 250.
[8] Max. Tyr. 21. 7; *Anth. Pal.* 7. 24, 5 ff.

οὐδ' αὖ μ' ἐάσεις μεθύοντ' οἰκάδ' ἀπελθεῖν;[1]

'will you not allow me, now that I am drunk, to go home?', and indeed his poems on drink have their own skill and inventiveness. In one poem at an earlier stage he proclaims his desire to drink like a Bacchant, 'with no heel-taps', but even so he qualifies his desire with a respect for decorum:

ἄγε δή, φέρ' ἡμίν, ὦ παῖ,
κελέβην, ὅκως ἄμυστιν
προπίω, τὰ μὲν δέκ' ἐγχέας
ὕδατος, τὰ πέντε δ' οἴνου
κυάθους, ὡς ἀνυβρίστως
ἀνὰ δεῦτε βασσαρήσω.

Come boy, bring us a jar, that I may drink without taking breath; put in ten ladles of water to five of wine that I may play the Bacchant decorously.

But as the poem continues he changes his mood and calls for a more seemly conduct of the proceedings:

ἄγε δηῦτε μηκέθ' οὕτω
πατάγῳ τε κἀλαλητῷ
Σκυθικὴν πόσιν παρ' οἴνῳ
μελετῶμεν, ἀλλὰ καλοῖς
ὑποπίνοντες ἐν ὕμνοις.[2]

Come again, let us no longer tope like Scythians with din and uproar over the wine, but drink in moderation between beautiful hymns.

Even on a literally Dionysiac occasion Anacreon enjoys the preparations and pays attention to the correct performance of the rites:

ἐπὶ δ' ὀφρύσιν σελίνων στεφανίσκους
θέμενοι θάλειαν ἑορτὴν ἀγάγωμεν
Διονύσῳ.[3]

let us set little garlands of celery on our brows and hold a hearty feast for Dionysus.

Wine and feasting played a large part in Anacreon's life, but he

---

[1] Fr. 49 D. See Wilamowitz, *S.u.S.* p. 90 n. 2.

[2] Fr. 43 D. That the two pieces, despite P. Von der Muehll, *Hermes*, lxxv (1940), pp. 422 ff., come from the same poem is clear from Athenaeus' quotation 10. 427 a, in which after quoting the first piece, he uses the word προελθών of going on to the second; see E. Fraenkel, *Horace*, p. 179 n. 2.

[3] Fr. 37 D.

had a nice taste for their ceremonial variations and accommodated his art to them.

On such occasions Anacreon sang of his boy-loves. This seems
to have been the established custom in the circle of Polycrates,
and there may have been an air of artificiality about it. Poets
were expected to conform to their patron's taste and to show their
affinity with him. Anacreon certainly made much of the subject;
for, as Maximus of Tyre says:

> So too Anacreon made Polycrates more gentle to the Samians by
> mingling love with tyranny—the hair of Smerdies and Cleobulus, the
> beauty of Bathyllus, and Ionian song.[1]

The fragments contain nothing from Anacreon's songs to Bathyllus, but his relations with other boys are not without interest.
Megistes, to whom he writes about the μυθιῆται, seems to have
stirred in him feelings not unlike those which Theognis felt for
Cyrnus. In one place Anacreon praises him to his face for his
quiet ways:

> ἐγὼ δὲ μισέω
> πάντας, ὅσοι χθονίους ἔχουσι ῥυσμούς
> καὶ χαλεπούς· μεμάθηκά σ', ὦ Μεγίστη,
> τῶν ἀβακιζομένων.[2]

I hate all who have underground and difficult ways. I have learned,
Megistes, that you are one who is quiet.

So too he takes pride in Megistes' part in the worship of Dionysus,
whose cult was brought by the Carians[3] and may have been the
special concern of boys who had reached the age of puberty:

> ⟨ὁ⟩ Μεγιστῆς δ' ὁ φιλόφρων δέκα δὴ μῆνες ἐπείτε
> στεφανοῦταί τε λύγῳ καὶ τρύγα πίνει μελιηδέα.[4]

Ten months have passed since warm-hearted Megistes has crowned
himself with willow and drunk the honey-sweet wine.

In this there is a note of affectionate pride. If Anacreon conformed to current conventions, he was none the less sincere in the
expression of his love.

Of Smerdies too we know something. Anacreon's love for him

[1] 37. 5.
[2] Fr. 65 D. See Weber, p. 99. That Anacreon praises Megistes is clear from *Et.
Mag.* 2. 47 ἀντὶ τοῦ τῶν ἡσυχίων καὶ μὴ θορυβωδῶν.
[3] Athen. 15. 672 d.   [4] Fr. 21 D.

brought him into conflict with Polycrates, who was a rival for his affection and in a fit of temper cut off his hair.[1] Anacreon did not blame Polycrates, but accused the boy of cutting off his own hair, and wrote more than one poem on the subject. At one place he seems to have spoken of the boy as

$$\Theta\rho\eta\iota\kappa\acute{\iota}\eta\nu \ \sigma\iota\acute{o}\nu\tau\alpha \ \chi\alpha\acute{\iota}\tau\eta\nu^2$$

'tossing his Thracian hair', and at another to have blamed him for cutting it off:

$$\mathring{a}\pi\acute{e}\kappa\epsilon\iota\rho\alpha s \ \delta' \ \mathring{a}\pi\alpha\lambda\mathring{\eta}s \ \mathring{a}\mu\omega\mu\text{ov} \ \mathring{a}\nu\theta\text{os}^3$$

'You have cut off the perfect flower of your soft hair.' A recently published papyrus deals with the same subject and cannot be the work of anyone but Anacreon. The first surviving eight lines lament what has happened:

κⲁⲓ̀ κ[όμη]s, ἤ τοι κατ' ἀβρὸν
2   ἐσκία[ζ]εν αὐχένα.

νῦν δὲ δὴ σὺ μὲν στολοκρός,
ἡ δ' ἐς αὐχμηρὰς πεσοῦσα
χεῖρας ἀθρόη μέλαιναν
6   ἐς κόνιν κατερρύη,

τλῆμον[ο]s τομῇ σιδήρου
περιπεσοῦσ', ἐγὼ δ' ἄσῃσι
τείρομαι· τί γάρ τις ἔρξῃ
10   μηδ' ὑπὲρ Θρηίκης τυχών;⁴

And of the hair which shadowed your delicate neck. But now indeed you are cropped, and all your hair has fallen into coarse hands and flowed down into the black dust, having encountered the cleaving stroke of the ruthless iron. I am distressed with sorrow. For what is a man to do who has failed even for Thrace's sake?

This version of what has happened is rather different from the later tradition or from what Anacreon himself says in fr. 46.

---

[1] Stob. Ecl. 4. 21; Athen. 12. 540 e; Ael. V.H. 9. 4.

[2] Fr. 47 D. So far as the metre is concerned, this could come from the same poem as either fr. 46 D. or Ox. Pap. 2322.   [3] Fr. 46 D.

[4] Ox. Pap. xxii. 2322; see W. Peek, W.Z.M.–L.H. v (1955–6), pp. 200–2. C. Gallavotti, P.P. xl (1955), pp. 41–47, does not convince me that the poem is the work of an Alexandrian imitator. In 7 τλημόν[ω]s is possible in the sense of 'miserably', as at Eur. Tro. 40 and Hesych. τλημόνως· ἐλεεινῶς, but perhaps τλῆμον[ο]s is more apt in the sense of 'ruthless', as at Aesch. Cho. 384; Theog. 196; Soph. El. 439; Eur. Med. 865. For the application of such an epithet to iron cf. Soph. Trach. 886 στονόεντος ἐν τομᾷ σιδάρου.

Here Smerdies is not reproached for cutting off his own hair; for, when Anacreon says that it has fallen ἐς αὐχμηρὰς χεῖρας, he surely means that it has fallen into the squalid hands of some barber's assistant.[1] If the boy had cut off his own hair, it would not have fallen into his own hands, and they would hardly be called αὐχμηράς. The obvious solution is that he has got someone to do it for him, and that when Anacreon accuses him elsewhere of doing it himself, he means that it was done by his choice. Nor does Anacreon's temper suggest upbraiding. The words ἄσῃσι τείρομαι come from the language of love and its anguish.[2] He is saddened and distressed by the loss of something which he loved.

In 9–10 the reference to Thrace is undeniably puzzling. The words are in the papyrus and make sense grammatically. The question is rather of their implications. We may perhaps find a clue in the consideration that Smerdies' hair was regarded as characteristically Thracian. Anacreon certainly does so at fr. 46, and the same implication may be seen in a line about him by Antipater of Sidon

ἢ Κίκονα Θρηκὸς Σμερδίεω πλόκαμον[3]

'for the Ciconian lock of Thracian Smerdies', and in another epigram which mentions Anacreon's loves:

καὶ τὸν Σμερδίεω Θρῆκα λέλοιπε πόκον,[4]

'and he has left the Thracian lock of Smerdies'. The Thracians wore their hair long, and this was regarded as one of their charms, but the appeal to Anacreon may have been more than this, and his insistence on the Thracian character of Smerdies' hair may have referred to its colour or texture or both. The lines then reveal their meaning. Anacreon has fought for Smerdies' hair as if he were fighting for Thrace and its national honour, but he has failed and cannot see what he can do now. The slight exaggeration is typical of him and shows that, despite his distress, he is still able to introduce a small touch of absurdity.

The papyrus goes on without any sign of a break with two more stanzas:

[1] For αὐχμηρός in this sense cf. Eur. *Alc.* 947; *Hel.* 1540; Plat. *Symp.* 203 d.
[2] For ἄσῃσι cf. Sappho fr. 1. 3 L.–P.; Eur. *Med.* 245; for τείρομαι cf. Hes. fr. 105 R.; Telestes fr. 1. 7 D.
[3] *Anth. Pal.* 7. 27. 6.
[4] Ibid. 7. 25. 8.

οἰκτρὰ δὴ φρονεῖν ἀκού[ω
τὴν ἀρίγνωτον γυναῖ[κα,
πολλάκις δὲ δὴ τόδ' εἰπ[εῖν
14   δαίμον' αἰτιωμέ[ν]η[ν·

ὡ]ς ἂν εὖ πάθοιμι, μῆτερ,
εἰ] μ' ἀμείλιχον φέρουσα
π]όντον ἐσβάλοις θυίοντα
18   π]ορφ[υρ]έοισι κύμασι.¹

I hear that the lady, easy to recognize, has pitiful thoughts, and often, as she blames her destiny, she says this: 'How well would be my case, mother, if you were to carry me and cast me into the pitiless sea that rages with purple waves.'

It is not clear what connexion this has with what precedes, or whether it has any connexion at all. We might at first think that it comes from the same poem, since it is in the same metre and there is no sign in the papyrus that a new poem begins. But at this point the edge of the papyrus is cut so closely that, even if such a sign had existed, we should not see it. The question is therefore open and must be settled on grounds of sense or coherence. First, let us assume that this is a single poem and that Anacreon turns from his grief on the loss of Smerdies' hair to the mention of τὴν ἀρίγνωτον γυναῖκα. It has been suggested that she is Thrace personified or some eponymous heroine with the same name.² Such were certainly known in Hellenistic times,³ but we may doubt whether she is in question here. First, the reference to such an abstraction is unlike Anacreon's usually concrete and factual manner. He does not seem to have been interested in mythological figures of this kind and does not elsewhere mention them. Secondly, if Thrace is referred to in this way, we should expect some word of explanation, but all we get is τὴν ἀρίγνωτον γυναῖκα, and whatever γυναῖκα may mean, it cannot mean 'heroine'. Thirdly, if it is Thrace who laments the loss of Smerdies' hair, who is the mother of whom she speaks, and what are we to make of her lament? Thrace had indeed a mother called

¹ In 11 ἀκούω is not certain but seems on most hypotheses to be more direct and pointed than ἀκούεις. It is remarkable, as H. Lloyd-Jones points out to me, that the first syllable of θυίοντα should be short. I know of no parallel to this, but can think of no suitable emendation for a word which in itself makes excellent sense.

² Lobel, ad loc.

³ Schol. Aesch. P.V. 185; Tzetz. in Lyc. 894; Steph. Byz. s.v. Θρᾴκη.

Parthenope,[1] and presumably her words mean that she wishes her land to be engulfed in the sea. This is surely too cold and too inhuman an hyperbole for Anacreon and suggests that we should look for another explanation.

If we still assume that all comes from a single poem, we might argue that the words refer not to the abstraction of Thrace but to a real woman, and this is the natural meaning of γυναῖκα in the context. Anacreon, then, refers to 'the famous lady', and leaves it to his audience to identify her, just as in fr. 5 he does not give the name of the 'girl with motley slippers', because presumably everyone knows who she is. She might be some woman well known at Samos for her devotion to Smerdies. She may be assumed to be still young, since she complains like a child to her mother and blames her δαίμων for what has happened. Her complaint indicates an unqualified despair, and when Anacreon tells of it, he may in part reveal through her some of his own feelings or at least his commiseration with her. Yet even this does not seem very satisfactory. ἀρίγνωτος does not in fact mean so much 'well known' as 'easily known', and the hint is that Anacreon has in mind some woman who will be recognized by his audience at once, and though this is not inconsistent with the view that she is in love with Smerdies, it leaves open the possibility that the words are in some degree ironical. But what really troubles us is the abrupt change of sense. Though δή can be used in a connective sense,[2] it is not often so used, and we should expect something more coherent. This leads to the third possibility that here begins a new poem, and this is at least not inconsistent with the evidence of the papyrus.

If we try this hypothesis, we can see that it has certain advantages. It not only rids us of the need to identify the woman with Thrace, but it gives to the eight lines a perfectly satisfactory coherence in themselves. The poem begins dramatically, and δή serves a proper purpose in drawing attention to οἰκτρά and setting the note of the poem at the start. Anacreon goes straight for his main subject without preliminaries, and repeats what he has heard. His subject is of some young woman, not indeed a girl but still young enough to behave very like one, who laments her sad state and wishes to be cast into the sea. We must assume that

---

[1] She was one of the Sirens, *De Mir. Ausc.* 103; Steph. Byz. s.v. Σειρηνοῦσσαι.
[2] J. D. Denniston, *The Greek Particles²*, p. 240.

everyone will know at once who she is and that Anacreon does not mention her name because it is not necessary and might even spoil the effect of his words, by removing the air of news which they convey. The woman blames her δαίμων, as Deianira does in her last moments before killing herself,[1] or Plato makes the man who has made the wrong choice of becoming a tyrant and regrets it too late blame not himself but his fortune and his δαίμονες and everything except himself.[2] Yet though this is natural enough, we may suspect that Anacreon is not quite so sympathetic as we might think and that his words have in them a slight touch of malice or mockery. The woman in question longs for death in the sea, but the words which describe it with so pictorial a brilliance are hardly heart-broken and suggest that Anacreon is exaggerating the woman's grief in order to discredit it quietly. We have no notion how the poem continued, and it remains a tantalizing fragment, which shows how Anacreon's delicate art could be put to more than one kind of purpose and exploit its own shades of subtlety.

Boys and youths provided Anacreon not only with objects for his affection but to some degree with an audience. At least in one place he claims that his songs have an appeal for them:

> ἐμὲ γὰρ λόγων ⟨ἐμῶν⟩ εἴνεκα παῖδες ἂν φιλοῖεν·
> χαρίεντα μὲν γὰρ ᾄδω, χαρίεντα δ' οἶδα λέξαι.[3]

Boys would love me for my words; for I sing what is charming and I know how to say what is charming.

This element of χάρις is prominent in Anacreon's work. He is more eager to please than to impress, to catch the gaiety of the moment than to touch on solemn issues. But because he has strong emotions and is not always ready to display them in all their strength, he exercises that kind of imaginative wit which comes from disguising them in some graceful or fantastic image, or from making them look not too important by stopping just at the point where they might become disturbing and by turning them aside with something that is almost a joke. Indeed, much of his poetry may be summed up in his own words:

---

[1] Soph. *Trach.* 910 αὐτὴ τὸν αὑτῆς δαίμον' ἀνακαλουμένη.

[2] *Rep.* 10. 619 c οὐ . . . ἑαυτὸν αἰτιᾶσθαι τῶν κακῶν, ἀλλὰ τύχην τε καὶ δαίμονας καὶ πάντα μᾶλλον ἀνθ' ἑαυτοῦ.

[3] Fr. 32 D. Blass suggested ⟨μελέων τε⟩ after λόγων.

ἐρέω τε δηὖτε κοὐκ ἐρέω
καὶ μαίνομαι κοὐ μαίνομαι.[1]

'Again I am in love and not in love, am mad and not mad.' Half
of him watches the other half, and is amused by the spectacle.
Just as Suckling writes, with an assumption of surprise, 'Out
upon it, I have loved Three whole days together', so Anacreon
treats love as something not of paramount importance and is
able to keep it in hand. His method is neatly exemplified in a
complete little poem:

ὦναξ, ᾧ δαμάλης Ἔρως
καὶ Νύμφαι κυανώπιδες
    πορφυρέη τ᾽ Ἀφροδίτη
συμπαίζουσιν· ἐπιστρέφεαι δ᾽
ὑψηλὰς ὀρέων κορυφάς,
    γουνοῦμαί σε, σὺ δ᾽ εὐμενὴς
ἔλθ᾽ ἡμῖν, κεχαρισμένης δ᾽
    εὐχωλῆς ἐπακούειν.
Κλευβούλῳ δ᾽ ἀγαθὸς γενεῦ
σύμβουλος, τὸν ἐμὸν δ᾽ ἔρωτ᾽,
    ὦ Δεύνυσε, δέχεσθαι.[2]

Master, with whom Love the subduer and the blue-eyed Nymphs and
rosy Aphrodite play, who hauntest the high peaks of the mountains,
I beseech thee. Come to us with kindly heart, and let our prayer
please thee, and hearken to it. Be a good counsellor to Cleobulus, and
may he, O Dionysus, receive my love.

This is no formal hymn for a ceremony but a song among friends.
Wilamowitz may well be right when he suggests that it is sung
in the spring, when over the wine Anacreon turns his thoughts to
love.[3] He addresses Dionysus, as suits the festive moment, and
offers a prayer to him. He imagines the god with his joyous company of Eros, Aphrodite, and the Nymphs, and presents a vivid
picture of them as they rove the hills. He makes them vivid not
by the stock epithets derived from the epic but by new epithets of
his own minting. Eros is δαμάλης, the subduer of men;[4] Aphrodite

[1] Fr. 79 D. In the surviving fragments Anacreon uses δηὖτε five times with
reference to love. B. Snell, *The Discovery of the Mind*, p. 58, comments, 'we suspect
his heart is not in it'. But Sappho uses δηὖτε hardly less often, and we should hardly
make the same comment of her. It looks as if δηὖτε did not quite have the full force
of our 'again' but simply drew attention to a new situation.
[2] Fr. 2 D; see Weber, p. 27.   [3] *S.u.S.* p. 113.
[4] Wilamowitz translates 'der Jungstier', but cf. Hesych., δαμάλην· τὸν Ἔρωτα.
ἤτοι τὸν δαμάζοντα.

is πορφυρέη because of the glow that shines from her;[1] the Nymphs, who reared Dionysus and taught him song,[2] are κυανώπιδες, perhaps because blue eyes are a rarity in Greece and have a special distinction. The adjectives create a brilliant scene in a very few words. Then comes the climax. Dionysus is asked to be a good σύμβουλος to Κλεύβουλος and the deliberate play on the words shows that, when Anacreon comes to his own emotions, he is not going to make too grand a parade of them. The vernal parade of the gods leads up to this little joke, and though there is something serious behind it, Anacreon covers it with a smile.

A similar humour may be seen in three other lines to Cleobulus:

> Κλευβούλου μὲν ἔγωγ' ἐρέω,
> Κλευβούλῳ δ' ἐπιμαίνομαι
> Κλεύβουλον δὲ διοσκέω.[3]

Cleobulus I love, for Cleobulus I am mad, on Cleobulus I gaze.

Here the gaiety is in the form. The name Cleobulus is repeated, first in the genitive, then in the dative, finally in the accusative. This is an amusing trope, which Anacreon may have derived from Archilochus, who wrote of someone whose power he resented:

> νῦν δὲ Λεώφιλος μὲν ἄρχει, Λεώφιλος δ' ἐπικρατεῖ,
> Λεωφίλῳ δὲ πάντα κεῖται, Λεωφίλου δ' ἀκούεται.[4]

Now Leophilus rules, Leophilus has power, everything is in the grasp of Leophilus, Leophilus is listened to.

Anacreon improves upon this device and turns it from complaint to love. It helps to lessen the impact of the forceful words ἐρέω and ἐπιμαίνομαι, and the climax is simply that Anacreon gazes on Cleobulus. He takes the situation as it is, and is not too distressed that it ends in nothing but looks.

In these passages Anacreon keeps his emotions at a level of common experience by refusing to make too much of them. His eye is for the given moment, and even if it is one of defeat for him, he presents it with the same immediacy and reality. So he speaks of a girl:

---

[1] B. Marzullo, *Maia*, iii (1950), thinks it means 'of the sea', but see A. Castrignano, ibid. v (1952), pp. 118–21.

[2] Soph. *O.T.* 1109; Hor. *C.* 2. 19. 3.   [3] Fr. 3 D.

[4] Fr. 70 D. In 2 Λεωφίλου is Porson's emendation for Λεώφιλος.

σφαίρῃ δηὖτέ με πορφυρέῃ
βάλλων χρυσικόμης Ἔρως
νηνὶ ποικιλοσαμβάλῳ
συμπαίζειν προκαλεῖται.
ἦ δ'—ἔστιν γὰρ ἀπ' εὐκτίτου
Λέσβου—τὴν μὲν ἐμὴν κόμην,
λευκὴ γάρ, καταμέμφεται,
πρὸς δ' ἄλλην τινὰ χάσκει.[1]

Again gold-haired Love strikes me with a purple ball and summons me to play with a motley-slippered maiden. But she, for she comes from well-settled Lesbos, despises my hair, for it is white, and gapes after another girl.

Anacreon fancies that Eros, a beautiful youth with hair of gold, summons him by throwing a ball at him. An older, simpler fashion would have been to throw an apple, but here Eros is on the way to become the σφαιριστής which Apollonius[2] and Meleager[3] make him. He is conceived not as a small boy, but as a youth who would, like other Greek youths, often play with a ball. The challenge to Anacreon is that he must 'play', συμπαίζειν, with a girl who is designated as wearing motley slippers. The word συμπαίζειν can mean a good deal and does not exclude the play of lovers.[4] 'Motley-slippered' is not a stock epithet and must describe some definite person known to the company. Anacreon withholds her name, presumably because the description is quite enough to identify her. But she turns away from him because he has white hair and because she has the wrong tastes. She comes from Lesbos and shares the propensities of her island. In their quiet way the words are mocking and even malicious. The final χάσκει, is used for all kinds of gaping and is never very polite.[5] There is some mystery about εὐκτίτου. In a poem where everything else is pointed, it too should have a point. It is clearly derived from the Homeric ἐϋκτιμένῃ ἐνὶ Λέσβῳ,[6] but that does not explain why Anacreon uses it. Perhaps it is intended to convey a sense of security and established position, to show that the girl is not a slave who must do what Anacreon wants, but comes from a free home and can pick and choose. Or perhaps it is a sly

---

[1] Fr. 5 D. Cf. Wilamowitz, *S.u.S.* pp. 195 ff.; Page, *S. and A.* p. 143.
[2] 3. 135 ff. [3] *Anth. Pal.* 5. 214.
[4] Xen. *Symp.* 9. 2.
[5] Solon fr. 1. 36 D.; Aristoph. *Equ.* 804; *Nub.* 172; *Ran.* 990.
[6] *Od.* 9. 34; 17. 133.

dig at Lesbos, which is as well established in certain habits as it is in other ways. The poem combines a fresh transcript from life with a stroke of true fancy in the appearance of Eros, and the two elements are perfectly united.

In his concern with love Anacreon developed his own way of dealing with its different tones and tempers by image and metaphor, and drew freely on mythology, folk-lore, colloquial speech, and anything else which might help him to express himself in a lively and arresting fashion. In this respect his art is more sophisticated and more elaborate than Sappho's; for she was on the whole content with direct statement and with the accepted figures of religion and mythology. How elaborate this art can be may be seen from a papyrus which is indeed fragmentary but yields a more or less coherent sense. The poem is addressed to a boy:

> οὐδὲ[. . . .]ς, φ[. .]α
> φοβερὰς δ' ἔχεις πρὸς ἄλλῳ
> 3   φρένας, ὦ καλλιπρό[σ]ωπε παίδ[ων,
>
> καί σε δοκέει μὲν ἐ[ν δό]μοισιν
> πυκινῶς ἔχουσα [μήτηρ
> 6   ἀτιτάλλειν σ[ὺ
>
> τὰς ὑακιν[θίνας ἀρ]ούρας
> ἵ]να Κύπρις ἐκ λεπάδνων
> 9   ]. .α[ς κ]ατέδησεν ἵππους,
>
>]δ' ἐν μέσῳ κατῆξας
>]ῳ, δι' ἄσσα πολλοὶ
> 12   πολι]ητέων φρένας ἐπτοέαται.[1]

[1] *Ox. Pap.* xxii. 2321, fr. 1; see Peek, op. cit. pp. 196–8; P. Maas, *Acme,* viii (1955), pp. 113–14; Merkelbach, *Archiv f. Papyrusforsch.* xvi (1956), pp. 96–97. In 5 μήτηρ (Peek, Lloyd-Jones) must be right, as no other feminine word of this scansion makes sense. It strengthens the case for Lloyd-Jones's ἐν δόμοισιν in 4, where Maas wishes to read κρίνοισι, quoting Ibycus fr. 8 D., with the implication that the boy is nursed by Aphrodite in a spring meadow, but this conflicts with πυκινῶς ἔχουσα. In 9 the first word may have been an adjective for the mares, such as ἐροέσσας or χαριέσσας, but certainty is out of the question. In 10 the sense depends on what we make of κατῆξας. This could (*a*) come from κατάγω, as in Philum. *Ven.* 10. 4, but does not yield any clear sense, or (*b*) from κατάγνυμι, 'shattered', as in Hippocr. *Epid.* 5. 26, but this seems too violent, unless with Lloyd-Jones we supply ἄξονα at the beginning of the line, comparing Callim. fr. 260. 53, or (*c*) we could read κατῆξας in the sense of 'darted down'. For the beginning of 10 Peek's ἄστυ σύ is ungainly with its postponed δέ. ἄστυνδε is neater, but something like αὐτίκα is just as likely. In 11 Peek's δνοφερῷ is not appropriate, since the boy's beauty would not make much impression in the dark. B. Gentili suggests

In the presence of another you have a frightened heart, boy with the beautiful face. Your mother thinks that she keeps you fast at home and nurses you, but you . . . the fields of hyacinths, where the Cyprian has tethered her . . . mares from the yoke. In the middle of the . . . you darted down . . . wherefore many of the citizens have been fluttered in their hearts.

The art of these lines lies in the combination of quite simple statements with a striking and unusual imagery. They begin with an address to a beautiful boy, who seems to be shy or frightened. The precise meaning of the words depends on how we take πρὸς ἄλλῳ. This might mean, as Lobel suggests, 'as well', and this would imply that Anacreon has already said something else which this reinforces. If we feel this to be a little flat, we could take the words to mean 'in the presence of another', and though there is no close parallel to this before the fourth century,[1] it certainly makes good sense. Alternatively we might take the words to mean 'at something else',[2] with reference to some event or action, but it is less easy to see a neuter in ἄλλῳ than a masculine. In the present state of the text it is impossible to decide which, if any, of these interpretations is right, but it is clear that Anacreon is concerned with the boy's shyness.

The second surviving stanza tells simply and factually how his mother believes that she has the boy in safe keeping at home, and the word ἀτιτάλλειν implies that for her he is still a child, rather as Penelope brought up Dolios[3] or Chiron Achilles.[4] At the end of it Anacreon must surely have said that the boy has managed to escape from maternal surveillance, but the place of his escape, which appears in the third stanza, is a dazzling surprise. We are unexpectedly confronted with fields of hyacinth, where Aphrodite has unloosed her mares from the yoke and tethered them. The

ὁμάδῳ, which is more to the point, if it is not too short for the space. In that case θορύβῳ might be considered. Lloyd-Jones suggests δαπέδῳ. Merkelbach, p. 98, suggests persuasively that the lines should be rearranged to give a more familiar colometry:

$$-\cup\cup-\cup-\cup-$$
$$-\cup\cup-\cup-\cup-$$
$$-\cup\cup--\cup\cup-\cup--$$

This may well be right, and I have kept the papyrus scheme only because it indicates how the lines appear on it.

[1] Dem. 20. 98; 22. 28.
[2] Cf. Aristoph. *Nub.* 1010; Plat. *Rep.* 6. 500 b.
[3] *Od.* 18. 323.
[4] Pind. *Nem.* 3. 58.

word κατέδησεν is known from Homer, who, however, uses it for
tethering horses to mangers.[1] Anacreon uses the word for tethering horses in a field, as Hera tethers hers when she dismounts
from the chariot at the junction of Simois and Scamander.[2]
Such an action was too familiar to call for elaboration or explanation, and Anacreon introduces it nicely to give realism
and solidity to this sudden entry into a mythological scene. The
boy escapes to the field of hyacinths, where Aphrodite, no doubt
expecting him, is already present. The meadow can hardly be a
real meadow, though it is presented in a perfectly realistic way.
It is surely Aphrodite's counterpart to the unsullied meadow of
Artemis known from Euripides[3] and to the κᾶπος ἀκήρατος of
Ibycus.[4] It does for the awakening of desire, which is Aphrodite's
province, what these others do for the preservation of innocence.
The hyacinths suggest that this garden too enjoys the spring, and
the image of them conveys what it means in all its splendour to the
boy. He, who has been so carefully guarded at home, breaks away
into an entirely new world, which is presented in the language of
imaginative myth as something no less real than what he has just
left in a different order of things. There is no awkwardness in the
transition from the one order to the other, and the brilliant scene
conveys the radiance of the change which takes place in the boy.
In introducing the field of hyacinths Anacreon does in a more
striking way the same kind of thing as when he makes Eros a
youth with golden hair who throws a ball. He gives substance to
a state of mind by making it entirely visual and concrete and
enriching it with associations drawn from myth.

From this imaginative state Anacreon moves back to plainer
facts, which are no less dramatic. In the fourth stanza it is at
least clear that the boy has fluttered the hearts of the Samians.
This must be by his beauty, which is revealed as he appears
among them, and the situation is not very different from that in
Pindar, when Jason arrives at Iolcus

ἐν ἀγορᾷ πλήθοντος ὄχλου,[5]

and the onlookers are so struck by his appearance that they compare him with gods and heroes as they wonder who he can possibly be. Jason is a fully grown young man, and Anacreon's boy

---

[1] *Il.* 8. 434; 10. 567; *Od.* 4. 40.   [2] *Il.* 5. 775.
[3] *Hipp.* 74–81.   [4] Fr. 6. 4 D.   [5] *Pyth.* 4. 85.

is still only a boy, but the situations are similar in their vision of the crowd amazed at the new sight. Anacreon, however, stresses with some subtlety the special appeal which his boy makes. His word ἐπτοέαται recalls how Sappho's heart is set fluttering as she watches a girl[1] and perhaps finds an echo in Apollonius when he tells of the nymph whose heart is fluttered by Aphrodite at the sight of Hylas.[2] So in Anacreon the climax of the boy's adventure is when he makes his dramatic appearance among the citizens. With this the poem probably ends, and the extant lines fall into three stages—the boy's shy, restricted life at home, his discovery of Aphrodite, and his appearance in public. The first and last stages are presented realistically, and the second gains in contrast by being placed in a world of myth.

In the papyrus these lines are followed by another:

λεωφόρε, λεωφόρ' Ἡροτίμη.

It can hardly belong to the same poem, since the break in sense is too violent and the invocation of Herotime in the vocative suggests a fresh start in another poem on a different theme. This poem was evidently of quite a different kind. We know from ancient authorities[3] that Anacreon used the word λεωφόρος in the sense of πόρνη, and it is a sharp word of mockery, derived perhaps from vulgar speech. The word means 'highway', and there is no difficulty in seeing how it came to have the special meaning which Anacreon gives to it. Though it shows a very different temper from the images of the preceding poem, it is in its own way no less effective. It is perhaps developed from the notion that unfaithful lovers went astray κατ' ἀμάξιτον.[4] By an easy transposition the metaphor is shifted from what they do to what they are, and λεωφόρος conveys the idea with precision and contempt.

Anacreon also draws on current lore to give a new point or a dramatic interest to his feelings. So he writes:

ἀρθεὶς δηῦτ' ἀπὸ Λευκάδος
πέτρης ἐς πολιὸν κῦμα κολυμβέω μεθύων ἔρωτι.[5]

Again I climb up and dive from the Leucadian Rock into the hoary sea, drunk with love.

[1] Fr. 22. 14; cf. 31. 6 L.–P.   [2] 1. 1232.
[3] Eustath. 1329. 34; 1088. 38; 'Suid.' s.v. Μυσάχνη.
[4] Theogn. 599.   [5] Fr. 17 D.

The leap from the Leucadian Rock was thought to cure those
who suffered from unrequited love or to change the hearts of
their loved ones. So Calyce was said to have leapt from it out of
love for Euathlus,[1] and the story of Sappho's suicide is probably
due to a similar story told of her.[2] In it Anacreon finds an image
for himself. To gain his desire he proposes to leap into the sea of
love in the hope that his desperate risk may be rewarded. There
may even be a special point in μεθύων, for Euripides' Cyclops
proclaims his readiness

> ῥῖψαί τ' ἐς ἅλμην Λευκάδος πέτρας ἄπο,
> ἅπαξ μεθυσθεὶς καταβαλών τε τὰς ὀφρῦς.[3]

And once I'm drunk I'll close my eyes and leap
From the Leucadian Rock into the sea.

This suggests that those who made the leap sometimes comforted
or steeled themselves first with drink, and Anacreon may have
made use of the idea for his own purpose. His image illustrates,
not without humorous exaggeration, the state to which love has
reduced him.

In his avoidance of anything which might savour of pomposity
and to keep his usual air of not making too much show of his
feelings, Anacreon uses familiar phrases. If he has a special point
to make, he may combine two such images:

> μεγάλῳ δηῦτέ μ' Ἔρως ἔκοψεν, ὥστε χαλκεὺς
> πελέκει, χειμερίῃ δ' ἔλουσεν ἐν χαράδρῃ.[4]

Love, like a smith, smote me again with a great axe and soused me in
a wintry torrent.

Love has struck Anacreon a nasty blow and left him in trouble.
The blow is described in language which recalls the sacrifice of an
ox in Homer, when Thrasymedes stands by the victim and kills it
with a single blow from an axe.[5] Anacreon is not killed, but he
sees himself as at least stunned. This is combined with the different image of being soused in a wintry torrent. So too Theognis,

[1] Athen. 14. 619 e.
[2] Wilamowitz, S.u.S. pp. 29–30.
[3] Cyc. 166–7.
[4] Fr. 45 D. Cf. E. Schwyzer, Rh. Mus. lxxix, pp. 314 ff., where he argues that
πέλεκυς means 'hammer'.
[5] Od. 3. 442–50.

telling how badly he has been treated by his enemies, who have robbed him of his property, says:

$$\dot{\epsilon}\gamma\dot{\omega}\ \delta\dot{\epsilon}\ \kappa\dot{\upsilon}\omega\nu\ \dot{\epsilon}\pi\dot{\epsilon}\rho\eta\sigma\alpha\ \chi\alpha\rho\dot{\alpha}\delta\rho\eta\nu$$
$$\chi\epsilon\iota\mu\dot{\alpha}\rho\rho\omega\ \pi\sigma\tau\dot{\alpha}\mu\omega\ \pi\dot{\alpha}\nu\tau'\ \dot{\alpha}\pi\sigma\sigma\epsilon\iota\sigma\dot{\alpha}\mu\epsilon\nu\sigma\varsigma.[1]$$

I am the dog who crossed the torrent, having shaken off everything in the wintry river.

This image, presented as it is without introduction or explanation, must imply some fable or proverb or colloquial phrase. A dog, with a burden on its back, is caught in a torrent and gets out by abandoning the burden. The torrent is an image for trouble, and that is what Anacreon means. It is tempting to think that χαράδρη is chosen because it was used, as it was later in Attic comedy,[2] for a spate of words and that Anacreon has found himself deluged with abuse. But there is no solid evidence for this any more than there is for the view that these lines refer to his quarrel with Polycrates over Smerdies.[3]

Another, rather simpler, example of this method may be seen in the language with which Anacreon proclaims his belief in the Mean:

$$\dot{\epsilon}\gamma\dot{\omega}\ \delta'\ \sigma\ddot{\upsilon}\tau'\ \ddot{\alpha}\nu\ \mathcal{A}\mu\alpha\lambda\theta\dot{\epsilon}\eta\varsigma$$
$$\beta\sigma\upsilon\lambda\sigma\dot{\iota}\mu\eta\nu\ \kappa\dot{\epsilon}\rho\alpha\varsigma\ \sigma\ddot{\upsilon}\tau'\ \ddot{\epsilon}\tau\epsilon\alpha$$
$$\pi\epsilon\nu\tau\dot{\eta}\kappa\sigma\nu\tau\dot{\alpha}\ \tau\epsilon\ \kappa\dot{\alpha}\kappa\alpha\tau\dot{\sigma}\nu$$
$$T\alpha\rho\tau\eta\sigma\sigma\sigma\hat{\upsilon}\ \beta\alpha\sigma\iota\lambda\epsilon\hat{\upsilon}\sigma\alpha\iota.[4]$$

I would not wish for Amalthea's horn, nor to be king of Tartessus for a hundred and fifty years.

Here two disparate images are used as examples of what a sane man does not desire. The horn of Amalthea is known from an earlier contemporary of Anacreon. A couplet of Phocylides says:

$$\chi\rho\eta\dot{\iota}\zeta\omega\nu\ \pi\lambda\sigma\dot{\upsilon}\tau\sigma\upsilon\ \mu\epsilon\lambda\dot{\epsilon}\tau\eta\nu\ \ddot{\epsilon}\chi\epsilon\ \pi\dot{\iota}\sigma\nu\sigma\varsigma\ \dot{\alpha}\gamma\rho\sigma\hat{\upsilon},$$
$$\dot{\alpha}\gamma\rho\dot{\sigma}\nu\ \gamma\dot{\alpha}\rho\ \tau\epsilon\ \lambda\dot{\epsilon}\gamma\sigma\upsilon\sigma\iota\nu\ \mathcal{A}\mu\alpha\lambda\theta\epsilon\dot{\iota}\eta\varsigma\ \kappa\dot{\epsilon}\rho\alpha\varsigma\ \epsilon\hat{\iota}\nu\alpha\iota.[5]$$

If you desire wealth, take care of a fat field; for they say that a field is a horn of Amalthea.

The goat who nursed the infant Zeus was credited with miraculous horns, whose gifts provided later poets with opportunities for

---

[1] 347–8. J. Carrière, *Théognis*, p. 107, argues that there is no need to presuppose a fable (cf. Bergk *ad loc.*) and that the image is provoked naturally by the poet's circumstances. If so, it would surely be clearer than it is, and its appearance in two authors suggests a common source in lore or fable.

[2] Aristoph. *Vesp.* 1034; *Pax* 757.   [3] J. M. Edmonds, *L.G.* ii, p. 163.

[4] Fr. 8 D. Cf. Plin. *N.H.* 7. 48 (49). 154.   [5] No. 7 D.

ingenious fancy. It was said that one horn flowed with nectar and
the other with ambrosia,[1] while Ovid tells that, when the horn
was broken on a tree, the Nymphs filled it with fruits and brought
it to Zeus.[2] In Anacreon's time the powers of the horn need not
have been so clearly delineated, but for him it was clearly a
miraculous source of plenty. He refuses its gifts because he does
not want money, and this agrees with the story that, when pay
was offered to him, he refused it.[3] The second reference, to the
king of Tartessus, who reigned for a hundred and fifty years, is
likely to be a Samian story and suggests that the poem was written in Samos. Herodotus tells how in the seventh century the
Phocaeans penetrated to the far West of the Mediterranean and
formed a friendship with the king of Tartessus, who ruled for
eighty years and lived to be a hundred and twenty years old.[4]
He died before the fatal battle of Alalia in 535 which cut off the
West from Greek ships. But before the Phocaeans a Samian,
Colaeus, had made the first Greek voyage to Tartessus and
brought back a rich cargo.[5] His fame endured in Samos, and with
it the story of the old king. So when Anacreon, with pardonable
exaggeration, makes the king reign for a hundred and fifty
years, everyone would take his point.

Anacreon supplemented his colloquial phrases with metaphors
drawn from every day. Rather than see love as something super-
human, he saw that it could be related to common things and
described through images drawn from them. He knew, for instance, that it may lead to wild frenzy, but what he wrote was

$$\dot{a}\sigma\tau\rho\alpha\gamma\dot{a}\lambda\alpha\iota \ \delta' \ {}^{\prime\prime}E\rho\omega\tau\acute{o}s \ \epsilon\dot{\iota}\sigma\iota\nu$$
$$\mu\alpha\nu\acute{\iota}\alpha\iota \ \tau\epsilon \ \kappa\alpha\grave{\iota} \ \kappa\upsilon\delta\sigma\iota\mu\sigma\acute{\iota}.^{6}$$

'Love's dice are madness and turmoils.' Here a serious thought is
attached to a trivial image to lessen its weight. Anacreon, true to
the Greek tradition, regarded love as a dangerous and destructive
force, but he would not present it quite like this to his audience.
So he introduces the metaphor of knucklebones, which were the
ancient equivalent of dice. In giving this familiar disguise to his
subject he hints how incalculable love is when it treats madness

[1] Schol. Callim. *Hymn* 1. 49.
[2] *Fast.* 5. 115–28. Variant accounts are given by Antiphan. fr. 109 K.; Philoxenus
fr. 3. 5 B.; Lucian *Merc. Cond.* 13; Plut. *de Absurd. Stoic.* 5.
[3] Schol. Pind. *Isthm.* 2. 13.   [4] Hdt. 1. 163. 2.
[5] Id. 4. 152. 2.   [6] Fr. 34 D; see Weber, p. 50.

and turmoil as a game. His method is far removed from that of
Apollonius, who makes Eros and Ganymedes play with golden
dice.[1] Behind Anacreon's image lies an imaginative grasp of what
love means and costs. Conversely, when he wishes not to make too
much of a theme but to show it as part of common life, he will
catch just the right tone by some simple, short image. For
instance, he calls for wine:

> φέρ' ὕδωρ, φέρ' οἶνον, ὦ παῖ, φέρε δ' ἀνθεμόεντας ἡμῖν
> στεφάνους, ἔνεικον, ὡς δὴ πρὸς "Ερωτα πυκταλίζω.[2]

Bring water, bring wine, boy, bring garlands of flowers for us, bring
them at once, that I may box with love.

Here Eros is, as elsewhere, a youth, and Anacreon conceives that
he wishes to spar with him. So, speaking of some trouble, presumably love, through which he has passed and from which he
has recovered, he says:

> ὃς χα]λεπῶς δ' ἐπυκτάλιζ[ον
> νῦν] ἀνορέω τε κἀνακύπτω.[3]

I, who sparred painfully, now look up and lift my head.

Anacreon relates his sense of the pangs and struggles of love to an
image which does not minimize them but treats them almost
as a sporting event, and gains its colour from its context. How
powerful and solemn the same image could be when it applied
in a different spirit can be seen from two lines which Sophocles
gives to Deianira:

> "Ερωτι μέν νυν ὅστις ἀντανίσταται
> πύκτης ὅπως ἐς χεῖρας, οὐ καλῶς φρονεῖ.[4]

Whoso stands up to Love to have a round
Of fisticuffs with him, has lost his wits.

The difference of tone comes from Sophocles' conviction that
Love governs the gods as he wills and that human beings cannot
fight against him. Anacreon does not view the subject in so grave
and tragic a spirit. In fr. 27 he enters almost willingly into it, and
faces it almost as a pastime, not as a fight in which he is sure to be
worsted. Nor indeed does he admit that he cares whether he is
worsted or not. The fight is part of a carousal, and he is not prepared to be too solemn about it.

[1] *Arg.* 3. 117 ff.   [2] Fr. 27 D.
[3] *Ox. Pap.* 2321. 4 supplemented by Peek.   [4] *Trach.* 441-2.

Anacreon's images are chosen with a skill so deft and unobtrusive that we may not always realize their aptness at once or
appreciate the practised discrimination and insight which lie
behind them. If he is touched by something charming and simple,
he treats it in a charming and simple way, and lets his lyrical
fancy flow freely. So he writes:

$$\dot{\alpha}\gamma\alpha\nu\hat{\omega}s, \ o\dot{\imath}\acute{\alpha} \ \tau\epsilon \ \nu\epsilon\beta\rho\grave{o}\nu \ \nu\epsilon o\theta\eta\lambda\acute{\epsilon}\alpha$$
$$\gamma\alpha\lambda\alpha\theta\eta\nu\acute{o}\nu, \ \ddot{o}s \ \tau' \ \dot{\epsilon}\nu \ \ddot{\upsilon}\lambda\eta \ \kappa\epsilon\rho o\acute{\epsilon}\sigma\sigma\eta s$$
$$\dot{\alpha}\pi o\lambda\epsilon\iota\phi\theta\epsilon\grave{\imath}s \ \dot{\alpha}\pi\grave{o} \ \mu\eta\tau\rho\grave{o}s \ \dot{\epsilon}\pi\tau o\acute{\eta}\theta\eta.^{1}$$

Gently, like a young sucking fawn, who was afraid when he was left
away from his horned mother in a wood.

Since $\nu\acute{\epsilon}\beta\rho o\nu$ is masculine, it probably refers to a boy, and the
comparison with a fawn illustrates his frightened shyness. With-
out his mother, he does not know where he is. It is true that
Zenodotus wished to alter $\kappa\epsilon\rho o\acute{\epsilon}\sigma\sigma\eta s$ to $\dot{\epsilon}\rho o\acute{\epsilon}\sigma\sigma\eta s$ on the ground
that female deer do not have horns like males,[2] but his correction,
though true enough to natural history, leaves a hiatus in the verse
which Anacreon would not have tolerated, and it is safer to
assume that Anacreon was wrong on a point on which Pindar[3]
and Euripides[4] were also wrong. Indeed he may have gone
wrong on purpose. He does not choose his epithets lightly and
when he makes the mother horned, it is perhaps to show that she
is somehow formidable. The truth of the lines lies not in zoolo-
gical precision but in the way they hit off the gentle shyness of
a boy who is like a young fawn. Horace felt their beauty and
imitated them when he transferred them from a boy to a girl:

uitas inuleo me similis, Chloe,
quaerenti pauidam montibus auiis
matrem non sine uano
aurarum et siluae metu.[5]

He saw the essential truth of Anacreon's comparison and developed it in his own way. But even he seems to lack the immediate response to a charming young creature which Anacreon
feels so directly and so clearly.

Much of the success of an image depends on its skilful placing,
and Anacreon knows how to keep himself in full control until the

---

[1] Fr. 39 D. [2] Schol. Pind. *Ol.* 3. 52.
[3] *Ol.* 3. 29. [4] *Her.* 375; fr. 740 Nauck.
[5] *C.* I. 23. 1–4; cf. E. Fraenkel, *Horace*, pp. 183–4.

moment comes when he can let himself go with a word which both clinches and exalts what he has to say. A characteristic example is

ὦ παῖ παρθένιον βλέπων,
δίζημαί σε, σὺ δ' οὐ κοεῖς,
οὐκ εἰδὼς ὅτι τῆς ἐμῆς
ψυχῆς ἡνιοχεύεις.[1]

Boy with the look of a maid, I pursue you, but you pay no attention, not knowing that you are the charioteer of my soul.

The effect here depends on the transition from quite straightforward language to an unusually expressive metaphor. The first two lines are a delicate, careful statement of fact, in which no word is otiose and no idea unfamiliar. But when Anacreon moves to the image of the charioteer, he exalts his language to give fuller expression to his feelings. The image does not seem to be colloquial, though of course it has its roots in ordinary experience. In later times it was used of love by Plato,[2] and of madness by Aeschylus[3] and Euripides.[4] Anacreon does not make so much of it or work it so hard, but it does its task perfectly in catching the nature of the dominion which the boy has over him.

Anacreon adapts his imagery to his situations and makes it both suit and enforce the context. The sea can never have been very far from him, and he uses it more than once to illustrate a point, but in quite different ways. At one place he says of himself

ἀσήμων ὑπὲρ ἑρμάτων φορεῦμαι[5]

'I am borne over hidden reefs'. No doubt he speaks of the uncertain, even perilous passage of some love, in which he does not feel confident of success. The sense of risk is caught in the immediate associations which the words evoke in us. The sea which is traditionally associated with Aphrodite, could be used to illustrate less dignified activities than those for which she is responsible. In one place Anacreon addresses a woman:

μηδ' ὥστε κῦμα πόντιον
λάλαζε τῇ πολυκρότῃ
σὺν Γαστροδώρῃ καταχύδην
πίνουσα τὴν ἐπίστιον.[6]

[1] Fr. 4 D. In 2 κοεῖς is Bergk's emendation for κλαίεις of the MSS., comparing κοῶ in Epicharm. fr. 35, 14 K.
[2] Lach. 246 a; cf. Hermesianax fr. 7. 83–84 Powell.
[3] Cho. 1022.   [4] Hipp. 237; Or. 36; Her. 881.
[5] Fr. 31 D.   [6] Fr. 80 D.

Do not, like a wave of the sea, chatter with Gastrodora, while you drink profusely from the hearth-cup.

This is a frivolous piece, and the name Gastrodora has been thought to be a nick-name for someone called, for instance, Metrodora.[1] The point lies in the image of the sea, to whom the unnamed woman's chatter is compared, and suggests an unceasing flow of monotonous noise. In this context πολυκρότη is less likely to mean 'cunning', as it sometimes does,[2] than 'noisy', and the picture which emerges is of two garrulous women chattering over their drink.

This art relies for much of its success on the choice of the absolutely right words. Anacreon has left the formulaic style of the epic far behind him and chooses his words individually for their special merits. Just as his epithets are hardly ever otiose or conventional, or, if they seem to be, have in fact a new point, so he secures an effect of novelty and surprise by finding just the right word to hit off a situation. So in

$$\text{ἐκδῦσα χιτῶνα δωριάζειν}^3$$

'to put off her (? your) garment and behave like a Dorian', the word δωριάζειν carries a whole set of associations connected with the distaste and disapproval with which Ionians regarded the Spartan habit of allowing girls to exercise themselves naked. An equally deft choice of words may be seen in

$$\text{οὐδ' ἀργυρέη κ⟨ω τ⟩ότ' ἔλαμπε Πειθώ,}^4$$

'nor yet then did silver Attraction shine.' This must surely come from an amatory context, since Peitho is in some sense a divinity of love,[5] and what counts is the adjective ἀργυρέη. Goddesses like Aphrodite may be called 'golden',[6] but Anacreon is thinking of a lower kind of love and calls it silver to indicate that it is for hire.[7] There are more powerful undertones in the adjective of the phrase χθονίους ῥύσμους, which Anacreon tells Megistes that

---

[1] Wilamowitz, S.u.S. p. 155 n. 1.   [2] Hes. fr. 94, 22 R.; v. l. Od. 1. 1.
[3] Fr. 35 D.; cf. Eustath. 975. 38.   [4] Fr. 59 D.
[5] Sapph. fr. 96. 29 L.–P.; Pind. Pyth. 9. 39; frs. 107. 2 and 108. 9 Bo.; Aesch. Supp. 1040; Ibyc. 8. 3 D.
[6] Od. 8. 337, 342; 17. 37; 19. 54; Mimn. fr. 1. 1 D.
[7] Cf. Pind. Pyth. 11. 41–42,
    εἰ μισθοῖο συνέθευ παρέχειν
    φωνὰν ὑπάργυρον, ἄλλοτ' ἄλλᾳ ταρασσέμεν.

he does not like.[1] The word is very seldom used in a metaphorical sense, but here it conveys associations with things subterranean and hidden and menacing. Even the most unobtrusive adjectives as in ἄμωμον ἄνθος[2] or δακρυόεσσαν αἰχμήν[3] or πτερύγεσσι κούφαις[4] are both original and pointed, perfectly apt and at home. More adventurous and more impressive is the description of the sea in the lines on the lamenting girl, where it is not only ἀμείλιχον, as death is in Homer,[5] but also θυίοντα πορφυρέοισι κύμασι,[6] where the hint of a Maenad in θυίοντα makes it more personal and more uncontrolled, while it remains visibly itself in the adjective πορφυρέοισι. Though Anacreon learned something from Archilochus and something from Sappho and Alcaeus, he shaped his own use of words and showed a fine sense for their quiet, exact adaptation to his subjects.

Through this poetry dances a lyrical spirit which delights both in the emotions and in the visible world, but is tempered by imaginative wit and irony. Sometimes it disappears before them, and we are left with something sharp and almost savage, the outburst of a sensitive man, whose humour did not always protect him from dislike or indignation. When Anacreon's anger or contempt was aroused, he would forsake his graceful sweetness and write in harsher tones. His wit is still wit, but the more deadly because it is also satirical, as when he says

και θάλαμος, ἐν τῷ κεῖνος οὐκ ἔγημεν ἀλλ' ἐγήματο[7]

'and the chamber in which he did not marry, but was married', but there is a more uncontrolled savagery in his lines on Artemon:

πρὶν μὲν ἔχων βερβέριον, καλύμματ' ἐσφηκωμένα,
καὶ ξυλίνους ἀστραγάλους ἐν ὠσὶ καὶ ψιλὸν περὶ
    πλευρῇσι ⟨δέρριον⟩ βοός,
νήπλυτον εἴλυμα κακῆς ἀσπίδος, ἀρτοπωλίσιν
κἀθελοπόρνοισιν ὁμιλέων ὁ πονηρὸς Ἀρτέμων,
    κιβδηλὸν εὑρίσκων βίον,

---

[1] Fr. 65 D.   [2] Fr. 46 D.
[3] Fr. 57 D.   [4] Fr. 52. 1 D.
[5] Il. 9. 158, but κατὰ πόντον ἀμείλιχον is found at Hom. Hymn 33. 8.
[6] For purple waves cf. Hom. Hymn 28. 11–12 ἐκινήθη δ' ἄρα πόντος κύμασι πορφυρέοισι κυκώμενος, but Anacreon's substitution of θυίοντα for κυκώμενον entirely changes the temper of the scene and gives it a new wildness by making the sea active instead of passive.   [7] Fr. 87 D.

πολλὰ μὲν ἐν δουρὶ τιθεὶς αὐχένα, πολλὰ δ' ἐν τροχῷ,
πολλὰ δὲ νῶτον σκυτίνῃ μάστιγι θωμιχθεὶς κόμην
πώγωνά τ' ἐκτετιλμένος.
νῦν δ' ἐπιβαίνει σατινέων χρύσεα φορέων καθέρματα,
παῖς ⟨ὁ⟩ Κύκης, καὶ σκιαδίσκην ἐλεφαντίνην φορεῖ
γυναιξὶν αὔτως ⟨ἐμφερής⟩.[1]

Before, he used to wear a shabby garment and wasped head-dress, and wooden dice in his ears, and a bare ox-skin on his flanks that had been the unwashed cover of a miserable shield. He mixed with women who sell bread and with willing whores, the low Artemon. He sought a fraudulent living. His neck was often tied to the pillory, often to the wheel. His back was often seared by the leathern scourge, his hair and beard pulled out. Now the son of Cyce rides in carriages, wears golden ear-rings, and carries an ivory parasol, just like women.

A satirical piece of this kind calls for some elucidation. The first three sections deal with Artemon's earlier career and the low life in which he moved. The precise meaning of βερβέριον is uncertain, but it must be some sort of garment.[2] As a head-dress he wore καλύμματ' ἐσφηκωμένα, wrappings tightly bound round his head to keep his hair out of the way and fastened in a point at the back to resemble a wasp's hind-quarters.[3] This low-class style is implicitly contrasted with the normal Ionian habit of wearing long flowing hair.[4] The wooden dice in his ears are a cheap attempt at ear-rings, and the point is that even at this time Artemon, in his low and squalid way, had effeminate tastes. Like Megarian peasants,[5] he wore an ox-hide round his loins, and to deprive him of a peasant's dignity, Anacreon says that it was the unwashed cover of a shield. Artemon's company was women who sold bread and amateur whores. Bread-sellers had a name for bad language and were regarded as the dregs of society. When Hermippus wrote a comedy about Hyperbolus, who was notorious

---

[1] Fr. 54 D. See F. Blass, *Rh. Mus.* xxix, pp. 154 ff.; Weber, pp. 29 and 91; Smyth, *G.M.P.* pp. 290-1. In 3 δέρριον is an early conjecture of Bergk; later he preferred δέρμ' ἦει. In 4 Schoemann's νήπλυτον is vastly preferable in sense to νεόπλυτον, 'newly washed', of the MSS. In 12 ἐμφερής was supplied by Schoemann.

[2] Smyth suggests that it may be connected with the Arcadian Berbenii. B. Lavagnini, *Nuov. Ant.* p. 224, takes it to be 'un copricapo a punta, forse analogo al berretto frigio', but there seems to be no evidence for this.

[3] Weber, p. 56, quotes Aristoph. *Vesp.* 1072; cf. also *Il.* 17. 52; Soph. fr. 341 P.; Aristoph. *Pax* 1216.

[4] Asius fr. 13 K.; Duris 76 F 60 J.; Diog. Laert. 8. 47; E. Buschor, *Altsamischer Standbilder*, Taf. 5, 7, 8, 29, 31, 32.

[5] Theogn. 55.

for his abusive tongue, and his mother, he called it Ἀρτοπωλίδες,[1] and Aristophanes uses the word with the same implications.[2] In this low company Artemon came into conflict with the law. He had his neck tied to the δορύ, which was the same as the κύφων or pillory, to which fraudulent traders in the market were fastened.[3] He was also stretched on the wheel, a punishment given to those who aroused public anger, like the unfortunate barber who first spread the news at Athens of the Sicilian disaster in 413 B.C.[4] or the first men suspected of the mutilation of the Hermae.[5] Finally, he had his back scourged, which was a punishment for a variety of offences, and his hair pulled out, which was appropriate to adulterers.[6] This closes Artemon's early record, which was one of low company and copious convictions.

Contrasted with this murky past is Artemon's present splendour. He rides in a σατίνη, the cushioned carriage in which rich women rode.[7] He wears golden ear-rings instead of his old wooden dice. He has an ivory sun-shade such as the Persian Satrap has on the Nereid monument. He is now rich and luxurious, but what is the precise point of the contrast? A clue is to be found in two other lines of Anacreon:

$$\xi\alpha\nu\theta\hat{\eta}\ \delta'\ E\dot{\upsilon}\rho\upsilon\pi\dot{\upsilon}\lambda\eta\ \mu\dot{\epsilon}\lambda\epsilon\iota$$
$$\dot{o}\ \pi\epsilon\rho\iota\phi\dot{o}\rho\eta\tau os\ \dot{A}\rho\tau\dot{\epsilon}\mu\omega\nu.[8]$$

'fair-haired Eurypyle looks after the notorious Artemon'. This has caused some difficulty, because Chamaeleon says that περιφόρητος means 'borne in a litter'.[9] But this is probably due to a confusion with a second Artemon, a crippled engineer whom Pericles employed in the siege of Samos[10] and to whom the words περιφόρητος Ἀρτέμων were applied in a new, topical sense. We can hardly doubt that for Anacreon περιφόρητος means 'notorious', and that Artemon's notoriety comes from his relations with Eurypyle. This is to some extent confirmed by Aristophanes, who, in deriding a certain Cratinus, who surely is not the great comedian, accuses him of adultery and calls him περιπόνηρος Ἀρτέμων.[11] In this he combines two phrases of Anacreon with

[1] Frs. 8–13 K.   [2] Vesp. 1387–1416; Ran. 858.
[3] Poll. 10. 177.   [4] Plut. Nic. 30. 2.   [5] Andoc. 1. 43.
[6] Aristoph. Nub. 1083, Plut. 168.
[7] Hom. Hymn 5. 13; Sapph. fr. 44. 13 L.–P.; Eur. Hel. 1311.
[8] Fr. 16 D.   [9] Athen. 12. 533 e.
[10] Plut. Per. 27. 3.   [11] Ach. 850.

reference to Artemon, ὁ πονηρὸς Ἀρτέμων of our poem and περι-φόρητος Ἀρτέμων in the lines about Eurypyle, and shows that he knew the text well. From this we may deduce that Artemon's prosperity comes from being kept by Eurypyle, and the sharp edge of Anacreon's satire is that in this affair Artemon is more like a woman than a man. There is no need to assume that Artemon defeated Anacreon in his pursuit of Eurypyle. What offends him is that the low-born Artemon now thrives on his immoral earnings.

Much of Anacreon's mature poetry must have been written in Samos. The gaiety and the wit, the brilliance and the elegance, are well suited to that sophisticated and intelligent society. Anacreon accepted its conventions because they chimed with his own character, and made the most of them. But this delightful sojourn came to an end. About 522 Polycrates was treacherously captured and crucified by the Persians, and Anacreon went to Athens. The story was that Hipparchus sent a fifty-oared galley to fetch him,[1] and in Athens Anacreon passed a large part of his remaining years. He was nearly fifty when he went there, but he seems to have found no difficulty in accommodating himself to his new surroundings. In Hipparchus he found a patron who shared the erotic tastes of Polycrates[2] and welcomed a famous poet who brought renown to his court. The life which Anacreon found in Athens cannot, at least at first, have been very different from what he had enjoyed in Samos. He made friends in influential circles and won a name for his convivial tastes.

This stay in Athens was broken by the expulsion of Hippias in 510, if not by the murder of Hipparchus in 514. Anacreon, like Simonides, seems to have profited by the friendship of the Peisistratids with the princes of Thessaly and to have found a home with them. Light on this Thessalian sojourn may be thrown by two epigrams, though we may feel certain reservations about their value as evidence. The first is a dedicatory inscription attributed to Anacreon and written for Echecratidas, king of Pharsalus, who after the destruction of the Aleuads, made himself ταγός or High King of Thessaly:

σάν τε χάριν, Διόνυσε, καὶ ἀγλαὸν ἄστεϊ κόσμον
Θεσσαλίας μ' ἀνέθηκ' ἀρχὸς Ἐχεκρατίδας.[3]

---

[1] 'Plat.' Hipparch. 228 b; Ael. V.H. 8. 2.
[2] Aristot. Const. Ath. 18; Thuc. 6. 54. 2.
[3] No. 107 D.

To thy pleasure, Dionysus, and to be a fine ornament to the city I was
set up by Echecratidas, ruler of Thessaly.

We cannot doubt that this comes from about the time when
Anacreon was in Thessaly, and its simple manner accords with
such a date. But we may doubt whether he wrote it, not merely
because all such attributions of inscriptions are open to question,
but because we should expect it to be in his usual Ionic dialect,
which it is not. The second concerns Dyseris, the wife of Echecratidas, and also accompanied a dedication:

$$\Pi\rho\eta\xi\iota\delta\iota\kappa\eta \ \mu\grave{\epsilon}\nu \ \grave{\epsilon}\rho\epsilon\xi\epsilon\nu, \ \grave{\epsilon}\beta\sigma\upsilon\lambda\epsilon\upsilon\sigma\epsilon\nu \ \delta\grave{\epsilon} \ \varDelta\upsilon\sigma\eta\rho\iota\varsigma$$
$$\epsilon\grave{\iota}\mu\alpha \ \tau\delta\delta\epsilon\cdot \ \xi\upsilon\nu\grave{\eta} \ \delta' \ \grave{\alpha}\mu\phi\sigma\tau\grave{\epsilon}\rho\omega\nu \ \sigma\sigma\phi\iota\eta.^1$$

Prexidice made, and Dyseris designed, this robe. Its art belongs to
them both alike.

Here the unquestionably Ionic language suggests that it may well
be the genuine work of Anacreon, since no local poet is likely to
have written with just these forms and words. It accompanies the
ritual offering of a robe to a goddess, such as the women of Troy
make to Athene.[2] There is quiet skill in the neat contrast between
$\grave{\epsilon}\rho\epsilon\xi\epsilon\nu$ and $\grave{\epsilon}\beta\sigma\upsilon\lambda\epsilon\upsilon\sigma\epsilon\nu$, and the order of words secures that the
name of the queen comes at the end of the line. $\sigma\sigma\phi\iota\eta$ is the
nearest word which the Greeks had at this period for 'art', and is
used alike for painting, sculpture, and poetry.[3] Anacreon evidently felt justified in using it for skilful embroidery.

Anacreon's visit to Thessaly seems to have been only an inter-
lude. He returned to Athens, where his former friendship with
Hipparchus does not seem to have counted against him. Among
his friends was Xanthippus, the father of Pericles, and when in
later times his statue stood by that of Anacreon on the Acropolis,[4]
it need not have been by mere chance. Their friendship is im-
plied in a muddled sentence of Himerius, $\grave{\epsilon}\chi\alpha\iota\rho\epsilon \ \mu\grave{\epsilon}\nu \ \grave{A}\nu\alpha\kappa\rho\grave{\epsilon}\omega\nu \ \epsilon\grave{\iota}\varsigma$
$\Pi\sigma\lambda\upsilon\kappa\rho\grave{\alpha}\tau\sigma\upsilon\varsigma \ \sigma\tau\epsilon\lambda\lambda\delta\mu\epsilon\nu\sigma\varsigma \ \tau\grave{\sigma}\nu \ \mu\grave{\epsilon}\gamma\alpha\nu \ \varXi\grave{\alpha}\nu\theta\iota\pi\pi\sigma\nu \ \pi\rho\sigma\sigma\phi\theta\grave{\epsilon}\gamma\xi\alpha\sigma\theta\alpha\iota.^5$ It
seems unlikely that Anacreon went to the court of Polycrates to
greet Xanthippus, and Wilamowitz ingeniously emended $\tau\grave{\sigma}\nu$
$\mu\grave{\epsilon}\gamma\alpha\nu \ \varXi\grave{\alpha}\nu\theta\iota\pi\pi\sigma\nu$ to $\tau\grave{\sigma}\nu \ \xi\alpha\nu\theta\grave{\sigma}\nu \ M\epsilon\gamma\iota\sigma\tau\eta\nu$, and referred the words to
Anacreon's love,[6] Megistes. But the change neglects the context in

---

[1] No. 108 D.   [2] Il. 6. 286 ff.
[3] Pind. Pyth. 4. 248; Nem. 7. 23. See B. Snell, Der Begriff das Wissens in der
vorplatonischen Philosophie, pp. 5–20.
[4] Paus. 1. 25. 1.   [5] Or. 39. 2 Colonna.
[6] Ind. Lect. Gött. 1889, p. 22.

Himerius. He is addressing the Emperor Julian before he himself
sets out for Thessalonica, and he compares himself with poets, like
Anacreon and Pindar, who had great men to celebrate. The comparison is appropriate enough if the emperor is compared with
the famous soldier Xanthippus, but grotesque if he is compared
with the Samian boy Megistes. It looks as if Himerius, who knew
Greek poetry better than Greek history, had misunderstood some
poem of Anacreon in which Xanthippus was mentioned, and
connected it, quite wrongly, with Samos on the assumption that
Anacreon normally wrote about Samos. If Anacreon was the
friend of Xanthippus, he would have had an entry into aristocratic Athenian society, and this would suit the tastes of a man
who said of himself:

> οὐ δηῦτ' ἔμπεδός εἰμι
> οὐδ' ἀστοῖσι προσηνής.[1]

'I am not now stiff-necked nor easy-going with the citizens.' He
had been at home with Polycrates, and now in Athens he found
a society no less to his taste.

The part played by Anacreon in Athens was remembered in at
least one family. Critias, the friend of Socrates and a member of
the Thirty, must have known that his grandfather and namesake,
the son of Dropides, was as a young man admired by Anacreon;[2]
for he celebrated the poet in a short poem:

> τὸν δὲ γυναικείων μελέων πλέξαντά ποτ' ῳδὰς
> ἡδὺν Ἀνακρείοντα Τέως εἰς Ἑλλάδ' ἀνῆγεν,
> συμποσίων ἐρέθισμα, γυναικῶν ἠπερόπευμα,
> αὐλῶν ἀντίπαλον, φιλοβάρβιτον, ἡδύν, ἄλυπον.
> οὔποτέ σου φιλότης γηράσεται οὐδὲ θανεῖται,
> ἔστ' ἂν ὕδωρ οἴνῳ συμμειγνύμενον κυλίκεσσι
> παῖς διαπομπεύῃ προπόσεις ἐπιδέξια νωμῶν,
> παννυχίδας θ' ἱερὰς θήλεις χοροὶ ἀμφιέπωσιν,
> πλάστιγξ θ' ἡ χαλκοῦ θυγάτηρ ἐπ' ἄκραισι καθίζει
> κοττάβου ὑψηλοῦ κορυφαῖς Βρομίου ψακάδεσσιν.[3]

Teos brought to Hellas sweet Anacreon, who once wove songs for
women's melodies, the awaker of revels, the deceiver of women, the
rival of flutes, lover of the lyre, sweet anodyne of sorrow. Never shall
love of you grow old or die, so long as the boy carries round water
mingled in cups with wine, and passes the drinks to the right, so long

---

[1] Fr. 19 D.   [2] Plat. *Char.* 157 e; Schol. Aesch. *P.V.* 128.
[3] Fr. 3 Diels.

as the maiden companies keep their holy night-long festivals, and the scale, daughter of bronze, sits on the top of the kottabos-pole for the throwing of the drops of Bromius.

These lines, written by an unimpeachable authority, show that in Athens Anacreon kept his love of wine, women, and song. In his own lifetime he was famous enough to be depicted by the first painters of red-figured vases, and three of these, by Oltos,[1] the Gales Painter,[2] and the Cleophrades painter,[3] show him playing his lyre, while young men dance with a certain abandonment to it. We must not expect these pictures of him to be close likenesses, but they show what view the Athenians took of him. His statue on the Acropolis has perished, but something of its character may be deduced from a later copy in the Ny Carlsberg Glypothek at Copenhagen, which shows him singing to the lyre in dignified nakedness.[4] Later pictures of Anacreon may well have turned him into a drunken sot,[5] but the Athenians, who knew him, saw him differently. He was indeed a master of the revels, but he led them with authority and style.

Critias' lines are relevant to Anacreon's art as well as his life. They show him as a member of that section of Athenian society which sang σκόλια at its feasts. Of the songs which Anacreon composed in these conditions we have a good specimen. Elegiac couplets and quatrains were often sung among more lyrical types of verse after dinner, and such is a quatrain of Anacreon:

> οὐ φιλέω ὃς κρητῆρι παρὰ πλέῳ οἰνοποτάζων
> νείκεα καὶ πόλεμον δακρυόεντα λέγει,
> ἀλλ' ὅστις Μουσέων τε καὶ ἀγλαὰ δῶρ' Ἀφροδίτης
> συμμίσγων ἐρατῆς μνήσκεται εὐφροσύνης.[6]

I like not him, who, when he quaffs wine over a full bowl, talks of strifes and tearful war, but him who mixes the glorious gifts of the Muses and Aphrodite and recalls the good times which he loves.

---

[1] Beazley, A.R.V. p. 40, no. 69, in British Museum. Photograph in M. Platnauer, Fifty Years of Classical Scholarship, fig. 5.
[2] Beazley, ibid. p. 31, no. 2, in Syracuse. Drawing in J. C. Hoppin, A Handbook of Attic Red-figured Vases, i, p. 465.
[3] Beazley, ibid. p. 123, no. 29, in Rome. In general see S. Papaspyridi-Karouzou, B.C.H. lxvi–lxvii (1942–3), pp. 248–54.
[4] F. Poulsen, Iconographic Studies in the Ny Carlsberg Glypothek, p. 15, fig. 12; G. Hafner, J.D.A.I., lxxi (1956), pp. 1–28.
[5] Leonidas of Tarentum, Anth. Pal. 16. 306 and 307.
[6] Fr. 96 D.

In the circles where rich men drank and sang there was naturally much talk and song about war, but Anacreon, who knew what war was, disapproved of such themes and said so politely but firmly. The lines were almost certainly composed in Athens, since their use of εὐφροσύνη for the delights of feasting is specially Attic. Its history may be traced back to Solon who wrote of the leaders of the people:

οὐ γὰρ ἐπίστανται κατέχειν κόρον οὐδὲ παρούσας
εὐφροσύνας κοσμεῖν δαιτὸς ἐν ἡσυχίῃ.[1]

They do not know how to curb their insolence or how to order the delights they have in peaceful feasting.

The word reappears about 490 in the Attic σκόλιον to Pan,[2] and there can be little doubt that it was a good colloquial Attic word for a 'good time'.

Critias also refers to 'maiden companies who keep night-long festivals', and the existence of παννυχίδες, especially in connexion with the Panathenaea on the 28th day of Hekatombaion, is known from inscriptions.[3] No extant specimen survives of a song sung at them, and though their essential character may have resembled that of similar songs at Thebes or Sparta, they seem to have been less important and less often to have attracted famous poets. The words of Critias are to some small degree amplified by a fragmentary papyrus of the Homeric commentator Ammonius, who seems to refer to παρθενεῖα and to quote a passage from one in which Anacreon mentions a son of that Asteropaeus who attacked Achilles.[4] It is too mutilated to yield any coherent sense, but the language looks more elaborate than is usual with Anacreon. Among his other remains are one or two which may conceivably come from Maiden-songs. Since such songs were often sung at sunrise, we might possibly refer to them the address to the sun:

῾Ήλιε καλλιλαμπέτη,[5]

'fair-shining sun'. Another quotation, which is in the same metre

---

[1] Fr. 3. 9–10 D.   [2] No. 4 D.

[3] *I.G.* i². 334. 34 τοὺς δὲ ἱεροποίους τοὺς διοικοῦντας τὰ Παναθήναια τὰ κατ' ἐνιαυτὸν ποιεῖν τὴν παννυχίδα ὡς καλλίστην τῇ θεῷ καὶ τὴν πομπὴν πέμπειν ἅμα ἡλίῳ ἀνιόντι.

[4] *Ox. Pap.* ii. 221. For attempted restorations see O. Schroeder, *Pindari Carmina,* ed. mai, 1900, p. 389, and Edmonds, *L.G.* ii, p. 432.

[5] Fr. 50 a D.

and uses the first personal singular feminine, may come from a similar poem:

$$ἐκ ποταμοῦ 'πανέρχομαι$$
$$πάντα φέρουσα λαμπρά,^1$$

'I come up from the river, bringing everything bright.' This looks as if it was connected with the Attic Πλυντήρια, which was held on the 25th day of Thargelion, when the clothes of Athene's statue were washed.[2] Neither of these cases can be ascribed to Maiden-songs with positive assurance, but the little that they say is not inconsistent with such a possibility.

In Athens Anacreon grew old and wrote about old age. It does not seem to have diminished his taste for pleasure, and we find him addressing a girl:

$$κλῦθί μευ γέροντος, εὐέθειρα χρυσόπεπλε κούρη,^3$$

'Listen to me who am old, girl with the beautiful hair and the golden robe.' He feels that love passes him by, and he gives to the situation a dramatic, half-mythological splendour:

$$⟨"Ερως,⟩ ὅς μ' ἐσιδὼν γένειον$$
$$· ὑποπόλιον χρυσοφαέννων πτερύγων ἀήταις$$
$$παραπέταται.^4$$

Love, who has seen my chin going white, flies past me on the wind of his wings agleam with gold.

This is not Anacreon's usual way of treating Love as a handsome youth. He aims at something more exalted and more exciting, and the measure of his success may be seen from his influence on other poets, as when Euripides calls Love πτανὸς χρυσοφαής[5] and in the parabasis of the *Birds* Aristophanes speaks of him as στίλβων νῶτον πτερύγοιν χρυσαῖν.[6] It is possible that the same poem also contained the lines in which Anacreon proclaims that, since his approaches are rejected by some boy, he flies to Olympus, no doubt to entreat Love to put things right for him:

$$ἀναπέτομαι δὴ πρὸς "Ολυμπον πτερύγεσσι κούφαις$$
$$διὰ τὸν "Ερωτ'· οὐ γὰρ ἐμοὶ ⟨παῖς ἐ⟩θέλει συνηβᾶν.^7$$

---

[1] Fr. 73 D.
[2] *I.G.* ii.[2] 842; Xen. *Hell.* 1. 4. 12; Lycurg. fr. 43; Plut. *Alc.* 34.
[3] Fr. 91 D.   [4] Fr. 53 D.
[5] *Hipp.* 1265.   [6] *Av.* 698.
[7] Fr. 52 D. This may be the poem to which the pseudo-Julian refers *Ep.* 18, p. 237. 263 Bidez–Cumont, εἰ δέ μοι θέμις ἦν κατὰ τὸν Τήϊον ἐκεῖνον μελοποιὸν εὐχῇ

On light wings I fly up to Olympus for the sake of Love; for a boy refuses to enjoy his youth with me.

Perhaps too this was the song, mentioned by Himerius, in which Anacreon threatened the Loves that, if they did not punish a boy who had rejected him, he would strike up no more songs in their honour.[1] It is clear that advancing years did not deter or discourage him from his favourite pursuits.

At the same time he knew that death could not be far off, and he viewed the prospect with distaste. Old age was bad enough, but what came after it might be worse:

πολιοὶ μὲν ἡμὶν ἤδη
κρόταφοι κάρη τε λευκόν,
χαρίεσσα δ' οὐκέθ' ἤβη
πάρα, γηράλεοι δ' ὀδόντες.
γλυκεροῦ δ' οὐκέτι πολλὸς
βιότου χρόνος λέλειπται.

διὰ ταῦτ' ἀνασταλύζω
θαμὰ Τάρταρον δεδοικώς·
Ἀίδεω γάρ ἐστι δεινὸς
μύχος, ἀργαλέη δ' ἐς αὐτὸν
κάτοδος· καὶ γὰρ ἑτοῖμον
καταβάντι μὴ ἀναβῆναι.[2]

My temples are already hoary, and my head is white; no longer is graceful youth with me, and my teeth are old. No more is a long span of sweet life left to me. Often in fear of Tartarus I lament this; for dread is the pit of death, and hard the way down to it. For there is no way by which a man who has gone down can come up.

Anacreon allows himself no illusions and no consolations about old age or death. What troubles him in the first is the decay of his body, and in the second the unknown horrors that may be in store. He does not comfort himself with the common Greek notions that age makes amends by the experience which it brings and that death is at least a release from troubles. But even so he is not too solemn about it, but speaks of it without exaggeration, almost with acceptance. He lived to be eighty-five,[3] and then, the legend says, he died from swallowing a grape-pip.[4] The story is

τὴν τῶν ὀρνίθων ἀλλάξασθαι φύσιν..., but the same image occurs at Ox. Pap. 2321, fr. 6. 4 πάννυχος πετοίμην, and Anacreon clearly used it more than once.

[1] Or. 48. 4 Colonna. [2] Fr. 44 D.
[3] 'Luc.' Macr. 26. [4] Val. Max. 9. 12. 8.

dubious, but it shows the conviction of posterity that he enjoyed himself to the last. He probably survived Marathon but died soon afterwards, having kept his intellectual faculties well enough to be able to enjoy the lyrics of Aeschylus.[1] He might not have felt entirely at ease in the new world which came into being after Salamis and Plataea, and he had lived for a span long even for a Greek.

Anacreon's personality emerges clearly from his fragments and has little resemblance to the senile and bibulous rake who was created in his name by his imitators. He loved pleasure and sang unaffectedly of it. He had little interest in war or politics. Yet he is usually dignified and decorous. He smiles at his own pleasures as much as at his own decaying body, and knows that after all both are human. The choice of convivial subjects, and his treatment of them, were no doubt congenial to his character, but they were also influenced by the conditions in which he sang.[2] Both with Polycrates and with Hipparchus the right time for singing was over the wine, and the most favoured subjects were drink and love. But even at his most relaxed and unabashed Anacreon has a reserve of strength and detachment which saves his character and his art. There is always a hint that he does not treat his amusements too seriously, that he knows their true worth. And when this reserve is present, there is no question of his poetry being degraded or degrading.

---

[1] Schol. Aesch. *P.V.* 128 καὶ ἠρέσθη λίαν τοῖς μέλεσι τοῦ τραγικοῦ.

[2] Athen. 10. 429 b ἄτοπος δ' ὁ Ἀνακρέων ὁ πᾶσαν αὐτοῦ τὴν ποίησιν ἐξαρτήσας μέθης. τῇ γὰρ μαλακίᾳ καὶ τῇ τρυφῇ ἐπιδοὺς ἑαυτὸν ἐν τοῖς ποιήμασι διαβέβληται, οὐκ εἰδότων τῶν πολλῶν ὅτι νήφων ἐν τῷ γράφειν καὶ ἀγαθὸς ὢν προσποιεῖται μεθύειν οὐκ οὔσης ἀνάγκης.

VIII. SIMONIDES

SOME fifteen miles across the water east of Cape Sunium lies the island of Ceos. High and rocky, it is no home for horses and cattle, but in its valleys and on the slopes of its hills vines grow plentifully, and it still deserves the adjective ἀμπελο-τρόφος given to it by Bacchylides,[1] still answers to the description put by Pindar on its own lips:

> ε]ἰ καί τι Διω[νύσ]οι᾽ ἄρουρα φέρει
> βιόδωρον ἀμαχανίας ἄκος,
> ἄνιππός εἰμι καὶ βουνομίας ἀδαέστερος.[2]

If my soil bears something of Dionysus' life-giving remedy for misery, I have no horses and know not the tending of oxen.

It has, on its north-west coast, an excellent harbour in a sea where harbours are few, and its position on the direct route from the Dardanelles to Peiraeus is still a source of livelihood to its inhabitants. Its chief town, Iulis,[3] lay inland among hills beyond the reach of pirates and developed its own distinctive life. The Ceans had close connexions with Euboea[4] and were for Herodotus 'an Ionian people from Athens'.[5] Their speech and culture conformed to the main Ionian pattern, but they had their local peculiarities. The chief god of the island was Apollo. Festivals in his honour were held in both towns,[6] and the Ceans kept a guest-house on Delos,[7] to which they sent choirs of boys to sing hymns to Apollo. From Carthaea comes an inventory of the temple's treasures, which include the dedication of a gold crown by the leader of such a choir,[8] and Bacchylides' Ode XVII, despite its place among his Dithyrambs, seems to have been sung by such a choir at Delos, while Pindar's *Paean* IV was composed for Apollo's feast at Carthaea. Besides Apollo there were at least two other important gods. One was the bees' protector, Aristaeus, an old vegetation deity, who was said to have saved the island

---

[1] 6. 5. [2] *Paean* 4 (fr. 38 Bo.). 22–24.
[3] For the legendary history cf. Callim. fr. 75. 51 ff. P.
[4] Strab. 448. [5] 8. 46. 2.
[6] Strab. 486. [7] Hdt. 4. 35. 4.
[8] Michel, *Rec. d'Inscr. Gr.* 834.

from a pest in hot weather by bringing etesian winds for forty days and was transformed into Zeus as Ζεὺς Ἀρισταῖος;[1] the other was Dionysus, whose image appears on Cean coins and who was suitably honoured in a vine-growing land. The strict conditions of life led to some simplicity and even severity. Suicide was said to be compulsory for men who reached the age of sixty,[2] and an extant inscription imposes severe penalties on luxurious living.[3] The high tone of the island was proverbial, and there were said to be neither flute-girls nor harlots on it.[4] This combination of an enforced simplicity with the spirit of Apolline and Dionysiac worships may have helped to shape the character of Cean poetry and sculpture. In both there is the same enjoyment of life and the same intellectual discipline; in both fire and inspiration have found an expressive outlet in respect for style. The remains of early Cean sculpture are scanty, but the sixth-century kouros in Athens[5] and the colossal lion carved out of the rock facing Simonides' own town of Iulis show that technique had surmounted its first obstacles and found adequate means to convey life and majesty in stone. A similar success was to be won in poetry.

Simonides, the son of Leoprepes, of the deme Hylichidai, came of a good Cean family.[6] He was born at Iulis in 556 B.C.[7] Of his childhood and beginnings we have no information except two tantalizing metrical γρῖφοι attributed to him on the none too good authority of Chamaeleon.[8] If they are indeed his work, they would show that in his youth he affected an enigmatic style and made use of it for local and topical events. But their authenticity is uncertain, and we cannot put too much trust in them. It is possible that Simonides learned something from the poetry of Stesichorus, which he certainly knew,[9] and which he followed in

---

[1] Schol. Ap. Rhod. 2. 498; Diod. Sic. 4. 82.1; see Farnell, *G.H.C.* pp. 50–51.
[2] Strab. 486.   [3] *I.G.* xii. 5. 1. 593.   [4] Strab. 486.
[5] Richter, *A.G.A.* p. 94 (fig. 158), dates it 530–520 B.C.
[6] For his father Leoprepes, fr. 77. 6 D.; Hdt. 7. 228. 4; Callim. fr. 64. 8 P.; for his family, Callim. fr. 222. 2 P.; for the name, *I.G.* xii. 5. 609. 102 ff. and 637.
[7] This follows from fr. 77. 6 D., where Simonides speaks of himself as eighty years old. Since the dedication was made in the archonship of Adeimantus, which fell in *Ol.* 74. 4 (477–6 B.C.) (Diod. 11. 41; Plut. *Them.* 5; *Mar. Par.* 55) the date of Simonides' birth is fixed with some assurance. R. F. Stella, *R.F.C.* 1946, pp. 1–24, argues for bringing it down to 532–529 B.C.
[8] Frs. 69–70 D. Reitzenstein, *E.u.S.* pp. 118–19, argues that 69 is concerned with the death of two poets, the one a writer of dithyrambs, the other of tragedies, and that 70 is concerned with a literary competition in which the prize was a cup.
[9] Fr. 32 D.

placing the murder of Agamemnon at Sparta[1] and in dividing
the night into five watches instead of three.[2] But his first known
successes were in an art not known to have been practised by
Stesichorus, the composition of ἐπινίκια, choral songs in honour of
victors in the great games. The Epinician, so familiar from
Pindar, seems to have owed much to Simonides, and he may have
been partly responsible for its transformation from a short im-
promptu catch into a full-scale choral song with many characteristics of a hymn. In the seventh century a short song with a
triple refrain of τήνελλα καλλίνικε was attributed to Archilochus,[3]
and this was sung by the victor and his friends when they went to
the temple of the presiding deity to get the prize. But the increasing prestige of athletic victories demanded celebrations more
elaborate than this, especially as the victor's home-coming became an occasion for public rejoicing and justified, for its full
recognition, something like a hymn. The need was emphasized
by the importance which Greek nobles of the sixth century
attached to athletic prowess. It was not merely that success in
the games proved a man's ἀρετή and showed his triumphs over
difficulties by endurance and courage, but every victory meant
the success of the victor's city over other cities and gave a prestige which everyone respected; for the games were an outward
symbol of the spiritual and national unity which the Greeks
were so slow to embody in their politics but of which they were
none the less conscious. The games at Olympia were founded in
776 B.C., but the sixth century added the Pythian Games in 588,
the Isthmian in 582, and the Nemean in 573. Tyrants, like those
of Corinth and Sicyon, saw their importance both as a means
for amusing their own subjects and for displaying their own
wealth and power to strangers. The result was that a victory in
one of the great games came to be regarded as the goal of
every healthy man's desire. The victor might have no prize
but a crown of wild olive, but at home he received special
privileges and rewards. At Athens he was given a sum of money
and was kept at the public charge.[4] In Simonides' own island
of Ceos a list of athletic victors was inscribed in the temple
of Apollo,[5] and all over Greece victors received honours and

---

[1] Schol. Eur. Or. 46.　　　　[2] Schol. Eur. Rhes. 5.
[3] Pind. Ol. 9. 1 ff. with scholia; Archilochus fr. 120 D.
[4] Plat. Apol. 36 a.　　　　[5] I.G. xii. 5. 608.

privileges.[1] In the sixth century the games were a foremost feature of Greek life, and in celebrating the men who won in them poets found a renown that spread far beyond their own cities.

A consequence of the honour in which the games were held was the development of the Epinician ode. It became serious and stately; it assumed characteristics which had hitherto belonged to the hymn; it told instructive or illuminating stories; it contained aphorisms on man's relations with the gods. All these can be found in Pindar's odes, and we cannot doubt that Simonides did something to prepare the way for them. His work was eclipsed by Pindar's, and the fragments are too few to allow any close analysis of his methods,[2] but enough remains to point a few comparisons and contrasts and to suggest that the manner of Simonides was not that of Pindar and may have been closer to the simpler songs from which the full-fledged Epinician grew.

In 520 B.C. Glaucus of Carystus won the boys' wrestling-match at Olympia,[3] and Simonides wrote an Epinician for him. Glaucus grew to be a famous athlete, who later won a victory in the Pythian Games and seven in the Nemean and Isthmian.[4] His punch was said to drive the coulter into the plough.[5] Of Simonides' poem for him we have both a quotation and some information. The quotation comes from Lucian, who says that in praise of Glaucus Simonides used the words:

οὐδὲ Πολυδεύκεος βία
χεῖρας ἀντείναιτ' ἂν ἐναντίον αὐτῷ
οὐδὲ σιδάρεον Ἀλκμήνας τέκος.[6]

Neither strong Polydeuces nor the iron son of Alcmene would lift hands against him.

If Simonides said this of Glaucus, there are, it is claimed, two difficulties.[7] First, could he possibly have used praise so excessive and claimed that a mere boy could defeat the heroic prototypes

[1] Xenophan. fr. 2 D.; Eur. fr. 282 N.; see Bowra, *Problems*, pp. 15 ff.
[2] The broken scraps of a papyrus at Strasburg, published by B. Snell, *Euripides: Alexandros*, which come from Simonides' Ἐπίνικοι δρομέῦσιν, suggest that they were arranged according to the types of victory celebrated, but nothing can be made of the text; cf. also *Ox. Pap.* 2430.1.
[3] 'Suid'. s.v. Γλαῦκος Καρύστιος; Bekker, *An. Gr.* i. 232. The text is not certain, but Brunn's emendation of 'Ολ. βε' to ξε' looks right. *c.* 490 Glaucus was in Sicily, where he died *c.* 480. See P. Maas, *R.-E.* iii A, 1. 186.
[4] Dem. 18. 319; Paus. 6. 10. 1–3; Aeschin. 3. 189.
[5] Paus. 6. 10. 1.   [6] Fr. 23 D.
[7] H. J. Rose, *C.R.* xlvii (1933), pp. 165–7.

of athletic prowess, Polydeuces and Heracles? Surely such praise
would sound both impious and absurd to Greek ears. Secondly, a
statement of Quintilian[1] implies that in this same poem Simonides
praised the Dioscuri, and this seems to be inconsistent with the
words quoted from it. It is therefore argued that the quotation
is not from this poem but from a different poem, probably later
and not necessarily written for Glaucus in this hyperbolical
manner. The objections to this are, first, that Lucian's words are
quite explicit. He quotes the lines knowing well that they compare a man favourably with the gods, and comments that nobody
minded; for he goes on to say:

> Do you see to what gods he likened him, or rather declared him to
> be superior? And neither was Glaucus himself annoyed at being
> praised at the expense of the gods who watch over athletes, nor did
> they punish either Glaucus or the poet for his impiety.[2]

Lucian was a well-read man, who was not likely to make so
emphatic a point without being sure of his text. Nor is the second
argument any more weighty. Quintilian indeed mentions a poem
written *pugili coronato* which had a long digression in honour of the
Dioscuri, but adds that there was a great division of opinion
among his authorities whether it was written to Glaucus or Leo-
crates or Agatharchus or Scopas.[3] A poem whose subject was so
disputed cannot be the same as that which Lucian knew as
praising Glaucus. The situation surely is that Simonides wrote
these words as the highest praise he could think of. Pindar would
never have written them, nor perhaps would Simonides in his
later years. But in 520 he seems to have caught the popular
excitement at a victory which greatly impressed the onlookers.
Nor need he have meant his words to be taken too seriously.
They clearly exaggerate, and the exaggeration was not necessarily
meant to deceive.

An equal lack of restraint, though of a different kind, may be
seen in another Epinician of Simonides, which may belong to the
beginning of the fifth century. In the *Clouds* of Aristophanes
Strepsiades says:

---

[1] *Inst. Or.* 11. 2. 11 'cuius uulgata fabula est: cum pugili coronato carmen, quale
componi uictoribus solet, mercede pacta scripsisset, abnegatam ei pecuniae partem,
quod more poetis frequentissimo digressus in laudes Castoris ac Pollucis exierat.'

[2] *Pro Imag.* 19.

[3] Loc. cit. 'est autem magna inter auctores dissensio Glauconi Carystio an Leo-
crati an Agatharcho an Scopae scriptum sit id carmen.'

πρῶτον μὲν αὐτὸν τὴν λύραν λαβόντ' ἐγὼ 'κέλευσα
ᾆσαι Σιμωνίδου μέλος, τὸν Κριὸν ὡς ἐπέχθη.[1]

I bade him bring his lyre, and sing, the supper to adorn,
Some lay of old Simonides, as, how the Ram was shorn.[2]

This proves that the song was popular and suggests that it was
cheerful. We have the opening lines:

ἐπέξαθ' ὁ Κριὸς οὐκ ἀεικέως
ἐλθὼν ἐς εὔδενδρον ἀγλαὸν Διὸς
τέμενος.[3]

The Ram was fleeced in no unnatural way when he came to the
glorious wooded precinct of Zeus.

The Ram here named is Crius, who was a famous Aeginetan
figure and largely responsible for turning king Cleomenes of
Sparta out of Aegina.[4] Cleomenes sent him with nine other
hostages into custody at Athens, and, though, after the king's
death, Aegina demanded their restoration, it was refused.[5] We
can hardly doubt that Simonides mocks Crius, not, as has been
thought, for having cut his long hair, since this makes no point
and has nothing to do with the games, but for some other reason.[6]
The words ἐπέξαθ' ὁ Κριός are a joke, 'the Ram was fleeced', and
Simonides is deriding him for some defeat. We cannot be quite
certain that this defeat was in the games, though the context
certainly suggests that it was, since the wooded precinct of Zeus
must be that of Olympia or Nemea. If so, the poem looks as if
it was written for his victorious opponent or takes advantage of
some other occasion to deride Crius. The words came at the
beginning of the poem and were clearly intended to get a laugh.
That Simonides should gibe at an unsuccessful athlete is not
contrary to the Greek conception of sport. Even Pindar, who
treats it with consistent gravity, says of defeated competitors:

κατὰ λαύρας δ' ἐχθρῶν ἀπάοροι
πτώσσοντι, συμφορᾷ δεδαγμένοι.[7]

In back-streets, out of their enemies' way,
They cower; for disaster has bitten them.

---

[1] Nub. 1355–6. [2] Trans. B. B. Rogers. [3] Fr. 22 D.
[4] Hdt. 6. 73. 2. [5] Id. 6. 85. 3.
[6] D. L. Page, J.H.S. lxxi (1951), pp. 140–1, disposes of Wilamowitz's suggestion
A.u.A. ii, p. 284 n. 4, that the words mean 'when he came to Nemea he had a
smart hair-cut'. He does not, however, examine the nature of the failure for which
Simonides derides him. [7] Pyth. 8. 86–87.

The quality of Simonides' mockery can be assessed only by deciding what exactly he means by οὐκ ἀεικέως. If this means, as we might expect, 'not shamefully', then the implication is that Crius' failure was not disgraceful, but it could also mean 'not unnaturally',[1] and in that case the point is that Crius got what he deserved, and is less generous.

Simonides' treatment of Crius may owe something to political passions. Crius was a leading figure in Aegina when it medized in 490 and when in the years between Marathon and Salamis it was hostile to Athens. As such, he may have been a target for Simonides, who was at this period deeply engaged in Athens and loyal to it. This is not to say that he took the opportunity provided by an athletic failure to deride Crius for his political misadventures, since the song may well have been written before these, but it may mean that his failure to win in the games brought an existing dislike to the surface, and that is why the song was remembered in Athens. The joke which Simonides makes on Crius' name is similar to one made by Cleomenes himself when, on finding himself opposed in Aegina, he asked Crius what his name was, and on learning it commented ἤδη νῦν καταχαλκοῦ τὰ κέρεα, ὦ Κριέ, ὡς συνοισόμενος μεγάλῳ κακῷ.[2] Just as Cleomenes found his retort in the idea of a ram whose horns are gilded before sacrifice, so Simonides found his jest in the idea that Crius was properly fleeced when he appeared in the games.

In his Epinician Odes Simonides seems to have been gayer and more light-hearted than Pindar. He displays an element of excitement, natural to the mood of victory but alien to Pindar's solemn warnings against pride. Among those whom he celebrated was Astylus of Croton, who won the δίαυλος at Olympia in 492, 484, and 480 and whose statue, by Pythagoras of Rhegium, was erected there.[3] Of him Simonides wrote:

$$τίς δὴ$$
$$τῶν νῦν τοσάσδ' ἢ πετάλοισι μύρτων$$
$$ἢ στεφάνοισι ῥόδων ἀνεδήσατο νίκας$$
$$ἐν ἀγῶνι περικτιόνων;[4]$$

Who among those of today has bound so many victories with leaves

---

[1] For this meaning cf. Hdt. 3. 33; 6. 98. 3; Aesch. *P.V.* 1042.
[2] Hdt. 6. 50. 3.
[3] Paus. 6. 13. 1; Dion. Hal. 8. 1. 77; Diod. 11. 1. 2. For his austere habits cf. Plat. *Laws* 8. 840 a.   [4] Fr. 21 D.

of myrtle or crowns of roses in contest against the men who dwell around?

This is a compliment, whose slight air of exaggeration would be alien to Pindar's careful enumeration of victories. The tribute is indeed to victories won not in the great games but in local championships, as περικτιόνων shows, but it is none the less handsome. So too there is an un-Pindaric ring in the words which Simonides uses to celebrate a chariot-victory:

$$\pi\hat{\imath}\nu\epsilon\ \pi\hat{\imath}\nu'\ \dot{\epsilon}\pi\grave{\imath}\ \sigma\upsilon\mu\phi\circ\rho\alpha\hat{\imath}\varsigma,^1$$

'Drink, drink over good fortunes.' The gaiety of the mood is guaranteed by the appearance of the words in Aristophanes' *Knights*, where the Chorus use them in an exhilarated mood,[2] and it is very unlike the grave restraint with which Pindar introduces a festal occasion.[3] The playfulness of Simonides was recognized by the Greeks and became part of his legend. Aristotle tells that, when Anaxilas of Rhegium asked Simonides to celebrate his victory in the mule-race, the poet refused on the plea that he could not write about mules, but, when the fee was raised, he wrote:

$$\chi\alpha\acute{\imath}\rho\epsilon\tau'\ \dot{\alpha}\epsilon\lambda\lambda\circ\pi\acute{\circ}\delta\omega\nu\ \theta\acute{\upsilon}\gamma\alpha\tau\rho\epsilon\varsigma\ \ddot{\imath}\pi\pi\omega\nu^4$$

'Hail, daughters of storm-footed steeds.' The story may well be apocryphal, but it conceals a sound literary instinct. The periphrasis for the prosaic mules is ingenious and half humorous. They could hardly be exalted to true poetic grandeur and are given instead a playful solemnity.

It may be doubted whether Simonides' Epinician Odes ever reached the heights to which Pindar sometimes soared. In two places we may compare the poets in their treatment of similar themes, and the comparison shows how differently they worked. Simonides wrote for some victor in the pentathlon:

$$\dot{\omega}\varsigma\ \dot{\circ}\pi\acute{\circ}\tau\alpha\nu\ \chi\epsilon\iota\mu\acute{\epsilon}\rho\iota\circ\nu\ \kappa\alpha\tau\grave{\alpha}\ \mu\hat{\eta}\nu\alpha\ \pi\iota\nu\acute{\upsilon}\sigma\kappa\eta$$
$$Z\epsilon\grave{\upsilon}\varsigma\ \ddot{\alpha}\mu\alpha\tau\alpha\ \tau\acute{\epsilon}\sigma\sigma\alpha\rho\alpha\ \kappa\alpha\grave{\imath}\ \delta\acute{\epsilon}\kappa\alpha-$$
$$\lambda\alpha\theta\acute{\alpha}\nu\epsilon\mu\circ\nu\ \tau\acute{\epsilon}\ \mu\iota\nu\ \ddot{\omega}\rho\alpha\nu\ \kappa\alpha\lambda\acute{\epsilon}\circ\upsilon\sigma\iota\nu\ \dot{\epsilon}\pi\iota\chi\theta\acute{\circ}\nu\iota\circ\iota$$
$$\dot{\imath}\rho\grave{\alpha}\nu\ \pi\alpha\iota\delta\circ\tau\rho\acute{\circ}\phi\circ\nu\ \pi\circ\iota\kappa\acute{\imath}\lambda\alpha\varsigma$$
$$\dot{\alpha}\lambda\kappa\upsilon\acute{\circ}\nu\circ\varsigma.^5$$

---

[1] Fr. 14 D.   [2] *Equ.* 406.
[3] *Ol.* 1. 11; *Nem.* 1. 21 ff.
[4] Fr. 19 D.; Aristot. *Rhet.* 1405 b 24.   [5] Fr. 20 D.

As when in a winter month Zeus makes fourteen days of calm —men on earth call it the holy season, which forgets the winds and nurses the young of the pied halcyon.

This is a simile, and though we do not know its context, it must refer in some way to a sudden glory in a dark season.[1] As such it has something in common with Pindar's words to Hieron:

> ὁ νικῶν δὲ λοιπὸν ἀμφὶ βίοτον
> ἔχει μελιτόεσσαν εὐδίαν
> ἀέθλων γ' ἕνεκεν.[2]

The victor all the rest of his life
Breathes a delicious and serene air
When he remembers the games.

In both the imagery is drawn from fine, calm weather, but there is a notable point of difference. Simonides gives a piece of natural history as he knew it. The halcyon was said to nest at the winter-solstice, and the halcyon days were the seven days before and the seven after it.[3] This is neat, exact, and, for its time, scientific. Pindar, however, creates a magnificent phrase, resonant and imaginative, but not neat or exact. The εὐδία, the calm of the summer sea, is, pedantically speaking, not μελιτόεσσα. Pindar aims at conveying the more than human joy which the victor finds in his glory, and to do so he strains at the bounds of speech. In Simonides all is quite simple and illustrated by an apt parallel from nature.

Another comparison may be made between two passages in which both poets speak of the Pleiads, but here the comparison is more of style than of outlook, Simonides, introducing perhaps a myth, wrote:

> δίδωτι δ' εὖχος Ἑρμᾶς ἐναγώνιος,
> Μαιάδος οὐρείας ἑλικοβλεφάρου παῖς. ἔτικτε δ' Ἄτλας
> ἑπτὰ ἰοπλοκάμων φιλᾶν θυγατρῶν τάν γ' ἔξοχον εἶδος,
> ταὶ καλέονται Πελειάδες οὐράνιαι.[4]

Hermes, lord of the games, grants the prayer, he the child of mountain

---

[1] H. Fränkel, *Wege und Formen*, p. 70 n. 1, suggests that the lines may refer to a victory in war and compares Pind. *Isthm.* 4. 18, but the parallel is not very close, since Pindar speaks of the spring and Simonides of the halcyon days in winter.

[2] *Ol.* 1. 97–99.

[3] Aristot. *H.A.* 142 b 4 ff.; Aristoph: *Av.* 1594; Theocrit. 7. 57, with Gow's note. See Thompson, *Glossary of Greek Birds*, p. 30.

[4] Fr. 30 D. The lines are not explicitly quoted as coming from an Epinician, but ἐναγώνιος indicates that they do. Cf. Pind. *Pyth.* 2. 10.

Maia of the black eyes. Atlas bred her, the fairest in beauty of his
seven dear dark-haired daughters, who are called Doves of the sky.

This is based on an Arcadian story. In Cyllene Maia gave birth
to Hermes,[1] and in Arcadia she and her six sisters were pursued
by Orion and turned, for their own safety, into doves.[2] If the
victor, for whom the poem was written, came from Arcadia, he
would be pleased to hear a legend from his own land. The words
tell their own story, and we need look for no secondary or symbolical significance. Not so Pindar. Wishing to praise a pancratiast
from Acharnae, he says suddenly and unexpectedly:

$$\text{ἔστι δ' ἐοικὸς}$$
$$\text{ὀρειᾶν γε Πελειάδων}$$
$$\text{μὴ τηλόθεν 'Οαρίωνα νεῖσθαι.}[3]$$

It is right
That Orion should follow
Not far behind the mountain Pleiads.

The point is that the victor, Timodamus, follows in the wake of
the glory of his athletic relatives, as Orion follows the Pleiads,
and the point is made sharper by the verbal assonance between
ὀρειᾶν and 'Οαρίωνα. This method is far more indirect and allusive than that of Simonides. A compliment, perhaps a little forced
but still graceful and imaginative, takes the place of a direct
presentation of mythological events. Pindar works his mythology
more closely into the texture of his poetry, because it is part and
parcel of his thought. Its effect is more intimate, more personal,
less detached.

Simonides came to Athens at the invitation of Hipparchus, who
is said to have kept him in continual attendance by high pay and
valuable gifts,[4] and Simonides, who was reputed to be fond of
money, must have been at home in this easy, cultivated life.
But on this period of his career we are curiously ill-informed. No
single fragment demonstrably belongs to it. All we can say is that
to it must belong some of the many dithyrambs which Simonides
wrote and for which, on his own statement, he won fifty-six
prizes. In 476, when he was eighty years old, he set up a dedicatory tablet with the inscription:

---

[1] Alcaeus fr. 308 L.–P.; Hom. Hymn 4. 3 ff.
[2] Hes. *Op.* 619 ff.   [3] *Nem.* 2. 10–12.
[4] 'Plat.' *Hipparch.* 228 c; Aristot. *Const. Ath.* 18; Ael. *V.H.* 8. 2.

ἐξ ἐπὶ πεντήκοντα, Σιμωνίδη, ἤραο ταύρους
καὶ τρίποδας, πρὶν τόνδ' ἀνθέμεναι πίνακα·
τοσσάκι δ' ἱμερόεντα διδαξάμενος χορὸν ἀνδρῶν
εὐδόξου Νίκης ἀγλαὸν ἅρμ' ἐπέβης.[1]

Fifty-six bulls and tripods, Simonides, did you win before you set up this tablet. So many times did you mount the shining chariot of glorious victory for teaching a delightful choir of men.

This shows that Simonides not only wrote the words but taught the choir, which consisted not of boys but of men. The natural assumption is that most, if not all, of these victories were won at Athens, since it was there that Lasus, under the patronage of the Peisistratids, had inaugurated dithyrambic performances or competitions,[2] for which the prize was a bull or a tripod. This agrees with a story of rivalry between Lasus and Simonides mentioned by Aristophanes:

Λᾶσός ποτ' ἀντεδίδασκε καὶ Σιμωνίδης·
ἔπειθ' ὁ Λᾶσος εἶπεν, ὀλίγον μοι μέλει.[3]

Simonides and Lasus once competed,
And then said Lasus, 'I don't care a bit.'

Lasus' apparent indifference to the result may perhaps be interpreted as an admission that Simonides' victory was a foregone conclusion. But of all these Dithyrambs we have only a single name, Μέμνων, and even this presents a difficulty. Strabo says that 'Memnon is said to have been buried near Paltus in Syria, on the banks of the river Badas, as is told by Simonides in his dithyramb *Memnon* included among his *Deliaca*.'[4] There is nothing surprising in Dithyrambs being sung at Delos, and the poem on Memnon was presumably composed for some Delian festival, as was the 'Ηίθεοι of Bacchylides, which, though in effect a Paean, was classed as a Dithyramb. There is no known connexion between Memnon and Dionysus, and the poem may have been a straightforward narrative like some of Bacchylides' Dithyrambs, in which Dionysus is not mentioned. It is curious too that Strabo uses the archaic form Δαλιακῶν, which some scholars have attempted to emend. But it is possible that Simonides preferred the

---

[1] No. 79 D. No. 77 refers to the same occasion.
[2] 'Suid.' s.v. Λᾶσος . . . διθυραμβώδεις ἀγωγὰς εἰσήγαγεν, where Bekker, not perhaps necessarily, emends to διθύραμβον εἰς ἀγῶνα εἰσήγαγεν, see A. W. Pickard-Cambridge, *Dithyramb, Tragedy, Comedy*, pp. 23-24.
[3] *Vesp.* 1410-11.　　　　　　　　　[4] Strab. 728.

archaic name for this part of his work, and it survived because he had used it. The story of Memnon was as old as Hesiod[1] and the *Aethiopis*[2] and was not uncommonly depicted on Attic black-figure vases,[3] while in Simonides' own time the fight between Achilles and Memnon was a favourite theme,[4] and the removal of his dead body by the Dawn appears on a fine cup of Douris in the Louvre.[5] The story seems to have had no specially local associations, and there is no means of discovering why Simonides told it in a poem meant for performance at Delos.

This amounts to almost all that can be said about Simonides' Dithyrambs. It has indeed been assumed that a poem of his called Εὐρώπη[6] was one, but there is no ancient statement to this effect, and the mere presence of a bull does not provide cogent proof of the poem's character. But a curious statement of 'Suidas' that Simonides wrote τραγῳδίαι,[7] tragedies, may perhaps throw a small ray of light on his Dithyrambs. It is most unlikely that he wrote tragedies in the proper sense, since no trace of them and no word about them have survived. On the other hand, if he did not write them, it is odd that 'Suidas' should say that he did, and a possible solution is that by τραγῳδίαι 'Suidas' meant the dramatic form of the Dithyramb such as we find in Bacchylides' Ode XVIII. This poem may well have been influenced by the forms of Attic drama, but, since Aristotle expressly derives tragedy from the leaders of the Dithyramb, it seems at least possible that the *Theseus* is a survival from a transitional form, which was still a choral poem but in which the leader took a special part and the rest of the performers behaved much like a tragic chorus. Such poems had enough in common with tragedies for an inaccurate editor to class them as such, and a mistake of this kind might account for 'Suidas'' statement.

The Dithyramb was so closely associated in antiquity with

---

[1] *Theog.* 984.

[2] Proclus *ap.* Allen, Hom. *Op.* V, p. 106.

[3] Memnon with negro attendants: Beazley, *A.R.V.* p. 144, No. 8 (Exekias); p. 149 (near Exekias); p. 375, No. 207 (Leagros Group); p. 393, No. 11 (Nikosthenes Painter).

[4] Beazley, *A.R.V.* p. 23 (Phintias); p. 138, No. 102 (Berlin Painter); p. 185, No. 1 (Tyskiewicz Painter); p. 246, No. 4 (Brygos Painter); p. 258, No. 3 (manner of Brygos Painter); p. 281, No. 21 (Douris); p. 412, No. 8 and p. 413, No. 9 (Altamura Painter).

[5] Ibid. p. 288, No. 71; Pfuhl, iii, Taf. 466.

[6] Bergk, *P.L.G.* iii⁴, p. 399.　　　　　[7] s.v. Σιμωνίδης.

narrative in lyrical form[1] that we might expect Simonides to have
told stories in it. His methods of lyrical narrative may receive
some faint illustration from a papyrus which contains the fragmentary remains of the last thirty-six lines of one poem and
the first three of another.[2] They are not certainly the work of
Simonides, but there is a possibility that they may be. The first
poem describes women or girls in some place by the sea. They
are in a parlous plight:

$$υ]πὲρ ἀμετέρ[ας νεό-$$
$$τατος ἐρατύ[ει ὄ]μματα$$
$$δ]υσμενέω[ν· ἀν]εχοίμεθα$$
$$ἀκρίτοις ἀν[$$
$$ὑπὸ πένθε[σιν ἤ]μεναι·$$
$$κρυόεντι γὰρ [ἐμ π]ολέμῳ . . .$$

. . . in defence of our youth keeps off the eyes of our enemies; we could
endure to sit under unceasing griefs, for in chilling war . . .

Their situation recalls some words of Plutarch:

If a man is wise and remembers this, and is not completely brain-
struck, he will choose to live in exile on an island such as Gyaros or
Cinaros . . . without losing heart or lamenting like the women in
Simonides

$$ἴσχει δέ με πορφυρέας$$
$$ἁλὸς ἀμφιταρασσομένας ὀρυμαγδός.[3]$$

the din of the purple sea holds me as it breaks around.[4]

The situation here described is similar to that in the papyrus, and
the metre of both seems also to be similar.[5] There is then a chance
that this piece and the following are by Simonides.[6] Even so it is
not clear from what kind of poem they come. It is improbable that
they are dirges,[7] since the first poem ends with ἰὴ ἰή, which is

[1] Plat. Rep. 3. 394 c; 'Plut.' Mus. 10.
[2] A. Vogliano, P.S.I. x (1932), No. 1181, pp. 169 ff.; Page, Gk. Lit. Pap. i, pp.
382-7.
[3] Fr. 28 D.   [4] Plut. Exil. 8.
[5] J. A. Davison, C.R. xlviii (1934), pp. 205-7, but it must be admitted that it is
hard to establish any exact metrical correspondence between the papyrus and
fr. 28.
[6] A possible alternative is that the lines are by Bacchylides, especially as the
title Λευκιππίδες might be a continuation of his Dithyrambs, which are arranged
alphabetically in the British Museum papyrus. But the papyrus is not by the same
hand, nor was it found in the same place, and any coincidence may be quite
fortuitous.
[7] So Snell, Euripides: Alexandros, p. 99, but he offers no arguments.

usually a cry of joy. Since the second piece has the title Λευκιπ-πίδες it looks like a Dithyramb, for Dithyrambs often have titles of this kind with reference to the stories told in them. Perhaps the simplest solution is that these pieces are poems with some narrative characteristics of the Dithyramb, like Bacchylides' Ἠίθεοι. The beginning of the Λευκιππίδες suggests a gay occasion, and indicates that it is sung in honour of Aphrodite. Choral songs to her are indeed rare, and a Greek editor would be hard put to classify them. But perhaps we can see how Simonides began a poem which must have had a certain element of narrative:

> ἰοδερκέϊ τελλόμεναι
> Κύπριδι νεοκέ[λ]αδον
> ε]ὐειδέα χόρον.

Fulfilling for the Cyprian of the violet glances our new-sounding shapely song.

The fragments present far more problems than can be solved, and even if they are the work of Simonides, they do not throw much light on his methods.

Simonides' sojourn in Athens under the patronage of the Peisistratids received a severe blow when Hipparchus was murdered in 514, and it is remarkable that Simonides is credited with a couplet in praise of the tyrannicides:

> ἦ μέγ' Ἀθηναίοισι φόως γένεθ', ἡνίκ' Ἀριστο-
> γείτων Ἵππαρχον κτεῖνε καὶ Ἁρμόδιος.[1]

Truly a great light came to the Athenians, when Aristogeiton and Harmodius killed Hipparchus.

Hephaestion, who quotes the couplet, says that it came from Simonides' ἐπιγράμματα,[2] and the word indicates that it was not an elegiac σκόλιον but an inscription. As such, its authenticity is open to doubts, since many such were attributed to Simonides in later days, and he does not seem to have made a collection of them himself.[3] We know now that the lines, followed by two others too fragmentary to restore, were cut on the base of the statue of Harmodius and Aristogeiton made by Critius and Nesiotes in 477 B.C. to replace the statue by Antenor which had been removed by Xerxes to Persia.[4] We do not know if the verses were on

---

[1] Fr. 76 D.   [2] p. 15. 3 Consbruch.
[3] Wilamowitz, S.u.S. pp. 192 ff.; J. Geffcken, R.-E. iii A, 1. 192–6.
[4] Paus. 1. 8. 5; Mar. Par. 54. For the inscription see A.J.A. xl (1936), p. 190; Hesp. v (1936), pp. 355 ff.; Friedländer, Epigrammata, p. 141, No. 150. It contains

the earlier statue, though it is possible that they were, since the second seems to have been a free restoration of the first. Such lines were probably attributed to Simonides in later days, when he was regarded as the writer *par excellence* of elegiac inscriptions in the early part of the fifth century. Since the evidence for his authorship is at least dubious, we need not defend him from the charge of disloyalty and ingratitude to his former hosts.

There are two other more relevant pieces of evidence about Simonides' relations with the house of Peisistratus. The fragment of an ancient commentary,[1] possibly by Didymus, says that Simonides called Peisistratus a Siren and that Pindar referred to this in the words

$$οὔτε \ πελέκεις \ οὔτε \ Σηρήν^2$$

'neither axes nor Siren'. No context is given, and we can only guess Simonides' intention from the meaning which the word Σηρήν had for the Greeks. It was indeed double-edged. For Alcman it meant simply the divine perfection of singing which even his maidens could not claim for themselves,[3] and in a Maidensong Pindar makes his choir say:

$$σειρῆνα \ δὲ \ κόμπον$$
$$αὐλίσκων \ ὑπὸ \ λωτίνων \ μιμήσομ' \ ἀοιδαῖς.^4$$

On reed-pipes I shall copy
The Siren voice in my songs.

Just as this may have been suggested by the notion that the Sirens' songs calmed the sea,[5] so Simonides' comparison of Peisistratus may have been no more than a tribute to the tyrant's charms which lulled even his enemies to peace. But the image suggests more than this. The Sirens lured to death and became a symbol of it for Sophocles[6] and for Euripides.[7] So it looks as if Simonides meant to compare Peisistratus with a Siren in the sense that, just because he exerted remarkable charms, he might be dangerous to those who paid attention to them. What Pindar meant in picking up the word we do not know, but he may well

the final word Ἁρμόδιος from our couplet, and then another couplet of which the end survives, πατρίδα γῆν ἐθέτην.

[1] G. Zuntz, *C.R.* xlix (1934), pp. 4–6.
[2] Fr. 160 Bo. Zuntz suggests that the words come from a Dirge for Hippocrates the Alcmaeonid, 486 b.c. Cf. Pind. fr. 122 Bo.
[3] Fr. 1. 96–97 D.   [4] Fr. 84, 10–11 Bo.
[5] Schol. *Od.* 11. 169.   [6] Fr. 861 P.   [7] *Hel.* 169.

have referred to someone who was unmoved alike by the blandishments and by the threats of Peisistratus. There is no reason to think that Simonides failed to maintain his personal dignity and independence with the Peisistratids, and it is quite conceivable that he spoke freely about their father. Some light on his attitude may be thrown by an epitaph on the daughter of Hippias, which is credited to him. The authorship is not certain,[1] but the style and the sentiments would suit him:

> ἀνδρὸς ἀριστεύσαντος ἐν Ἑλλάδι τῶν ἐφ' ἑαυτοῦ
> Ἱππίου Ἀρχεδίκην ἥδε κέκευθε κόνις,
> ἣ πατρός τε καὶ ἀνδρὸς ἀδελφῶν τ' οὖσα τυράννων
> παίδων τ' οὐκ ἤρθη νοῦν ἐς ἀτασθαλίην.[2]

This dust hides Archedice, daughter of Hippias, foremost man among those in Hellas in his time. Though she had tyrants for father, husband, brother, and sons, she did not lift up her thoughts to pride.

The danger of tyrants was that they might fall into ὕβρις, and here Simonides shows that he recognized this and honoured those who escaped it. He consorted with tyrants, but there is no reason to think that he was servile to them.

From Athens after the fall of the Peisistratids Simonides went to Thessaly, and the mere fact shows that his connexion with Hipparchus was a possible source of danger. Thessaly gave him a respite in which to recover his position before he emerged as a truly Panhellenic figure in the Persian Wars, and there too he wrote some of the works which won him his greatest fame in antiquity. Among his hosts was Echecratidas of Crannon, the ταγός, or High King, of Thessaly, and the host of Anacreon. His son, Antiochus, died young, and for him Simonides wrote a Dirge, which came to be regarded as a classical example of its kind. Simonides seems to have been inspired by the theme of the love which Antiochus' mother, Dyseris, felt for her son. For Aristides, in his funeral speech on Eteoneus, refers to the Dirge with high praise:

What Simonides, what Pindar shall bewail such a thing as this? . . . What Dyseris of Thessaly ever made such a lament for the death of an Antiochus as this mother makes for her son?[3]

---

[1] Thucydides, 6. 59. 3 who quotes it, gives no name of an author, but Aristotle, *Rhet.* 1367 b 19, ascribes it to Simonides. See Wilamowitz, *S.u.S.* p. 213; M. Boas, *De Epigr. Simon.* pp. 70 ff. A. Hauvette, *Epigrammes de Simonide*, pp. 48–49, points out that the structure is like that of the unquestionably authentic epitaph on Megistias.   [2] No. 85 D.   [3] *Or.* 1. 127.

A no less famous Dirge was that which Simonides wrote for a calamity which proved almost fatal to him.[1] At Pharsalus or Crannon[2] the whole family of the Scopads was destroyed by the collapse of their banqueting-hall, and Simonides was said to have been saved only because he was at the time outside owing to the miraculous intervention of the Dioscuri.[3] Simonides' Dirges were much admired in antiquity. Quintilian says: 'His chief excellence lies in his pathos; indeed some critics consider that in this quality he surpasses all other writers in this class of literature.'[4] Dionysius passes a similar judgement: 'Moreover, and here he surpasses Pindar, he is remarkable for his expression of pity, not by using the grand style but by appealing to the emotions.'[5] Though neither of these tributes mentions the Dirges, we can hardly doubt that Simonides' power of pathos was manifest in them. Nor was it appreciated only by critics. When Catullus wishes to console a friend in a great loss, he says that he wishes he could send something worthy of Simonides:

> paulum quid lubet allocutionis
> maestius lacrimis Simonideis.[6]

That Simonides was a master of pathos is clear from his epitaphs and his lines on Danaë, but in the extant fragments of the Dirges we are struck by somewhat other qualities, which show how seriously he took his task.

Simonides saw death and disaster in a typically Greek spirit. He knew that at any moment they might come, and he believed that men must be ready for them. He expresses this sense of uncertainty in his own remarkable fashion:

> ἄνθρωπος ἐὼν μή ποτε φάσῃς τί γενήσεται αὔριον,
> μηδ᾽ ἄνδρα ἰδὼν ὄλβιον, ὅσσον χρόνον ἔσσεται·
> ὠκεῖα γὰρ οὐδὲ τανυπτερύγου μυίας
> οὕτως ἁ μετάστασις.[7]

[1] Favorin. ap. Stob. *Ecl.* 4. 41. 9 says that it commemorated τὴν τῶν Σκοπαδῶν ἀθρόαν ἀπώλειαν.

[2] At Crannon according to Callim. fr. 64. 13 P.; Apollas 266 F 6 J; Cic. *de Or.* 2. 86. 352; at Pharsalus according to Apollodorus 244 F 67 J; Eratosthenes 241 F 34 J; Euphorion, fr. 55 Scheidweiler.

[3] Callim. fr. 64. 11–14 P.; Ovid. *Ibis* 511 ff.; Val. Max. 1. 8. 7; Phaedr. 14. 23.

[4] *Inst. Or.* 10. 1. 64.   [5] *Vet. Script.* 420 Reiske.

[6] 38. 7–8.

[7] Fr. 6 D. In 1, where the MSS. give ὅ τι γίνεται, a future is needed to balance ἔσσεται in 2. So I have changed to τί γενήσεται.

Being a man, never say what tomorrow will be, nor, when you have seen a man happy, how long he will be so. For not even the turning of the long-winged fly is so swift a change as this.

The theme is old, but the image of man's fortune turning like a dragon-fly's wing is miraculously apt and right. By it Simonides conveys just that sense of the unpredictable insecurity of human life which he had seen, for instance, in the destruction of the Scopads. We do not know that these lines come from his Dirge on them, but they communicate a mood which would have suited such a subject.

Other fragments of the Dirges show that Simonides shared with Pindar a temper which has often been called pessimism. He was deeply impressed by the impartiality and the omnipresence of death. He saw power and wealth suddenly brought to an end by it, and he wrote:

πάντα γὰρ μίαν ἱκνεῖται δασπλῆτα Χάρυβδιν,
αἱ μεγάλαι τ' ἀρεταὶ καὶ ὁ πλοῦτος.[1]

For all things come to a single hideous Charybdis,—even great achievements and wealth.

The statement is again simple and straightforward, and again the chief effect comes from a surprising, striking phrase, δασπλῆτα Χάρυβδιν. Simonides finds his notion of death in the terrible whirlpool from which even Poseidon cannot save a man,[2] and he adds to it Homer's epithet for the avenging Fury.[3] For him death is indeed dark and frightening, and he drives home his point by two words. For a man who had such thoughts, and is not known to have believed in any Orphic or other scheme for life beyond the grave, it was at times inevitable that the spectre of death should darken his vision, and that in such a mood he should write:

ἀνθρώπων ὀλίγον μὲν
κάρτος, ἄπρακτοι δὲ μεληδόνες, αἰῶνι δ' ἐν παύρῳ πόνος ἐπὶ πόνῳ.
ὁ δ' ἄφυκτος ὁμῶς ἐπικρέμαται θάνατος·
κείνου γὰρ ἴσον λάχον μέρος οἵ τ' ἀγαθοὶ
ὅστις τε κακός.[4]

Little is men's strength, and their cares may not be accomplished, and in their short life trouble upon trouble is theirs. Without distinction

---

[1] Fr. 8 D.   [2] Od. 12. 107.   [3] Od. 15. 234.   [4] Fr. 9 D.

unescapable death hangs over them. For in him noble and base alike have an equal lot.

Few Greeks would have thought this unusual. Despite their ardent love of life and their sense of the divine glory which from time to time irradiates it, death was never very far from their thoughts and provided a background, a contrast, and a challenge to their soaring fancies and unleashed ambitions.

Before disaster fell on the Scopads, Simonides wrote some famous poems for them. One was supposed to have been performed in the dining-hall before it collapsed.[1] Little is known of it except that it praised the Dioscuri and may have been an Epinician. In the judgement of Theocritus the fame of the Scopads in after ages owed much to the songs which Simonides wrote for their victories in chariot-races, worthy of the princes of a horse-breeding land:

ἄμναστοι δὲ τὰ πολλὰ καὶ ὄλβια τῆνα λιπόντες
δειλοῖς ἐν νεκύεσσι μακροὺς αἰῶνας ἔκειντο,
εἰ μὴ θεῖος ἀοιδὸς ὁ Κήιος αἰόλα φωνέων
βάρβιτον ἐς πολύχορδον ἐν ἀνδράσι θῆκ' ὀνομαστοὺς
ὁπλοτέροις· τιμᾶς δὲ καὶ ὠκέες ἔλλαχον ἵπποι
οἵ σφισιν ἐξ ἱερῶν στεφανηφόροι ἦλθον ἀγώνων.[2]

Though they left behind them all that wealth, they would have lain among the unhappy dead unremembered for long ages, if the skilled singer of Ceos had not sung various lays to his many-stringed lyre and made them renowned among men of later days; and their swift horses also won honour and brought home to them crowns from the holy games.

Nothing more is known of these Epinicians, and we can attribute to Simonides' Thessalian period scarcely any of the few fragments of his Epinicians which survive.[3]

More revealing for this stage of his career is a poem to Scopas, preserved by Plato.[4] It seems to be an ἐγκώμιον and consists of four verses, each composed on the same metrical plan, of which we have the beginning of the first, the whole of the second and third, and the latter part of the fourth.[5] The meaning has been

---

[1] Cic. de Or. 2. 352; Quint. 11. 2. 14.
[2] 16. 42–47.   [3] Ox. Pap. 1431 was written for Thessalians, the sons of Aeatius.
[4] Prot. 339 a–347 a.
[5] The poem has been discussed by Wilamowitz, S.u.S. pp. 159–83; J. T. Sheppard, The Oedipus Tyrannus of Sophocles, pp. xxx–xxxii; H. Gundert, Festschrift Otto Regenbogen, pp. 71–93; H. D. Verdam, Mnem. lvi (1928), pp. 299–310.

much discussed, and conclusions unflattering to the poet, accusing him of a low standard of morality, have been drawn from it, but if we follow the text closely, we are forced to a different interpretation, and see that Simonides was in the van of ethical thought in his day. The background of the poem seems to be that Scopas asked Simonides what he thought of a saying of the sage Pittacus, χαλεπὸν ἐσθλὸν ἔμμεναι, hoping no doubt that Simonides would answer that, though of course it was difficult to be ἐσθλός, yet Scopas had succeeded. The answer he got was not this, but almost a lecture on the true meaning of the word 'good'. The explanations which Plato's Socrates gives of the poem are hardly serious. Words are wrongly construed, and the main purport of the poem is distorted. Taken verse by verse without reference to Socrates, its meaning is revealed.

The first verse states the problem as it has been presented to Simonides:

> ἄνδρ' ἀγαθὸν μὲν ἀλαθέως γενέσθαι
> χαλεπὸν χερσίν τε καὶ ποσὶ καὶ νόῳ
> τετράγωνον ἄνευ ψόγου τετυγμένον.[1]

It is hard to become a man truly noble, in hands and feet and mind, fashioned foursquare without blemish.

Simonides takes the saying of Pittacus that it is hard to be really ἐσθλός and elaborates what the word meant for Pittacus. He first, as it were, clears up the terminology of what has been said, and fairly assumes that by ἐσθλός Pittacus meant what in Simonides' day was called ἀγαθός, that is 'noble'. The idea of the ἀνὴρ ἀγαθός was not strictly or exclusively ethical. Its abstract noun was ἀρετή, which included far more than moral excellence. The 'noble' man must have mental and bodily excellence, and therefore, in his explanation of what the word means, Simonides mentions hands and feet and mind. Such a combination would not sound in the least strange to his hearers. Pindar admires the combination of mental and physical fitness and says that it is through the gods that men χερσὶ βιαταὶ περίγλωσσοι τ' ἔφυν.[2] This was a recognized and familiar ideal among Greek aristocrats, and Simonides is justified in assuming that Pittacus' ideal of the ἀνὴρ ἀγαθός is the same. He then adds the word τετράγωνος, 'four-square', to emphasize the completeness of the ideal. This

---

[1] Fr. 4. 1–3 D. [2] Pyth. 1. 42.

may be a Pythagorean notion; for the Pythagoreans thought that the square was the perfect figure and the image of divinity,[1] and Aristotle, who knew their doctrine, accepted the identification of the four-square man with the good man, because 'both are perfect'.[2] The notion may also have derived some support from the concept of the four cardinal virtues, courage, temperance, justice, and wisdom, as they were known to Pindar[3] and Aeschylus.[4] This concept indeed said nothing about physical qualities except in so far as they are implied in courage, but it is not ultimately far removed from the Pythagorean belief, and in all notions of this kind a certain elasticity is permissible. In the opening lines Simonides describes the noble man as Pittacus would have accepted him, and as Scopas would recognize him. What follows shows that this was not Simonides' own view. We do not know what was said in the rest of the first verse, but perhaps the traditional notion was elaborated and illustrated at greater length. So far Simonides is not yet stating his own views but clearing up the problem for further discussion.

The second verse develops the argument. Simonides shows that the old ideal is in fact impossible and can never be attained as a permanent state:

οὐδέ μοι ἐμμελέως τὸ Πιττάκειον
νέμεται, καίτοι σοφοῦ παρὰ φωτὸς εἰ-
 ρημένον· χαλεπὸν φάτ᾽ ἐσθλὸν ἔμμεναι.
θεὸς ἂν μόνος τοῦτ᾽ ἔχοι γέρας, ἄνδρα δ᾽ οὐκ
 ἔστι μὴ οὐ κακὸν ἔμμεναι,
ὃν ἀμάχανος συμφορὰ καθέλῃ.
πράξας γὰρ εὖ πᾶς ἀνὴρ ἀγαθός,
κακὸς δ᾽ εἰ κακῶς τι,
κἀπὶ πλεῖστον ἄριστοι
οὕς κε θεοὶ φιλῶσιν.[5]

Nor do I think that the word of Pittacus was said harmoniously, although said by a wise man. He said that it is hard to be noble. God alone can have this privilege, and man cannot but be base, whomsoever irresistible misfortune has overtaken. For in good fortune every man is noble, and in bad fortune base, and for the most part they are the noblest whom the gods love.

---

[1] Procl. ad Eucl. El. 48 g δοκεῖ δὲ καὶ τοῖς Πυθαγορείοις (τὸ τετράγωνον) εἰκόνα φέρειν τῆς θείας οὐσίας.   [2] Rhet. 1411 b 27.
[3] Nem. 3. 74–75.   [4] Sept. 610.   [5] Fr. 4. 4–12 D.

Simonides makes a good point, though it is obscured by the many irrelevant associations which our minds have for all words to do with good and bad. He says in effect that it is impossible to be ἐσθλός in Pittacus' sense of the word, because the position of an ἐσθλός may be changed, and then he becomes κακός. In other words Simonides takes the accepted, aristocratic view that the ἀγαθοί are the rich, the beautiful, and the fortunate, and points out that so soon as they lose their money or their looks or their good luck, they cease to be ἀγαθοί in the old sense. A god can keep his blessed state for ever, but human beings sooner or later suffer misfortune, and then they become 'base' because they are ugly or poor or unlucky. The only hope is that a fortunate few will, through the gods' love for them, escape some of these evils, but there is always a chance that the gods will change their attitude, and good fortune is not a thing that men can command for themselves. This, then, is Simonides' answer to the saying of Pittacus. It is more than a verbal refutation; it is a realistic and practical criticism of a code of honour which regarded the born aristocrat as the only 'good' man. The flaw which causes Simonides to find Pittacus' saying οὐκ ἐμμελέως εἰρημένον is precisely that in this view 'goodness' can neither be won nor kept by men. It is a gift beyond control and comes from the gods, and those who consider that it is the only true form of goodness must admit that they are in no position to command it.

The paradox which Simonides propounds is not entirely his own. It had been noticed before him by such champions of the old régime as Alcaeus and Theognis, even if they did not draw such far-reaching conclusions from it. Alcaeus confessed bitterly that 'Money makyth man',[1] and Theognis saw that the rise of a new moneyed class undermined the old notion that the rich and the noble were necessarily the same:

Κύρνε, πόλις μὲν ἔθ' ἥδε πόλις, λαοὶ δὲ δὴ ἄλλοι,
   οἳ πρόσθ' οὔτε δίκας ᾔδεσαν οὔτε νόμους,
ἀλλ' ἀμφὶ πλευραῖσι δορὰς αἰγῶν κατέτριβον,
   ἔξω δ' ὥστ' ἔλαφοι τῆσδ' ἐνέμοντο πόλεος.
καὶ νῦν εἰσ' ἀγαθοί, Πολυπαΐδη, οἱ δὲ πρὶν ἐσθλοὶ
   νῦν δειλοί· τίς κεν ταῦτ' ἀνέχοιτ' ἐσορῶν;[2]

Cyrnus, this city is still a city, but its people are others, who before knew neither justice nor laws, but on their flanks wore out hides of

[1] Fr. 360. 2 L–P.   [2] 53–58.

goats, and they pastured like deer outside this city. And now, son of Polypaus, they are noble, and those who before were noble are now base. Who can look on this and endure it?

This is a partisan but not incorrect view of the situation. Theognis sees that the social order which he has taken for granted is changing before his eyes, that the rich are no longer the same as the noble, and he deplores the change. Simonides sees the change, accepts it, and points out to the advocates of the old order that their notion of nobility cannot be securely realized in this world, since it leaves too much outside a man's own control. When he closes by saying that those are best whom the gods love, he means simply that the aristocratic conception of nobility divorces all tests of noble and base from a man's character and founds them on his circumstances. Therefore the tests must be wrong.

In the third stanza Simonides begins by disowning the old ideal and then proceeds to offer his own substitute for it:

> τοὔνεκεν οὔποτ' ἐγὼ τὸ μὴ γενέσθαι
> δυνατὸν διζήμενος κενεὰν ἐς ἄ-
> πρακτον ἐλπίδα μοῖραν αἰῶνος βαλέω,
> πανάμωμον ἄνθρωπον, εὐρεδοῦς ὅσοι
> καρπὸν αἰνύμεθα χθονός,
> ἐπί τ' ὔμμιν εὑρὼν ἀπαγγελέω.
> πάντας δ' ἐπαίνημι καὶ φιλέω,
> ἑκὼν ὅστις ἔρδῃ
> μηδὲν αἰσχρόν· ἀνάγκᾳ δ'
> οὐδὲ θεοὶ μάχονται.[1]

Therefore shall I never, in a search for what cannot exist, waste my span of life in an empty, impracticable hope—the all-blameless man, among all of us who win the fruit of the broad-based earth. If I find him, I shall tell you the news. But I praise and love all, whosoever does nothing base of his own free will; but against necessity not even the gods fight.

The opening words, which describe the futility of the search, are politely ironical. Simonides knows that he will never find the perfect man of the aristocratic ideal because he cannot exist; no man can have all the gifts which it demands. Then he becomes entirely serious and states with authority his own theory in succinct and pregnant words. He admires the man who of his own accord does nothing shameful. This doctrine may seem

[1] Fr. 4. 13–21 D.

platitudinous to us, but in Simonides' time it was revolutionary, because it establishes a new standard of goodness. It removes the emphasis from what a man has or is and places it on what he does. First, he must do nothing αἰσχρόν and secondly, what matters is what he does of his own free will, ἑκών.

In Homer and other early writers αἰσχρός means 'ugly'. Thersites is αἴσχιστος of the men who came to Troy.[1] It was easy and natural to apply the word to other things than personal appearance, and Pindar could speak of a man whose athletic prowess matched his looks, ἄγει τ' ἀρετὰν οὐκ αἴσχιον φυᾶς.[2] But in the early years of the fifth century the word had already assumed a more specialized meaning and could be applied to things morally shameful. Aeschylus gives a clear example of this, when he describes the warrior Melanippus:

> μάλ' εὐγενῆ τε καὶ τὸν Αἰσχύνης θρόνον
> τιμῶντα καὶ στυγοῦνθ' ὑπέρφρονας λόγους.
> αἰσχρῶν γὰρ ἀργός, μὴ κακὸς δ' εἶναι φιλεῖ.[3]

Truly well-born and honouring the throne of Shamefastness, and hating presumptuous words. For in shameful things he is idle, and he loves not to be base.

Here αἰσχρόν is whatever offends αἰσχύνη and is essentially different from Pindar's view of it. An ethical meaning has taken the place of an aesthetic, and this meaning is largely negative. Here too Theognis shows the change at work:

> σοὶ δ' ἐγὼ εὖ φρονέων ὑποθήσομαι, οἷά περ αὐτός,
> Κύρν', ἀπὸ τῶν ἀγαθῶν παῖς ἔτ' ἐὼν ἔμαθον.
> πέπνυσο, μηδ' αἰσχροῖσιν ἐπ' ἔργμασι μηδ' ἀδίκοισιν
> τιμάς, μηδ' ἀρετὰς ἕλκεο μηδ' ἄφενος.
> ταῦτα μὲν οὕτως ἴσθι· κακοῖσι δὲ μὴ προσομίλει
> ἀνδράσιν, ἀλλ' αἰεὶ τῶν ἀγαθῶν ἔχεο.[4]

With good intent I will give you counsels which I learned as a boy, Cyrnus, from the noble. Be wise and draw not to yourself honours or successes or wealth on account of shameful or unjust deeds. Know this in this way. Consort not with base men, but cling to the noble always.

Cyrnus is to avoid 'shameful and unjust deeds' because these are what the κακοί would do, and the injunction is given on the principle of noblesse oblige. But even so the word has an ethical tinge, and though it is not so precise as in Aeschylus, it has

---

[1] Il. 2. 216.   [2] Isthm. 7. 22.   [3] Sept. 409–11.   [4] 27–32.

moved far from its first meaning. Theognis knows that certain
actions are ugly and repellent; Aeschylus goes a step farther and
says that they are those which shock a man's sense of shame.
With him Simonides agrees.

The word ἑκών is no less emphatic and important. It is a new
moral point to say that it matters whether a thing is done
voluntarily or not. The point had indeed been recognized in the
laws of Dracon, which distinguished between voluntary and involuntary homicide;[1] but in the ordinary vocabulary of aristocratic morality the word had little place because it had little
meaning. Good looks and high birth are neither voluntary nor
involuntary. Once, however, goodness had become a question
of acts, the distinction is real and important. Aeschylus, who was
interested in the nature and functions of law, is well aware of it.
In case he should be excused on the plea of acting involuntarily
when he stole fire from heaven, Prometheus says:

$$\text{ἑκὼν ἑκὼν ἥμαρτον, οὐκ ἀρνήσομαι,}^{[2]}$$

and, true to the spirit of Dracon's Law, the Chorus of the
Agamemnon hold it against Aegisthus that on his own admission
he has slain Agamemnon of his own will:

$$\text{σὺ δ' ἄνδρα τόνδε φῂς ἑκὼν κατακτανεῖν.}^{[3]}$$

To this order of thought Simonides' words belong. He sees that
it is important whether a man does a thing willingly or not; he is
indeed forced to it by his decision that the good man is he who
does not act against his sense of shame. If through accident or
ignorance or even passion a man does something which he usually
thinks wrong he is not to blame.[4]

Simonides closes this stanza with a reservation. When he says
that 'against Necessity not even the gods fight', most Greeks
would accept his words without cavil, but they have an important place in his argument. He admits the part played in human
life by incalculable elements and is far from thinking man the
sole arbiter of his own destiny. But once he has admitted the
element of choice, he has to define its limits, and he does so simply
by saying that there is a sphere in which not choice but necessity rules. Here again Aeschylus was not far from him. In the

---

[1] S.I.G.³ 111.11 καὶ ἂν μὴ ἐκ προνοίας κτείνῃ τις.   [2] P.V. 266.
[3] Ag. 1613.   [4] Cf. Ox. Pap. 2432. 8–11.

Eumenides the Furies, in the process of their transformation from
the Erinyes into the Kindly Ones, proclaim:

> ἑκὼν δ' ἀνάγκας ἄτερ δίκαιος ὤν
> οὐκ ἄνολβος ἔσται.[1]

He who is righteous willingly and without constraint shall be not un-
blessed.

Here the elements that we find in Simonides are brought together in a slightly different way. Aeschylus says that a good
action must be voluntary, Simonides that a man's involuntary
actions must not be held against him. Both attach decisive importance to choice in moral action.

The opening lines of the fourth stanza are missing, and we
have no hint what they contained. In what follows Simonides
develops his views and shows what they mean in practice:

> οὐκ
> εἰμ' ἐγὼ φιλόμωμος· ἐξαρκεῖ γ' ἐμοὶ
> ὅ τε μὴ κακὸς μηδ' ἄγαν ἀπάλαμνος, εἰ-
> δώς γ' ὀνησίπολιν δίκαν,
> ὑγιὴς ἀνήρ· οὐδὲ μή μιν ἐγὼ
> μωμήσομαι· τῶν γὰρ ἠλιθίων
> ἀπείρων γενέθλα·
> πάντα τοι καλά, τοῖσί τ'
> αἰσχρὰ μὴ μέμεικται.[2]

I am no lover of carping. Sufficient for me is the man who is not base,
nor too witless, if he has in his heart the justice which helps the city,
a sound man; nor shall I blame him, for the generation of fools is past
counting. All things are fair in which base things are not mingled.

Simonides fears that he may be misunderstood, and his new
standards be thought too exacting and too difficult to follow. So
he explains his position and shows that it is not really intolerant,
even if it has its obvious limits. First, his good man must not be
κακός, 'base', and though by this he does not imply all the political and social associations that the word had for Alcaeus, he
admits that some forms of κακία, as generally understood, are no
more to his liking than to that of old-fashioned aristocrats. Again,
he is not far from Theognis:

[1] *Eum.* 550–1. ἑκὼν δ' is Wiesseler's correction of ἐκ τῶνδ' in the MSS.
[2] Fr. 4. 22–29 D.

οὐδεμίαν πω, Κύρν', ἀγαθοὶ πόλιν ὤλεσαν ἄνδρες·
ἀλλ' ὅταν ὑβρίζειν τοῖσι κακοῖσιν ἅδῃ,
δῆμον τε φθείρωσι δίκας τ' ἀδίκοισι διδῶσιν
οἰκείων κερδέων εἵνεκα καὶ κράτεος,
ἔλπεο μὴ δηρὸν κείνην πόλιν ἀτρεμιεῖσθαι,
μηδ' εἰ νῦν κεῖται πολλῇ ἐν ἡσυχίῃ,
εὖτ' ἂν τοῖσι κακοῖσι φίλ' ἀνδράσι ταῦτα γένηται
κέρδεα δημοσίῳ σὺν κακῷ ἐρχόμενα.
ἐκ τῶν γὰρ στάσιές τε καὶ ἔμφυλοι φόνοι ἀνδρῶν
μούναρχοί θ', ἃ πόλει μήποτε τῇδε ἅδοι.[1]

Never yet, Cyrnus, have noble men ruined a city, but when it pleases the base to be arrogant, and they destroy the people, and give judgement for the unrighteous for the sake of private gain and power, think not that this city will remain long in peace, even if now it rests in great tranquillity, yes, then, when these things become dear to the base, even profits that come with public harm. For of such come discords and internecine murders of men, and tyrants—may these things never please this city.

Simonides believed in law, order, and justice, and had no sympathy for those who attacked or perverted them. Therefore he makes it clear that his good man has none of the qualities associated by an older generation with the κακὸς ἀνήρ.

Next, Simonides will not allow his man to be a fool. He is tolerant, but the helpless nincompoop, even though he acts on the best of motives, is not the man for him; there are too many fools in the world, and he will not allow that his good man can be one of them. He still regards wisdom as one of the cardinal virtues. His critics might argue that, in laying so much stress on avoiding what is αἰσχρόν, he makes the fool the equal of the wise man. Here too he answers an objection that arises naturally from aristocratic ways of thinking. The nobles arrogated the name of wise to themselves, and thought their democratic adversaries fools. Theognis, if it be he, makes the point clear:

εἰκὸς τὸν κακὸν ἄνδρα κακῶς τὰ δίκαια νομίζειν,
μηδεμίαν κατόπισθ' ἁζόμενον νέμεσιν·
δειλῷ γάρ τ' ἀπάλαμνα βροτῷ πάρα πόλλ' ἀνελέσθαι
πὰρ ποδός, ἡγεῖσθαι θ' ὡς καλὰ πάντα τίθει.[2]

It is natural that the base man should have a base view of justice and have no respect for retribution to come. For before a craven's feet

<hr>

[1] 43–52.   [2] 279–82.

lie many foolish things for him to pick up, and make him think that he fashions everything fair.

For Simonides, who was himself accounted a wise man, there was no defence to be offered on behalf of fools who could do as much harm as the genuinely wicked.

Thirdly, and this is the crux of the matter, the good man must have civic justice in his heart. Simonides reflects the spirit of his time in rejecting alike the heroic ideal of the unfettered individual and the aristocratic ideal, which had much in common with it, for a specifically social conception of ἀρετή. It is realized in service to the city, and this is its most characteristic feature. He anticipates Sophocles:

> ἄλλοτ' ἐπ' ἐσθλὸν ἕρπει·
> νόμους περαίνων χθονὸς
> θεῶν τ' ἔνορκον δίκαν,
> ὑψίπολις· ἄπολις, ὅτῳ τὸ μὴ καλὸν
> ξύνεστι τόλμας χάριν.[1]

At another time he advances to the good. When he fulfils the laws of the land and the sworn justice of the gods, high is his city. No city has he who in rashness consorts with what is not fair.

Sophocles agrees with Simonides in seeing civic virtue as the main and most important part of goodness. Finally, Simonides clinches his thesis with the words ὑγιὴς ἀνήρ. This ethical use of ὑγιής is common enough in the second half of the fifth century[2] but Simonides is a pioneer in it. Aeschylus too saw its implications, when he made his reformed Furies say:

> ἐκ δ' ὑγιείας
> φρενῶν ὁ πᾶσιν φίλος
> καὶ πολύευκτος ὄλβος.[3]

From health of mind comes the happiness which is dear to all and prayed for by many.

In this, as in other respects, he was a child of the same intellectual movement as Simonides and operated with some of the same ideas and words.

Simonides' last line sums up the situation and recapitulates what has already been said in the third stanza. All is καλόν, good,

---

[1] *Ant.* 367–71. I follow Jebb's punctuation.
[2] Soph. *Phil.* 1006; Eur. *Andr.* 448; *Bacch.* 948; frs. 496, 821; Hdt. 1. 8. 3; 6. 100. 1; Thuc. 4. 22. 2.   [3] *Eum.* 534–6.

in which there is no admixture of αἰσχρόν, what is morally repulsive. The emphatic repetition of this theme shows what importance he attached to it. This was the ideal which he set up against the old notion of the ἐσθλὸς ἀνήρ. He held that the goal of human endeavour was still ἀρετή, but he gave the word a more strictly ethical meaning than it had hitherto possessed. Instead of its being an hereditary excellence belonging to a single class, he saw it as something that any man could find by his own efforts. Its special sphere was in the life of a city, and that a man learned it there is clear from Simonides' statement in some other poem that πόλις ἄνδρα διδάσκει.[1] He does not anticipate future notions of conscience, but he assumes that the average man knows what is base and what is not. His definition of goodness begins with a negative and leaves a large class of action undefined. It is a social virtue which lies in the sane performance of anything that does not shock a reasonable man, but it has also its positive side, which is that it helps the city in which a man lives. Simonides is both tolerant and constructive.[2]

It may have been in Thessaly that Simonides wrote some other lines, his account of Danaë floating in a chest at sea with her small child, Perseus. Stories of such chests are widely spread, but the Thessalians were interested in Perseus, and it was at Pharsalus that in *Pythian* X Pindar told of Perseus' adventures with the Gorgon's head. Tradition told that in Larissa Perseus accidentally killed Acrisius,[3] and later the coins of Larissa showed him with the Gorgon's head.[4] The piece has, naturally enough, been thought to come from a Dirge because of its pathos, but this kind of pathos is not really connected with mourning. The grief and despair of Danaë were soon to be turned to joy, and there is no connexion between the story and death. On the other hand the piece may conceivably have been written for a Thessalian prince, like Pindar's patron, and in that case it might come from almost any kind of choral song performed at his court.

The text of the piece is full of unsolved and perhaps insoluble problems. Dionysius, who quotes it, does so to illustrate a point which has nothing to do with the poem's merits. His purpose is

---

[1] Fr. 53 D. That Simonides had his own ideas on birth and breeding seems clear from Aristot. fr. 92 R. Σιμωνίδην δέ φασι διερωτώμενον τίνες εὐγενεῖς τοὺς ἐκ πάλαι πλουσίων φάναι.

[2] Simonides treated a similar theme to that of this poem in the recently published *Ox. Pap.* 2432.   [3] Apollodor. *Bib.* 2. 4. 4.   [4] B. Head, *H.N.* p. 301.

to show that, if it is read as it comes without reference to its metrical units, we shall not know where we are:

Please read the piece carefully by divisions; be sure that the rhythm of the song will escape you and you will not be able to grasp strophe, antistrophe, or epode; it will read like a piece of continuous prose.[1]

If he intended to keep us guessing, he has succeeded beyond all expectation. It seems almost impossible to arrange the fragment in strophe, antistrophe, and epode, though Dionysius seems to imply that they are there, and it is possible that, though all three are represented in it, only one of them is complete, and therefore we should not look for metrical correspondence but just take the lines as they come from the manuscripts with the smallest possible number of changes. If we do this, we get something like the following, but we must recognize that the text may well be more corrupt than we know:

> ὅτε λάρνακι
> ἐν δαιδαλέᾳ
> ἄνεμός τε μέμηνε πνέων,
> κινηθεῖσα δὲ λίμνα
> 5 δεῖμά τ' ἔρειπεν, οὐκ
> ἀδιάντοισι παρειαῖς
> ἀμφί τε Περσέϊ βάλλε φίλαν χέρα
> εἶπέν τ'· ὦ τέκος, οἶον ἔχω πόνον·
>
> σὺ δ' ἀωτεῖς, γαλαθηνῷ
> 10 δ' ἤτορι κνώσσεις ἐν ἀτερπέϊ
> δούρατι χαλκεογόμφῳ
> τῷδε νυκτιλαμπεῖ
> κυανέῳ δνόφῳ ταθείς·
> ἄλμαν δ' ὕπερθεν τεᾶν
> 15 κομᾶν βαθεῖαν παριόντος
> κύματος οὐκ ἀλέγεις
> οὐδ' ἀνέμου φθόγγον
> πορφυρέᾳ κείμενος ἐν χλανίδι,
> πρόσωπον καλὸν προφαίνων· εἰ δέ τοι
> 20 δεινὸν τό γε δεινὸν ἦν,
> καί κεν ἐμῶν ῥημάτων
> λεπτὸν ὑπεῖχες οὖας.

---

[1] de Comp. 26 πρόσεχε δὴ τῷ μέλει καὶ ἀναγίνωσκε ταῦτα κατὰ διαστολάς, καὶ εὖ ἴσθ' ὅτι λήσεταί σε ὁ ῥυθμὸς τῆς ᾠδῆς καὶ οὐχ ἕξεις συμβαλεῖν οὔτε στροφὴν οὔτε ἀντιστροφὴν οὔτ' ἐπῳδόν, ἀλλὰ φανήσεταί σοι λόγος εἰς εἰρόμενος.

κέλομαί σ' εὗδε, βρέφος,
εὑδέτω δὲ πόντος, εὑδέ-
25   τω δ' ἄμετρον κακόν·
μεταβουλία δέ τις φανείη,
Ζεῦ πάτερ, ἐκ σέο·
ὅττι δὲ θαρσαλέον ἔπος εὔχομαι
ἢ νόσφι δίκας,
30   σύγγνωθί μοι.[1]

When on the carven chest the wind raved as it blew, and the troubled
sea and fear cast her down, with cheeks not unwet she cast her loving
arm round Perseus and said: 'My child, what trouble is mine, but
you sleep and in your baby heart slumber in this joyless craft bronze-
bolted, shining in the night, as you are stretched out in the dark-blue
gloom. The deep brine of the wave passing above your head you reck
not, nor the voice of the wind as you lie in your purple mantle, revealing
your lovely face. If for you terror were really terrible, then you would
turn your little ear to my words. But sleep, I bid you, my child, and
sleep the sea, and sleep our immeasurable ill. May some change of
heart, father Zeus, be revealed from you. Whatever word of prayer I
utter in boldness or without justice, forgive me.'

These deservedly famous lines show how well justified was
Simonides' reputation for pathos and how much broader was its
scope than in reference to death. The effect is secured by an
explicit account of Danaë's sufferings, but nothing is overdone,
and the poet passes no comment. The pathos is truly dramatic.
This is the crucial point of the story, the period of uncertainty
between Danaë's brutal expulsion from Argos and her arrival on
Seriphos with its frightening consequences. The crude story is
transformed by the skill with which Simonides brings it within the
range of human experience in his understanding of the despairing
mother's feelings. Nor is his approach merely through the emotions. He makes also an appeal to the eye. The chest is a real
chest, carved and fitted with bolts of bronze. The child sleeps, as

[1] Fr. 13 D. I have in the main followed the text as reconstructed by Page,
J.H.S lxxi (1951), pp. 133 ff. In 3 I welcome his tentative suggestion of τε
μέμνηνε for τε μήν. In 10 ἤτορι of the MSS. of Athenaeus seems more effective than
ἤθει, and κνώσσεις is less forbidding than κνοώσσεις. In 14 Bergk's ἄλμαν is perfectly appropriate to the scene, while Page's ἄχναν seems a little too precise and
precious. In 19 I feel that a verb is needed to govern πρόσωπον καλόν and accept
Ahrens's προφαίνων, which may perhaps give a hint that the child's face shines in
the darkness. Useful work in clearing the text of unnecessary accretions was done
by J. A. Davison *C.Q.* xxix (1935), pp. 85–95, and other suggestions may be found
in G. Perrotta, *Maia*, iv (1951), pp. 1–37.

the son of a princess should, in his purple cloak. In the darkness, which is called 'blue', Danaë sees his face, and it stirs her love. Outside the wind and the waves are loud. But it is not a static picture that Simonides gives. There is a psychological, dramatic development in Danaë's words. Beginning with fear, she sees her child sleeping calmly and recovers enough self-command and strength to pray for deliverance. Like a modest woman, she fears that her prayer may be presumptuous, and, if it is, she asks that she may be forgiven. Simonides displays an accomplished art of narrative, as he changes his tone with the changes of action in his story, and sees all as a real chapter of human experience.

Though it is possible that these lines were written for Thessalians, there is almost equally good reason to connect them with Athens, where the story of Danaë and Perseus had a certain vogue in the early years of the fifth century. A red-figure hydria by the Gallatin Painter, in Boston,[1] shows the chest being made by a workman. To the right stands Danaë holding her child, while to the left an old man, who must be Acrisius, gives orders. A fourth figure, a woman, seems to be an attendant of Danaë. A variation of the same theme may be seen on a calyx-crater of the Triptolemus Painter in Leningrad,[2] and on it Perseus is a small boy playing with a ball. The other end of the story appears on a stamnos of the Eucharides Painter, also in Leningrad,[3] which shows a graceful young woman carrying a child on her left arm, while she receives the salutations of a bearded man, who must be her rescuer Dictys, after she has arrived on Seriphos. This part of the story is now known to have been treated by Aeschylus in a Satyric drama, the *Dictyulci* or *Net-Drawers*, in which the second fragment tells how, when Danaë and Perseus have come to land, Dictys looks after her, while the Satyrs play with the child and foretell what a future awaits him. Aeschylus' scene is gay and lively, but at one point he may pick up a hint from Simonides. When Danaë replies to Dictys' welcome, the broken lines of the papyrus suggest that she feels that she has made amends for any fault which she has committed:

$$Ζεῦ, τῶνδε] \ πέμπ' \ ἀρωγόν, \ εἰ \ δοκεῖ, \ τινά·$$
$$σὺ \ μὲν \ γὰρ] \ εἶχες \ αἰτίας \ τῆς \ μείζονος$$

[1] Beazley, *A.R.V.* p. 163, No. 1; illustration in *A.R.V.A.M.* p. 51, fig. 32.
[2] Id. *A.R.V.* p. 239, No. 1.
[3] Ibid. p. 155, No. 26; illustration in *A.R.V.A.M.* p. 47, fig. 28.

βλάβης, δίκη]ν δὲ πᾶσαν ἐξέτεισ' ἐγώ.
θεῖναι τάδ'] εὖ σ' ἔλεξα· πάντ' ἔχεις λόγον.[1]

It is possible that Aeschylus knew Simonides' poem, and though his own play dealt with a later stage in the story and treated it, naturally enough, in a different temper, he provides a sequel to the dark imprisonment in the chest at sea.[2]

It is not known how long Simonides stayed in Thessaly, and none of his Thessalian poems can be dated at all closely. In due course he returned to Athens, and was certainly there in 490, when, according to the anonymous *Life of Aeschylus* prefixed to the plays,[3] he defeated Aeschylus in writing an epitaph εἰς τοὺς ἐν Μαραθῶνι τεθνηκότας. Such a success is not surprising in this very special form of art in which Simonides was a master, but in this case we can perhaps form a very faint idea of the difference between the two poets. In the excavations of the Agora at Athens the remains of a stone have been found on which are inscribed two epigrams, both of which relate to the Persians and to men who fought against them. Neither appears in the *Palatine Anthology* or any other collection, and we may assume that no transcripts were made because the originals were lost in the Persian destruction of Athens in 480, and nothing was known of them when the 'Simonidean' epigrams were collected from stones for editing. The lower of the two epitaphs is written by the same hand as the upper, but whereas the upper seems to have been carved in the sculptor's workshop, the lower seems to have been carved when the stone was already in position, and looks as if it were added by an afterthought, since it occupies a part of the stone which we should expect to be left blank. Here are two epigrams in memory of the men who fell at Marathon, and it looks as if the upper were the winning poem of Simonides, and the lower the poem of Aeschylus, added very soon afterwards on the insistence of an Athenian public, which perhaps felt that it had unduly slighted its own poet who had himself fought in the battle. Both epigrams are deplorably incomplete, and restorations are

---

[1] *Ox. Pap.* xviii. 2161, col. i. 782–4; H. Lloyd-Jones, *Aeschylus*, ii (Loeb ed.[2]), p. 538; see also E. Fraenkel, *P.B.A.* xxviii (1942), pp. 237–61.

[2] Lucian, *Dial. Mar.* i. 12. 1, presents a dialogue between Thetis and the sea-nymph Doris, in which they speak about the plight of Danaë and Perseus while they are still in the chest, but if it owes anything to Simonides, the debt is very general.

[3] *Vit. Aesch.* 8.

extremely hazardous.[1] It is, however, characteristic of Simonides that he praises the ἀρετή of the fallen, while Aeschylus seems to refer to their ἀδάμαστος θυμός, and more noteworthy that, while for Aeschylus the victory is won for the city, for Simonides it is won

$$h\epsilon\lambda\lambda\acute{a}[\delta a\ \mu]\grave{\epsilon}\ \pi\hat{a}\sigma a\nu\ \delta o\acute{\nu}\lambda\iota o[\nu\ \check{\epsilon}\mu a\rho\ \grave{\iota}\delta\hat{\epsilon}\nu.$$

He revealed himself, as indeed he was to remain for the rest of his life, a truly Hellenic poet who was limited by no specifically local loyalties.

In Athens Simonides attached himself to no single set or circle. A four-lined σκόλιον attributed to him was, as we shall see, probably closely related to the circle of Miltiades. Another σκόλιον may be seen in an elegiac couplet addressed to Callias on the death of his friend Megacles:

$$\sigma\hat{\eta}\mu a\ \kappa a\tau a\phi\theta\iota\mu\acute{\epsilon}\nu o\iota o\ M\epsilon\gamma a\kappa\lambda\acute{\epsilon}o\varsigma\ \epsilon\hat{\upsilon}\tau'\ \mathring{a}\nu\ \check{\iota}\delta\omega\mu a\iota,$$
$$o\mathring{\iota}\kappa\tau\acute{\iota}\rho\omega\ \sigma\epsilon,\ \tau\acute{a}\lambda a\nu\ Ka\lambda\lambda\acute{\iota}a,\ o\mathring{\iota}'\ \check{\epsilon}\pi a\theta\epsilon\varsigma.[2]$$

Whenever I see the tomb of dead Megacles, I pity you, unhappy Callias, for your lot.

Megacles, son of Hippocrates, was ostracized in 487/6,[3] and in his exile won the chariot-race in the Pythian Games, for which Pindar wrote *Pythian* VII with its reference to φθόνον ἀμειβόμενον τὰ καλὰ ἔργα, and since Megacles seems to have died soon afterwards, Simonides' couplet may have been written at this time. Callias too was a prominent figure at Athens. The son of Hipponicus, he fought at Marathon[4] and married Miltiades' granddaughter and Cimon's daughter, Elpinice.[5] He may have been born between 530 and 520, and he won the chariot-race at Olympia in 496, 492, and 488.[6] His family had close associations with the Alcmaeonids, to whom Megacles belonged, in their opposition to Peisistratus and his sons. They had combined in the expulsion of Hippias, and Herodotus regarded both their houses as prominent examples of μισοτύραννοι.[7] At Marathon there was probably a split between them, as Megacles may have been

---

[1] J. Oliver, *Hesperia*, ii, pp. 480–94; F. Hiller von Gaertringen, *Hermes*, lxix, pp. 204–6; W. Peek, ibid. pp. 339–43; P. Maas and L. Wickert, ibid. lxx, pp. 235–8; J. Kirchner, *Imag. Inscr. Att.* p. 12, No. 18, pl. ix; A. Wilhelm, *Anz. Ak. Wien.* 1934, pp. 89–107; J. Oliver, *A.J.P.* pp. 193–201.

[2] No. 84 D. Cf. Wilamowitz, *S.u.S.* p. 211.

[3] Aristot. *Const. Ath.* 22; Lys. *Alc.* 1. 39.

[4] Plut. *Aristid.* 5. 5; Schol. Aristoph. *Nub.* 64.

[5] Plut. *Cim.* 4. 7.

[6] C. Robert, *Hermes*, xxxv, p. 177.

[7] 6. 121. 1.

z

associated with those Alcmaeonids who were ready to com-
promise with Persia,[1] and that would account for his ostracism
later, while Callias fought in the battle. That this division led to
no personal breach between Megacles and Callias may be seen
from our couplet. Simonides honoured both when he wrote it.

The position which Simonides held in 490 was strengthened
and confirmed when Xerxes came in 480. He was now the
laureate of the Hellenic cause and gave his support and allegiance
to its champion, Themistocles. While the poet admired the statesman, the statesman must have seen that the poet could be useful
to him in making his policies and purposes known. The two were
indeed personal friends. Plutarch tells how Themistocles mocked
Simonides for reviling the Corinthians who dwelt in a fine city
while he himself was so ugly;[2] Cicero tells how Themistocles said
to the poet that, so far from needing an art of memory such as
Simonides professed to teach, he needed an art of forgetfulness
—'for I remember what I would not and cannot forget what I
would.'[3] These stories are trivial and probably apocryphal, but
they are part of the Simonides legend, and the connexion between
him and Themistocles must be an historical fact. The poet who
wrote the epitaphs for 480 was too important not to be noticed by
Themistocles, and, what is more significant, his poetical activities
in that and succeeding years are best explained by a personal
attachment to the statesman.

In 480 and 479 Simonides did not limit his poetical activity to
writing epitaphs for the fallen. These perfect works of art were
almost beyond the claims of city or party, but a more personal
note may be suspected in two poems known to antiquity as *The
Sea-fight of Artemisium* and *The Sea-fight of Salamis*.[4] Both must have
been choral odes sung on public occasions, and both celebrated
events in which Themistocles had taken a leading part. The
fragments ἐβόμβησεν θάλασσα and ἀποτρέποισι Κῆρας[5] from *The
Sea-fight of Artemisium* show that it was composed in a lyric metre
and not, as 'Suidas' says, δι' ἐλεγείας. Both its origin and the
occasion of its performance have been well demonstrated by
Wilamowitz, who shows that it was concerned with the so-called
victory of the Greek fleet over the Persian off Artemisium, when
the North Wind, Boreas, was asked to intervene on the Greek

---

[1] Hdt. 6. 115.   [2] Plut. *Them.* 5. 5.   [3] *de Fin.* 2. 32. 104.
[4] 'Suid.' s.v. Σιμωνίδης.   [5] Frs. 1–2 D.

behalf and did so to their great advantage. Herodotus says of the Greeks:

When they were anchored at Chalcis in Euboea and saw the storm increasing, or even before this, they sacrificed and summoned Boreas and Oreithyia to come to their help, and destroy the ships of the barbarians as before about Athos. I cannot say if it was for this reason that Boreas had helped them before and then worked this destruction, but when they went away they built a temple of Boreas by the river Ilissus.[1]

From this Wilamowitz concludes that this temple was founded very soon after the battle and Simonides' poem was the hymn sung at the foundation.

Wilamowitz also assumes that two passages from Himerius, which concern Simonides, are derived from this poem.[2] In one Himerius says:

The wind, doubtless recognizing the Cean song which Simonides sang to it after the sea, comes straightway at the call of the music, and blowing strong and full astern drives on the bark with its breath.[3]

The wind here has not the same characteristics as that which scattered and smashed the Persian ships off Artemisium. It is strong, but it is following and favourable, κατὰ πρύμνης οὔριος, while the wind at Artemisium came from the north and, though it helped the Greeks indirectly, it was hardly favourable in any real sense. The same image of a friendly wind is used elsewhere by Himerius in a similar context:

For now desiring to call the wind poetically but being unable to utter poetic speech, I wish to address the wind according to the Cean Muse . . . Softly spreading above the waves it cleaves the purple waves about the prow.[4]

Here the wind is ἁπαλός, and the word is inappropriate to Boreas. These passages, then, are unlikely to refer to *The Sea-fight of Artemisium*, but it is possible that they refer to *The Sea-fight of Salamis*. From the accounts of Salamis it is plain that in the evening of the battle a wind rose which damaged the defeated and retreating Persians. Herodotus expressly says that this was Zephyrus, the West wind,[5] and Aeschylus tells how the Persians sailed raggedly κατ' οὖρον,[6] which agrees with this. This wind had

[1] 7. 189. [2] *S.u.S.* pp. 206–8. [3] *Or.* 47. 14 Colonna.
[4] *Or.* 12. 32 Colonna. [5] 8. 96. 2. [6] *Pers.* 481.

not the force and violence of that at Artemisium, but was no less helpful to the Greeks and worthy of honourable mention.

It seems, then, that at Salamis the wind played a helpful part and was mentioned by Simonides in his poem on the battle. He is said to have described the Greeks as enduring till the evening,[1] and since it was then that the wind arose, his reference to it may have occurred at this point. We may also surmise when *The Sea-fight of Salamis* was performed. Himerius precedes his first statement with the words:

A song shall loose the moorings of the vessel, the song which the chorus of Athenians sing when they call the wind to the ship that it may be present and fly along with the procession.[2]

The vessel here mentioned is the car which represented a ship in the Panathenaic procession and had the πέπλος of Athene hung on it like a sail.[3] It looks as if Himerius got his notion from the same source as his reference to the wind, and since he speaks both of the θεωρίς and of προσᾴδουσιν, the natural conclusion is that *The Sea-fight of Salamis* was sung as a προσόδιον in the Panathenaic procession, and its choral character is confirmed by 'Suidas'' comment that it was composed μελικῶς. The revival of the Panathenaea after the Persian evacuation of Attica must have been an occasion for high rejoicing and a natural time for a hymn which celebrated the victory of Salamis.

Almost nothing is known of two poems, which Simonides may have composed at this time, *The Kingdom of Cambyses and Darius*, said by 'Suidas' to be written in elegiacs, and *The Sea-fight with Xerxes*, which need not necessarily be the same as *The Sea-fight of Salamis*.[4] But the fullest specimen of his choral poetry on these events is a fragment on the fallen of Thermopylae. He had personal ties with Sparta, and when his friend Megistias was killed in the battle, he honoured his memory with four unforgettable lines.[5]

---

[1] Plut. *Them.* 15. 2, where the words μέχρι δείλης ἀντισχόντας are probably a quotation.

[2] *Or.* 47. 14 Colonna.

[3] Schol. Aristoph. *Eq.* 566; Paus. 1. 29. 1; *I.G.* ii². 657; Harpocrat. s.v. τοπεῖον.

[4] *Ox. Pap.* xxii. 2137 contains the very fragmentary remains of what must have been quite a long poem in elegiacs. It refers to the sea, war, Medes, Persians, Phrygians, and Phoenicians, and may conceivably be the work of Simonides. But the remains do not allow the certain restoration of a single line, and there is no evidence, external or internal, for its authorship. Cf. W. Peek, *W.Z.M.–L.U.* v (1955–6), pp. 202–6, for suggested supplements.

[5] No. 83 D.

Nor can we lightly reject his claim to the authorship of the epitaph on the Spartan Three Hundred who fell with their king.[1] That he had some position in Sparta is clear from the stories which connect him with Pausanias,[2] and though these suffer from the usual moralizing note of apocryphal anecdote, it is hard to ignore the statement of the second Platonic epistle that the friendship of Pausanias and Simonides was already a stock case of association between king and poet,[3] or to dismiss out of hand the tradition that Simonides wrote for the king the inscription for the dedication of the Persian spoils at Delphi which played a large part in his prosecution at Sparta:

ʿΕλλήνων ἀρχηγός, ἐπεὶ στρατὸν ὤλεσε Μήδων,
    Παυσανίας, Φοίβῳ μνῆμ' ἀνέθηκε τόδε.[4]

Pausanias, leader of the Hellenes, set up this memorial to Phoebus, when he had destroyed the army of the Medes.

As a truly Hellenic poet, Simonides was well fitted to celebrate the fallen of Thermopylae not only by an epitaph for their grave, but by a choral song which honoured their memory.

Diodorus says that the lines are an ἐγκώμιον,[5] but he is surely using the word not in the technical sense which it had in the fifth century but in its later sense of any piece of praise. Others have thought that they come from a σκόλιον,[6] but they are too stately and too hieratic for that. Bergk ascribed them to *The Sea-fight of Artemisium*,[7] but that was concerned with Athens, and so emphatic a tribute to Sparta might be out of place in it. A possible alternative is that they belong to a θρῆνος, but to this too there are objections. Normally a θρῆνος was sung immediately after death over the dead. In the words of Simonides there is no note of lamentation; funeral rites are not mentioned; the song cannot have been sung over the dead at Thermopylae, for the Persians were in occupation of it. We must look for another explanation.

The men who fell in the Persian Wars were soon exalted to the rank of heroes, and shrines were erected to them, at which rites suitable to heroes were conducted. To the celebration of some such rites the words of Simonides seem to belong. At Marathon the

---

[1] No. 92 D. See Bowra, *E.G.E.* pp. 193–5.
[2] Plut. *Cons. Apoll.* 6; Ael. *V.H.* 9. 41.
[3] 311 a.
[4] No. 105 D.; Thuc. 1. 132. 2.
[5] 11. 11. 6.
[6] Bernhardy, quoted by Smyth *G.M.P.* p. 308.
[7] *P.L.G.* iii⁴, p. 383.

local inhabitants honoured as heroes those who fell in the battle.[1]
At Plataea every year the Plataeans honoured the tombs of the
fallen with a public festival, bringing them clothing and the first
fruits of their crops.[2] In the rite a banquet was prepared for the
dead, prayers were offered to the god of heaven and the god of
earth, and the archon, clothed in a blood-red tunic and girded
with a sword, pledged the souls of the dead with a cup of wine and
said: 'I drink to the men who died for the liberty of Greece.'[3]
Such rites were not necessarily confined to the actual graves, but
could be held *in absentia*, at some suitable cenotaph or monument.
At Sparta the two soldiers, Maron and Alpheus, whom Herodotus
names as the best fighters at Thermopylae after Leonidas,[4] had
a ἱερόν or shrine,[5] but they were not buried in it, since all the
Spartan dead were buried at Thermopylae,[6] and the shrine must
have been a place for the cult of them in absence. If we look at
the lines carefully, we shall see that they imply some sort of cult
and that each phrase is carefully meditated and makes its own
point:

> τῶν ἐν Θερμοπύλαισι θανόντων
> εὐκλεὴς μὲν ἁ τύχα, καλὸς δ' ὁ πότμος,
> βωμὸς δ' ὁ τάφος, πρὸ γόων δὲ μνᾶστις, ὁ δ' οἶκτος ἔπαινος.
> ἐντάφιον δὲ τοιοῦτον εὐρὼς
> 5   οὔθ' ὁ πανδαμάτωρ ἀμαυρώσει χρόνος·
> ἀνδρῶν ἀγαθῶν ὅδε σηκὸς οἰκέταν εὐδοξίαν
> Ἑλλάδος εἵλετο. μαρτυρεῖ δὲ καὶ Λεωνίδας
> κοσμὸν ὁ Σπάρτας βασιλεὺς ἀρετᾶς μέγαν λελοιπὼς
> ἀέναόν τε κλέος.[7]

Of those who died at Thermopylae glorious is the fortune and fair the
doom. For tomb they have an altar, for lamentations they have remembrance, for pity praise. Such a funeral rite nor rust nor all-
conquering time shall obliterate. This holy place of noble men has
won the glory of Hellas as its household spirit. Leonidas, too, is witness, the king of Sparta, who has left a great ornament of valour and
an everlasting fame.

The poem cannot have been sung at Thermopylae, and that is
why the emphatic ἐν Θερμοπύλαισι takes the place of some such

---

[1] Paus. 1. 32. 4.   [2] Thuc. 3. 58. 4.   [3] Plut. *Aristid.* 21.
[4] Hdt. 7. 227.   [5] Paus. 3. 12. 9.   [6] Hdt. 7. 228. 1.
[7] Fr. 5 D. See Wilamowitz, *S.u.S.* pp. 140–1, and for the metre A. M. Dale,
C.Q. n.s. i (1951), pp. 119–20. I follow Bergk in punctuating after χρόνος in 5,
because it gives a more impressive emphasis to what follows. In 7–8 I follow the
order of words suggested by Wilamowitz.

word as ἐνθάδε. It follows that the words βωμὸς δ' ὁ τάφος mean not that 'their tomb is an altar', but 'for a tomb they have an altar', and are parallel to ὁ δ' οἶκτος ἔπαινος, which means not 'pity for them is praise', but 'for pity they have praise'. The τάφος is not where they are buried at Thermopylae, but somewhere else, presumably at Sparta, where their memory is held in honour. The character of the place is made clearer by being called a σηκός. Strictly a σηκός was a sacred enclosure or precinct, and Ammonius and others say that it was sacred to a hero, while a ναός was sacred to a god.[1] If the dead Spartans were honoured as heroes, σηκός was the appropriate word for the place of their cult, and it remained appropriate even if their bodies were elsewhere, since it had no definite associations with burial or the tomb. The presence of an altar was indispensable if there were rites like those at Plataea. Simonides' point in βωμὸς δ' ὁ τάφος is that here an altar takes the place of a tomb.

Simonides begins by making a distinction between τύχα and πότμος. τύχα is the chance which the Spartans had of winning κλέος, glory, at Thermopylae, and πότμος is the doom which gave it to them and is therefore called καλός. It prepares the way for the rites and honours which they now receive. The words πρὸ γόων δὲ μνᾶστις do not simply mean that the dead have died so nobly that they find lasting remembrance instead of tears. That is a later and more sophisticated idea which appeals to Hyperides, who says of his dead warriors οὐ γὰρ θρήνων ἄξια πεπόνθασιν, ἀλλ' ἐπαίνων μεγάλων πεποιήκασι,[2] 'for they have not suffered what deserves lamentation but they have done what deserves great praise.' Since the dead of Thermopylae are celebrated away from their tombs some time after their death, they cannot have γόοι or οἶκτος, tears wept over them or pity showed for their passing, but what they can have is μνᾶστις, remembrance, and ἔπαινος, praise. A similar consolation is offered by Pericles in his funeral speech:

κοινῇ γὰρ τὰ σώματα διδόντες ἰδίᾳ τὸν ἀγήρων ἔπαινον ἐλάμβανον καὶ τὸν τάφον ἐπισημότατον, οὐκ ἐν ᾧ κεῖνται μᾶλλον, ἀλλ' ἐν ᾧ ἡ δόξα αὐτῶν παρὰ τῷ ἐντυχόντι αἰεὶ καὶ λόγου καὶ ἔργου καιρῷ ἀείμνηστος καταλείπεται.[3]

[1] Diff. p. 94 Valcknaer; Pollux 1. 6; Schol. Thuc. Ox. Pap. 853, col. x. 3, quoting Callim. fr. 694 P.; Ptolem. de Voc. Diff. ed. E. Heylbutt, Hermes, xxii (1887), p. 402. 17.
[2] Epitaph. 42.   [3] Thuc. 2. 43. 2.

So they gave their bodies to the commonwealth and received each for his memory praise that will never die, and with it the grandest of all sepulchres, not that in which their mortal bones are laid, but a home in the minds of men, where their glory remains fresh to stir to speech or action as the occasion comes by.[1]

Pericles speaks at the funeral ceremony, but he knows that the dead are remembered elsewhere and have a second memorial in men's thoughts. His ideas are fundamentally similar to those of Simonides, and he too makes praise an essential element in such remembrance.

The words that follow are less easy to interpret, and there is a special difficulty in ἐντάφιον. It has been taken to mean 'shroud' or 'winding-sheet', and the most apt parallel are the words which a companion said to Dionysius of Syracuse, when there seemed to be no hope of deliverance from the Carthaginians, καλὸν ἐντάφιον ἡ τυραννίς,[2] which presumably means that it is glorious to die a king. Something of the same kind may be seen much later when Polybius writes κάλλιστον ἐντάφιον ἕξουσι τὸν ὑπὲρ τῆς πατρίδος θάνατον.[3] If we press the meaning of Simonides' words in the light of such passages, they must imply that the glory of the dead is like a shroud which will last for ever. But this is surely a little strained, as the shroud is not an image which suggests all that Simonides has in mind. It is therefore tempting to seek another meaning for ἐντάφιον, and though there is no certain solution, there is perhaps a hint of one. The plural ἐντάφια is used by Sophocles[4] and others[5] for offerings made to the dead. The scholiast explains it as ἐναγίσματα, and since the singular ἐνάγισμα means 'offering', ἐντάφιον may possibly mean something of the kind. If this is the case, the point is that the ceremony at the shrine includes a rite to the dead which will never fall into decay.

The shrine has won εὐδοξίαν Ἑλλάδος as its οἰκέταν, and this has been taken to mean that it has Hellenic renown as its inhabitant;[6] that is, personified Fame dwells in it. This receives some support from the words of Pericles, already quoted, in which ἡ δόξα is itself a memorial, and is in the main correct. But the meaning of οἰκέταν can hardly be 'inhabitant', since this is

[1] Trans. A. Zimmern.
[2] Isocr. 6. 44.
[3] 15. 10. 3.
[4] *El.* 326.
[5] Eur. *Hel.* 1420; Isae. 8. 38.
[6] Wilamowitz, *S.u.S.* p. 141.

not a testified use of it. It seems rather to have a technical religious significance. It appears on a Spartan inscription as a title of Apollo,[1] and the combination Κάρνειος οἰκέτας was thought by Pausanias to be a survival from Achaean times.[2] οἰκέτας seems to mean 'god of the household', and to be a title of Apollo comparable to his title of δωματίτας, 'builder of the home', in Aegina.[3] It follows that when Glory is οἰκέτας of the shrine, she is a protecting divinity and will look after it. Though it is easy to alter the masculine form to the feminine οἰκέτιν,[4] there is probably no need to do so, since the masculine form had clear associations for Spartans and is best kept intact.

The poem, then, seems to have been sung at Sparta at a shrine dedicated to the fallen of Thermopylae. That such a shrine existed is not surprising; for the ἱερόν of Maron and Alpheus proves that even individual fighters had their special cult. The cenotaph of the fallen host which Simonides celebrates seems to have been near that of Leonidas; for it was here that Pausanias saw the στήλη which contained the names of those who fell at Thermopylae. Leonidas too was buried at Thermopylae, but had his own shrine at Sparta,[5] and like all dead Spartan kings was regarded as a hero,[6] in whose honour games, τὰ Λεωνίδεια, were held.[7] Because he has his own shrine, he is cited as witness to the prowess of those who fell with him, rather as, when Pindar's Epharmostus wins in the games at Thebes, the tomb of Iolaus is cited as a σύνδικος, or witness, to his victory.[8] The part played by Leonidas in Simonides' lines becomes more intelligible when we think of him as a neighbour of the shrine where the poem is sung.

To the years immediately after the Persian War must belong a curious chapter of literary history, which involves both Simonides and Themistocles. There was a Rhodian poet, Timocreon of Ialysus, a poor enough fellow, part blackguard and part buffoon, famed for his prowess as an athlete and as a trencher-man. When the Persians occupied Rhodes, he sold his services to them and

[1] I.G. v. i. 497 Καρνείου βοικέτα.　　　　　　　　　　[2] 3. 13. 4.
[3] Schol. Pind. Nem. 5. 81.
[4] So Thiersch, Edmonds, Lavagnini.
[5] Paus. 3. 14. 1. The remains were brought to Sparta forty years after the battle.
[6] Xen. Resp. Lac. 15. 9.
[7] I.G. v. 1. 18 A 8; 19. 15; 658. 12.
[8] Ol. 9. 98–9.

σύνδικος δ' αὐτῷ 'Ιολάου
τύμβος ἐνναλία τ' 'Ελευσὶς ἀγλαΐαισιν.

was taken to Susa, where he amused the Great King by his boasts and his gluttony.[1] But he lived to regret his treachery and wrote a σκόλιον in which he deplored the evil effects of money. This won a great vogue and was remembered even in the seventh century A.D., when Isidore of Pelusium says that it was an ancient custom to sing to the lyre the words ἀπόλοιο, ὦ Πλοῦτε, καὶ μήτε ἐν γῆ φανείης μήτ' ἐν θαλάσσῃ.[2] Timocreon's song runs:

ὤφελέν σ', ὦ τυφλὲ Πλοῦτε,
μήτε γῆ μήτ' ἐν θαλάσσῃ
μήτ' ἐν ἠπείρῳ φανῆμεν,
ἀλλὰ Τάρταρόν τε ναίειν
κἀχέροντα· διὰ σὲ γὰρ πάντ'
ἔστ' ἐν ἀνθρώποις κακά.[3]

Would that, o blind Wealth, you had never appeared on land or sea or the continent, but dwelt in Tartarus and Acheron; for because of you all evils exist among men.

Timocreon was not the first to sing of the evils of Wealth, and before him Hipponax had called Wealth blind.[4] His song looks like a variation on an old theme, but a particularly personal turn has been given to it by the words ἐν ἠπείρῳ. These have often been thought otiose or an anti-climax and have been altered to ἐν οὐρανῷ or the like; but they are not only in all the manuscripts which quote the poem but are embedded in Aristophanes' account of Pericles' Megarian decrees:

ἐτίθει νόμους ὥσπερ σκόλια γεγραμμένους,
ὡς χρὴ Μεγαρέας μήτε γῆ μήτ' ἐν ἀγορᾷ
μήτ' ἐν θαλάττῃ μήτ' ἐν ἠπείρῳ μένειν.[5]

Enacting laws which ran like drinking-songs,
That the Megarians presently depart
From earth and sea, the mainland and the mart.[6]

The words ἐν ἠπείρῳ are unquestionably what Timocreon wrote, and they must have a point. They mean 'on the continent' and refer to the Persian realm, which was the cause of his troubles.[7] Because he had taken money from the Persians, he was, after their defeat, kept out of his home because of his collaboration with the enemy, and had good reason to lament the evil influence of Wealth.

---

[1] Athen. 10. 415 e.   [2] Ep. 2. 146.   [3] Fr. 5 D.
[4] Fr. 29 D.   [5] Ach. 532-4.   [6] Trans. B. B. Rogers.
[7] H. T. Wade-Gery, J.H.S. liii (1933), p. 85.

After Salamis Timocreon hoped to get home through the influence of Themistocles, but failed. The result is a curious little hymn of hate:

ἀλλ' εἰ τύ γα Παυσανίαν ἢ καὶ τύ γα Ξάνθιππον αἰνεῖς
ἢ τύ γα Λευτυχίδαν, ἐγὼ δ' Ἀριστείδαν ἐπαινέω
ἄνδρ' ἱερᾶν ἀπ' Ἀθανᾶν λῷστος ὃς ἦλθεν, ἐπεὶ
Θεμιστοκλῆν ἤχθαρε Λατώ,

ψεύσταν, ἄδικον, προδόταν, ὃς Τιμοκρέοντα ξεῖνον ἐόντα
ἀργυρίοισι κοβαλικοῖσι πεισθεὶς οὐ κατᾶγεν
ἐς πατρίδ' Ἰάλυσον, λαβὼν δὲ τρί' ἀργυρίου
τάλαντ' ἔβα πλέων εἰς ὄλεθρον,

τοὺς μὲν κατάγων ἀδίκως, τοὺς δ' ἐκδιώκων, τοὺς δὲ καίνων·
ἀργυρίου δ' ὑπόπλεως Ἰσθμοῖ γελοίως πανδόκευε,
ψυχρὰ κρέ' ἐμπαρέχων· οἱ δ' ἤσθιον εὐχόμενοι
μὴ ὥραν Θεμιστοκλέος γενέσθαι.[1]

But if you, sir, praise Pausanias, and you, sir, Xanthippus, and you, sir, Leotychidas, I praise Aristides, who was the best man to come from holy Athens, when Lato formed a hatred for Themistocles, liar, unjust, traitor, who in obedience to ill-gotten bribes did not bring his guest-friend Timocreon to his land of Ialysus, but took three talents of silver and went sailing to the devil, bringing some unjustly home, persecuting others, killing others, and, gorged with silver, kept ridiculous hospitality at the Isthmus, providing cold meats. They ate, praying that no attention be paid to Themistocles.

The poem may well be complete, but it raises problems both technical and historical.

First, what sort of poem is it? In most editions it is presented in the triadic form of strophe, antistrophe, and epode, which implies that it was sung by a choir. But this is surely out of the question. It must be some kind of *σκόλιον* sung by the poet himself among

[1] Fr. 1 D. A reasonable degree of correspondence between the three strophes can be secured without too great a violation of the text on the scheme

– – ⏑ ⏑ – ⏑ ⏑ – – – ⏑ – – – ⏑ – –
– ⏑ ⏑ – ⏑ ⏑ – ⏓ – ⏑ – – – ⏑ – –
– ⏑ ⏑ – ⏑ ⏑ – ⏓ – ⏑ ⏑ – ⏑ ⏑ –
⏓ – ⏑ – – – ⏑ – –.

In 3 the MSS. vary between *ὃς ἦλθε λεκτὸς* and *ἐλθεῖν ἕνα λῷστον*, which can be satisfactorily combined in *λῷστος ὃς ἦλθεν*, as suggested by Maas. In 7 for the scansion *Ἰάλυσον* cf. Dionysius of Rhodes, *Anth. Pal.* 7. 716 *πόλιν Ἰαλύσοιο*. In 11 correspondence is secured by altering *κηὔχοντο* to *εὐχόμενοι*. Since the final syllable of *κρέα*, which, to satisfy the metre, should be long, is elsewhere short, except perhaps at Antiphan. fr. 20. 1 K, I suggest *ἐμπαρέχων*. In general see P. Maas, *Hermes*, lxix (1934), p. 460.

his cronies. The repeated τύ γα suggests that the occasion is informal and convivial, and ἐγώ of 2 indicates that Timocreon speaks for himself. Indeed, as he goes round the company, he recalls how Bdelycleon begins his lesson to Philocleon in the art of singing songs after dinner with the words

$$\text{οὐδεὶς πώποτ' ἀνὴρ ἔγεντ' Ἀθήναις.}^{1}$$

In the same way Timocreon announces that his own hero is Aristides, but uses this really as a cover to attack Themistocles for treachery, a form of accusation which comes suitably in σκόλια, which are often concerned with loves and hates. It is true that in the manuscripts there is not an exact metrical correspondence between the third strophe and the first two, but there is sufficient to suggest that it was not different, and it can be brought into line by quite easy changes. Once this is done the poem is recognizable as a σκόλιον.

The poem also raises historical questions. When was it written, and to what does it refer? First, there is the old view of Kirchhoff,[2] restated with some variations by Beloch,[3] that the poem was written late in the seventies, when, it is alleged, Themistocles went to Rhodes with a Greek fleet and failed to keep his promise to restore Timocreon to Ialysus. The objection to this is that there is no evidence for Themistocles being with a fleet in the Aegean at any time in the seventies or after his assault on Andros and Paros in 480. Nor does it help to quote Plutarch's statement that 'he was unpopular with the allies when he sailed round the islands and got money from them.'[4] The words precede an account of the siege of Andros and are no more than a summary of Herodotus' narrative.[5] Indeed it is unlikely that Themistocles was ever in charge of a fleet in the seventies; for he soon lost the popularity which he had won in the war, and was displaced in Athenian favour by Aristides and Cimon.

Moved by these difficulties, Wilamowitz placed the poem in the autumn of 480,[6] when Themistocles was still in command of the Greek fleet and certainly went as far as Paros. He assumes that Themistocles had encouraged Timocreon to think that the fleet would sail to Rhodes, and Timocreon was furious when it came back from Paros to the Isthmus. The virtue of this theory is the

---

[1] Aristoph. *Vesp.* 1226.
[2] *Hermes*, xi, p. 44.
[3] *Gr. Gesch.* ii. 2, p. 144.
[4] *Them.* 21. 1.
[5] 8. 109 ff.
[6] *A.u.A.* i, p. 138.

point which it gives to the mysterious words ἐπεὶ Θεμιστοκλῆν
ἤχθαρε Λατώ, which Wilamowitz refers to Corinth, where there
was a temple of Lato in which the Corinthian admiral Diodorus
dedicated booty from Salamis, with an inscription which survives in the form:

ταῦτ' ἀπὸ δυσμενέων Μήδων ναῦται Διοδώρου
ὅπλ' ἀνέθεν Λατοῖ μνάματα ναυμαχίας.[1]

The collapse of Themistocles, over which Timocreon is so jubilant,
is then his failure to win the prize for valour at the Isthmus. This,
says Timocreon, is due to the Corinthian Lato's hatred for him.
This theory takes account of most of the relevant facts, but it can
be emended and supplemented in such a way as to give a more
coherent picture of what happened.

First, Timocreon makes play with the name of Aristides and
indicates that he had something to do with the fall of Themistocles.
When Timocreon praises him so fulsomely, we may assume that he
is in some way grateful to him. Now this can have no connexion
with the failure of Themistocles to win the prize at the Isthmus;
for in 480 Aristides was his loyal colleague. Secondly, Wilamowitz,
by making the hatred of Lato contemporary with the events at
the Isthmus described in the third strophe, neglects a nice point
of language. On his explanation we should expect not the aorist
ἤχθαρε but the imperfect ἤχθαιρε. If Lato's hatred of Themistocles
is contemporaneous with his failure, then it should be in the same
tense. There must be some special point in the aorist ἤχθαρε, and
it can only mean 'formed a hatred for' and refer to something in
the relations of Aristides and Themistocles. It looks as if this was
the immediate occasion of the poem, and the events of the third
strophe came a little earlier. In other words, we have to deal with
an occasion after Themistocles' voyages in the Aegean and his
failure at the Isthmus.

We may try to be more precise on the occasion which inspired
the poem. The important clues are Aristides and Lato. First,
Aristides. In the years after 479 Themistocles rapidly lost prestige
and popularity in comparison with him. The crisis came when
by a stroke of luck Aristides was at Byzantium, and the allies,
highly incensed by the tyrannical manners of Pausanias, asked
Athens to succeed Sparta as their leader. The result was the

[1] 'Simon.' No. 108 D.

foundation of the Delian League in 478–477, and in this Aristides played the chief part. From all this Themistocles was excluded, and his exclusion could not but be noted as a sign of his decline from power. To Timocreon his exclusion was an omen of his downfall and an occasion for malicious rejoicing. We may, then, conclude that the prominence which Timocreon gives to Aristides means that Aristides has replaced Themistocles in power and popularity, and the date of this may be placed at the foundation of the Delian League in 478–477.

This is confirmed by the mention of Lato. Delos, far more than Corinth, was inextricably associated with her. There she was said to have given birth to Apollo, and there she was honoured with him. The mention of Lato would suggest Delos to anyone in Timocreon's company. So, when he ranks her first in the downfall of Themistocles, we may infer that the poem was inspired by events in Delos. This is a natural conclusion to draw from the words ἱερᾶν ἀπ' Ἀθανᾶν λῷστος ὃς ἦλθε, which are applied to Aristides. They might of course mean that he is a fine specimen of Athenian manhood, but it is easier to take them literally and to assume that Aristides has come from Athens and is called λῷστος because of his character and reputation. That he was in Delos in 478–477 is almost incontrovertible in view of his part in founding the League, and his presence there bore witness to his new importance. Leotychidas and Xanthippus are perhaps mentioned with him because they had recently been busy in the Aegaean liberating Samos and collecting allies from Ionia and Aeolis,[1] while Pausanias was still remembered from his recent behaviour at Byzantium. These men would be known personally or by name to Timocreon's circle and were among the most prominent figures of their time. The mention of them suggests that they too, no less than Aristides, have eclipsed Themistocles, and Timocreon, rejoicing in what has happened, regards them as legitimate objects of praise.

Timocreon's σκόλιον is certainly a strange and uncomfortable poem. Of course hymns of hatred are liable to show the marks of age, and even the best abuse wears thin with the years, but the difficulties of appreciating Timocreon's art are increased by his combination of attempts at a grand manner with something else much less dignified. For instance, the phrase εἰς ὄλεθρόν has

[1] Hdt. 9. 90 ff.

a tragic smack and recalls Oedipus' outburst to Teiresias.[1] The words ἱερᾶν ἀπ' Ἀθανᾶν have a lyrical ring like that of Pindar's praise of Acragas or Sicyon or Delphi.[2] Timocreon was after all a lyrical poet, who could not quite exclude the lyrical manner from his poem, but he matched it with phrases which come from a lower level of speech. The adjective κοβαλικός, used of the bribes taken by Themistocles, has few parallels outside comedy, where both κόβαλος and κοβαλίκευμα are used by Aristophanes to vilify Cleon and his kind.[3] Again, both ἀργυρίου ὑπόπλεως and ψυχρὰ κρέα are on the edge of slang, for ὑπόπλεως implies that Themistocles has glutted himself with money, while ψυχρά suggests that his entertainments were a 'frost'.[4] In πανδόκευε the notion is that of an inn-keeper who fleeces his guests.[5] Indeed all this part of the poem recalls Archilochus or Hipponax rather than any lyric poet. The odd mixture in Timocreon's style suggests that the σκόλιον was not usually turned to such purposes and that he had no clear precedents to guide him.

The decline of Themistocles' influence was soon to be followed by his ostracism, exile, and condemnation in absence to death. This too delighted Timocreon. Plutarch quotes two fragments of what looks like a single poem:

> Μοῦσα, τοῦδε τοῦ μέλεος
> κλέος ἀν' Ἕλληνας τίθει,
> ὡς ἐοικὸς καὶ δίκαιον.

and

> οὐκ ἄρα Τιμοκρέων μοῦνος
> Μήδοισιν ὁρκιατομεῖ·
> ἔντι κἄλλοι δὴ πονηροί·
> οὐκ ἐγὼ μόνα κόλουρις·
> ἔντι κἄλλαι ἀλώπεκες.[6]

Muse, spread the fame of this song among the Hellenes, as is fit and right. . . . Not only Timocreon, it seems, swears oaths with the Medes. There are other blackguards too. I am not the only curtail. There are other vixens too.

The metre, which resembles that of the lines on Wealth, indicates that this also is a σκόλιον. It must have been written after

---

[1] Soph. O.T. 430.
[2] Ol. 2. 9; Nem. 9. 53; Pyth. 11. 9.
[3] Equ. 332, 450; Ran. 1015.
[4] Aristoph. Thesm. 170, 848.
[5] Plat. Laws 11. 918 d; Theophr. Char. 6. 5.
[6] Frs. 2–3 D; Plut. Them. 21.

Themistocles had escaped to Persia and entered the service of King Artaxerxes. Timocreon feels that he is now all square with his old enemy; for Themistocles, who in the past harmed him for taking money from the Persians, has now been caught at the same thing himself. In comparing himself with a fox, Timocreon might claim the example of Archilochus,[1] but the comparison was hardly to his credit, when popular songs could say:

οὐκ ἔστιν ἀλωπεκίζειν,
οὐδ' ἀμφοτέροισι γίγνεσθαι φίλον.[2]

Timocreon is quite shameless about himself and is delighted that the theme of double-dealing foxes who lose their tails can now be applied to his old enemy as well as to himself.

So far Timocreon had, in his own way, not done badly. Themistocles was discredited, and Timocreon could take his verbal revenge on him. But at some point Simonides seems to have been involved in the controversy. That he was a friend and supporter of Themistocles would be enough to earn him Timocreon's hostility, and later generations remembered them as enemies.[3] One small piece of evidence suggests that Simonides struck a shrewd and sharp blow at Timocreon. The *Palatine Anthology* preserves under the name of Simonides a magnificent couplet:

πολλὰ πιὼν καὶ πολλὰ φαγὼν καὶ πολλὰ κάκ' εἰπὼν
ἀνθρώπους κεῖμαι Τιμοκρέων 'Ρόδιος.[4]

Athenaeus knew the lines and said that they were written on Timocreon's grave.[5] That, alas, is pure fancy, since Greek propriety would not have tolerated such plain speech about the dead. Athenaeus' words have less truth perhaps than the delightful superscription in the *Anthology*, which says: 'Simonides on Timocreon, whose inclinations and habits were those of my uncle.' The lines are in fact not an epitaph but an elegiac σκόλιον, and for this reason their ascription to Simonides is far more likely

---

[1] Plat. *Rep.* 2. 365 c; Dio Chrys. *Or.* 55. 10.
[2] Aristoph. *Vesp.* 1240–1.
[3] For this cf. Diog. Laert. 2. 46; 'Suid.' s.v. Τιμοκρέων ... διεφέρετο δὲ πρὸς Σιμωνίδην τὸν τῶν μελῶν ποιητὴν καὶ Θεμιστοκλέα τὸν Ἀθηναῖον, εἰς ὃν ἐξύφανε ψόγον δι' ἐμμελοῦς τινος ποιήματος. ἔγραψε δὲ κωμῳδίαν εἴς τε τὸν Θεμιστοκλέα καὶ εἰς Σιμωνίδην τὸν μελοποιὸν καὶ ἄλλα. It is not clear what is meant by κωμῳδίαν.
[4] No. 99 D. (*Anth. Pal.* 7. 348).   [5] Athen. 10. 415 f.

to be right than if they had been written on a stone.[1] The couplet
is derisive and intended to wound, and much of its point lies in
κεῖται. This word, appropriate to a man lying dead, could also be
used of someone struck by misfortune, who is, so to speak,
'down'. So Sophocles uses it, when in the *Philoctetes* the Chorus
sing of the hopeless state of the heroic castaway:

πάντων ἄμμορος ἐν βίῳ
κεῖται μοῦνος ἀπ' ἄλλων.[2]

Here κεῖται cannot mean 'lies'; for Philoctetes is known to be
out of his cave looking for food. Nor can it mean 'is dead'. It is
closely associated with ἐν βίῳ and means that, though he is in
fact alive, he is so stricken that he might as well be dead. This is
how Simonides uses the word in his pseudo-epitaph on Timocreon. Under the guise of a sepulchral inscription he raises a cry
of triumph that Timocreon is 'stricken' or 'down', and in these
masterly lines the mocker has his own weapon turned against him.

It is just possible that we have Timocreon's reply to this. The
Palatine Anthology ascribes two lines to him:

Κηία με προσῆλθε φλυαρία οὐκέτ' ἐόντα,
οὐκέτ' ἐόντα με προσῆλθε Κηία φλυαρία.[3]

The Cean nonsense came to me who am no longer; to me, who am
no longer, the Cean nonsense came.

The use of the same words to form first a dactylic hexameter and
then a trochaic tetrameter catalectic appears in another couplet,
attributed to Simonides:

Μοῦσά μοι Ἀλκμήνης καλλισφύρου υἱὸν ἄειδε·
υἱὸν Ἀλκμήνης ἄειδε Μοῦσά μοι καλλισφύρου.[4]

Muse, of fair-ankled Alcmene's son sing to me; sing to me, Muse, of
fair-ankled Alcmene's son.

If these ascriptions are genuine, two possible conclusions follow.
First, the couplet of Timocreon looks like an attempt to reply to
Simonides' crushing 'epitaph' on him. Its point would be that,
since he is 'dead', what Simonides says cannot trouble him.
Secondly, for his answer Timocreon uses a form used by Simonides,

[1] Bowra, *E.G.E.* pp. 182 ff.   [2] *Phil.* 182–3.
[3] *Anth. Pal.* 13. 31. Bergk's correction of οὐκ ἐθέλοντα in both lines to οὐκέτ'
ἐόντα is necessary to the metre and much improves the sense.
[4] Ibid. 30.

evidently because he thinks it suitable for controversy. Why
Simonides used this form in the first place, it is hard to say,
though it is tempting to think that his first line is quoted from
Timocreon[1] and that Simonides transposes it into a different
metre to show up something that he feels to be heavy or coarse in
its rhythm. But it is not certain, and perhaps not even likely, that
either of these couplets is authentic. What little we know of
Timocreon suggests that he would have answered Simonides'
gibe in harsher and ruder words. Moreover, the Hellenistic age
took pleasure in such metrical ingenuities, but there is no good
reason to think that Simonides did, since one or two attributed to
him are of doubtful authenticity.[2] The hostility between the two
poets was sufficiently known for ingenious versifiers to make their
own contributions to it. It is not absolutely impossible that either or
both of the couplets are genuine, but we must at least question it.

We know little else of Simonides' life in Athens. Three pieces
ascribed to Theognis address Simonides, and it is tempting to
think that this is the poet. The first, 467–96, contains advice on
how to behave under the influence of drink; the second, 667–82,
is a variation on the image of the ship of state; the third, 1345–
50, is on an erotic theme. But we cannot be certain that this
Simonides is the poet, and even if he were, the pieces would tell
us nothing important about him.[3] What is more important is
that in 476, when he was eighty years old, Simonides took a big
decision and went to Sicily, where he stayed until his death in
468/7. He may have been tempted by generous offers from Hieron,
but it is worth noting that 476 marked the last important public
appearance of Themistocles. In the spring of this year he appeared
as χοραγός for the *Phoenissae* of Phrynichus,[4] and it looks as if

---

[1] Edmonds *L.G.* ii, p. 345.   [2] Nos. 152, 159 D.

[3] In favour of this Simonides being the poet we might argue (*a*) that the language
of 481–3 with its ἀπάλαμνα and αἰσχρά recalls his poem to Scopas, (*b*) that the reference to the Melian Sea in 672 may be connected with the events of 480–479. On the
other hand, since 472 is quoted, with the variant of χρῆμ᾽ for πρᾶγμ᾽, by Aristot.
Met. 1015 a 28 and ascribed to Euenus of Paros, it looks as if he was the author of
all three poems. The famous Euenus, who was a member of the Socratic circle
(Plat. *Apol.* 20 b; *Phaed.* 60 d; *Phaedr.* 267 a), cannot have known Simonides, and
is unlikely, as J. Carrière suggests, *Théognis*, p. 110, to have addressed poems to
him after his death. There was indeed another Euenus, whose *floruit* is given in the
Armenian version of Eusebius as 460. But in mentioning Euenus Aristotle may
have referred to the better known of the two poets who bore the name. Cf. Harpocr.
s.v. Εὔηνος. γνωρίζεσθαι δέ φησιν ('Ερατοσθένης) τὸν νεώτερον μόνον. See Bowra,
C.R. xlviii (1934), pp. 2–4.   [4] Plut. *Them.* 5. 4.

his patronage of a patriotic play was dictated by a desire to re-
habilitate his waning prestige by reminding the Athenian public
of events in which he had taken a leading part. Soon after 476
his collapse began, and it is not unreasonable to assume that
among Simonides' reasons for leaving Athens was the change in
the circumstances of his life there.

In Syracuse Simonides established a considerable position.
The stories of his conversations with Hieron are futile enough,
but at least they indicate that he treated his patron with an easy
equality.[1] His prestige and experience of public affairs enabled
him to reconcile Theron and Hieron when they were on the
brink of war.[2] But of his poetical activities in this last period few
traces remain. His Epinician for Xenocrates of Acragas may have
been written soon after his arrival; for it celebrated a victory
mentioned by Pindar in *Olympian* II in 476.[3] Simonides certainly
wrote something for Hieron; for Himerius says:

Simonides of Ceos, when sending Hieron from Sicily to another
land, touched the lyre and mingled tears with the notes as he played.[4]

This looks like a προπεμπτικόν, but nothing else is known of it.
In Sicily Simonides was accompanied or joined by his nephew
Bacchylides, and in the year that he went there Pindar also
came and wrote his first three *Olympians* for Hieron and Theron.
The Alexandrian scholars liked to find in Pindar's poetry traces
of references to Simonides, and though there is no evidence for
anything like a quarrel, the tradition is good and the evidence
worth attention. That the two poets were on friendly enough
terms follows from Pindar's *Paean* IV, where he makes the island
of Ceos speak of its poets:

γινώσκομαι δὲ καὶ
Μοῖσαν παρέχων ἅλις.[5]

I am known from providing the Muse also in abundance.

Such differences as we can detect are on points of art and not
without interest for the views of poetry that existed in their time.

Writing *Isthmian* II for Xenocrates of Acragas, who also
patronized Simonides, Pindar says:

---

[1] *Pap. Hib.* 17; Aristot. *Rhet.* 1391a8; Cic. *N.D.* 1. 22. 60.
[2] Schol. Pind. *Ol.* 2. 29.
[3] *Ol.* 2. 50; Schol. Pind. *Isthm.* 2 Inscr. a.
[4] *Or.* 31. 2 Colonna.   [5] Fr. 38. 20–21 Bo.

ἁ Μοῖσα γὰρ οὐ φιλοκερδής πω τότ᾽ ἦν οὐδ᾽ ἐργάτις,
οὐδ᾽ ἐπέρναντο γλυκεῖαι μελιφθόγγου ποτὶ Τερψιχόρας
ἀργυρωθεῖσαι πρόσωπα μαλθακόφωνοι ἀοιδαί.[1]

For the Muse was not yet a lover of gain, nor a hireling, nor did soft-voiced songs pass for sale, with silvered faces, from honey-voiced Terpsichore.

The scholiast refers this to Simonides, who was said to be the first poet to take money for his work. The tradition was as old as Aristophanes,[2] and known to Callimachus[3] and the pseudo-Platonic *Hipparchus*.[4] How justified it was we cannot say, and it may have been partly due to Simonides' well-known fondness for money.[5] That poets made money before him is clear from Herodotus' account of Arion, who went to Sicily and amassed a large fortune.[6] Nor was Pindar himself averse from being paid for his work. Indeed the whole beginning of *Isthmian* II reads like an apology for asking for pay when in the old days he would have given his services for nothing, and elsewhere he admits that his Muse lends herself for hire.[7] Even if the words of *Isthmian* II are a reference to Simonides which everyone would recognize, and they are perhaps a little too general for that, they do not so much imply hostility or criticism as recognize a state of affairs for which Simonides may indeed have been partly responsible but could not seriously be blamed.

More mysterious, and more troubling, is the end of *Olympian* II, written in 476 for Theron of Acragas, where Pindar says:

πολλά μοι ὑπ᾽ ἀγκῶνος ὠκέα βέλη
ἔνδον ἐντὶ φαρέτρας
φωνάεντα συνέτοισιν· ἐς δὲ τὸ πᾶν ἑρμανέων
χατίζει. σοφὸς ὁ πολλὰ εἰδὼς φυᾷ·
μαθόντες δὲ λάβροι
παγγλωσσίᾳ κόρακες ὣς ἄκραντα γαρύετον
Διὸς πρὸς ὄρνιχα θεῖον.[8]

Many are the swift arrows in the quiver under my elbow, that speak to the wise, but for the crowd they need interpreters. Wise is he who

---

[1] *Isthm.* 2. 6–8.   [2] *Pax* 698 ff.
[3] Fr. 222 P.   [4] 228 c.
[5] Chamael. ap. Athen. 14. 656 d; *Ox. Pap.* 1800, fr. 1. 40; Stob. 10. 62; *Pap. Hib.* 17; Plut. *Sen.* 5; Aristot. *Rhet.* 1391 a 8.
[6] Hdt. 1. 24. 1.   [7] *Pyth.* 11. 41 ff.; cf. Schol. *Nem.* 5. 1.
[8] *Ol.* 2. 83–89.

knows much by nature; but the two, mere learners, wag noisy tongues like ravens and talk in vain against God's holy bird.

The scholiast says that the ravens are Simonides and Bacchylides, and the holy bird, the eagle, is Pindar. In favour of this there are two arguments. First, the dual γαρύετον must refer to two people,[1] and second, Pindar is clearly saying something which Theron will understand, though it is cryptically expressed. In 476 all three poets were probably in Sicily[2] and may well have been at Acragas to celebrate Theron's victory in the chariot-race at Olympia. That Pindar despised Bacchylides is clear from *Pythian* II,[3] and he may have allowed this to influence him into associating Simonides with him. The point at issue is the true nature of poetry. Pindar distinguishes between himself with his inborn σοφία, and the others who are mere learners. For him poetry was a gift of the gods and could not be made by mere intellectual effort. There is nothing in the fragments of the legends of Simonides to suggest that he held an opposite view, and if Pindar thought poorly of his art, it was no doubt because contemporary poets often fail to appreciate one another, since each is occupied with his own special problems. In the last resort, perhaps, Pindar felt that Simonides was not truly inspired but relied too much on the traditional devices of his craft. This is at least a legitimate deduction from a passage in *Olympian* IX, which Pindar wrote in 466, after the death of Simonides:

> αἴνει δὲ παλαιὸν μὲν οἶνον, ἄνθεα δ' ὕμνων
> νεωτέρων.[4]

Praise an old wine, but the flower of songs that are new.

He must surely have intended a comment on some words of Simonides which use the same image

> ἐξελέγχει
> ὁ νέος οἶνος οὔπω τὸ πέρυσι δῶρον ἀμπέλου. μῦθος
> κενεόφρων κούρων ὅδε.[5]

---

[1] The MSS. agree on the form of γαρύετον and the scholia refer it to Simonides and Bacchylides. It can only be the dual of the present indicative. The simplest correction would be Bergk's γαρύετων, which would be the plural of the imperative, but such a form is not found in Pindar, despite *Od.* I. 273 ἔστων and Aesch. *Eum.* 32 ἴτων. It seems a counsel of despair to follow Farnell, *The Works of Pindar*, ii, p. 22, in keeping the dual and attributing it to 'two local critics'.

[2] Pindar for *Olympians* I–III, and Bacchylides for Ode IV.

[3] See Bowra, *Problems*, pp. 62–92.   [4] 48–49.   [5] Fr. 49 D.

Not yet does the new wine convict last year's gift of the vine. This is an empty-witted tale of boys.

In poetry Simonides stood for more old-fashioned methods than Pindar, and in this Pindar seems to have seen evidence for a lack of inborn genius.

In Sicily Simonides died in 468 and was buried in Acragas.[1] He was nearly ninety and had had a full life. Though posterity remembered him no less as a wise man than as a poet and liked little anecdotes about him, the surviving fragments of his work show that he was a poet of rare quality. A generation older than Pindar, he seems to be in many ways a younger man. In his personal independence, his Hellenic outlook, his translucent style, he was a true son of the Ionian world. But in Athens he learned something more. He moved in the same world as Aeschylus, and was sincere and serious in a time of enormous changes, which he observed and understood in the amplitude of their possibilities and related to his own special outlook and convictions.

The enlightenment of Simonides may be seen in his approach to poetry. There is no evidence that he denied the importance of inspiration, and indeed he implied something like a Platonic notion of it, when he said that wine and music have the same origin.[2] But he was not prepared to make a mystery of his art, and is quite candid about its processes. He knew that once the Muse visited him, there was no holding her:

> ἁ Μοῦσα γὰρ οὐκ ἀπόρως γεύει τὸ πάρον μόνον, ἀλλ' ἐπέρχεται
> πάντα θεριζομένα.[3]

For the Muse does not helplessly taste only what lies before her, but goes forth harvesting everywhere.

The Muse carried him on, and he could not or would not resist her. In this Pindar, at least in his earlier days, would have agreed with him.[4] But Simonides none the less believed that the poet's

---

[1] Callimach. fr. 64. 4 P.; 'Suid.' s.v. Σιμωνίδης. The tomb was destroyed by an Acragantine general called Phoenix in a war with Syracuse, of which the date is not certain. Diod., 19. 3. 70 ff. and 20. 56. 62, puts it in the time of Agathocles (361–289 B.C.), and probably draws on Duris and Timaeus.

[2] Athen. 2. 40 a.

[3] Fr. 46 Bergk. I see no reason to doubt the ascription to Simonides. The notion of the Muse on the move is different from the Homeric notion of the Muses as static repositories of wisdom, Il. 2. 485, ὑμεῖς γὰρ θεαί ἐστε πάρεστέ τε ἴστε τε πάντα.

[4] Pyth. 10. 53–54 ἐγκωμίων γὰρ ἄωτος ὕμνων
ἐπ' ἄλλοτ' ἄλλον ὥτε μέλισσα θύνει λόγον.

task has its own purpose and its own end. He expressed this by comparing poetry with the bee:

ὁμιλεῖ δ' ἄνθεσιν
ξανθὸν μέλι μηδομένα.[1]

She consorts with flowers, contriving her yellow honey.

It is clear from the contexts in which the words occur[2] that Simonides is not troubled by the apparent vagaries of the creative spirit but regards the poet as gathering sweetness where he can find it. On the means by which this end was to be reached he has left at least one illuminating statement. He said: 'Painting is silent poetry; poetry is painting that speaks.'[3] This close association of the two arts in an age which had no single word for art, but regarded the several arts and most handicrafts as different forms of σοφία, 'wisdom', or τέχνη, 'handicraft', is itself evidence for an original approach to the subject. It may be amplified by another saying attributed to Simonides that 'the word is the image of things'.[4] By image, εἰκών, he means an almost visible representation, such as is to be seen in painting and sculpture; for that is what εἰκών meant to Aeschylus[5] and would mean to Simonides. When we examine his poetry, we see that he often appeals to the mind's eye, often creates an effect which is certainly visual, if not actually visible.

To this particular gift and its worth the author of *On the Sublime* bears eloquent witness. In a discussion of the value of images in poetry he first praises the closing scene of Sophocles' *Oedipus at Colonus* with its portents in the sky, and then goes on to say:

Magnificent too is the passage where the Greeks are on the point of sailing away and Achilles appears above his tomb to those who are putting out to sea—a scene which I doubt whether anyone has depicted more vividly than Simonides.[6]

Nothing is known of the poem but this, but the critic's words ὄψιν ἐναργέστερον εἰδωλοποίησε leave no doubt that he had its

---

[1] Fr. 43 D.
[2] Plut. *Prof. in Virt.* 8; Cramer, *An. Ox.* iii. 173. 12.
[3] Plut. *Glor. Ath.* 3 τὴν μὲν ζωγραφίαν ποίησιν σιωπῶσαν προσαγορεύει, τὴν δὲ ποίησιν ζωγραφίαν λαλοῦσαν. M. Treu, *Von Homer zur Lyrik*, p. 303, compares Parmenides, fr. 4 D–K.
[4] Mich. Psell. π. 'Ενεργ. Δαιμ. 821, Migne, ὁ λόγος τῶν πραγμάτων εἰκών ἐστι.
[5] *Sept.* 558–9.　　　　　　　　　[6] *de Sub.* 15. 7.

pictorial effect in mind. In it Simonides must have given a fine example of the doctrine 'ut pictura poesis'. Some of the fragments show a similar spirit at work. He liked, for instance, to mention colours, such as the scarlet reins of a charioteer:

$$\mu\grave{\eta} \ \beta\acute{a}\lambda\eta \ \phi o\acute{\iota}\nu\iota\kappa\alpha\varsigma \ \acute{\epsilon}\kappa \ \chi\epsilon\iota\rho\hat{\omega}\nu \ \acute{\iota}\mu\acute{a}\nu\tau\alpha\varsigma^{1}$$

'lest he throw the scarlet reins from his hands'; or the sail of Theseus' ship, which he made scarlet, though tradition made it white:

$$\phi o\iota\nu\iota\kappa\acute{\epsilon}o\nu \ \acute{\iota}\sigma\tau\acute{\iota}o\nu \ \acute{\upsilon}\gamma\rho\hat{\omega}$$
$$\pi\epsilon\phi\upsilon\rho\mu\acute{\epsilon}\nu o\nu \ \pi\rho\iota\nu\grave{o}\varsigma \ \acute{a}\nu\theta\epsilon\iota$$
$$\acute{\epsilon}\rho\iota\theta\alpha\lambda o\hat{\upsilon}\varsigma.^{2}$$

The scarlet sail dyed with the wet flower of the sturdy holm-oak.

For him nightingales are $\chi\lambda\omega\rho\alpha\acute{\upsilon}\chi\epsilon\nu\epsilon\varsigma$,[3] the swallow $\kappa\upsilon\alpha\nu\epsilon\acute{a}$,[4] the halycon $\pi o\iota\kappa\acute{\iota}\lambda\alpha$.[5] His description of a young girl singing,

$$\pi o\rho\phi\upsilon\rho\acute{\epsilon}o\upsilon$$
$$\acute{a}\pi\grave{o} \ \sigma\tau\acute{o}\mu\alpha\tau o\varsigma \ \acute{\iota}\epsilon\hat{\iota}\sigma\alpha \ \phi\omega\nu\grave{a}\nu \ \pi\alpha\rho\theta\acute{\epsilon}\nu o\varsigma,$$

'a maiden sending forth her voice from red lips', was admired by Sophocles, who claimed that $\pi o\rho\phi\upsilon\rho\acute{\epsilon}o\upsilon$ was an example of the rightness of a word in such a context.[6]

Simonides' pictorial powers go farther than this. He sometimes composes a scene like a picture. The fate of Danaë in her chest or the appearance of Achilles over his tomb might well be subjects for painters. So on a smaller scale he writes of the miraculous singing of Orpheus:

$$\tau o\hat{\upsilon} \ \kappa\alpha\grave{\iota} \ \acute{a}\pi\epsilon\iota\rho\acute{\epsilon}\sigma\iota o\iota$$
$$\acute{o}\rho\nu\iota\theta\epsilon\varsigma \ \acute{\upsilon}\pi\grave{\epsilon}\rho \ \kappa\epsilon\phi\alpha\lambda\hat{a}\varsigma \ \pi\omega\tau\hat{\omega}\nu\tau', \ \acute{a}\nu\grave{a} \ \delta' \ \acute{\iota}\chi\theta\acute{\upsilon}\epsilon\varsigma \ \acute{o}\rho\theta o\grave{\iota}$$
$$\kappa\upsilon\alpha\nu\acute{\epsilon}\alpha\varsigma \ \acute{a}\lambda\grave{o}\varsigma \ \acute{\epsilon}\xi\acute{a}\lambda\lambda o\nu\tau o \ \kappa\alpha\lambda\hat{a}\varsigma \ \acute{\upsilon}\pi' \ \acute{a}o\iota\delta\hat{a}\varsigma.^{7}$$

Over his head flew innumerable birds, and to his beautiful song fish leapt straight out of the blue sea.

This has life and movement as well as design and colour, and shows that Simonides aimed at much more than a purely static effect. In some other lines, which may possibly come from the

---

[1] Fr. 17 D.   [2] Fr. 33 D. Cf. Plut. *Thes.* 17.
[3] Fr. 45 D.   [4] Fr. 46 D.
[5] Fr. 20 D.   [6] Fr. 44 D.; Athen. 13. 604 b.
[7] Fr. 27 D. For the subject cf. Aesch. *Ag.* 1629–30; Eur. *Bacch.* 560 ff.; *I.A.* 1211 ff.; Ap. Rhod. 1. 26–31; Conon 45. I follow the text as given by Wilamowitz, *Pindaros*, p. 393.

same poem,[1] he conveys an effect not so much of sight but of atmosphere, of silence in a physical setting:

οὐδὲ γὰρ ἐννοσίφυλλος ἀήτα τότ' ὦρτ' ἀνέμων,
ἅτις κ' ἀπεκώλυε κιδναμένα μελιαδέα γάρυν
ἀραρεῖν ἀκοαῖσι βροτῶν.[2]

For then not even a breath of wind arose to stir the leaves, which would by its quivering movement prevent the honey-sweet voice from being fixed in the ears of men.

Here indeed much depends on the wonderful aptness of ἀραρεῖν, which is exactly designed to suggest the effect of a sudden sound in the middle of silence. We can well understand what Dionysius meant when he praised Simonides for τὴν ἐκλογὴν τῶν ὀνομάτων, τῆς συνθεσέως τὴν ἀκρίβειαν.[3] His 'precision in arrangement' is indeed part of the γλαφυρὰ σύνθεσις, for which Dionysius classes him with Sappho and Anacreon[4] and which is handsomely displayed in his lines on Danaë. His 'choice of words' is no less remarkable, especially when he appeals to the eye. The effect is often unobtrusive, but none the less exactly right, whether it is the wind over the water

εἰσ' ἅλα στίζοισα πνοιά,[5]

'the wind comes stippling the sea', where στίζοισα catches the precise impression of the first stirring of the waves, or the dust rising around a chariot:

κονία δὲ παρὰ τροχὸν μεταμώνιος ἀέρθη,[6]

'and, borne by the wind, the dust rose by the wheel', where the description is economical and exact and dramatic.

Like Pindar, Simonides varied his verse with maxims, and it is characteristic of his art that he sometimes presents them in a homely guise, as if he recognized their affinity with popular saws. In what seems to be a statement that everything has its own characteristics and we must know them for what they are, he said:

χρὴ κορυδαλλαῖς πάσαισιν ἐμφῦναι λόφον,[7]

---

[1] Schneidewin combined them with fr. 20.
[2] Fr. 40 D., with Page's correction of the MSS. κατεκώλυε to κ' ἀπεκώλυε.
[3] Vet. Script. 420 Reiske.   [4] de Comp. 23.
[5] Fr. 41 D.   [6] Fr. 16 D.
[7] Fr. 3 D. Plutarch, Pr. Reip. Ger. 14, who quotes it, continues ἐπεὶ ... καὶ πᾶσα πολιτεία φέρει τινὰς ἔχθρας καὶ διαφοράς, οὐχ ἥκιστα καὶ περὶ τούτων ἐσκέφθαι τὸν πολιτικόν.

'every lark must have its crest'. In contrasting the pretence of loyalty with the reality, he stresses the absolute difference between them:

> παρὰ χρυσὸν ἄπεφθον ἀκήρατον
> οὐδὲ μόλυβδον ἔχων,[1]

'having not even lead at the side of refined, unmixed gold'. In this he picks up a theme which Ibycus used of physical beauty[2] and Theognis of friendship,[3] and gives it a new neatness and point. When he says

> μόνος ἅλιος ἐν οὐρανῷ,[4]

'the sun alone in the sky', he may anticipate the opening of Pindar's *Olympian* I by making the sun stand for something unique and radiant and overwhelming.[5] He chooses his images with the same aptness as his single words and through their proverbial character keeps his poetry in touch with the common world.

His love of the physical scene did not prevent Simonides from seeing invisible forces at work in it. Too little remains of his Hymns and references to the gods for us to see how he treated them, but one passage of Himerius suggests that Simonides saw divine powers at work in his art and claimed their sanction for it:

For this reason I listen to Simonides in what he sang in his lyrical poems about the Muses; for this, I think, is what he said: 'The Muses are always dancing, and it is dear to the goddesses to be engaged in songs and music. When they see Apollo beginning to lead the dance, then more than before they put forth their best in song and send down from Helicon an all-harmonious sound.'[6]

This shows that for Simonides, as for Pindar, the gods could indeed have a visible shape. But in him this was matched by something else. Cicero tells that, when Hieron asked Simonides about the nature and the attributes of the gods, he kept putting off the answer, until, when pressed for it, he said that the longer he thought about the matter, the obscurer it became.[7] This story

---

[1] Fr. 50. D. The text is uncertain. I follow Herwerden's ἄπεφθον for ἔφθον and keep ἔχων of the MSS.　　　　　　　　[2] Fr. 3. 42 D.

[3] 447 ff.　　　　　　　　　　　　　　　[4] Fr. 52 D.

[5] *Ol.* 1. 5–6　　　μηκέθ' ἀλίου σκόπει
　　　　　　　　　ἄλλο θαλπνότερον ἐν ἀμέ-
　　　　　　　　　ρᾳ φαεινὸν ἄστρον ἐρήμας δι' αἰθέρος.

[6] *Or.* 62. 7 Colonna.　　　　　　　　[7] *N.D.* 1. 22.

may represent something in his treatment of the gods and the beliefs which he expressed in his poetry. He seems to have been feeling his way towards a conception of a single power, omnipotent and beyond criticism. When he wrote

μηδὲν ἁμαρτεῖν ἔστι θεοῦ καὶ πάντα κατορθοῦν[1]

'it is of God to make no mistakes and always to succeed' and

Ζεὺς πάντων αὐτὸς φάρμακα μοῦνος ἔχει,[2]

'Zeus himself alone has remedies for all things', he was not far from a conception of divinity which was beyond the range even of Aeschylus. If the gods were omnipotent, they controlled human life for better or for worse, and this was accepted by Simonides, who attributed to them both men's successes and men's disasters. It is the gods who give success, even if this means that men must make great efforts to win it:

οὔ τις ἄνευθε θεῶν
ἀρετὰν λάβεν, οὐ πόλις, οὐ βροτός.
θεὸς ὁ πάμμητις. ἀπήμαντον δὲ
οὐδέν ἐστιν ἐν ἀνθρώποις.[3]

Without the gods no one has found success, no city, no man. The all-deviser is God. There is nothing without trouble among men.

Equally we must accept the evil that the gods send no less than the good:

οὐκ ἔστιν κακὸν
ἀνεπιδόκητον ἀνθρώποις, ὀλίγῳ δὲ χρόνῳ
πάντα μεταρρίπτει θεός.[4]

There is no evil which men may not expect, and in a little while God turns everything upside down.

For Simonides this was the lesson taught by life and the essential assumption in all human calculations and endeavours.

Like most Greeks, Simonides had his moments of defeat and melancholy. These were naturally prompted by such subjects as inspired his Dirges, but he had read the lessons of the past and knew that

οὐδὲ γὰρ οἳ πρότερόν ποτ' ἐπέλοντο,
θεῶν δ' ἐξ ἀνάκτων ἐγένονθ' υἷες ἡμίθεοι,
ἄπονον οὐδ' ἄφθιτον οὐδ' ἀκίνδυνον βίον
ἐς γῆρας ἐξίκοντο τελέσσαντες.[5]

[1] Fr. 63 D.   [2] Fr. 66 D.   [3] Fr. 10 D.   [4] Fr. 11 D.   [5] Fr. 7 D.

For not even those who lived once of old and were begotten, half-divine sons, from the master gods, came to old age without passing a life of sorrow and destruction and peril.

His vision taught him that the span of human life is negligible and thousands of years are but a moment or the fraction of a moment.[1] But despite his misgivings, or even because of them, he never lost his sense of the good things of life. What he valued most were the finer and nobler pleasures, and in them of course he included effort and fame. For him a life without pleasure was not worth living:

> τίς γὰρ ἁδονᾶς ἄτερ
> θνατῶν βίος ποθεινὸς ἢ ποία τυραννίς;
> τᾶσδ' ἄτερ οὐδὲ θεῶν ζαλωτὸς αἰών.[2]

For what life of man is desirable without pleasure, or what kingly power? Without this not even the life of the gods is to be envied.

His roots were firmly fixed in the earth, and he knew that health was a primary good:

> οὐδὲ καλᾶς σοφίας ἐστὶν χάρις,
> εἰ μή τις ἔχει σεμνὰν ὑγίειαν.[3]

Nor is there any delight in beautiful art, if a man have not holy health.

Simonides countered his moments of gloom with a firm belief in the good things of life.

For him, as for Pindar, among these were noble toil and achievement. He looked into the matter with care and was not content to state his conclusions in bald maxims or simply to lecture his public. He was much concerned with the issues of human conduct, and he not only wrote of them with passion and imagination but found his own symbols for them. He saw the goal of human life as ἀρετά, manly success, and his treatment of it is well illustrated by his adaptation of an old theme from Hesiod. Hesiod had spoken of the hardness of human life, and his words are a complaint:

> τῆς δ' ἀρετῆς ἱδρῶτα θεοὶ προπάροιθεν ἔθηκαν
> ἀθάνατοι· μακρὸς δὲ καὶ ὄρθιος οἶμος ἐς αὐτὴν
> καὶ τρηχὺς τὸ πρῶτον· ἐπὴν δ' εἰς ἄκρον ἵκηται,
> ῥηιδίη δὴ ἔπειτα πέλει, χαλεπή περ ἐοῦσα.[4]

---

[1] Plut. Cons. Apoll. 17 τὰ γὰρ χίλια καὶ τὰ μυρία κατὰ Σιμωνίδην ἔτη στιγμή τις ἐστὶν ἀόριστος, μᾶλλον δὲ μόριόν τι βραχύτατον στιγμῆς.

[2] Fr. 57 D.   [3] Fr. 56 D.   [4] Op. 289-92.

But in front of Virtue have the deathless gods set sweat; long is the way thereto and steep and rough at first. But when a man has reached the summit, then it is easy, despite all its hardness.

This was a fair estimate of what Hesiod held to be valuable in a farmer's life. Simonides' notion of ἀρετά is more advanced, but he makes use of Hesiod to say something which touches him deeply:

> ἔστι τις λόγος
> τὰν Ἀρετὰν ναίειν δυσαμβάτοισ' ἐπὶ πέτραις,
> νυμφᾶν δέ μιν θοᾶν χορὸν ἁγνὸν ἀμφέπειν.
> οὐ δὲ πάντων βλεφάροις θνατῶν ἔσοπτος,
> 5 ᾧ μὴ δακέθυμος ἱδρὼς ἔνδοθεν μόλῃ,
> ἵκῃ τ' ἐς ἄκρον ἀνδρείᾳ.[1]

There is a tale that Virtue dwells on rocks which are hard to climb, and that a holy company of swift Nymphs attends her, nor may she be seen by the eyes of all mortal men, but only by him whose heart-devouring sweat rises from the marrow, and he comes to the summit by daring.

The main image comes from Hesiod, and it may perhaps have been reinforced by a recollection of the proverbial ἄκρον ἀρετῆς which is found in Tyrtaeus[2] and Pindar.[3] On this foundation Simonides constructs his little myth of Ἀρετά. He clarifies and strengthens the implications of Hesiod's imagery by making the rocks where she dwells hard to climb, by surrounding her with Nymphs such as accompany Artemis on the mountains,[4] and by making her invisible except to those who climb to the summit by their own courage. Each little touch brings her nearer to the gods, and she becomes a special case of the old rule

> οὐ γάρ πως πάντεσσι θεοὶ φαίνονται ἐναργεῖς.[5]

What might have been a mere abstraction has gained a new, vivid reality, and this is done by transforming the old theme of Hesiod into something like a religious belief.[6]

In Plato's *Republic* Socrates calls Simonides σοφὸς καὶ θεῖος ἀνήρ,[7] and there is no reason for thinking that he does not mean what he says, or that Simonides was not to Socrates' liking. At

---

[1] Fr. 37 D. I give the text as corrected by Wilamowitz, *S.u.S.* p. 170, but keep θοᾶν in 3.   [2] Fr. 9. 43 D.   [3] *Nem.* 6. 23.
[4] *Od.* 6. 105 ff.   [5] *Od.* 16. 161.
[6] Perhaps Simonides had something similar in mind when he made To-morrow a deity, Menand. *Encom. Rhet. Gr.* 9. 133 Walz. ὥσπερ Σιμωνίδης τὴν Αὔριον δαίμονα κέκληκεν.   [7] *Rep.* 1. 331 e.

one point indeed he anticipates the doubts which Plato felt about the arts,[1] and especially about their ability to do all that was claimed for them. The contemporaries of Simonides assumed, as indeed Theognis did[2] and Pindar after him,[3] that, whatever a man's life may be after death, he is able to win a special immortality in the memory of men, through song or stone. The notion was known to Simonides, who dealt with it decisively. One of the Seven Sages, Cleobulus of Rhodes, was said to have written some hexameters on the tomb of Midas. They speak of the bronze monument on the tomb and boast that it will last as long as nature herself:

χαλκῆ παρθένος εἰμί, Μίδεω δ' ἐπὶ σήματι κεῖμαι.
ἔστ' ἂν ὕδωρ τε νάῃ καὶ δένδρεα μακρὰ τεθήλῃ,
ἠέλιός τ' ἀνιὼν λάμπῃ λαμπρά τε σελήνη,
καὶ ποταμοί γε ῥέωσιν ἀνακλύζῃ τε θάλασσα,
αὐτοῦ τῇδε μένουσα πολυκλαύτου ἐπὶ τύμβου
ἀγγελέω παριοῦσι Μίδης ὅτι τῇδε τέθαπται.[4]

A bronze maiden am I, and I lie on Midas' tomb. So long as water runs and tall trees grow, and the sun rises and shines, and the bright moon, and rivers flow, and the sea swells high, I shall remain here on this much-wept tomb and proclaim to passers-by that Midas is buried here.

It is clear that Simonides did not know this in precisely this form, since he says nothing about a bronze figure and indeed implies that he has not heard about it, but he certainly knew some lines very like these and dealt with their claims firmly and categorically.

τίς κεν αἰνήσειε νόῳ πίσυνος Λίνδου ναέταν Κλεόβουλον
ἀενάοις ποταμοῖσ' ἄνθεσί τ' εἰαρινοῖς
ἀελίου τε φλογὶ χρυσέας τε σελάνας
καὶ θαλασσίαισι δίναις ἀντία θέντα μένος στάλας;
ἅπαντα γάρ ἐστι θεῶν ἥσσω· λίθον δὲ
καὶ βρότεοι παλάμαι θραύοντι. μωροῦ φωτὸς ἅδε βουλά.[5]

Who that trusts in his wits would praise Cleobulus who dwelt in Lindos, when against the everflowing rivers and the flowers of the spring, the fire of the sun and of the golden moon, and the sea's eddies

---

[1] Plat. Phaedr. 275 d; cf. Xen. Mem. 3. 10. 3. It is quite likely that in fr. 55 D. τὸ δοκεῖν καὶ τὴν ἀλάθειαν βιᾶται Simonides agrees with Pindar, Ol. 1. 30 ff., Nem. 7. 20 ff., on the deceiving influence of art.
[2] 237 ff.
[3] Pyth. 1. 92 ff.
[4] Diog. Laert. 1. 90.
[5] Fr. 48 D.

he set the might of a gravestone? For all things are inferior to the gods, and stone even mortal hands shatter. The man who thought this was a fool.

Though Simonides believed in the beauty of art, he knew that he must not claim too much for it, and he shows his scorn for a man who hoped to challenge the powers of nature by a monument as enduring as they are. Against this boast Simonides turns his sense of the majesty of natural forces, and lavishes his poetry on them. Rivers, flowers, sun, moon, and sea are presented in their essential grandeur. The flowers are, the rich carpet that is the glory of Greek lands in spring. The rivers are 'everflowing', as Aeschylus[1] and Euripides[2] also call them. The sun is seen as the flaming thing that it is, and the moon is golden like Pindar's χρυσάρματος μήνα.[3] The sea with its hidden springs and currents is a power far beyond mortal man and his creations. Against this array of unperishing glories Simonides sets the solitary, contemptuous word στάλας. The single spondee comes emphatically and derisively at the end of a series of dactylic sequences and trochaic dipodies. The single spondee is rare in the 'dactylo-epitrite' metre, and its introduction here is a triumph of metrical skill. The contrast could not be made better between the hollow boasts of man and the recurring pageant of visible nature, behind which lies the unreckonable power of the gods.

It is, then, not surprising that posterity regarded Simonides as a σοφὸς ἀνήρ, wise alike in his knowledge of life and in his presentation of it in poetry. His fragments suggest that ideas were essential to the full realization of his art, and he presented them in an Ionian way. His restraint and his candour are well matched by his style, which never says too much and makes every word do its task with what seems to be an effortless ease but is of course a triumph of art. Though he loved pleasure and beautiful things, he knew that they were not everything, and he knew that at times men must face hardship and that in so doing they master it. When he said that 'in time of necessity even harshness is sweet',[4] he spoke of what he understood; for he had lived through dangerous struggles and shared in their anxieties and their exultation. If he really said that 'we should play in our lives and never

---

[1] *Supp.* 553. [2] *Ion* 1083; fr. 594 1. N.
[3] *Ol.* 3. 19.
[4] Plut. *Arat.* 45. 5 ἐν ἀνάγκαις γλυκὺ γίνεται καὶ τὸ σκληρόν.

be entirely in earnest',[1] he cannot have intended it to be taken quite literally, but surely meant that we must be on our guard against treating ourselves too solemnly. His quick, receptive intelligence was combined with senses which observed keenly the physical scene and saw that it was a fitting stage for the doings of men. This was indeed encompassed by a great darkness, but on it there shone a bright light from noble achievements and the affections of the human heart. Simonides praised what he admired, knowing it to be good.

[1] Theon, *Progn.* 1. 215 Walz. βλαβερῶς παραινεῖ Σιμωνίδης παίζειν ἐν τῷ βίῳ καὶ περὶ μηδὲν ἁπλῶς σπουδάζειν.

IX. ATTIC DRINKING-SONGS

THE rapid and vigorous development of painting and sculpture in the sixth century at Athens seems to have had little counterpart in poetry. At the beginning of the century Solon had written his political and patriotic elegiacs, less skilful indeed than those of his friend Mimnermus but noble and undeniably moving. But after him there is hardly a trace of poetry until the patronage of the Peisistratids gradually helped into existence the majestic forms which were to dominate the succeeding century. With the emergence of Dithyramb and Tragedy came also a new kind of lyrical song, which under the influence of Lesbian example and of distinguished visitors like Anacreon and Simonides covers the transition from the sixth to the fifth century and from tyranny to democracy. A small collection of such songs is preserved by Athenaeus and called by him σκόλια Ἀττικά.[1] An Attic σκόλιον was not identical in form or in function either with the drinking-songs of Alcaeus or with the type of σκόλιον represented by Simonides' poem to Scopas. Its special character was due to the peculiar circumstances in which it grew to maturity. It was formal, and it was aristocratic. Its origins lay in those gatherings which were held by Athenian nobles in the Prytaneum, or Town Hall, of Athens, when they wished to celebrate some notable occasion. At these gatherings women were not present, and perhaps for this reason these songs are more serious than some of the drinking-songs of Alcaeus and Anacreon. The company consisted of men of good family, and the songs are on the whole decorous and public-minded. They were, moreover, sung in a peculiar way, which explains certain features in the songs themselves and in the character of the collection. The evidence for their manner of performance is of reputable antiquity and goes back to Dicaearchus[2] and Aristoxenus,[3] who were serious antiquarians and had excellent material at their disposal. They agree

[1] 15. 693 ff.
[2] Schol. Plat. *Gorg.* 451 e; Schol. Aristoph. *Nub.* 1364; id. *Vesp.* 1239. Cf. Plut. *Quaest. Symp.* 1. 1. 5.
[3] Schol. Plat. *Gorg.* 451 e; see Reitzenstein, *E.u.S.* pp. 3–13.

that at an Athenian feast there were three stages of song. First came a choral song sung by the whole company; next a song sung round the company in turn; last οἱ συνετώτατοι each sang a song. This last was a σκόλιον. Different explanations were given of its name, of which the most convincing is that the word 'crooked' applied to the zigzag course taken by the proceedings as one member took up a song from another and capped it, at the same time taking a myrtle bough from him.[1]

These σκόλια developed a specifically Attic quality, but they probably owed something at the start to Lesbian and Ionian influences. Aristophanes makes it clear that pieces by Ibycus, Alcaeus, and Anacreon were sung at feasts and festal occasions,[2] and it is at least possible that parts of them were sung in this 'crooked' fashion. More illuminating evidence comes from No. 8 in Athenaeus' collection. As it stands, it is anomalous in that it consists of a single Alcaic stanza which has no parallel elsewhere in the collection. The text is imperfect:

$$\text{ἐκ γῆς χρὴ κατίδην πλόον}$$
$$\text{εἴ τις δύναιτο καὶ παλάμην ἔχοι,}$$
$$\text{ἐπεὶ δέ κ' ἐν πόντῳ γένηται,}$$
$$\text{τῷ παρεόντι τρέχειν ἀνάγκη.}^{[3]}$$

The metre, the forms πλόον and κατίδην, and the imagery drawn from seafaring have long suggested that this may be the work of Alcaeus, and its appearance on a papyrus now proves this to be, within limits, true:

$$\text{ἐ]κ γᾶς χρῆ προΐδην πλό[ον}$$
$$\text{αἴ τις δύνατα]ι καὶ π[αλ]άμαν ἔ[χ]ηι,}$$
$$\text{ἐπεὶ δέ κ' ἐν π]όν[τῳ γ]ένηται}$$
$$\text{τώι παρέοντι . . . . . ἀνά]γκα.}^{[4]}$$

This quatrain was detached from the poem to which it belongs and sung as a σκόλιον, but by the time it was included in the Attic song-book it had undergone some changes. First, κατίδην was substituted for προΐδην, to the detriment of the sense, since

---

[1] Pollux 6. 108, καὶ παροίνια δ' ἄσματα ἦν καὶ σκόλια· καὶ μυρρίνην ἐπὶ δεξιὰ περιφέροντές τινες καὶ ἔκπωμα καὶ λύραν ᾄδειν ἠξίουν.

[2] *Thesm.* 160–3 (Ibycus, Anacreon, Alcaeus); fr. 223 K. (Alcaeus and Anacreon).

[3] In 3 κ' ἐν is Dindorf's correction of the MSS. reading καὶ ἐν.

[4] Fr. 249. 6–9 L.–P.

κατίδην means 'to catch sight of',[1] whereas προΐδην means 'to foresee' and is much more to the point. Secondly, the substitution of optatives for subjunctives in the second line is the kind of mistake that might occur when a song was passed orally from singer to singer, even if it somewhat impairs the syntax. Thirdly, though we do not know what followed τῶι παρέοντι in the fourth line of the original text, it cannot have been τρέχειν (Aeolic τρέχην), since this would spoil the metre by lengthening the final syllable of παρέοντι. The point of this verse, if we may judge by a possible allusion in Plutarch,[2] may have been that, though before setting out to sea you should show foresight, yet when you are at sea, you must accept circumstances and make the best of them. The Attic τρέχειν does not suit this, and looks as if it were either a correction or a corruption. In the first case, it might mean that a man at sea must travel before whatever wind there is. The original verse of Alcaeus would appeal to Athenian singers of σκόλια, especially if it had a political reference, and that may be the reason for its appearance in the collection.[3]

Athenaeus preserves twenty-five σκόλια, and there can be little doubt that they form the whole or part of a song-book intended for those participants at feasts who felt that they could not improvise songs for themselves and thought it easier to sing an old favourite.[4] To this extent the collection is like that of the Homeric Hymns, which seem to have been προοίμια intended for rhapsodes to sing before proceeding to the actual Homeric poems.[5] The collection of Attic σκόλια was probably known to Dio Chrysostom[6] and other ancient authorities. It is arranged on recognizable principles. The first seven pieces are quatrains in the same metre, and the first four of them are addressed to various gods and goddesses, rather as are the first four pieces of the elegiacs attributed to Theognis.[7] The other three follow easily

---

[1] Lobel, quoted by Page, *S. and A.* p. 197.

[2] *Praec. Reip. Ger.* 2. 798 d ἔξω βλέπουσι ναυτιῶντες καὶ ταραττόμενοι μένειν τε καὶ χρῆσθαι τοῖς παροῦσιν ἀνάγκην ἔχοντες. From this Lobel suggests μένην, but χρῆσθαι suggests that we should perhaps have some word that means 'make use of'.

[3] It is pleasing to note that Diogenes Laertius 1. 78 attributes a similar sentiment to Pittacus συνετῶν ἀνδρῶν, πρὶν γενέσθαι τὰ δυσχερῆ, προνοῆσαι ὅπως μὴ γένηται, ἀνδρείων δὲ γενόμενα εὖ θέσθαι.

[4] Wilamowitz, *A.u.A.* ii, pp. 316-22.

[5] Pind. *Nem.* 2. 3; Thuc. 3. 104. 4, but see Allen and Halliday, *Homeric Hymns*, pp. xciii-xciv.   [6] 2. 63.   [7] F. Jacoby, *Theognis*, pp. 8-25.

and look as if they belonged to the same section. Then come two
odd pieces, one of which is the stanza of Alcaeus. After them
come four quatrains of Harmodius and Aristogeiton, which are
clearly closely related. Then come nine couplets in similar but
not identical metres, whose technique may display some Lesbian
influence, on a variety of subjects. The last three pieces are dis-
ordered. Nos. 23 and 24 are to be found in Aristotle's *Constitution
of Athens*.[1] One is an elegiac couplet, and as such is unique in the
collection, and the other is a quatrain like Nos. 1–7. The probability is that they were added to the collection from the text
of Aristotle. No. 25 seems to belong to the same section as Nos.
14–22 and to round off the whole series with a good general
sentiment.

The arrangement is formal and not chronological, and if we
wish to study the development of Attic σκόλια, we must try to
rearrange them in an approximately temporal order. This is not
impossible, as certain indications of date can be found, but the
validity of the attempt lies in the arrangement of the songs in
groups. Because σκόλια were sung in succession one after another,
it follows that, when we have a series of them composed in the
same or similar metres or displaying similar characteristics, then
we have a series of verses which may come from the same section
of society and from approximately the same period. In Athenaeus'
collection Nos. 1–7, 10–13, and 14–22 present such homogeneous
series and may be treated as separate collections, each of which
may be traced to a single time and a single social group. On this
assumption we may take each series and see what can be made
of it.

We may begin with Nos. 14–22 and add to them No. 25. It
consists of couplets in colloquial Attic, and there is no trace of
Lesbian or other dialects. The couplets are composed in Asclepiad and other closely related metres, and the absence of
quatrains increases the appearance of unity. Their external
similarity suggests that all come from a single social group, since,
if one couplet was followed or capped by another, it was natural
that similar metres and themes should be used. The date and the
source of this section may be deduced from more than one point.
The first couplet, No. 14, announces that we must love the
ἀγαθοί and keep away from the δειλοί. This is an aristocratic

[1] 20. 5 and 19. 3.

doctrine, familiar from Theognis,[1] but its special interest here is that it is called Ἀδμήτου λόγος:

Ἀδμήτου λόγον, ὦ ἑταῖρε, μαθὼν τοὺς ἀγαθοὺς φίλει,
τῶν δειλῶν δ' ἀπέχου γνοὺς ὅτι δειλοῖς ὀλίγη χάρις.

Learn the saying of Admetus, comrade, and love the noble, but keep away from the base, knowing that the base have little gratitude.

Here a familiar sentiment is attributed to the Thessalian king Admetus, and the attribution is remarkable in an Attic song; for, except in the two plays of Phrynichus and Euripides, Admetus does not seem to have attracted much attention at Athens. Even his wife Alcestis seems not to have been depicted on Attic vases,[2] and in the vast mass of later legends only one connects Admetus with Athens, when the Atthidograph Phanodemus tells that, when in his old age Admetus was expelled from Pherae, he was given a home by Theseus.[3] His presence in Attica was certainly rare, and if we may judge by Euripides' *Alcestis*, he was not very highly honoured. Nor does the 'saying of Admetus', as the σκόλιον reports it, seem to have any bearing on the story of Alcestis. Eustathius, indeed, thought that τοὺς ἀγαθούς referred to Alcestis and τῶν δειλῶν to the father of Admetus,[4] while in modern times τοὺς ἀγαθούς has been taken to refer to Heracles.[5] But the words are so commonly combined in political contexts that it is hard not to read a political meaning into them here. Nor do such references to cowardice and courage come very well from Admetus if the poet had in mind the same stories of him as we have. He was hardly entitled to emphasize the virtue of loyalty. Once the later story had taken a hold,[6] it would have been difficult to attribute such a sentiment to him, and the couplet must surely have been composed at an earlier date.

The words μαθών and γνούς imply that the couplet is based on a maxim or proverb connected with Admetus. Such a proverb was probably Thessalian; for only in Thessaly was Admetus of any importance. Now Athenian relations with Thessaly were not normally significant or intimate, but there was one time when

---

[1] 31–32; 105. [2] Pfuhl, i, pp. 321 and 324.

[3] Schol. Aristoph. *Vesp.* 1239 (Phanod. 325 F 26, Jacoby); cf. Parthen. *Erot.* 5.

[4] 326. 30 ἔοικε δὲ διὰ μὲν τῶν ἀγαθῶν τὴν γενναίαν καὶ φίλανδρον ὑποδηλοῦν Ἄλκηστιν, διὰ δὲ τῶν δειλῶν τὸν Ἀδμήτου πατέρα, ὃς ὤκνησε θανεῖν ὑπὲρ τοῦ παιδός.

[5] Wilamowitz, *A.u.A.* ii, p. 321.

[6] For the treatment of Admetus in tragedy and comedy see A. M. Dale, *Euripides: Alcestis*, pp. xii–xiv.

they were, and that was when the Peisistratids made an alliance with the Thessalian princes and were well repaid by it. For when a Spartan army under Anchimolius invaded Attica and attempted to expel the Peisistratids, they were saved by the arrival of a thousand Thessalian horsemen under Cineas, who defeated the invaders.[1] The σκόλιον may actually come from this time or be a reminiscence of it. The supporters of Hippias had good reason to praise a Thessalian saying which urged them to cling to the ἀγαθοί. For the Thessalians had proved themselves good friends in contrast to those Athenians who tried to expel Hippias with Spartan support and in due course succeeded, when Cleomenes invaded Attica with his army.[2]

In favour of a Peisistratid origin for the Ἀδμήτου λόγος there is also some external evidence. By the time of Aristophanes it was assumed that some of the most popular σκόλια belonged to the time of the Peisistratids and had an old-fashioned, if not exactly tyrannical, flavour. When Bdelycleon teaches his father to sing σκόλια and says to him

> τούτοις ξυνὼν τὰ σκόλι' ὅπως δέξει καλῶς,

'in such company see that you cap the songs properly,' the old man replies:

> ἀληθές; ὡς οὐδεὶς Διακρίων δέξεται.[3]

'Indeed? No Diacrian will cap them better.' The Διάκριοι had been the political supporters of Peisistratus,[4] and these words show that in the last quarter of the fifth century certain σκόλια were still connected with the country people who had served him. Moreover, another passage of Aristophanes shows that the Ἀδμήτου λόγος was regarded with some distaste by true democrats. In his *Pelargi* he wrote:

> ὁ μὲν ᾖδεν Ἀδμήτου λόγον πρὸς μυρρίνην,
> ὁ δ' αὐτὸν ἠνάγκαζεν Ἁρμοδίου μέλος.[5]

the one was singing the Word of Admetus to a myrtle-bough, but the other compelled him to sing the Harmodius song.

Here there are two singers, of whom one wishes to sing the 'Word of Admetus', but the other stops him and forces him to sing the Harmodius song. This action is most easily understood if

---

[1] Hdt. 5. 63. 3.   [2] Id. 5. 64–65.   [3] *Vesp.* 1222–3.
[4] Aristot. *Const. Ath.* 13. 4.   [5] Fr. 430 K.

the second man disapproved of the political or social implications of the Word of Admetus and forced the first man to sing its antithesis, the popular song of the tyrannicides. There is then evidence, both internal and external, for the Peisistratid associations of the Ἀδμήτου λόγος.

The two couplets which follow, Nos. 15 and 16, do not certainly come from the same social origin, but they are not alien to it and have indeed what looks like some association with it. They tell of Aias, Telamon, and Achilles:

> παῖ Τελαμῶνος, Αἶαν αἰχμητά, λέγουσί σε
> ἐς Τροίαν ἄριστον ἐλθεῖν Δαναῶν μετ' Ἀχιλλέα.

Son of Telamon, warrior Aias, they say that after Achilles you were the best of the Danaans who came to Troy.

> τὸν Τελαμῶνα πρῶτον, Αἴαντα δὲ δεύτερον
> ἐς Τροίαν λέγουσιν ἐλθεῖν Δαναῶν μετ' Ἀχιλλέα.

They say that of the Danaans who came to Troy Telamon was first; and Aias second, after Achilles.

The second couplet caps the first on the principle that fathers are better than their sons. At first sight both look like variations of a theme of Homer:

> ἀνδρῶν αὖ μέγ' ἄριστος ἔην Τελαμώνιος Αἴας,
> ὄφρ' Ἀχιλεὺς μήνιεν· ὁ γὰρ πολὺ φέρτατος ἦεν.[1]

and so in some sense they are, though they may have been equally influenced by a line of Alcaeus:

> Κρονίδα βασίληος γένος Αἴαν τὸν ἄριστον πεδ' Ἀχίλλεα.[2]

This was a common enough theme, used amongst others by Pindar.[3] But our two couplets make a new point in introducing Telamon as well as Aias, and in so doing betray their origin. Aias and Telamon were Salaminian heroes, and Peisistratus was connected both with them and with Salamis. He was said to be descended from Aias' son, Philaus,[4] and his supporters had reason to remember this, since it was in the conquest of Salamis that he first revealed his military capacities.[5] Moreover, if the couplets

---

[1] *Il.* 2. 768–9.
[2] Fr. 387 L.–P. See Page, *S. and A.* p. 285.
[3] *Nem.* 7. 27. Reitzenstein, *E.u.S.* p. 16, suggests that the σκόλιον follows Pindar, but though Pindar follows Homer, he does not go beyond him and mention Telamon.
[4] 'Plat.' *Hipparch.* 228 b.   [5] Aristot. *Const. Ath.* 17. 7.

are in some sense Peisistratid, there is a real point in the mention of Troy; for Peisistratus fought Pittacus of Mytilene for the possession of the γῆ Ἀχιλλεῖτις of Sigeum in the Troad,[1] which was supposed to contain the graves of Aias[2] and of Achilles.[3] The couplet would be well suited to a circle which felt that it had a special connexion not only with Telamon and Aias but also with Troy, and this would suit the Peisistratids. There is no need to assume that the couplets are contemporary with the fighting at Sigeum, but they imply it as a background and are well suited to the traditions of Peisistratus and his sons.

Other couplets of this section have no obviously historical connexions, but they too may come from the same time and conditions. Peisistratus had popularized and reorganized the great festivals in honour of Dionysus and Athene, and Nos. 17 and 18 show how certain elements in these appealed to those who took part in them. No 17 was inspired by the solemn ceremonial which took place on the early morning of the eighth day of Elaphebolion—about 24 March.[4] After the sacrifice of oxen and the offering of first fruits came a procession of sons of men killed in war.[5] Sacred dances were performed to Dionysus, and Dithyrambs, such as those composed by Simonides and Lasos, were sung by choirs of fifty boys, gaily dressed for the occasion. Among them were players of the lyre,[6] and of such the poet thought when he wrote:

> εἴθε λύρα καλὴ γενοίμην ἐλεφαντίνη
> καί με καλοὶ παῖδες φοροῖεν Διονύσιον ἐς χόρον.

Would that I might become a fair lyre of ivory, and fair boys carry me to the dance of Dionysus.

This couplet was answered by another like it:

> εἴθ᾽ ἄπυρον καλὸν γενοίμην μέγα χρυσίον
> καί με καλὴ γυνὴ φοροίη καθαρὸν θεμένη νόον.

Would that I might become an unsmelted fair great vessel of gold, and that a fair woman carry me, who has set her thoughts to purity.

That this too refers to a ceremonial occasion we cannot doubt, but we cannot be quite sure what it is. It is just possible that the

---

[1] Hdt. 5. 94. 1. [2] Strab. 595. [3] Id. 596; Plin. N.H. 5. 30 (33). 125.
[4] E. Pfuhl, De Atheniensium Pompis Sacris, pp. 74–79.
[5] Isocr. 8. 82. [6] Harpocrat. s.v. Εὐνῖδαι.

χρυσίον is the golden basket carried by a maiden of noble birth in the same festival of Dionysus,[1] but we should expect it to be more precisely characterized, and it seems more likely that it refers to the sacred vessels of gold and silver, πομπεῖα χρυσᾶ καὶ ἀργυρᾶ, which were carried by virgins of noble origin and unblemished reputation in the Panathenaic procession.[2] Perhaps the words καθαρὸν νόον support this view.

The rest of this section is concerned with personal relations and problems, and has no political significance. Its interest is that it takes us into the inner sentiments of an aristocratic society and shows how it valued loyalty and truthfulness as Theognis and Alcaeus had valued them. No. 19 shows what a man expects from a friend:

σύν μοι πῖνε, συνήβα, συνέρα, συστεφανηφόρει,
σύν μοι μαινομένῳ μαίνεο, σὺν σώφρονι σωφρόνει.[3]

Drink with me, be young with me, love with me, wear garlands with me; be mad with me when I am mad, be sober with me when I am sober.

The easy, colloquial language and the neatness of the expression are an excellent guise for sentiments sincerely felt by men who feasted together. This belief in a whole-hearted friendship is balanced by a suspicion of unknown enemies and expressed in No. 20 by a traditional image:

ὑπὸ παντὶ λίθῳ σκορπίος, ὦ ἑταῖρ', ὑποδύεται·
φράζευ μή σε βάλῃ· τῷ δ' ἀφανεῖ πᾶς ἕπεται δόλος.

A scorpion, my friend, lurks under every stone; take care lest it strike you. Every deceit follows the unseen.

This is an expansion of a proverb known to Aristophanes as a παλαία παροιμία.[4] Its simplest form seems to have been ὑπὸ παντὶ λίθῳ σκορπίος εὕδει,[5] and poets had some affection for it. Sophocles turned it into an iambic line:

ἐν παντὶ γάρ τοι σκορπίος φρουρεῖ λίθῳ,[6]

---

[1] Schol. Aristoph. *Ach.* 242 κατὰ τὴν τῶν Διονυσίων ἑορτὴν παρὰ τοῖς Ἀθηναίοις αἱ εὐγενεῖς παρθένοι ἐκανηφόρουν. ἦν δὲ ἐκ χρυσοῦ πεποιημένα τὰ κανᾶ, ἐφ' ὧν τὰς ἀπαρχὰς ἁπάντων ἐτίθεσαν.

[2] Decrees of Stratocles, ap. Westermann, *Biog. Min.* p. 279. 184.

[3] For συνήβα cf. Alcaeus fr. 73. 9 L.-P. συνάβαις and Anacreon fr. 52. 2 D. οὐ γὰρ ἐμοὶ ⟨παῖς ἐ⟩θέλει συνηβᾶν and fr. 20 ἔραμαι δέ ⟨τοι⟩ συνηβᾶν, χαρίεν γὰρ ἦθος ἴσχεις, which may possibly reflect Attic usage. See Weber, pp. 97 ff.

[4] *Thesm.* 528–30.

[5] Hesych. s.v. ὑπὸ παντὶ λίθῳ.

[6] Fr. 37 P.

and Praxilla into an Asclepiad:

> ὑπὸ παντὶ λίθῳ σκορπίον, ὦ ἑταῖρε, φυλάσσεο.[1]

Because of the obvious similarity, the Attic line was attributed to her, but the theme was common, and there is no need to see her hand in our couplet.

Nos. 21 and 22 have a somewhat different spirit and are concerned with the waywardness of desire and of fortune. The first takes what looks like an old maxim, whose verbal forms suggest that it is not Attic but Atticized Doric or Aeolic, and adds a second line in the vernacular which applies the doctrine to the singer's own case;

> ἁ ὗς τὰν βάλανον τὰν μὲν ἔχει, τὰν δ' ἔραται λαβεῖν·
> κἀγὼ παῖδα καλὴν τὴν μὲν ἔχω, τὴν δ' ἔραμαι λαβεῖν.

The sow has this acorn and desires to get that; I have this pretty girl and desire to get that.

The sentiment is less dignified than usual in the collection, and is aptly matched by No. 22, in which a proverb or familiar saying again appears in the first line, to receive a new application in the second:

> πόρνη καὶ βαλανεὺς τωὐτὸν ἔχουσ' ἐμπεδέως ἔθος·
> ἐν ταὐτᾷ πυέλῳ τόν τ' ἀγαθὸν τόν τε κακὸν λόει.

The whore and the bath-man have constantly the same habit; each washes the good man and the bad man in the same trough.

In both of these there is more wit than poetry, but there is poetry none the less, even if it is somewhat pungent. No. 25, with which the whole collection closes, seems from its metre to belong to this section. It is a simple statement of the value of faithfulness before gods and men:

> ὅστις ἄνδρα φίλον μὴ προδίδωσιν, μεγάλαν ἔχει
> τιμάν ἔν τε βροτοῖσ' ἔν τε θεοῖσιν κατ' ἐμὸν νόον:

Whoso betrays not his friend has in my judgement great honour among mortals and among gods.

We cannot read these verses without seeing that they come from a delightful society, simple and sensitive, loyal and passionate. If indeed they come from the world of the Peisistratids, and certainly some of them seem to, they illustrate the curious irony

---

[1] Fr. 4 Bergk.

of history by which the fifth century, trained to hate the name of tyranny, still clung to its songs and honoured them as a national possession.

The chief enemies of the Peisistratids were the Alcmaeonids. Of ancient lineage and considerable wealth, they led the opposition. Condemned to exile, they maintained the struggle and eventually triumphed, when with Spartan help they expelled Hippias. No series in the collection seems to come purely from the Alcmaeonids, but they have left their mark on one or two pieces. No. 23 may indeed not be Alcmaeonid in origin, but certainly would win approval for its opposition to the Peisistratids:

$$\text{ἔγχει καὶ Κήδωνι, διάκονε, μὴ δ' ἐπιλήθου,}$$
$$\text{εἰ χρὴ τοῖς ἀγαθοῖς ἀνδράσιν οἰνοχοεῖν.}$$

Nothing is known of Cedon except Aristotle's short statement that he attacked the Peisistratids before the Alcmaeonids,[1] and the statement suggests that he was not himself one of them, though he may have been a friend or an ally. His attack must have been before the murder of Hipparchus in 514, and the couplet is not likely to be much later than the event which it commemorates. That it did not succeed is clear enough, and it looks as if Cedon lost his life in it; for otherwise he would hardly be honoured in this way.[2] His unsuccessful venture was almost forgotten in the greater glory of Harmodius and Aristogeiton.

The couplet is followed by a quatrain, No. 24, on the dead of Leipsydrion:

$$\text{αἰαῖ, Λειψύδριον προδωσέταιρον,}$$
$$\text{οἴους ἄνδρας ἀπώλεσας μάχεσθαι}$$
$$\text{ἀγαθούς τε καὶ εὐπατρίδας,}$$
$$\text{οἳ τότ' ἔδειξαν οἴων πατέρων ἔσαν.}$$

Alas, Leipsydrion, betrayer of comrades! what men have you destroyed, good at fighting and born of noble fathers, who showed then of what stock they were bred.

The dead of Leipsydrion were well remembered in Greek history. Herodotus[3] and Aristotle[4] place their activities between the

---

[1] *Const. Ath.* 20. 5 ἔτι δὲ πρότερον τῶν Ἀλκμεωνιδῶν Κήδων ἐπέθετο τοῖς τυράννοις, διὸ καὶ ᾖδον καὶ εἰς τοῦτον ἐν τοῖς σκολίοις. If the subject of ᾖδον is, as we might assume, οἱ Ἀλκμεωνίδαι, the song comes from their circle.

[2] Mittelhaus, in *R.-E.* xi. 110, thinks that the lines are addressed personally to Cedon, but in that case we should expect not a dative but a vocative.

[3] 5. 62. 2.   [4] *Const. Ath.* 19. 3.

murder of Hipparchus in 514 and the expulsion of Hippias in 510. The Alcmaeonids fortified Leipsydrion on the slope of Mount Parnes and from it tried to overturn Hippias' rule. They failed, and were routed in a battle on the mountain. The quatrain was composed in honour of those who fell, and not only comes from Alcmaeonid circles but may well have been composed soon after the battle; for in these years events moved so rapidly that later a lament of this kind would make little mark. It betrays its political antecedents. The men who fell were εὐπατρίδαι, and the word, which is the antithesis of κακοπάτριδαι which Alcaeus applies to his Lesbian opponents,[1] is used in the sense of 'well-born'. So Sophocles applies it three times to the children of Agamemnon,[2] and Euripides to Theseus[3] and to Admetus.[4] The Alcmaeonids traced their descent to Alcmaeon, the contemporary of Theseus,[5] and as early as the seventh century provided an archon in Megacles.[6] Men of such lineage might well call their brethren εὐπατρίδαι and boast οἵων πατέρων ἔσαν.

This is the only poem in the collection which can be referred with some confidence to the Alcmaeonids. Another oddity, of unknown origin, is No. 9. Written in two Telesillea followed by two Glyconics, it is unique in its metrical form, and has no verse to cap it. It tells a nice fable about a Crab and a Snake:

> ὁ καρκίνος ὧδ' ἔφα
> χαλᾷ τὸν ὄφιν λαβών·
> 'εὐθὺν χρὴ τὸν ἑταῖρον ἔμ-
> μεν καὶ μὴ σκολιὰ φρονεῖν.'

Thus spoke the Crab, when he caught the Snake in his claw: 'A comrade should be straight and not have crooked thoughts'.

This accords with Greek notions of natural history; for, according to Aelian,[7] there was at Ephesus a cave in which large venomous serpents lived and, as they came out of the water, were caught by crabs who throttled them with their claws. This song is not a variation on the theme of the Pot calling the Kettle black; its point is not that, just as the Crab ought to go straight instead of sideways, so he tells the Serpent that he ought to be straight and not crooked. εὐθὺν ἔμμεν does not mean 'walk straight', nor is

---

[1] Frs. 67. 4; 75. 12; 348. 1 L.–P.　　　　[2] El. 162, 859, 1081.
[3] Hipp. 152.　　　[4] Alc. 920.　　　[5] Paus. 2. 18. 8.
[6] Hdt. 6. 125. 1.　　　[7] N.H. 16. 38.

σκολιά the right word for the Crab's sideway progress. This is a moral tale in which the Crab is the hero and the Snake the villain, and the cream of the joke is the word εὐθύν; for when a snake dies, it literally stiffens out straight. A story which makes the same point is attributed to Aesop.[1] There a kind and gentle Crab makes friends with a Snake, and finding him intolerably treacherous kills him, and at the end of it says: τοῦ δὲ ὄφεως μετὰ θάνατον ἐκταθέντος ἐκεῖνος εἶπεν· "οὕτως ἔδει καὶ πρόσθεν εὐθὺν καὶ ἁπλοῦν εἶναι· οὐδὲ γὰρ ἂν ταύτην τὴν δίκην ἔτεισας." The quatrain gives the climax and the main point of the story, which is that the only straight snake is a dead snake. A comrade must be straight or he will be punished for his crookedness.

We may now turn to a more solid block of σκόλια. Nos. 1–7 are all composed on the same metrical plan and present a convincing air of unity. A date may be inferred from No. 4, which implies a charming chapter of Athenian history. It is addressed to Pan:

> ὦ Πάν, Ἀρκαδίας μέδων κλεεννᾶς,
> ὀρχηστά, Βρομίαις ὀπαδὲ νύμφαις,
> γελάσειας, ὦ Πάν, ἐπ' ἐμαῖς
> εὐφροσύναις, ἀοιδαῖς κεχαρημένος.[2]

O Pan, ruler of renowned Arcadia, dancer who accompaniest the Nymphs of Bromius, take delight in my songs, Pan, and smile on my merry-making.

Pan seems to have played very little part in Attic belief or cult before the battle of Marathon. He is not represented on black-figured vases or mentioned in poetry. But in 490 he sprang into fame. Herodotus tells that, when the Athenians heard of the destruction of Eretria by Datis and Artaphrenes, the Athenian generals, of whom Miltiades was one, sent Philippides to Sparta with the news. On Mount Parthenion above Tegea in Arcadia Philippides saw Pan, who declared his good will to the Athenians despite their neglect of him. Later, after the battle but probably not long after, since Herodotus says καταστάντων σφι ἤδη τῶν πραγμάτων, the Athenians built a shrine to him in a grotto on the north-west slope of the Acropolis.[3] In 472 Aeschylus made him

---

[1] *Fab.* 346 Halm, 290 Chambry.

[2] In 4 the MSS. are in confusion, and any reconstruction is uncertain. Bergk read εὐφροσύναισι, ταῖσδ' ἀοιδαῖς κεχαρημένος, which gives a metre different from the rest of this section but in itself unexceptionable. Wilamowitz suggested εὔφροσι ταῖσδ' ἀοιδαῖς κεχαρημένος. I follow Hermann.

[3] Hdt. 6. 105. 3.

haunt Psyttalea,[1] and about the same time he makes a dramatic appearance on the splendid bell-krater of the Pan Painter in Boston.[2] By 458 he was sufficiently acclimatized for Aeschylus to associate him with Zeus and Apollo.[3] The Homeric Hymn to Pan looks as if it was of Athenian origin, when it shows the new regard in which he was held by making him enter Olympus.[4] Our song sings of him soon after his appearance to Philippides, when he is still specifically an Arcadian god and has not been fully assimilated in Attica.

As Miltiades was one of the generals who sent Philippides on his errand and was preeminently the victor of Marathon, it is tempting to connect the poem with him and his circle or his associates in victory. The connexion is strengthened by a dedicatory inscription ascribed, like so many others, to Simonides:

τὸν τραγόπουν ἐμὲ Πᾶνα, τὸν Ἀρκάδα, τὸν κατὰ Μήδων,
τὸν μετ' Ἀθηναίων στήσατο Μιλτιάδης.[5]

The Simonidean authorship is of course open to the usual objections, but the simplicity of the style, so unlike Meleager's adaptation,[6] suggests an early date, and the repetition of τόν in asyndeton seems almost a mannerism of Simonides himself, since it recalls the repetition in ἓν πέλαγος, μία νύξ, εἷς τάφος in his lines on the men who were shipwrecked when bringing spoils from the Tyrrhenians.[7] In any case the couplet represented a tradition which connected Miltiades with the newly established cult of Pan, and our quatrain looks as if it belonged to the same social sphere.

The connexion of this section with Marathon receives some additional, if tantalizing, support from No. 5. Unfortunately it is almost certainly mutilated. The manuscripts give:

ἐνικήσαμεν, ὡς ἐβουλόμεσθα,
καὶ νίκην ἔδοσαν θεοὶ φέροντες,
παρὰ Πανδρόσου ὡς φίλαν Ἀθηνᾶν.

This is unsatisfactory for two reasons. First, though the first two lines conform to the metrical scheme of the preceding pieces, the third line does not, and though it can be taken as another Phalaecian hendecasyllable, it is more likely that it contains the imperfect remains of two lines on the usual plan. Secondly, as it

---

[1] *Pers.* 448-9. [2] J. D. Beazley, *Der Pan-Maler*, pp. 10-11, Taf. 2.
[3] *Ag.* 56. [4] Hom. Hymn 19. 42 ff. [5] No. 143 D.
[6] *Anth. Pal.* 7. 207. [7] No. 97 D.

stands, it hardly makes sense. If the gods gave victory, it is an anti-climax, if not worse, to say that it came from Pandrosos, who was herself a goddess, and the words ὡς φίλαν Ἀθηνᾶν, which must presumably be taken with νίκην, are not very effective as meaning 'as dear to Athens', and anyhow we should expect not a genitive but a dative. The lines are beyond cure, since too much is missing, but it is at least clear that they refer to a victory, and it is not unreasonable to think that this was Marathon. That this was connected with Pandrosos need not surprise us. She had a shrine on the Acropolis, and in its precinct was the sacred olive-tree.[1] Since this was burned by the Persians in 480, a reference to Pandrosos would be more likely in 490 when the shrine was intact and was an important centre of Athenian national religion.

No. 3 may also be connected with the same time and circumstances. It concerns Apollo and Artemis:

> ἐν Δήλῳ ποτ᾽ ἔτικτε τέκνα Λατώ,
> Φοῖβον χρυσοκόμαν, ἄνακτ᾽ Ἀπόλλω,
> ἐλαφηβόλον τ᾽ ἀγροτέραν
> Ἄρτεμιν, ἃ γυναικῶν μέγ᾽ ἔχεις κράτος.

In Delos once Lato gave birth to children, to golden-haired Phoebus, lord Apollo, and to the shooter of deer, the huntress Artemis, who hast great power over women.

The important clue is ἀγροτέραν, in which Wilamowitz saw no more than a natural invocation of Artemis as the goddess of wild things.[2] But we are well informed on the cult of Artemis ἀγροτέρα, and our information provides a more illuminating conclusion. She had a shrine at Agrai across the Ilissus, and on the sixth day of Thargelion, the anniversary of the battle of Marathon, three hundred goats were sacrificed to her in accordance with a vow made by Miltiades.[3] The sacrifice, as befitted its national character, was conducted by the polemarch.[4] Plutarch tells that the procession to Agrai was still performed in his day,[5] and an inscription of the first century B.C. refers to it in the significant words ἐπειδὴ οἱ ἔφηβοι . . . ἐπόμπευσαν τῇ Ἀρτεμίδι τῇ Ἀγροτέρᾳ ἐν ὅπλοις.[6] There was an intimate connexion between

---

Artemis Agrotera and the battle of Marathon, and the mention of her in this song indicates that it too belongs to this period. In giving so prominent a place to the goddess in her special role the quatrain looks as if it was composed soon after the establishment of the rite.[1]

Another piece, No. 1, which begins both the whole collection and this special section, certainly has nothing in it inconsistent with a like date, and indeed looks as if it came from much the same circumstances. It addresses Athene:

> Παλλὰς Τριτογένει᾽, ἄνασσ᾽ Ἀθάνα,
> ὄρθου τήνδε πόλιν τε καὶ πολίτας
> ἄτερ ἀλγέων καὶ στάσεων
> καὶ θανάτων ἀώρων, σύ τε καὶ πατήρ.

Pallas, Triton-born, queen Athene, guide this city aright, and its citizens, without pains and quarrels and untimely deaths, thou and thy father.

Each word makes a point, and the impression which emerges is that Athens is in danger and calls on her guardian goddess for help. Pallas Τριτογένεια, despite the unknown meaning of the title, was summoned specially in time of need. In the *Iliad* the epithet is given three times to Athene, and in each has some reference to her warlike prowess.[2] Hesiod associates it closely with her prowess in battle.[3] When the women in Aristophanes' *Lysistrata* attempt their *coup d'état*, they pray

> καί σε καλῶ ξύμμαχον, ὦ
> Τριτογένει᾽.[4]

The word had militant and patriotic associations, and would be thoroughly suitable to a prayer in time of war. In the second line ὄρθου, 'guide aright', recalls Pindar's use of ὀρθωθεῖσα for the island of Salamis in the sea-battle of 480.[5] In the third line Athene is asked to save the city from στάσεις and ἄλγη, from civil and foreign wars. The first was apt enough for a city which

---

[1] The mention of Delos, Lato, and Apollo may be due to no more than their usual association with Artemis, but it is worth noticing that in the year of Marathon Delos won a great fame because of an earthquake of which Herodotus 6. 98. 1 says καὶ τοῦτο μέν κου τέρας ἀνθρώποισι τῶν μελλόντων ἔφηνε ὁ θεός. If the earthquake was interpreted as an omen of disaster to the Persians, there would be good reason for the Athenians to remember Delos and Apollo when they celebrated Marathon.   [2] 4. 515; 8. 39; 22. 183.   [3] *Theog.* 895–6.
[4] 346–7.   [5] *Isthm.* 5. 48.

in 490 was not united against the enemy; the second recalls how Aeschylus speaks of war as παγκλαύτων ἀλγέων[1] and κακά τ' ἄλγη πολέμους θ' αἱματόεντας.[2] The sense of threatening disaster is increased by the final words, which recall the wish of the Eumenides that Athens may have peace and prosperity:

> ἀνδροκμῆτας δ' ἀώ-
> ρους ἀπεννέπω τύχας.[3]

The quatrain does not demonstrably belong to the time of Marathon, but since it precedes others which do and is certainly not incompatible with such a date, we may tentatively place it there.

No. 2 is interesting less for political than for social reasons. It is addressed to Demeter and Persephone:

> Πλούτου μητέρ', 'Ολυμπίαν ἀείδω
> Δήμητρα στεφανηφόροις ἐν ὥραις,
> σέ τε, παῖ Διός, Φερσεφόνη,
> χαίρετον, εὖ δὲ τάνδ' ἀμφέπετον πόλιν.

I sing the mother of Wealth, Olympian Demeter, in the season when garlands are worn, and thee, daughter of Zeus, Persephone; hail, both, and tend this city well.

It is possible that behind this lies the Athenian festival of the Ἁλῷα which was held in the month of Posideon,[4] roughly the equivalent of December, as a kind of thanksgiving, for getting in the fruits of the earth,[5] to Demeter, Kore, and 'the other gods in accordance with national custom.'[6] As such it suits our song in more than one respect. At it Demeter and Persephone were honoured together, which was by no means as common as we might expect. Secondly, it was a national festival, honoured with other such festivals,[7] and at it sacrifices were offered for the Athenian people[8] and an ἀγὼν πάτριος was held. Thirdly, though it took place in the winter, it might reasonably be described as στεφανηφόροις ἐν ὥραις, for it seems to have been customary to crown important participants with a crown of myrtle.[9] Such

---

[1] Sept. 367–8. [2] Supp. 1044–5.
[3] Aesch. Eum. 956–7. [4] Philochorus ap. Harpocr. s.v. Ἁλῷα.
[5] Bekker, Anec. Graec. i, p. 385 ἐπὶ συγκομιδῇ τῶν καρπῶν; Schol. Lucian Dial. Meretr. 7. 4 ἐπὶ τομῇ τῶν ἀμπέλων καὶ τῇ γεύσει τοῦ ἀποκειμένου ἤδη οἴνου.
[6] S.I.G³. 485. 9 and 23; 661. 8. [7] Ibid. 485. 30.
[8] Ibid. 13.
[9] Ibid. 661. 19 καὶ στεφανῶσαι μυρρίνης στεφάνῳ, ὧι πάτριόν ἐστι.

a festival, with its thanksgiving for the good things of the earth, appealed primarily to those who lived on the land and was to this degree an aristocratic occasion. Its social implications were clear to the song-writer when he called Demeter 'mother of Wealth'. This had indeed the authority of Hesiod,[1] but its emphatic position in the song shows that it is really meant. Nor was it usual to call Demeter 'Olympian'. This indeed she was, but the adjective exalts her to a special dignity, and makes her as august as possible. The song looks as if it came from aristocratic, land-owning circles, like the γνώριμοι whose leader was Miltiades.[2]

The house of Miltiades was indeed renowned for its generous conviviality. Herodotus pays a tribute to the hospitality of the grandfather,[3] and a relic of the family's life may be seen in the fine plate by the Cerberus Painter in the Ashmolean Museum, which dates from c. 520–510 and shows a young archer in foreign dress on horseback and has the inscription Μιλτιαδες καλος.[4] The tradition of good living was inherited by Miltiades' son, Cimon, of whom Eupolis wrote:

κακὸς μὲν οὐκ ἦν, φιλοπότης δὲ κἀμελής.[5]

'He was not bad, but fond of drink and careless.' In such a family it was natural that σκόλια should be sung about the great events in which its members had played an active part. Such a circle, and others like it, resembled the circle of the Peisistratids in insisting upon high standards of truth and loyalty. No. 6 is concerned with them:

εἴθ' ἐξῆν, ὁποῖός τις ἦν ἕκαστος,
τὸ στῆθος διελόντ', ἔπειτα τὸν νοῦν
ἐσιδόντα, κλείσαντα πάλιν
ἄνδρα φίλον νομίζειν ἀδόλῳ φρενί.

Would that it were possible to open a man's breast, just as each man is, then to see his mind, and, closing it again, to think him a true friend from his guileless heart.

Here, as in the quatrain on the Crab and the Snake, the point comes from a fable, of which the outline is given by Eustathius.[6]

---

[1] Theog. 969.   [2] Aristot. Const. Ath. 28. 2.   [3] 6. 35.
[4] C.V.A. Oxford, i, pl. I, No. 5. See H. T. Wade-Gery, Essays in Greek History, p. 155.   [5] Fr. 208 K.   [6] Od. 1574, 16.

The main tenor of the idea is common enough,¹ but it had a special point at a time when Athenian society had many divisiosn, and faithfulness to a cause or a party was held in special esteem.

No. 7 is a famous piece concerned with the 'four best things':

ὑγιαίνειν μὲν ἄριστον ἀνδρὶ θνατῷ,
δεύτερον δὲ φυὰν καλὸν γενέσθαι,
τὸ τρίτον δὲ πλουτεῖν ἀδόλως,
καὶ τὸ τέταρτον ἡβᾶν μετὰ τῶν φίλων.

For a mortal man it is best to be healthy; second to have been born beautiful in body; third to be rich without deceit; and fourth to be young with friends.

Ancient authorities,² none of them very good, say that this quatrain was variously assigned to Epicharmus and to Simonides. Epicharmus' authorship may be ruled out, since there is plainly a confusion with a line of his on the same subject quoted by Aristotle:

ἀνδρὶ δ' ὑγιαίνειν ἄριστόν ἐστιν, ὥς γ' ἡμῖν δοκεῖ.³

It is, however, not impossible that Simonides wrote the quatrain. He certainly admired health, for he wrote:

οὐδὲ καλᾶς σοφίας ἐστὶν χάρις,
εἰ μή τις ἔχει σεμνὰν ὑγίειαν.⁴

Nor is there any grace in beautiful art, if a man have not holy health.

He may well have admired good looks, and would hardly have been a Greek of his time if he had not. The anecdotes about his fondness for money would agree with his praise of wealth, and his taste for good living would include feasting.⁵ It is perhaps more to the point that he was at Athens at the time of Marathon and knew Miltiades and the other leading figures, when he wrote his epitaph for the fallen. It is not impossible that he composed this little song for this society.

A third important section in this collection of σκόλια is taken up by Nos. 10–13, which celebrate the murder of Hipparchus by Harmodius and Aristogeiton:

¹ Theogn. 121 ff.; Eur. Hipp. 925 ff.; Med. 516–19; Aristot. Eth. Eud. 1237 b 15.
² Schol. Plat. Gorg. 451 e; Steph. ad Arist. Rhet. 1394 b 13.
³ Rhet. 1394 b 13 (fr. 262 Kaibel). ⁴ Fr. 56 D.
⁵ This is clear from what look like remains of convivial elegiacs in fr. 72 D. οὐ γὰρ ἀπόβλητον Διονύσιον οὐδὲ γίγαρτον and fr. 73 D. οἶνον ἀμύντορα δυσφροσυνάων.

ἐν μύρτου κλαδὶ τὸ ξίφος φορήσω,
ὥσπερ Ἁρμόδιος καὶ Ἀριστογείτων
ὅτε τὸν τύραννον κανέτην
ἰσονόμους τ' Ἀθήνας ἐποιησάτην.

φίλταθ' Ἁρμόδι', οὔ τί που τέθνηκας,
νήσοις δ' ἐν μακάρων σέ φασιν εἶναι,
ἵνα περ ποδώκης Ἀχιλεὺς
Τυδεΐδην τέ φασιν ἐσθλὸν Διομήδεα

ἐν μύρτου κλαδὶ τὸ ξίφος φορήσω,
ὥσπερ Ἁρμόδιος καὶ Ἀριστογείτων
ὅτ' Ἀθηναίης ἐν θυσίαις
ἄνδρα τύραννον Ἵππαρχον ἐκαινέτην.

αἰεὶ σφῷν κλέος ἔσσεται κατ' αἶαν,
φίλταθ' Ἁρμόδιος καὶ Ἀριστόγειτον,
ὅτι τὸν τύραννον κανέτην
ἰσονόμους τ' Ἀθήνας ἐποιησάτην.

I shall take the myrtle branch and carry my sword,[1] like Harmodius and Aristogeiton, when they slew the tyrants and gave equal laws to Athens.

Dearest Harmodius, you are not dead, I think, but they say that you are in the Islands of the Blest, where is fleet-footed Achilles, and, they say, the son of Tydeus, noble Diomedes.

I shall take the myrtle-branch and carry my sword, like Harmodius and Aristogeiton, when at the festival of Athene they slew the tyrant Hipparchus.

Their fame shall live on the earth for ever, dearest Harmodius and Aristogeiton, since they slew the tyrant and gave equal laws to Athens.

To modern eyes this looks like a complete poem, and can be enjoyed as such, but since it occurs in the collection of σκόλια, where each is a unit waiting to be capped by another, we must pay attention to this in any discussion of its structure and its authorship.

In antiquity a Ἁρμοδίου μέλος was attributed to Callistratus.[2]

---

[1] The reference to the myrtle branch does not imply that the assassins of Hipparchus hid their swords in such branches, but means simply that the singer takes the branch before starting his song. See J. C. Vollgraff, *Mnemosyne*, xlix (1921), pp. 246–50.

[2] Hesych. s.v. Ἁρμοδίου μέλος· τὸ ἐπὶ Ἁρμοδίῳ ποιηθὲν σκόλιον ὑπὸ Καλλιστράτου οὕτως ἔλεγον.

Though nothing is known of him, the song must have borne some relation to ours. We might of course entertain the notion that he wrote the four quatrains intending them to be sung in the usual manner of σκόλια and that his work was not so much a single poem as a series of variations on a given theme. But this solution is too easy. First, though each quatrain is indeed a variation on a theme, the differences are very small and look rather like the kind of changes that singers themselves might have made. Secondly, in our manuscripts the fourth line of the second quatrain

$$Τυδείδην τέ φασιν ἐσθλὸν Διομήδεα$$

does not conform metrically to the fourth lines of the other stanzas.[1] It is in itself a perfectly good metrical unit like that of the first lines in Nos. 15–18, but if a single poet composed all four stanzas, we should expect him to make this one on exactly the same model. Nor is it easy to emend. If we omit ἐσθλόν, it is metrically beyond cavil, but weaker in sense; if we omit φασιν, it spoils the metre and the syntax. The line looks sound and suggests some variety of authorship.

There is, moreover, some external evidence that, by the time of Aristophanes, what was known as the Harmodius Song was not exactly the same as our text. When Bdelycleon teaches his father how to sing σκόλια, he begins his lesson with the words:

$$ᾄδω δὲ πρῶτος Ἁρμοδίου· δέξαι δὲ σύ·$$
$$οὐδεὶς πώποτ' ἀνὴρ ἔγεντ' Ἀθήναις....[2]$$

I start with the Harmodius Song. You cap it.
'No man ever yet was born in Athens . . .'.

This shows that the song had at least another verse which is not in our version, and was regarded as its start. Again, the scholiast on *Acharnians* 980 quotes the first line of the second verse

$$φίλταθ' Ἁρμόδι', οὔ τι που τέθνηκας$$

and says that it is the beginning of a song called Ἁρμοδίου. Of course, with the passage of the fifth century, new verses may well have been added to the original, and it must always have been difficult to maintain a constant order in a series of quatrains which are so easily interchangeable. None the less the song, as we

---

[1] The repetition of φασιν in the second and fourth lines looks, and is, awkward, but is perhaps not out of place in a verse of this kind with its air of improvisation.

[2] *Vesp.* 1225–6.

have it, looks more like a series of quatrains meant to cap each other than a single poem. Of these Callistratus presumably wrote some, but we can hardly doubt that his work was supplemented and changed by singers who liked his song and wished to make more of it.

The date of the song is not easy to fix. Harmodius and Aristogeiton killed Hipparchus in 514, but the tyranny did not come to an end until Hippias was expelled with Spartan help in 510. This is the earliest possible date for the song or for any parts of it. That the cult of the tyrannicides began soon after this is clear from the erection of a statue to them by Antenor almost immediately afterwards.[1] The reasons for this cult may be surmised. Hippias had in fact been expelled by Spartan troops, and it was necessary for those who had taken part in this to find some more glorious and more national myth. This was found in the pair of tyrannicides, who in fact did very little to free Athens and whose motives were by no means purely patriotic or democratic,[2] but at least the popularization of their memory would distract attention from the actual facts, and it is quite likely that powerful Athenian families had a hand in this effective campaign of propaganda. It is by no means impossible that the song began its career at this date. On the other hand, some years later, after the defeat of the Persians, the cult of Harmodius and Aristogeiton received a new impetus. The statue by Antenor, removed by Xerxes, was replaced by a new statue by Critius and Nesiotes in 477,[3] and from this period the murder of Hipparchus became a subject for vase-painters. The stamnos by the Copenhagen Painter in Würzburg dates from c. 475;[4] the small black-figured lekythos by the Emporion Painter in Vienna from c. 470;[5] the Villa Giulia fragment from 460–450.[6] The subject was also treated on coins and tesserae and continued to be popular with artists for a long time.[7] Unfortunately we do not know when certain rites were decreed for them, such as the sacrifices and libations which were offered to them as if they were real heroes[8] and were conducted by the

---

[1] Plin. *N.H.* 34. 4 (9). 17: 'hoc actum est eodem anno quo et Romae reges pulsi' (509 B.C.).   [2] Thuc. 6. 54. 3.
[3] *Mar. Par.* 54; Paus. 1. 8. 5.
[4] Langlotz, quoted by Beazley, *J.H.S.* lxviii (1949), p. 27.
[5] Haspels, *A.B.L.* pl. 48. 5, with p. 167 and p. 264, no. 39.
[6] Beazley, op. cit. p. 27.
[7] O. M. Washburn, *A.J.A.* xxii (1918), pp. 146–53.   [8] Dem. 19. 280.

polemarch,[1] or when it was forbidden by law to say or sing anything evil of them.[2] Our series of quatrains may date from about
510 or from 477 or be a mixture from both dates with perhaps
some later additions or changes.

When Nos. 10 and 13 both say that Harmodius and Aristogeiton made Athens ἰσονόμους, they anticipate a famous concept
of Athenian democracy. The notion does not appear again until
Herodotus speaks of ἰσονομίη as the essential characteristic of
democratic government,[3] and it is perhaps difficult to believe
that such a notion was already current in 510, when the struggle
for power was between the oligarchic party of Isagoras and the
more democratic party of the Alcmaeonids. We do not know
what catch-words Cleisthenes used when he 'took the people
into partnership',[4] but it is quite possible that he referred to the
establishment of 'equal laws'. Such a notion need not yet have
developed the full meaning that it had later, but might well have
appealed to those families who had resisted the tyrants and felt
that at least they themselves should be equal before the law.[5]
Nor need we necessarily be too troubled when No. 11 speaks of
Harmodius dwelling in the Islands of the Blest. It was indeed
a high compliment to pay him, but it would be no more unlikely
soon after his death, when his glory was at its height, than later,
when his memory had been revived. Finally, though in 510
there were good reasons for paying attention to the tyrannicides,
it would be obvious to many that in fact it was not they who had
liberated Athens. But martyrs collect their own legends soon
enough, and, though later Herodotus knew the truth,[6] these
men who were the forerunners of liberation may have received
their first recognition soon after their death. There is no final
reason why the song should not have started its career about 510,
and indeed it seems likely to have done so, while the names of
the tyrannicides still evoked recent memories in many Athenian
minds. Once this had happened, the song could receive additions, and it is tempting to think that the second stanza, with its
slight difference of metre, is such. Perhaps the original song of
Callistratus consisted of the first and fourth stanzas, which
balance each other neatly in the traditional manner of σκόλια.

---

[1] Aristot. *Const. Ath.* 58. 1. [2] Hyperid. 2. 3.
[3] 3. 80. 6. [4] id. 5. 66. 2.
[5] V. Ehrenberg, *Historia*, i (1950), pp. 530 ff. [6] 6. 123. 2.

The third stanza, with its reference to the ἄνδρα τύραννον "Ἱπ-
παρχον instead of τὸν τύραννον,[1] may be a later addition, and the
second may belong to the time when the tyrannicides received
heroic honours. The question of the date is almost insoluble in a
song like this which was liable to be expanded, and we can only
mark the possibility that its career may have begun quite soon
after the events which it celebrated.

The collection in Athenaeus gives us almost all the Attic
σκόλια that we possess, but outside it lies another, which seems
to have had a considerable vogue, and was known as the 'Cleitagora'. It is this which Bdelycleon teaches to Philocleon:

χρήματα καὶ βίαν
Κλειταγόρᾳ τε κἀ-
μοὶ μετὰ Θετταλῶν.[2]

'money and violence for Cleitagora and me with the Thessalians'.
The tradition on this is confused and looks suspiciously like
guess-work. It is, for instance, impossible for it to refer to the
war against the tyrants,[3] since in this the Thessalians were on the
side of Hippias. Nor can we make much of the tradition that
Cleitagora was a Laconian poetess,[4] since the song plainly points
to the pleasures of war and loot in Thessalian company. There
are two possible origins for the song, first that it comes from the
Peisistratid side when the Thessalians helped to expel Anchimolius, the second that it comes from 476 B.C., when Menon of
of Pharsalus sent a subsidy of 10 talents and 300 horsemen to
Cimon's expedition against Eion.[5] Two references in comedy
concern it, but raise as many questions as they answer. The first
is from the Χίρωνες of Cratinus:

Κλειταγόρας ᾄδειν, ὅταν Ἀδμήτου μέλος αὐλῇ,[6]

to sing the 'Cleitagora', when he plays the tune of Admetus.

The second is from Aristophanes, when in the Lysistrata the
Second Athenian tells the First Athenian of the effects of wine at
Sparta:

---

[1] V. Ehrenberg, *Wiener Studien*, lxix (1956), p. 66.

[2] Aristoph. *Vesp.* 1245 ff.

[3] Schol. ibid. Κλειταγόρας μέλος λέγουσι τὸ εἰς αὐτὴν Κλειταγόραν, ἥτις ἐγένετο
Θετταλή τις γυνή . . . ἐκ σκολίου τινός ἐστιν. Ἀθηναίοις δὲ συνεμάχησαν Θετταλοὶ ἐν
τῷ πρὸς τοὺς τυράννους πολέμῳ.

[4] Schol. *Lys.* 1237 ἡ γὰρ Κλειταγόρα ποιήτρια ἦν Λακωνική, ἧς μέμνηται καὶ ἐν
Δαναΐσιν Ἀριστοφάνης.   [5] Dem. 23. 199.   [6] Fr. 236 K.

νυνὶ δ᾽ ἅπαντ᾽ ἤρεσκεν, ὥστ᾽ εἰ μὲν γέ τις
ᾄδοι Τελαμῶνος, Κλειταγόρας ᾄδειν δέον,
ἐπῃνέσαμεν ἂν καὶ προσεπιωρκήσαμεν.[1]

Now everything gives pleasure; if a man
When he should sing Cleitagora, strike up
With Telamon's song, we'd clap him on the back,
And say 'twas excellent; ay, and swear it too.[2]

There is plainly a contrast between the 'Cleitagora' on the one
hand and the 'Admetus' and the 'Telamon' on the other. It is
conceivable that in both passages the reference gets its point
from the songs coming from different political and social worlds,
but it is no less possible that the failure to sing the right song is
simply a sign of intoxication. Since the metre of the 'Cleitagora'
is different from that of both the 'Admetus' and the 'Telamon',
it presumably had a different tune, and to sing it instead of them
argues for a considerable confusion of mind. The song looks as
if it was rather wilder and less decorous than most of the other
known σκόλια, and that perhaps is why it did not find a place in
the song-book known to Athenaeus. If it was composed *c.* 476, it is
possible that it came from the circle of Cimon and continued the
tradition of such songs in his family.

These σκόλια were well known in the time of Aristophanes, but
by that of Antiphanes (*c.* 388–*c.* 311 B.C.) they were passing out of
fashion. One of his characters says:

ἔπειτα μηδὲν τῶν ἀπηρχαιωμένων
τούτων περάνῃς, τὸν Τελαμῶνα, μηδὲ τὸν
Παιῶνα, μηδ᾽ Ἁρμόδιον.[3]

Next, don't perform any of these antiquated turns, the Telamon or
the Paeon or the Harmodius.

The great day of the σκόλια was in the latter part of the sixth
century and the first part of the fifth. They were essentially an
aristocratic art which was not ideally suited to democratic
conditions. Bdelycleon and Pheidippides show no sign of the
formality by which a myrtle-branch was passed round and
compelled its recipient to sing a song. These drinking-songs were
at first supplemented and then superseded by new songs of a
choral character, by selections from the older lyric poets and
from Euripides. They were still remembered, but they no longer
played a distinctive part in Athenian life.

[1] *Lys.* 1236–8.　　　[2] Trans. B. B. Rogers.　　　[3] Fr. 85. 3–5 K.

APPENDIX I

The Song of Hybrias the Cretan

At the end of his collection of Attic σκόλια Athenaeus[1] quotes a poem, on which his only comment is σκόλιον δέ φασί τινες καὶ τὸ ὑπὸ τοῦ Ὑβρίου τοῦ Κρητὸς ποιηθέν. The same poem is mentioned by Eustathius 1574. 7, who adds nothing to our knowledge of the author, and very little to that of the text. Until the discovery of the Hymn of the Curetes, the Song of Hybrias was our sole specimen of Cretan lyrical poetry, and even now it stands apart from the main currents of Greek literature and raises its own peculiar questions. Its author's name, its date, its text, and its character are subjects of doubt and dispute.

Athenaeus calls the author Ὑβρίου, and it has been commonly assumed that the nominative was Ὑβρίας, but a passage in Hesychius, cited by Wilamowitz,[2] throws doubt even on this. The entry says Ἰβικτήρ· ὁ παρὰ Κρησὶν Ἴβριος ἐμβατήριον ποιησάμενος, ὅπερ ὁ ᾄδων οὕτω καλεῖται. The natural meaning of this is that a Cretan called Ἴβριος composed a marching-song, and that the singer of this was called ἰβικτήρ. The connexion between Ἴβριος and ἰβικτήρ looks too aetiological to be true, and Wilamowitz connects the entry with two others in Hesychius, ἰβύ· τινὲς τὸ βοᾶν· οἱ δὲ τὸ πολύ. ἔστι δὲ Λυδῶν and ἰβύει· τύπτει, βοᾷ. From these it might perhaps be deduced that the name Ὑβρίας is really a corruption of a title given by the Cretans to a man who led them in their marching-songs. But Ὑβρίας may be related to such names as Ὑβρέας and Ὕβρων, if not to Ὑβρίστας, Ὑβρέστας, and Ὕβριμος.[3] It looks like a real name, even if ἰβικτήρ is a real title. It is perfectly possible that the poet was really called Ὑβρίας and that advantage was taken of this to associate him with the singers of marching-songs.

Hybrias is said by Athenaeus to have been a Cretan, and presumably his song is Cretan too. It is therefore remarkable that it shows hardly any trace of the Cretan dialect except the Doric genitive ἀμπέλω, the nominative singular δεσπότας, and the verbal form κυνέοντι. On the other hand certain forms are recognizably not Cretan. Neither ἀρῶ, nor οἶνον, without a digamma, nor κέκλημαι is of the same dialect as the Gortyn Code. But this absence of a Cretan exterior need not necessarily mean that the poem was not composed

---

[1] 15. 695 f.   [2] *Gr. Versk.* pp. 498–9.
[3] F. Bechtel, *Griechische Personennamen*, p. 270.

by a Cretan or sung in Crete. It may well have suffered from its later popularity and have been altered into a familiar κοινή, or it may have from the first have been composed in the more or less international language of lyric poetry. Flach thought that 'the poem is written in the conventional Doric of the younger choral lyric and can hardly have been composed before Simonides'.[1] But the poem has few traces of the ripe choral style. It has indeed its own rhetorical devices, but they may be old and are not demonstrably choral. For instance, the four times repeated τούτῳ recalls in structure, if not in sense, the triple repetition of ἐν δορί in a couplet of Archilochus,[2] and if the apposition of πρόβλημα χρωτός seems to have a sophisticated look, a parallel may be found in Alcaeus' λάμπραι κνάμιδες, ἄρκος ἰσχύρω βέλεος.[3] So far as the style is concerned, there is no need to bring the poem down to the time of Simonides, though equally the style provides no certain evidence of an earlier date. Soldiers' songs do not necessarily display all the marks of the finer literature of the age to which they belong.

There is a similar uncertainty about conclusions to be drawn from the metre. If we take the first strophe, which seems to be reasonably intact, we get something like the following plan:

– ∪ – – | – ∪ – ∪ ∪ – ∪ –	Epitrite, Glyconic
– ∪ ∪ – – | – ∪ – – | – ∪ – –	Adonius, 2 Epitrites
– – ∪ ∪ – – | – ∪ – –	Reizianum, Epitrite
– – ∪ ∪ – ∪ – | ∪ – ∪ ∪ – ∪ –	2 Telesillea
– – – ∪ – ∪ ∪ – | ∪ – –	Choriambic dimeter, Bacchius

The combination struck Wilamowitz as elaborate, and he concluded that it 'is the technique of the Doric and dramatic lyric; the poem derives at least from the fourth century, but in its present state it was sung by the Κρηταιεῖς of the third or second centuries'.[4] On examination this conclusion seems to be unwarranted. The main metrical combinations of the poem can be found in quite early lyric poetry. The use of the Adonius as a colon is paralleled by Sappho,[5] that of the Reizianum by the Rhodian swallow-song.[6] The combination of a Choriambic Dimeter and a Bacchius recalls Sappho's combination of a Glyconic and a Bacchius,[7] and the placing of an Epitrite before a Glyconic is not unlike the way in which Alcaeus prefixes an Iambic Dipody.[8] These parallels come from monody or folk-song, but when we turn to choral poetry, we find, for instance in Alcman, combinations considerably more elaborate than in Hybrias. He may have

[1] *Geschichte der griechischen Lyrik*, p. 55.
[2] Fr. 2 D.; see Bowra, *An. Fil. Clas.* vi (1954), pp. 7 ff.
[3] Fr. 357. 5 L.–P.
[4] *Gr. Versk.* p. 499.
[5] Fr. 158 L.–P.
[6] Athen. 8. 360 c.
[7] Fr. 96 L.–P.
[8] Fr. 70 L.–P.

learned something from the choral style, but there seems to be no good argument from metre to place his song in the fourth century.

If neither language nor metre gives much help with the poem's date, we must look to its contents. The text of the first verse looks sound and may be presented in its usual form:

> ἔστι μοι πλοῦτος μέγας δόρυ καὶ ξίφος
> καὶ τὸ καλὸν λαισήϊον, πρόβλημα χρωτός·
> τούτῳ γὰρ ἀρῶ, τούτῳ θερίζω,
> τούτῳ πατέω τὸν ἀδὺν οἶνον ἀπ' ἀμπέλω,
> τούτῳ δεσπότας μνοίας κέκλημαι.

My great wealth is my spear and sword, and the fine targe, which guards my skin; with this I plough, with this I reap, with this I tread the sweet wine from the vine, with this I am called master of the serfs.

Here there is at least an indisputable piece of evidence that the song is connected with Crete. The μνοία are familiar to ancient history as the publicly owned serfs who cultivated the land in Crete.[1] The poet proclaims that he is their master and that by means of his spear and sword and targe he gets the fruit of their toil in harvest and vintage. If we press the words, they must mean that Hybrias is in charge of these slaves and in some sense their master, not indeed as their owner, but as the man who gets all that he wants from them.

Athenaeus quotes the opinion of 'some people' that the poem was a σκόλιον and no doubt in later times it was sung over the wine. But a σκόλιον in any strict sense it can hardly have been, since it must have been accompanied by gestures with the weapons which it names. Only on this assumption is the repeated τούτῳ intelligible. We have to deal with some war-song or weapon-song. This may be taken with Hesychius' statement that it is an ἐμβατήριον or marching-song. Little enough is known of Greek marching-songs, and six lines quoted from Sparta by Dio Chrysostom[2] are all that we possess. Our song is not quite like them. It boasts the prowess of a single man, while the Spartan song is a summons to all to be brave. Nor is it easy to envisage how the song of Hybrias could be sung actually on the march. It looks as if it were accompanied by weapon-play and recalls Hector's words to Aias

> οἶδα δ' ἐνὶ σταδίῃ δηΐῳ μέλπεσθαι Ἄρηι[3]

or Pindar's account of Bellerophon mounted on Pegasus:

> ἀναβὰς δ' εὐθὺς ἐνόπλια χαλκωθεὶς ἔπαιζεν.[4]

That weapon-dances existed in Crete we know from Plato's mention

---

[1] Strab. 541; Athen. 6. 263 f.; Pollux 3. 83; Hesych. s.v. μνῴα.
[2] Or. 2. 59.   [3] Il. 7. 241.   [4] Ol. 13. 86.

of Κουρήτων ἐνόπλια παίγνια¹ and though the Curetan dance may have
had a religious significance it need not have been very different from
the dances of Hector and Bellerophon. The song of Hybrias may
belong to this class.

The Curetan dance was choral, but the other weapon-dances look
as if they were performed by a single man, Such must have been the
song of Hybrias. He calls himself δεσπότας and brooks no rivals or even
partners. His song resembles the μολπή of Hector and Bellerophon
and not the later πυρρίχη, and this may be an argument for an early
date. Most war-dances are choral,² and it is hard to believe that,
if Ephorus is telling the truth about Crete in the fourth century,³
an arrogant individualism on this scale would have been tolerated.
But the point can hardly be pressed. Ephorus idealizes, and Hybrias
boasts, and their worlds may not have been so different as the records
suggest.

So far as sentiment, style, and metre are concerned, the song could
be placed in the sixth century, but of course it might still be later. At
this point the word λαισήϊον holds out an alluring hope that it may
help to fix the chronology. What λαισήϊον means can be seen from an
account of general fighting which appears twice in the *Iliad*:

> δῄουν ἀλλήλων ἀμφὶ στήθεσσι βοείας
> ἀσπίδας εὐκύκλους λαισήϊά τε πτερόεντα.⁴

The λαισήϊα are distinct from the ἀσπίδες, and it is perhaps a legitimate
assumption that the first are used by the Trojans, the second by the
Greeks. In that case λαισήϊα were regarded by Homer as a peculiarly
Asiatic means of defence, and that is no doubt why they were used by
the Cilicians in the army of Xerxes: λαισήϊα . . . εἶχον ἀντ' ἀσπίδων
ὠμοβοέης πεποιημένα.⁵ There is no evidence that they were used by
Greeks. Even on Dipylon vases warriors carry round shields, and the
reliefs from Prinia show the same armament in Crete at an early
date.⁶ We might then conclude that Hybrias served as a mercenary
in Asia Minor or some adjacent region and there learned to use the
λαισήϊον. This sounds attractive, but we may doubt its validity. First,
no warrior of any eminence would use a λαισήϊον if he could possibly
use the far more efficient ἀσπίς. Secondly, we may suspect that
Hybrias uses the word with a sense of its antique, heroic air, not to

¹ *Laws* 7. 796 b.
² Plat. *Laws* 7. 815 a; 816 b; Poll. 4. 96; Xen. *Anab.* 6. 1. 5; Athen. 14. 628 c;
Ael. *V.H.* 3. 8; Eur. *Andr.* 1135.
³ 70 F 149 Jacoby.
⁴ *Il.* 5. 452–3; 12. 425–6; cf. H. L. Lorimer, *Homer and the Monuments*, pp. 194–6.
⁵ Hdt. 7. 91.   ⁶ Richter, *A.G.A.* pl. 54.

describe a modern weapon. We cannot therefore press the meaning of
the word in trying to fix a date for the poem.

On the other hand there seems to be good reason to think that
Hybrias had soldiered abroad. The presence of Greek mercenaries in
foreign lands in the seventh and sixth centuries is well known, and in
later centuries Crete was a great source of supply of them. That
Hybrias was a successful soldier of fortune receives additional con-
firmation from the second stanza, but before we examine its contents
we must look at the text. In Athenaeus it is presented as

τοὶ δὲ μὴ τολμῶντ' ἔχειν δόρυ καὶ ξίφος
καὶ τὸ καλὸν λαισήϊον, πρόβλημα χρωτός,
πάντες γόνυ πεπτηῶτες ἐμὸν κυνέοντι δεσπόταν
καὶ μέγαν βασιλῆα φωνέοντες.

Here there is clearly something wrong. First, γόνυ needs a preposition
such as ἀμφί to bring it into the sentence, and a word for 'me' seems
to be missing as the object of κυνέοντι. With some small additions the
text can be made perfectly grammatical. A second difficulty is that the
responsion between the second strophe and the first is not complete.
The first two lines correspond very nicely, but after that the correspondence is very vague. Either we must assume that much more
has fallen out than the sense seems to require or we must accept the
difference between the two strophes and regard it as quite appropriate
for a poem of this kind. Exact correspondence is not always found in
strophic songs. For instance, in Aristophanes' *Ecclesiazusae* we expect
900–5 to correspond with 906–10, 911–17 with 918–23, and 952–9
with 960–8, but none of them does, and no satisfactory way has been
found to make them do so. It seems that at a certain popular level of
composition exact correspondence was not demanded, and we can
understand that in a song like that of Hybrias the difference of metre
might reflect some difference in the actual movement of the dance
and the weapon-play. In that case we have only to make the minimum
alterations to the second stanza, and we get:

πάντες γόνυ πεπτηῶτες ἀμφ' ἐμὸν
κυνέοντί με δεσπόταν
καὶ μέγαν βασιλῆα φωνέοντες.

The meaning is then quite clear. Hybrias announces his contempt for
those who have not won a place like his own through their weapons
and must therefore do obeisance to him as if he were a great king.
There is no specific reference to Crete or to serfs. Hybrias' claim is
more exorbitant than when he started, and his contempt embraces
all who are not so successful as he is.

The chief interest lies in the last line with its mention of μέγαν βασιλῆα. These words can only refer to some oriental monarch, whose ways are known to Hybrias and whose titles and ceremonies he appropriates to himself. Nor is there any reason to think that this was other than the Persian king. Indeed this seems to follow from the following points. First, the word κυνέοντι describes a practice familiar at the Persian court. It is known to Herodotus[1] and deplored by Aristotle[2] and Demosthenes[3] as barbarian and unworthy of Greeks. Secondly, δεσπότας is commonly used of the Persian king, whether by Herodotus of Cambyses,[4] or by Thucydides of Asiatic rulers in general,[5] and in the form δέσποτα δεσποτᾶν by Persian Elders of the Ghost of Darius.[6] Thirdly, the appellation βασιλεὺς μέγας is thoroughly appropriate to the Persian king. Herodotus calls him by this title,[7] and Aeschylus refers to satraps as βασιλῆς βασιλέως ὕποχοι μεγάλου.[8] These three claims made by Hybrias are expressed in language normally applied to the Persian monarchy, and though it is conceivable that they might have been applied to the kings of Babylon or Assyria or Lydia, there is no evidence that they were. They suggest that the song was written after the accession of Cyrus. How long after we cannot say, but it need not have been very long. The song seems to have been written by a Cretan soldier of fortune who had seen service under the Persian king and returned home to glory in his success and declared his intention of applying his Asiatic methods in Crete.

[1] 1. 119. 1; 3. 86. 2.; 8. 118. 4.   [2] *Rhet.* 1361 a 36.
[3] 21. 106.   [4] 3. 89. 3.   [5] 6. 77. 1.
[6] Aesch. *Pers.* 666.   [7] 1. 188. 1.   [8] *Pers.* 24.

A Prayer to the Fates

I N his choice of quotations concerning fate and the good ordering of events Stobaeus (*Ecl.* 5. 10–12) gives in succession three passages which the manuscripts ascribe to the *Peleus* of Euripides and the *Phaedra* of Sophocles; but, as Wilamowitz[1] and Nauck[2] saw, all three form a single piece, and the ascriptions to Euripides and Sophocles do not concern them. The text so recovered may be presented as follows:[3]

Κλῦτε, Μοῖραι, Διὸς αἵ τε παρὰ θρόνον ἀγχοτάτω θεῶν
ἑζόμεναι περιῶσι' ἄφυκτά τε μήδεα
παντοδαπᾶν βουλᾶν ἀδαμαντίναισιν ὑφαίνετε κερκίσιν,
Αἶσα καὶ Κλωθὼ Λάχεσίς τ' εὐώλενοι
5 Νυκτὸς κόραι,
εὐχομένων ἐπακούσατ', οὐράνιαι χθόνιαί τε
δαίμονες ὦ πανδείματοι,
πέμπετ' ἄμμιν ῥοδόκολπον
Εὐνομίαν λιπαροθρόνους τ' ἀδελφάς, Δίκαν
10 καὶ στεφανηφόρον Εἰρήναν, πόλιν τε τάνδε βαρυφρόνων λελάθοιτε
συντυχιᾶν.

3 ὑφαίνεται codd., corr. Wilamowitz.   4 καὶ supp. Nauck.   5 κοῦραι Νυκτός codd., corr. Wilamowitz.   7 πανδείμαντοι codd., corr. Wachsmuth.

Hearken, Fates, who sit nearest of the gods by the throne of Zeus, and on shuttles of adamant weave countless, inescapable devices for counsels of every kind, Aisa and Clotho and Lachesis, fair-armed daughters of Night, listen to our prayers, goddesses of heaven and earth, all-terrible; send us rose-bosomed Lawfulness and her brightly throned sisters, Right and crowned Peace, and make this city forget the misfortunes which lie heavily on her heart.

Since the metre is relevant to the discussion of the poem it may be displayed schematically:

$$-\cup-\ |\ -\cup\cup-\cup\cup-\cup\cup-\cup\cup-\cup-$$
$$-\cup\cup-\cup\cup-\cup\cup-\cup\cup-\cup\cup$$
$$-\cup\cup--\ |\ -\cup\cup-\cup\ |\ -\cup\cup-\cup\cup-\cup\cup$$
$$-\cup--\ |\ -\cup\cup--\ |\ -\cup-$$
$$5\qquad --\cup-$$

[1] *Isyllos von Epidauros*, pp. 16 ff.
[2] *Tr. Gr. Fr.*, 2nd ed., p. xx.
[3] Diehl, *Anth. Lyr. Gr.* ii. 159–60. There is a good, short commentary in H. W. Smyth, *Greek Melic Poets*, pp. 473–4.

–◡◡–◡◡–◡|–◡◡–◡◡–◡
–◡◡––|–◡–
–◡–|–◡◡–◡
–◡◡–◡◡–◡|–◡–|–◡–
10   –◡◡–◡◡––|–◡–◡|–◡◡–◡|–◡◡–◡
–◡◡–

Nobody will deny that the greater part of this is dactylo-epitrite. The only uncertainty of scansion is at the end of 1, where θεῶν can be either a disyllable as usual, or a monosyllable as less usual.[1] The first alternative would mean that we have a scansion rather like that of *Ol.* 6 Str. 3; the second that the dactylic series ends in, a spondee. This is an unimportant detail. What matter are more striking divergences from the usual practice of dactylo-epitrites.

The first of these, which struck Wilamowitz, is that the final syllables of the different *metra* are nearly as often short as long. Thus we find –◡◡–◡◡–◡ instead of –◡◡–◡◡–– in 6 (twice) and 9, –◡◡–◡ instead of –◡◡–– in 3, 8, and 10 (twice), and –◡–◡ instead of –◡–– in 10. This is not the practice of either Pindar or Bacchylides and makes it unlikely that either is the author. For this reason Wilamowitz decided that, by process of exhaustion, the lines must be the work of Simonides. He does not argue for this in detail, but the extant remains of Simonides' dactylo-epitrites support his case. In fr. 5 D –◡◡–◡◡–◡ appears in 4, 6, and 7 and –◡–◡ in 2 (twice) and 7; while in fr. 20 –◡◡–◡◡–◡ appears in 3 and –◡–◡ in 2 and 4. Other fragments in the same metre suggest a similar usage, and we cannot doubt that Wilamowitz's instinct was sound when he assigned the lines to Simonides because of this metrical peculiarity.

The metrical analysis reveals another abnormality of which Wilamowitz says nothing, perhaps because he did not anticipate Nauck in seeing that 1–2 are an integral part of the fragment. In 1–3 we have successions of dactyls, preceded indeed in 1 by –◡– and in 3 by –◡◡–––◡◡–◡, but none the less striking and unexpected in the company of dactylo-epitrites. To this Bacchylides presents no parallel, and Pindar only when he uses –◡◡–◡◡–◡◡–– at *Pyth.* 4 Str. 4, *Nem.* 1 Ep. 3 and 5 Ep. 9, and *Isthm.* 5 Ep. 8, and in a catalectic form at *Pyth.* 4 Str. 5, or the longer –◡◡–◡◡–◡◡–◡◡–– at *Pyth.* 3 Str. 4. Pindar's practice varies in two important respects. First, his dactylic series always end in one or two long syllables, and secondly he never has so many as five dactyls in succession. He seems not so much to introduce dactyls for their own sake as to extend the usual dactylic *metron* which is basic to dactylo-epitrites. Nor is the free

---

[1] At fr. 4. 21 D. Simonides almost certainly scans θεοί as a monosyllable.

intrusion of dactyls any commoner in choral passages of tragedy or comedy. It is true that at *Ajax* 172 (182) Sophocles begins an almost purely dactylo-epitrite strophe with a dactylic series and that at *Peace* 775–95 (796–816) Aristophanes uses mainly dactylo-epitrites, but at 790–1 (814–15) he uses first a dactylic hexameter and then a dactylic tetrameter. But both these cases are mild mixtures compared with our fragment. We cannot say that it is characteristic of Simonides, whose extant fragments provide nothing like it, but it is none the less likely that the poet who introduces dactyls in this way operates with an earlier form of dactylo-epitrites than that of Pindar or Bacchylides, in both of whom practice has hardened into a more rigorous shape.

It might of course be argued that the lines come not from lyric poetry proper but from a choral ode in tragedy. It is true that their style and manner bear little relation to anything extant in the works of the three tragedians, but there remains the possibility that they come from some other tragedian whose manner is not known to us. In the last resort this is impossible to disprove, but surely most will share Nauck's conclusion that the fragment does not come from a lost play because 'a tragoedia alienum est'. What is lacking is anything that smacks of the stage or drama, not merely the individual references which keep a play going but the air of fictitious urgency which has to be more emphatic in a play than in a theme drawn from life. It is true that some choral songs of tragedy are modelled on authentic ritual songs, and that such a piece as the Parodos of the *Oedipus Tyrannus* has many characteristics of a prayer in time of need, but our piece is simpler, more direct, and more closely related to actual events. It deals with a pressing crisis, but has no need to explain the setting, and this suggests that it comes from lyrical song.

A second argument for Simonides' authorship may perhaps be found in the style. Difficult as such matters are to prove, we know enough of his manner to see that he deserved Dionysius' appreciation of his ἐκλογὴν τῶν ὀνομάτων (*Vet. Script.* 420 Reiske). So here the poet picks his words with delicate precision and makes them suit the situation exactly. The abundant adjectives, for instance, do their work with unobtrusive skill, when they suggest the vast scope of the Fates' designs in περιῶσι' ἄφυκτά τε, or the irrevocable nature of their decrees in ἀδαμαντίναισιν, or their formidable and final character in πανδείματοι. In contrast with these suggestions of power are the adjectives given to the Hours, which come from the traditional vocabulary of praise and worship and present images of plastic and visible appeal in ῥοδόκολπον, λιπαροθρόνους, στεφανηφόρον. This is characteristic not only of Simonides' doctrine that poetry is 'painting which speaks' (Plut. *de Glor. Ath.* 3), but of his way of making unseen powers more vivid by giving them visual epithets, as when he calls the Muses

καλλικόμων (fr. 26. 2 D.) or Maia οὐρείας ἑλικοβλεφάρου (fr. 30. 1 D.) or
the Pleiads ἰοπλοκάμων (ibid. 3). The simplicity of this art lies in preferring the single, significant word to periphrasis or allusive elaboration. Something of the kind may indeed be found in Bacchylides, but
hardly on this scale or with quite this concentration of strength.

Dionysius also praises Simonides for τῆς συνθέσεως τὴν ἀκρίβειαν,
and it is instructive to test our lines in the light of this judgement.
The whole piece consists of two sentences, of which the first addresses
the Fates in their awful majesty, and the second, which is, structurally,
closely connected with it, beseeches them to send the Hours to the
unhappy city for which the poet speaks. He begins with an exalted
vision of the Fates in their glory, recites their names with hieratic
solemnity, and then becomes more human and more intimate in
words of actual prayer. The subtlety of his art can be illustrated by the
phrase περιῶσι᾽ ἄφυκτά τε μήδεα παντοδαπᾶν βουλᾶν. The Fates weave
μήδεα, devices, by which their decisions, βουλαί, are put into action,
and the decisions are of every kind just as the devices are beyond
counting. The phrase, which might at first sight seem a little inflated,
has a precise meaning and is indeed an example of precision in arrangement in that it says in a few words just what the poet means.

This style is informed by a powerful emotion, a deep and troubled
anxiety. The poet controls it and rises above it, but it makes itself felt
in the outburst of εὐχομένων ἐπακούσατ᾽, in the appeal πέμπετ᾽ ἄμμιν,
and in the final words with their urgent prayer that the city may forget its βαρυφρόνων συντυχιᾶν. This powerful undercurrent of feeling
recalls Dionysius' comment that Simonides βελτίων εὑρίσκεται καὶ
Πινδάρου, τὸ οἰκτίζεσθαι μὴ μεγαλοπρεπῶς ὡς ἐκεῖνος ἀλλὰ παθητικῶς
(Vet. Script. 420 Reiske) and Quintilian's judgement that praecipua . . .
eius in commovenda miseratione virtus (Inst. Or. 10. 1. 64). If we may judge
by the lines on Danaë (fr. 13 D.), the secret of Simonides' pathos was
the restraint which he exercised in its presentation. His appeals to pity
are the more powerful because they are almost statements of fact
which need no elaboration or comment. So here, the poet, faced by
a disastrous situation, lets it speak for itself as he prays to the gods for
succour.

There are, then, good reasons for agreeing with Wilamowitz that the
lines may have been written by Simonides, but of course on such a
question there can be no final certainty. What looks reasonably sure
is that the piece was written by a poet whose art is simpler and more
straightforward than that of Pindar or even Bacchylides, and who
practised the γλαφυρά rather than the αὐστηρὰ ἁρμονία. At the start it
is clear that he casts his words in the form of a prayer to the Fates,
and what we have is surely the beginning of his poem, since the
words κλῦτε, Μοῖραι conform to the habitual language of prayers,

and such an appeal to the gods usually comes at the start, as when Glaucus prays to Apollo:

> κλῦθι, ἄναξ, ὅς που Λυκίης ἐν πίονι δήμῳ
> εἰς ἢ ἐνὶ Τροίῃ . . . .　　　　　　　　　(Il. 16. 514–15.)

So Odysseus, cast up from the sea on Phaeacia, prays to whatever god may guard the place:

> κλῦθι, ἄναξ, ὅτις ἐσσί· πολύλλιστον δέ σ' ἱκάνω
> φεύγων ἐκ πόντοιο Ποσειδάωνος ἐνιπάς.　　(Od. 5. 445–6.)

The form passed from the epic into other kinds of verse, as when Archilochus, in what looks like the beginning of a poem, says:

> κλῦθ', ἄναξ Ἥφαιστε, καί μοι σύμμαχος γουνουμένῳ
> ἵλαος γενεῦ, χαρίζευ δ' οἷά περ χαρίζεαι.　　(fr. 75 D.)

Or Pindar starts a Dithyramb on a note of war:

> κλῦθ', Ἀλαλά, Πολέμου θύγατερ . . . .　　(fr. 66. 1 Bo.)

So our poet goes straight to work and addresses his prayer to the Fates. The actual address could be postponed till later, as Pindar does in Ol. 14. 4–5 to the Graces of Orchomenus, but it is more effective at the beginning and gives a greater sense of urgency in a time of crisis.

Since the lines are cast in the form of a prayer, we may ask from what kind of poem they come. It is tempting to think that this may have been a Paean. Didymus, who had a vast knowledge of Greek poetry, says that the Paean was sung to secure an end to famine and other troubles (Et. Gud. 446. 50 Sturz), and since among these στάσις is expressly mentioned (Schol. Lond. Dion. Thrac. p. 451. 13 Hilg.), it would be suitable for the situation in our poem. Indeed, the propriety of a Paean to a time of trouble may be seen from Pindar's Paean 4, written for the Thebans in 463 B.C., when an eclipse of the sun seemed to foretell unknown disasters. In it Pindar prays for the well-being of Thebes and hopes that the omens do not portend στάσιν οὐλομέναν (fr. 44. 15 Bo.). Its background has enough in common with our piece to suggest that this too was a Paean. On the other hand the Paean was normally connected with Apollo (Schol. Aristoph. Plut. 636; Schol. Plat. Symp. 177 a; Schol. Eur. Phoen. 1102), and it was not till the fourth century that it began to lose the connexion. Since our lines mention Zeus and not Apollo, they are more likely to come from a ὕμνος. The term could be applied to songs which contained more than mere ascription of praise and were akin to prayer. An anonymous author gives a helpful definition ὕμνος· ἔστιν ὁ μετὰ προσκυνήσεως καὶ εὐχῆς κεκραμένης ἐπαίνῳ λόγος εἰς θεούς (Et. Gud. 540. 46) and among various kinds of ὕμνοι Menander mentions οἱ μὲν εὐκτικοί, οἱ δὲ ἀπευκτικοί (p. 331. 1 Spengler), which would, if combined, cover our piece, since it asks that evils may depart and that good things may come in their stead. That a Hymn in this sense should be addressed to the Fates is not surprising. If a Chorus of the *Thesmophoriazusae* 700 could pray ὦ πότνιαι Μοῖραι or a Chorus of the *Choephoroe* 306 begin a song with ἀλλ' ὦ μεγάλαι Μοῖραι, there is no great difficulty about our poet writing a ὕμνος εἰς Μοίρας, which he begins, naturally enough, by addressing them.

A Hymn to the Fates presupposes a cult of them at which it is sung. Such cults were not uncommon, and the Fates had temples of their own at Corinth (Paus. 2. 4. 7)[1] and Thebes (id. 9. 25. 4). But we may none the less be surprised that the Fates are invoked instead of the high gods who usually watch over cities. It is true that here they are associated with Zeus, but it is to them, and not to him, that the words are addressed, and this suggests a cult more stately than any on which we have information. Nor are the Fates normally regarded as important civic deities. They have much to do with individuals but not with cities. But it would not be difficult or anomalous to extend their scope to families and even countries. So Pindar speaks of the Μοῖρα which guides the house of the Emmenidae (*Ol.* 2. 35 ff.). More strikingly, the Chorus of the *Eumenides* addresses the Fates as undeniably civic deities when it calls them

> δαίμονες ὀρθονόμοι,
> παντὶ δόμῳ μετάκοινοι.   (963-4.)

So in our poem the Fates are approached on behalf of a city which is in dire straits and suffers from internal dissensions. In this the Fates have a special duty. They are concerned with kinship and withdraw their presence when domestic sanctities are outraged, as Pindar says:

> Μοῖραι δ' ἀφίσταντ', εἴ τις ἔχθρα πέλει
> ὁμογόνοις αἰδῶ καλύψαι.   (*Pyth.* 4. 145-6.)

The same would apply to a city. If it suffers from internal discords, it means that the Fates are hostile to it, and the poet begs that they will restore their favour. Nor would he do this if they were not important divinities and honoured with more than usual respect.

The poet builds his supplication with a quiet assurance, and each step marks something new in his approach. He begins by saying that the Fates sit nearest of the gods to Zeus, and this conforms to tradition as Hesiod presents it:

> Μοίρας θ' ᾗς πλείστην τιμὴν πόρε μητιέτα Ζεύς.   (*Theog.* 903.)

---

[1] Mr. W. G. G. Forrest points out to me that at Corinth they appear on the pediment of Temple E, *Corinth*, i. 2, p. 226.

Behind the tradition lay rites in which Zeus was connected with the Fates. As Μοιραγέτης he had a temple at Delphi (Paus. 10. 24. 4), a cult at Athens (*I.G.* i². 80. 12), and an altar at Olympia (Paus. 5. 15. 5), and as such he was depicted on the shrine of Despoina at Akakesion in Arcadia (id. 8. 37. 1) and named with the Fates at Chios.[1] At Halicarnassus an oracle of Apollo commanded sacrifices to be made to the Fates together with Ζεὺς πατρῷος, Apollo, and the Mother of the Gods (*S.I.G.*³ 1044. 5) ; at Thebes their shrine was next to that of Zeus ἀγοραῖος (Paus. 9. 25. 4). Zeus and the Fates were closely connected in worship, and it is perfectly appropriate to bring them together in this supplication.

The Fates make their decisions, βουλαί, and on their adamantine shuttles spin the devices, μήδεα, which put these into effect. In this fine image the poet picks up an old idea and gives it a new force. The notion that a man's life is a thread spun at his birth is widely spread in many countries, and in Greece it was responsible for the names of two of the Fates, Clotho and Lachesis, whom popular etymology connected with κλώθειν and λαχεῖν. This notion can be seen, at an early stage, in Homer, who not only attributes the thread of life or fortune to gods (*Il.* 24. 525; *Od.* 1. 17; 8. 579; 16. 64), but more explicitly says that Αἶσα span his life for Achilles (*Il.* 20. 127–8), Μοῖρα for Hector (*Il.* 24. 209), and Αἶσα Κλῶθές τε for Odysseus (*Od.* 7. 197). At this date the Fates were not necessarily three in number, nor fully differentiated from one another. They are still birth-goddesses, and Atropos, who deals only with death, has not yet taken a place among them. Our poet differs from Homer in accepting the existence of three Fates and in applying their dominion not to the life of an individual but to the existence of a city.

He had to some extent Hesiod behind him. Hesiod presents the Fates as Clotho, Lachesis, and Atropos (*Theog.* 219, 905), and our poet cannot have failed to know this. When he substituted Αἶσα for Atropos, he must have done so deliberately, and we may surmise his reasons. Atropos is concerned with death, and on this occasion the poet is concerned not with death but with the fortunes of a city, to which Atropos is irrelevant. He therefore introduces Αἶσα, whose functions are less closely defined and who has Homeric authority behind her. He also picks up the Homeric notion of Κλῶθες and clarifies it as Clotho and Lachesis. He thus not only rejects one of Hesiod's names for the Fates but contradicts the view of a Hesiodic poet that of the Fates Atropos was προφερὴς πρεσβυτάτη τε (*Scut.* 260). It is possible that our poet chooses Αἶσα because she has a special

---

[1] G. Zolotas, Ἐπιγραφαὶ Χῖοι Ἀνέκδοτοι, p. 225. I owe this reference to Mr. W. G. G. Forrest.

role in the relations of gods and men. Just as Aeschylus calls her
Αἶσα φασγανουργός (*Cho.* 647) and gives her a task of vengeance, so
here the poet may summon her to a like task in the restoration of civic
order. We need feel no surprise at seeing the names of the Fates
handled in this way. Hesiod's list was ancient but not obligatory or
universally accepted. Even at Athens one of the Fates seems to have
been Ἀφροδίτη οὐρανία (Paus. 1. 19. 2). In general their existence was
more important than their individual names, and many Greeks would
probably think of them, as the painter of the François Vase suggests,
simply as Μοῖραι. In such matters Greek poets took considerable
liberties, and it is instructive to note that, when Pindar deals with a
similar topic, he goes his own way. In his Hymn εἰς Τύχην he not only
makes Τύχη one of the Fates, for which he has no precedent in Homer
or Hesiod, but says that she has power over her sisters (fr. 21 Bo.). It is
also relevant to our passage that he treats Τύχη as a social, rather than
as a personal, power when he calls her φερέπολις (fr. 19 Bo.). The
names of the Fates allow some variation, and clearly when a city's
future was in question, some adaptation and adjustment of old ideas
might be necessary. So our poet, well within his rights, substitutes
Αἶσα for Atropos.

There were two views about the parentage of the Fates, both of
which may be found in Hesiod, who at one place makes them the
daughters of Night without any father (*Theog.* 217 ff.) and at another
daughters of Zeus and Themis (ibid. 904 ff.). So glaring a contra-
diction suggests that one of the passages is an interpolation, but it
is almost impossible to say which. What matters is that both views
existed, and each represented a different approach. The first sees the
Fates as incalculable beings who belong to the world of darkness, the
second as agents of divine order working for the will of the gods.
Ancient poets were aware of the difficulty, and at one place Pindar
reveals his embarrassment when he makes the Fates bring Themis to
wed Zeus (fr. 10. 3 Bo.), thereby rejecting the notion that they are the
daughters of this marriage. It looks as if he were trying to harmonize the
two stories of their origin by giving them an independent birth but at
the same time making them creatures of light and happiness. Our
poet must have been aware of this problem, since he too attempts a
harmony, when he sets the Fates on Olympus next to Zeus but at the
same time makes them daughters of Night, as does the Orphic Hymn
when it calls them

$$\text{Μοῖραι ἀπειρέσιοι, Νυκτὸς φίλα τέκνα μελαίνης.} \quad (59.\ 1.)$$

There must have been good reasons for keeping Night as their mother.

A clue may be found in the words οὐράνιαι χθόνιαί τε, which imply
that the Fates have a dual character. On the one hand, they are

enthroned at the side of Zeus and carry out his will; on the other hand, they belong to the underworld of darkness and death and perform very different functions. This side has to be emphasized, since the poet is concerned with the eradication of evil as well as with the establishment of good. That perhaps is why he makes the Fates daughters of that Νὺξ ὀλοή, whom Hesiod supplies with so mixed and so forbidding a progeny (*Theog.* 211 ff.). The Fates are both Olympian and chthonic, and when they are addressed as daughters of Night, we are reminded that Night is also the mother of the Furies, who call her μᾶτερ at *Eumenides* 321 ff. Our poet stresses this relation and is fully entitled to do so; for the Fates are closely connected in rite and myth with the Erinyes or Eumenides. At Sicyon in the grove of the Eumenides there was an altar of the Fates, at which yearly sacrifices were made of sheep, wine mixed with honey, and flowers (Paus. 2. 11. 4); at Amyclae the Fates had an altar, and at Corinth a temple, next to those of Demeter, Kore, and Pluto (Paus. 3. 19. 4; 2. 4. 7); at the Piraeus they received bloodless offerings (*C.I.A.* 2. 1622; 3. 357), like the Eumenides. This association was recognized by Epimenides, who makes

$$\text{Μοῖραί τ' ἀθάνατοι καὶ 'Ερινύες αἰολόδωροι}\qquad\text{(fr. 9 Kinkel)}$$

the children of Cronos and Aphrodite. The genealogy is bold, but it keeps the ancient association between the Fates and the Furies. So, too, Aeschylus makes Prometheus class the two together:

$$\text{Μοῖραι τρίμορφοι μνήμονές τ' 'Ερινύες.}\qquad\text{(P.V. 516.)}$$

Though he seems to have held that the Eumenides are subordinate to the Fates, who grant them power (*Eum.* 334–5, 392 ff.), yet in the end he calls them both ματροκασίγνηται (ibid. 962). The close association of the two is implied in Homer, who makes an Erinys silence the horse of Achilles when it has foretold what is fated, μόρσιμον, for its master (*Il.* 19. 418). The Fates are daughters of Night and χθόνιαι because they are closely connected with the Furies and bring vengeance as well as rewards.

By making Night the mother of the Fates the poet secures an important point, but at the cost of creating a small difficulty; for it means that they cannot be sisters of the Hours, whom the Fates are asked to summon. The Hours are the daughters of Themis (Hes. *Theog.* 901; Pind. fr. 10. 6; 36. 6 Bo.), and whatever control the Fates have over them, it cannot be as sisters. But this need not cause very much trouble. The Fates and the Hours were sufficiently connected for any precision about family ties to be superfluous. They were brought together at Megara above the statue of Zeus in his temple (Paus. 1. 40. 4), and at Amyclae on the altar of Hyacinthus (id. 3.

19. 4). The association is easily understood; for if the Furies represent the darker side of the Fates as χθόνιαι, the Hours represent the brighter side as οὐράνιαι. The Hours belong to Olympus, where Themis bore them to Zeus, and Pindar attaches them to him as his special attendants (Ol. 4. 2). In their high position the Fates can work either through the Furies, when they send destruction, or through the Hours, when they send prosperity.

The Hours were originally goddesses of the earth, and such they remained, even when new duties were assigned to them. In Attica they were known as Auxo, Karpo, and Thallo (Paus. 9. 35. 2), and Pindar speaks of them as ἀγλαοκάρπους (fr. 10. 6 Bo.) and φοινικεάνων (fr. 63. 15). But though this view of them persisted, it had been rationalized and made more civic and social by the time of Hesiod when he used a popular etymology of their name to connect them with political virtues:

Εὐνομίην τε Δίκην τε καὶ Εἰρήνην τεθαλυῖαν
αἳ ἔργ᾿ ὡρεύουσι καταθνητοῖσι βροτοῖσι.   (Theog. 902–3.)

The transition from one function to another would be easy enough in a society which connected good government with the success of the harvest (Hes. Op. 225 ff.), and Hesiod's conception of the Hours is not at absolute variance with the popular conception. It is rather a difference of emphasis and intention. So our poet, who on this point follows Hesiod closely, still insists on the beauty of the Hours in the adjectives which he gives to them. But he is no less concerned with their power and majesty and shows his hand when he calls Right and Peace λιπαροθρόνους rather as Pindar acclaims Hera as χρυσόθρονον (Nem. 1. 37) or Aphrodite as εὐθρόνου (Isthm. 2. 5). The old goddesses of the earth are turned into august civic powers, Olympian presences who bestow the best things of life upon men.

In this treatment of the Fates and the Hours there is nothing which would be obviously alien to Simonides. This adaptation of a theme from Hesiod recalls his treatment of Ἀρετά in fr. 37 D. The sense of the vast powers of the Fates is like such a sentiment as

τὸ γὰρ γεγενημένον οὐκέτ᾿ ἄρεκτον ἔσται   (fr. 54 D.)

The dexterous handling of divine genealogies is suitable enough to the man who made Αὔριον a goddess (Men. Encom. Rhet. 9. 133 Walz). But the lines have also a more strictly political significance, which raises special problems. The Hesiodic conception of the Hours, as it is here presented, was used more than once in the first half of the fifth century. Writing for Pytheas of Aegina, probably not after 485 B.C.,[1] Bacchylides says of the island:

[1] A. Severyns, Bacchylide, pp. 41–54.

Εὐνομία τε σαόφρων,
ἃ θαλίας τε λέλογχεν
ἄστεά τ' εὐσεβέων
ἀνδρῶν ἐν εἰρήνᾳ φυλάσσει.   (13. 186–9.)

Δίκα is not mentioned, but she cannot be far from his thoughts. In another poem, of which unfortunately we know neither the occasion nor the date, he tells how Menelaus makes a speech at Troy and says:

ἀλλ' ἐν μέσῳ κεῖται κιχεῖν
πᾶσιν ἀνθρώποις Δίκαν ἰθεῖαν, ἀγνᾶς
Εὐνομίας ἀκόλουθον καὶ πινυτᾶς Θέμιτος.   (15. 53–55.)

Even more relevant to our passage are the lines which Pindar wrote for Xenophon of Corinth in 464 B.C.:

ἐν τᾷ γὰρ Εὐνομία ναίει κασί-
γνηταί τε, βάθρον πολίων ἀσφαλές,
Δίκα καὶ ὁμότροφος Εἰρήνα, τάμι' ἀνδράσι πλούτου,
χρύσεαι παῖδες εὐβούλου Θέμιτος.   (Ol. 13. 6–9.)

We cannot assert with confidence that either Bacchylides or Pindar had our poem in mind, though it is not impossible, but it is clear that both are concerned with the Hours as political powers of order and justice, and it is possible that this was almost a *communis locus* in choral poetry when it dealt with the fortunes of cities. What is more important is that both for Bacchylides and for Pindar the mention of the Hours, and especially of Εὐνομία, implies an aristocratic or oligarchic background. This is obvious in the cases of Aegina and Corinth, and it is confirmed by the general use of εὐνομία as the catchword of those systems of government which rejected the ἰσονομία claimed by democracies. The question is whether our poet calls upon the Hours in this partisan spirit. It is true that in the sixth century εὐνομία did not have so specialized a sense. Solon uses it for his own reformed society, which is to counter the δυσνομίη of the existing system (fr. 3. 30 ff. D.), and Xenophanes applies it to the good order which is disturbed when honours are paid to the wrong men (fr. 2. 19 D.). Even Pindar is not quite precise in his use of it; for when in 462 B.C. he addresses King Arcesilas of Cyrene, he includes among the gifts of Apollo peaceful lawfulness in the heart:

ἀπόλεμον ἀγαγὼν
ἐς πραπίδας εὐνομίαν,   (Pyth. 5. 66–67.)

and if this has any political reference, it is rather to hereditary monarchy than to aristocracy or oligarchy. The word may have hardened and become more limited as the fifth century advanced, and we cannot be certain that our poet sees in the Hours the same political implications as Pindar did at Corinth.

None the less it is at least possible that he did, that the repetition of the names of the Hours in their Hesiodic form suggests a conservative standpoint, that two poets, ours and Pindar, would not have used them without some similarity of political intention, that after all they are not what we should expect from a poem written for a democracy or a tyranny. On the whole we may conclude that our poet, like Pindar, invokes the Hours because of their aristocratic associations and that in the prayer which he makes for a city rent by στάσις, he is acting for the nobles. The matter is relevant to the question of authorship, since, though Simonides seems to have been equally at home with tyrants and democratic leaders, there is not much evidence that he worked for aristocracies, and to Aegina at least, as the enemy of Athens, he was hostile.

The problem would be simpler if we knew for what city the lines were written. The only clue is that the Fates are given a striking prominence, and this would be possible both in Thebes and in Corinth. Now it happens that immediately after the Persian Wars Themistocles was associated with Thebes, and since Simonides was his friend, he also may have been involved in its affairs. Themistocles saved Thebes from being expelled, as the Spartans proposed, from the Delphic Amphictyony (Plut. *Them.* 20). Moreover, Thebes was rent by civil strife after Plataea, when the δυναστεία ὀλίγων ἀνδρῶν was transformed into an ὀλιγαρχία ἰσόνομος (Thuc. 3. 62. 3), or even for a time into some sort of democracy ('Xen.' *Resp. Ath.* 3. 11). But it is hard to believe that in such a struggle Simonides would take the side of the Theban aristocrats unless he was under strong compulsion to do so, and for this there is no evidence; for we do not hear that Themistocles supported the Theban nobles against their adversaries. The case for Corinth is perhaps a little stronger. For Simonides paid a handsome tribute to the Corinthians who fought at Plataea (fr. 64 D.), and this was quoted in later days to correct the false impression given by Herodotus of their behaviour (Plut. *de Mal. Herod.* 42). If Simonides was on good terms with the Corinthians, they may have asked him to write a Hymn for them, but we know too little of their politics in the years after 479 B.C. to say whether the situation called for such lines as ours. But all this is to carry speculation too far. Even if the poem is the work of Simonides, and we cannot be certain that it is, we do not know for whom he wrote it. It remains a striking and impressive piece of Greek poetry.

GENERAL INDEX

(Abbreviations: n., note; qu., quoted; text., quotation and textual discussion; comp., compared with.)

in Prytaneum, 373; and Thessaly, 377–8, 396, and Sicyon, 246, 6th-c. society, 301 ff., Spartan attacks on Peisistratids, 378, 383, 394, Cleomenes on Acropolis, 113, politics in 510, 395, tyrannicide cult, 394–5, divisions at time of Marathon, 341–2, 389, 391, and Aegina, 313, 314, 415, Persian destruction, 340, 387, post-480 politics, 352, 353 ff., and Delian League, 353–4, isonomia and democracy, 395.

Atreus, house of, 114, 115.

Atropus, 410.

Atthis, 179, 193–4.

Attic dialect: and 'Hector and Andromache', 227–8; εὐφροσύνη, 304; and Attic Scolia, 374, 376.

Attic Scolia: emergence and character, 373; name, 374; manner of performance, 373–4; capping, 169, 376, 384, 392; and Anacreon, 303, 373; and Simonides, 373, 391; verses of Ibycus, Anacreon, Alcaeus as scolia, 374; No. 8 corrupt verse of Alcaeus, 374–5; Lesbian influence, 228, 373, 374, 376, (Alcaeus) 379; Athenaeus' collection, 373, a song book, 375, known to ancient scholars, 375, arrangement, 375–6; 'Cleitagora' not included, 396, 397, series within, 376, Peisistratid? (Nos. 14–22, 25), 376–83—metre and dialect, 376, date and source, 376 ff., still treasured in 5th c., 383; Alcmaeonid? (23, 24), 383–4—quoted in Ath. Pol., 376; Marathon and Miltiades? (1–7), 385–91; 'Harmodius Song' (10–13), 391–6—authorship and character, 392–4, 395–6, extra verse, 393, date, 394–6, contrasted 'Admetus' in Aristophanes, 378–9; 'Cleitagora', 396–7; metre, 374, 375, 376, 382, 384, 385, 386, 393, 397; heyday and decline of scolia, 397.

— No. 1 (in Athenaeus) (Athene Tritogeneia): 388 qu.–9. 2 (to Demeter and Persephone): 389 qu.–90. 3 (to Artemis Agrotera): 387 qu.–8. 4 (to Pan): 385 qu.–6, 304. 5: 386 qu.–7. 6: 390 qu.–1. 7: 391 qu., 341. 8: 374, text., etc.–5. 9: 384 qu.–5. 10–13, 'Harmodius Song':

392 qu.–6. 14, 'Admetus': 376–9, 377 qu., 397. 15, 16, 'Telamon': 379 qu.–80, 397. 17, 18: 380 qu.–1. 19: 381 qu. 20: 381 qu.–2. 21, 22: 382 qu. 23 (Cedon): 383 qu. 24 (Leipsydrion): 383 qu.–4. 25: 382 qu., 376.

Autoleon, of Croton, 108.

Babylon, 135, 139, 241.

Bacchants, 37–38.

Bacchylides: included in Alexandrian Nine, 2; flute accompaniment, 3; Alexandrian classification, 4; choral scolia, 6; encomia, 8; main features of choral ode seen in, 12; metre, 11, 87, 405; and dithyramb-naming, 83, 88, narrative pieces dissociated from Dionysus, 318, 321, 'Theseus' represents transitional form?, 319; and Stesichorus' Suotherai, 96, 97, 98; echoes Ibycus, 259; possible author 'Simonides' lamenting women pap. frag., 320 n.; in Sicily with Simonides, 359; and Pindar, 361; and Prayer to Fates—metrical practice different, 405–6, and style, 407, political use of Hours compared, 414.

— Ode xvii composed for Ceans at Delos, 308.

— 5. 26–27: 259 qu. 5. 124–6: 98 qu. 5. 128–9: 97. 6. 5: 308. 13. 186–9: 413–14 qu. 15. 53–55: 414 qu.

— Fr. 25. 8 Snell: 96.

Bathyllus, 277.

Beattie, A. J., 142 n.

Beauty competitions, 147, 178.

Beazley, J. D., 123, 177 n.

Bellerophon, weapon-dance, 400–1.

Beloch, J., 352.

Bentley, R., 52 n.

Bergk, T., 8 n., 40 n., 159 n., 186 n., 257 n., 295 n., 298 n., 338 n., 345, 346 n., 357 n., 361 n., 385 n.

Bion, lament for Adonis possibly echoes Sappho, 212.

Birds, in imagery, 24, 61, 65, 70, 265; in Alcman—Halcyon-choir, 24, Dove-choir, 56–57, and myth of discovery of music, 29–30; in Alcaeus, 172; in Sappho, 233; in Ibycus, 264–6; dances, 24; dresses, 56.

Blass, F., 24, 40 n., 191 n.

Blomfield, C. J., 218 n.
Boeotia, and Stesichorus, 118.
Boreas, 342–3.
Bread-sellers, as term of abuse, 298–9.
Brunn, H., 311 n.
Bucolic poetry, and Stesichorus, 84.
Bycchis, loved by Alcaeus, 163.

Cadmus, 99.
Caeneus, 96, 97.
Callias, son of Hipponicus, 341–2.
Callimachus, Fr. 222 P.: 360. 414 P.:
    266 n. 693 P.: 56.
Callinus, 13.
Calliope, 29.
Callistratus, 392–4, 395.
Calpurnius, L. Piso Frugi, 2.
Calyce, 85–86, 290.
Calydonian boar hunt, 95–98, 120, 242.
Capaneus, 100–1.
Carians, 275, 277.
Carneia, and early foreign poets, 20.
Carrère, J., 291 n., 358 n.
Carthaea, 308.
Carthage, 76.
Cassandra, 105, 255.
Castor, 121.
Catane, 76, 118, 242.
Catullus, and Alcman, 67; and Sappho,
    187, 217, 219–21; and Simonides, 324.
— C. 13:67. 38. 7–8:324 qu. 51:187.
    61. 120:217. 62. 1–2: 219 qu. 62.
    38–44:220 qu. 62. 57–58: 220 qu.
Cedon, 383.
Centaurs, 93, 119.
Ceos, 308–9, 310.
Cerberus, fetching of, 94, 120.
Cerberus Painter, 390.
Cercylas, of Andros, 176.
Chamaeleon, 266, 299, 309.
Chantraine, P., 68 n.
Charaxus, 209–11.
Chariot, in Sappho, 183; as image, 49,
    65, 182 n.; charioteer, 295.
Charybdis, death-image, 325.
Chios, Zeus and Fates at, 410.
Choir: undeveloped form of, 6, 8;
    speaks for poet, 25, as entity, 32, in
    singular and plural indiscriminately,
    46; character influences poet, 25, 31,
    32, 38, interplay choir, choir-master,
    31, 65; composition for Maiden-
    songs, 30, 47, for Epithalamia, 217,

220, 222, for Dithyrambs, 318, 380,
of Ceans at Delos, 308; ritual duties,
55, 56, 58; divided choir, 11, 64;
leader, 5–6, 8, 49, 62, 67, 319.
Choral song: forms known to Homer,
    4, 5, other early forms, 7–9, war- and
    weapon-songs, 401, to Aphrodite,
    321; and monody, 4–5, 6–7, 13;
    characteristic features, 12–13, 39, 41,
    language, 252, 266, 399, and narra-
    tive, 87, 104, 106, 126–7, personal
    elements, 7, 13, 31, 67, 87, metre,
    6–7, 10–11, 134, 399; and religion,
    11–13, 258; and music, 9–11, 20,
    82; and epic, 9, 12, 13, 21, 81, 87,
    127, 232; and Alcman, 16, 25, 39, 81,
    87, and Stesichorus, 77, 81, 87, 127,
    241, and Ibycus, 251, 252, 255, 258;
    Ibycus' poem to Polycrates choral,
    251, Timocreon's on Themistocles
    not, 351.
Cicero, on Ibycus, 264, on Simonides,
    342, 366.
— de Fin. 2. 104: 342.
— N.D. 1. 22: 366. Tusc. Disp. 4. 71:
    264 qu.
Cimmerians, 16, 27.
Cimon, displaces Themistocles, 352;
    Thessalian help against Eion, 396;
    ? connected with 'Cleitagora', 397;
    Eupolis on, 390.
Cineas, 378.
Circe, 22.
Clazomenae, and Alyattes, 141.
Clearchus, on Locrian local song, 83,
    and Mill-song, 132.
Cleis, Sappho's mother, 176, daughter,
    176, 207–9.
Cleisthenes, in 510, 395.
Cleisthenes, of Sicyon, 246.
Cleitagora, 396.
Clement, on Hippocoontids, 41.
Cleobulus, 284.
Cleobulus, of Rhodes, 370; Midas
    epitaph, 370 qu.
Cleomenes, of Sparta, on Acropolis,
    113, and Crius, 313, 314.
Cleophrades Painter, 303.
Clitias, 95.
Clonas, 10.
Clotho, 410.
Clymene, 104.
Clytaemestra, 111, 114–17.

— Epigrams: No. 77: 318 n. 79 (on his dithyrambic victories): 317–18 qu. 83 (on Megistias): 344. 84 (to Callias): 341 qu. 85 (on Archedice): 323 qu. 92 (on Spartan 300): 345. 97: 386. 99 (on Timocreon): 356 qu. 105 (dedication of Persian spoils): 345 qu. 108 (Salamis dedication at Corinth): 353 qu. 143 D. (Pan dedication): 386 qu. 152, 159: 358.

— *Ox. Pap.* 2137: 344 n. 2431: 326 n. 2432: 336 n.

— *P.S.I.* x, No. 1181, pp. 169 ff.: 320–1 qu.

— Plut. *Arat.* 45, ἐν ἀνάγκαις γλυκὺ γίνεται καὶ τὸ σκληρόν: 371.

— Theon, *Progn.* 1. 215. παίζειν ἐν τῷ βίῳ . . . : 371–2.

Simonides, grandfather of poet, 75.

Sirens, as image, 29, 57, 322; Simonides calls Peisistratus, 322.

Sirius, 59, 63 (Alcm. fr. 1 D.), 267 (Ibycus).

Sisyphus, 162.

Sitzler, J., 191 n., 196 n.

Smerdies, 277–81, 291.

Smyrna, 141.

Smyth, H. W., 298 n., 404 n.

Snell, B., 96 n., 283 n., 320 n.

Socrates, comp. Sappho, 182; and Simonides, 369.

Solon, comp. Pittacus, 136; poetry, comp. Alcaeus, 150, comp. Mimnermus, 373, comp. personal poets, 240; use of εὐνομία, 414.

— Fr. 3. 9–10 D.: 304 qu. 3. 30 ff.: 414. 7. 4: 239. 10: 150.

Sophocles: view of love, 293; Siren death-symbol for, 322; ideal of civic virtue, 335; on Simonides, 364; and Stobaeus' lines on fate, 404; characteristics of prayer in *Oedipus Tyrannus* parodos, 406; εὐπατρίδης in, 384.

— *Ajax* 172 (182): 406.

— *Ant.* 367–71: 335 qu.

— *El.* 25–26: 264. 326: 348. 417 ff.: 116.

— *O.C.* 1248: 27.

— *O.T.* 56–57: 156 qu. 430: 355.

— *Phil.* 182–3: 357 qu. 436: 270 n.

— *Trach.* 144–7: 261 qu. 441–2: 293 qu. 910: 282 qu.

— Fr. P. 37, 381 qu. 724: 270 n. 861: 322.

— *Heracles at Taenarus*, 94.

Sosibius, 40–41.

Sosiphanes, 55.

Sparta: in 7th c., 16, 19, 66, 67, 72–73; trade, 19; art, 19, 69–70; music, 16, 20, 82, 115; Maiden-songs, 30, 304; marching-songs, 400; early foreign poets at, 18, 20; epic at, 20–21; and Homeric Hymns, 23; and Alcman, 16, 19, 20, 38, 66–67, 72–73; and Stesichorus, 111–18, 254; and Ibycus, 246–7, 264; and Simonides, 344–5, 349 (ode on Thermopylae dead performed at); religion, 19, 20, 34–37, 46, 51, 52–55, 58, 72, 111, 115, 118, 346–7, 349; 2nd Messenian War, 19; 6th-c. policy, 112–15, 246, 254; and Croesus, 247; loses hegemony to Athens, 353.

Sport, Greek view of, 313.

Statius, *Silu.* 5. 3. 154: 128.

Stella, R. F., 309 n.

Stesichorus, 2, 11, 12, 17, 39, 74–129, 241, 242–3, 244, 245, 252–3, 309–10.

— Date, 74–76, younger than Alcman, 17, 76, than Mimnermus, 90, older than Simonides, 74, 76; name, 76; background, 76, Locri, 82, 83, 86, 119, Himera, 84, 89, 119, on mainland, 107, 118, at Sparta, 111, 112 ff., 118; death, 76, 118; personality, 91, 104, 128 (heroic temper and lack of), 87, 94 (seriousness), 115, 128 (gaiety), 111 (moral judgements); influences and debts, 76–77, 82–84, 85–87, local, 76, 77, 83–87, 95, 107, epic, 77, 79, 81, 87, 127, Homer, 77–79, 94, 95, 100, 101, 103, 104, 109, Hesiod, 79–81, 89, 95, 104, 108, 110, 118, Mimnermus, 90, 92, Alcman, 81–82, 102, Xanthus, Xenocritus, Arion, 82–83, 102, Sacadas, 103; art, 126–9—fusion of elements, 76–77, 87, epic reshaped in lyric, 81, 87, 126–8; scale of composition, 11, 93, 102, 104, 108, 115, 126; innovatory treatment of traditional stories, 80–81, 89–90, 92, 98, 99, 100–1, 103, 104, 112 ff., 123, 124; narrative, 81, 87, 88, 108–9, 126–7; metre, 87, and triad, 11, 39; romantic tendencies, 98, 103–4, 245;

INDEX OF GREEK WORDS